The American Presidency

Eighth Edition

Sara Miller McCune founded SAGE Publishing in 1965 to support the dissemination of usable knowledge and educate a global community. SAGE publishes more than 1000 journals and over 800 new books each year, spanning a wide range of subject areas. Our growing selection of library products includes archives, data, case studies and video. SAGE remains majority owned by our founder and after her lifetime will become owned by a charitable trust that secures the company's continued independence.

Los Angeles | London | New Delhi | Singapore | Washington DC | Melbourne

The American Presidency

Origins and Development, 1776–2018

EIGHTH EDITION

SIDNEY M. MILKIS
University of Virginia

MICHAEL NELSON
Rhodes College

Los Angeles | London | New Delhi
Singapore | Washington DC | Melbourne

FOR INFORMATION:

CQ Press

An Imprint of SAGE Publications, Inc.

2455 Teller Road

Thousand Oaks, California 91320

E-mail: order@sagepub.com

SAGE Publications Ltd.

1 Oliver's Yard

55 City Road

London EC1Y 1SP

United Kingdom

SAGE Publications India Pvt. Ltd.

B 1/I 1 Mohan Cooperative Industrial Area

Mathura Road, New Delhi 110 044

India

SAGE Publications Asia-Pacific Pte Ltd

18 Cross Street

#10-10/11/12

China Square Central

Singapore 048423

Printed in the United States of America

Library of Congress Cataloging-in-Publication Data

Names: Milkis, Sidney M., editor. | Nelson, Michael, 1949- editor.

Title: The American presidency : origins and development, 1776-2018 / Sidney M. Milkis, University of Virginia, Michael Nelson, Rhodes College, editors.

Description: Eighth Edition. | Los Angeles : SAGE / CQ Press, [2019] | Includes bibliographical references and index.

Identifiers: LCCN 2018042301 | ISBN 9781544323121 (Paperback : acid-free paper)

Subjects: LCSH: Presidents—United States—History. | Executive power—United States—History. | Constitutional history—United States. | United States—Politics and government.

Classification: LCC JK511 .M56 2019 | DDC 352.23/50973—dc23 LC record available at https://lccn.loc.gov/2018042301

This book is printed on acid-free paper.

Senior Acquisitions Editor: Lauren Schultz

Acquisitions Editor: Monica Eckman

Editorial Assistant: Sam Rosenberg

Production Editor: Kelle Clarke

Copy Editor: Pam Schroeder

Typesetter: C&M Digitals (P) Ltd.

Proofreader: Barbara Coster

Indexer: Beth Nauman-Montana

Cover Designer: Scott Van Atta

Marketing Manager: Erica DeLuca

Certified Chain of Custody
SUSTAINABLE FORESTRY INITIATIVE
Promoting Sustainable Forestry
www.sfiprogram.org
SFI-01268

SFI label applies to text stock

19 20 21 22 23 10 9 8 7 6 5 4 3 2 1

Contents

Preface

Nearly three decades ago, we wrote and CQ Press published the first edition of *The American Presidency: Origins and Development*. Encouraged by the strong response that it and the next six editions received, we have undertaken an eighth edition with three important objectives in mind. First, we wanted to take account of recent events and developments, especially the latter part of the Obama presidency, the 2016 election, and the first twenty months of the Trump presidency. Second, we wanted to incorporate the best of the new scholarship on the origins and development of the presidency. And third, we wanted to flesh out our coverage of issues involving race and the presidency.

At its launch, *The American Presidency* was the first comprehensive, one-volume history of the presidency to be written by political scientists in more than fifty years. One advantage of a historical approach to the presidency is that it fills the enormous gap that has arisen in the education of most contemporary students of the office. Because the historical profession (with notable exceptions) has in recent years deemphasized political history in favor of social history, we political scientists have had to step into the breach. So be it: the historians' self-inflicted misfortune has become our good fortune.

Another reason for political scientists to approach the presidency with an eye to history is that in doing so, we supplement the approach taken by most standard textbooks. Instead of artificially segregating the presidency into its discrete parts—the president and Congress, presidential elections, party leadership, and so on—a historical approach necessarily integrates every aspect of the office in a way that accurately reflects the dynamic interaction of the various parts. We see, for example, how Franklin D. Roosevelt's attempt to seize control of the Supreme Court in 1937 simultaneously affected—and was affected by—his relations with Congress, his party, the public, and the media. The same can be said of Donald J. Trump's use of social media and early resort to unilateral executive action, which deeply influenced public opinion, public policy, and the bureaucracy.

As we have developed this narrative over the past thirty years, our most important task has been to bring to light the history of how the institution of the presidency was created and how it has developed during its more than two centuries of existence. We describe what has remained constant in the office, mostly because of its constitutional design. We also discuss those historical innovations that have endured.

We are less concerned about describing what is idiosyncratic about particular presidents. Abraham Lincoln and Millard Fillmore, for example, receive a chapter and a few paragraphs, respectively, but more because of how they affected the presidency and the political system than because of the kinds of people they were. We believe that the institutional history of the presidency is a sufficiently important and neglected topic to merit a book all its own.

Some readers may ask: how pertinent is the presidency's first century and a half to its most recent eight decades? The answers of many political scientists, at least until recently, have ranged from "hardly" to "not at all." Students of the modern presidency typically mark 1933, the year of FDR's first inauguration, as year one of presidential history.

Our argument—and our evidence—is different. Many of the most important institutional characteristics of the presidency date from the Constitutional Convention and the earliest days of the Republic, which we chronicle in Chapters 1–3. During the nineteenth century, highly significant patterns and practices of presidential conduct took shape; these we discuss in Chapters 4–7. As for the era of the modern presidency—that is, the era in which the president has replaced Congress and the political parties as the leading instrument of popular rule—we trace its origins to Theodore Roosevelt and Woodrow Wilson as much as to Franklin Roosevelt and his successors (Chapters 8–16). Put simply, TR and Wilson began the practices that strengthened the president as the nation's popular and legislative leader; FDR then consolidated, or institutionalized, the president's new leadership roles in ways that subsequent presidents have continued.

This book is an interpretive political history of the presidency (and, in Chapter 17, the vice presidency) as well as a factual one. We have worked hard to get our facts straight and to make our interpretations sound. Research scholars, we think, will continue to be stimulated by much of what we report about the deep roots of modern American political institutions. Students will gain a solid undergirding for their study of the presidency, the Constitution, political development, and contemporary American politics and government. We also hope that this book will continue to find its home not only in reading rooms and classrooms but also in living rooms. After all, in a system of republican government such as ours, political history means our politics, our history.

We take pleasure and pride in the long friendship and colleagueship that underlie our continuing collaboration on *The American Presidency*. The book is truly a joint intellectual endeavor.

We have many thanks to offer, not least to our wives and children, to whom this book is dedicated. Keith Bolte, William Jessup University, David Darmofal, University of South Carolina, Jasmine Farrier, University of Louisville, Jeffrey W Ladewig, University of Connecticut, Michael Petersen, Utah State University, Ted Ritter, Virginia Union University, and Kenneth R. Stevens, Texas Christian University, reviewed the seventh edition and provided several helpful suggestions for improvement. We also thank Jesse H. Rhodes of the University of Massachusetts, Amherst and Emily Charnock of the University of Cambridge for sharing with us their excellent research and penetrating insights on President Barack Obama. Nicholaus Jacobs of the University of Virginia offered excellent suggestions for themes and events that should be addressed in the new edition. We are indebted to Beth Nauman-Montana for her excellent index. For their work or encouragement (or, in most instances, both) on previous editions, we thank these members of CQ Press's extraordinarily able staff: Charisse Kiino, director of college editorial; Monica Eckman, Executive Publisher, Social Sciences, Sage Publishing; Sarah Calabi, acquisitions editor; Davia Grant, editorial assistant; Pam Schroeder, freelance copy editor; and Catherine Forrest, production editor manager.

Sidney M. Milkis and Michael Nelson

Dedicated, with love and gratitude, to

Carol Milkis	*Linda E. Nelson*
Lauren Milkis	*Michael C. L. Nelson Jr.*
David Milkis	*Samuel M. L. Nelson*
Jonathan Milkis	*McClain Alexander Nelson*
	Chau Nelson

CHAPTER 1

The Constitutional Convention

The Constitutional Convention of 1787 was, as Connecticut governor Samuel Huntington told the delegates to his state's ratifying assembly,

> a new event in the history of mankind. Heretofore, most governments have been formed by tyrants and imposed on mankind by force. Never before did a people, in time of peace and tranquility, meet together by their representatives and, with calm deliberation, frame for themselves a system of government.[1]

In the midst of this "new event," nothing was newer than the American presidency, an invention unlike any other national executive in history. In designing the office, the fifty-five convention delegates drew on their personal and professional experience, study of history and philosophy, understanding of political reality, and individual and collective wits.

The constitutional presidency that the convention created may be regarded as, in a sense, the office's genetic code. Because of the Constitution, the presidency is a one-person office, and the president, who is elected for a fixed four-year term by the entire country, shares virtually all the powers of the national government with an equally distinct and independent Congress.

The constitutional presidency contains, as does an individual's configuration of DNA molecules, some ingredients whose meaning has been clear and unchanging from the moment of conception, such as eye color of and the thirty-five-year minimum age requirement for the president. The Constitution also includes sentences and phrases that are the legal equivalent of genetically rooted baldness: their meaning, although determined at the very beginning, could only be discovered later. For example, "He shall take Care that the Laws be faithfully executed" first appeared as a passing constitutional reference—the fifth of six clauses in the single sentence that constitutes Article II, section 3. But in later

1

years this provision afforded the president a strong legal claim to powers as varied as acting against secession by the southern states and directing the activities of the extensive federal bureaucracy. Finally, there are those attributes whose meaning could be found only in the vagaries of individual choice and environmental circumstance. Just as the relation of physical strength to well-being varies from person to person and situation to situation, for example, so has the president's constitutional power to "recommend to [Congress's] consideration such Measures as he shall judge necessary and expedient" been of varying importance to different presidents at different times.[2]

Antecedents

As is true of any invention, the presidency had antecedents, all of which influenced the form the office took in the Constitution. The delegates to the Constitutional Convention had long experience with British executives—namely, the king in London and his appointed governors in the American colonies. And ever since independence was declared in 1776, delegates had the benefit of a decade's worth of experience with governments of their own design, both the state constitutions and the Articles of Confederation, which created and defined a kind of national government. These experiences, more than anything else, set the stage for the calling of the convention and the creation of the presidency in the late spring and summer of 1787.

British and Colonial Executives

During their long years as colonists of Great Britain, Americans became well acquainted with the British form of government, which is best described as a constitutional monarchy. Great Britain was headed by a king (or, less frequently, a queen) who assumed the throne through inheritance and reigned for life. The monarch's power was limited by Parliament, the British legislature. Although the king could order the nation into war, his order prevailed only if Parliament was willing to appropriate the funds needed to finance the effort. Conversely, Parliament could pass laws, but the king could veto them. Parliament, a bicameral legislature, consisted of the House of Commons, an elected body, and the House of Lords, which was made up of hereditary peers with lifetime tenure.

The British form of government was more than just the most familiar one to the American colonists. Many of them also regarded it as the best that human beings ever had devised. Basic liberties seemed better safeguarded by Great Britain's constitutional monarchy than by any other government in history. British wealth and power were first among the nations of the world. Indeed, Great Britain seemed to have solved what traditionally had been regarded as an insoluble problem of classical political philosophy—that is, the inherent limitations of each of the three basic forms of government identified by Aristotle: monarchy (rule by one person), aristocracy (rule by an elite group), and democracy (rule by the people).[3] As the problem usually was formulated, because those who were entrusted to govern on behalf of the whole society ended up using power for their own selfish ends, monarchy soon degenerated into despotism, aristocracy into oligarchy, and democracy into anarchy, then tyranny. The British remedy, developed over several centuries, was to ameliorate these tendencies by blending elements of all three forms of government into one—monarchy in the king, aristocracy in the House of Lords, and democracy in the House of Commons—and then allowing each element to check and balance the others.

The governments of most of Great Britain's American colonies resembled the British government—that is, they had a governor chosen by the king and a legislature composed of an upper house, which in most colonies was appointed by the governor, and a lower house, which was elected by the people—that is, the "people" as defined in Colonial America: the roughly two-thirds of white males who owned at least a small farm or shop.[4] Royal governors were armed with substantial powers, including the right to cast an absolute veto over colonial legislation, the right to create courts and appoint judges, and even the right to prorogue, or dissolve, the legislature. But politically astute governors exercised these powers cautiously because only the legislature was empowered to appropriate the funds required to finance a colony's government and pay the governor's salary.

For all their virtues, the British and colonial governments were prone to abuse by executives who were hungry for power. King George III, who reigned during the American Revolution, used government contracts, jobs, and other forms of patronage as bribes to ensure the support of members of Parliament. Some colonial governors employed similar practices to influence their legislatures.[5] The king and his governors also stubbornly resisted the colonists' pleas to respect their rights as Englishmen, dismissing Parliament member Edmund Burke's argument that force would be "a feeble instrument, for preserving a people so numerous, so active, so growing, so spirited" as the Americans.[6] In 1776 the colonists' anger about these abuses of power was expressed fervently in the Declaration of

Independence. The Declaration is best known for its ringing preamble ("all men are created equal," "Life, Liberty and the pursuit of Happiness"), but it consists mainly of a long, detailed indictment of executive "injuries and usurpations, all having in direct object the establishment of an absolute Tyranny over these States."

The lesson many Americans learned from their experience with the British and colonial governments was that liberty is threatened by executive power and safeguarded by legislative power. As James Wilson, a Scottish-born Pennsylvanian who signed the Declaration, fought in the Revolutionary War, and later served as a delegate to the Constitutional Convention and a justice of the Supreme Court, observed:

> Before [the Revolution], the executive and judicial powers of the government were placed neither in the people, nor in those who professed to receive them under the authority of the people. They were derived from a different and a foreign source: they were regulated by foreign maxims; they were directed to a foreign purpose. Need we be surprised, then, that they were objects of aversion and distrust? . . . On the other hand, our assemblies were chosen by ourselves: they were guardians of our rights, the objects of our confidence, and the anchor of our political hopes. Every power which could be placed in them, was thought to be safely placed: every extension of that power was considered as an extension of our own security.[7]

State Constitutions

During the course of the Revolutionary War, seventeen constitutions were written by the thirteen newly independent states. (Some states began with one constitution, then replaced it with another.) Revulsion against their experience with the British executive—the king in London and his royal governors in the colonial capitals—led almost all the authors of state constitutions to provide for weak governors and strong legislatures. As Wilson wryly observed, under independence,

> the executive and the judicial as well as the legislative authority was now the child of the people; but to the two former, the people behaved like stepmothers. The legislature was still discriminated by excessive partiality; and into its lap, every good and precious gift was profusely thrown.[8]

In the decade after independence was declared, state governors typically were elected by the legislature for a brief term (one year, in most cases) and were ineligible for reelection. They were forced to share their powers with a council whose members were appointed by the legislature or elected by the people. This arrangement made the governors, in the assessment of historian Gordon S. Wood, "little more than chairmen of their executive boards."[9] Indeed, at the Constitutional Convention, Virginia governor Edmund Randolph opposed the proposal to make the presidency a unitary office by saying that as governor, he was merely "a member of the executive."

The powers the governors did have were meager. Most state constitutions made vague grants of authority to their executives and, by specifically denying them the right to veto legislation and make appointments, rendered them incapable of defending even that modest influence from legislative encroachment. In his *Notes on the State of Virginia,* Thomas Jefferson described the result in his home state:

> All the powers of government, legislative, executive and judiciary, result to the legislative body. The [state constitutional] convention, which passed the ordinance of government, laid its foundation on this basis, that the legislative, executive and judiciary departments should be separate and distinct, so that no person should exercise the powers of more than one of them at the same time. But no barrier was provided between these several powers. The judiciary and executive members were left dependent on the legislative for their subsistence in office and some of them for their continuance in it.[10]

The constitution of the historically pro-British state of New York offered a striking exception to the general practice of weak governors and strong legislatures. New York's governor was elected by the people, not the legislature, for a term of three years, not one, and, rather than being confined to a single term, could be reelected as often as the voters wanted. George Clinton, the first governor to be chosen under the New York constitution, was elected seven times for a total of twenty-one years. The executive power in New York's government was unitary, exercised by the governor alone and not shared with a council. The governor was empowered to veto legislation, subject to override by the legislature, and to make appointments, subject to legislative confirmation. Finally, these and other powers of New York's governor (which were extensive) were defined by the state's constitution in detail.

The Articles of Confederation

The decision by the Continental Congress to declare independence from Great Britain in the summer of 1776 was accompanied by another important decision. Congress adopted the Virginian Richard Henry Lee's motion that "a plan of confederation be prepared and transmitted to the respective Colonies for their consideration and approbation." Such a step was militarily necessary. Although the Declaration of Independence made each of the states, in effect, an independent nation, they could not fight a common war against the British without some sort of common government.

The states, jealous of their independence and reluctant to substitute even a homegrown central government for the British government they had just rejected, surrendered power grudgingly. They stipulated to their delegates in Congress that the confederation was to be no stronger than was absolutely necessary to wage the war for independence. Reacting against their experience with British rule, the states also made clear that the confederation's executive component must be minimal. Nothing remotely resembling a king would be tolerated.

On June 11, 1776, the Continental Congress formed the Committee of Thirteen (one delegate from each state) to draft a plan of confederation. The committee acted expeditiously, submitting its recommendation on July 12. More than a year later, on November 15, 1777, Congress adopted a revised version of the plan, calling it the Articles of Confederation and Perpetual Union. Ratification by the states came slowly, with the last state not voting its approval until March 1, 1781. But because the articles so much resembled the ad hoc arrangement the states were already using under the Continental Congress, the delay in ratification made little difference.

The Articles of Confederation more than embodied the states' dread of central government and executive power. Indeed, they created less a government than an alliance or, as the articles themselves put it, a "league of friendship." Each state, regardless of wealth or population, was represented equally in Congress: one state, one vote. The president, chosen by Congress, was merely its presiding officer, not an executive at all. Eventually, after the burden of making all financial, diplomatic, and military decisions and executing all legislative enactments became more than the legislators could handle, Congress created small executive departments headed by appointed officials. The activities of these departments, however, were closely monitored by Congress. In truth, Congress enacted few laws of consequence because passage required the support of nine of the thirteen states. Amendments to the articles had to be approved by all the states.

In addition to setting forth a weak institutional structure, the Articles of Confederation undermined the power of the national government in other ways. Technically, Congress was empowered to declare war, make treaties and enter alliances, raise an army and navy, regulate coinage, borrow money, supervise American Indian affairs, establish a post office, and adjudicate disputes between states. Funds and troops were supposed to be supplied by the states according to their wealth and population. But Congress had no power to tax the states or to enforce its decisions, generating "a massive collective-action problem."[11] When, as often happened, one or two states balked at meeting an obligation, other states followed suit. "Each state sent what was convenient or appropriate," historians Christopher Collier and James Lincoln Collier have observed, "which usually depended on how close to home the fighting was."[12] After the Revolutionary War was won, states felt even less reason to honor Congress's requests.

National Problems

For all its weakness, the Articles of Confederation did not prevent the United States from winning independence. The war effectively ended on October 17, 1781, when Gen. George Washington's American army and a French fleet, anchored off Yorktown, Virginia, forced the British forces led by Charles Lord Cornwallis to surrender.

The problems of a weak, purely legislative national government became more apparent in the half-decade after victory. No longer bound together by the threat of a common foe, the states turned their backs almost completely on Congress and each other.

Overlapping claims to western lands brought some states into conflict. Connecticut settlers and Pennsylvania troops clashed in one disputed area. The western territories, which extended as far as the Mississippi River, were the nation's most valuable resource, but until the states' rival claims were settled, it was difficult to develop the land and profit from it. On the Atlantic coast, some states with port cities placed taxes on goods imported from overseas by merchants in neighboring states. Caught between New York and Pennsylvania, Rep. James Madison of Virginia wrote, New Jersey was like "a cask tapped at both ends." North Carolina, also lacking a deep-water port and trapped between Virginia and South Carolina, was "a patient bleeding at both arms."[13] The new nation was burdened by a crippling debt. By 1789 foreign creditors held more than $10 million in promissory notes and were owed $1.8 million in unpaid interest. Unless paid, they were unwilling to engage in further trade with the United States. Yet Congress was unable to persuade the states to contribute to the Treasury.

By 1786 states were withholding 98 percent of congressionally requisitioned funds.[14] The total income of the national government in 1786 was less than one-third of the interest due that year on the national debt. Only a series of loans from Dutch bankers, negotiated by John Adams, kept the new nation solvent.

The United States also faced numerous problems on its borders. The nation's northern, southern, and western boundaries were under siege, with only an ill-equipped, poorly financed army of seven hundred to defend them. British soldiers continued to occupy two Great Lakes forts that their government had promised to vacate under the Treaty of Paris, which formally ended the Revolutionary War in 1783. Similarly, Spain closed the Mississippi River to American ships and made claim to land east of the river that according to the treaty belonged to the United States. Both Spain and Great Britain encouraged American Indian tribes to raid frontier settlements. (Spain, in particular, roused the Creeks in Florida to harass settlers in Georgia.) Returning from a trip to the interior, Washington lamented, "The Western settlers . . . turn on a pivot; the touch of a feather would turn them any way"—perhaps toward an alliance with Spain or Great Britain that would secure their safety.[15] Abroad, American ships were preyed on by Mediterranean pirates based in the Barbary states of Algiers, Morocco, Tripoli, and Tunis. Great Britain denied them access to its colonies in Canada and the West Indies, two lucrative markets for trade.[16]

In the midst of foreign and domestic difficulties, another problem developed that mixed elements of both. A currency crisis engulfed the United States, largely because Americans had gone on a buying spree, importing luxury items such as clocks, glassware, and furniture from Great Britain that they had been unable to get during the war. As specie—gold and silver, the only American currency acceptable to foreign creditors—flowed out of the country to pay for these goods, it became scarce at home. Meanwhile, many debtors, especially farmers who had left the land to fight for independence and still had not been paid by the financially destitute national government, faced bankruptcy or foreclosure. In response, these debtors pressured their state legislatures to print vast sums of paper money that they could use to pay their debts. Creditors, unwilling to be reimbursed in depreciated currency, fought back politically but with limited success. The state legislatures were highly democratic by the standards of the late seventeenth century and therefore often were more responsive to the greater number of debtors among their constituents than to the smaller number of creditors.

Lessons of Experience

Fear of executive power remained strong among Americans during the decade after independence was declared. But the problems that beset the United States under the strong legislative governments of the states and the weak legislative government of the Articles of Confederation taught certain lessons, particularly to people of property.[17] As political scientist Charles C. Thach Jr. wrote, "Experience with the state governments during the period following the cessation of hostilities served . . . to confirm the tendencies toward increasing confidence in the executive and increasing distrust of the legislature." Experience also taught several things about the proper design of an effective executive:

> It taught that executive energy and responsibility are inversely proportional to executive size; that, consequently, the one-man executive is best. It taught the value of integration; the necessity of executive appointments, civil and military; the futility of legislative military control. It demonstrated the necessity of the veto as a protective measure . . . [for] preventing unwise legislation. . . . It demonstrated the value of a fixed executive salary which the legislature could not reduce. It discredited choice [of the executive] by the legislature, though without teaching clearly the lesson of popular choice. . . . And, above all, it assured the acceptance of, if it did not create, a new concept of national government—the fundamental principles of which were the ruling constitution, the limited legislature, and the three equal and coordinate departments.[18]

The Constitutional Convention

Of all the problems that plagued the new nation after independence, none seemed more amenable to solution than those involving commerce among the states. Few benefited, and many suffered from the protectionist walls that individual states built around their economies. The Virginia Assembly, at the urging of James Madison, one of its youngest members, called for a trade conference to be held at Annapolis, Maryland, in September 1786 and urged all the other states to send delegations.

The Annapolis Convention was a failure. Only Virginia, New Jersey, and Delaware sent full delegations, and seven states, suspicious of Virginia's intentions, boycotted the meeting altogether. The convention proposed no remedies to the nation's trade difficulties. But the delegates who did come to Annapolis, notably Madison and Alexander Hamilton of New York, rescued the enterprise by issuing a bold call to Congress to convene an even more wide-ranging meeting. They urged that the states be enjoined to choose delegates to

> meet at Philadelphia on the second Monday in May next [1787], to take into consideration the situation of the United States, to devise such further provisions as shall appear to them necessary to render the constitution of the Federal Government adequate to the exigencies of the Union.

Initially, Congress was cool to the summons of the Annapolis Convention. But within weeks an event occurred that lent urgency to the nationalist cause. A mob of farmers in western Massachusetts, saddled with taxes and debts and unable to persuade the state legislature to ease credit, closed down courts and stopped sheriffs' auctions to prevent foreclosure orders from being issued and executed against their lands. Although similar outbreaks had occurred in about half the other states, they had been suppressed easily.[19] This one, dubbed Shays's Rebellion after one of its leaders, Revolutionary War veteran Daniel Shays, threatened for a time to rage out of control.

The reaction around the country among people of property was shock and horror, not just at the class warfare that seemed to be erupting and the inability of the national government to help states maintain the peace but also at several states' subsequent decision to avert future rebellions by allowing debtors to pay off their creditors with newly printed, nearly worthless paper money. Thomas Jefferson's private comment to Madison that "a little rebellion now and then is a good thing" was very much the exception in this regard. "What, gracious God, is man!" declared the usually stoic George Washington after hearing of the Massachusetts riots. "That there should be such inconsistency and perfidiousness in his conduct. We are fast verging to anarchy and confusion."[20]

On February 21, 1787, Congress decided to act on the Annapolis Convention's request by passing a resolution:

> RESOLVED, That in the opinion of Congress it is expedient that on the second Monday in May next a Convention of delegates who shall have been appointed by the several states be held in Philadelphia for the sole and express purpose of revising the

Articles of Confederation and reporting to Congress and the state legislatures such alterations and provisions therein as shall when agreed to in Congress and confirmed by the states render the federal constitution adequate to the exigencies of government and the preservation of the Union.

The states were no more compelled to obey this congressional summons than to follow any other. But when a sufficient number—whether frightened by the prospect of further uprisings, concerned about the nation's growing domestic and international weakness, or inspired by the example of the nationally revered Washington, who decided to attend as a delegate from his native Virginia, selected delegations, all the other states but Rhode Island fell into line for fear of having their interests ignored.

The Delegates

The Constitutional Convention has been variously described as an "assembly of demigods" (Jefferson), a "miracle at Philadelphia" (author Catherine Drinker Bowen), a "nationalist reform caucus" (political scientist John P. Roche), and a "coup" (legal scholar Michael Klarman), to cite but four descriptions.[21] The convention may have been all of these things. But, mundanely, it also was a gathering of fifty-five individuals.

Who were the delegates? Self-selection had much to do with determining who was chosen by the states to represent them at the convention and who actually went. Political leaders who were committed to the idea that the national government must be dramatically improved embraced the opportunity to attend. Most of those who were basically satisfied with the status quo—including prominent Americans such as Patrick Henry and Richard Henry Lee of Virginia, Samuel Adams of Massachusetts, and George Clinton of New York—chose to stay away. Henry, a strong defender of the Confederation, reputedly said that he "smelt a Rat."[22] If they had attended and fought stubbornly for their position, observed political scientist Clinton Rossiter, the convention "would have been much more perfectly representative of the active citizenry of 1787. It would also, one is bound to point out, have been crippled as a nation-building instrument."[23]

The fifty-five delegates were generally united in their belief that a stronger national government was vital to the health of the new American nation. In part, this agreement stemmed from their similar experiences in the national arena. Forty-two were current or former members of Congress. Thirty had risked life and livelihood by fighting in the Revolutionary War.

Eight had signed the Declaration of Independence. All were republican, at least to the extent that they opposed a hereditary monarchy and supported some form of representative government.

Collectively, the convention was young. Many of the delegates were, in the words of historians Stanley Elkins and Eric McKitrick, "the young men of the Revolution," who had come of age during the revolutionary decade of the 1770s, when the idea of building a nation was more inspiring than traditional state loyalties.[24] Madison, at thirty-six, was older than eleven other delegates, including Gouverneur Morris of Pennsylvania (thirty-five), Edmund Randolph of Virginia (thirty-three), and Charles Pinckney of South Carolina, who was twenty-nine but said he was twenty-four, so he could claim to be the youngest delegate. (That distinction belonged to Jonathan Dayton of New Jersey, who was twenty-six.) The average age of the delegates—even counting Benjamin Franklin of Pennsylvania, who, at age eighty-one, was sixteen years older than the next-oldest delegate—was forty-three.

Other shared characteristics contributed to the delegates' common outlook on many fundamental issues. All were white; all were men. Almost all lived in the long-settled coastal regions of their states; the backcountry frontier was hardly represented at the convention. Almost all were prosperous—about half were lawyers, and another quarter owned plantations or large farms. Only two delegates were small farmers, a group that accounted for 85 percent of the nation's white population. The wealth of most of the delegates derived from personal property—government securities and investments in manufacturing, shipping, and land speculation. The prosperity of other delegates lay in real property, notably large farms and, in the South and elsewhere, fellow human beings. Twenty-five delegates—nearly half—were slave owners.[25]

Rules and Procedures

Congress had summoned the convention to assemble on Monday, May 14, 1787. But not until Friday, May 25, were the seven state delegations needed for a quorum present in Philadelphia. Although most of the other delegations arrived within a few days, some came much later. Others left early. Never were all fifty-five delegates present at the same time.

The first order of business on May 25 was to elect a president, a word that in the usage of the day, suggested a "presiding officer" more than a "leader" or "chief executive." Not surprisingly, George Washington was the delegates' unanimous choice. Washington spoke on only one issue during the convention. Fearing that the new Constitution would be attacked as antirepublican, he rose on the last day to support a proposal requiring that each member of the House of Representatives represent at least thirty thousand people rather than the previously agreed-to forty thousand.[26] The delegates approved unanimously. This intervention was not the only evidence that Washington played more than a ceremonial role. According to the Colliers, "during that long, hot summer, this gregarious man was constantly having dinner, tea, supper with people, and one must assume of course that he was actively promoting his position"—namely, a strong national government and a strong executive within that government.[27] Even Washington's last-minute speech on representation was meaningful in symbolic terms. As Gordon Wood points out, "It was his way of saying to his colleagues that he favored the Constitution"—and that he and his fellow authors believed it must embody republican principles.[28]

After Washington was elected president of the convention, a secretary was chosen—Maj. William Jackson of Pennsylvania. Jackson kept the convention's official journal, which was little more than a record of motions and votes. Fortunately, James Madison decided to keep a more extensive record of the delegates' debates and deliberations. Madison had been frustrated in his studies of other governments by the near impossibility of determining what their founders intended when creating them. Although he was acting on his own initiative, the other delegates knew what he was doing because he sat up front next to Jackson, instead of with the Virginia delegation, so that he would not miss a word. In fairness to his colleagues, Madison decided to keep his notes secret until the last delegate died. That delegate turned out to be Madison, who died in 1836, at the age of eighty-five. Along with the rest of Madison's papers, his notes on the Constitutional Convention were purchased by Congress in 1837 and published in 1840.

The only other business of the convention's first day was to accept the credentials of the state delegations. In doing so, the delegates implicitly agreed to follow the then-customary procedure of having each state cast one vote. James Wilson was displeased by this arrangement (he felt the more populous states should have a greater voice), but he was persuaded by Madison and others that to alienate the small-state delegates at such an early stage could abort the entire proceeding.

On Monday, May 28, the delegates adopted additional rules and procedures. None was more important to the success of the convention than the rule of secrecy. The rule was simple: no delegate was allowed to communicate anything to anyone except a fellow delegate about the convention's discussions and deliberations.

Thomas Jefferson, then the U.S. ambassador to France, wrote John Adams, the ambassador to Great Britain, that he was appalled by "so abominable a precedent. . . . Nothing can justify this but the innocence of their intentions and ignorance of the value of public discussions." But in a letter to Jefferson, Madison explained the delegates' decision: "It was thought expedient in order to secure unbiased discussion within doors, and to prevent misconceptions & misconstructions without, to establish some rules of caution which will for no short time restrain even a confidential communication of our proceedings."[29] In other words, secrecy permitted the delegates to speak candidly about issues without fearing immediate public retribution as well as to change their minds without appearing weak or vacillating. It also kept opponents of a stronger national government from sensationalizing particular proposals or decisions as a means of discrediting the whole undertaking. Years later, Madison told historian Jared Sparks that "no Constitution would ever have been adopted by the Convention if the debates had been made public."[30]

Another important rule the convention adopted was to permit any of its decisions to be reconsidered at the request of even a single delegate. Because issues could always be raised and decided again, those who were on the losing side of a crucial vote were encouraged to stay and try to persuade the other delegates to change their minds rather than to walk out and return home in protest.

An Overview of the Convention

The Constitutional Convention was not a scripted or even an especially orderly proceeding. The delegates' decision to allow issues to be reconsidered, reinforced by their twin desires to build consensus among themselves and to create a government whose parts would mesh with one another, meant that the convention "could not, and did not, proceed in a straight line, neatly disposing of one issue after the next until all were dealt with. It moved instead in swirls and loops, again and again backtracking to pick up issues previously debated."[31] Historian Jack N. Rakove has compared the constitution-writing process to "the solution of a complex equation with a large number of dependent variables: change the value of one, and the values shift throughout."[32]

Students of mathematics know that not all such equations are solved. Once the convention was called, the risk of failure was great. As Franklin wrote to Jefferson on April 19, 1787, "If it does not do good it will do harm, as it will show that we have not the wisdom among us to govern ourselves."[33] Nor did the delegates' work proceed smoothly. Near the midway point, Washington wrote, "I almost despair of seeing a favourable issue to the proceedings of the Convention, and do therefore repent having had any agency in the business."[34] Nevertheless, from May to September the delegates used drafts, debates, compromises, and committees to organize their deliberations and help them work through the many issues that faced them. These plans and committees structured the work of the convention into seven main stages:

- Introduction of the Virginia Plan (May 29)

- Decision by the convention to recast itself as the Committee of the Whole, originally for the purpose of considering the Virginia Plan in detail but later to evaluate the New Jersey Plan and Alexander Hamilton's plan as well (May 30–June 19)

- Clause-by-clause debate by the delegates of their decisions when meeting as the Committee of the Whole (June 20–July 26)

- Work of the five-member Committee of Detail, which was appointed by the convention to produce a draft of the new constitution that reflected the delegates' previous decisions on multiple issues (July 24–August 6)

- Consideration by the delegates of each provision in the report of the Committee of Detail (August 7–31)

- Recommendations of the eleven-member Committee on Postponed Matters, which was created to propose acceptable solutions to problems that continued to stalemate the delegates (August 31–September 8)

- Final adjustments, including the work of the Committee of Style, which was charged to write a polished draft of the Constitution, and last-minute tinkering by the delegates, culminating in their signing of the proposed plan of government (September 9–17)

Virginia Plan (May 29). The Virginia Plan, introduced on May 29 by Governor Randolph but written mainly by Madison, offered a radical departure from the Articles of Confederation. The plan proposed to create a three-branch national government and to elevate it to clear supremacy over the states, partly by grounding its authority squarely in the sovereignty of the people.[35]

According to the Virginia Plan, the heart of the national government would be a bicameral legislature. The lower house would be apportioned according to some combination of wealth and population and elected by the people. Members of the upper house would be elected for a longer term by the lower house from a list of candidates nominated by the states. The legislature's powers would include broad authority not just to pass laws but also to conduct foreign policy and to appoint most government officials, including judges.

A national judiciary, organized into "one or more supreme tribunals" and "inferior tribunals" and appointed by the legislature to serve "during good behavior"—that is, with life tenure—would form the second branch. One of its broad-ranging powers was "impeachments of any National officers."

The government also would have an executive branch, although it was vaguely defined in the Virginia Plan. The "national executive" (the plan left unresolved the question of whether this would be a person or group of people) was "to be chosen by the National Legislature for a term of _____ years." Its powers were obscure: "besides a general authority to execute the National laws, it ought to enjoy the Executive rights vested in Congress by the [Articles of] Confederation." No one knew exactly what the phrase "Executive rights" meant.

Another element of the proposed new government was a "Council of revision" consisting of "the executive and a convenient number of the National Judiciary." The council would be empowered to veto laws passed by the national legislature, subject to override if a vetoed law was passed again by an unspecified legislative majority.[36]

Finally, the new government would have the power to veto state laws that were in conflict with the Constitution or with national legislation. For Madison, argues Gordon Wood, the worst thing about the Articles of Confederation was not the weakness of the national government but "the vices within the several states" that had produced an abundance of unjust and inconsistent laws. When the convention later rejected this provision of the Virginia Plan, Madison was for a time "convinced that the Constitution was doomed to fail."[37]

The delegates' response to the Virginia Plan was remarkably placid, especially considering that it proposed to replace the weak national government of the Articles rather than amend the document. "So sharp a break was Virginia asking the other states to make with the American past that one wonders why at least one stunned delegate . . . did not rise up and cry havoc at the top of his lungs," Rossiter wrote. "Instead, the delegates ended this [May 29] session by resolving to go into a 'committee of the whole house'" on the next day to "consider the state of the American union."[38]

Committee of The Whole (May 30–June 19). In becoming the Committee of the Whole, the convention was, in a sense, simply giving itself a different name. The same group of delegates made up the committee as made up the convention. But as the Committee of the Whole, they could operate more informally. To symbolize this change, Washington temporarily stepped down as president, and Nathaniel Gorham of Massachusetts was chosen to preside. In addition, any decision made by the delegates while meeting as the committee would be in the form of a recommendation that the convention would debate and vote on at least once more.

From May 30 to June 13 the Committee of the Whole spent most of its time going over the Virginia Plan, clause by clause. Much of the plan was accepted, but parts of it were altered, and some ambiguous provisions were clarified.[39] The executive was defined as a unitary, or one-person, office. This person would be elected by the legislature for a single, seven-year term and would be subject to impeachment and removal on grounds of "malpractice or neglect of duty." The executive alone, not a council of revision, was empowered to veto laws passed by the legislature, subject to override by a two-thirds vote of both houses. The requirement for a supermajority here and elsewhere in the new plan of government was an American innovation unknown to the British Parliament but used widely in the states.[40]

In deference to the states, the Committee of the Whole decided that members of the upper house of the national legislature (who had to be at least thirty years old) would be chosen by the state legislatures. They would serve seven-year terms and be eligible for reelection. Members of the lower house, also eligible for reelection, would serve three-year terms. All members of the national legislature would be barred from holding any other government office, mainly to prevent the emergence of conflicts of interest. As for the courts, there would be one "supreme tribunal," and the judges who served on it or on such "inferior tribunals" as the national legislature might decide to create would be appointed by its upper house for a lifetime term.

The New Jersey Plan. One plank of the Virginia Plan was especially controversial: the provision that both houses of the national legislature be apportioned according to population. Delegates from the states that thought of themselves as large (Virginia, Massachusetts, Pennsylvania, and the three states whose populations were growing most rapidly—Georgia,

North Carolina, and South Carolina) favored the idea. They fought sharply with the delegates from the other states who feared that their constituents would be hopelessly outnumbered in the legislature and wanted to preserve the existing arrangement of equal representation in Congress for each state. A compromise plan, proposed by Roger Sherman of Connecticut on June 11, would have apportioned the lower house of the legislature according to population and the upper house on the basis of one state, one vote. But few delegates were ready yet for compromise. Instead, small-state delegates responded to the Virginia Plan with a sweeping counterproposal. It was introduced on June 15 by William Paterson of New Jersey.

The New Jersey Plan came in the form of amendments to the Articles of Confederation rather than as a new constitution. It proposed to add two branches to the one-branch national government of the Articles: a plural, or committee-style, executive, to be elected by Congress for a single term and "removeable by Cong[ress] on application by a majority of the Executives [governors] of the several States," and a supreme court consisting of judges appointed by the executive for lifetime terms. The plan also declared national laws and treaties to be "the supreme law of the respective States" and authorized the executive to use force if necessary to implement them. In addition, Congress would be empowered to regulate interstate and international commerce and impose taxes. But the main purpose of the New Jersey Plan was unstated: to preserve the structure of Congress under the Articles as a single-house legislature in which each state, regardless of size, cast one vote.[41]

Hamilton's Plan. On June 18 Alexander Hamilton delivered a four- to six-hour speech to the delegates in which he urged them to consider his plan for an avowedly British-style government.[42] "He had no scruple in declaring," according to the notes kept by Madison, "supported as he was by the opinions of so many of the wise & good, that the British Government was the best in the world: and that he doubted much whether any thing short of it would do in America."[43]

Specifically, Hamilton proposed that as in Great Britain, the national government would be supreme in every way to the states. State governors would be appointed by the national legislature and granted the right to veto laws passed by their own assemblies. Members of the upper house of the national legislature, like members of the British House of Lords, would serve for life. As for the executive, "the English model is the only good one on this subject," Hamilton asserted.[44] Although he did not suggest that the United States create a hereditary monarchy, Hamilton did propose that the executive be chosen by electors and granted lifetime tenure and vast powers, including "a negative on all laws about to be passed, . . . the direction of war when authorized or begun, the sole appointment of the heads of the departments, the power of pardoning all offences except Treason," and, along with the Senate, the treaty-making power. In truth, argues biographer Ron Chernow, Hamilton's proposal was for "a new hybrid form of government that would have the continuity of a monarchy combined with the civil liberties of a republic."[45]

Hamilton's speech was dismissed by most of the delegates as being far beyond the bounds of what the people or the states would accept. Some scholars have suggested that his real purpose was to offer a plan so extreme that the Virginia Plan would seem moderate by comparison.[46] Yet several of Hamilton's specific proposals were adopted later in the convention, notably those concerning the president's power to grant pardons and to negotiate treaties. As for the New Jersey Plan, it was defeated on June 19 by a vote of seven states to three. Later that day, the Virginia Plan, as already modified, was approved by the Committee of the Whole and referred to the convention for further consideration. But the conflict between the delegates from the large states and the small states over apportionment in the national legislature was far from resolved.

Convention Debate (June 20–July 26). On June 20, with Washington again in the chair as president of the convention, the delegates began their clause-by-clause evaluation of the plan of government they had tentatively laid out while meeting as the Committee of the Whole. Among the changes they voted in the plan were these:

- Members of the lower house of the legislature would be elected for a term of two years, not three, and would have to be at least twenty-five years old.

- Members of the upper house would serve a six-year rather than a seven-year term. Terms would be staggered so that one-third were elected every two years.

- The national legislature would not have the power to veto state laws, much to Madison's dismay. But, borrowing a plank from the New Jersey Plan, national laws and treaties would be "the supreme law of the respective States."

- A property-owning requirement for members of the executive, legislative, and judicial branches would be established. (This idea later was abandoned.)

- Delegates expressed enough displeasure with the provision for legislative election of the president to a single, seven-year term to guarantee that it would not remain in the final document, but they failed to agree on an alternative.

More than any other issue, deciding how the legislature would be apportioned consumed the convention's time, attention, and endurance during these five weeks of debate. Delegates from the small states pressed relentlessly for equal representation of the states. Large-state delegates just as adamantly insisted that representation in both houses reflect population, wealth, or some combination of the two.

A special committee, with members from every state, was appointed on July 2 to propose a compromise. On July 5, after a break to celebrate Independence Day, the committee recommended a plan of equal representation for each state in the upper house and apportionment according to population in the lower house. As a sop to delegates from the large states who feared that the small, state-dominated upper house would push for spending programs that would impoverish the large states, the committee vested exclusive power in the lower house to originate all legislation dealing with money.

For more than a week, the delegates engaged in a complex and sometimes bitter debate about the compromise over representation. New questions were raised about whether states yet to be admitted to the Union should receive as much representation as the original thirteen, how often a national census should be taken to measure population changes, and whether apportionment in the lower house should reflect a state's wealth as well as its population. On July 16 the convention voted narrowly to approve the main points of the special committee's proposal, sometimes called the Connecticut Compromise in honor of its author, Roger Sherman. One week later the delegates undermined the idea that the upper house would represent the states in the new government by deciding that every state would have two members, each of them free to vote independently of each other and of their state governments.

This happy mixture of principle and practicality was tarnished by a dreadful, if unavoidable, compromise with America's "peculiar institution." In one of the three constitutional clauses that protected forced servitude, each enslaved individual was counted as three-fifths of a person for purposes of representation in the lower house. These three clauses, which also included both a guarantee that slaves could continue to be imported for twenty years and a fugitive slave provision requiring states to return escaped slaves to their owners, would cast a long, dark shadow over the republic.

As terrible as these concessions to slavery were, they could have been worse. Although allowing the continuation of slavery and even abetting it by promising to help catch fugitive slaves—a Faustian bargain that most Framers feared was necessary to prevent the dissolution of the Union—the delegates refrained from providing slavery with a moral stamp of approval. Indeed, the word *slavery* is never mentioned in the document; instead, they resorted to euphemisms such as "persons held to service," a tacit acknowledgment of their embarrassment in acquiescing to it. By depriving the defenders of slavery of moral ground to stand on, the Constitution's wording also allowed later opponents of slavery, such as the abolitionist Frederick Douglass and President Abraham Lincoln, to claim that the Framers regarded slavery as a necessary evil rather than a positive good.

Committee of Detail (July 24–August 6). As fraught as these compromises were, by July 24 the convention resolved to appoint a Committee of Detail to review all of its decisions and draft a constitution that incorporated them. The five-member committee included representatives of the three main regions of the country—Nathaniel Gorham of Massachusetts and Oliver Ellsworth of Connecticut (a protégé of Sherman) from New England, James Wilson of Pennsylvania from the middle states, and Edmund Randolph of Virginia and John Rutledge of South Carolina from the South. The committee worked, while the rest of the convention adjourned until August 6.

One indication of the committee's influence is that it took convention-passed resolutions amounting to 1,200 words and transformed them into a draft constitution of 3,700 words.[47] The committee also drew from a wide range of other sources in compiling its report: the New Jersey Plan, the Articles of Confederation, the rules of Congress, some state constitutions (notably those of New York and Massachusetts), and a plan of government proposed by Charles Pinckney of South Carolina.[48]

Most of the memorable phrases in the Constitution were written by the Committee of Detail, including "state of the Union" and "We the People." Institutions were named. The executive became the president; the national tribunal, the Supreme Court; and the legislature, Congress, with its upper house called the Senate and its lower chamber, the House of Representatives.

For the most part, the committee, in keeping with its name, simply fleshed out the details of earlier convention decisions. It established procedures for the president's veto, defined the jurisdiction of the courts, and adjusted certain relations among the states. In some instances, however, the committee substituted its own judgment for the convention's. For example, it vested the power to impeach in the House and omitted the property requirement for officeholders.

Perhaps the most important decision by the Committee of Detail was to transform general grants of power for each branch into specific ones. What previously had been Congress's broadly stated authority "to legislate in all cases for the general interests of the Union" became instead a list of eighteen enumerated powers, including the power to lay and collect taxes, regulate interstate commerce, establish post offices, "make war," elect a national treasurer, and create inferior courts—all culminating in a sweeping grant "to make all Laws that shall be necessary and proper for carrying into Execution" these and "all other Powers vested" in the new government. The states were forbidden certain powers, notably to make treaties with other nations, to print money, and to tax imports.

The committee granted the president the authority to recommend legislation to Congress, make executive appointments, receive ambassadors from other nations, issue pardons, "take care" that the laws be executed, and command the armed forces. An oath to "faithfully execute the office" of president also was included, as was a provision that the Senate's own elected leader would exercise the powers and duties of the presidency if the president died, resigned, or became disabled. The judiciary—the Supreme Court and the other inferior courts to be created by law—was given jurisdiction in cases arising under the laws of the national government as well as in controversies between states or between citizens of different states.

Finally, responding to a threat to walk out by Gen. Charles Cotesworth Pinckney of South Carolina (an older cousin of Charles Pinckney), the committee not only forbade Congress to tax or ban the importing of slaves and the exporting of goods but also placated southern delegates' fears that Congress might enact navigation laws requiring that American exports be transported on American ships (a boon to northern shipbuilders but a burden to southern agricultural exporters). The committee recommended that Congress would have to pass such laws by a two-thirds vote in both houses.

Convention Debate (August 7–31). As they had with the Virginia Plan and the report of the Committee of the Whole, the delegates reviewed the draft constitution proposed by the Committee of Detail clause by clause. Much of the draft was approved. Some parts, however, were modified, and others became matters of serious controversy.

Modifications. The delegates tinkered with several provisions of the Committee of Detail's draft:

- They enacted minimum citizenship requirements for members of Congress (seven years for members of the House, nine years for senators), along with a requirement that legislators be inhabitants of the states they represent.

- They raised the majority needed in both houses of Congress to override a president's veto from two-thirds to three-fourths. (Near the end of the convention, the delegates restored the two-thirds requirement.)

- They judged Congress's power to make war too sweeping to protect the nation if it was attacked when Congress was out of session. The clause was revised to read "declare war."

- They forbade Congress to pass ex post facto laws (retroactive criminal laws) or bills of attainder (laws that declare a person guilty of a crime without a trial).

- They barred the government from granting "any title of nobility" to any person and forbade government officials to receive "any present, emolument, office, or title of any kind whatever from any king, prince, or foreign state."

- They empowered Congress to activate the militia of any state "to execute the laws of the Union, suppress insurrections, and repel invasions."

- They dropped the two-thirds requirement for Congress to pass navigation acts.

- They created a convention-based procedure for amending the Constitution: "on the application of the legislatures of two-thirds of the states in the Union for an amendment of this Constitution, the legislature of the United States shall call a convention for that purpose."

- They prohibited any religious test as a requirement for holding office.

- They expanded the president's oath to include these words: "and will to the best of my judgment and power preserve, protect, and defend the Constitution of the United States." (Later, "to the best of my judgment and power" became "to the best of my ability.")

- The Committee of Detail had proposed that the new constitution take effect when ratified by state conventions, not state legislatures that might resent the plan's dilution of their powers. The delegates now voted to set the number of states needed for ratification at nine, or two-thirds—a number "familiar to the people" from the Articles of Confederation.

Controversies. The draft constitution's slavery provisions came under fierce assault from several northern delegates, especially the three-fifths rule for counting enslaved people as part of the population and the prohibition against laws banning the importation of slaves. The North's concern derived less from moral considerations than from fear of slave rebellions, which might attract foreign intervention and, in any event, probably would require northern arms and money to put down. Southern delegates not only defended the provisions to protect slavery but also confirmed that their states would not ratify any constitution that placed slavery in jeopardy.

Adopting the same approach used to settle the controversy between the large and small states, on August 22 the convention appointed a special committee to find a compromise solution. Two days later, the committee proposed that Congress be authorized, if it so decided, to end the importation of slaves after 1800. In the meantime, Congress could tax imported slaves at a rate no greater than ten dollars each. As noted, euphemisms— not "slave" but "other Persons"—were used in the Constitution. General Pinckney persuaded the convention to change 1800 to 1808. The committee's recommendation, as amended, was passed.

Controversies over two other matters caused the convention to bog down: the powers of the Senate, which delegates from the large states wanted to minimize and delegates from the small states wanted to maximize, and a cluster of issues concerning presidential selection. On August 31, nearing the end of its labors, the convention appointed a Committee on Postponed Matters, with a member from each state delegation, to propose solutions to these vexing problems.

Committee on Postponed Matters (August 31–September 8). Beginning on September 4, the Committee on Postponed Matters, chaired by David Brearley of New Jersey, made several recommendations about the presidency.[49] The committee, sometimes referred to as the Committee on Unfinished Parts or, because it had one member from each state delegation at the convention, the Committee of Eleven, proposed a presidential term of four years rather than seven, with no restriction on the president's eligibility for reelection. The president was to be chosen not by Congress but by the Electoral College. To constitute the Electoral College, each state would select, by whatever means it chose, electors equal in number to its representatives and senators in Congress. The candidate who received the largest majority of electoral votes would become president. The candidate who finished second would become vice president. (This was the first mention of the vice presidency at the convention.) If no candidate received a majority, the Senate would select the president and vice president from among the five candidates who received the greatest number of electoral votes.

As a corollary to its proposal for the Electoral College, the committee recommended that certain responsibilities be assigned to the vice president: to preside over the Senate, with the right to cast tie-breaking votes, and to act as president if the office became vacant before the president's term expired. Finally, the committee recommended that qualifications for president be stated in the Constitution. The president would have to be at least thirty-five years old, a natural-born citizen of the United States or a citizen at the time of the Constitution's enactment, and a resident of the United States for at least fourteen years.

For several days the delegates carefully considered the committee's complex proposal for presidential selection. On September 7 they passed it after making just one substantial change: the House of Representatives, not the Senate, would choose the president in the event of an Electoral College deadlock, with each state delegation casting one vote. The Senate still would choose the vice president if the electoral vote for that position was tied.

Having approved the Electoral College, the convention quickly acted to reduce the powers of the Senate, mostly in response to demands by the large states. The president was granted the authority to make treaties and to appoint ambassadors, public ministers, consuls, Supreme Court justices, federal judges, and all other officers whose appointments were not otherwise provided for. Senate confirmation would be required for all of these appointments. A two-thirds vote by the Senate was stipulated for ratifying treaties.

On September 8 the convention approved the final proposals of the Committee on Postponed Matters. The president was to be impeached by the House on grounds of "treason or bribery or other high crimes and misdemeanors against the United States" and removed from office if convicted by the Senate. The delegates added the vice president and other civil officers to the roster of those who were subject to impeachment, but they raised the majority needed for Senate conviction from a simple majority to two-thirds. In addition, the House was empowered to originate "all bills for raising revenue."

Having completed (or so they believed) their work on the Constitution, the delegates ended their business later that day by voting to create a five-member Committee of Style to write a polished final draft of the document for them to sign. The committee's leading members were Madison, Hamilton, and Gouverneur Morris, who seems to have done most of its work.

Final Adjustments (September 9–17). Even as the Committee of Style labored, the convention continued to modify some of its earlier decisions. On September 10 Madison urged that special constitutional conventions not be a part of the process of amending the Constitution. Instead, he argued, amendments should be initiated by a two-thirds vote of Congress or by two-thirds of the state legislatures, with approval by three-fourths of the states needed for ratification. Two days later, Hugh Williamson of North Carolina successfully moved that the requirement for overriding a presidential veto be reduced from a three-fourths vote of each house of Congress to a two-thirds vote. The Committee of Style incorporated these changes into its draft.

Meanwhile, some delegates were expressing more fundamental reservations about the Constitution. Randolph worried that the convention had gone far beyond its original charge from Congress to propose revisions in the Articles of Confederation. He urged that the proposed constitution be approved not just by state ratifying conventions but also by Congress and the state legislatures, even if this process necessitated a second constitutional convention. His fellow Virginian, George Mason, and Elbridge Gerry of Massachusetts objected to the absence of a bill of rights from the Constitution. So convinced were the other delegates that such an enumeration was unnecessary, observes historian Richard Beeman, that "not a single state delegation in the Convention supported the idea of a federal bill of rights."[50]

The Committee of Style reported to the convention on September 12.[51] Its draft not only reduced the number of articles from twenty-three to seven but also included some significant innovations. The most memorable of these was the preamble:

> We the People of the United States, in Order to form a more
> perfect Union, establish Justice, insure domestic Tranquility,
> provide for the common defence, promote the general Welfare,
> and secure the Blessings of Liberty to ourselves and our Posterity,
> do ordain and establish this Constitution for the United States of
> America.[52]

The committee also added a provision that barred states from passing laws to impair the obligations of contracts. Finally, it wrote vesting clauses for Congress and the president that, intentionally or not, suggested that the president might have executive powers beyond those enumerated in the Constitution.

The committee's draft met with widespread approval from the delegates, but they continued to tinker. Congress was stripped of its power to choose the national treasurer in favor of the president. A provision was added that the Constitution could not be altered to deprive a state of equal representation in the Senate without the state's consent. And, at the initiative of Gouverneur Morris and Elbridge Gerry, a compromise procedure for amending the Constitution was created that incorporated both the Committee of Detail's recommendation and Madison's plan. As finally agreed, a constitutional amendment could be proposed by either a two-thirds vote of both houses of Congress or a convention that Congress was required to call if two-thirds of the state legislatures requested one. In either case, three-fourths of the states would have to ratify an amendment for it to become part of the Constitution.

Despite these alterations, Randolph, Gerry, and Mason remained unhappy, expressing doubts about the magnitude of the changes that the convention was recommending. But their motion for another constitutional convention to consider any objections and recommendations that might be offered by the states was defeated by a vote of eleven states to none. As Jack Rakove has noted, the delegates realized from experience that "a second federal convention would assemble encumbered by proposals for amendments of all kinds and bound by instructions that would make it impossible to replicate the process of persuasion, compromise, and bargaining from which the completed Constitution had so laboriously emerged."[53]

The convention's work finished, the delegates assembled on September 17 to sign an engrossed, or final, copy of the Constitution. Forty-two of the original fifty-five delegates were still present in Philadelphia, and all but Randolph, Mason, and Gerry signed the document. Even then, the delegates could not resist some fine-tuning, unanimously approving at this time the Washington-supported motion to alter the apportionment formula for the House of Representatives.

Speaking first before and then during the signing ceremony, Benjamin Franklin offered the convention's most memorable benediction. To the delegates, he presented a long speech that—as read by Wilson because of Franklin's frailty—said in essence:

George Washington presiding at the signing of the Constitution in Philadelphia on September 17, 1787.
Source: Library of Congress.

Mr. President, I confess that there are several parts of this constitution which I do not approve, but I am not sure that I shall never approve them. For having lived long, I have experienced many instances of being obliged by better information, or fuller consideration, to change opinions even on important subjects, which I once thought right, but found to be otherwise. . . . I doubt too whether any other convention we can obtain may be able to make a better constitution. . . . It therefore astonishes me, Sir, to find this system approaching so near to perfection as it does; and I think it will astonish our enemies. . . . Thus I consent, Sir, to this constitution because I expect no better, and because I am not sure it is not the best.[54]

Later, as the last few delegates waited to affix their signatures to the Constitution, Franklin gestured to Washington's chair and said to those standing nearby,

Painters have found it difficult to distinguish in their art a rising from a setting sun. I have often in the course of this session and the vicissitudes of my hopes and fears as to its issue, looked at that sun behind the President without being able to tell whether it was rising or setting. But now, at length, I have the happiness to know that it is a rising and not a setting sun.

Notes

1. Max Farrand, ed., *The Records of the Federal Convention*, 3 vols. (New Haven: Yale University Press, 1911), 2: 641–643.

2. The idea is elaborated on in Erwin C. Hargrove and Michael Nelson, *Presidents, Politics, and Policy* (Baltimore: Johns Hopkins University Press, 1984), chap. 2.

3. Aristotle, *The Politics*, trans. Carnes Lord (Chicago: University of Chicago Press, 1984), bks. 3.14–18 and 4.

4. Alan Taylor, *American Revolutions: A Continental History, 1750–1804* (New York: W.W. Norton, 2016), 33.

5. Jack P. Greene, *Peripheries and Center: Constitutional Development in the Extended Polities of the British Empire and the United States, 1607–1788* (Athens: University of Georgia Press, 1986), chap. 2.

6. Thomas P. Slaughter, *Independence: The Tangled Roots of the American Revolution* (New York: Hill and Wang 2014), 406.

7. Quoted in Charles C. Thach Jr., *The Creation of the Presidency, 1775–1789* (Baltimore: Johns Hopkins University Press, 1969), 27.

8. Ibid.

9. Gordon S. Wood, *The Creation of the American Republic, 1776–1787* (Chapel Hill: University of North Carolina Press, 1969), 138.

10. Thomas Jefferson, *Notes on the State of Virginia*, ed. William Peden (Chapel Hill: University of North Carolina Press, 1955).

11. Michael J. Klarman, *The Framers' Coup: The Making of the United States Constitution* (New York: Oxford University Press, 2016), 18.

12. Christopher Collier and James Lincoln Collier, *Decision in Philadelphia: The Constitutional Convention of 1787* (New York: Ballantine, 1986), 5.

13. Lynne Cheney, *James Madison: A Life Reconsidered* (New York: Viking, 2014), 116.

14. Klarman, *The Framers' Coup*, 20.

15. Edward J. Larson, *The Return of George Washington, 1783–1789* (New York: William Morrow, 2014), 48.

16. To a large degree, British hostility to the United States was caused, or at least rationalized, by the American failure to comply with two provisions of the Treaty of Paris. One provision compelled the United States to reimburse British loyalists for property that had been seized from them during the war; the other required that prewar debts to British merchants be paid. Individual states actively resisted both of these requirements, and the national government was powerless to enforce them.

17. Wood, *Creation of the American Republic*.

18. Thach, *Creation of the Presidency*, 49, 52–53.

19. Woody Holton, *Unruly Americans and the Origins of the Constitution* (New York: Hill & Wang, 2007), 145–146.

20. George Washington to David Humphries, December 26, 1786, http://gwpapers .virginia.edu/documents/constitution/1784/index.html; George Washington to James

Madison, November 5, 1786, http://www.loc.gov/teachers/classroommaterials/connections/george-washington/file.html.

21. Lester Cappon, ed., *The Adams-Jefferson Letters* (Chapel Hill: University of North Carolina Press, 1959), 1: 196; Catherine Drinker Bowen, *Miracle at Philadelphia* (Boston: Little, Brown, 1966); and John P. Roche, "The Founding Fathers: A Reform Caucus in Action," *American Political Science Review* 55 (December 1961): 799–816; Klarman, *The Framers' Coup.*

22. Quoted in Collier and Collier, *Decision in Philadelphia*, 74.

23. Clinton Rossiter, *1787: The Grand Convention* (London: MacGibbon and Kee, 1968), 141.

24. Stanley Elkins and Eric McKitrick, "The Founding Fathers: Young Men of the Revolution," *Political Science Quarterly* 76 (June 1961): 181–216.

25. Taylor, *American Revolutions*, 373–375. Historian Charles A. Beard believed that the enactment of the Constitution, more than anything else, was a triumph of the "personality"—that is, financial and commercial—interests over the "realty," or landed interests. See Beard, *An Economic Interpretation of the Constitution* (New York: Macmillan, 1913). A powerful critique of this once-influential theory was offered by Forrest McDonald in *We the People: Economic Origins of the Constitution* (Chicago: University of Chicago Press, 1958).

26. Washington was right: even with the adoption of the change he prescribed, Anti-Federalist opponents of the proposed Constitution attacked it severely during the ratification debates for requiring each House member to represent too many people.

27. Collier and Collier, *Decision in Philadelphia*, 108.

28. Gordon S. Wood, *Revolutionary Characters: What Made the Founders Different* (New York: Penguin Press, 2006), 46.

29. Cappon, *Adams-Jefferson Letters*, 1: 196; Farrand, *Records*, 3: 35. All of Madison's notes on the convention are included in Farrand. A one-volume edition is James Madison, *Notes of Debates in the Federal Convention of 1787* (Athens: Ohio University Press, 1966).

30. Roche has argued that the preservation of secrecy by the delegates testifies to their sense of shared enterprise: even when they disagreed strongly about particular issues, they were sufficiently committed to the effort to keep their objections within the convention's walls. See Roche, "Founding Fathers."

31. Collier and Collier, *Decision in Philadelphia*, 120.

32. Jack N. Rakove, *Original Meanings: Politics and Ideas in the Making of the Constitution* (New York: Knopf, 1996), 14.

33. Walter Isaacson, *Benjamin Franklin: An American Life* (New York: Simon and Schuster, 2003), 445.

34. Quoted in Joseph J. Ellis, *His Excellency, George Washington* (New York: Knopf, 2004), 178.

35. The Virginia Plan can be found in Farrand, *Records*, 1: 20–22.

36. The Virginia Plan was one of two that were offered to the convention on May 29. Madison recorded in his notes for that day that Charles Pinckney of South Carolina also introduced a plan. But because Madison (who had long loathed Pinckney from their days together in Congress) neither described the Pinckney Plan nor included its text, scholars have had to reconstruct it as best they could from other documents—in particular, some notes found in the papers of James Wilson. The Pinckney Plan probably resembled the Virginia Plan in many ways. It, too, provided for a strong, three-branch national government. It seems to have been more specific regarding the executive, however. The executive was to consist of a single person (called "president") who would serve a seven-year term and be empowered, among other things, to recommend laws to the legislature, oversee the executive branch, and act as commander in chief of the military. Pinckney borrowed most of the elements of his plan from the Articles of Confederation, the Massachusetts Constitution,

and especially, the New York Constitution. Even though his plan was rejected, somewhere between twenty-one and forty-three specific contributions to the U.S. Constitution (depending on how one does the counting) seem to have been made by Pinckney. See S. Sidney Ulmer, "James Madison and the Pinckney Plan," *South Carolina Law Quarterly* 9 (Spring 1957): 415–444; Ulmer, "Charles Pinckney: Father of the Constitution?" *South Carolina Law Quarterly* 10 (Winter 1958): 225–247; and Collier and Collier, *Decision in Philadelphia*, 97.

37. Wood, *Revolutionary Characters*, 157, 160.

38. Rossiter, *1787*, 171.

39. The resolution of the Committee of the Whole can be found in Farrand, *Records*, 1: 235–237.

40. Richard J. Ellis, ed., *Founding the American Presidency* (Lanham, Md.: Rowman and Littlefield, 1999).

41. The New Jersey Plan can be found in Farrand, *Records*, 1: 242–245.

42. Hamilton's Plan can be found in ibid., 1: 291–293.

43. Ibid., 1: 288.

44. Ibid., 1: 289.

45. Ron Chernow, *Alexander Hamilton* (New York: Penguin Press, 2004), 232.

46. Clinton Rossiter dismisses this view in *Alexander Hamilton and the Constitution* (New York: Harcourt, Brace and World, 1964).

47. The Committee of Detail report can be found in Farrand, *Records*, 2: 177–189.

48. See note 29.

49. The recommendations of the Committee on Postponed Matters can be found in Farrand, *Records*, 2: 497–499, 508–509.

50. Richard Beeman, *Plain, Honest Men: The Making of the American Constitution* (New York: Random House, 2009), 342. James Wilson of Pennsylvania argued that any attempt to enumerate the rights of the people would necessarily be incomplete, posing the risk that "everything not expressly mentioned will be presumed to be purposely omitted" (343).

51. The Committee of Style draft can be found in Farrand, *Records*, 2: 590–603.

52. The preamble it replaced was blander and more state centered: "We the people of the states of New Hampshire, Massachusetts," and so on.

53. Rakove, *Original Meanings*, 107.

54. Farrand, *Records*, 2: 641–643.

Creating the Presidency

During the course of the Constitutional Convention, the presidency developed along two main lines. First, the loosely designed executive of the Virginia Plan took on greater clarity and specificity. Second, the plan's weak executive, which was subordinate to the legislature and initially seemed to be favored by most delegates, was made stronger. These two developments manifested themselves at the convention in a variety of specific issues of executive design. The issues included the number of the executive, the methods of executive selection and succession, the length and character of the term of office, the means of removing the executive in extraordinary circumstances, the institutional separation of the executive from the legislature, and the enumerated powers of the executive.

The Making of the Presidency: An Overview

The design of the executive was one of the most vexing problems of the Constitutional Convention, and solving it was the convention's most creative act. Other issues were more controversial, but they typically lent themselves to compromise solutions, such as the small states agreeing to split the difference with the large states and provide for a bicameral legislature and northern and southern delegates working out the three-fifths rule for counting enslaved people. When it came to the nature and powers of the executive, however, the delegates labored in a realm of such intellectual and political uncertainty that the politics of compromise was largely irrelevant. The result, although long in coming, was that "the presidency emerged not from the clash of wills to gain a long-contested point, but from a series of ingenious efforts to design a new institution that would be suitably energetic but safely republican."[1]

One problem the delegates encountered was that their experience offered several models of what they did not want in an executive but few models that they found attractive. The British monarch and the royal colonial governors had been, in their eyes, tramplers of liberty. The constitutions that nearly all of the states wrote after independence provided for governors who were unthreatening but also weak to the point of impotence. The national government of the Articles of Confederation, such as it was, had no chief executive at all.

A second problem that stymied the delegates derived from their general ambivalence about executive authority. They wanted an executive that was strong enough to enforce the law and check a runaway legislature but not so strong as to become despotic. This ambivalence was shared by the American people, whose hatred of monarchy existed side by side with their longing to make George Washington king. As political scientist Seymour Martin Lipset showed, Washington was a classic example of what the German sociologist Max Weber called a charismatic leader, one "treated as endowed with supernatural, superhuman, or at least specifically exceptional powers or qualities."[2] Historian Marcus Cunliffe records:

> Babies were being christened after him as early as 1775, and while he was still President, his countrymen paid to see him in waxwork effigy. To his admirers he was "godlike Washington," and his detractors complained to one another that he was looked upon as a "demigod" whom it was treasonous to criticize. "Oh Washington!" declared Ezra Stiles of Yale (in a sermon of 1783). "How I do love thy name! How have I often adored and blessed thy God, for creating and forming thee into the great ornament of humankind!"[3]

But the public's longing for Washington was just that: a longing for Washington, not for a hereditary monarchy. As Stanley Elkins and Eric McKitrick have pointed out, Washington's wide-ranging responsibilities as commander in chief during the Revolutionary War meant that "he had in a certain sense been acting as President of the United States since 1775."[4] Delegates and citizens alike knew that Washington would wield power responsibly and relinquish it voluntarily—he had already done so once. But would his successors? "The first man put at the helm will be a good one," Benjamin Franklin told the convention. "No body knows what sort may come afterwards."[5]

Despite the delegates' difficulties, the presidency gradually took shape as the convention wore on. For all their intellectual uncertainty, the delegates moved steadily in the direction of a more clearly defined executive. For all their ambivalence about power, they made the executive stronger than they were initially inclined to do.

Greater Clarity

Charles Thach noted in his classic book *The Creation of the Presidency* that Virginia delegate James Madison "has with much justice been called the father of the Constitution." But even as admiring a scholar as Thach conceded that "the claims for his paternity do not extend to the fundamentals of Article II," the executive article.[6]

Madison himself claimed no role in creating the presidency. As he wrote to Washington on April 16, 1787, less than a month before the scheduled opening of the convention, "I have scarcely ventured as yet to form my own opinion either of the manner in which [the executive] ought to be constituted or of the authorities with which it ought to be cloathed."[7] Madison's Virginia Plan offered the convention a shadowy and vaguely defined national executive. Even the basic structure of the executive—whether it would be a single person, a chaired board, or a committee—was unclear. In addition, the length of the executive's term was not specified, and its powers were not enumerated.[8]

Madison's fellow delegates seem to have shared his uncertainty. The only issues they resolved to their satisfaction during the convention's first two months were the unitary nature of the executive and its power to veto laws passed by the legislature, subject to override. The Committee of Detail, which began its work on July 24, helped matters some: it gave the executive the name *president*, provided for succession

George Washington, hero of the American Revolution and presiding officer of the Constitutional Convention, was to many people the personification of the new republic and of the presidency.

Source: Library of Congress.

if the office became prematurely vacant, and enumerated its powers. But the main issues that divided the delegates—the method of selecting the president, the length of the term, and the president's eligibility for reelection—were not resolved until September, when the Committee on Postponed Matters proposed selection by an Electoral College, a four-year term with no limit on reeligibility, and the creation of the vice presidency.

Greater Strength

For all the vagueness of its conception, the national executive of the Virginia Plan generally accorded with what most delegates at the start of the Constitutional Convention seem to have been seeking: an agent of restraint in a basically legislative government. The executive in Madison's proposal was weak (it was bound by a council and devoid of enumerated powers), but it certainly was stronger than in the one-branch legislative government of the Articles of Confederation. The executive also was subordinate to the legislature, which was empowered to elect it. But it was not subservient, as demonstrated by its fixed term, the veto power, and the bar on legislative reductions of the executive's salary.

Dissatisfied with the convention's early inclination toward a subordinate executive, a coterie of committed and talented delegates worked diligently and effectively to strengthen the office's constitutional power. They were led by two Pennsylvania delegates: James Wilson, who envisioned the executive as "the man of the people," and Gouverneur Morris, who regarded a properly constituted executive as "the great protector of the Mass of the people."[9] Although Wilson and Morris both favored a strong executive, they did so for different reasons. Morris thought that a strong executive would serve the people best by restraining public opinion.[10] Wilson thought that such an executive would enhance public influence. Historian Richard Beeman accurately describes Wilson as the only delegate who envisioned presidents "much like those we have today—vigorous and powerful, but based firmly on the will of the people."[11]

Despite these differences, during the course of the convention, the pro-executive group won victory after victory. Once the architects of the Constitution resolved to strengthen the national government—to create self-government on a grand scale—they had no recourse, it seemed, but to attempt to reconcile it with executive power. Their halting efforts to construct an energetic and independent executive became more decisive once they decided to give every state equal representation in the Senate. It was at that point, political scientist David Robertson has written, that "Madison began to assert that the president should have more power to pursue the nation's interest."[12]

Number of the Executive

The number of the executive was the first issue to rouse the delegates. The debate on number followed two tracks. First, should the executive be unitary or plural—that is, a single person or a board? Second, should the executive be forced to consult with a council before exercising some or all of its powers?

Unitary or Plural?

The Virginia Plan said nothing about the number of the executive, perhaps because Madison had no clear opinion on the matter or perhaps because, like Roger Sherman of Connecticut, he initially felt that the legislature should be free to define and then redefine the shape of the executive as it saw fit.

On June 1 the convention, meeting as the Committee of the Whole, heard a motion from Wilson that the executive be a single person. According to Madison's notes, "a considerable pause ensu[ed]" as the usually talkative delegates lapsed into silence.[13] They were discomforted by the prospect of discussing the issue in the presence of George Washington, whom everyone assumed would be the first leader of whatever executive branch they created.[14] After Franklin admonished his colleagues to speak freely, however, the debate was joined. The issue became an early test for the pro-executive delegates at the convention.

Edmund Randolph of Virginia and Sherman led the fight against Wilson's motion. Randolph, arguing that a single executive, by its nature, would be the "foetus of monarchy," proposed instead a three-person committee, with one member from each region of the country. Sherman, who regarded the ideal executive "as nothing more than an institution for carrying the will of the Legislature into effect," said he "wished the number might not be fixed, but that the legislature should be at liberty to appoint one or more as experience might dictate."[15] Franklin argued that the policies pursued by an executive board would be less easily changed and, therefore, more stable and consistent than those of an individual. In addition, he pointed out that the death or disability of an executive board member would not pose problems of succession, unlike the death or disability of a single executive.[16]

Wilson defended his motion shrewdly. To be sure, he argued, a single executive would be a source of "energy" and "dispatch"—that is, of vigorous and timely action—in the new government. But Wilson also claimed that a single executive was indispensable to controlling executive power—how could responsibility for incompetence or abuses of power be assigned to a committee?[17] These arguments were persuasive to most delegates. They feared monarchy, but they also realized how much the national government had suffered under the Articles of Confederation from the diffuseness of executive responsibility. As property owners, they worried about threats to the social order such as Shays's Rebellion and regarded a single executive as more likely than a committee to respond quickly and effectively to riot and discord.

On June 4 the convention voted strongly for a unitary executive. One of Washington's few recorded votes was in favor of this motion. Washington's concern to unify executive responsibility was born of his experience as the wartime commander in chief of the revolutionary forces. Lacking clear administrative authority, even in the appointment of his own officers, Washington complained bitterly of having "power without the means of execution when these ought to be coequal at least."[18] On average, the most vocal proponents of a unitary executive at the convention were nearly fifteen years younger than the opponents. The reason for this discrepancy, political scientist Richard J. Ellis has argued, is that

> the views of executive power of the older delegates were colored
> by their battles against the royal governors. The younger
> delegates who had come of age during the 1770s and 1780s were
> more worried about the weakness of executive power in the state
> constitutions and the Articles of Confederation.[19]

A Council?

The Virginia Plan provided that a "council of revision" consisting of the executive and "a convenient number of the National Judiciary" be created to veto laws passed by the legislature. All thirteen state constitutions provided for councils of some sort, most of which were legislatively selected. Sherman, who voted in the end for the single executive, said that he had done so only because he assumed it would be forced to share power with a council. Wilson, however, opposed a council because he believed that such a body would dilute the virtues of the unitary executive—energy, dispatch, and responsibility.

The proposal for a council was tabled on June 4 after two Massachusetts delegates, Elbridge Gerry and Rufus King, injected a new argument into the debate. Gerry and King questioned the wisdom of having judges participate in making laws on which they later would be asked to rule. Delegates also wondered what effect a council would have on executive power. Some saw it as a check on the executive, but others, including Madison, thought a council would buttress the executive with the support of the judiciary, thereby strengthening it in its relations with the legislature.

The council idea recurred in several guises throughout the convention. Morris and others tried to persuade the delegates to enact a purely advisory council, consisting mainly of the heads of the executive departments.[20] As late as September 7, George Mason of Virginia suggested that the House of Representatives or the Senate be charged to appoint an executive council with members from all regions of the country. "The Grand Signor himself had his Divan," Mason noted, drawing from Ottoman history.[21] But because no consensus ever formed about either the wisdom of having a council or the form it should take, the idea was abandoned.

Selection and Succession

Wilson was as much opposed to the clause in the Virginia Plan that provided for the executive "to be chosen by the National Legislature" as he was in favor of a unitary executive. Legislative selection would make the executive a creature of (and therefore subservient to) the legislature, Wilson believed. On June 1 he proposed instead that the executive be elected by the people. Wilson said he realized that his idea "might appear chimerical," but he could think of no better way to keep the executive and legislative branches "as independent as possible of each other, as well as of the states."[22]

The delegates dismissed Wilson's proposal for popular election. To some, the idea was just too democratic. (They thought democracy was suited only for small polities.) In addition, by requiring voters to pass judgment on candidates from distant states of whom they knew little or nothing, popular election seemed impractical. Mason stated both of these objections cogently: "It would be as unnatural to refer the choice of a proper character for chief Magistrate to the people, as it would, to refer a trial of colours to a blind man."[23] Speaking on behalf of the southern delegates, Madison added a more overtly political point: in direct elections, candidates from the more populous North almost always would win.[24]

Undiscouraged, Wilson returned to the convention on June 2 with a proposal for an Electoral College to select the executive. For purposes of election, each state would be divided into a few districts. The voters in these districts would choose electors, who in turn would gather at a central location to elect the executive. A plan similar to Wilson's was accepted in principle on July 19 and a modified version ultimately was adopted in September. But in the early days of the convention it still seemed too novel.[25] Delegates feared the mischief that might ensue when the electors met, perhaps instigated by agents of foreign governments. They also doubted whether "men of the 1st nor even of the 2d. grade" would be willing to serve as electors.[26] The delegates voted instead to affirm the legislative selection provision of the Virginia Plan.

The convention's decision to adopt legislative selection of the executive, although it was reaffirmed in several votes taken in July and August, was less a happy one than a return to its "default mode."[27] The source of the unhappiness was that in the delegates' minds a legislatively selected executive could not be allowed to stand for reelection lest executive powers and patronage be used, in effect, to bribe legislators for their votes. But the delegates also believed that the prospect of reelection was a valuable incentive to good performance in office and regretted that legislative selection ruled out executive reeligibility.

The result was an ongoing search for a selection process that was desirable in its own right and also allowed for reelection. This was no easy task. In the memorable description of political scientist Robert A. Dahl, "The Convention twisted and turned like a man tormented in his sleep by a bad dream as it tried to decide."[28] Of the ideas the delegates considered and rejected, wrote Clinton Rossiter, some were rather far-fetched:

> [E]lection by the state governors or by electors chosen by them, neither a scheme that could muster any support; nomination by the people of each state of "its best citizen," and election from this pool of thirteen by the national legislature or electors chosen by it, an unhelpful proposal of John Dickinson; election by the national legislature, with electors chosen by the state legislatures taking over whenever an executive sought reelection, a proposal of [Oliver] Ellsworth that found favor with four states; and, most astounding of all, election by a small group of national legislators chosen "by lot."[29]

The search for an alternative to legislative selection became more urgent after August 24. Until that day, no consideration had been given to how the legislature would choose the president. Now, by a vote of seven states to four, the convention approved a motion that Congress would elect the president by a "joint ballot" of all the members of the House of Representatives and Senate, following the practice most states used to elect their governors. This decision, by giving the large states a clear majority in the presidential selection process, threatened to reignite the controversy between large and small states that had already split the convention once. To avert this catastrophe, Sherman, the chief author of the Connecticut Compromise between the large and small states on legislative apportionment, moved on August 31 to refer the whole issue of presidential selection to the Committee on Postponed Matters.

On September 4 the committee proposed the Electoral College as a method to elect the president, with no restriction on the president's right to seek reelection. The president would be selected by a majority vote of the electors, who would be chosen by the states using whatever method each state decided to adopt. (The delegates expected that in time most states would entrust the selection of electors to the people.[30]) Every state would receive electoral votes equal in number to its representation in Congress. If no presidential candidate won the votes of a majority of electors, the Senate would elect the president from among the five highest electoral vote recipients. To prevent a cabal from forming in the Electoral College, electors would never meet as a national body. Instead, they would vote in their state capitals and then send the results to the Senate for counting. Finally, to ensure that the electors would not simply support a variety of home-state favorites, each was required to vote for two candidates for president, at least one from a different state, an idea first proposed by Gouverneur Morris on July 25. The runner-up in the presidential election would fill the newly created office of vice president.

The proposal for an Electoral College was generally well received by the delegates, who realized, as committee member John Dickinson later wrote, that "the Powers which we had agreed to vest in the President were so many and so great that I did not think the people would be willing to deposit them with him unless they themselves would be more immediately concerned in his Election."[31] As political scientist Andrew Rudalevige has noted, "The Electoral College [was] very much a salesman's straddle, allowing proponents of popular election and legislative selection both to tout its provisions."[32] Fred Barbash has listed several ways in which the proposal was "baited" with something for virtually every group at the convention:

For those in the convention anxious for the President to be allowed reelection, the committee made him eligible without limit.

For those worried about excessive dependence of the President on the national legislature, the committee determined that electors chosen as each state saw fit would cast ballots for the presidency.

For the large states and the South, the committee decided that the number of electors would be proportioned according to each state's combined representation in the House and Senate. . . .

For the small states, the committee determined that when no candidate won a majority of electoral votes, the Senate would choose the president from among the leading contenders.[33]

Only one aspect of the proposed Electoral College proved controversial among the delegates: Senate selection of the president in the absence of an Electoral College majority for any candidate. Large-state delegates objected because the Senate underrepresented them in favor of the small states. Moreover, not foreseeing the development of a two-party system, some delegates believed that after Washington (the obvious choice as the first president), majorities seldom would form in the Electoral College, and the Senate would choose most presidents. George Mason estimated that the Electoral College would fail to reach a majority "nineteen times in twenty."[34]

Sherman proposed what historian Carol Berkin has called "a brilliant solution": let the House of Representatives elect the president if the Electoral College failed to produce a majority but assign each state's House delegation a single vote.[35] The Senate still would choose the vice president in the event of a tie. Quickly, on September 6, the convention agreed.

One issue that the creation of the vice presidency resolved, at least partially, was what would happen if the president died, resigned, became disabled, or was impeached and removed. The Committee of Detail was the first to deal with the matter. It recommended that the president of the Senate "discharge the powers and duties of [the presidency] . . . until another President of the United States be chosen, or until the disability of the President be ended." When Madison and other delegates objected that this proposal might give the Senate an incentive to remove the president in favor of one of its own members, the issue was referred to the Committee on Postponed Matters.

The committee proposed that the vice president, not a senator, be president of the Senate. It also designated the vice president as the person to step in if a vacancy occurs in the presidency. The convention agreed but only after passing an additional motion, discussed later in this chapter, that seemed to call for a special presidential election before the expiration of the prematurely departed president's term. Somehow this intention was lost when the Committee of Style wrote its final draft of the Constitution. No one caught the error. As a result, the convention left the Constitution vague on two important matters. First, in the event of the president's death, resignation, disability, or removal, did the vice president become president or merely assume the powers and duties of the office as an acting president? Second, would the vice president serve out the unexpired balance of the president's term or only fill in until a special election could be held to pick a new president?

Term of Office

Questions about length of term, eligibility for reelection, and selection were so interwoven in the minds of the delegates that they could not resolve any one of them without resolving the others. Indeed, one political scientist has compared their efforts to sort out these questions to a game of "three-dimensional chess."[36]

The Virginia Plan left the length of the executive's term of office blank—literally: "Resolved, that a National Executive be . . . chosen by the National Legislature for the term of _____ years." The plan also stipulated that the executive was "to be ineligible a second time." When these provisions came before the Committee of the Whole on June 1, a variety of alternatives was proposed, including a three-year term with no limit on reeligibility, a three-year term with two reelections allowed, and a seven-year term with no reeligibility at all. Although the delegates approved the single seven-year term, the vote was close, five states to four.

Underlying the delegates' uncertainty was the relationship between two aspects of the executive that they eventually came to regard as incompatible: eligibility for reelection and legislative selection. Mason explained why the Constitution could not include both: if the legislature could reelect the executive, there would be a constant "temptation on the side of the Executive to intrigue with the Legislature for a re-appointment," using political patronage and illegitimate favors to buy legislators' votes.[37] Nevertheless, on July 17 the convention voted for both legislative selection and reeligibility. When James McClurg of Virginia pointed out the contradiction between these two decisions, the one-term limit on the executive was reinstated. McClurg, supported by Morris and by Jacob Broom of Delaware, offered a different way out of the dilemma: election of the executive by the legislature for a life term. But this proposal smacked too much of monarchy to suit most of the other delegates.

On July 24 and 26 the convention voted again to have the legislature select the executive for a single seven-year term. But the advantages the delegates saw in reeligibility were so powerful that the issue remained alive. Reeligibility would allow the nation to keep a good executive in office and give the executive what Morris called "the great motive to good behavior, the hope of being rewarded with a re-appointment."[38] In that era, "Ambition was neither a Christian nor a republican virtue," biographer Fred Kaplan has written. "Honor and rewards should search out deserving men, not be sought after."[39] Nevertheless, Alexander Hamilton later argued in *Federalist* No. 72, even an executive whose behavior was governed by personal motives such as "ambition," "avarice," or "the love of fame" would do a good job in order to hold onto the office that could fulfill those desires.[40] More ominously, Morris warned: "Shut the Civil road to Glory & he may be compelled to seek it by the sword."[41]

To complicate their task further, the delegates' choice between legislative selection and reeligibility implied a related decision between a short term and a long term. If the executive were chosen by the legislature for a single term only, the delegates believed, the term should be long. If the executive were eligible for reelection, it should be short.

In late August the convention changed course for the last time. Effectively deciding against legislative selection of the president, the delegates created the Committee on Postponed Matters to propose an alternative. The committee's recommendation, adopted by the convention, was that the Electoral College choose the president for a four-year term with no limit on reeligibility. Even this relatively short term was longer than that of any state governor.

Removal

As the convention unfolded, the delegates realized they ought to provide for situations in which the executive should be removed from office before the four-year term expired.[42] Serious abuse of power was one such situation. The remedy was impeachment. Disability was the other, but even at convention's end, the delegates were less than clear about what ought to happen if the executive became disabled.

Impeachment

Impeachment, a traditional practice of the British political system, has deep historical roots. During the seventeenth century, as Richard Ellis has written, impeachment of the king's ministers and councilors by the House of Commons, with trial by the House of Lords, "became a tool in Parliament's struggle to rein in the power of the monarchy and to make ministers of the Crown accountable to Parliament."[43] In the eighteenth century, when the House of Commons gained the power to force ministers to resign after a vote of no confidence, impeachment waned in importance. But the tradition of executive accountability remained.

Although the Virginia Plan made no detailed provision for impeaching the executive (it merely said that the "supreme tribunal" would "hear and determine . . . impeachments of any National officers"), most of the delegates agreed that some mechanism should be included in the Constitution. Even proponents of a strong executive realized that their goal could be achieved only if the other delegates were assured that an out-of-control president could be removed from office.

The convention's consensus on impeachment became apparent on June 2, when the Committee of the Whole passed North Carolina delegate Hugh Williamson's motion that the executive be "removable on impeachment and conviction of malpractice or neglect of duty."[44] Impeachment is analogous to indictment by a grand jury. For the impeached official to be removed from office, it must be followed by a trial and conviction.

The consensus was confirmed and strengthened on July 19, when Gouverneur Morris suggested that if the executive was assigned a short term of office, there would be no need for impeachment because the passage of time would lead to the executive's removal soon enough. Morris was answered the next day by Gerry, Randolph, Franklin, and Mason, all of whom made clear that they regarded impeachment not only as a vital safeguard against and punishment for abuses of power but also (at least in Franklin's view) as a way to remove tyrants without "recourse . . . to assassination." Morris retreated, declaring that he was persuaded by his colleagues' arguments. Unlike a king who has "a life interest" in the nation's welfare, Morris added, "our Magistrate . . . may be bribed by a greater interest to betray his trust," especially by "foreign pay."[45]

The Committee of Detail tried to clarify Williamson's definition of the grounds for presidential impeachment, changing it from the vague "malpractice or neglect of duty" to the somewhat more specific "treason, bribery, or corruption." It also created a mechanism for removal: "impeachment by the House of Representatives and conviction in the Supreme Court."

The convention did not take up the impeachment provision of the committee's report until August 27, when Morris asked that it be tabled. He argued that if as still seemed possible, the convention decided to create an executive council that included the chief justice of the United States, the Court should not be involved in the impeachment process. The delegates agreed to Morris's motion without objection. Later that week, on August 31, the Committee on Postponed Matters was formed and took charge of the impeachment issue.

The committee made its three-part recommendation on September 4: first, impeachment by the House; second, trial by the Senate, with the chief justice presiding; and third, impeachment and conviction on grounds of treason or bribery but not the broad offense of "corruption." On September 8 Mason complained that to bar only treason and bribery "will not reach many great and dangerous offenses," including certain "attempts to subvert the Constitution." Drawing from the constitutions of six states, including his own state of Virginia, Mason proposed that "maladministration" be added to the list of impeachable actions.[46] After Madison objected that in practice maladministration would mean nothing more than unpopularity with Congress, Mason moved to substitute "other high crimes and misdemeanors," a term from fourteenth-century English common law that referred to serious abuses of constitutional authority. This definition passed, despite Madison's continuing objection to its breadth.

The delegates made three other modifications to the committee's impeachment proposal on September 8. The majority required for Senate conviction was raised to two-thirds. The vice president and "all civil officers of the United States" were made subject to impeachment in the same way as the president. Finally, to remind senators that they should vote impartially, the delegates decided that "they shall be on Oath or Affirmation" during impeachment trials.

Disability

Although the delegates were thorough and deliberate in considering the grounds for and process of impeachment, they treated presidential disability carelessly. The matter was first put before the convention on August 6 as part of a provision of the Committee of Detail report that dealt mainly with succession. It read: "In the case of his . . . disability to discharge the powers and duties of his office, the President of the Senate shall exercise those powers and duties, until another President of the United States be chosen, or until the disability of the President be removed."

On August 27, when this provision of the committee's report came before the convention, John Dickinson of Delaware complained that "it was too vague. What is the extent of the term 'disability' & who is to be the judge of it?"[47] The delegates decided to postpone their discussion of disability until another time, presumably intending to supply answers to these questions. But that time never came. Disability was left undefined in the Constitution, and no process was created either to determine if a president is disabled or to transfer the powers and duties of the presidency to someone else. Instead, the Committee on Postponed Matters merely named the vice president, rather than the president of the Senate, as the successor to a disabled president and substituted "inability" for "disability," without explaining what difference, if any, this substitution made.

Institutional Separation from Congress

Many of the delegates were strongly influenced by the idea that to preserve liberty, government should incorporate the principle of separation of powers. Political philosophers of the Enlightenment, including England's John Locke, had articulated this idea, but no version was more familiar than that of French writer Baron de Montesquieu. As the author of *L'Esprit des lois* (The Spirit of the Laws) in 1748, Montesquieu was "the oracle who is always consulted and cited" on the subject of separation of powers, wrote Madison in *Federalist* No. 47. One passage in Montesquieu's book, which the delegates knew well and Madison quoted, stated:

> When the legislative and executive powers are united in the same person or body, there can be no liberty because apprehensions may arise lest *the same* monarch or senate should enact *tyrannical laws to execute* them in a tyrannical manner. . . . Were the power of judging joined with the legislative, the life and liberty of the subject would be exposed to arbitrary control, for *the judge* would then be *the legislator.*[48]

Montesqui

As applied in the Constitution, the separation of powers principle did not require a strict division of labor in which each branch of the government is assigned complete and exclusive power to perform certain functions. Indeed, the Constitution assigns few powers to the federal government that are not shared by two or more branches. To the delegates, separation of powers actually meant something more like "separated institutions sharing powers"—that is, a joint exercise of the government's powers by an executive and legislature whose membership does not overlap.[49] Some blending of executive, legislative, and judicial powers was necessary, Madison argued in *Federalist 48*, "to give to each a constitutional control over the others."[50] Defenders of a strong executive were especially concerned that the president be given specific grants of power, including the veto, to prevent Congress from encroaching on its authority.

From the beginning, the convention imposed two prohibitions to preserve institutional separation within the government. The first banned alterations in the incumbent executive's salary. The second forbade simultaneous membership in the legislative and executive branches. Both prohibitions were in the Virginia Plan and remained substantially unaltered in the final Constitution.

Salary

Immediately after the clause stating that the executive shall be chosen by the legislature, the Virginia Plan provided that the executive shall "receive punctually at stated times, a fixed compensation for the services rendered, in which no increase or diminution shall be made so as to affect the Magistracy existing at the time of increase or diminution." In view of the Virginia Plan's brevity and generality, the level of detail in this provision is remarkable, as is the priority Madison assigned to it. Clearly, Madison feared that the legislature might either infringe on executive independence by lowering the executive's salary or reward or entice the executive by increasing the salary.

During the course of the convention, the provision for executive salary was modified only slightly. The delegates eventually added stipulations that "he shall not receive within [his term of office] any other Emolument from the United States, or any of them" or from "any King, Prince, or foreign State." On June 2 Franklin urged that the executive not be compensated at all. To attach a salary to the position, he said, "united in view of the same object" two "passions which have a powerful influence on the affairs of such men. These are ambition and avarice, the love of power, and the love of money. . . . Place before the eyes of men a post of *honor* that shall be at the same time a place of *profit,* and they will move heaven and earth to obtain it."[51] The delegates gave Franklin's words courteous attention but no more. Their concern was to protect the executive from the legislature, not to create an office that only the rich could afford to occupy.

Membership

The delegates' commitment to separating membership in Congress from the executive branch did not waver. The Virginia Plan said that legislators were "ineligible to any office established by a particular State, or under the authority of the United States, except those peculiarly belonging to the functions of the first branch [the legislature], during the term of service, and for the space of _____ after its expiration." The final document, although lifting the restriction on legislators holding executive office after they left Congress, included essentially the same provision: "no Person holding any Office under the United States, shall be a Member of either House during his Continuance in Office." The Constitution also prohibited members of Congress from serving as electors in presidential elections.

The delegates wanted to keep the membership of the legislative and executive branches separate to prevent the executive from, in effect, bribing members of Congress with jobs and salaries. On June 22 Pierce Butler of South Carolina, supported by Mason, "appealed to the example of G[reat] B[ritain] where men got into Parl[iamen]t, that they might get offices for themselves or their friends. This was the source of corruption that ruined their Govt."[52] On June 23 Butler added:

> To some of the opposers he [George III] gave pensions—others offices, and some, to put them out of the house of commons, he made lords. The great Montesquieu says, it is unwise to entrust persons with power, which by being abused operates to the advantage of those entrusted with it.

The office-holding issue was raised again on August 14, when John Mercer of Maryland took the opposite side of the question. He argued that because "governments can only be maintained by *force* or *influence*" and the president lacks force, to "deprive him of influence by rendering the members of the Legislature ineligible to Executive offices" would reduce the president to "a mere phantom of authority."[53] Unpersuaded, the delegates did not alter their earlier decision, either then or on September 3, when Wilson and Charles Pinckney argued that honorable people would be reluctant to serve in the new government under a constitution that presumed they were too corrupt to faithfully fulfil the responsibilities of more than one office.[54]

Nothing was said during the convention about judges holding executive offices. The New Jersey Plan would have prohibited them from doing so, but the subject never was discussed on the convention floor. Indeed, most of the proposals that delegates made for an executive council included one or more federal judges as members. Political scientist Robert Scigliano has argued that allowing judges to hold executive office was not an oversight on the delegates' part. Instead, they regarded the executive and judicial powers as joined because both involved carrying out the law. According to Scigliano, the delegates also believed that Congress would be the most powerful branch in the new government unless the executive and the judiciary could unite when necessary to restrain it.[55]

Enumerated Powers

The convention was slow to enumerate the powers of either the presidency or the other branches of the government. Indeed, the delegates' initial inclination seems to have been to give each branch a general grant of power rather than a specific list. The Virginia Plan empowered the legislature simply "to legislate in all cases to which the separate states are incompetent, or in which the harmony of the United States may be interrupted by the exercise of individual [state] Legislation." The executive, in addition to sharing the veto with a council, was to execute the national laws.

The advantage the delegates saw in a general grant of power (which they approved both while meeting as the Committee of the Whole and soon afterward in convention) was that the alternative, a specific enumeration, risked limiting the government to a list of powers that the passage of time would render obsolete. But the convention was uneasy with its choice. "Incompetent" was a vague word, easily subject to abuse, and so was any other word or phrase they might devise for a general grant.

Reading the delegates' mood, the Committee of Detail enumerated each branch's powers in the draft constitution that it presented to the convention. The delegates' reaction confirmed the committee's judgment. Although they debated each proposed power separately, they never questioned the decision to enumerate.

All the powers of the presidency are detailed in Article II of the Constitution except the veto power, which is in Article I, section 7. The powers are discussed below in the order they appear in the Constitution. So are three other provisions of Article II: the president's title, oath of office, and qualifications.

Veto

The right to veto acts passed by the legislature was the only specific grant of power to the executive proposed in the Virginia Plan. The states' recent experience with weak governors and powerful legislatures was proof enough to most delegates that the veto was indispensable to executive self-defense against legislative encroachments. Even so, they were initially reluctant to cede too much responsibility to the executive. After all, as legal historian Michael Klarman has pointed out, "the first three grievances listed in the Declaration of Independence had been directed at abuses of the veto power by the king."[56]

The Virginia Plan provided that the executive could cast a veto only with the cooperation of a council of judges. Madison believed that support from such a council would buttress the executive's willingness to cast vetoes. He based this belief on the contrasting experiences of New York, where the governor alone had the veto power and almost never used it, and Massachusetts, where council-supported governors vetoed bills freely.[57] The plan also stipulated that a vetoed act would become law if an unspecified majority of both houses of the legislature voted to override it.

On June 4 Wilson and Hamilton urged the delegates, then meeting as the Committee of the Whole, to grant the executive an absolute veto—that is, a veto not subject to legislative override. Franklin, Sherman, Mason, and others rose in opposition to this suggestion, invoking their own and the public's memories of the king and his royal governors, who had cast absolute vetoes against acts passed by colonial legislatures. "We are not indeed constituting a British Government, but a more dangerous monarchy, an elective one," warned Mason, who wanted to empower the executive merely to postpone the enactment of an offensive law in the hope that the legislature would decide to revise it.[58] Elbridge Gerry found a middle ground that was acceptable to most of the delegates: an executive veto, subject to override by a two-thirds vote of each house of the legislature. The recommendation that the executive share the veto power with a council was tabled.

In its report of August 6 the Committee of Detail, although faithfully reflecting the recommendations of the Committee of the Whole concerning the veto, also sought to settle an unresolved issue. The committee stipulated that after a bill was passed and presented, the president would have seven days in which to respond. If the president neither signed nor vetoed the bill during that week, it would become law. But the committee made an important exception to prevent Congress from getting its way by adjourning before the president had a chance to cast a veto. If Congress adjourned during the seven-day period, the president had merely to ignore the bill for it to be vetoed. Such vetoes later became known as "pocket vetoes," the image being of the president sticking the bill in a back pocket.

On August 15 and 16 the convention voted to modify the Committee of Detail's report in ways that strengthened the president's veto power. The two-thirds requirement for congressional override of a veto was raised to three-fourths. In addition, the period in which a president could cast a veto was lengthened from seven days to ten days, not including Sundays. Finally, to prevent Congress from evading a veto by passing legislation and calling it something other than a "bill," the veto power was extended to "every order, resolution, or vote" of Congress.

Only one further modification was made to the veto. On September 12, in a gesture designed to persuade delegates suspicious of presidential power to sign the Constitution, the convention voted to make veto overrides easier by restoring the two-thirds requirement. Even so, the president's veto power, like the appointment power discussed later in this chapter, exceeded that of any state governor at the time.

"The Executive Power"

The Virginia Plan began the executive article by stating "that a national Executive be instituted." The Committee of the Whole modified this provision of the plan by adding "to consist of a single person." The Committee of Detail, however, proposed "vesting" clauses to introduce the articles for all three branches of government:

> The legislative power shall be vested in a Congress. . . .
>
> The Executive Power of the United States shall be vested in a single person. His stile shall be, "The President of the United States of America," and his title shall be, "His Excellency."
>
> The Judicial Power of the United States shall be vested in one Supreme Court, and in such inferior courts as shall, when necessary, from time to time, be constituted by the Legislature of the United States.

The vesting clause that the Committee of Detail proposed for the president was particularly important because it made clear that the powers of the presidency derive directly from the Constitution, not from discretionary grants by Congress. But the clause was less instructive on another important aspect of presidential power. As political scientist Richard M. Pious has noted, "'Executive Power' was a general term, sufficiently ambiguous so that no one could say precisely what it meant. It was possible that the words referred to more than the enumerated powers that followed, and might confer a set of unspecified executive powers."[59] First among these unspecified powers was prerogative, which John Locke had discussed at length in his *Second Treatise of Government*, a book that was widely familiar among the delegates. Locke argued that in times of crisis, laws that are inadequate to the challenges at hand should temporarily "give way to the executive power, viz., that as much as may be, all the members of society are to be preserved." Prerogative, according to Locke, is "the people's permitting their rulers to do several things of their own free choice, where the law was silent, or sometimes, too, against the direct letter of the law, for the public good, and their acquiescing in it when so done."[60]

The theory that the powers of the presidency extend beyond those listed in the Constitution is supported by the language of the document itself, thanks to a "joker," as Charles Thach called it, that Morris, the chief drafter for the Committee of Style, tossed into the final version. The committee's charge was merely to put the Constitution into polished language. "Positively with respect to the executive article," noted Thach, Morris "could do nothing." His pro-executive biases were so well-known that any changes involving the presidency would have been detected quickly. Morris left the vesting clause for the executive unaltered ("the executive Power shall be vested in a President of the United States of America"), but he changed the vesting clause for Congress to read: "All legislative Powers *herein granted* shall be vested in a Congress of the United States" (emphasis added).

Thach suspected that Morris did his tinkering "with full realization of the possibilities"—that is, presidents could later claim that the different phrasing of the two branches' vesting clauses implies that there are executive powers beyond those "herein granted." Otherwise, why would the Constitution not apply those restricting words to the president in the same way it does to Congress? "At any rate," Thach concluded, "whether intentional or not, it [the difference between the two vesting clauses] admitted an interpretation of executive power which would give the president a field of activity wider than that outlined by the enumerated powers."[61]

Commander in Chief

Because the Virginia Plan said nothing about who would direct the armed forces, the delegates took for granted during the early stages of the convention that Congress would be the controlling branch, as it had been under the Articles of Confederation. The issue did not come up for debate in the Committee of the Whole. The Committee of Detail, however, suggested a military role for the president in its enumeration of the powers of each branch.

The committee proposed that the president "shall be commander in chief of the Army and Navy of the United States, and of the Militia of the several States." Commander in chief was a title nearly all state governors had. It involved authority not to initiate a war but rather to direct the fighting once a war was under way. Not willing to leave such an important act of sovereignty open to misinterpretation, however, the committee also recommended that Congress be empowered "to make war; to raise armies; to build and equip fleets; to call forth the aid of the militia, in order to execute the laws of the Union; enforce treaties; suppress insurrections, and repel invasions."

The meaning of these provisions confused the delegates when they took them up for consideration on August 17. Clearly, Congress's power to "make" war included directing the actual conduct of the fighting, but so did the president's power as "commander in chief of the Army and the Navy." Which branch actually would order soldiers and sailors into action? Which would tell them where to go and what to do when they got there?

The debate on the convention floor about the powers of war was brief and went only part way toward resolving the ambiguities created by the Committee of Detail. Pierce Butler, doubting that Congress would be able to react quickly enough if an urgent need for military action should arise, urged the convention to vest the power to make war in the president, "who will have all the requisite qualities, and will not make war but when the Nation will support it." Madison and Gerry agreed that Congress might be unable to respond to a foreign invasion promptly, perhaps because it was not in session. But, unwilling to entrust the president with such vast military powers, they "moved to insert 'declare' [war], striking out 'make' war; leaving to the Executive the power to repel sudden attacks." Sherman agreed: "The Executive shd. be able to repel and not to commence war."[62] Madison and Gerry's motion passed.

As for control of the state militia, on August 27 the convention approved without discussion a motion by Sherman that the president act as commander in chief of the militia only "when called into the actual service of the U.S." The clause as finally written in the Constitution reads: "The President shall be Commander in Chief of the Army and Navy of the United States, and of the Militia of the several States, when called into the actual Service of the United States."

"Require the Opinion"

The Constitution authorizes the president to "require the Opinion, in writing, of the principal Officer in each of the executive Departments, upon any Subject relating to the Duties of their respective Offices."[63] This curious provision (Hamilton described it in *Federalist* No. 74 "as a mere redundancy in the plan, as the right for which it provides would result of itself from the office"[64]) was proposed on September 4 by the Committee on Postponed Matters and adopted by a unanimous vote on September 7. But the clause's origin lay in the Virginia Plan's proposal for an executive council, an idea that recurred frequently during the convention.

Although most delegates seem to have favored some sort of council, they never created one because they held such varied opinions about who should be on it and whether its relationship to the president should be merely advisory or involve the shared exercise of executive powers. One version of the council idea was included in a sweeping plan for the organization of the executive branch that Gouverneur Morris and Charles Pinckney introduced on August 20. The Morris–Pinckney plan provided for the creation of five departments: domestic affairs, commerce and finance, foreign affairs, war, and marine. The "principal officers" of each department would be appointed by the president and serve at the president's pleasure. Together with the chief justice of the United States, they would constitute a Council of State whose purpose would be to

> assist the President in conducting the Public affairs. . . . The President may from time to time submit any matter to the discussion of the Council of State, and *he may require the written opinions of any one or more of the members:* But he shall in all cases exercise his own judgment, and either Conform to such opinions or not as he may think proper; and every officer abovementioned shall be responsible for his opinion on the affairs relating to his particular Department (emphasis added).[65]

The Morris–Pinckney plan was not debated by the delegates, and although the Constitution presumed that executive departments would be created, none were provided for or named. But the proposal to empower the president to require written opinions from individual department heads on matters relating to their responsibilities seems to have been the basis for the September 4 recommendation of the Committee on Postponed Matters. On September 7, after Mason, Franklin, Wilson, Dickinson, and Madison again urged that a council be created, their colleagues, frustrated by their inability to agree on a specific proposal and eager to conclude the convention's business, approved the committee's recommendation as written.

Pardon

Hamilton was the first delegate to suggest that the delegates grant the president the power to pardon criminals. In his long speech to the convention on June 18, he urged that the executive "have the power of pardoning all offences except Treason; which he shall not pardon without the approbation of the Senate."[66] Perhaps persuaded by Hamilton's proposal, the Committee of Detail recommended that the president "shall have power to grant reprieves and pardons; but his pardon shall not be pleadable in bar of an impeachment" (that is, to prevent an impeachment).

The pardon power is a power of kings. In Great Britain all crimes were regarded as offenses against the Crown. Accordingly, the power to forgive was a royal prerogative. Crimes in the United States were regarded as offenses against the law, not the executive, which is why no state constitution allowed governors a unilateral pardon power.[67] It is therefore remarkable that the delegates resisted efforts to modify the committee's recommendation in any substantial way. Sherman's August 25 motion to require the president to gain the Senate's consent for a pardon was defeated by a vote of eight states to one. Two days later Luther Martin of Maryland moved to allow pardons only "after conviction." He withdrew the motion when Wilson, using the crime of forgery as an example, objected that "pardon before conviction might be necessary in order to obtain the testimony of accomplices."

On September 12 the Committee of Style clarified one aspect of the pardon power by limiting it to "offences against the United States"—that is, to violations of federal rather than state law. A September 15 motion by Randolph to disallow pardons for treason ("The President may himself be guilty. The Traytors may be his own instruments") was defeated by a vote of eight states to two after Wilson argued that if the president "be himself a party to the guilt he can be impeached and prosecuted."[68] The pardon entered the Constitution as the president's only important unchecked power.

Although no thorough case for granting the pardon power to the president was ever offered at the convention, Hamilton's defense of it in *Federalist* No. 74 may reflect the delegates' thinking. Hamilton began by pleading the need for leeway in the criminal justice system to "make exceptions in favor of unfortunate guilt." As to pardons for treason, he wrote, perhaps with Shays's Rebellion in mind,

> The principal argument for reposing the power of pardoning in
> this case in the Chief Magistrate is this: in seasons of insurrection

or rebellion there are often critical moments when a well-timed offer of pardon to the insurgents or rebels may restore the tranquility of the commonwealth; and which, if suffered to pass unimproved, it may never be possible afterwards to recall.[69]

"Make Treaties"

At the start of the convention, most delegates seemed to assume that the power to make treaties with other sovereign nations would be vested in Congress. That had been the practice under the Articles of Confederation, and although the Virginia Plan said nothing specific about treaties, it did provide that "the National Legislature ought to be impowered to enjoy the Legislative Rights vested in Congress by the Confederation."

The first suggestion that the treaty power be shared between the legislative and executive branches came from Hamilton. One provision of the plan of government he proposed on June 18 was that the executive should "have with the approbation and advice of the Senate the power of making all treaties."[70] The delegates did not discuss Hamilton's suggestion on the convention floor, and it appeared to be dead when the August 6 report of the Committee of Detail provided instead that "the Senate shall have power to make treaties."

The committee's proposal sparked heated debate, much of it spawned by changes in the design of the Senate that had occurred during the convention. The conclave of national statesmen envisioned by the Virginia Plan had become a states-dominated body, a smaller and perhaps more easily manipulated cousin of the Articles' congress.[71] Mason argued that an exclusive treaty-making power would enable the Senate to "sell the whole country by means of treaties."[72] Madison thought that the president, who would represent the entire country, should make treaties.

Regional concerns also were expressed. Southern delegates worried that their states' right to free navigation of the Mississippi River might be surrendered in a treaty. New Englanders expressed similar fears about their right to fish in the waters near Newfoundland. Having reached an impasse, the delegates referred the treaty issue to the Committee on Postponed Matters.

On September 4 the committee recommended that the president, "with the advice and Consent of the Senate," be granted the treaty-making power and that no treaty be approved "without the consent of two-thirds of the members [of the Senate] present." The provision for a two-thirds majority was designed to assuage the separate concerns of southerners and New

Englanders that they would be outvoted on issues of regional importance. It was highly controversial and provoked numerous motions to revise. One proposal would have deleted the two-thirds requirement for ratification in favor of a simple majority. Another would have strengthened the requirement by stipulating two-thirds approval by the entire membership of the Senate, not just those who were present for the vote. Another would have included the House of Representatives in the treaty ratification process. Yet another proposal—which initially passed and then was rejected—would have applied the simple majority rule to treaties whose purpose was to conclude a war. In the end, however, the committee's recommendation of a two-thirds vote of the senators present was accepted.

Only one motion was made to modify the president's role in treaty making. Madison moved to allow two-thirds of the Senate, acting alone if it chose to do so, to conclude peace treaties. Madison worried that the president, who inevitably would derive unusual power and prominence from a state of war, might be tempted to "impede a treaty of peace." His motion failed when Nathaniel Gorham of Massachusetts pointed out that Congress could end a war by simply refusing to appropriate funds to continue the fighting.[73]

Appointment and Commissioning

Article II, section 2, of the Constitution provides three methods for appointing federal judges and other unelected government officials: presidential appointment with Senate confirmation (the ordinary method); presidential appointment without Senate confirmation (when the Senate is in recess); and when Congress so determines by statute, appointment of certain "inferior Officers" (that is, officers subordinate to the heads of the departments or the courts of law) by the relevant department heads or courts. Clearly, the delegates moved a long way from both the Articles of Confederation, which vested the appointment power entirely in Congress, and the Virginia Plan, which proposed to continue that practice.

From start to finish, the appointment power was one of the most contentious issues at the convention. Although, as Richard Ellis has shown, no delegate doubted that "it was the legislature and not the executive that should have the power to create offices, there the agreement ended."[74] On June 1 the delegates, meeting as the Committee of the Whole, approved Madison's motion to modify the Virginia Plan slightly by adding to the then-limited powers of the executive the ambiguous phrase "to appoint to offices in cases not otherwise provided for."[75] But this decision simply opened the door to stronger advocates of executive power, such as Wilson and Hamilton, who wanted to make the appointment of judges, ambassadors, and other government officials a purely executive responsibility, with no involvement by the legislature.

Heated debates erupted periodically in June and July about issues such as which branch of government would be most prone to favoritism in appointments and which would know best the qualifications of prospective appointees. Many delegates, mindful of how George III and his colonial governors had used government appointments as patronage plums to curry support among legislators, dreaded giving this power to even a homegrown executive.

On July 21 the delegates voted to assign the Senate sole responsibility for judicial appointments. The Committee of Detail added the appointment of ambassadors to the Senate's list of powers and then stipulated that Congress as a whole would elect the national treasurer. The committee also confirmed the convention's earlier decision that the president "shall appoint officers in all cases not otherwise provided for by this Constitution" and authorized the president to "commission all the officers of the United States." It remained unclear, however, where responsibility would lie for appointing the heads of the departments and other departmental officials and employees.

On August 24, at a time in the convention when the large-state delegates were doing their best to trim back the powers of the small state-dominated Senate, they passed a motion that although not altogether clear seemed to expand the president's right to make most appointments while still leaving complete responsibility for choosing judges and ambassadors in the Senate's jurisdiction. The motion, which was offered by John Dickinson, stated that the president "shall appoint to all offices established by this Constitution, except in cases herein otherwise provided for, and to all offices which may hereafter be created by law."[76] But the delegates did not revisit their August 17 rejection of Delaware delegate George Read's motion to allow the president to appoint the treasurer. They still wanted anything to do with money firmly in Congress's hands.

As it had for the treaty power, the Committee on Postponed Matters proposed in early September to extend even further the president's role in the appointment process. Judges, ambassadors, ministers, and officers that the delegates had not already provided for would be appointed by the president with the advice and consent of the Senate. A simple majority vote of the senators present would suffice to confirm a presidential appointment. Wilson tried again to persuade the delegates to make appointments a unilateral power of the president. To involve the Senate, he argued, would foster "a dangerous tendency to aristocracy." But his motion failed.[77]

The convention accepted the committee's recommendation after making three additions: the president was given the power to fill vacancies that occur while the Senate is in recess (September 6); the power to appoint the treasurer at last was transferred from Congress to the president (September 14); and control of certain forms of patronage was distributed between the two branches by giving Congress the power to "vest the appointment of such inferior officers as they think proper" in the president, the courts, or the heads of the departments (September 15).

Advisory Legislative Powers

In enumerating the proposed powers of the presidency, the Committee of Detail specified: "He shall, from time to time, give information to the Legislature, of the state of the Union; he may recommend to their consideration such measures as he shall deem necessary, and expedient." The latter of these two provisions, both of which were uncontroversial, was modified slightly in response to an August 24 motion by Morris. He argued that the Constitution should make it "the *duty* of the President to recommend [measures to Congress], & thence prevent umbrage or cavil at his doing it." In other words, Congress would be less likely to resent presidential recommendations if the president had no constitutional choice but to offer some.

The convention approved Morris's suggestion that the words "he may" be replaced by "and."[78] The Constitution as finally written reads, "He shall from time to time give to the Congress Information of the State of the Union, and recommend to their Consideration such Measures as he shall judge necessary and expedient."

Convene and Adjourn Congress

The Committee of Detail recommended that the president be allowed to "convene them [the House and Senate] on extraordinary occasions"—that is, to call Congress into special session. Furthermore, "in case of disagreement between the two Houses, with regard to the time of adjournment, he may adjourn them to such time as he thinks proper."

James McHenry of Maryland was among those who wanted to grant the president the flexibility to call only the Senate back into session, presumably to consider a matter in which the House had no authority, such as a treaty or an urgent presidential appointment. He persuaded the delegates to amend the special session clause to that effect on September 8. The Constitution therefore reads: "he may, on extraordinary Occasions, convene both Houses, or either of them."

"Receive Ambassadors"

The president's power to "receive Ambassadors" was proposed by the Committee of Detail. The committee joined this power to another— permission to "correspond with the supreme Executives of the several States"—which the convention rejected on August 25 as being, according to Morris, "unnecessary and implying that the president could not correspond with others."[79] As for receiving ambassadors, the absence of debate or discussion leaves unclear whether the delegates meant this power to be substantive or merely ceremonial. In practice, the power to receive or, in particular cases, to refuse to receive ambassadors has made the president the sole official recipient of communications from foreign governments and the sole determiner of which governments the United States recognizes diplomatically. Joined with the convention's later decisions to transfer the treaty-making and ambassador-appointing powers from the Senate to the president, it underscored the primacy of the presidency in matters of diplomacy.

"Take Care"

According to the Virginia Plan, the executive was to have "general authority to execute the National Laws." On June 1 Madison sought to revise this provision to read: "power to carry into effect the national laws . . . and to execute such other powers not Legislative nor Judiciary in their nature as may from time to time be delegated by the national Legislature." The stipulation about legislative and judicial powers reflected Madison's acceptance of a suggestion by Charles Cotesworth Pinckney, who felt it was important to explicitly prohibit "improper powers" from being delegated to the executive. The other South Carolina Pinckney (Charles) persuaded the delegates to strike the amendment as "unnecessary."[80] No further controversy over the "take care" clause ensued. The Committee of Detail's formulation—"he shall take care that the laws of the United States be duly and faithfully executed"—was adopted without discussion by the convention and survived virtually intact in the final Constitution: "he shall take Care that the Laws be faithfully executed."

Title

During the first two months of their deliberations, the delegates usually referred to the head of the executive branch as the "national executive," "supreme executive," or "governor." On August 6 the Committee of Detail included the term "president" in its report to the convention. The title had been used for the presiding officer of Congress and other legislative bodies, including the convention itself. It was familiar and seemed reassuringly innocuous to those who feared that the delegates might be creating a monarchical or tyrannical office. Once proposed by the committee, the title "president" was accepted without debate by the convention.

Oath of Office

"Before he enter on the Execution of his Office," the Constitution requires the president to "take the following Oath or Affirmation:—'I do solemnly swear (or affirm) that I will faithfully execute the Office of President of the United States, and will to the best of my Ability, preserve, protect and defend the Constitution of the United States.'" Although another provision of the Constitution states that all legislators, judges, and other officials of both the national government and the state governments "shall be bound by Oath or Affirmation, to support this Constitution," the language of only the president's oath is included in the document. Some regard the wording of the oath (it pledges the president to execute "the office" rather than the laws) as further support for the claim that there are implied powers of presidential prerogative in the Constitution.

Virtually no debate or discussion accompanied the writing of the president's oath by the Constitutional Convention. The first half of the oath was proposed by the Committee of Detail on August 6: "I _____ solemnly swear (or affirm) that I will faithfully execute the office of President of the United States of America." On August 27 Mason and Madison moved that the phrase "and will to the best of my judgment and power preserve, protect and defend the Constitution of the U.S." be added. Wilson objected that a special presidential oath was unnecessary, but Mason and Madison's motion passed handily.[81] On September 15 the delegates substituted "abilities" for "judgment and power," but no discussion was recorded that explains this alteration.

Departing from the practice that prevailed in most of the states at the time, the convention barred the imposition of a religious oath on the president and other officials of the national government. Some state constitutions required public adherence to Christianity as a condition for serving as governor, others an adherence to the Protestant form of Christianity. North Carolina insisted that its governor affirm the existence of God and the truth of Protestantism and hold no religious beliefs that were inimical to the "peace and safety" of the state. On August 30 Charles Pinckney moved that "no religious test shall ever be required as a qualification to any office or public trust under the authority of the U. States." Sherman said he thought the proposal was "unnecessary, the prevailing liberality being a sufficient security agst. such tests." Nevertheless, Pinckney's motion was approved.[82]

Qualifications

No statement of qualifications for president was included in the Constitution until September 7, just ten days before the convention ended. In all likelihood, the lateness of the convention's actions on presidential qualifications was the result of deliberation, not neglect. Throughout their proceedings, the delegates seem to have operated on the principle that qualifications for an office needed to be established only if qualifications for those choosing the person to fill the office were not.[83] Qualifications, which were not stated for voters or state legislators, were included for members of the national legislature: members of the House of Representatives must be at least twenty-five years old, seven years a citizen, and an inhabitant of the state they represented; and senators must be at least thirty years old, nine years a citizen, and an inhabitant of the state. Conversely, qualifications for judgeships and other appointed offices never were included in the Constitution because these officials are selected by other government officials for whom qualifications were stated.[84]

Through most of the convention's deliberations, the majority of delegates remained wedded to the idea that Congress, a body of constitutionally qualified members, would elect the president. The delegates thus saw no need to include qualifications for president in the Constitution. By mid-August, however, it was obvious that most had changed their minds about legislative selection of the executive. Although they had not yet decided on an alternative, whatever procedure they eventually devised to choose the president would involve selection by an unqualified body because members of Congress were the only officials for whom constitutional qualifications were stated. This new election procedure, in turn, would necessitate the writing of qualifications for president. These qualifications would have to be high because the delegates also seem to have agreed that the greater the powers of an office, the more stringent the qualifications to hold it should be.

On August 20 Gerry moved successfully that the Committee of Detail be revived for the purpose of proposing a list of qualifications for president. Two days later, the committee did so: the president was to be thirty-five years old or older, a U.S. citizen, and an inhabitant of the United States for at least twenty-one years. On September 4 the Committee on Postponed Matters submitted a revised statement of qualifications: at least thirty-five, a natural-born citizen or a citizen at the time of the Constitution's adoption, and fourteen years a resident. The delegates approved the revised recommendation on September 7.

Each element of the presidential qualifications clause was grounded in its own rationale. The age requirement had two justifications. First, the delegates presumed that age would foster maturity. As Mason said in the debate on establishing a minimum age for members of the House of Representatives, "Every man carried with him in his own experience a scale for measuring the deficiency of young politicians; since he would if interrogated be obliged to declare that his political opinions at the age of 21 were too crude & erroneous to merit an influence on public measures."[85] Second, the passage of years would leave in its wake a record for the electorate to assess. According to John Jay, the author of *Federalist* No. 64,

> By excluding men under 35 from the first office [president], and those under 30 from the second [senator], it confines the electors to men of whom the people have had time to form a judgment, and with respect to whom they will not be liable to be deceived by those brilliant appearances of genius and patriotism which, like transient meteors, sometimes mislead as well as dazzle.[86]

The residency and citizenship requirements for president were grounded less in principles of good government than in the politics of the moment. The stipulation that the president must be at least fourteen years a resident of the United States was designed to eliminate both British sympathizers who fled to England during the Revolutionary War and popular foreign military leaders, notably Baron Frederick von Steuben of Prussia, who emigrated to the United States to support the revolutionary cause. As for the length of the residency requirement, the Committee of Detail's recommendation of twenty-one years probably was reduced to fourteen because the longer requirement—but not the shorter one—might have been interpreted to bar three of the convention's delegates from the presidency: Alexander Hamilton, Pierce Butler, and James McHenry.

The reason for requiring that the president be a natural-born citizen also was tied to contemporary politics. In early August rumors spread that the delegates were plotting to invite a European monarch to rule the United States. The Duke of Osnaburgh, who was King George III's second son, was the most frequently mentioned pretender.[87] The practice of importing foreign rulers was not unknown among European monarchies and would not have seemed preposterous to Americans who heard the rumor. The delegates, aware that the mere existence of an independent executive in the Constitution was going to provoke attacks by opponents who suspected that the presidency was a latent monarchy, seem to have believed that they could squelch the foreign king rumor by requiring that the president be a natural-born citizen of the United States.[88]

No property qualification for president was included in the Constitution, even though most state constitutions required that the governor own property and the delegates had approved a similar requirement for the president more than a month before they enacted the presidential qualifications clause. On July 26, the convention adopted a motion by Mason and the Pinckneys that a property qualification be stated for judges, legislators, and the executive. The Committee of Detail neglected the motion in its proposed draft of the Constitution, which provoked both a complaint and another motion from Charles Pinckney on August 10. John Rutledge of South Carolina, the chair of the committee, apologized and seconded Pinckney's motion. He said the committee had made no recommendation about property "because they could not agree on any among themselves, being embarrassed by the danger on one side of displeasing the people by making them high, and on the other of rendering them nugatory by making them low."[89] Pinckney suggested $100,000.[90]

In response, Franklin rose to attack the very idea of property qualifications. As Madison paraphrased Franklin's argument in his notes, "Some of the greatest rogues he was ever acquainted with, were the richest rogues." Pinckney's motion, Madison recorded, quickly "was rejected by so general a no, that the States were not called."[91] In truth, the practical difficulty of establishing an acceptable property requirement, more than the belief that such a requirement should be rejected as a matter of principle, explains why the Constitution was silent about property ownership by the president.

The Vice Presidency

The idea of an office like the vice presidency was not unknown among the delegates to the Constitutional Convention. During the period of British rule, several colonies had lieutenant governors (sometimes known as deputy governors or by another title) whose ongoing duties were minor but who stood by to serve as acting governor if the governor died, was removed from office, was ill, or was absent from the colony.

After independence, five states—Connecticut, Massachusetts, New York, Rhode Island, and South Carolina—included lieutenant governors in their constitutions. Each lieutenant governor was elected in the same manner as the governor and was charged to act as governor when needed. New York's lieutenant governor was also the ex officio president of the state senate and was allowed to break tie votes. Other states handled the matter of gubernatorial death, absence, or inability differently. In Georgia and Virginia the head of the privy council, a cabinet-style body, was the designated gubernatorial successor; in Delaware and North Carolina it was the Speaker of the upper house of the legislature; in New Hampshire, the senior member of the state senate.[92]

It is difficult to say whether the experience of the states had much influence on the convention's decision to create the vice presidency. No one referred to the state lieutenant governors in the debates. Nor was any proposal made to include a vice president in the Constitution until very late in the proceedings. Instead, the invention of the vice presidency was an afterthought of the convention, a residue of its solution to the problem of presidential selection.

As noted earlier, the delegates initially decided that the legislature should choose the executive, but they eventually replaced legislative selection with the Electoral College, providing that each state pick electors, who in turn would elect the president by majority vote. A possibly fatal defect of this procedure was that the electors would simply vote for a variety of local favorites, preventing the choice of a nationally elected president. But the committee remedied this potential problem by assigning each elector two votes for president, requiring that they cast at least one of their votes for a candidate who "shall not be an inhabitant of the same State with themselves" and attaching a consequence to both votes: the runner-up in the election for president would be awarded the newly created office of vice president.

As Hugh Williamson, a member of the Committee on Postponed Matters, testified, "Such an office as vice-President was not wanted. He was introduced only for the sake of a valuable mode of election which required two to be chosen at the same time."[93] But, having invented the vice presidency, the committee proposed that the office be used to solve two other problems that troubled the convention.

Senate President

The first problem was the role of president of the Senate. Some delegates had fretted that if a senator were chosen for this position, one of two difficulties would arise. If the senator were barred from voting except in the event of a tie (which was customary for presiding officers because it guaranteed that tie votes would be broken), the senator's state would be denied half its representation on most issues. If the senator were allowed to vote on all matters, the state would be effectively overrepresented in the Senate, occupying two voting seats and the presiding officer's chair. As a way around this dilemma, the Committee on Postponed Matters recommended that the vice president serve as president of the Senate, voting only to break ties. An exception was made for presidential impeachment trials, when the chief justice of the United States presides. In an oversight, vice presidents were not barred from presiding at their own impeachment trials.

Succession

The second problem that the committee used the vice presidency to solve was succession when the presidency unexpectedly became vacant. This, too, was a matter to which the convention turned rather late. The Virginia Plan and the New Jersey Plan were silent about succession. On June 18, as part of his sweeping proposal for a national executive chosen by electors to serve for life, Hamilton suggested that in the event of the executive's death, resignation, impeachment and removal, or absence from the country, the senator who served as president of the Senate should "exercise all the powers by this Constitution vested in the President, until another shall be appointed, or until he shall return within the United States, if his absence was with the Consent of the Senate and Assembly [House of Representatives]." But Hamilton's proposal was never formally discussed.

Sustained attention was first given to the succession question by the Committee of Detail. Knowingly or not, the committee followed Hamilton's lead in its August 6 report to the convention, providing that

> in the case of his [the president's] removal as aforesaid, death, resignation, or disability to discharge the powers and duties of his office, the President of the Senate shall exercise those powers and duties, until another President of the United States be chosen, or until the disability of the President be removed.

When the delegates discussed this provision on August 27, considerable dissatisfaction was voiced. Madison feared that the Senate would have an incentive to create presidential vacancies if its own president was the designated successor. He suggested instead that "the persons composing the Council to the President" fill that role.[94] (Of course, despite Madison's hopes, there was no such council.) Morris offered the chief justice as successor. Finally, Williamson asked that the question be postponed. The convention agreed, placing the issue in the hands of the Committee on Postponed Matters.

Reporting to the convention on September 4, the committee proposed that "in the case of his [the president's] removal as aforesaid, death, absence, resignation, or inability to discharge the powers or duties of his office the Vice President shall exercise those powers and duties until another President be chosen, or until the inability of the President be removed." Three days later Randolph, in an effort to supplement the committee's proposal with one that provided a method of presidential succession if there were no vice president, moved: "The Legislature may declare by law what officer of the United States shall act as President in the case of the death, resignation, or disability of the President and Vice President; and such Officer shall act accordingly until the time of electing a President shall arrive." Madison then moved to replace the last nine words of Randolph's motion with "until such disability be removed, or a President shall be elected." The motion passed, as amended.[95]

Madison's reason for amending Randolph's motion is clear: he wanted Congress to call a special presidential election to replace a departed president or, in his words, to permit "a supply of vacancy by an intermediate election of the President." Other evidence from the records of the convention suggests that most of the delegates intended that the president's successor serve merely as acting president and only until a special election could be called.[96] But sometime in the period September 8 to 12, when the Committee of Style was working to fulfill its charge to produce a smooth, final draft of the Constitution, that intention was lost, probably unwittingly. The committee took the September 4 motion of the Committee on Postponed Matters and Randolph's September 7 motion and merged them into one provision, which with minor modification, became paragraph 6 of Article II, section 1, of the Constitution:

In Case of the Removal of the President from Office, or of
his Death, Resignation, or Inability to discharge the Powers
and Duties of the said Office, the Same shall devolve on the

Vice President, and the Congress may by Law provide for the Case of Removal, Death, Resignation or Inability, both of the President and Vice President, declaring what Officer shall then act as President, and such Officer shall act accordingly, until the Disability be removed, or a President shall be elected.[97]

Clearly, the delegates' intentions regarding succession were obscured by the Committee of Style. Grammatically, it is impossible to tell—and in its rush to adjournment, the convention did not notice the ambiguity—whether "the Same" in this provision refers to "the said office" (the presidency) or, as the delegates intended, only to its "powers and duties." Nor can one ascertain if "until . . . a President shall be elected" means until the end of the original four-year term or, again as intended, until a special election is held.[98]

The vice presidency was not a controversial issue at the Constitutional Convention. On September 4, when the delegates were considering the Committee on Postponed Matters' proposal for the Electoral College, Nathaniel Gorham worried that "a very obscure man with very few votes" might be elected because the proposal required only that the vice president be the runner-up in the presidential election, not the recipient of a majority of electoral votes. Sherman replied that any of the leading candidates for president would likely be distinguished.

The role of the vice president as president of the Senate was discussed on September 7. Gerry, seconded by Randolph, complained about mixing legislative and executive elements: "We might as well put the President himself at the head of the Legislature. The close intimacy that must subsist between the President & vice-president makes it absolutely improper." Morris responded wryly that "the vice president then will be the first heir apparent that ever loved his father." Sherman added that "if the vice-President were not to be President of the Senate, he would be without employment." He also reminded the convention that for the Senate to elect a president from among its own members probably would deprive that senator of a vote. Mason ended the brief debate by branding "the office of vice-President an encroachment on the rights of the Senate; . . . it mixed too much the Legislative & Executive, which as well as the Judiciary departments, ought to be kept as separate as possible."[99]

Despite these objections, the convention voted overwhelmingly to approve the vice presidency. In doing so, however, the delegates gave no serious attention to the vice president's responsibilities as successor to the president.

Ratifying the Constitution

Congress's original call for a convention in Philadelphia charged the delegates only to propose amendments to the Articles of Confederation, not to design an entirely new system of government. By itself, the delegates' decision to ignore this charge ensured that controversy would ensue when, having met so long in secret, they published their proposed plan of government in September. In addition, several provisions of the draft Constitution, including the enhanced powers of the national government and the design of the legislative branch, were certain to be controversial. But nothing astonished the nation more than the convention's decision to recommend that a strong national executive be established—unitary, independently elected for an unrestricted number of terms, and entrusted with a substantial grant of powers.

In the debates that the state ratifying conventions held on the Constitution, Anti-Federalists (the label attached to those who opposed the plan) were quick to attack the Constitution in newspaper essays, concentrating much of their fire on the presidency. Organized to answer them by Alexander Hamilton, Federalists rose to the office's defense. Most state conventions debated at least one aspect of the proposed executive.[100]

The Anti-Federalist Critique of the Presidency

Anti-Federalists attacked the presidency as a disguised monarchy that in collaboration with an allegedly aristocratic Senate would rule the United States much as the British king, assisted by the House of Lords, was said to rule England.

The most strident opposition to the presidency was registered by Patrick Henry of Virginia. On June 7, 1788, speaking with unvarnished fervor, Henry voiced the Anti-Federalists' fears of a presidential monarchy to his state's ratifying convention:

> This Constitution is said to have beautiful features, but when
> I come to examine these features, Sir, they appear to me to be
> horridly frightful: Among other deformities, it has an awful
> squinting; it squints towards monarchy: And does this not raise
> indignation in the breast of every American?
>
> Your President may easily become a King; . . . if your
> American chief, be a man of ambition, how easy it is for him to
> render himself absolute: The army is in his hands, and if he be

a man of address, it will be attached to him; . . . I would rather infinitely, and I am sure most of these Convention are of the same opinion, have a king, Lords, and Commons, than a Government so replete with such insupportable evils. If we make a King, we may prescribe the rules by which he shall rule his people, and interpose such checks as shall prevent him from infringing them: But the President, in the field, at the head of his army, can prescribe the terms on which he shall reign master, so far that it will puzzle any American ever to get his neck from under the galling yoke. . . . And what have you to oppose this force? What will then become of you and your rights? Will not absolute despotism ensue?[101]

Other Anti-Federalists focused their criticisms on the close relationship they thought the Constitution fostered between the "monarchical" president and the "aristocratic" Senate, the two bodies that shared the powers of appointment and treaty making without the involvement of the "democratic" House of Representatives. A group of delegates at the Pennsylvania ratifying convention published a report on December 18, 1787, asserting that the Constitution's treaty-making provisions virtually invited foreign meddling. The Senate would consist of twenty-six members, they noted, two from each of the thirteen states. Fourteen senators would constitute a quorum for that body, of whom only ten were needed to provide a two-thirds vote to ratify a treaty proposed by the president. "What an inducement would this [small number] offer to the ministers of foreign powers to compass by bribery *such concessions* as could not otherwise be obtained," the Pennsylvania dissenters warned.[102]

Although monarchy was the Anti-Federalists' main fear, few features of the presidency were immune from their attack. The North Carolina and Virginia ratifying conventions urged the enactment of a constitutional amendment that would limit each president to no more than eight years in office in any sixteen-year period. The Anti-Federalist Cato, who is often but not conclusively identified as New York governor George Clinton, argued in the *New York Journal* in November 1787 that the president's term was too long and cited Montesquieu's endorsement of annual elections. In addition, Cato charged, the absence of a council meant that the president would "be unsupported by proper information and advice, and will generally be directed by minions and favorites." Instead of direct election by the people (which Cato favored), the president "arrives to this office at the fourth or fifth hand."[103]

Some of the most pointed criticisms of the proposed constitution came from disaffected delegates to the Constitutional Convention. George Mason told the Virginia-ratifying convention that the "mode of [presidential] election is a mere deception . . . on the American people." Because, after George Washington's certain election as the first president, the Electoral College almost never would produce a majority for a candidate; the House of Representatives would end up selecting nearly all presidents.[104] In a widely published article, Mason also decried the absence of a council and the president's "unrestrained power of granting pardons for treason."[105] Luther Martin complained to the Maryland convention that the veto allowed the president to prevail over all but a two-thirds majority of both houses of Congress.[106]

The presidency also drew criticism from two future presidents. Thomas Jefferson warned in private correspondence that a president "may be reelected from 4 years to 4 years for life." Vacancies will seldom occur in the presidency, and when they do, the stakes will be so high as to make "every succession worthy of intrigue, of bribery, of force, and even of foreign interference."[107] James Monroe also worried about the possibility of a president being reelected into life tenure.

The Federalist Defense of the Presidency

Article II posed a political challenge for Federalists who were trying to persuade the states to ratify the Constitution. Not only was the presidency the most obvious innovation in the new plan of government, but its unitary nature aroused fears of a British-style monarchy. The Anti-Federalists fanned these fears.

Proponents of the Constitution at the state ratifying conventions stressed both the virtues of the presidency and the restraints the Constitution placed on the office. In doing so, they relied heavily on the explanations and defenses of the Constitution that Hamilton, Madison, and Jay were putting forth in a series of eighty-five newspaper articles that Hamilton commissioned. These articles, soon gathered in a two-volume book called *The Federalist*, appeared pseudonymously in several New York newspapers under the name "Publius," after the Roman statesman Publius Valerius, who is celebrated in Plutarch's *Parallel Lives* for stabilizing the nascent republic even though he was falsely criticized as a monarchist.[108] Hamilton wrote about fifty of the articles, Madison about twenty-five, and Jay, who became ill after writing four of the first five numbers in the series, five. Hamilton and Madison collaborated on the rest. The articles were reprinted and disseminated widely throughout the states.[109]

In March 1788 Hamilton wrote *Federalist* Nos. 69 to 77, which dealt with the presidency.[110] In the constitution he would have preferred, the president would be elected for life, have an absolute veto and undiluted appointment powers, and in general be much more powerful than in the Constitution the convention actually wrote. But like fellow delegate Pierce Butler, Hamilton resolved to "follow the example of Solon who gave the Athenians not the best Government he could devise but the best they would receive."[111] In his essays urging ratification, Hamilton defended every provision of Article II without reservation.

Federalist No. 69 squarely addressed the Anti-Federalist charge that the presidency was a latent monarchy. Hamilton argued that in contrast to the British king who secured his office by inheritance and served for life, the president is elected for a limited term. The king had an absolute veto on laws passed by Parliament; the president's veto could be overridden by Congress. The king could both declare war and raise an army and navy; the president could do neither. The king could prorogue Parliament for any reason at any time; the president could adjourn Congress only when the House of Representatives and the Senate could not agree on an adjournment date. The king could create offices and appoint people to fill them; the president could not create offices and could fill them only with the approval of the Senate. Finally, Hamilton noted that the president, unlike the king, could be impeached and removed. In *Federalist* No. 65, he described impeachable offenses as "the abuse or violation of some public trust. They are of a nature which may with peculiar propriety be denominated POLITICAL, as they relate chiefly to injuries done immediately to the society itself."

Hamilton dissembled to some degree in drawing these contrasts. The powers he ascribed to the British monarch were more characteristic of the seventeenth century than of the eighteenth century, during which the influence of Parliament and the prime minister had grown. For example, the last British monarch to veto an act of Parliament was Queen Anne in 1707. But *Federalist* No. 69 was effective in deflating the Anti-Federalists' caricature of the presidency. Indeed, Hamilton deftly argued that in many cases the president's power was less than that wielded by the governor of New York, the staunchly Anti-Federalist Clinton.

Federalist No. 70, less defensive in tone than No. 69, described the virtues of the presidency. Its theme was "energy," a quality that according to Hamilton, is requisite to good government:

> It is essential to the protection of the community against foreign attacks; it is not less essential to the steady administration of

the laws; to the protection of property against those irregular and high-handed combinations which sometimes interrupt the ordinary course of justice; to the security of liberty against the enterprises and assaults of ambition, of faction, and of anarchy.

Energy in the government created by the Constitution was provided by the president, Hamilton argued, mostly because of the office's unitary character. Unity provided the presidency with a whole host of virtues—"decision, activity, secrecy, and dispatch . . . vigor and expedition." In contrast, a plural executive would be riven by disagreements among its members that would render it slow to act and prone to faction. It also would be hard for the people to hold a plural executive responsible for failures because each member could blame the others.

In *Federalist* Nos. 71 to 73, Hamilton defended the presidency as having additional qualities indispensable to energy. "Duration," the theme of No. 71, was one. The four-year term provided the president with enough time to act firmly and with resolve but was not so long as "to justify any alarm for the public liberty." Hamilton shrewdly added in No. 72 that the provision for reelection acknowledged that "the desire of reward is one of the strongest incentives of human conduct." Without that incentive, a president would be tempted either to slack off or, at the opposite extreme, to usurp power violently. With it, a national leader would be prompted "to plan and undertake extensive and arduous enterprises for the public benefit." Presidential reeligibility also allowed the nation to keep a president in office if it so desired. "There is an excess of refinement in the idea," he insisted, "of disabling the people to continue in office men who had entitled themselves, in their opinion, to approbation and confidence."

"Adequate provision for its support" was a third energy-inducing quality of the presidency, according to Hamilton. He attached great importance to the prohibition that the Constitution placed on Congress not to raise or lower an incumbent president's salary.

Later in No. 73, and continuing in Nos. 74 to 77, Hamilton defended the enumerated powers of the presidency, which along with unity, duration, and adequate support, were for him the indispensable ingredients of presidential energy. Far from being threatening, Hamilton argued, the office's constitutional powers were modest and essential to the operations of good government.

VETO. "The propensity of the legislative department to intrude upon the rights, and to absorb the powers, of the other departments has been already more than once suggested. . . . [Without the veto, the president] might gradually be stripped of his authorities by successive resolutions or annihilated by a single vote. . . . But the power in question has a further use. It not only serves as a shield to the executive, but it furnishes an additional security against the enaction of improper laws."

COMMANDER IN CHIEF. "Even those [constitutions] which have in other respects coupled the Chief Magistrate with a council have for the most part concentrated the military authority in him alone. Of all the cares or concerns of government, the direction of war most peculiarly demands those qualities which distinguish the exercise of power by a single hand."

TREATIES. "With regard to the intermixture of powers [between the president and the Senate] . . . the essence of the legislative authority is to enact laws, or, in other words, to prescribe rules for the regulation of the society; while the execution of the laws and the employment of the common strength, either for this purpose or for the common defense, seem to comprise all the functions of the executive magistrate. The power of making treaties is, plainly, neither the one nor the other. . . . It must indeed be clear to a demonstration that the joint possession of the power in question, by the President and Senate, would afford a greater prospect of security than the separate possession of it by either of them."

APPOINTMENT. "I proceed to lay it down as a rule that one man of discernment is better fitted to analyze and estimate the peculiar qualities adapted to particular offices than a body of men of equal or perhaps even of superior discernment. The sole and undivided responsibility of one man will naturally beget a livelier sense of duty and a more exact regard to reputation. He will, on this account, feel himself under stronger obligations, and more interested to investigate with care the qualities requisite to the stations to be filled, and to prefer with impartiality the persons who may have the fairest pretensions to them. . . . To what purpose then require the co-operation of the Senate? I answer, that the necessity of their concurrence would have a powerful, though, in general, a silent operation. It would be an excellent check upon a spirit of favoritism in the President, and would tend greatly to prevent the appointment of unfit characters. . . . The possibility of rejection would be a strong motive to care in proposing."[112]

OTHER POWERS. "The only remaining powers of the executive are comprehended in giving information to Congress on the state of the Union; in recommending to their consideration such measures as he shall judge expedient; in convening them, or either branch, upon extraordinary occasions; in adjourning them when they cannot themselves agree upon the time of adjournment; in receiving ambassadors and other public ministers; in faithfully executing the laws; and in commissioning all the officers of the United States. Except some cavils about the power of convening *either* house of the legislature, and that of receiving ambassadors, no objection has been made to this class of authorities; nor could they possibly admit of any."

The Vice Presidency in the Ratification Debates

"Post-convention discussion of the vice presidency was not extensive," legal scholar John D. Feerick has noted.[113] The only mention of the office in *The Federalist* is in No. 68, written by Hamilton. Like the delegates'

Alexander Hamilton, one of the authors of The Federalist Papers, *defended the Constitution's provisions for a strong executive office.*

Source: Library of Congress.

debate at the Constitutional Convention, this passage is concerned mainly with the vice president's role as president of the Senate:

The appointment of an extraordinary person, as Vice-President, has been objected to as superfluous, if not mischievous.
It has been alleged, that it would have been preferable to have authorized the Senate to elect out of their own body an officer answering to that description. But two considerations seem to justify the ideas of the Convention in this respect. One is, that to secure at all times the possibility of a definitive resolution of the body, it is necessary that the President should have only a casting [tie-breaking] vote. And to take the Senator of any State from his seat as Senator, to place him in that of President of the Senate, would be to exchange, in regard to the State from which he came, a constant for a contingent vote. The other consideration is, that, as the Vice-President may occasionally become a substitute for the President, in the supreme Executive magistracy, all the reasons which recommend the mode of election prescribed for the one, apply with great if not with equal force to the manner of appointing the other.[114]

Hamilton may have been responding in part to concerns raised by the Anti-Federalist Cato, who argued that the vice presidency was both "unnecessary" and "dangerous." "This officer," warned Cato, "for want of other employment is made president of the Senate, thereby blending the executive and legislative powers, besides always giving to some one state, from which he is to come, an unjust preeminence."[115]

Luther Martin of Maryland, who opposed ratification, expressed concern that large states like Pennsylvania and Virginia typically would benefit from the vice president's Senate role:

> After it is decided who is chosen President, that person who has the next greatest number of votes of the electors, is declared to be legally elected to the Vice-Presidency; so that by this system it is very possible, and not improbable, that he may be appointed by the electors of a *single large state;* and a very undue influence in the Senate is given to that State of which the Vice-President is a citizen, since, in every question where the Senate is divided, that State will have two votes, the President having on that occasion a casting voice.

George Mason, another convention delegate who opposed ratification, also complained about the vice president's right to vote in the Senate and the office's admixture of legislative and executive responsibilities. His fellow Virginia Anti-Federalist Richard Henry Lee worried about the absence of stated qualifications for the vice president.[116]

Defenders of the vice presidency made a virtue of the office's role as Senate president. In their view, the vice president's election by the nation as a whole would be good for the Senate. "There is much more propriety to giving this office to a person chosen by the people at large," urged Madison, "than to one of the Senate, who is only the choice of the legislature of one state." William R. Davie of North Carolina expressed confidence that a nationally elected vice president would cast tie-breaking votes "as impartially as possible," not favoring any section of the country. Answering another argument of the Constitution's critics, Connecticut delegates Oliver Ellsworth and Roger Sherman wrote separately that the vice president did not wield a mix of legislative and executive powers but rather that the vice presidency was part of the legislative branch except in the event of a succession, at which time it entered the executive branch.[117]

In all, as Feerick has concluded, the vice presidency "received scant attention in the state ratifying conventions. . . . The discussion of the vice-presidency that did occur centered mostly on the fact that the office blended legislative and executive functions."[118] As at the Constitutional Convention, little was said in the state debates about the vice president's duties as successor to the president.

Notes

1. Jack N. Rakove, *Original Meanings: Politics and Ideas in the Making of the Constitution* (New York: Knopf, 1996), 82.

2. Seymour Martin Lipset, *The First New Nation* (New York: Basic Books, 1963), chap. 1; Max Weber, *The Theory of Social and Economic Organizations* (New York: Oxford University Press, 1947), 358.

3. Marcus Cunliffe, *George Washington: Man and Monument* (New York: New American Library, 1958), 15.

4. Stanley Elkins and Eric McKitrick, *The Age of Federalism: The Early American Republic, 1788–1800* (New York: Oxford University Press, 1993), 34.

5. Max Farrand, ed., *The Records of the Federal Convention*, 3 vols. (New Haven: Yale University Press, 1911), 1: 103. Contemporaries often compared Washington to Cincinnatus, the ancient Roman who left his plow when called to lead Rome against Carthage and then returned to it as soon as the victory was won. See Garry Wills, *Cincinnatus: George Washington and the Enlightenment* (Garden City, N.Y.: Doubleday, 1984), 36–37.

6. Charles C. Thach Jr., *The Creation of the Presidency, 1775–1789* (Baltimore: Johns Hopkins University Press, 1969).

7. Robert A. Rutland and William M. E. Rachal, eds., *The Papers of James Madison* (Chicago: University of Chicago Press, 1975), 9: 385.

8. Political scientist Calvin C. Jillson argues that Madison's fellow Virginia delegates, not Madison himself, brought what little clarity there was to the executive provision of the Virginia Plan. See Jillson, *Constitution Making: Conflict and Consensus in the Federal Convention of 1787* (New York: Agathon Press, 1988), 42–47.

9. Farrand, *Records*, 2: 52, 523.

10. Richard J. Ellis, ed., *Founding the American Presidency* (Lanham, Md.: Rowman and Littlefield, 1999), 12–13.

11. Richard Beeman, *Plain, Honest Men: The Making of the American Constitution* (New York: Random House, 2009), 129.

12. David Brian Robertson, *The Original Compromise: What the Constitution's Framers Were Really Thinking* (New York: Oxford University Press, 2013), 106.

13. Farrand, *Records*, 1: 65.

14. Charles L. Mee Jr., *The Genius of the People* (New York: Harper and Row, 1987), 118.

15. Farrand, *Records*, 1: 66, 65.

16. Ibid., 1: 102.

17. Ibid., 1: 65.

18. W. B. Allen, ed., *George Washington: A Collection* (Indianapolis, Ind.: Liberty Classic, 1988), 230.

19. Ellis, *Founding the American Presidency*. See also Beeman, *Plain, Honest Men*, 27.

20. See, for example, Farrand, *Records*, 2: 487–488.

21. Ibid., 2: 541.

22. Ibid., 2: 68, 69.

23. Ibid., 2: 30.

24. Ibid., 2: 57.

25. Ibid., 2: 100.

26. Indispensable to the eventual adoption of the Electoral College was Wilson's conversion of Madison, who declared on July 19 that "it is essential then that the appointment of the Executive should either be drawn from some source, or held by some tenure, that will give him a free agency with regard to the Legislature. This could not be if he was appointable from time to time by the Legislature" (ibid., 2: 56).

27. Ray Raphael, *Mr. President: How and Why the Founders Created a Chief Executive* (New York: Alfred A. Knopf, 2012), 88.

28. Robert A. Dahl, *Pluralist Democracy in the United States: Conflict and Consent* (Chicago: Rand-McNally, 1967), 84.

29. Clinton Rossiter, *1787: The Grand Convention* (London: MacGibbon and Kee, 1968), 199.

30. Richard P. McCormick, *The Presidential Game: The Origins of American Presidential Politics* (New York: Oxford University Press, 1982), 25. Shlomo Slonim has argued that in many ways, the Electoral College was "a second round of the Connecticut Compromise in settling large state–small state differences." Slonim, "The Electoral College: The Evolution of an Ad Hoc Congress for the Selection of a President," *Journal of American History* 73 (June 1986): 55.

31. James H. Hutson, ed., *Supplement to Max Farrand's The Records of the Federal Convention of 1787* (New Haven: Yale University Press, 1987), 300.

32. Andrew Rudalevige, *The New Imperial Presidency: Renewing Presidential Power after Watergate* (Ann Arbor: University of Michigan Press, 2005), 25.

33. Fred Barbash, *The Founding: An Account of the Writing of the Constitution* (New York: Linden Press/Simon and Schuster, 1987), 182.

34. Farrand, *Records*, 2: 500.

35. Carol Berkin, *A Brilliant Solution: Inventing the American Constitution* (New York: Harcourt, Brace, 2002), 143–144.

36. John P. Roche, "The Founding Fathers: A Reform Caucus in Action," *American Political Science Review* 55 (December 1961): 810.

37. Farrand, *Records*, 1: 68.

38. Ibid., 2: 33.

39. Fred Kaplan, *John Quincy Adams: American Visionary* (New York: Harper, 2014), 79.

40. Alexander Hamilton, James Madison, and John Jay, *The Federalist Papers,* with an introduction by Clinton L. Rossiter (New York: New American Library, 1961), 437–448.

41. Farrand, *Records*, 2: 53.

42. For a fuller treatment of presidential removal, see Michael Nelson, "'The Firing, Retiring, and Expiring of Presidents': Impeachment, Disability, Resignation, and Death—From the Constitutional Convention to Donald Trump," in *The Presidency and the Political System*, 11th ed., ed. Michael Nelson (Washington, D.C.: CQ Press, 2018), 542–563.

43. Ellis, *Founding the American Presidency*, 233.

44. Farrand, *Records*, 1: 88.

45. Ibid., 2:

46. Ibid., 2: 550.

47. Ibid., 2: 427.

48. Hamilton, Madison, and Jay, *Federalist Papers*, 301, 303.

49. Richard E. Neustadt, *Presidential Power* (New York: Wiley, 1960), 35.

50. Alexander Hamilton, James Madison and John Jay, *The Federalist Papers*, ed. Charles Kessler (New York: Signet Classics, 2003), 305.

51. Farrand, *Records*, 1: 82.

52. Ibid., 1: 376.

53. Ibid., 2: 284.

54. The bar to overlapping membership strongly distinguishes the American system of government from parliamentary systems, in which executive offices are customarily held by legislators. James Sundquist, *Constitutional Reform and Effective Government*, rev. ed. (Washington, D.C.: Brookings, 1992), 232–244.

55. Robert Scigliano, "The Presidency and the Judiciary," in *The Presidency and the Political System*, 3rd ed., ed. Michael Nelson (Washington, D.C.: CQ Press, 1990), 471–499.

56. Michael J. Klarman, *The Framers' Coup: The Making of the United States Constitution* (New York: Oxford University Press, 2016), 213.

57. Robert J. Spitzer, *The Presidential Veto: Touchstone of the American Presidency* (Albany: State University of New York Press, 1988), 10.

58. Farrand, *Records,* 1: 101.

59. Richard M. Pious, *The American Presidency* (New York: Basic Books, 1979), 29.

60. John Locke, *Second Treatise of Government* (Indianapolis, Ind.: Bobbs-Merrill, 1952), 91–96.

61. Thach, *Creation of the Presidency*, 138–139.

62. Farrand, *Records*, 2: 318.

63. Political scientist Anthony J. Bennett has interpreted the phrase "their respective Offices" to mean that the convention did not intend for the department heads to constitute a cabinet. See Bennett, *The American President's Cabinet: From Kennedy to Bush* (New York: St. Martin's Press, 1996), 2.

64. Hamilton, Madison, and Jay, *Federalist Papers*, 447.

65. Farrand, *Records*, 2: 343–344.

66. Ibid., 1: 292.

67. Ellis, *Founding the American Presidency*, 220–221.

68. Farrand, *Records*, 2: 426, 626.

69. Hamilton, Madison, and Jay, *Federalist Papers*, 447, 449.

70. Farrand, *Records*, 1: 292.

71. Rakove, *Original Meanings*, 89, 267.

72. Farrand, *Records*, 2: 309.

73. Ibid., 2: 540.

74. Ellis, *Founding the American Presidency*, 190.

75. Farrand, *Records*, 1: 67.

76. Ibid., 2: 405.

77. Ibid., 2: 522.

78. Ibid., 2: 405.

79. Ibid., 2: 419.

80. Ibid., 1: 67.

81. Ibid., 2: 427.

82. Ibid., 2: 468. In 1853 Franklin Pierce affirmed—rather than swore—to faithfully execute the office of president. At the first inaugural ceremony, on April 30, 1789, George Washington began the practice of adding the words "so help me God" at the conclusion of the oath. See Charles C. Euchner and John Anthony Maltese, *Selecting the President* (Washington, D.C.: CQ Press, 1997), 142.

83. Michael Nelson, "Constitutional Qualifications for the President," *Presidential Studies Quarterly* 17 (Spring 1987): 383–399.

84. During most of the convention, the appointment power belonged mainly to senators; toward the end, the president's role in appointments was enhanced substantially.

85. Farrand, *Records*, 1: 375.

86. Hamilton, Madison, and Jay, *Federalist Papers*, 391.

87. Edward J. Larson, *The Return of George Washington, 1783–1789* (New York: William Morrow, 2014), 136. See also Beeman, *Plain, Honest Men*, 263.

88. Another reason the convention decided to include a requirement of natural-born citizenship for the president may be found in a letter John Jay sent to George Washington on July 25. "Permit me to hint," Jay wrote, "whether it would not be wise and reasonable to provide a strong check on the admission of foreigners into the administration of our National Government, and to declare expressly that the command in chief of the American Army shall not be given to, nor devolve upon, any but a natural *born* citizen." On September 2, two days before the Committee on Postponed Matters proposed the natural-born citizen requirement to the convention, Washington replied to Jay, "I thank you for the hints contained in your letter." See Farrand, *Records*, 4: 61, 76.

89. Ibid., 2: 249.

90. Beeman, *Plain, Honest Men*, 280.

91. Farrand, *Records*, 2: 249.

92. John D. Feerick, *From Failing Hands: The Story of Presidential Succession* (New York: Fordham University Press, 1965), chap. 2.

93. Farrand, *Records*, 2: 537.

94. Ibid., 2: 427.

95. Ibid., 2: 535.

96. See ibid., 2: 137, 146, 163, 172.

97. On September 15, 1787, delegates discovered a clerical error in the committee's draft and changed "the period for chusing another president arrive" to "a President shall be elected."

98. For a thorough comparison of the convention's decisions on succession with the Committee of Style's rendering of them, see Feerick, *From Failing Hands*, 48–51. Feerick speculates that the committee may have omitted presidential "absence" from the list of situations that require a temporary successor because it was covered by the term *inability*.

99. Farrand, *Records*, 2: 537. In truth, it still is constitutionally unclear whether the vice president is part of the legislative branch, the executive branch, both branches, or neither. See Michael Nelson, *A Heartbeat Away* (Washington, D.C.: Brookings, 1988), chap. 4.

100. Pauline Maier, *Ratification: The People Debate the Constitution* (New York: Simon and Schuster, 2010), passim.

101. Quoted in Ralph Ketcham, ed., *The Anti-Federalist Papers and the Constitutional Convention Debates* (New York: New American Library, 1986), 213–214.

102. Ibid., 251.

103. "Cato, 'Letter No. 4,'" in *The Evolving Presidency: Landmark Documents* 5th ed., ed. Michael Nelson (Washington, D.C.: CQ Press, 2019), 17–19.

104. Ellis, *Founding the American Presidency*, 117.

105. "George Mason, 'Objections to This Constitution of Government,'" in *The Evolving Presidency*, ed. Nelson, 16–17.

106. Ellis, *Founding the American Presidency*, 145.

107. Jon Meacham, *Thomas Jefferson: The Art of Power* (New York: Random House, 2012), 213.

108. Plutarch, *Lives*, vol. 1 (New York: Modern Library, 2001). Noah Feldman notes that Hamilton, who chose the pseudonym, identified with Publius as a republican accused of being a monarchist. Feldman, *The Three Lives of James Madison: Genius, Partisan President* (New York: Random House, 2017), 178.

109. Voices of other famous people were raised in defense of the Constitution as well. See, for example, Tenche Cox, "An American Citizen I," and Noah Webster, "A Citizen of America," in *The Debate on the Constitution*, part 1 (New York: Library of America, 1993), 20–25 and 129–163, respectively.

110. All quotations from the *Federalist* may be found in Hamilton, Madison, and Jay, *Federalist Papers*, 415–464.

111. Alan Taylor, *American Revolutions: A Continental History, 1750–1804* (New York: W.W. Norton, 2016), 378.

112. In a passage in *Federalist* No. 77 that would prove embarrassing a year later, Hamilton wrote that the Senate's consent "would be necessary to displace as well as to appoint" an executive official.

113. Feerick, *From Failing Hands*, 51.

114. Hamilton, Madison, and Jay, *Federalist Papers*, 414–415.

115. Quoted in Cecelia M. Kenyon, ed., *The Antifederalists* (Indianapolis, Ind.: Bobbs-Merrill, 1966), 305.

116. Feerick, *From Failing Hands*, 52–54.

117. Quotes are drawn from ibid., 52–55.

118. Ibid., 52.

CHAPTER 3

Bringing the Constitutional Presidency to Life

George Washington and John Adams

The Constitution provides a broad outline of the powers and duties of the president, leaving considerable leeway for individual presidents and future events to shape the executive office. By stating that "the executive Power shall be vested in a President of the United States of America" and that "he shall take Care that the Laws be faithfully executed," without in many instances stipulating what those executive responsibilities would be, the Constitution gives rise to unending conflict about the proper scope of presidential authority. "The executive article fairly bristles with contentious matter," Charles Thach has written, "and, until it is seen what decision was given to these contentions, it is impossible to say just what the national executive meant."[1]

From the words of the Constitution alone, for example, one cannot determine what the relationship of the chief executive to the chief officers of the executive departments is supposed to be or that of Congress to the executive branch. Similarly, the Constitution leaves unclear the extent of the powers that are implied by the president's responsibilities in war, peace, and diplomacy.[2]

In large measure, presidents have been able to fill the interpretive void, as "presidentialists" at the Constitutional Convention such as James Wilson, Gouverneur Morris, and Alexander Hamilton had hoped. As political scientist Richard Pious has observed, "The president claims the silences of the Constitution."[3] The expansion of executive power did not come easily, however. The institutional design of the Constitution created congressional as well as presidential partisans, including influential political leaders such as Thomas Jefferson and James Madison. Depending on which political forces controlled which branch of government at a particular time, these partisans sometimes switched sides on the constitutional debate only to switch again in response to shifting electoral tides. This chapter and those that follow chronicle the major developments that have shaped both the idea of presidential power, including some furious debates about the proper definition of executive authority, and the institutional changes that have occurred in the presidency.

The Election of George Washington

Many of the most important questions about the character and breadth of presidential authority were settled during the two terms served by George Washington. The nation's first chief executive was very much aware that his actions could establish enduring precedents. "Few who are not philosophical spectators," Washington wrote early in his first term,

> can realize the difficult and delicate part which a man in my
> situation has to act. . . . In our progress towards political
> happiness my station is new; and, if I may use the expression,
> I walk on untrodden ground. There is scarcely any part of my
> conduct which may not hereafter be drawn into precedent.[4]

Significant precedents for the proper conduct of the executive office were settled not only by the first president but also by the First Congress. As Thach has noted, its work from 1789 to 1791 "was simply the continuation of that done at the Constitutional Convention two years before."[5] Many of those who framed the Constitution in Philadelphia were on hand in New York, the government's first temporary capital, to put the new instrument into operation. The First Congress included eighteen delegates to the convention: eight in the House of Representatives, including Madison, and ten in the Senate. "It is safe to say," historian Charles A. Beard has written, "that four-fifths of the active, forceful leaders of the Convention helped to realize as a process of government the paper constitution they had drafted."[6] Because Anti-Federalist opponents of ratifying the document were slow to engage in the electoral process, they secured only eleven of fifty-nine House seats in the First Congress and just two of twenty-two seats in the Senate.[7] As a result, although Congress and the states followed Madison's lead in adding the first ten amendments to the Constitution (later known as the Bill of Rights), legislators refused to consider the proposed structural changes that mattered even more to the Anti-Federalists, including a term limit on the president and restrictions on the pardon power.

The delegates bestowed expansive powers on the executive office in no small measure because they expected George Washington to be the first president. As James Monroe wrote to Thomas Jefferson, who was deeply troubled by the failure of the Convention to put limits on the president's tenure, "be assured [Washington's] influence carried this government; for my own part I have a boundless confidence in him nor have I any reason to believe he will ever furnish occasion for withdrawing it."[8]

Although the election of Washington as the first president was never in doubt, the forbearance he displayed in grasping the reins of power revealed an acute understanding of the challenges he faced in conferring legitimacy on institutional arrangements that were fiercely contested during the ratification of the Constitution. As one historian has observed, "Never was the election of a president so much a foregone conclusion and yet so tortuous in consummation."[9] Although the Electoral College met in the state capitals on February 4, 1789, its unanimous vote for Washington was not official until the president of the Senate, temporarily elected for the purpose, opened the ballots in the presence of both the House and the Senate. One of the final acts of the outgoing Congress of the Articles of Confederation had been to summon the new Congress to convene in New York on March 4. But the newly elected legislators were slow to arrive, and a quorum still was not reached by the end of the month. Anyone other than Washington might have been in the capital in time for the opening of Congress, which finally occurred when the House obtained a bare quorum on April 1 and the Senate on April 6. But Washington wanted to fulfill the strictest requirements of correct behavior. Because he would not be elected officially until a joint session of Congress tallied the votes of the electors, he waited for formal notification at his Mount Vernon, Virginia, home and worried about the "stupor or listlessness" being displayed by the members of Congress on whom the success of the Constitution would largely depend.[10]

Nevertheless, the start of the new government was further delayed by Washington himself who, when he finally received official notice of his election on April 14 from Secretary of the Congress Charles Thompson, took his time riding from Virginia to New York "lest unseemly haste suggest that he was improperly eager for the office."[11] Because the president-elect believed that the future of the government required its acceptance by the people, he was concerned with how his progress through the states to the capital would be received.

Washington's caution, however, went deeper than an awareness of the American people's fear of executive power. Washington, both as general and as president, sought to fulfill the Cincinnatus myth of Roman legend, which celebrates the disinterested patriot who devotes his life to his country. Washington's diffidence, although studied, was not disingenuous.

Self-denial came naturally to him: in 1783, toward the end of the Revolutionary War, Washington had faced down the Newburgh Conspiracy, a cabal of army officers who were prepared to act against Congress for failing to meet its financial obligations to the military. Although the exact plans of the conspiring officers were never stated clearly, they apparently discussed displacing Congress and ruling the country themselves.

Revered by most of the officers and soldiers, Washington could have emulated famous generals-turned-dictator such as Julius Caesar, Oliver Cromwell, and Napoleon by taking advantage of this uprising to advance his personal power. Instead, at a hastily called meeting he prevailed on the conspirators to reaffirm their loyalty to Congress. At a time when the relationship between the army and the legislature was still unsettled, Washington established a critical precedent that strengthened the fragile tradition of military subordination to civilian authority. The Newburgh incident also enhanced Washington's reputation for honesty and unshakable devotion to republican government and the ideals of the Revolution, at least those not compromised by his ownership of slaves.[12] Thomas Jefferson expressed the general feeling when he observed that "the moderation and virtue of a single character had probably prevented this revolution from being closed as most others have been by a subversion of that liberty it was intended to establish."[13]

After the signing of the Treaty of Paris, which ended the Revolutionary War and secured British recognition of American independence, Washington surrendered his sword to Congress on December 23, 1783, and retired to Mount Vernon. His retirement from power had a profound effect throughout the Western world. "It was extraordinary, it was unprecedented in modern times," Wood has written, for "a victorious general [to surrender] his arms and [return] to his farm."[14] English war heroes such as William of Orange and the Duke of Marlborough had all sought political rewards commensurate with their military achievements. In contrast, Washington sincerely wanted, both for himself and his soldiers, to "return to our Private Stations in the bosom of a free, peaceful and happy country."[15]

The American people recognized Washington's sincerity and responded with respect, admiration, even awe. As classicist Garry Wills has noted, Washington "gained power from his willingness to give it up."[16] Hearing of Washington's post-war decision to retire to private life, King George III reputedly said, "If he does that he will be the greatest man in the world."[17] The popular adulation that greeted Washington in every hamlet as he traveled to New York to become president revealed his country's devotion.

As he entered Philadelphia, surrounded by military horsemen who had formed an escort fifteen miles from the city, some twenty thousand citizens "lined every fence, field, and avenue." At the city limits, infantry wheeled, and artillery fired their cannon. The units then fell into line behind Washington, as did squads of citizens on every block until, as one newspaper account had it, "the column swelled beyond credibility itself." The parade finally reached the City Tavern, where Washington was honored with "a very grand and beautiful banquet." The evening was topped off by fireworks.[18] The nation's first president arrived at last in New York in time to be inaugurated on April 30, 1789.

The long and complicated business of Washington's election and his assumption of the responsibilities of the presidency foretold the major task of his administration: "to make the government which had been adopted, often by the thinnest of majorities, and in only eleven out of thirteen states, happily acceptable to the overwhelming majority of the entire population."[19] This was an ambitious task. It required the construction of a unified and energetic national government on a political landscape that was traditionally inhospitable to strong central authority. That the "more perfect Union" promised by the Constitution included a strong presidency was particularly notable, even radical, in the American context, in which executive power had long been the object of public distrust. In view of this tradition, bringing the constitutional presidency to life may have been an impossible task without Washington's great popularity and propriety. Indeed, Washington was, or so James Madison wrote in 1789, the only aspect of the government that caught the imagination of the people at the outset.[20]

Making the Presidency Safe for Democracy

As America's first "republican monarch," historian Joanne B. Freeman has written, "Washington had an exceedingly difficult role: somehow he had to embody the new government's dignity and authority without rising to monarchical excess."[21] Washington's awe-inspiring personality and popularity made him an indispensable source of unity and legitimacy for the newly formed government. At the same time, those who were suspicious of strong executive power found these qualities dangerous. The result was that many of the conflicts that arose during Washington's administration and that of his successor, John Adams, involved efforts to make executive power compatible with republican government.

Some of these conflicts concerned the most routine matters. For example, Washington's schedule became the subject of controversy at the start of his administration, prompting him to distribute queries to trusted advisers "on a line of conduct most eligible to be pursued by the President of the United States." The challenge, as Washington understood it, was to establish precedents for presidential conduct that would allow the executive enough "time for all the official duties of his station" and enough distance to retain the "respectability" of the office, without giving the impression that through "superciliousness, and seclusion" and "too great a withdrawal of himself from company" he disdained contact with the people.[22] The course that Washington decided on satisfied neither those, such as Vice President John Adams and Treasury Secretary Alexander Hamilton, who wanted to insulate the president from excessive popular influence, nor zealous republicans who wished to see an open executive office. Nevertheless, Washington revealed his great sensitivity to the importance of attaining public support and respect for the presidency through activities that no matter how mundane were of great symbolic importance.

Washington established two occasions a week when any respectably dressed person could, without introduction, invitation, or any prearrangement, be ushered into his presence. One was the president's "levee," for men only, every Tuesday from three to four o'clock. The other was Martha Washington's tea party, for men and women, held on Friday evenings. Washington also would stage dinners on Thursdays at four o'clock in the afternoon. To avoid any charges of favoritism or contests for invitations, only officials and their families were asked to the dinners in an orderly system of rotation.[23]

Washington's effort to strike the right balance between "courtly formality and republican simplicity" was broadly, but not universally, successful.[24] As historian Catherine Allgor has written, "To Jefferson these entertainments embodied European practices characteristic of the court systems that republicanism meant to overthrow . . . the deep corruption of monarchies."[25]

An even more controversial issue of etiquette was how the president should be addressed in official communications. A committee of the House of Representatives wanted to address him simply as "the President of the United States." But in May 1789 the Senate, at the urging of Vice President Adams, who was presiding over the upper chamber, rejected the House report. Adams believed that "titles and politically inspired elegance were essential aspects of strong government" (even ambassadors were addressed as "Most Illustrious and Most Excellent") and that a plain title for the president would earn "the Contempt, the Scorn and the Derision of all Europe." He urged the adoption of "His Elective Majesty," "His Mightiness," or even "His Highness the President of the United States and Protector of the Rights of the Same."[26] But these proposals and others (such as one that future presidents be addressed as "Washington" in the same way that Roman emperors were addressed with the first emperor's family name of Caesar) proved controversial. Madison led the opposition in the House to what he perceived as the Senate's effort to apply nomenclature to the executive that would be "dangerous to republicanism," as well as being "phantom, ridiculous, and absurd."[27]

At first, Washington favored a title for the president as grand as Adams's suggestions: "His High Mightiness, the President of the United States and Protector of Their Liberties."[28] But when he realized the extent of the controversy, Washington threw his support to Madison, even expressing annoyance at Adams's efforts "to bedizen him with a superb but spurious title." On May 27, in a letter to Jefferson, Madison reported with relief that calm had been restored in Congress; the episode's only result was the facetious presentation to the heavy-set Adams of the title "His Rotundity."[29] Thereafter, it was agreed that the chief executive should have no more elaborate title than president of the United States.

Beneath all the bickering over etiquette and nomenclature lay serious matters of state. Some political leaders, such as Adams and Hamilton, believed that a strong executive was necessary to make the American experiment in self-government successful. Other important figures in the new government, especially Jefferson and Madison, were concerned that too much reliance on the presidency would undermine the delicate system of checks and balances that had been worked out in Philadelphia in 1787. Madison had led the effort to strengthen the national government at the convention, and he played a critical role during Washington's presidency in fighting off some early legislative attempts to encroach on the executive domain. Yet concern about the domestic policies and international objectives that Hamilton pursued as Washington's secretary of the Treasury spurred Madison to join Jefferson in opposing the further expansion of executive power in the decade after 1790.

Even minor controversies became important when they touched on the central principles of how a republican government ought to work. The fundamental issues that animated battles over such matters underlay virtually all of the conflicts that made the task of forming a new government so delicate. It was to Washington's great credit that he was able to mediate effectively the disputes that surrounded the creation of the American presidency and, in doing so, build a strong foundation for national unity.

Forming the Executive and Judicial Branches

During Washington's first term, Congress passed bills to establish three major executive departments: state, treasury, and war. In accordance with the Constitution, the heads of these departments were nominated by the president and confirmed by the Senate. For secretary of state, Washington chose Jefferson, who as minister to France had shown himself to be an excellent diplomat. Hamilton, a widely recognized expert on finance and commerce, became secretary of the Treasury. Henry Knox, a diligent administrator who had served General. Washington reliably as chief of artillery during the Revolutionary War, was President Washington's choice to be secretary of war.

Washington selected Edmund Randolph of Virginia as the first attorney general. At that time, the office of attorney general occupied a unique position in the executive branch. It did not yet possess the status and dignity of a department, but the attorney general served as legal adviser to the president and the department heads.[30]

In forming the executive branch, the Washington administration employed highly informal procedures. No rigid division of labor was established among the departments, nor did formal rules or strictly defined codes of behavior govern their internal operations. In general, executive administration was ad hoc and personal. The Constitution authorized the president to "require the Opinion in writing" of individual department heads "upon any Subject relating to the Duties of their respective Offices." But Washington wanted "to compare the opinions of those in whom I confide with one another," especially on controversial matters.[31] Still, he did not convene formal meetings of "the Heads of the Great Departments" and the attorney general until almost the end of his first term, and he did not use the word *cabinet* until April 1793, near the start of his second term.

Administrative informality did not mean that no purpose animated the appointments and procedures of Washington's presidency. Recognizing the need to invest his administration with talented and respected leaders whose presence would advance the acceptability of the new government, Washington sought the most admired people available to carry out its functions. His three principal counselors—Hamilton, Jefferson, and in Congress, Madison—formed a remarkable constellation of advisers, and the latter two later were elected president in their own right. Nevertheless, strong disagreements arose among them, with Madison and Jefferson often allied against Hamilton. Washington recognized the varied talents of these three independent-minded leaders and, for a time, was able to yoke them in a "single harness." His ability to do so and the general success that he achieved as an administrator helped "to plant in the minds of the American people the model of a government which commanded respect by reason of its integrity, energy, and competence" as well as its openness to competing views.[32]

Washington's appointments to other jobs also were intended to enhance the legitimacy of the fledgling national government. As the bills to create departments became law during his first term, the president found himself with nearly a thousand offices to fill. Considering all of these appointments to be important, Washington devoted an enormous amount of time to them. According to administrative historian Leonard D. White, "No collector of customs, captain of a cutter, keeper of a lighthouse, or surveyor of revenue was appointed except after specific consideration by the President."[33]

Although besieged by applicants, directly or through intermediaries, Washington "scrupulously declined to exploit the opportunity to create a patronage system." His appointments were made with little regard to personal relations or family connections. They were partisan only in the sense that he chose persons "of known attachment" to the Constitution. Especially during the first two years of his administration, Washington took care not to appoint former British loyalists or other persons whose support for the Constitution was doubtful.[34]

In general, White has written, "Washington's rules of selection shone in statesmanlike splendor. The dominating standard was the rule of fitness."[35] In screening applicants for jobs Washington did not employ the criteria of "merit" and "neutral competence" that have dominated civil service procedures since the late nineteenth century. He was concerned less with his appointees' expertise than with their reputations for good character. Apart from personal integrity, standing in one's local community was a principal ingredient of fitness, reflecting Washington's desire to cultivate a favorable opinion of the national government in the far-flung sections of the Union. As Stanley Elkins and Eric McKitrick have observed, Washington routinely referred to his appointees as "first Characters . . . who by virtue of their abilities and records of public service stood first, as it were, in the respect of their neighbors."[36]

In every way, Washington's personnel policies manifested his concern for the requirements of building a nation. Not just an executive branch but also a judicial branch had to be created and staffed. The Constitution stated that there would be "one supreme Court" (but nothing of its size and little of its structure) and "such inferior Courts as the Congress may from time to time ordain and establish." These matters were resolved by the Judiciary Act of 1789, which created a six-member Supreme Court consisting of a chief justice and five associate justices; thirteen district courts (essentially one per state); and three regional courts of appeal, where individual Supreme Court justices "rode circuit" hearing cases. Washington's initial nominees to the supreme tribunal—all of them distinguished, each from a different state, half from the North and half from the South—won easy Senate confirmation. When Chief Justice John Jay retired in 1795, however, senators rejected Washington's choice of John Rutledge, who was eminently qualified but whose views on foreign policy had become politically controversial. Washington's waning influence during his second term also helps explain Rutledge's rejection by the Senate, auguring further rejections at future times of relative presidential weakness.

The first cabinet, selected by President George Washington, far left, included Secretary of War Henry Knox (on Washington's left), Secretary of the Treasury Alexander Hamilton, Secretary of State Thomas Jefferson, and Attorney General Edmund Randolph.

Source: Library of Congress.

Presidential "Supremacy" and the Conduct of the Executive Branch

In addition to his hiring policies, Washington established the critical precedent that authority over the executive branch belongs primarily to the president. He subscribed to a theory of administration that viewed the heads of the departments as "assistants or deputies" of the president. As Hamilton had written in *Federalist* No. 72, such persons "ought to derive their offices from his appointment, at least from his nomination, and ought to be subject to his superintendence." Washington's theory of national administration prevailed against competing views that foresaw either the Senate or individual cabinet officers sharing fully in the direction of the executive departments.[37]

The belief that the upper house of the legislature should be involved in the details of administration was especially strong in the American tradition, reaching far back into the colonial era. Indeed, a bill nearly passed Congress during Washington's first term that would have severely restricted the president's administrative authority. The bill, which involved the creation of the Department of State, raised the issue of where the power to dismiss an executive official should lie. Significantly, Hamilton's advocacy of the "deputy" theory of administration originally did not extend to the removal of executive officeholders. In *Federalist* No. 77, he had cited the principle of "steady administration" to contend that the Senate's approval would be needed to remove an official, just as it was to appoint one.

Washington and Madison, his chief congressional ally in this matter, responded to *Federalist*-quoting critics of a strong executive by arguing that presidents would be rendered powerless if they were not masters of their own domain. As Madison argued during the House debate on the State Department bill, "Vest [the removal power] in the Senate jointly with the President, and you abolish at once the great principle of unity and responsibility in the executive department, which was intended for the security of liberty and the common good."[38] In other words, how could the president be held responsible for the actions of incompetent or disobedient executive officials if denied the authority to fire them?

Madison successfully led the fight in the House against senatorial interference with presidential removals, but in the Senate the final vote was tied. Vice President Adams, as president of the Senate, broke the tie in favor of the president's unilateral power to remove executive appointees from office. From then on, the First Congress followed Madison's lead by passing laws establishing the other major departments of the government that were carefully designed to minimize legislative influence in how the executive branch was led.[39] Indeed, Madison regarded it as important that the new laws treat the removal power as one granted to the president by the Constitution, not by congressional choice. Not only was this power implied by the provision that vested "the executive power" in the president but also by the clause that established the president's responsibility "to take Care that the Laws be faithfully executed."[40] Resistance by obstreperous but unremovable subordinates, Madison argued, would prevent the president from fulfilling this constitutional responsibility.

The decision to acknowledge that the Constitution vested the removal power in the president was a critical prelude to Washington's dominance of administration. As the most comprehensive account of public administration in the early days of the Republic concludes, "All major decisions in matters of administration, and many minor ones, were made by the President. No department head, not even Hamilton, settled any matter of importance without consulting the President and securing his approval."[41]

Congress's eventual acquiescence to presidential supremacy over the departments was probably a tribute to Washington's demonstrated devotion to the principle of separation of powers. The president shared Madison's conviction that the chief executive should be supreme in matters pertaining to the conduct of the executive branch but restrained in matters that are rightfully the legislature's. Washington did recommend legislation to Congress, albeit sparingly, but he applied no pressure to get his program enacted. "Nor," Washington biographer James Thomas Flexner has observed, "did he attempt during his first term to achieve by executive orders any matter that the strictest interpretation of the Constitution could regard as within the legislative domain."[42]

Hamilton had argued in *Federalist* No. 73 that aggressive use of the veto was essential for the president to protect the office from legislative usurpation and to "furnish security against the enaction of improper laws." But Washington believed that the president's veto power should be applied only to bills of doubtful constitutionality, not unwise policy.[43] He signed "many Bills with which my Judgment is at variance," Washington explained, "from motives of respect to the legislature (and I might add, from my interpretation of the constitution)."[44] Washington's caution, which resulted in only two vetoes in eight years, was understandable in the context of the times. Memories were fresh of controversial vetoes by the king and royal governors in the colonial era.[45]

Washington's circumspect use of the veto did not mean that he was a weak president intent on avoiding conflict with the legislature at all costs.

Rather, the first president sought to win the trust of Congress and the people so that he and future presidents would be able to exercise power forcefully when it seemed most appropriate—that is, when managing the affairs of the executive branch, conducting foreign policy, and upholding the law. In view of the inherently uneasy relationship between executive power and popular rule, Washington feared that aggressive presidential efforts to dominate the legislative process might vindicate the fears of the Anti-Federalists that the presidency would tend toward monarchy. Washington's respect for Congress won him the trust of most legislators, which eventually enabled him to carve out significant spheres of presidential influence in his own domain. Just as Washington's self-denial at the end of the revolution had set the stage for his ascent to the presidency, so did his restraint as the first president bestow legitimacy on the office he occupied.[46]

Washington's propriety in executive–legislative relations extended even to foreign policy. The president did not hesitate to assert his primacy in diplomatic affairs, but he also tried hard to develop a line of communication with the Senate, which he believed was required by the Constitution's stipulation that the president seek that body's "Advice and Consent" on treaties. Washington initially interpreted this requirement to include consultation with the Senate before treaty negotiations with another sovereign nation began. But his first effort to involve the Senate fully in the making of a treaty occasioned an awkward and embarrassing incident that caused a different precedent to be established.

Washington began by drafting instructions for a commission he appointed, with Senate approval, to negotiate a treaty with the Creek Indians, who controlled much of west Georgia and what later would become Alabama. He then accompanied acting secretary of war Knox to the Senate chamber in August 1789 to seek the senators' advice. Vice President Adams began the session by reading the proposed treaty to the Senate. But the president's appeal for consultation was greeted with an awkward silence that was broken only reluctantly by the senators, who proceeded to engage in a confused and tentative discussion of the treaty. Finally, Sen. William Maclay of Pennsylvania, certain that there was "no chance of a fair investigation of subjects while the President of the United States sat there, with his Secretary of War, to support his opinions and overawe the timid and neutral part of the Senate," spoke in favor of a motion that the president's papers be submitted to a Senate committee for study. As the senator sat down, Washington started up in what Maclay described as a "violent fret" and cried out: "This defeats every purpose of my coming here."[47] Although Washington achieved his purpose in the end—the Senate later ratified the treaty with only minor changes—he had to sit for a long time, listening to what seemed to him a dull and irrelevant debate. When the president left the Senate chamber, he reportedly was overheard saying that he would "be damned if he ever went there again."

The Creek Indian treaty incident revealed the great difficulty of establishing a forum for formal consultations between the chief executive and the legislature within the constitutional system of "separated institutions sharing powers." Washington in effect "slammed the door" on similar encounters in the future, and as a result, neither he nor any later president ever consulted the Senate in the same way.[48] Most significant, Washington's failure to obtain the Senate's active cooperation in the preliminary work of making treaties ended up firmly establishing the president's supremacy in matters of diplomacy. To be sure, presidents never did come to possess an unhampered treaty-making power. But the Washington administration created a precedent that relegated the Senate to approving or rejecting treaties that the executive already had negotiated.

Presidential Nonpartisanship and the Beginning of Party Conflict

Washington's conduct as president embodied his understanding that the presidency was a nonpartisan office. Like most of the Framers of the Constitution, he disapproved of "factions" and did not regard himself as the leader of any political party. Washington believed that Article II of the Constitution encouraged the president to stand apart from the jarring conflict that was inherent in a legislative body. As such, the president could provide a strong measure of unity and stability to the political system. This was a task that by temperament and background Washington was well suited to perform. Although he insisted on being master of the executive branch, it was contrary to his principles to try to influence either congressional elections or the legislative process. The primary duty of the president, he believed, was to execute the laws.[49]

Washington's conception of the presidency did not survive even his own administration. Disagreements within his brilliant constellation of advisers led to the early demise of the nonpartisan presidency. Party conflict arose from the sharp differences between Hamilton and Jefferson that emerged during Washington's first term and became irreconcilable during his second term. These differences became obvious in the reaction to Hamilton's financial measures for the "adequate support of public credit," which he proposed in a series of reports to Congress in 1790 and 1791. In the reports, Hamilton called on Congress to assume the debts incurred by the states and the national government during the war, to create a national bank, and to enact a system of tariffs to protect infant manufacturing industries in the United States.

All of these proposals, save for the protectionist tariff, were supported by Washington and passed by Congress. Once implemented, Hamilton's innovations allowed the United States, so lately on the verge of bankruptcy, to establish sounder credit and a more stable financial system than all but a few European nations. They also gave creditors a direct financial stake in the success of the new national government. Yet these measures, successful as they were, pushed Jefferson into barely disguised opposition to the Washington administration's domestic program, sowing seeds of formal party conflict that blossomed as soon as Washington retired from the presidency.

Jefferson did not oppose all of Hamilton's measures; indeed, he approved of the plan to assume the national government's domestic and foreign debts. Although Jefferson had grave reservations about the national government paying the states' debts, believing that such a policy would unduly benefit securities speculators, he acquiesced even to this policy as part of a deal he worked out with Hamilton. The two agreed that the nation's capital would be transferred from New York to Philadelphia in 1790 for ten years, pending permanent removal in 1800 to the new federal city of Washington, which would be built on the Potomac River between Maryland and Jefferson's home state of Virginia. The new capital, Jefferson hoped, would become as much the center of national life as London was in England and Paris in France.[50] But he, and eventually Madison, opposed Hamilton's proposal for a national bank, which was contained in the Treasury secretary's December 1790 report to Congress. According to Jefferson and Madison, Hamilton's plan would establish national institutions and policies that exceeded the constitutional powers of the new government. Did the word *necessary* in the Constitution's "necessary and proper" clause mean essential, as Jefferson argued in a memorandum requested by the president, or merely "conducive to," as Hamilton insisted in his own memo? Washington accepted Hamilton's broader construction. So did northern members of Congress, who voted almost unanimously for the bank even as most southern members, fewer in number, opposed it.

Apart from their economic importance, Hamilton's initiatives presupposed a principal role for the executive in formulating public policies and carrying them out. This view, Jefferson and Madison believed, made the more decentralized and republican institutions—Congress and the states—subordinate to the executive, thereby undermining popular sovereignty and starting the United States down the path toward a British-style monarchy whose "increasing splendor and [the] number of its prerogatives . . . might prove excitements to ambition . . . and consequently strengthen the pretext for an hereditary designation of the magistrate."[51]

Neutrality Proclamation 1793

When war broke out in 1793 between Great Britain and France, a difference of opinion about the executive's proper role in foreign affairs aggravated the growing rift between Hamilton and Jefferson. Convinced that the French Revolution of 1789 had gotten out of hand, degenerating into mob rule, Hamilton took the side of England, a nation for which he had deep sympathies. Jefferson and Madison endorsed what they believed to be the sacred republican cause of the French Revolution. They regarded Hamilton's support of England as evidence of his supposed preference for monarchy.

Conflicts over foreign affairs, like those over domestic policy, were inextricably joined to contrasting beliefs about the proper extent of presidential power. As political scientist Fred Greenstein has observed, Washington was supremely confident of his ability to chart the new nation's course through dangerous international waters because, as commander in chief during the Revolutionary War, he had "perfected his political and diplomatic skills in the course of his dealings with the [independent] state governments, Congress, and France."[52] But when Washington issued the Neutrality Proclamation of 1793, the Anglo–French question provoked a bitter exchange of views about the executive's proper role in foreign policy. The proclamation declared that the duties and interests of the United States required the government to "with sincerity and good faith adopt and pursue a conduct friendly and impartial to the belligerent powers." It prohibited Americans from "committing, aiding, or abetting hostilities against any of the said powers, or by carrying to them any of those articles which are deemed contraband by the modern usage of nations."[53]

Even before Washington's policy was announced, Hamilton and Jefferson took predictable stands on the merits of the Neutrality Proclamation. In private councils, Jefferson advised the president against it on two grounds. First, he believed such a unilateral executive action to be unconstitutional. A declaration of neutrality was, in effect, a declaration that there would be no war, a decision that rightfully belonged to Congress. Second, the 1778 treaty that secured French support for the American Revolution obligated the United States to provide France with any necessities of war that had to be brought across the Atlantic. In reply, Hamilton told the president that in the absence of a declaration of war by Congress, the executive had full power to proclaim and enforce American neutrality. Moreover, he defended neutrality between Great Britain and France on its merits, claiming that the tumultuous events in France had deprived that nation of any permanent government, thereby abrogating the obligations of the 1778 treaty.

Washington sided with Hamilton on the neutrality issue, but he took pains to unify his administration in public support of the proclamation. To mollify Jefferson, the word *neutrality* was not used in the text, although the sense clearly was there. Jefferson won a more substantial concession when Washington, against Hamilton's recommendation, decided to receive France's ambassador to the United States, Edmond Genet, which made the United States the first nation to receive an emissary from the new Republic of France. These concessions to the secretary of state notwithstanding (Genet became a troublemaker by publicly recruiting Americans to fight the British), the proclamation was a victory for Hamilton. It boldly asserted the president's power of initiative in the conduct of foreign affairs.[54]

The controversy over the neutrality proclamation became public after Washington announced his policy, prompting Hamilton to write a series of newspaper articles under the pseudonym "Pacificus." Madison, at Jefferson's urging, replied to these postings in articles written as "Helvidius." The issues that the erstwhile coauthors of *The Federalist Papers* broached in this exchange illuminate the fundamental nature of a conflict that has occupied the nation's attention time and time again, not only in foreign affairs but also in other matters pertaining to the president's authority.

In defending the neutrality proclamation, Hamilton offered a sweeping justification for discretionary presidential power that sharply distinguished between the Constitution's separate "vesting clauses" for legislative and executive authority. Article I, Hamilton pointed out, states that "all legislative Powers herein granted shall be vested in a Congress of the United States." Article II seems to provide a much more general grant: "The executive Power shall be vested in a President of the United States of America." The absence from Article II of the words "herein granted," Hamilton argued, meant that the executive power is both wide-ranging and vested exclusively in the president, "subject only to the exceptions and qualifications which are expressed in the Constitution."[55]

In foreign affairs, the explicit constitutional restrictions on presidential power extended no further than the right of the Senate to ratify treaties and of Congress to declare war. These rights of the legislature, Hamilton insisted, did not hinder the executive in other matters of foreign policy, which "naturally" were the domain of the president.[56] Indeed, Hamilton set forth a theory of presidential power that not only delegates to the executive nearly absolute discretion in the conduct of foreign affairs but also proposes a broad conception of emergency powers that later presidents, especially those in the twentieth and twenty-first centuries, would draw on generously.[57]

Madison, replying in a rival newspaper as Helvidius, denied that foreign policy was "naturally" an executive power. The tasks of foreign policy—to declare war, to conclude peace, and to form alliances—were among "the highest acts of sovereignty; of which the legislative power must at least be an integral and preeminent part." In foreign as in domestic matters, Madison argued, republican government requires that the president's power be confined to executing the laws. To suggest, as Hamilton did, that foreign policy is within the proper definition of executive power was to imply that the executive branch has a legislative power. Such an argument was "in theory an absurdity—in practice a tyranny."[58]

The precedent Washington established that a president can unilaterally enunciate a policy of neutrality was important but limited. He never challenged Congress's right to overturn such a decision by declaring war and even secured congressional endorsement of his specific action with passage of the Neutrality Act of 1794. Far more significant was the larger issue in the debate between his leading advisers: whether the president is limited by the letter of the Constitution or is a sovereign head of state with discretion to act independently unless the Constitution specifically spells out exceptions and limitations. The fundamental and contentious debate between Pacificus and Helvidius signaled that Washington's hope of establishing a presidency above parties was unrealistic, thwarted by fundamental conflicts about the constitutional interpretation of presidential power. Indeed, in the face of the bitter partisanship aroused by the Neutrality Proclamation, Hamilton and his political allies organized a series of mass meetings throughout the country to generate public support for the president's policy.[59]

The Whiskey Rebellion

The strains created by the controversy over the neutrality proclamation led inevitably to an outbreak of open party conflict. Federalists shared Hamilton's support for commerce and manufacturing, an independent and energetic executive as the anchor of a strong national government, and a foreign policy that established strong ties with Great Britain. In contrast, Democratic-Republicans shared Jefferson's devotion to agriculture, a strong legislature in a weak national government, and France. Aggravating the tension, historian Alan Taylor has argued, was that Federalists and Democratic-Republicans alike disdained the concept of political parties, which meant that both claimed "exclusively to speak for the American people" and "cast rivals as insidious conspirators bent on destroying freedom and union."[60] Although the Federalists were strongest in the North and the Democratic-Republicans in the South, the partisan polarization of the 1790s transcended regional loyalties. Most Anti-Federalists—the opponents of the Constitution—migrated into the Democratic-Republican Party, which echoed the fears expressed during the ratification fight about executive aggrandizement and national consolidation. In joining the opposition to the Federalists, they did not repeat the mistake made in 1788 of sitting out the congressional elections. Indeed, in 1792, as Washington was elected unanimously to a second term, the Democratic-Republicans became the stronger party in Congress.

The full implications of rising partisan conflict became clear during the presidency of John Adams, who took office in 1797. But even Washington, during his second term, was confronted with serious problems born of partisan differences. These problems culminated in the first significant test of the president's constitutional power to "take Care that the Laws be faithfully executed."

In 1794 militant opposition to a national excise tax on the production of whiskey arose in several parts of the country, particularly in the four westernmost counties of Pennsylvania, where whiskey was so important to the local economy that it was used, like money, as a medium of exchange. Backcountry Pennsylvanians had avoided paying the hated whiskey tax since it was first levied in 1791.[61] In the summer of 1794 resistance turned into mass defiance, stimulated at least in part by a local Democratic-Republican organization, the Mingo Creek society. A federal marshal and an excise inspector were forced to flee the area in July, and for two weeks western Pennsylvania was agitated by impassioned meetings, radical oratory, threats to drive all federal authority from Pittsburgh by force, and occasional acts of violence.

President Washington's response to the so-called Whiskey Rebellion was to issue a stern proclamation on August 7, 1794, demanding that the rebels "disperse and retire peaceably to their respective abodes" and warning "all persons whomsoever against aiding, abetting, or comforting the perpetuators of the . . . treasonable acts."[62] Almost simultaneously, after satisfying the law by securing from Supreme Court justice James Wilson a certification that the situation was beyond the control of federal marshals and courts, Washington asked the governors of Maryland, New Jersey, Pennsylvania, and Virginia to supply a militia army to put down the rebellion.

The governors complied with Washington's request. An army of thirteen thousand was assembled in Harrisburg, Pennsylvania, in September. It promptly marched into western Pennsylvania, with Washington himself in command—"the first and only time," historian Joseph J. Ellis has pointed out, "a sitting American president led troops in the field."[63] Pennsylvania governor Thomas Mifflin had argued against federal intervention, insisting that his state's militia was adequate to cope with the outbreak of lawlessness. But Washington was persuaded by Hamilton to suppress the insurrection with a massive display of force.

Hamilton was convinced that Washington had to assert unequivocally the supremacy of the national government when in conflict with local claims of independence as well as to establish the president's leadership in such situations. But the secretary of the Treasury and leader of the Federalists also was motivated by partisan considerations. Hamilton viewed the insurrection in rural Pennsylvania as an opportunity to discredit and crush his political enemies by branding them as traitors. The Mingo Creek society was one of several that had sprung up throughout the states in 1793 in response to the heightened polarization spawned by disagreements between the Federalists and Democratic-Republicans over the war in Europe. Although not formally associated with the Democratic-Republican Party, these societies militantly supported most of its policies. Referring to the local Democratic-Republican societies, Hamilton averred in a letter to Washington on August 2, 1792, that "formal public meetings of influential individuals" had "fomented" the "general spirit of opposition" that produced the violence in the western counties.

Democratic-Republican leaders, including Jefferson and Madison, did not actively oppose the national government's intervention in the insurrection; indeed, many members of the Democratic-Republican societies in Philadelphia and Baltimore volunteered to join the federal force against the Whiskey Rebellion. Nevertheless, the Democratic-Republicans found themselves in a politically vulnerable position because of the activities of their brethren in the West. Most Americans seemed convinced that treason and rebellion had arisen from the opposition societies. "The[ir] game," wrote Madison of the Federalists' strategy, "was to connect the Democratic societies with the odium of insurrection, to connect the Republicans in Congress with those societies," and to place President Washington "in opposition to both."[64] The immediate result was that the Federalists won back control of Congress in the 1794 midterm elections.[65]

For his part, Washington delayed using federal force in Pennsylvania until his protracted efforts to conciliate the rebels were rejected, reflecting "his earnest wish to avoid a resort to coercion."[66] In the face of a Washington-led army, the rebellion dissolved. Only twenty rebels were found; they were taken to Philadelphia and charged with treason. Two were convicted, but Washington, with his usual determination to show that a strong executive need not be despotic, pardoned them.[67]

Although his display of force in Pennsylvania ended anticlimactically, Washington reported to Congress on November 19, 1794, that suppressing the insurrection had demonstrated that the prosperity of the United States rested "on solid foundations, by furnishing an additional proof that [citizens embraced] the true principles of government and liberty."[68] "The first president clearly understood that a government which cannot enforce its laws is no government at all," historian William M. Goldsmith has written, "and he also realized that within the framework of our complex political system, with its deliberate distribution of power, it is the responsibility of the executive to see that the laws are obeyed."[69]

Nevertheless, the Whiskey Rebellion and Washington's response exacerbated rather than ended the political conflicts that divided Americans in the 1790s. Jefferson and Madison became even more convinced that Hamilton intended to establish an overweening executive, including a large standing army, that would subvert the Constitution. Moreover, as word of the actual events in western Pennsylvania spread throughout the country, the prestige of the Federalist Party began to erode. Jefferson wrote to Madison on December 28, 1794, that "the information of our militia, returned from the Westward, is uniform, that tho the people there let them pass quietly, they were objects of their laughter, not of their fear, . . . that their detestation of the excise law is universal, and has now associated to it a detestation of government." Jefferson added that the time was coming when the Democratic-Republicans would "fetch up the leeway of our vessel."[70]

Fortunately, the conflict between the Federalists and the Democratic-Republicans never became as raw and disruptive as the framers of the Constitution feared partisan strife would be. The enduring restraint on factionalism in the United States may be attributed in part to the forceful example of nonpartisanship that was offered by George Washington at a time when maintaining unity was critical to the survival of the new government. To some extent, Washington sought to deal with the divisions between the Hamiltonians and the Jeffersonians by avoiding them, choosing to preside over the government rather than to dominate it.[71] To be sure, as his response to the Whiskey Rebellion makes clear, Washington at times took forceful stands on controversial issues, usually on the Hamiltonian side. Yet his extraordinary stature and popularity, combined with his commitment to a strong and independent legislature, restrained partisan strife for as long as he was president. Moreover, Washington's renunciation of party leadership left his successors a legacy of presidential impartiality that has never been eclipsed. Even after a formal two-party system emerged, the precedent set by Washington demanded that the chief executive strive to lead the nation, not just the party that governs the nation.

Washington's Retirement and the Jay Treaty: The Constitutional Crisis of 1796

Near the end of 1795, the paramount political question for most public figures in the United States was whether Washington would accept a third term as president. The Constitution imposed no limit on presidential reeligibility, and although Washington's political reputation was slightly tarnished by the partisan animosities that divided his cabinet and Congress, he could easily have remained in office had he chosen to do so.

Washington, however, was eager to return to Mount Vernon. In September 1796 he announced his retirement, marking the event by releasing his Farewell Address, which was published rather than spoken to an audience. Washington did not want his voluntary retirement to set a precedent limiting future presidents to two terms. Rather, he wanted the country to learn that the Constitution would function without him as president.

Washington's decision to retire eased somewhat the Jeffersonians' concerns about the dangerous aggrandizement of executive power. So did the absence of an heir: George and Martha Washington had no children. As biographer Richard Brookhiser has pointed out, to a nation as familiar with monarchy and besotted with Washington as the United States was in its early years, "The dynastic temptation was very real. The country was lucky that there was so little material for temptation to work with."[72] At the Constitutional Convention, delegate Hugh Williamson had worried that the president would become "an elective king" who would "lay a train of succession of his children."[73] Fortunately, perhaps, of the first five presidents, only John Adams had sons who survived to adulthood. His eldest son, John Quincy Adams, became the sixth president.

Washington's retirement cleared the way for a more partisan form of presidential politics. As long as he was president, Washington was able by dint of his prestige to restrain open party conflict. But Vice President Adams, although a distinguished and respected political leader, lacked Washington's stature as well as his reputation for impartiality. In the division between Federalists and Democratic-Republicans, Adams was clearly identified with the Federalists. His role in the controversy over the president's title and his well-known admiration for the British form of government marked him as a "monarchist" in the eyes of Jeffersonians. When Washington's decision to retire became known and Adams stepped forward as the heir apparent, the presidential campaign of 1796 began in earnest.

The 1796 election is generally regarded as one of the bitterest and most acrimonious in American history. The election matched Adams and Thomas Pinckney, the Federalist candidates for president and vice president, against the Democratic-Republican ticket of Thomas Jefferson and Aaron Burr. The divisions between the parties were crystallized by the controversial Jay Treaty, which had been signed in London in November 1794.

In the Jay Treaty, Great Britain pledged that it would evacuate the northwestern military posts that had sustained British power on American soil since the Revolution. The treaty also won a limited right for American vessels to trade with the British West Indies. As such, it promised to secure the territorial integrity of the United States and to ameliorate dangerous conflicts at sea, where several skirmishes, the by-product of Great Britain's ongoing war with France, had brought the United States and Great Britain to the brink of war. Yet when some secret terms of the Jay Treaty were leaked to the Democratic-Republican press in late June 1795, a political firestorm ensued that made John Jay (the chief justice of the United States, who acting as a presidential envoy, negotiated the treaty) and, by implication, Washington the targets of vicious partisan attacks.

Democratic-Republican opposition to the Jay Treaty was animated by an intense dislike of the British, which was reinforced by Great Britain's use of its eight northwestern posts to stir American Indian tribes to attack settlers in the Northwest Territory. Southern Democratic-Republicans also were enraged because the treaty provided no compensation to slave owners for the slaves seized by the British at the end of the Revolution. Nor did it create a mechanism to settle the pre-Revolutionary War debts that Americans owed to British citizens, which placed southerners, especially, in jeopardy of having to repay loans of long standing. In effect, then, the

Jay Treaty became the issue through which the emerging tensions between Federalists and Democratic-Republicans hardened into an enduring and organized two-party conflict.[74]

The Constitution required a two-thirds vote of the Senate to ratify a treaty. On June 24, 1795, the Federalist-dominated majority ratified the Jay Treaty by 20 to 10, with not a vote to spare. What made the treaty an election issue in 1796 was Madison's subsequent battle to undermine it in the House of Representatives. Because the treaty required that arbitration commissions be established to settle disagreements between the United States and Great Britain that were not resolved by the document itself, it could not be carried into effect without congressional appropriations. "Money bills," as the Constitution clearly specified, could originate only in the House of Representatives. Whether the House, by virtue of its power over appropriations, would share the Senate's role in foreign affairs was a constitutional issue that had not yet been settled. Madison sought to weld the widespread popular opposition to the treaty to the lower chamber's ingrained resentment of executive and senatorial power. In doing so, he enjoyed the full support of Jefferson, who wrote on November 30, 1795, in a letter to Edward Rutledge, a friend in the South Carolina legislature:

> I trust the popular branch of our legislature will disapprove of it [the Jay Treaty], and thus rid us of this infamous act, which is really nothing more than a treaty of alliance between England and the Anglomen of this country, against the legislature and people of the United States.[75]

On March 24, 1796, the Democratic-Republicans succeeded in passing a House resolution requesting the president to provide the House with all papers pertaining to the negotiation of the Jay Treaty. Albert Gallatin, one of the party's most persuasive leaders, argued that representatives had the authority to make this request

> because their cooperation and sanction was necessary to carry the Treaty into full effect, to render it a binding instrument, and to make it properly speaking, a law of the land; because they had full discretion either to give or to refuse that cooperation; because they must be guided, in the exercise of that discretion, by the merits and expediency of the treaty itself, and therefore had a right to ask for every information which could assist them in deciding the question.[76]

Gallatin's aim was not merely to see the papers or even to defeat the Jay Treaty and pave the way for the election of a Democratic-Republican president in 1796.[77] Along with Madison and Jefferson, he also wanted to assert the House's right to participate in the treaty-making process. They believed that if this power belonged exclusively to the president and two-thirds of the Senate, the president conceivably could act in concert with just twenty-two of the then thirty-two senators to usurp all the powers of the House. Treaties, they noted, had the same constitutional status as the laws enacted by Congress.

In view of the Jay Treaty's unpopularity, the Democratic-Republicans had a real chance to scuttle it, which would have severely limited the president's power to conduct foreign affairs. But Washington, on the verge of retirement, chose to make the House's request for papers the last great constitutional issue of his presidency. He replied to the resolution with "a thunderous refusal," as historian Forrest McDonald has described it.[78] "To admit . . . a right in the House of Representatives to demand . . . papers respecting a negotiation with a foreign power," Washington asserted, "would be to establish a dangerous precedent." Except in matters pertaining to impeachment, "it does not occur that the inspection of papers asked for can be relative to any purpose under the cognizance of the House of Representatives."

Washington also lectured Congress on the Constitution. "Having been a member of the General Convention and knowing the principles on which the Constitution was formed," he observed pointedly, "the power of making treaties is exclusively vested in the President, by and with the advice and consent of the Senate, provided two-thirds of the senators present concur; and . . . every treaty so made and promulgated thenceforward became the law of the land."[79]

A constitutional impasse had been reached. The House claimed a right to see the papers, but it had no means to pry them loose from the president. A debate followed, consuming the entire month of April 1796, about whether the House would appropriate the funds (roughly $90,000) that were needed to carry the treaty into effect. In the end, Washington's resolute stand eroded the Democratic-Republicans' initial House majority. The enabling legislation for the treaty was approved at the end of April by the narrow vote of 51–48.

The Democratic-Republicans' effort to transform hostility to the Jay Treaty into a central campaign issue backfired. Their opposition to the treaty probably contributed to Adams's election as president in 1796 and to the Federalist's gains in that year's congressional elections. The only solace the Democratic-Republicans could find in this latest defeat was that it rested on George Washington's influence, not the Federalist Party's. Even the Federalists must have realized, wrote Jefferson, "that nothing can support them but the colossus of the President's merits with the people, and the moment he retires, that his successor, if a monocrat, will be overborne by the republican sense of his Constituents."[80]

With the final enactment of the Jay Treaty, a constitutional crisis, underlain with bitter partisan strife, was averted. The incident did not settle permanently the question of the House's proper role in foreign affairs. "But the precedent and correlative implications of the decision that Washington established in 1796," William Goldsmith has observed, "would be difficult to erase."[81]

The 1796 Election

In spite of the strong disagreements that divided Democratic-Republicans from Federalists, the contestants in the partisan strife of the 1790s were reluctant warriors. Partisanship was still not considered respectable in American politics, and candidates for president were not expected to seek the office actively. "Neither Adams nor Jefferson," historian John Ferling has noted, "left their farms that autumn, and neither issued public statements or wrote so much as a single letter in an effort to round up support."[82]

Nevertheless, disdain for parties in theory had become rancorous partisanship in practice, with each side viewing its opponents as enemies of republican government. Local party organizations dominated the 1796 election, conducting their campaigns through newspaper polemics, pamphlets, and political rallies.[83] The issues that the grassroots partisans raised so divided the country that the hard-won national unity the Constitutional Convention and the Washington administration had achieved was threatened. The Federalists branded Jefferson an atheist who would destroy all organized religion. He was accused of being a radical democrat who as president would allow republican government to deteriorate into the sort of mob rule that recently had brought the Reign of Terror to revolutionary France. Democratic-Republicans excoriated Adams as a monarchist who neither believed in democracy nor respected the Constitution.

Hamilton, who despised both Jefferson and Adams, complicated matters further by trying to manipulate the Electoral College so that neither candidate would become president. In 1789 Hamilton had privately urged several Federalist electors not to cast their second presidential votes for John

Adams, lest the vice-presidential candidate somehow outpoll Washington. Although Adams received the second-highest number of electoral votes, he was named on fewer than half the ballots, a result so embarrassing that he considered refusing the office.[84] Now, seven years later, Hamilton secretly sought to persuade southern Federalist electors to mark their ballots for Jefferson and Pinckney, not to help Jefferson but to deny Adams the largest majority. Pinckney's home state of South Carolina did so, but this time Adams's supporters in New England caught on to Hamilton's scheme, and eighteen Federalist electors withheld their own second votes from Pinckney, who ended up finishing third.

The 1796 election ended with a narrow Federalist victory. Adams was elected president with seventy-one electoral votes. He swept New England and, except for Pennsylvania, the Mid-Atlantic states while losing the South. Jefferson's sixty-eight electoral votes made him the vice president. Because the avowedly nonpartisan constitutional mechanism for selecting the president and vice president had not yet been changed to accommodate the emergence of partisan competition, the election of 1796 yielded an administration that was headed by the leaders of two hostile political organizations. Only their strong mutual respect kept the first party-fought battle under the new Constitution from tearing the country apart. "I can particularly have no feelings which would revolt at a secondary position to Mr. Adams," wrote Jefferson. "I am his junior in life, was his junior in Congress, his junior in the diplomatic line, his junior lately in our civil government."[85] Political tensions between the two men emerged later, but the transition from contested election to consolidated government was a smooth one.

The Embattled Presidency of John Adams

John Adams became president in extraordinarily difficult circumstances. No other chief executive would ever have the unenviable task of succeeding a leader of Washington's stature. More significant, the international situation that Adams faced in 1797 was perilous. The Jay Treaty had greatly worsened American relations with an aggressive French government that was, after Napoleon Bonaparte defeated Austria in October 1797, at the height of its power. French harassment of American commerce at sea made Great Britain's interference with American shipping in 1793 seem mild. As Jefferson said of George Washington, "The President is fortunate to get off just as the bubble is bursting, leaving others to hold the bag."[86]

The naval war with France escalated when Adams's diplomatic attempts to maintain Washington's policy of neutrality received an insulting and humiliating response from the French foreign ministry. The American mission to France, composed of John Marshall, Charles Cotesworth Pinckney, and Elbridge Gerry, a Democratic-Republican whom Adams included to convince the opposition of his good intentions, was subjected to high-handed manipulation by Talleyrand, the French foreign minister. Talleyrand dispatched three representatives of the French government, referred to in secret dispatches as "X, Y, and Z," to meet with Adams's emissaries. Their mission was to discover how much the United States was willing to pay in bribes to French officials and loans to the French government to secure a treaty.

When the so-called XYZ Affair became public in early 1798, a furor erupted in the United States that seemed to make war with France inevitable. The more extreme Federalists, the "Arch-Federalists" or "Ultra-Federalists" as they were known, urged that a large army be created to deter an invasion by France. Although Adams was far more moderate than the extremists in his party, he also supported war preparations, especially the development of a larger navy. The naval budget in 1798 was $1.4 million, more than in the previous ten years combined. Meanwhile, war fever prompted Americans to "rally 'round the flag" in support of their president. Historian Sean Wilentz has noted that "Adams suddenly became, for the only time in his life, the focus of popular enthusiasm as the heroic American commander-in-chief."[87] He even took to wearing a full military uniform adorned by a sword.

Adams's surge of popularity was short-lived, deflated by the higher taxes he and Congress imposed to pay for the expanded military. The resentment triggered by these levies, especially the increased impost on whiskey, became a potent political issue for the Democratic-Republicans. Growing animosity between Federalists and Democratic-Republicans even led to rumors of civil discord and southern secession. At the end of June 1797, an alarmed Jefferson wrote to Edward Rutledge:

> The passions are too high at present, to be cooled in our day.
> You and I have formerly seen warm debates and high political
> passions. But gentlemen of different politics would then
> speak to each other, and separate the business of the Senate
> from that of society. It is not so now. Men who have been
> intimate all their lives, cross the street to avoid meeting, and
> turn their heads another way, lest they should be obliged to
> touch their hats.[88]

Adams's efforts to deal with the domestic and international crises of the late 1790s were hindered as much by members of his own party as by the opposition. Although everyone expected the Democratic-Republicans, led behind the scenes by Vice President Jefferson, to oppose Adams's actions, "the Federalists were often as recalcitrant or bitter toward the president."[89] The president's most influential critic within the party was Hamilton, who regarded Adams as too moderate politically and therefore incapable of dealing with the nation's problems.

Although Adams was a Federalist, he intended to follow Washington's example of remaining above party as much as possible. The president was willing to accept a war with France, but he hoped to avoid one. His primary objectives were to protect American commerce through diplomacy and an expanded navy and to force the French to respect the American flag. Hamilton and his Arch-Federalist allies, however, wanted to declare war on France. Ultimately, these differences caused an irreconcilable split within the Federalist Party. Jefferson noted in May 1797 that the "Hamiltons" were "only a little less hostile [to Adams] than to me."[90]

Hamilton severely tested Adams's authority as chief executive in several ways.[91] He was determined to guide the policy of the administration, even though he was not part of it. Hamilton had retired from the Treasury Department at the end of January 1795, but during the latter days of Washington's second term and throughout Adams's tenure, he remained the dynamic center of the Federalist Party as a private citizen. Indeed, Hamilton's influence was enhanced in 1797 by Adams's decision to retain Washington's cabinet, a policy that the new president pursued both in deference to his predecessor and because he believed that good government required able and experienced administrators.[92] The tradition that each new president appoints a new cabinet had not yet been established.

Three members of Washington's final cabinet—Secretary of State Timothy Pickering, Secretary of War James McHenry, and Oliver Wolcott, who succeeded Hamilton as secretary of the Treasury—owed their positions in the government mostly to Hamilton, who persuaded Washington to appoint them. In all important matters they looked to Hamilton, not to President Adams, to guide their actions. Only Charles Lee, who as attorney general was the least powerful member of the cabinet, and Benjamin Stoddert, who joined the administration as the secretary of the newly established Navy Department in 1798, were Adams loyalists. Disunity prevailed in executive policy except on those rare occasions when the president happened to agree with Hamilton.

As a result, the Adams administration suffered "an extraordinary situation in which the control of public policy became the prize of a struggle between a New York lawyer and a president who apparently was not fully aware of the activity of his rival."[93] The situation was aggravated by Adams's tendency to retreat for as long as seven months from the capital (still in Philadelphia) in the erroneous belief that he could manage the affairs of government from his home in Quincy, Massachusetts.[94]

The conflict between Adams and Hamilton's Arch-Federalists culminated in 1799, when the president decided to send a second mission to France in an effort to avoid war. In February, without consulting the cabinet or even the secretary of state, he nominated William Vans Murray, the American minister to the Netherlands, as minister plenipotentiary to the French Republic. Adams chose Murray because of his good relations with France. It was through Murray, in fact, that Adams learned France was willing to receive a new American mission and wanted to avoid war with the United States. The Federalist-controlled Senate, which was sympathetic to Hamilton's views, probably would have rejected the nomination, but Adams's quick, unilateral action caught its members by surprise. Senators compromised by asking for a three-member mission. The president consented.

Thwarting attempts by Secretary of State Pickering and others to postpone the sailing of the second mission, Adams first indicated that he was not opposed to a delay and then hurried the peace mission aboard an American frigate. The mission arrived in time to take advantage of France's uncertain political situation in the aftermath of a series of military defeats by the British. Although Adams's bold course aggravated his problems with the cabinet and the Federalist Party, on September 30, 1800, he achieved a commercial agreement with France that removed the threat of war, thereby preserving the principle of neutrality toward Europe that he inherited from George Washington. Adams's attempt to assume Washington's mantle of impartiality did not succeed politically, however. News of the diplomatic breakthrough reached the United States too late to affect the outcome of his bid for reelection.

Nevertheless, Adams rescued the authority of the presidency. His political position was shaken by the peace mission controversy. In all likelihood it cost him any chance for reelection. But as Leonard White has written,

> The outcome was a resounding affirmation of the authority
> of the President as chief executive and of the subordination of
> the department heads to his leadership and direction. Adams

confirmed the character of the presidency as the Constitutional Convention had outlined it and as Washington had already formed it—but only after events which stirred grave doubts concerning its future.[95]

Solidifying his leadership in the aftermath of the peace mission, Adams rid the cabinet of the two men who were most disloyal to him. In May 1800 he asked for the resignation of McHenry, who gave it, and summarily fired Pickering when he refused to resign because, according to John Ferling, "he expected Jefferson to be elected in the fall and wished to remain in charge of the last gasp of Federalist foreign policy."[96] Pickering was the first cabinet officer to be removed from office by a president. Adams appointed John Marshall to replace him as secretary of state.

The Alien and Sedition Acts

Scholars frequently praise John Adams for upholding the authority of the presidency in the face of a badly divided cabinet and party. But Adams also is widely condemned for his part in the passage and enforcement of the Alien and Sedition Acts of 1798. The Alien Act gave the president authority to expel foreigners who were suspected of subversion. The Sedition Act made it a crime, punishable by fine or imprisonment, to bring "false, scandalous and malicious" accusations against the president, Congress, or the government. Both acts were the product of war fever, which the Ultra-Federalists in Congress regarded as an opportunity to discredit Democratic-Republicans as anti-American. But Adams signed them into law without demurral.

The Sedition Act, in particular, was widely denounced as unconstitutional. Although the act, which imposed on the prosecution the burden to prove an "intent to defame" and required a jury trial to convict, was not as oppressive as similar European statutes, it was enforced in ways that treated legitimate political opposition as if it were a conspiracy against the government. As such, the Sedition Act violated the First Amendment to the Constitution, which had been added in 1791 and, among other things, forbade Congress to pass any law abridging freedom of speech or press.

The passage and enforcement of the Sedition Act was an unhappy chapter in American history. Although Jefferson's fear that it presaged the creation of a hereditary monarchy and a "Senate for life" was not realized,[97] the statute was motivated by partisan intolerance. Fourteen people were sentenced under the act, and suits were filed against five of the six leading Democratic-Republican newspapers. Most sedition cases came to trial in 1800 and were tied directly to the presidential election. The law degenerated into a Federalist instrument to stifle and even destroy the Democratic-Republican Party.

But the Sedition Act was not simply an opportunistic partisan campaign tool. It represented a clash of views about the foundation of executive authority.[98] Was the personal reputation and character of the president the ultimate source of the office's authority, as the Federalists claimed? Or did the executive office's legitimacy properly rest in public opinion, as the Democratic-Republicans argued? The Federalists insisted that they were not attempting to restrict free speech, properly understood, but only false and malicious opinions that would destroy the reputation of national leaders. As President Adams put the Federalists' case, "The man or the nation without attachment to reputation, or honor, is undone."[99]

Democratic-Republicans warned that it was all too easy in the heat of political battle to exploit restrictive measures like the Sedition Act for partisan purposes. Why, for example, were "malicious" attacks on Vice President Jefferson not forbidden by the act?[100] More fundamentally, they argued that opinions about government were intrinsically contentious and that judges and juries were incapable of distinguishing between legitimate and seditious points of view. Jefferson and his Democratic-Republican allies believed that all political opinions had a right to be heard, even those that were "false, scandalous, and malicious" or might "dissolve the Union or change its republican form." Such opinions should be allowed to "stand undisturbed as monuments of the safety with which the error of opinion may be tolerated where reason is left free to combat it."[101]

The partisan and intellectual dispute about the fundamental basis of presidential authority would have been much more damaging to the Union had Adams not resisted the most militant inclinations of his fellow Federalists. The president had little sympathy for the more extreme purposes of the Alien and Sedition Acts. He resisted Secretary of State Pickering's desire to use the alien laws to deport large numbers of immigrants, especially Irishmen whose votes went strongly Democratic-Republican.[102] Indeed, Adams deported no one. He also opposed the Arch-Federalists' proposal to establish a large army. Adams's restraint was not unimportant. As historian Richard Hofstadter has written, "If we can imagine a determined High Federalist President in the White House seizing upon the most intense moment of Anti-French feeling to precipitate a war, we can imagine a partisan conflict that would have cracked the Union."[103] Nevertheless, although Adams's efforts to rise above partisan politics helped prevent civil discord, they did not save him from defeat in the election of 1800. The Democratic-Republican victory sealed the fate of the Federalist Party and the Federalists' hope of withstanding the growing influence of popular opinion on the executive office.

Notes

1. Charles C. Thach Jr., *The Creation of the American Presidency, 1775–1789* (Baltimore: Johns Hopkins University Press, 1969), 140.

2. Richard M. Pious, *The American Presidency* (New York: Basic Books, 1979), 38.

3. Ibid., 333.

4. *The Writings of George* Washington, ed. John C. Fitzpatrick, 39 vols. (Washington, D.C.: Government Printing Office, 1931–1944), 30: 496. For a comprehensive account of Washington's contribution to the constitutional presidency, see Glen A. Phelps, "George Washington: Precedent Setter," in *Inventing the American Presidency*, ed. Thomas E. Cronin (Lawrence: University Press of Kansas, 1989).

5. Thach, *Creation of the American Presidency*, 141.

6. Charles A. Beard, *The Economic Origins of Jeffersonian Democracy* (New York: Macmillan, 1915), 105.

7. Alan Taylor, *American Revolutions: A Continental History, 1750–1804* (New York: W.W. Norton, 2016), 392.

8. James Monroe to Thomas Jefferson, July 12, 1788, https://founders.archives.gov/documents/Jefferson/01-13-02-0256.

9. James Thomas Flexner, *George Washington and the New Nation: 1783–1793* (Boston: Little, Brown, 1970), 171.

10. *Writings of George Washington*, 30: 280.

11. Forrest McDonald, *The Presidency of George Washington* (Lawrence: University Press of Kansas, 1974), 24.

12. Richard H. Kohn, "The Inside History of the Newburgh Conspiracy: America and the Coup d'Etat," *William and Mary Quarterly* 28 (April 1970): 187–220.

13. Jefferson is quoted in Gordon S. Wood, *Revolutionary Characters: What Made the Founders Different* (New York: Penguin Press, 2006), 42.

14. Gordon S. Wood, "The Greatness of George Washington," *Virginia Quarterly Review* 68 (Spring 1992): 196–197.

15. Quoted in ibid., 197.

16. Garry Wills, *Cincinnatus: George Washington and the Enlightenment* (Garden City, N.Y.: Doubleday, 1984), 23.

17. Alan Taylor, *American Revolutions: A Continental History, 1750–1804* (New York: W.W. Norton, 2016), 320.

18. This description of Washington's journey is based on the account provided in Flexner, *George Washington and the New Nation*, 174–181.

19. Ibid., 398. North Carolina and Rhode Island did not ratify the Constitution until November 21, 1789, and May 29, 1790, respectively. See also "George Washington's First Inaugural Address," in *The Evolving Presidency: Landmark Documents*, 6th ed., ed. Michael Nelson (Washington, D.C.: CQ Press, 2019), 43–46.

20. Flexner, *George Washington and the New Nation*, 193.

21. Joanne B. Freeman, *Affairs of Honor: National Politics in the New Republic* (New Haven: Yale University Press, 2001), 43.

22. Fergus Bordewich, *The First Congress: How James Madison, George Washington, and a Group of Extraordinary Men Invented the Government* (New York: Simon and Schuster, 2016), 80.

23. Flexner, *George Washington and the New Nation*, 196.

24. Joseph J. Ellis, *His Excellency, George Washington* (New York: Knopf, 2004), 193.

25. Catherine Allgor, *Parlor Politics, in Which the Ladies of Washington Help Build a City and a Government* (Charlottesville: University Press of Virginia, 2000), 20–21.

26. Ellis, *His Excellency, George Washington*, 193, and Bordewich, *The First Congress*, 47

27. Noah Feldman, *The Three Lives of James Madison: Genius, Partisan, President* (New York: Random House) 2017, 264.

28. Wood, *Revolutionary Characters*, 54.

29. Flexner, *George Washington and the New Nation*, 182–183; McDonald, *Presidency of George Washington*, 29–31; John Zvesper, *Political Philosophy and Rhetoric: A Study of the Origins of the American Party System* (New York: Cambridge University Press, 1977), 66; James Madison to Thomas Jefferson, May 27, 1789, in *The Writings of James Madison*, 9 vols., ed. Gaillard Hunt (New York: Putnam's, 1904), 5: 370–372. See also Madison's letter to Jefferson of May 23, 1789, in 5: 369–370.

30. On the early history of the office of attorney general, see Leonard White, *The Federalists: A Study in Administrative History* (New York: Macmillan, 1948), 164–172. The Department of Justice was established as an executive department of government in 1870.

31. Richard J. Ellis, *The Development of the American Presidency* (New York: Routledge, 2012), 249.

32. Flexner, *George Washington and the New Nation*, 399; White, *Federalists*, 101.

33. White, *Federalists*, 106.

34. McDonald, *Presidency of George Washington*, 39.

35. White, *Federalists*, 258–259.

36. Stanley Elkins and Eric McKitrick, *The Age of Federalism: The Early American Republic 1788–1800* (New York: Oxford University Press, 1993), 54.

37. McDonald, *Presidency of George Washington*, 39.

38. "James Madison's Defense of the President's Removal Power," in Nelson, *Evolving Presidency*, 47–50.

39. Flexner, *George Washington and the New Nation*, 222; Thach, *Creation of the American Presidency*, 140–165. See also "James Madison's Defense of the Removal Power," in Nelson, *Evolving Presidency*.

40. "James Madison's Defense of the President's Removal Power."

41. White, *Federalists*, 370.

42. Flexner, *George Washington and the New Nation*, 221.

43. Washington made one exception to the rule that the veto power should be confined to bills of doubtful constitutionality. Claiming only that it was bad military policy, he vetoed legislation to reduce the size of the army by dismissing two specific companies serving at outposts on the western frontier. Washington thereby implicitly claimed that presidential deference to Congress was less appropriate in foreign affairs and military policy than in domestic matters. See Phelps, "George Washington: Precedent Setter," 268–269.

44. Ellis, *Development of the American Presidency*, 135.

45. Richard Beeman, *Plain, Honest Men: The Making of the American Constitution* (New York: Random House, 2009), 137.

46. Phelps, "George Washington: Precedent Setter," 266.

47. "Account by William Maclay of President George Washington's First Attempt to Obtain the Advice and Consent of the Senate to a Treaty," August 22, 1789, in *The Growth*

of Presidential Power: A Documented History, 3 vols., ed. William M. Goldsmith (New York: Chelsea, 1974), 1: 392–396.

48. Flexner, *George Washington and the New Nation,* 215–218.

49. Ibid., 398–399.

50. "Known as a lover of rural life, Jefferson was also, by this time, a connoisseur of cities." John B. Boles, *Jefferson: Architect of American Liberty* (New York: Basic Books, 2017), 237.

51. "Consolidation," from the *National Gazette,* December 5, 1791, in Hunt, *Writings of James Madison,* 6: 67. As political scientist John C. Koritansky has noted, Jefferson's and Madison's fears about Hamilton's thoughts and practices were not without foundation: "The picture of the United States government that emerges from reflecting on Hamilton's thoughts is that of a constitutional monarchy. Jefferson [and Madison] knew whereof they spoke when they branded Hamilton a 'monarchist' and 'monocrat,' even if Hamilton never himself referred to his own thought in those words after he had respectively repudiated the avowedly monarchical stance he had taken in the Philadelphia convention." Koritansky, "Alexander Hamilton and the Presidency," in Cronin, *Inventing the American Presidency,* 296.

52. Fred I. Greenstein, *Inventing the Job of President: Leadership Style from George Washington to Andrew Jackson* (Princeton: Princeton University Press, 2009), 15.

53. Printed in *Letters of Pacificus and Helvidius on the Proclamation of Neutrality of 1793* (Washington, D.C.: Gideon, 1845), 3. See also "The Pacificus-Helvidius Letters," in Nelson, *Evolving Presidency,* 51–58.

54. McDonald, *Presidency of George Washington,* 126–127.

55. As described in Chapter 2, the Framers probably did not intend for the vesting clauses to differ in this way.

56. *Letters of Pacificus and Helvidius,* 5–15.

57. Goldsmith, *Growth of Presidential Power,* 1: 398.

58. *Letters of Pacificus and Helvidius,* 53–64.

59. Gary J. Schmitt, "President Washington's Neutrality Proclamation," in *The Constitutional Presidency,* eds. Joseph Bessette and Jeffrey Tulis (Baltimore: Johns Hopkins University Press, 2009).

60. Taylor, *American Revolutions,* 412.

61. The discussion of the Whiskey Rebellion relies heavily on McDonald, *Presidency of George Washington,* 145–147.

62. President George Washington, Proclamation of August 7, 1794, "Final Warning of a Resort to Force," in Goldsmith, *Growth of Presidential Power,* 1: 246–248.

63. Ellis, *His Excellency, George Washington,* 225.

64. Quoted in Sean Wilentz, *The Rise of American Democracy: Jefferson to Lincoln* (New York: Norton, 2005), 65.

65. Alexander Hamilton to George Washington, August 2, 1794, in *The Papers of Alexander Hamilton,* ed. Harold C. Syrett (New York and London: Columbia University Press, 1986), 15–19. See also Thomas P. Slaughter, *The Whiskey Rebellion: Frontier Epilogue to the American Revolution* (New York: Oxford University Press, 1986), 163, 190–229; and Leland D. Baldwin, *Whiskey Rebels: The Story of a Frontier Uprising* (Pittsburgh: University of Pittsburgh Press, 1939), 259–272.

66. James D. Richardson, ed., *Messages and Papers of the Presidents,* 20 vols. (New York: Bureau of National Literature, 1897), 1: 156.

67. McDonald, *Presidency of George Washington,* 145.

68. President George Washington, "Report to Congress on Success of Operation," November 19, 1794, in Goldsmith, *Growth of Presidential Power,* 1: 253–255.

69. Ibid., 1: 255.

70. *The Writings of Thomas Jefferson,* 10 vols., ed. Paul Leicester Ford (New York: Putnam's, 1895), 6: 516–519; Wilfred E. Binkley, *President and Congress* (New York: Knopf, 1947), 287–288.

71. McDonald, *Presidency of George Washington*, 114.

72. Richard Brookhiser, *Founding Father: Rediscovering George Washington* (New York: Free Press, 1996), 164–165.

73. Michael J. Klarman, *The Framers' Coup: The Making of the United States Constitution* (New York: Oxford University Press, 2016), 215.

74. McDonald, *Presidency of George Washington*, 160.

75. Jefferson to Edward Rutledge, November 30, 1795, in Ford, *Writings of Thomas Jefferson*, 7: 39–40.

76. *Annals of the Congress of the United States* (Washington, D.C.: Gales and Seaton, 1849), 4th Cong., part 1 (1795–1796), 465.

77. McDonald, *Presidency of George Washington*, 173.

78. Ibid., 173.

79. Richardson, ed., *Messages and Papers of the Presidents*, 1: 186–188.

80. Jefferson to James Monroe, July 10, 1796, in Ford, *Writings of Thomas Jefferson*, 7: 88–90.

81. Goldsmith, *Growth of Presidential Power*, 1: 420–421. The power of the House in foreign affairs has become especially controversial since the Vietnam War, which undermined confidence in the presidency and prompted a rise in congressional assertiveness during the 1970s and 1980s. The Carter administration learned, to its dismay, that it could not ignore the House in the pursuit of its diplomatic initiatives. Although House approval was not necessary to ratify treaties, the lower chamber influenced treaty making during the Carter years through both the appropriations process and committee investigations, thereby raising concerns about illegitimate House intrusion into the president's right to conduct foreign affairs. During the ratification process for the two Panama Canal treaties in 1977 and 1978, for example, three House committees held hearings that served as important and controversial forums to generate support for and opposition to the treaties. The debate over House intervention in the details of foreign affairs intensified during the Reagan years as partisan differences sharpened the constitutional struggles between the executive and legislative branches. The House's "micromanagement" of foreign policy toward Central America, especially, became the subject of considerable political conflict and public controversy. The Boland Amendment, a prohibition on the expenditure of federal funds to aid the contra rebels in Nicaragua, was a House rider to an appropriations bill, which the Reagan administration considered an abuse of Congress's budgetary power. By the 1990s the House had come to play a routine part in the treaty-making process, requiring presidents to take greater care in building political support for important or controversial treaties. As political scientist Robert Spitzer has observed, "The president cannot ignore the House. Through the appropriations process, committee investigations, and the ability to gain public attention, the House (especially the key committees) can have a profound effect on the treaty process." Robert Spitzer, "The President and Congress," in *Congressional Quarterly's Guide to the Presidency*, 2nd ed., ed. Michael Nelson (Washington, D.C.: Congressional Quarterly, 1996), 1301.

82. John Ferling, *Adams v. Jefferson: The Tumultuous Election of 1800* (New York: Oxford University Press, 2004), 85.

83. Jeffrey L. Pasley, *The First Presidential Contest: 1796 and the Founding of American Democracy* (Lawrence: University Press of Kansas, 2013).

84. Larson, *Return of George Washington*, 255–256.

85. Ibid., 407.

86. Jefferson to James Madison, January 8, 1797, in Ford, *Writings of Thomas Jefferson*, 7: 104–105.

87. Wilentz, *Rise of American Democracy*, 77.

88. Jefferson to Edward Rutledge, June 24, 1797, in Ford, *Writings of Thomas Jefferson*, 7: 152–155.

89. Ralph Adams Brown, *The Presidency of John Adams* (Lawrence: University Press of Kansas, 1975), 25.

90. Jefferson to Elbridge Gerry, May 13, 1797, in *The Portable Thomas Jefferson*, ed. Merrill D. Peterson (New York: Viking Press, 1975), 471–474.

91. Leonard White, *The Federalists: A Study in Administrative History* (New York: Macmillan, 1948), 237–252.

92. Brown, *Presidency of John Adams*, 26–27.

93. White, *Federalists*, 241.

94. See, for example, David McCullough, *John Adams* (New York: Simon and Schuster, 2001), 508–514, 526–529.

95. White, *Federalists*, 237.

96. John Ferling, *John Adams: A Life* (Knoxville: University of Tennessee Press, 1992), 394.

97. Jon Meacham, *Thomas Jefferson: The Art of Power* (New York: Random House, 2012), 313.

98. Freeman, *Affairs of Honor*.

99. John Adams, Address to New Jersey College, 1798, in John Morton Smith, *Freedom's Fetters: The Alien and Sedition Laws and American Civil Liberties* (Ithaca: Cornell University Press, 1956), 99.

100. Lynne Cheney, *James Madison: A Life Reconsidered* (New York: Viking, 2014), 275.

101. "Thomas Jefferson's First Inaugural Address," in Nelson, *Evolving Presidency*, 67–71.

102. Taylor, *American Revolutions*, 423.

103. Richard Hofstadter, *The Idea of a Party System: The Rise of Legitimate Opposition in the United States* (Berkeley: University of California Press, 1969), 110. For a balanced account of Adams's role in the passage and enforcement of the Alien and Sedition Acts, see Brown, *Presidency of John Adams*, 122–127.

CHAPTER 4

The Triumph of Jeffersonianism

Like George Washington, Thomas Jefferson would be counted among the leading Americans in history even if he had never been president. French writer Alexis de Tocqueville celebrated the author of the Declaration of Independence "as the greatest democrat ever to spring from American democracy."[1] Jefferson's contributions as president deepened his reputation as the first champion of popular rule to occupy the executive office. Neither Washington nor John Adams considered himself a democratic leader; instead both understood the president's constitutional responsibility as requiring them to stand above the clashes of opinion and partisan conflict that jarred American politics during the 1790s.

Although Jefferson presided over much of the democratization of the country's norms and institutions, his commitment to popular rule was far from complete. With the indispensable support of James Madison, Jefferson formed and led America's first great democratic political party, but he never acknowledged the legitimacy of party government. As political scientist Harvey Mansfield has observed, Jefferson "never intended the public coexistence, permanent establishment, and occasional alternation of two parties."[2] Rather, Jefferson defended the Democratic-Republican Party as a temporary instrument of the people, its purpose being to defeat the Federalist attempt to impose centralized "consolidation" on a fundamentally decentralized nation. Once the Federalists and their program of executive aggrandizement were beaten, Jefferson hoped, his own party could safely wither away, restoring the nonpartisan character of the government created by the Constitution. The country, he assured an anxious political ally, would then see a "rapid return of general harmony," and its people would move "in phalanx in the paths of regular liberty, order, and sacrosanct adherence to the constitution."[3] The Democratic-Republican Party, as historian Richard Hofstadter argued, was to be a "party to end party."[4]

In practice, however, Jefferson proved a better builder than architect. Under him and the two presidents who followed, fellow Virginians James Madison and James Monroe, the Federalist Party faded into inconsequentiality and, by 1820, extinction, leaving the Democratic-Republicans uncontested on the field of political battle. At first blush, this was Jefferson and Madison's dream since the time of the founding come true: a national consensus so all-embracing as to eliminate any need for parties. But in as large, complex, and dynamic a society as the United States, the triumph of the Democratic-Republican Party did not bring an end to partisanship. Instead, politics was reborn in the form of factional and personal competition within the party. Monroe's nearly unanimous reelection in 1820 was followed four years later by a bitterly divisive four-candidate contest that elected John Quincy Adams of Massachusetts to the presidency but tainted his administration and effectively brought an end to the Democratic-Republican Party. It also set the stage for a new era of two-party competition between Democrats and Whigs.

Led by Jefferson in its early years, however, the Democratic-Republican Party endeavored to use partisanship to strengthen the decentralizing, supposedly more democratic institutions of the Constitution—that is, Congress and the states. Once in office the Democratic-Republicans tried, at least initially, to constrain the power of the executive, as well as to limit the scope of the national government's authority so that it rarely intersected with the lives of the people.

With the triumph of the Jeffersonians, the national government shrank and remained small until the Civil War. Even today, despite its size, the United States retains a combination of qualities that is unique, at least in degree, among modern democracies: a constitutional commitment to the rights of individuals, a mistrust of elites, and a lack of centralized rule. Jefferson's contribution to American governance was both stylistic and substantive: he made the presidency look democratic, and he championed policies that moved the new nation in an antielitist direction. By the end of his eight years in office, Jefferson had weakened the connection between governance and economic privilege that the Federalists had sought to establish.

The "Revolution" of 1800

The engine of Jefferson's victory in the presidential election of 1800 was the Democratic-Republican Party. Creating the party had been the work of many hands, but Jefferson was its undisputed leader. Although Jefferson disavowed partisan ambitions, his public stature and behind-the-scenes maneuvers were vital for maintaining the unity and commitment that made the Democratic-Republican triumph over the Federalists possible. But the coming of the Democratic-Republican Party to power was preceded by an odd set of occurrences that precipitated a constitutional crisis and nearly abrogated the results of the presidential election.

As noted in Chapter 2, the original Constitution, which was written without political parties in mind, provided that the candidate with the largest majority of electoral votes would become president and the runner-up in the presidential election would become vice president. In 1796 Federalists and Democratic-Republicans understood that Adams and Jefferson were the heads of their respective party tickets, and widespread agreement existed about the identity of each party's candidate for vice president: Thomas Pinckney and Aaron Burr, respectively. But the nominating process that the parties had devised was not yet sufficiently developed to enforce party discipline in support of a complete ticket. Adams was elected president in 1796, but his opponent, Jefferson, became the vice president when Pinckney received fewer votes than the Virginian.

The House of Representatives decided the outcome of the election of 1800 after Thomas Jefferson (left) and Aaron Burr received the same number of electoral votes for president. The Twelfth Amendment, which required that separate ballots be cast for president and vice president, was subsequently passed to avoid similar deadlocks.

Source: (both) Library of Congress.

By 1800, however, formal party organizations were fully in place. Each party's members of Congress caucused to choose its nominees for president and vice president. The caucus's decision was then coordinated with party organizations in the states so that electors functioned as instructed agents of the party, pledged to cast their two constitutionally mandated ballots for president for its presidential and vice-presidential candidates. The 1800 election broke along the same North–South divide as in 1796, but this time, with Aaron Burr of New York again on the ticket, the Democratic-Republicans carried New York, giving them seventy-three electoral votes to the Federalists' sixty-five. Jefferson expected that one or two of Georgia's and South Carolina's electors would cast their votes for him and for someone other than Burr.[5] When that did not happen, Jefferson and Burr ended up with the same number of electoral votes for president. According to the Constitution, it then fell to the lame-duck Federalist majority in the House of Representatives to decide which Democratic-Republican—Jefferson or Burr—would become president.[6]

Federalist leaders in Congress saw an advantage in making Burr president: in their view, he was a less principled and, therefore, a more pliable politician than the "fanatic," Jefferson. Burr, for his part, refused to take the honorable steps required to correct the results of the Electoral College, even though everyone clearly understood that Jefferson was the head of the ticket. Instead, as historian Sean Wilentz has written, when Burr "fully realized that he had a credible chance to win the presidency, he decided to play out the string, come what may."[7] The result was a deadlock. Under the Constitution, a majority of the representatives in nine of the sixteen state delegations was needed to elect the president, and neither party could produce the votes. The stalemate lasted through thirty-five ballots. Not until February 17, 1801, on the thirty-sixth ballot, was Jefferson elected.

Ironically, Jefferson's leading Federalist supporter in the House election was Alexander Hamilton, who not many months before had urged Gov. John Jay of New York to change the state's election laws in the Federalists' favor "to prevent an *atheist* in religion and a fanatic in politics from getting possession of the helm of State." Faced with a choice between Burr and Jefferson, however, Hamilton assured Federalist House members that Jefferson was the safer man. Writing to Delaware senator James A. Bayard in January 1801, Hamilton portrayed Jefferson in remarkably astute terms, foretelling much about the Virginian's presidency: "I admit that his politics are tinctured with fanaticism; that he is too much in earnest with his democracy; that he has been a mischievous enemy to the principal measures of our past administration." But, Hamilton added, Jefferson was neither an enemy of executive authority nor a slave to his principles. On the contrary, he was likely "to temporize" and acquiesce in the prevailing, mainly Federalist, governing arrangements. Jefferson was also incapable of being corrupted, unlike Burr, whom Hamilton regarded as "the most unfit man in the U.S. for the office of President."[8] With tacit assurances from Samuel Smith, a Democratic-Republican representative from Maryland, that Jefferson would neither scuttle the navy, destroy the national bank, nor summarily purge Federalist officeholders from the executive branch, Bayard, Hamilton, and a few other Federalist leaders were able to persuade enough Federalist members of the House to abstain that Jefferson was elected by a vote of ten states to four.[9] The new president denied the deal with Bayard but governed in a way consistent with it.

Although Jefferson was willing to "temporize" on certain matters, his victory in the 1800 election marked the beginning of a critical realignment in American politics. To be sure, he outpolled Adams only because his party dominated the South, whose electoral clout was inflated by the Constitution's three-fifths rule for counting slaves as part of the population. The rule gave southern states more seats in the House of Representatives and therefore more electoral votes than was warranted by their share of the electorate, turning what would have been a two-vote defeat for Jefferson into a three-vote victory.[10] But by sweeping the congressional as well as the presidential elections, the Democratic-Republicans became the nation's leading political party and remained so until the 1820s, by which time the three-fifths rule was giving southern states eighteen extra seats in the House (fully 10 percent of the total membership) and an equal number of extra votes in the Electoral College. Although this reliance on the South belied the egalitarian aspects of Jeffersonian democracy, the election brought about the first important transfer of power in American history. During the last decade of his life, in a letter to Spencer Roane, an eminent lawyer and legal scholar, Jefferson said that the "revolution of 1800," although it came about peacefully through a national election, was "as real a revolution in the principles of our government as that of 1776 was in its form."[11] As historian Joanne B. Freeman has pointed out, the peaceful revolution may have forestalled a violent one. If the Federalists in Congress had persisted in their efforts to deny him the presidency, Jefferson wrote, "the certainty is that a legislative usurpation would be resisted by arms."[12] President Adams agreed that a civil war was expected, not unlike the one triggered sixty years later by the election of Abraham Lincoln.[13]

In Jefferson's view, the principles of the Revolutionary War had been perverted by the Federalists in their ardent commitment to expanding the responsibilities of the national government. He believed that the Federalists' domestic and international initiatives required the executive to assume so dominant a role in formulating and implementing public policy that the president eventually would be transformed into a monarch. The task of the Democratic-Republican revolution was to restore republican government by casting off the Federalist institutions and, according to historian Forrest McDonald, by "instill[ing] the people with the historical knowledge and true principles that would prevent them from losing their liberties again."[14]

The importance of the Democratic-Republican task was revealed clearly in Jefferson's first inaugural address, which pronounced a party program of reform that included a strictly limited role for the national government and "support of the state governments in all their rights"; a "frugal" administration, dedicated to economy in public expenditures; and the encouragement of agriculture over commerce. In laying out this program, Jefferson stressed that it commanded the allegiance of a majority of the people. Although he took care to pay homage to the rights of the minority against the "unreasonable will of the majority," Jefferson called for "a jealous care of the right of election by the people" and "absolute acquiescence in the decisions of the majority."[15]

Jefferson's War with the Judiciary

Jefferson's desire to pursue majority rule by his party animated his war with the federal judiciary, the only branch of government the Democratic-Republican Party did not control. In a desperate attempt to maintain a foothold in the national government, the Federalists packed the courts with judges of their own party before Adams left office. The Judiciary Act of 1801, enacted by the Federalist Congress and signed by Adams shortly before the new president was inaugurated, reduced the size of the Supreme Court from six justices to five to deny Jefferson an appointment while creating two dozen new federal judgeships, which were hurriedly filled through so-called midnight appointments by the outgoing Adams administration and Federalist Senate. Adams also was able to rush Secretary of State John Marshall's nomination as chief justice through the lame-duck Federalist Senate five weeks before his term ended. To the Jeffersonians, the judiciary constituted "the final barrier to be assaulted in the advance of popular government and political liberty." To the Federalists, the courts represented "the last bastion of moderation and sanity arresting the progress of mob rule and anarchy."[16]

More was at stake in this dispute than partisan power. The Democratic-Republicans opposed the doctrine that the Constitution implicitly vests the courts with broad authority to overturn the actions of elected officials on constitutional grounds. The Federalists supported the judiciary's claim to be the ultimate arbiter of the Constitution. Although Jefferson and his followers did not challenge the courts' right of judicial review, they insisted that each branch of the government shares equally the responsibility to decide matters of constitutionality.

These issues of power and principle came to a head in the case of *Marbury v. Madison* (1803).[17] The case involved a request by one of the Federalists' midnight appointees, William Marbury, that the Supreme Court issue a writ of mandamus forcing Jefferson's secretary of state, James Madison, to deliver Marbury's commission as a justice of the peace in the new capital city, Washington, D.C. Although the commission had been ratified by the Senate and signed by Marshall, who was still secretary of state at the time, it never was delivered to Marbury. Madison, scorning the midnight appointments as part of a Federalist plot to control the government, simply held on to it. The unenviable task of mediating this bitter and symbolically important dispute fell to Marshall, the new chief justice and an ardent Federalist.

The Jefferson administration expected the Supreme Court to lay itself open to political attack by issuing the writ that Marbury requested. But in a brilliant piece of judicial statecraft, Marshall outmaneuvered the Democratic-Republicans, sidestepping the case's narrow partisan issues to establish the authority of the Supreme Court. Writing for a unanimous Court, all of whose members had been appointed by Washington or Adams, Marshall scolded the administration for refusing to deliver the commission to which Marbury was legally entitled, noting that even the president is not above the law. But Marshall denied Marbury his writ of mandamus by ruling that Section 13 of the Judiciary Act of 1789, under which Marbury had brought his suit, was unconstitutional because it presumed to give the Supreme Court original jurisdiction in the matter, even though the Constitution provided that the Court's jurisdiction is purely appellate in all but a few kinds of cases. In effect, Marshall gave Jefferson a free hand to bar a few Federalist appointees from office but only on the condition that the president concede the Court's power to judge the constitutional validity of acts of Congress.[18]

Jefferson was reluctant to accept victory on these terms. But so adroit was Marshall's ruling that the president could find no way to disobey the Court, as he had hoped to do. When he failed in a subsequent effort to persuade the Senate to remove the highly partisan but indisputably competent justice Samuel Chase, Jefferson's war with the judiciary came to an end. In any event, other developments seemed to make the war unnecessary. By 1804 much of the Democratic-Republican program that Jefferson heralded in his inaugural address was completed. The judiciary weathered the storm of Jefferson's first term, although he did manage to disemploy a number of Federalist judges by abolishing their positions, an approach Congress endorsed by repealing the Judiciary Act of 1801. But the question that gave rise to the conflict between the president and the Court was never fully resolved. That question—whether ultimate authority on matters of constitutionality rests with elected officials in Congress and the White House or in the interpretations of the judiciary—would arise time and time again in American history.[19]

The Democratic-Republican Program and the Adjustment to Power

In important respects, the Democratic-Republican program was negative. A great deal of it aimed at repealing Federalist policies that the Jeffersonians believed had undermined the Constitution. In 1801 the Democratic-Republican-controlled Congress removed the last vestiges of the Sedition Act. The act expired the day before Jefferson took office, but wanting to underscore his fierce opposition to it, he pardoned everyone (mostly Democratic-Republican newspaper publishers) who had been convicted of sedition. Moreover, at Jefferson's request Congress voted to repay with interest most of the fines that were levied as part of their sentences. During Jefferson's first term, Congress also abolished most internal taxes, including the unpopular whiskey and direct property taxes, which the Federalists had enacted in 1798 to prepare for a possible war with France. It reduced the size of the already small military establishment by severely cutting army and naval appropriations, even as it created a new military academy at West Point to fulfill Jefferson's vision of a republican officer corps.[20]

Although Jefferson emphasized the importance of restraining the national government, he was not narrowly doctrinaire about government's proper limits. His main concern was to make Washington more responsive to the will of the people. "His faith in the people," historian Robert M. Johnstone Jr. has written, "gave to his views on power a flexibility that permitted the use of power in positive ways to emphasize the freedom *from* government."[21] In those areas in which actions by the national government were proper—that is, in matters pertaining to foreign affairs and the relations among the states—Jefferson believed that its powers should be exercised energetically.

When circumstances required, Jefferson was even willing to tolerate government actions that seemed to contradict his stated principles. In 1801 he launched a successful naval war against the Barbary pirates, who had long preyed on American ships in the Mediterranean from their bases on the North African coast. In 1803 he purchased the massive Louisiana Territory from France, even though, as he conceded in a letter to Sen. John Breckinridge of Kentucky, he did not think the Constitution provided "for our holding foreign territory," still less for incorporating foreign nations into our union."[22] "The less we say about constitutional difficulties respecting Louisiana the better," Jefferson told Madison.[23] In 1807, seeking to prevent the United States from being drawn into the war between Great Britain and France, the president persuaded a Democratic-Republican Congress to enact legislation that imposed an embargo on all foreign commerce. Enforcing the embargo involved coercion by the federal government on a scale rivaling the notorious Alien and Sedition Acts. As Jefferson argued in a September 1810 letter, written seventeen months after leaving the presidency,

> A strict observance of the written laws is doubtless *one* of the high duties of a good citizen, but it is not the *highest*. The laws of necessity, of self-preservation, of saving our country when in danger, are of higher obligation. To lose our country by a scrupulous adherence to written law, would be to lose the law itself, with life, liberty, property and all those who are enjoying them with us; thus absurdly sacrificing the end to the means.[24]

Jefferson's actions as president reflected a "duality that was to underlie the whole of the [Democratic-Republican] era and to account for many of its frustrations."[25] Contrasting conceptions of executive power lay at the heart of the bitter conflict between the Federalists and the Democratic-Republicans. The Federalists had invested the president with broad responsibilities, fretted about legislative encroachments on executive power, and especially in matters pertaining to foreign affairs, tried to minimize the checks on the president that the Constitution granted to Congress. In contrast, the Democratic-Republicans, at least when out of power, placed their faith in the people's representatives, believing that important decisions should originate in Congress. They also sought to restrict executive discretion severely, not only in domestic matters but in foreign affairs as well. As noted in Chapter 3, during the battle over the Jay Treaty, Democratic-Republicans asserted the right of the House of Representatives to deny the funds necessary to implement treaties, thereby claiming for the lower house of Congress a virtual veto in foreign policy making.

In view of these differences, one might have expected important changes to occur in the conduct of the presidency when Jefferson and his party took control in 1801. But the Democratic-Republicans soon realized that a wholesale dismantling of executive power would make governing in pursuit of their agenda virtually impossible. Jefferson, with able support from his secretary of the Treasury, Albert Gallatin, exercised as much control of domestic policy as Alexander Hamilton had during the Washington administration. Hamilton's assurance to his Federalist colleagues in 1801 that Jefferson was "no enemy to the power of the executive" predicted accurately how Jefferson would act as president. To enforce his embargo policy, Jefferson secured authority from a Democratic-Republican Congress that exceeded any grant of executive power ever made by the Federalists. Moreover, Jefferson used this power with the kind of energy he once had denounced as the mark of tyranny.[26] In important respects, then, the "revolution of 1800" brought sweeping alterations less in how the government functioned than in the cast of characters who ran it.

Nevertheless, Jefferson's presidency marked an important change in the relationship between the president and the people.[27] His predecessors, Washington and Adams, had believed that the power of the presidency derived from its constitutional authority. Jefferson, although not rejecting this view, maintained that the strength of the office ultimately depended on the "affections of the people." He strongly implied in his first inaugural address that the program of the Democratic-Republican Party should be enacted simply because a majority of the country endorsed it in the 1800 election.[28]

Washington and Adams believed that some distance from the people was essential if presidents were to perform their proper task, which was to moderate the clash of parties and interests that inevitably would occur in Congress. But Jefferson felt that the most effective and responsible way for the president to lead the national government was by guiding the institutions that were rooted most firmly in a popular base—the House and, to a lesser extent, the Senate. Rather than stand apart from developments in Congress, Jefferson sought to direct them. In contrast to Hamilton's concept of a strong presidency, which emphasized the need for independent executive initiatives, Jefferson assumed the mantle of party leader in an effort to yoke the separate branches of the government in service to his and the Democratic-Republican Party's agenda.

Informed by a clear conception of the presidency, Jefferson's administration brought other important institutional changes in pursuit of a closer relationship between the president and the people. One such change was to reduce the ceremonial trappings of the executive office. Jefferson stripped away much of the pomp and ceremony to which Washington and Adams had adhered; he regarded excessive formality in the conduct of the presidency as incompatible with a popularly based government. Unlike Washington, Jefferson rode around the capital not in a coach attended by liveried outriders but on his own horse, with only one servant in attendance. He was the first president not to strap on a sword at his inauguration or powder his hair.[29] His clothing expressed republican simplicity, even to the point of offending some who regarded his appearance as unsuitable for a head of state. As one critic described Jefferson, "The President was in an undress—Blue coat, red vest . . . white hose, ragged slippers, with his toes out, clean linen, but hair disheveled."[30]

Jefferson's interest in removing the "monocratic" features from the executive led him to simplify his relationship with the legislature. His decision to fulfil the president's constitutional duty to "give to Congress information of the State of the Union" in writing rather than deliver it as a speech, as Washington and Adams had done, was "a calculated political act, designed to . . . reduce the 'relics' left by the Federalists and underline the return to sound republican simplicity."[31] (It also reflected his acute discomfort at public speaking.) Jefferson began what turned out to be the century-long practice of presidents sending written annual messages to Congress to be read aloud by the clerk of the House.

Jefferson's adoption of a simpler presidential etiquette corresponded nicely with the transfer of the capital from Philadelphia to Washington in 1800. As secretary of state in the Washington administration, Jefferson had insisted on this transfer as the price for supporting Secretary of the Treasury Hamilton's plan to have the national government assume the states' debts. The move left members of Congress, executive officials, judges, and foreign diplomats, who were accustomed to Philadelphia's culture and comforts, feeling stranded on the muddy banks of the Potomac. Historian Merrill D. Peterson has described the new city of Washington as "a village pretending to be a capital, a place with a few bad houses, extensive swamps, hanging on the skirts of a too thinly peopled, weak and barren country."[32] Yet Jefferson appreciated the change in setting. His informal style was compatible not just with his view of the presidency but also with Washington's relatively rustic character.

The move to the new capital also symbolized the growth in people and territory under way in the United States. The nation's population increased by more than one-third between 1800 and 1810. Geographically, the acquisition of the Louisiana Territory roughly doubled the country's size at the bargain price of only four cents per acre. Jefferson's Democratic-Republican successors continued to support territorial expansion, committed as they were to encouraging agriculture over manufacturing. In this view, the nation had to expand whenever the opportunity arose "to make room for the generation of farmers yet unborn."[33] Furthermore, the political ascendance of the Democratic-Republican Party represented the rise of the agrarian and frontier interests of the South and West to political parity with the older commercial and financial interests of the Northeast, which had controlled national politics under the Federalists.

Besides the favorable financial terms, the close relationship between territorial expansion and the Democratic-Republican program explains Jefferson's willingness to make the Louisiana Purchase in disregard of his oft-expressed commitment to a strict construction of the Constitution. After reaching the deal with France, he pushed the Louisiana Treaty through the Senate, certain that constitutional niceties were less important than the opportunity to contribute on such a scale to the public good. The purchase of Louisiana, and the overwhelmingly favorable reaction it received around the country, sustained the Democratic-Republican effort to define the president as the agent of the people's best interests.[34]

Although it marked an important change in the politics and practices of the executive office, Jefferson's "empire of liberty" was indifferent to the rights of African Americans. One unfortunate consequence of the move to Washington was that it embedded the seat of government in the heart of slave country. Indeed, Jefferson felt comfortable bringing enslaved people into the Executive Mansion. Of the four Jeffersonian presidents, only John Quincy Adams was not a slaveholder. The others—Jefferson, Madison, and Monroe—faced less criticism in Washington than they would have in the nation's previous capitals, Philadelphia and New York, and therefore felt less pressure to consider the justice of slavery as an institution. Congress Jefferson-inspired decision to ban the further importation of slaves, which the Constitution forbade it to do until 1808, was not only a testament to the president's acknowledgment that slavery was an institution of "unremitting despotism" but also an expression of the widespread fear that too great a concentration of newly arrived Africans would increase the likelihood of a slave rebellion.[35]

The Limits of "Popular" Leadership

The limits on popular presidential leadership during the Jeffersonian era went beyond the Democratic-Republicans' tolerance of slavery. Neither Jefferson nor his successors tried to enhance their power by bartering patronage or other favors for legislation in Congress. Indeed, until Andrew Jackson took office in 1829, presidents seldom used the spoils of federal appointments either to enhance party unity or to obtain legislation.

In spite of the bitter competition between the Federalists and the Democratic-Republicans, Jefferson did not purge all of his partisan opponents from the executive branch. Instead he filled vacancies with Democratic-Republicans as they occurred. The rate of turnover among federal jobholders was only one-third during his first two years in office and one-half during his entire first term. On the whole, the Democratic-Republicans continued to use Federalist methods of administration. As Leonard D. White has written, "After a brief period of transition, during which new men took over the most important posts, the same expectation of nonpartisan, lifetime service prevailed."[36] In appointing the heads of the executive departments, Jefferson valued steadiness of administration so highly that after choosing his team with unusual care, he experienced less turnover in the cabinet than any two-term president in history.[37]

Nor was it considered appropriate during the Jeffersonian era for the president to appeal over the heads of Congress to the people.[38] Until the early twentieth century, presidents who tried to arouse popular support for their politics usually did so through their influence on party mechanisms in Congress and the state governments.

Jefferson's refusal to "go public" on the controversial embargo issue illustrates the limits on the era's acceptable techniques of presidential persuasion.[39] Initially, he was able to persuade Congress to enact the embargo by using his enormous popularity to exert influence indirectly on Democratic-Republican leaders. His hope was that keeping the country out of the conflict between France and Great Britain would avert the sort of executive aggrandizement for which he had indicted the Federalists when they prepared for war with France during the Adams administration. Yet during the course of its fourteen-month existence, the embargo began to unravel. The severe restrictions it placed on foreign trade wreaked havoc on business owners in New England and planters in the South. The embargo also deprived the government of millions of dollars in revenue by barring nearly all imports. Perhaps most significant, it made a travesty of the Democratic-Republicans' traditional opposition to a broad constitutional interpretation of the authority vested in the national government and, especially, in the executive. By its unprecedented concentration of power in the president, by its deployment of the navy for law enforcement, and by its disregard of the Fourth Amendment's protection against "unreasonable searches and seizures," the embargo "carried the administration to the precipice of unlimited and arbitrary power as measured by any American standard then known."[40] In a reversal of their own, previously nationalistic Federalists began "asserting states' rights to resist what they deemed federal decrees."[41]

Even after the embargo became hotly controversial, Jefferson never took the issue directly to the people. To have done so would have violated the custom that presidents not use oratory to influence public opinion directly. But Jefferson did not face the growing opposition to the embargo with an "an imperturbable, almost sphinxlike silence."[42] Instead, as presidential scholar Mel Laracey has noted, from late 1807 to early 1809, Jefferson sent at least nineteen public letters to citizen groups, Democratic-Republican Party meetings, and state legislatures explaining and defending his unpopular policy and urging continued support for it. Jefferson's most strongly worded letter was published on March 1, 1809, the same day he reluctantly signed the Non-Intercourse Act, which ended the embargo and replaced it with a bill that forbade trade only with Great Britain and France.[43] "Thus we were driven from the high and wise ground we had taken," Jefferson complained privately.[44] In truth, when it came to Britain and France, he had always "overestimated their need for American goods," both as secretary of state and as president.[45]

The Twelfth Amendment

The paragraphs in Article II, section 1, of the Constitution that created the Electoral College were among the document's least controversial provisions, both during the late stages of the Constitutional Convention and in the ratification debates that followed. "The mode of appointment of the Chief Magistrate of the United States," wrote Alexander Hamilton in *Federalist No. 68*, "is almost the only part of the system of any consequence, which has escaped without severe censure, or which has received the slightest mark of approbation from its opponents." It is all the more ironic, then, that the Electoral College was the first institution of the new system of government to undergo a major constitutional overhaul.

The source of the irony was the convention's faulty assumption that political parties would not arise to contest presidential elections. Instead, the delegates believed that states and ad hoc groups would nominate candidates for president. Individual electors would then vote for two of these candidates, one of them perhaps a local favorite but the other a leader of national stature. The most respected and, presumably, the best-qualified candidate would be elected as president and the second-most respected as vice president.

The delegates' expectations were soon disappointed. The two political parties that formed during the Washington administration began within a few years to nominate complete national tickets. In 1800 the inevitable happened: the perverse tie vote in the presidential election between Jefferson and his Democratic-Republican running mate, Burr. To make matters worse, partisan mischief in the House almost overturned the voters' intentions. Some disgruntled Federalists then began hatching plots for the 1804 election. If the Democratic-Republican ticket won, they resolved, Federalist electors would cast one of their votes for the opposition party's vice-presidential nominee, thereby electing him instead of the presidential nominee as president and the presidential nominee as vice president.[46]

Aware of both the unsuitability of the original Constitution's presidential election process to the new realities of party politics and the Federalists' willingness to exploit the process's weaknesses, the Democratic-Republican–controlled Congress decided in December 1803 to propose the Twelfth Amendment. All but Connecticut, Delaware, and Massachusetts, the most ardent Federalist states, quickly voted to ratify, and the Twelfth Amendment became part of the Constitution in June 1804, just in time for the presidential election. Jefferson and his new vice president, George Clinton, won by 162 electoral votes to 14 electoral votes with no confusion about which candidate had been elected to which office. No amendment except the Twenty-Sixth, which in 1971 gave eighteen-year-olds the right to vote, has been ratified as rapidly.

The main effect of the Twelfth Amendment was to change a system in which electors cast two votes for president, with the candidate receiving the largest majority elected as president and the second-place finisher as vice president, to a system in which the electors were charged to vote separately for president and vice president, with a majority of electoral votes required to win each office. The amendment also reduced the number of candidates from which the House would elect the president in the event that no one received a majority of electoral votes. The reduction from the five highest electoral vote recipients to the three highest was an acknowledgment that a two-party system had developed in which even three candidates were unlikely to receive electoral votes in most elections as well as that the parties had taken charge of the presidential nominating function.

The authority to select a vice president in the event of an Electoral College failure was lodged exclusively in the Senate, not partially as in the original Constitution. The amendment empowered senators to choose from the two highest electoral vote recipients for vice president, with a majority of the entire membership of the Senate required for election. The Constitution's age, residency, and citizenship requirements for the president were extended to the vice president, correcting an oversight in the original document. Finally, the new amendment stated that if a vice president, but not a president, has been chosen by the March 4 following the election, "the Vice President shall act as President as in the case of the death or other constitutional disability of the President."

The Twelfth Amendment reinforced the unitary character of the executive by eliminating the possibility that the vice president would be the leader of the opposition party.[47] For reasons discussed in Chapter 17, the amendment also severely diminished the prestige that the original Constitution conferred on the vice presidency.

Jefferson's Mixed Legacy

Like the Federalists, Jefferson understood the need for presidential power. But Jefferson altered the tone and manner of executive authority to make it consistent with popular rule. In place of the wide-ranging unilateral authority the Federalists found for the executive in Article II of the Constitution, Jefferson substituted a party program that would be implemented by the president but shaped by Congress and sanctioned by popular election.

Unlike Washington and Adams, therefore, Jefferson de-emphasized the constitutional powers of his office, governing mainly through his extra-constitutional role as party leader. The Jefferson administration encouraged the development of a disciplined party organization in Congress, with the president relying on his floor leaders in the House and Senate to advance his program. Another source of presidential influence was the party caucus, which was created by the Federalists but used more extensively by the Democratic-Republicans. During Jefferson's tenure as president, conclaves of party leaders from the executive and legislative branches formulated policy and encouraged party unity. Secretary of the Treasury Gallatin played an important role in these caucuses, and the president himself occasionally presided. In short, Jefferson constructed a highly centralized political party within the government but one that operated for the most part through consultation and free discussion.[48]

The development of party machinery within the government made possible, as legislative historian Ralph Volney Harlow has written, "a radical change in the relationship between executive and legislature." Jefferson exercised considerable influence over his party's legislative caucus, but should the party's leaders in Congress ever take charge of the machine, they would be in a position to control the executive.[49] That is precisely what happened when Jefferson left office. The institutions he developed for presidential leadership were turned to the advantage of Congress. Ironically, then, it was only after Thomas Jefferson's administration that the presidency shrank to the limited constitutional office that long had been prescribed by the Democratic-Republican Party's chief theorist, Thomas Jefferson.

The Presidency of James Madison and the Rise of the House of Representatives

The decline of presidential influence was evident during James Madison's administration and those of Jefferson's other Democratic-Republican successors, James Monroe and John Quincy Adams. While Madison was president, major institutional developments transferred power from the executive to the legislative branch, especially the House of Representatives. One such development was the evolution of the congressional party caucus into an independent bastion of power.

The Democratic-Republican caucus's nomination of Jefferson for president in 1800 and 1804 had been a foregone conclusion, but the caucus of 1808 had a real decision to make. Although Secretary of State Madison generally was regarded as Jefferson's heir apparent, the leader of the small anti-Jefferson faction in the Democratic-Republican Party, Rep. John Randolph of Virginia, tried to secure the nomination for James Monroe. In the end, with Jefferson's strong endorsement, Madison was nominated with votes from eighty-three of the caucus's ninety-four members and was elected in a 122–47 electoral vote landslide that reduced support for his opponent, Charles Cotesworth Pinckney, to the Federalist Party's New England base.

But the promises Madison had to make to his party's members in Congress to win their endorsement suggested that subsequent presidential nominations might well become occasions "to make explicit executive subordination to congressional president-makers." Indeed, some scholars believe that Madison's renomination by the Democratic-Republican Party in 1812 was delayed until he assured the "War Hawks" in the congressional caucus that he supported their desire for war with Great Britain.[50]

The congressional caucus also had a divisive effect on the president's official family. Even during a president's first term, but especially during the second, ambitious cabinet officers would spend more time currying favor on Capitol Hill than in the Executive Mansion in hopes of securing caucus members' support for a presidential nomination.[51] The frustrated Madison appointed a total of eighteen secretaries in the five departments in hopes of finding leaders who would place his administration's interest above their own.

The emergence of the Speaker of the House as an important leader in Congress, and Kentuckian Henry Clay's extraordinary use of the office during the Madison presidency, further reduced executive power in relation to Congress. Until Clay's election as Speaker in 1811, party leadership in the House had been shared among several members. Clay was able to change this practice dramatically. According to Leonard White,

> Clay was chosen Speaker on an issue that President Madison
> was unable to grip, and with the intention of forcing national
> action despite the president's incapacity to act—war with Great
> Britain. Clay succeeded in this purpose, and until the last day of
> Madison's administration the initiative in public affairs remained
> with Clay and his associates in the House of Representatives.[52]

At Clay's direction, the House also strengthened its capacity to meet its broader legislative obligations by expanding the number and influence of its standing committees, which enabled each representative to specialize in an area of interest. Because the committees' activities were coordinated by the Speaker, the House became an effective legislative instrument. Indeed, from 1811 to 1825 Clay was arguably the most powerful man in Washington.

The decline of presidential influence was demonstrated most dramatically during the War of 1812. War sentiment had been aroused by evidence that the British were supplying arms to American Indians, who were already angry about frontier settlers encroaching on historic tribal lands in the Indiana and Michigan territories, as well as by British seizure of American ships and impressment of crew members, and to some degree, by a desire to acquire territory in British Canada and Spanish Florida. The War Hawks, most of them Democratic-Republican members of Congress from the South and West, whose constituents were suffering from Indian attacks and falling agricultural prices, fanned the flames of anti-British feeling. New England Federalists, traditionally pro-British and commercially tied to Great Britain through shipping and trade, opposed war but were severely outnumbered in Congress and around the country.

Madison's message of June 1, 1812, which urged Congress to declare war against Great Britain, was the first war message by an American president and commanded the least support: the vote to declare war was only 79–49 in the House and 19–13 in the Senate, with every Federalist member opposed. Madison's command of the military effort as the nation's first wartime commander in chief was singularly undistinguished. He was hampered not only by his inability to influence Congress but also by personal qualities that were poorly suited to the task at hand. Madison's figure was slight, his speaking voice was weak, and the force of his personality was, at best, moderate. As Gaillard Hunt, a generally sympathetic Madison biographer, has written of the president's war leadership,

> The hour had come but the man was wanting. Not a scholar in governments ancient and modern, not an unimpassioned writer of careful messages, but a robust leader to rally the people and unite them to fight was what the time needed, and what it did not find in Madison.[53]

From a military standpoint, the War of 1812 was among the least successful in American history. Congress and the president rushed into war with a small, poorly trained army of less than seven thousand men and a sixteen-vessel navy, partly because Madison assumed that Canadians, many of them of French origin, would happily abandon their status as a British colony in favor of the United States. Jefferson predicted that the conquest of Canada would be "a mere matter of marching."[54] Far from it: at the beginning of the war, a relatively small British detachment stationed in Canada administered a series of disastrous defeats to the disorganized American army. The low point of the conflict occurred in August 1814, when Madison had to evacuate the capital for three days to escape a modest British force that had moved unchallenged up the Chesapeake Bay and marched with little resistance into the heart of Washington, burning the Capitol, the White House, the Navy Yard, and most other public buildings.

Only Great Britain's decision not to prosecute the war on a massive scale for fear of diluting its focus on Europe saved the United States from further disaster. Public morale was boosted belatedly by Gen. Andrew Jackson's victory in the Battle of New Orleans on January 8, 1815. Although the battle had no effect on the outcome of the war (a peace treaty—the Treaty of Ghent—had been concluded two weeks earlier), it enabled Madison to retire as president in 1817 with some measure of honor. New Orleans also rendered a fatal political blow to the New England-based, pro-British Federalists, many of whom had opposed the war from the beginning and some of whom had gathered in December 1814 at the Hartford Convention to threaten secession from the Union. "The confident nationalist party of Washington, Hamilton, and Adams," Wilentz has observed, "had shriveled into [a] phobic sectional party."[55]

Federalist defeat did not translate automatically into Democratic-Republican triumph. In important respects, Madison's failures as president transcended his personal limitations. They were attributable not just to him but also to the legacies he inherited from the Jefferson administration and from the anti-executive, anti-military Democratic-Republican tradition of which he had been one of the major architects. By opposing the creation of anything more than a minimal army and navy, Madison and Jefferson, preaching economy in government, undid many of the military preparations that the Adams administration had undertaken. Their foreign policy depended on diplomacy to solve America's problems with France and Great Britain. When negotiations failed, the Democratic-Republicans were forced to rely on the 1807 embargo, an impractical attempt at peaceful coercion that proved disastrous for the economy without causing either Great Britain or France to stop interfering with American ships. The collapse of Madison's own embargo, enacted in 1812, left him no alternative but war when the British provocations continued, even though he knew that the country was neither prepared nor united for battle.

Years later, Madison recounted that he had hoped to overcome the nation's obvious unpreparedness by "throw[ing] forward the flag of the country, sure that the people would press onward and defend it."[56] Yet the rapid decline in the status of the presidency after Jefferson's tenure left Madison in a poor position to rally either Congress or the American people. Contrary to his expectations, Democratic-Republican legislators did not abandon their party's traditional doctrine of hostility to centralized power, even in wartime. Congress was willing to declare war but not to raise enough money to fight it. Moreover, the Madison administration's plan to mobilize the state militia was scuttled by some state governments' lack of cooperation. The governors of Connecticut and Massachusetts, for example, refused to release their militia to fight in the war. The president, long an advocate of states' rights, "offered no suggestion for stopping so grave a defiance of federal authority."[57] To Madison's credit, however, he held true to Jefferson's position that all political opinions have a right to be heard, even those that are "false, scandalous, and malicious" or might "dissolve the Union or change its republican form." The president did not use the war as a pretext to suppress dissent, even from Federalists urging secession. As legal historian Noah Feldman has noted, "Madison would not violate the principles of liberty to save liberty itself."[58]

Madison faced up to the limitations of Democratic-Republican principles in his seventh annual message in December 1815, which recommended several measures to solidify the national resolve, including chartering the Second Bank of the United States. (The Democratic-Republicans, with Madison's support, had allowed the first bank to expire in 1811.) With no national bank in operation during the War of 1812, the federal government had lacked a convenient and stable source of currency, exacerbating a financial crisis that saw the national debt grow from $45 million in 1811 to $127 million in 1815. Convinced by experience that a national bank was a necessary evil without which a sound currency was unattainable, Madison signed the bank bill into law in 1816. As political scientist James D. Savage has observed, it took the severe economic dislocations of the war to persuade Madison and his party to embrace "the ghostly presence of Hamilton's national bank, with all its potential for corrupting the republic."[59]

Madison never ceased to express profound concern, however, about the potential abuses of executive power that he believed Hamilton had committed during the 1790s. According to historian Ralph Ketcham: "in every one of his critical relationships and decisions—in bringing the nation face to face with war, in dealing with Congress, in arranging his Cabinet and in enduring near-treasonable dissent—[Madison] acted in view of [Democratic-Republican] principles of executive leadership."[60] In the final analysis, these principles simply were not conducive to effective presidential initiative.

The Presidency of James Monroe

Madison's Democratic-Republican successors, James Monroe and John Quincy Adams, were unable to restore to the presidency the strength that the office lost after Jefferson retired. Monroe, although a forceful man, was prone to formality and a stiffness of manner that ill qualified him for party leadership. He also was hindered by a growing split among Democratic-Republicans. With the Federalist Party dying (and soon dead), disagreements about policy necessarily were fought out within the only remaining party, the Democratic-Republicans. An important division emerged between "old" Democratic-Republicans, who inclined toward a strict construction of the Constitution, and "new" Democratic-Republicans, or National Republicans, who were more nationalist in outlook. Monroe was identified with the former group. The latter, which was led by prominent figures such as John C. Calhoun and Monroe's successor, John Quincy Adams, dominated the party after the War of 1812, even when Monroe was president.

Monroe, like Madison, was a protégé of Jefferson and therefore was regarded as the legitimate heir of the "Virginia Dynasty" that had supplied every president since 1801. Like both Madison and Jefferson, Monroe served as secretary of state, which was the main stepping-stone to the presidency throughout the Democratic-Republican era. But the fragmentation of their party ensured that Monroe would also be the last of his state's Jeffersonians. His nomination was a difficult affair. Two other contenders, Henry Clay and Secretary of the Treasury William Crawford of Georgia, were closely identified with the nationalist wing of the party. Although Monroe was nominated and easily elected in 1816, the trouble he had winning the endorsement of the congressional caucus foretold the difficulties that he would face in office.

One of the major domestic issues during the Monroe administration was "internal improvements." In his first annual message to Congress, the president declared that in his view a constitutional amendment was required before the national government could construct roads and canals. Congress, led by Clay, defied Monroe by passing a bill to repair the main east-west highway, known as the Cumberland Road. The president's veto of this bill signaled the breakdown of Democratic-Republican unity that was to plague him throughout his two terms.[61]

Monroe's strong response to the Cumberland Road controversy was the exception rather than the rule. Following the practice of presidents since Washington, he vetoed only legislation that he deemed unconstitutional. Indeed, Monroe's deference to Congress went beyond custom. More than any of his predecessors, he practiced as well as preached legislative supremacy. As a result, he mostly abstained from involvement in the greatest issue of the day: the admission of Missouri as a state, which for the first time forced Congress to debate the status of slavery in the Louisiana Territory.

As a private citizen, Jefferson observed the bitter debate about Missouri with great concern. Writing to Rep. John Holmes of Maine, he said, "This momentous question, like a fire-bell in the night, awakened and filled me with terror. I considered it at once the knell of the Union."[62] Congress allayed Jefferson's fears by enacting the Missouri Compromise of 1820. In effect, this compromise perpetuated the Constitution's original compromise with slavery: it admitted Missouri to the Union as a slave state, allowed Maine to enter as a free state, and temporarily resolved the issue of slavery in the Louisiana Territory by banning it from all other western territories north of Missouri's southern border, whose latitude is 36°30′. Monroe had little hand in the Missouri Compromise, save for signing the final bill. As Leonard White has written, "His course of action was perhaps politically wise, perhaps politically inevitable, but it abdicated leadership."[63] Indeed, the passive character of the Monroe administration prompted Supreme Court justice Joseph Story to remark in 1818 that "the Executive has no longer a commanding influence. The House of Representatives has absorbed all the popular feeling and all the effective power of the country."[64]

The Monroe Doctrine

Justice Story's lament was not as pertinent to foreign as to domestic affairs. The Constitution conferred powers on the president in foreign policy that remained essentially untarnished. Previous service as secretary of state made all the Jeffersonian presidents confident and for the most part confidence-inspiring in the diplomatic arena.[65]

Monroe reinforced the president's right to take the initiative in foreign affairs by issuing the Monroe Doctrine, which became one of the pillars of American foreign policy in the nineteenth and twentieth centuries. The revolt of Spain's Latin American colonies between 1815 and 1823 had nearly liquidated the Spanish empire. The Monroe administration was alarmed by reports that other European powers, France in particular, had designs on several of the newly independent South American nations. Simultaneously, Tsar Alexander I of Russia, noting the presence of a Russian trading station in Bodega Bay, near San Francisco, issued a decree claiming exclusive trading rights for Russia in the area north of the fifty-first parallel, including all of modern-day Oregon and Washington. Responding to these threats, on December 2, 1823, President Monroe included in his annual message to Congress a sweeping statement that proclaimed the Americas independent from European interference. "The occasion has been judged proper," he wrote, "for asserting, as a principle in which the rights and interests of the United States are involved, that the American continents, by the free and independent condition which they have assumed and maintain, are henceforth not to be considered as subjects for future colonization by any European powers."[66]

Although the Monroe Doctrine was neither confirmed by Congress nor enforced by Monroe, it was a significant document. As historian W. P. Cresson has written, "It was a sincere expression of the belief in the superiority of American institutions and ideals, and the right of self-preservation, grounded in the conviction that the extension of European principles would be dangerous to the peace and safety of the American system."[67]

The Monroe Doctrine was also an important statement, at a time of general executive weakness, that the president was paramount in the making of foreign policy. Monroe's defiant expression of hemispheric independence committed the United States to more burdensome diplomatic and military responsibilities, most of which inevitably would fall on the executive. For a time, this commitment was without important practical effect, but its potential to become a guiding influence on foreign policy was fulfilled in the late nineteenth and early twentieth centuries.[68]

The conclusion of the Monroe presidency in 1825 marked the end of a quarter-century-long political dynasty. Monroe was the last member of the Virginia "quadrumvirate"—Washington, Jefferson, Madison, and Monroe—to serve as president. Each of these men played an important role in the formation and early history of the Republic. During the 1790s, the country's first decade under the Constitution, all but Washington had been a founder of the Democratic-Republican opposition to the Federalists and a leader during its rise as a governing party. Each was elected to two full terms. Monroe was also the last president from the generation that won the War of Independence. With the end of the Virginia dynasty, the Democratic-Republicans no longer were led by national figures who could keep the party from dissolving.

Ironically, political unity became ever more difficult to achieve because of the party's extraordinary electoral success. Mobilizing popular support for a governing coalition requires a credible opponent.[69] But during Monroe's first term as president, the Federalist Party disappeared as a national organization. The Federalists had grown so weak by 1816 that they stopped fielding a ticket in presidential elections. As a result, Monroe was unopposed for reelection in 1820.

For a time, Jefferson's claim that the Democratic-Republicans would someday embody a new national consensus, a politics without parties, seemed justified. Their complete triumph over their Federalist rivals appeared to restore the nonpartisan character of the Constitution, this time on terms favored by Democratic-Republicans. But as political scientist James Roger Sharp has written, the Democratic-Republican Party did not wither away; instead it "became bloated and shapeless."[70] Triumph brought dissolution. Even as Monroe was inaugurated for the second time, his party was being torn apart by the ambitions of the many candidates who wanted to succeed him as president. In fact, as Catherine Allgor has pointed out, the 1824 campaign may have begun as early as 1817.[71] In 1818 John Quincy Adams, Monroe's secretary of state, observed that "political, personal and electioneering intrigues are intermingling themselves with increasing heat and violence." The result, Adams lamented, was that the government was "assuming daily more and more a character of cabal, and preparation, not for the next presidential election, but for the one after."[72]

Politics without Parties: The Controversial Election of 1824

With the Federalists vanquished and the Democratic-Republicans fragmented, the 1824 presidential election became a contest of individuals rather than of issues or parties. For the first time, no Virginian was in the race, further evidence that an era had passed. Rival leaders from New England, the South, and the West, each supported by his own organization and regional following, ran for president in one of the bitterest and most confusing campaigns in American history. The results of the election stirred a storm of controversy, prompting a revolt against the congressional caucus nominating process that had been used for a quarter century. John Quincy Adams, the eventual winner of the 1824 election, inherited an impossible governing situation. It was not improved by a personality that, in his own words, was "reserved, cold, forbidding, and austere."[73] When his one term in office was over, the Democratic-Republican era also came to an end amid conflicts so acrimonious that they endured for a generation.

In 1825, for the second time in twenty-four years, an election was decided not by the Electoral College but by the House of Representatives. Adams felt that as secretary of state, he was the logical heir to the presidency. In contrast to his predecessors as secretary, however, Adams had little experience wooing voters, and he finished second with eighty-four electoral votes. Monroe's secretary of the Treasury, William Crawford, was the nominee of the Democratic-Republican caucus in Congress. But the party machinery was badly run down by 1824, and its support no longer was tantamount to election. Crawford came in third with forty-one electoral votes. The powerful speaker of the House, Henry Clay, of Kentucky, was fourth with thirty-seven votes. Sen. Andrew Jackson of Tennessee, the hero of the Battle of New Orleans, received the most electoral votes, but with 99, he fell short of the 131 needed for a majority and election.[74] Jackson also won a strong plurality of popular votes in the eighteen states (all but six in the now twenty-four-state union) that in 1824 allowed voters to choose the electors.

Under the Twelfth Amendment, when any candidate fails to secure a majority of electoral votes, the House of Representatives chooses the president from among the three highest vote getters. This procedure eliminated Clay as a candidate. If the fourteen delegations from the states in which Jackson finished either first or second only to Clay in the election had supported the Tennessean, he would have become president.[75] But Clay used the influence he still had with his fellow representatives to help secure Adams's election. The new president, in turn, appointed Clay as secretary of state. Jackson's supporters were furious, charging that Adams and Clay had made a "corrupt bargain" to thwart the will of the people. Jackson himself branded Clay "the *Judas* of the West" and prophesied that "his end will be the same."[76] The charge of conspiracy was unfounded. Clay and Adams knew and respected each other, and both were National Republicans rather than Old Republicans like Jackson.[77] But the appearance of impropriety ensured the demise of what critics had come to call "King Caucus."

John Quincy Adams, the last president of the Jeffersonian era, was severely constrained by the general view that he was a minority president. But Adams was a statesman of considerable talent and accomplishment. Not content to stand in the shadow of Congress, he undertook to renew the strength of his office. In fact, Adams was the first president in history to openly attempt to lead Congress toward an active program of legislative achievement.

In his first annual message, Adams recommended a broad array of internal improvements, a national university, an observatory, scientific exploration, and voyages of discovery. His three Democratic-Republican predecessors had held strong reservations about the constitutional authority of Congress to create and fund such enterprises. Madison and Monroe followed Jefferson in believing that a constitutional amendment was needed before any of these things could be done. But Adams rejected both this narrow construction of the Constitution and the deference his recent predecessors had shown to Congress in domestic affairs. He also dismissed the reservations of his cabinet, whose members believed that his ambitious plans were impractical. After recounting the cabinet's resistance, Adams wrote in his diary, "Thus situated, the perilous experiment must be made. Let me make it with full deliberation, and be prepared for the consequences."[78]

Adams was the first president "to demonstrate the real scope of creative possibilities of the constitutional provision to 'recommend to their [Congress's] consideration such measures as he shall judge necessary and expedient.'"[79] But the combination of a disputed election, a divided party, and a stern and formal manner ill suited Adams for the task of building a political coalition. So, as political scientist Fred Greenstein has argued, did his failure to "moderate his proposals, establish priorities among them, and set about building support for the measures he deemed most important."[80] A quarter century of Jeffersonian presidents had not prepared the country for the sort of openly assertive executive leadership that Adams was attempting. As political scientist Richard Ellis has noted, "legislators received Adams's message with a mixture of scorn and disdain."[81]

Adams's influence, never very great, was effectively ended by the midterm congressional elections of 1826. His political foes, championing Andrew Jackson's opposition to the administration, won control of both the House and Senate. "General Jackson will be elected," Adams wrote in his diary, looking ahead to 1828.[82] The Democratic-Republican era ended with Congress, not the presidency, at the center of the national government but with the strongest president to date poised to seize control of Washington at the head of a new, democratic army.[83]

Notes

1. Alexis de Tocqueville, *Democracy in America*, ed. J. P. Mayer (Garden City, N.Y.: Doubleday, 1969), 203. Originally published in 1835 and 1840.

2. Harvey Mansfield, "Thomas Jefferson," in *American Political Thought: The Philosophic Dimensions of Statesmanship*, eds. Morton J. Frish and Richard G. Stevens (New York: Peacock, 1983), 49.

3. Jefferson to James Sullivan, February 9, 1797, in *The Writings of Thomas Jefferson*, ed. Paul Leicester Ford (New York: Putnam's, 1895), 7: 118.

4. Richard Hofstadter, *The Idea of a Party System: The Rise of Legitimate Opposition in the United States* (Berkeley: University of California Press, 1969), 122.

5. John Ferling, *Adams v. Jefferson: The Tumultuous Election of 1800* (New York: Oxford University Press, 2004), 161.

6. The method of voting added to the uncertainty of the House election. The Federalists controlled the House but did not control the congressional delegations of a majority of states. Of the sixteen states, eight could be counted on to support Jefferson, whereas six were controlled by the Federalists. The remaining two states were evenly divided. For a full account of the national trauma caused by the electoral gridlock of 1801, see ibid.; and James Roger Sharp, *American Politics in the Early Republic* (New Haven: Yale University Press, 1993), 250–275.

7. Sean Wilentz, *The Rise of American Democracy: From Jefferson to Lincoln* (New York: Norton, 2005), 93.

8. Hamilton to James A. Bayard, January 16, 1801, in *The Papers of Alexander Hamilton*, 27 vols., ed. Harold C. Syrett (New York: Columbia University Press, 1977), 25: 319–324. For a discussion of Hamilton's role in the 1800 election, see Hofstadter, *Idea of a Party System*, 136–140. See also Ferling, *Adams v. Jefferson*, 180.

9. Gordon S. Wood, *Empire of Liberty: A History of the Early Republic, 1789–1815* (New York: Oxford University Press, 2009), 285.

10. William W. Freehling, *The Road to Disunion: Secessionists at Bay, 1776–1854* (New York: Oxford University Press, 1990), 147.

11. Jefferson to Spencer Roane, September 6, 1819, in *The Writings of Thomas Jefferson*, 20 vols., ed. Albert Ellery Bergh (Washington, D.C.: Thomas Jefferson Memorial Association, 1903), 15: 212–216.

12. Joanne B. Freeman, *Affairs of Honor: National Politics in the New Republic* (New Haven: Yale University Press, 2001), 243.

13. James Roger Sharp, *The Deadlocked Election of 1800: Jefferson, Burr, and the Union in the Balance* (Lawrence: University Press of Kansas, 2010), 2, 4.

14. Forrest McDonald, *The Presidency of Thomas Jefferson* (Lawrence: University Press of Kansas, 1976), 34.

15. "Thomas Jefferson's First Inaugural Address," in *The Evolving Presidency: Landmark Documents*, 6th ed., ed. Michael Nelson (Washington, D.C.: CQ Press, 2019), 67–71.

16. Robert M. Johnstone Jr., *Jefferson and the Presidency* (Ithaca: Cornell University Press, 1978), 162.

17. *Marbury v. Madison*, 1 Cranch 137 (1803).

18. McDonald, *Presidency of Thomas Jefferson*, 50–51.

19. Indeed, for the rest of his life Jefferson regretted his failure to subdue the Marshall Court. As he told Spencer Roane, "The nation declared its will by dismissing functionaries of one principle, and electing those of another, in the two branches, executive and legislature, submitted to their election. Over the judiciary department, the Constitution deprived them of their control. That, therefore, has continued the reprobated system, and although new matter has been occasionally incorporated into the old, yet the leaven of the old mass seems to assimilate to itself the new, and after twenty years' confirmation of the federated system by the voice of the nation, declared through the medium of elections, we find the judiciary on every occasion, still driving us into consolidation." Jefferson to Roane, September 6, 1819, in Bergh, *Writings of Thomas Jefferson*, 5: 212.

20. McDonald, *Presidency of Thomas Jefferson*, 41; and John B. Boles, *Jefferson: Architect of American Liberty* (New York: Basic Books, 2017), 345–346.

21. Johnstone, *Jefferson and the Presidency*, 46 (emphasis in original).

22. Jefferson to John Breckinridge, August 12, 1803, in *The Portable Thomas Jefferson*, ed. Merrill D. Peterson (New York: Viking Press, 1975), 494–497.

23. Boles, *Jefferson*, 369.

24. Thomas Jefferson, "The Higher Law of Necessity," in *The President, Congress, and the Constitution: Power and Legitimacy in American Politics*, eds. Christopher H. Pyle and Richard M. Pious (New York: Free Press, 1984), 62–63 (emphasis in original).

25. Leonard D. White, *The Jeffersonians: A Study in Administrative History, 1801–1829* (New York: Macmillan, 1951), 3.

26. Ibid., 551.

27. The discussion of the change in the presidency during the Jeffersonian era is based on James Ceaser, *Presidential Selection: Theory and Development* (Princeton: Princeton University Press, 1979), 88–122; Johnstone, *Jefferson and the Presidency*, 52–75; and Jeremy Bailey, *Thomas Jefferson and Executive Power* (New York: Cambridge University Press, 2007).

28. Ceaser, *Presidential Selection*, 102.

29. John Ferling, *A Leap in the Dark: The Struggle to Create the American Republic* (New York: Oxford University Press, 2003), 477.

30. Quoted in Johnstone, *Jefferson and the Presidency*, 58.

31. Ibid., 58–59. See also Jefferson to Nathaniel Macon, May 14, 1801, in Ford, *Writings of Thomas Jefferson*, 8: 51–52.

32. Merrill D. Peterson, *Thomas Jefferson and the New Nation: A Biography* (New York: Oxford University Press, 1970), 653.

33. McDonald, *Presidency of Thomas Jefferson*, 22.

34. Johnstone, *Jefferson and the Presidency*, 67–75. Jeremy Bailey argues persuasively that Jefferson's view of executive power was as expansive as Hamilton's but that Democratic-Republicans added critical elements to the executive office that promoted its democratic character; see Bailey, *Thomas Jefferson and Executive Power*.

35. Thomas Jefferson, *Notes on the State of Virginia*, Quarry XVIII: Manners, http://teachingamericanhistory.org/library/document/notes-on-the-state-of-virginia-query-xviii-manners/; Thomas Jefferson to John Holmes, April 22, 1820, https://www.loc.gov/exhibits/jefferson/159.html.

36. White, *Jeffersonians*, 547.

37. Joyce Appleby, *Thomas Jefferson* (New York: Times Books, 2003), 41–42.

38. Jeffrey Tulis, *The Rhetorical Presidency* (Princeton: Princeton University Press, 1987).

39. Samuel Kernell, *Going Public: New Strategies of Presidential Leadership*, 3rd ed. (Washington, D.C.: CQ Press, 1997).

40. Leonard W. Levy, *Jefferson and Civil Liberties: The Darker Side* (Cambridge: Harvard University Press, 1963), 102.

41. Noah Feldman, *The Three Lives of James Madison: Genius, Partisan, President* (New York: Random House, 2016), 496.

42. Levy, *Jefferson and Civil Liberties*, 96.

43. Mel Laracey, "Dear America: Public Letters as an Early Form of Presidential Mass Communication," paper prepared for delivery at the 2009 Annual Meeting of the American Political Science Association, September 4, Toronto, Canada.

44. Jefferson to Thomas Mann Randolph, February 7, 1898, cited in Wilentz, *Rise of American Democracy*, 134.

45. Boles, *Jefferson*, 418.

46. Richard P. McCormick, *The Presidential Game: The Origins of American Presidential Politics* (New York: Oxford University Press, 1982), 82–87.

47. David E. Kyvig, *Explicit and Authentic Acts: Amending the U.S. Constitution, 1776–1995* (Lawrence: University Press of Kansas, 1996), 115–116.

48. White, *Jeffersonians*, 48–59.

49. Ralph Volney Harlow, *The History of Legislative Methods in the Period before 1825* (New Haven: Yale University Press, 1917), 192; and White, *Jeffersonians*, 52.

50. White, *Jeffersonians*, 53–54. A Madison biographer, Gaillard Hunt, exonerates Madison of striking any bargain with party leaders in Congress to secure his renomination. But there is no doubt that the Democratic-Republican caucus sought assurances about Madison's willingness to send a war message to Congress before agreeing to his renomination. See Hunt, *The Life of James Madison* (New York: Russell and Russell, 1902), 316–319.

51. Michael Nelson, "A Short, Ironic History of American National Bureaucracy," *Journal of Politics*, 44 (August 1982): 747–778.

52. White, *Jeffersonians*, 55.

53. Hunt, *Life of James Madison*, 325.

54. Wood, *Empire of Liberty*, 659–660, 677.

55. Wilentz, *Rise of American Democracy*, 165.

56. Hunt, *Life of James Madison*, 318–319.

57. Ibid., 329–330.

58. Feldman, *The Three Lives of James Madison*, 599.

59. James D. Savage, *Balanced Budgets and American Politics* (Ithaca: Cornell University Press, 1988), 98–99. See also Robert Allen Rutland, *The Presidency of James Madison* (Lawrence: University Press of Kansas, 1990), 68–70, 195–203.

60. Ralph Ketcham, "James Madison and the Presidency," in Cronin, *Inventing the American Presidency*, 360–361. Ketcham has argued that contemporary scholarly judgments of Madison as a weak president—such as his failure to be a dynamic leader, even during wartime—miss the philosophical and practical grounds of the president's conduct:

> It was not only uncongenial personally and in principle for Madison to move harshly against [the resistance to the war]; it was very nearly practically impossible as well. The federal system, which in Madison's own theory was the *only* republican way to govern a nation as large as the United States, gave state officials a multitude of ways to obstruct the national conduct of the war. Furthermore, republican theory forbade stifling the opposition or summarily denying civil liberties even during wartime; to do so was tantamount to losing the essential point (a free society) at the beginning and by default. (Ibid., 357–358 [emphasis in original].)

61. White, *Jeffersonians*, 38–41.

62. Jefferson to John Holmes, April 22, 1820, in Peterson, *Portable Thomas Jefferson*, 567–569.

63. White, *Jeffersonians*, 39. For a different, more appreciative view of Monroe as president, see Greenstein, *Inventing the Job of President*, chap. 6.

64. Quoted in ibid., 39.

65. William M. Goldsmith, ed., *The Growth of Presidential Power: A Documented History*, 3 vols. (New York: Chelsea, 1974), 1: 378–386.

66. "The Monroe Doctrine," in Nelson, *Evolving Presidency*, 75–78.

67. W. P. Cresson, *James Monroe* (Chapel Hill: University of North Carolina Press, 1946), 448.

68. Goldsmith, *Growth of Presidential Power*, 1: 455–456.

69. Ceaser, *Presidential Selection*, 102–103.

70. Sharp, *American Politics in the Early Republic*, 284.

71. Catherine Allgor, *Parlor Politics, in Which the Ladies of Washington Help Build a City and a Government* (Charlottesville: University Press of Virginia, 2000), chap. 4.

72. Charles Francis Adams, ed., *Memoirs of John Quincy Adams: His Diary from 1795 to 1848*, 12 vols. (Philadelphia: J. B. Lippincott, 1874–1877; New York: AMS Press, 1970), 4: 193.

73. Ibid., 7: 63.

74. In the absence of the three-fifths rule for counting slaves, Jackson "would have received 77 electoral votes and Adams 83." Daniel Walker Howe, *What Hath God Wrought: The Transformation of America, 1814–1848* (New York: Oxford University Press, 2007), 208.

75. Wilentz, *Rise of American Democracy*, 250.

76. Quoted in Sean Wilentz, *Andrew Jackson* (New York: Times Books, 2005), 49.

77. Fred Kaplan, *John Quincy Adams: American Visionary* (New York: Harper, 2014), 391.

78. Adams, *Memoirs of John Quincy Adams*, 7: 63.

79. Goldsmith, *Growth of Presidential Power*, 1: 325.

80. Greenstein, *Inventing the Job of President*, 80.

81. Richard J. Ellis, *The Development of the American Presidency* (New York: Routledge, 2012), 150.

82. Quoted in Wilentz, *Rise of American Democracy*, 294.

83. White, *Jeffersonians*, 42.

CHAPTER 5

The Age of Jackson

The presidency of John Quincy Adams took on the character of a long and acrimonious political campaign. Adams's own reelection effort began even before he was inaugurated in 1825 and continued for four years. As the president struggled in Washington with a recalcitrant Congress, a well-organized opposition formed around the country in support of Andrew Jackson, who was intent on rectifying the so-called corrupt bargain between Adams and Henry Clay that he believed had denied him the presidency in 1824.

By 1828 the confused political situation that underlay the previous presidential campaign, in which there were four candidates, was being replaced by a new party alignment. The Federalist Party was long defunct, and the Democratic-Republicans, who had dominated American politics since 1801, were now divided into two major factions. Adams and Clay led the National Republicans, as they sometimes were called because of their commitment to Washington-led economic development through high tariffs, the national bank, and funding for roads, canals, and other internal improvements. Jackson and John C. Calhoun, who was vice president during Adams's administration, led the opposition, which dedicated itself to the traditional Democratic-Republican principles of states' rights and a narrow interpretation of the national government's constitutional powers. By 1832 these factions had developed further into the Whig Party and Democratic Party, respectively. These two parties dominated the American political landscape until the eve of the Civil War, when the Whig Party died and the Republican Party arose to take its place.

The Jacksonian Democrats had the better of this rivalry. From 1828 until 1856 Democratic control of the presidency was interrupted only by the election of two Whig generals, William Henry Harrison in 1840 and Zachary Taylor in 1848, whose popularity as military heroes transcended party. Jackson's victory in the 1828 election was the culmination of a trend that began during the Jeffersonian era: the triumph of the emerging agrarian and frontier interests of the South and West over the commercial and financial interests of the Northeast. The purchase of the Louisiana Territory from France in 1803 and of Florida from Spain in 1819 not only added millions of acres to the United States but also afforded greater influence to many Americans who previously had stood outside the regular channels of political power.

Jackson, in fact, was the first political "outsider" to become president. All of his predecessors were from Virginia or Massachusetts and had undergone extensive apprenticeships in national politics and diplomacy as vice president, secretary of state, or both. The hero of the Battle of New Orleans was a Tennessean with little experience in Congress and none in executive administration. He was also, according to Sean Wilentz, "a social outsider, with an unpolished plebeian sensibility unlike any yet seen in an American president."[1] Jackson was a self-made man who had risen from a small cabin in the piney woods of South Carolina to a plantation near Nashville and eventually to the White House. Although his legacy has been tarnished by the historical memory of his administration's horrific treatment of Native Americans and fierce resistance to the Abolitionist movement, Jackson embodied political principles and personal qualities that held sway in the country for nearly three decades.[2] Appropriately, this period in American history has been called the "Age of Jackson."[3]

Jacksonian Democracy

The most important political theme of the Age of Jackson was the widespread desire for equality of opportunity, born of the conviction that no one should have special privileges at the expense of anyone else. Jackson followed Jefferson in believing that to eliminate privilege from society, political leaders must strictly limit the role of the national government. Rapid territorial expansion had been accompanied by dynamic economic growth, which seemed to foster unbounded opportunity in all parts of the country. Within that expansive environment, Jacksonians wanted to confine power as much as possible to the less obtrusive state governments. As Jackson's Democratic successor in the presidency, Martin Van Buren, stated in his first annual message to Congress in 1837,

> All communities are apt to look to government for too much. . . .
> But this ought not to be. . . . [T]he less government interferes

with private pursuits the better for the general prosperity. . . .
[I]ts real duty . . . is . . . to leave every citizen and every interest
to reap under its benign protection the rewards of virtue,
industry, and prudence.[4]

To be sure, the Jacksonian Democrats' concern for expanding equality of opportunity was limited to white males, especially those previously barred from voting because they did not own enough property. As historian Richard John has written, "The Jacksonians fully endorsed the post-Missouri [Compromise] consensus—sustained by nonslaveholders and slaveholders alike—that it was imperative to keep the slavery issue off the national political agenda."[5] When the militant abolitionist American Anti-Slavery Society (AASS), led by William Lloyd Garrison, sought to directly confront America's original sin in 1835 by mailing antislavery newspapers and other publications to religious and civic leaders throughout the South, the reaction was immediate and fierce. In his 1835 message to Congress, Jackson castigated "misguided" abolitionists for their "wicked attempts" to undermine the security and welfare of southern communities and urged Congress to pass legislation "to prohibit, under severe penalties, the circulation in the Southern States, through the mail, of incendiary publications intended to instigate the slaves to insurrection." When Congress did not pass the law, Jackson imposed the policy administratively, ordering postmasters to remove anti-slavery material from the mail.[6]

The Jacksonians' vigorous and unapologetic suppression of AAAS efforts to distribute antislavery materials reflected the political reality that southerners dominated not just the presidency but also Congress and the Supreme Court.[7] Their commitment to slavery, which the founding generation of tobacco-growing slaveholders thought was on the road to extinction because of its enervating effects on the soil, was strengthened by the invention and wide dissemination of the mechanical cotton gin, whose indispensability to labor-intensive, plantation-based cotton farming gave human bondage a new lease on life. From 1815 to 1826, annual cotton production rose from 210,000 to 730,000 bales, and the enslaved population doubled. Once viewed as a necessary evil to hold the Union together, slavery was now defended as a positive good.

Indeed, southern influence reinforced the Jacksonians' firm commitment to states' rights. Their political philosophy encouraged a much bolder assault on national institutions and programs than the generally more flexible Jeffersonians had undertaken. Jackson withdrew the federal government from the realm of internal improvements, not just highways and canals but also river dredging and harbor deepening. He kept the armed forces, especially the army, to a minimum. Jackson's fiscal policy was to hold down expenditures. The Bank of the United States, which Jeffersonians had learned to live with, was dismantled, and its deposits were reinvested in selected state banks.[8]

Still, the Age of Jackson had its contradictory and compensating aspects when it came to the authority of the national government. The Jacksonians regarded the president as the "tribune" of the people, an idea that invested the executive, in a period of democratic aspiration, with tremendous influence. During the Jeffersonian era, presidents had sometimes tried to develop a closer relationship with the people. But their modest efforts were made in the context of political principles and institutional arrangements that generally supported the supremacy of the legislature. Jackson tried to establish a direct connection between the president and the people, directly challenging Congress's status as the government's principal representative branch. As historian Major L. Wilson has observed, "This gave him [Jackson] independent power and made the presidency rather than the Congress, the true organ of the nation's will."[9] The Jacksonians' strengthened presidency "gave voice in a new age to the rising spirit of democratic nationalism," which sustained and strengthened the Union in the face of serious sectional conflicts over issues such as protective tariffs and slavery.[10]

Jackson's commitment to national sovereignty was never more apparent than in the nullification crisis that arose near the end of his first term. In an effort to compel the federal government to accede to its demand for a lower tariff, South Carolina's legislature summoned a state convention on November 24, 1832, to declare that the new 1832 tariff law was "null and void." South Carolina cited the nullification doctrine of its native son, Vice President John C. Calhoun. Calhoun had abandoned Adams's sinking political ship in 1828 and joined Jackson's ticket in hopes of eventually furthering his own presidential ambitions, only to find himself in such strenuous opposition to the president that he resigned.[11] The doctrine of nullification held that a state could declare any federal law that it deemed unconstitutional to be inapplicable within its borders. The ordinance of nullification that the South Carolina convention passed forbade federal officials to collect custom duties in the state after February 1, 1833, and threatened that the state's port cities would secede from the Union if the federal government responded by attempting to blockade Charleston or otherwise use force.

In the face of this threat, Jackson issued a ringing proclamation that vigorously rejected South Carolina's claim of a right to disobey a federal statute.

For a state to presume to annul a law of the United States, the president argued, was "incompatible with the existence of the Union, contradicted expressly by the letter of the Constitution, unauthorized by its spirit, inconsistent with every principle on which it was founded, and destructive of the great object for which it was formed."[12] The clash between Jackson and Calhoun was a critical precursor to the battle over slavery that exploded two decades later. In 1861, President Abraham Lincoln would base his response to southern secession on the same argument.

Jackson placed the responsibility to defend the Union squarely on the president's shoulders. It was the people, he believed, acting through the state ratifying conventions, who formed the Union in 1787–1788, and the president—not Congress or the states—who embodied most fully the will of the people. Jackson's conception of the presidency "transcended the older categories of nationalism versus states' rights" and offered a new understanding of national sovereignty.[13]

The idea that the president is the direct representative of the people lay at the heart of Jacksonian democracy. Although more supportive of popular rule than the Federalists, the Democratic-Republicans had demonstrated a restrained faith in democracy. The ongoing disputes between Democratic-Republicans and Federalists about the meaning of the Constitution overshadowed their basic agreement about the need to moderate democracy through formal relationships: among the legislative, executive, and judicial branches; between the state and national governments; and between the people and their representatives. The Jacksonians sought to reverse this equation by making the Constitution and its institutions the servant of public opinion. A leading Jacksonian journalist, John L. O'Sullivan, dismissed the founders' fears of democracy: "We are opposed to all self-styled 'wholesome restraints' on the free action of popular opinion and will." O'Sullivan believed in a system of checks and balances that prevented "precipitate legislation." But, he argued, all the branches of government, including the executive, "should be dependent with equal directness and promptness on the influence of public opinion."[14]

Alexis de Tocqueville, writing in the 1830s, identified this expanding doctrine of popular sovereignty as the cornerstone of Jacksonian democracy: "The people reign over the American political world as God rules over the universe. It is the cause and the end of all things; everything rises out of it and is absorbed back into it."[15] The dramatic surge of political reform in the 1830s had a profound effect on the presidency. Jackson's election in 1828 coincided with changes in state laws that replaced legislators with voters in the selection of presidential electors. In the first three presidential elections, most electors were chosen by the state legislatures. But by 1832 electors were selected by popular vote in every state except South Carolina, which retained legislative selection until the Civil War. More than four times as many people voted in both 1828 and 1832 as in 1824. The United States had become, historian Donald Cole has observed, "the world's first large-scale democracy."[16]

As a result, Jackson was the first president who could plausibly claim to have been elected by the people, strengthening his and his supporters' conviction that his mandate came directly from the source of all sovereignty.[17] As the efforts to undermine the Abolitionist movement make clear, the Jacksonian idea of sovereignty did not include women, Native Americans, or African Americans. Nor did Jacksonians' belief in expansive "self-rule" abate the Democratic Party's alliance with southern slaveholders. Yet it would be hard to deny that important political developments occurred in the 1830s that planted seeds of mass democracy.[18]

The president's claim to be the direct representative of the people also gained credence from the expansion of the electorate. His supporters worked successfully to persuade the states to eliminate property qualifications for voting, which meant that universal white manhood suffrage was virtually established by 1832. This development brought into the electorate farmers, mechanics, and laborers—"the humble members of society," as Jackson called them—who regarded the presidency under Old Hickory's superintendence as a rallying point. Their support freed the executive office from the congressional domination that had characterized presidential administrations from James Madison to John Quincy Adams, a trend that culminated in Adams's loss of Congress to Jackson's supporters in the midterm election of 1826—the first time that a president faced opposition-party control of both legislative houses.

With the collapse of the congressional nominating caucus in 1824, Jackson became the first president since George Washington to be chosen in a contest that did not involve Congress. In the 1828 election, Jackson defeated Adams by 178–83 in the Electoral College and won 56 percent of the popular vote, a figure unsurpassed by any presidential candidate until Theodore Roosevelt in 1904. Adams carried nearly all the states his father had in winning the 1796 election but lost all the states that had been added since then, including Ohio, Indiana, and Illinois in the Northwest and Alabama, Mississippi, and Louisiana in the Southwest. Taking office in 1829, Jackson found himself in a position to revitalize the presidency with a new independence and energy.

The Rise of the Party Convention

The advent of the Jackson presidency was accompanied by important developments in the party system. The demise of "King Caucus" left a vacuum in the presidential nominating process that soon was filled by national party conventions.[19] In 1832 the Democrats began using a convention to nominate their candidates for president and vice president, as did the Whigs. National convention delegates were selected by state-level conventions made up of local party members. Implicit in the idea of the national convention was the premise that the delegates' authority sprang directly from the rank and file or, as Jackson put it, "fresh from the people."[20] Taken together, the new and elaborate Whig and Democratic organizations reached far beyond the halls of Congress and eventually penetrated every corner of the Union. Sustained by his party's far-reaching political network, Jackson became the first president to appeal to the people over the heads of their legislative representatives.[21]

Party reform did not by itself ensure a strong presidency. The national party apparatus on which presidents depended for support was little more than a loose confederation of state and local organizations. Yet because the president and the national convention rather than Congress were at the heart of the party's identity and mission, strong leaders such as Jackson enjoyed an added source of political influence. Even though their organizational structure and practices were decentralized, the parties orchestrated presidential campaigns. As a consequence, their representatives in Congress muted, to some extent, sectional or local interests and supported national policies as expressed in the party platform. Moreover, with the formation of a stable two-party system during the Jacksonian era, partisan loyalties sank deep roots in the minds and habits of the American people. Presidents became the beneficiaries of an enduring foundation of popular support, enabling them to compete effectively with Congress for the public's attention.[22]

Jackson's Struggle with Congress

The transformation of the presidency from a congressionally to a popularly based office did not take place without a tremendous political struggle. The Whig Party, although it won only two of seven presidential elections between 1828 and 1852, offered vigorous opposition to the Democrats. Proclaiming the ideas of leaders such as Henry Clay and John Quincy

Adams, the Whigs took a national approach to national problems. They advocated Clay's program, known as the American Plan, to recharter the Second Bank of the United States, enact a protective tariff, and foster internal improvements. This program challenged the states-centered policies of the Democrats, resting instead on a broad, Hamiltonian construction of the Constitution.

Yet the Whigs, who originally formed as the party of opposition to Jackson, resisted the expansion of executive power and defended Congress's traditional status as the principal instrument of republican government. Jackson and the Democratic Party firmly controlled the House, but the Senate, led by forceful Whigs such as Clay and Daniel Webster, often challenged both the president's policies and his claims to executive primacy. Although the Whigs were seldom the majority party in Congress, they forged a coalition with Calhoun and some other states' right-oriented southern Democrats who resented Jackson's defense of the Union in the nullification crisis of 1832.

The conflict between the president and the Whigs came to a head in July 1832, when Jackson vetoed a bill to recharter the national bank four years before the existing charter expired. A generation earlier, as a central element of Alexander Hamilton's domestic program, the Bank of the United States had been a major point of contention between the Federalists and the Democratic-Republicans. Although Jefferson attacked the bank as an unconstitutional expansion of the national government, he and his Democratic-Republican successors became reconciled to it once they were in office, viewing the bank as a necessary evil to sustain a stable national currency. In 1816 the Second Bank of the United States received a twenty-year charter from Congress, but its president, Nicholas Biddle, decided to apply for an early recharter in 1832 at the urging of Clay and Webster. Clay, the Whigs' likely nominee for president in 1832, expected Jackson, whose dislike of the bank was well known, to veto the measure and thereby weaken his prospects for reelection. A considerable number of Democrats—especially in Pennsylvania, the home of the bank—supported the recharter legislation.

Jackson's veto of the bank bill on July 10, 1832, was, according to historian Robert V. Remini, "the most important veto ever issued by a president."[23] Jackson already had wielded the veto pen more freely than most of his recent predecessors, but the bank veto established a precedent that significantly strengthened the presidency. Beginning with Washington, Federalist and Democratic-Republican presidents alike had agreed that a veto should be cast only when the president believed that a piece of legislation was unconstitutional. In forty years under the Constitution, the first six presidents had vetoed only nine acts of Congress, and of these only three dealt with important issues. Jackson, in contrast, successfully vetoed twelve bills in eight years, even using the "pocket veto" for the first time. In his 1832 bank veto message to Congress, Jackson declared that a president should reject any bill he felt would injure the nation.

One implication of Jackson's interpretation of the veto power was that Congress now had to consider the president's opinions about bills before enacting them or else risk a veto. Even though the rechartering of the bank involved an "agent of the Executive branch of government," Jackson complained in his veto message, "neither upon the propriety of the present action nor upon the provisions of this act was the executive consulted."[24] In demanding the right to be involved in the development of important legislation, Jackson "essentially altered the relationship between the executive and legislative branches of government."[25]

Two other aspects of Jackson's veto message were significant. First, the message rearticulated Jefferson's belief that the president and Congress each possess coordinate power with the courts to determine questions of constitutionality. Jackson argued that the national bank was unconstitutional as well as unwise, a claim that his Whig opponents regarded as outrageous in view of Chief Justice John Marshall's decision in *McCulloch v. Maryland* (1819), which held that Congress had the constitutional power to charter a bank.[26] Webster charged that Jackson had claimed, in effect, "a universal power of judging over the laws and over the decisions of the judiciary" that was "nothing else but pure despotism."[27]

Jackson answered that in matters of constitutional interpretation, the president was no more bound by judicial rulings than by acts of Congress. Congress, the executive, and the Court, he asserted, "must each for itself be guided by its opinion of the Constitution." To rely solely on judicial precedent was to allow for "a dangerous source of authority, and should not be regarded as deciding questions of constitutional power except where the acquiescence of the people and the states can be considered as well settled."[28] Jackson's veto message dramatically reopened the controversy, which seemed to have been resolved in 1803 by *Marbury v. Madison*, over the authority of the federal courts. His claim that the president and Congress, the popularly elected branches, could reach their own judgments about the Constitution expressed his determination to forge a stronger connection between the people and their government.

The other notable aspect of Jackson's veto message was the manner in which he laid the controversy between himself and Congress before the

American people. The last paragraph of Jackson's message anticipated his campaign for reelection by stating that if he were "sustained by his fellow citizens," he would be "grateful and happy."

Concerned about the political effects of the bank war, Congress failed to override the president's veto. Jackson's 219–49 electoral vote defeat of Clay in the 1832 election, which was fought in large measure on the bank issue, convinced even his political opponents, as the respected Whig news-weekly *Niles' Register* reported, that when the president "cast himself upon the support of the people against the acts of both houses of Congress," he was sustained. Never before had a chief executive appealed to the people over the heads of their elected legislators. Jackson's victory confirmed his conviction that the president, not Congress, was the people's true representative in Washington.[29]

The Aftermath of the Bank Veto

The Jacksonian revolution was extended in the aftermath of the bank veto. Vindicated by his reelection, Jackson decided to kill off the bank once and for all by withdrawing the national government's deposits and placing them in selected state banks. But because Congress refused Jackson's request to remove the bank's funds, the power to do so remained with the secretary of the Treasury, who had been granted this authority in the law that chartered the Second Bank of the United States in 1816.

When Secretary of the Treasury Louis McLane rejected the president's request to transfer the deposits from the national bank to the state banks, Jackson nominated him to be secretary of state and replaced him at the Treasury with William J. Duane. But Duane also resisted Jackson's request and was dismissed within four months of taking office. His replacement, Roger B. Taney, formerly the attorney general, finally gave Jackson the cooperation he was looking for, which provoked the Senate to pass a censure resolution that accused the president of assuming "authority and power not conferred by the Constitution and laws."[30] Never before (or since) had a house of Congress voted to censure a president.

On April 15, 1834, Jackson countered the Senate's challenge with a written "Protest." In this message, which the offended Senate refused to enter in its journal, Jackson plainly stated his belief that "the President is the direct representative of the American people," not the Senate, which he dismissed as "a body not directly amenable to the people" because its members were elected by the state legislatures. Jackson further declared that the censure resolution was "wholly unauthorized by the Constitution, and in derogation of its entire spirit." He had been accused and, in effect, found guilty of an impeachable offense without the benefit of a trial, Jackson complained. Although the Senate's censure did not remove Jackson from office, it subjected him to a "solemn declaration" that threatened to undermine his authority and usurp the powers of the executive. The president concluded:

> I do hereby *solemnly protest* against the aforementioned proceedings of the Senate as unauthorized by the Constitution, contrary to its spirit and to several of its expressed provisions, subversive of that distribution of the powers of government which it has ordained and established, destructive of the safeguards by which those powers were intended on the one hand to be controlled and the other to be protected, and calculated by their character and tendency, to concentrate in the hands of a body not directly amenable to the people a degree of influence and power dangerous to their liberties and fatal to the Constitution of their choice.[31]

Taken together, Duane's dismissal, Taney's removal of public deposits from the national bank, and the Senate's censure of Jackson raised a fundamental constitutional question: Can the president, by firing someone, dictate how a discretionary power that Congress has vested exclusively in the head of a department shall be exercised? Whig leaders, notably Clay and Webster, defended Congress's right to vest independent authority in the Treasury secretary. Jackson claimed in response that the president was responsible "for the entire action of the executive department."

The Senate censure controversy—one battle in the long war between the president and Congress for control of executive administration—was won decisively by Jackson. His protest message became the leading issue in the next round of Senate elections, and Jackson's Democratic allies gained nine seats and took control of the upper house in 1837. At once, as historian H. A. Wise has written, the work of expunging from the record the Senate resolution of censure began. The effort "hurled senators from their seats in order to fill them with the pliant and supple tools of executive power to draw black lines on that journal around that resolution which dared to censure President Jackson!"[32]

On January 16, 1837, weeks before leaving office, Jackson had the satisfaction of seeing the Resolution of Censure formally expunged from the Senate journal. The Senate's decision to recant not only signified a personal political triumph for Jackson but also confirmed his broad interpretation of the president's power to control the executive branch.[33]

The Decline of the Cabinet

Within the executive branch, Jackson reduced the status of the cabinet. His dismissal of William Duane, in fact, merely capped the administration's unprecedented record of cabinet instability. During Jackson's two terms as president, he had four secretaries of state, five secretaries of the Treasury, two secretaries of war, three attorneys general, three secretaries of the navy, and three postmasters general.

Much of this turnover took place in 1831 when, for the first and only time in American history, the president forced an entire cabinet to resign. Jackson issued the resignation order in frustration over his inability to resolve the so-called Petticoat Affair.[34] The affair involved unsubstantiated rumors of scandal and immorality concerning Margaret Eaton, the wife of Secretary of War John Eaton, and the refusal of all the cabinet members' wives to associate with her. These snubs infuriated Jackson, who was a longtime friend of both Eatons and whose own recently deceased wife, Rachel, had also been the victim of vicious rumors. Jackson spent considerable time during his first two years as president establishing Margaret Eaton's innocence to his own satisfaction. He even presented a report of his findings to the cabinet—to no avail.

The impasse, which was poisoning both Washington society and the Jackson administration, was not resolved until Secretary of State Martin Van Buren, like Jackson a widower and a friend of the Eatons, persuaded the president to let him and Secretary Eaton resign as a way of triggering a wholesale turnover in the cabinet. Jackson's initial reaction to Van Buren's suggestion was "Never, sir! Even you know little of Andrew Jackson if you suppose him capable of consenting to such a humiliation of his friend by his enemies."[35] But the president soon came to see the political shrewdness of Van Buren's idea. Jackson told the other department heads that because he had formed the cabinet as a unit, the resignation of two members meant that he needed to replace them all. Van Buren's political star ascended in the eyes of the grateful president and his legions of devoted supporters. In contrast, the star of Van Buren's main rival to succeed Jackson as president, Vice President Calhoun, fell, in part because Calhoun's wife was among those who persisted in snubbing Margaret Eaton. Van Buren's deft handling of the Petticoat Affair, which led to his nomination as Jackson's running mate in 1832, brought cohesion and discipline to the executive branch; Jackson's new cabinet was much more clearly a creature of his democratic sentiments and political commitments than was the fractious body it replaced.

The cabinet's status in the Jackson administration also was diminished by the president's reliance on his "kitchen cabinet," a group of unofficial advisers with whom he conferred confidentially. They included Andrew J. Donelson, Jackson's ward and private secretary; Maj. William B. Lewis, a longtime friend whom Jackson invited to live in the White House; Van Buren, whom a grateful Jackson named as his second-term vice president; Amos Kendall, formerly a newspaper editor; and Francis P. Blair, the editor of the *Globe*, a newspaper whose pages he used from 1830 to 1845 to support Democratic policies and denounce the Whigs. The kitchen cabinet was depicted by Jackson's political enemies as slipping into the president's study by way of the kitchen stairs. In contrast, the traditional cabinet was sometimes called the "parlor cabinet."

According to critics of the administration, the kitchen cabinet consisted of men who were gifted in the arts of political manipulation but advised the president badly on matters of policy and government. Yet Jackson's reliance on informal advisers signified the dominant sway he held over public affairs more than any undue dependence on shadowy sources of influence. The only permanent member of the kitchen cabinet was Jackson himself. Membership in the group shifted from month to month and from issue to issue. The decline of the formal cabinet during the Jackson administration marked the unprecedented prominence of the presidency between 1829 and 1837, not the rise of a new advisory body.[36]

The Limits of the Jacksonian Presidency

According to the Whigs, the main legacy of Jackson's presidency was a dangerous expansion of presidential power. The bank controversy demonstrated, they argued, that the chief executive now possessed powers that dwarfed those of Congress and the judiciary, thereby undermining the constitutional separation of powers. Indeed, it was during this controversy that the anti-Jackson National Republicans assumed the name of "Whig." Historically, the label derived from the British political party that opposed the power of the king and supported parliamentary supremacy. Whigs in the United States meant by their name to imply that the Jackson wing of the Democratic-Republican Party—the Democrats—had abandoned

BORN TO COMMAND.

OF VETO MEMORY.

HAD I BEEN CONSULTED.

KING ANDREW THE FIRST.

Jackson's extension of executive power led his opponents to caricature him in this 1832 cartoon by an unknown artist as a monarch trampling the Constitution, a ledger of Supreme Court decisions, and the watchwords "Virtue," "Liberty," and "Independence."

Source: Library of Congress.

Jeffersonian principles in favor of an elected monarch, whom Whigs dubbed "King Andrew the First."[37]

Jackson's attitude toward the courts lent support to this indictment. His bank veto message had asserted that he reserved the right to question a Supreme Court decision if he thought it was based on an erroneous interpretation of the Constitution. Indeed, Jackson's response to the Supreme Court's ruling in *Worcester v. Georgia* (1832) nearly led to a direct clash between the president and the justices, especially Chief Justice Marshall.[38] In this case, the Supreme Court struck down a Georgia statute banishing the Cherokee Indians from the state's western territories on the ground that the law violated a federal treaty with the tribe. The issue was brought to the Court by two Christian missionaries, Samuel Worcester and Elizur Butler, who had ignored a provision in the Georgia law that prohibited whites from living in Cherokee territory without first obtaining a state license.

The *Worcester* legal battle posed a challenge to Jackson's Indian policy, as authorized by the Removal Act of 1830, which forced Eastern tribes to move west of Arkansas and Missouri. Jefferson had argued that Indian tribes in the Southeast should give up their land in exchange for territory in the West, but he did not force tribes from their homelands. More eager than his Jeffersonian predecessors to embrace executive power, Jackson developed a systematic approach to confiscate the land of Native Americans. By the end of his presidency, he signed into law almost seventy removal treaties, moving almost 50,000 eastern Native Americans to land west of the Mississippi. With the help of Worcester and Butler, the Cherokee nation resisted this forced exodus, and Marshall's opinion appeared to give constitutional sanction to the tribe's determination to remain in Georgia.

Yet Jackson maintained a deafening public silence in the face of the Court's ruling. Newspaper editor Horace Greeley later reported that Jackson's private response was "Well: John Marshall has made his decision: *now let him enforce it!*"[39] Although the authenticity of this statement has been questioned by some historians, Jackson certainly encouraged Georgia in its intransigence. His public actions, however, were more cautious. The president neither criticized the decision nor openly expressed support for Georgia's refusal to comply. Instead, with the help of Vice President-Elect Van Buren, he maneuvered behind the scenes to orchestrate a compromise. The two missionaries received a gubernatorial pardon in exchange for which they agreed to withdraw their legal challenge.[40]

Significantly, the *Worcester* controversy occurred during the national crisis aroused by South Carolina's passage of the ordinance of nullification. Jackson's cautious resolution of the court case enabled him to ask Congress for authorization to use force to suppress nullification in South Carolina without being embarrassed by his support of Georgia in its own clash with the national government.[41] In the debate on the Nullification Proclamation, Jackson's loud voice had been heard in support of democratic nationalism. His public silence in the *Worcester* controversy deflected attention from the terrible injustice of the removal policy. Although a majority of Cherokees continued to claim that the Jackson administration had no right to their land, their resistance gave way in 1838, when federal troops and Georgia state militia forced them to migrate to dry plains beyond the Mississippi. Between three and four thousand of the fifteen to sixteen thousand Cherokees died from the brutal conditions on this "Trail of Tears."

The institutional legacy of Jackson's two terms as president was much more ambiguous than his political opponents believed. Jackson's aggressive action in upholding the Union and, with respect to policies pertaining to the slavery and Native American controversies, denigrating the ideal of democratic nationalism did not simply expand the opportunities for unilateral executive action. His extension of executive power depended on the president's emergence as a popular leader, a role that was mediated in critical ways by his party. "More than any other American," Wilentz has written, "Jackson oversaw the decline and fall of the elitist, gentry order established by the Framers and its replacement with the ruder conventions and organization of democracy."[42] Seeking to tame the more dangerous tendencies of unfiltered democracy, Van Buren and other members of Jackson's kitchen cabinet built the first national party organization that was extensive enough to constrain any excesses of personal ambition that might arise among Jackson's presidential successors. As Van Buren wrote to Thomas Ritchie, the editor of the *Richmond Inquirer,* the ultimate objective was to "substitute party principle for personal preference."[43]

The Party Press

The bank war and other political struggles during the Jackson presidency were carried on through the party press that emerged during the 1830s. Jackson's relationship with Democratic journalists such as Amos Kendall and Francis Blair added an important dimension to his leadership. These editors provided the president with an acceptable tool for political influence by translating "executive decisions into forceful language and announc[ing] them with persuasive eloquence to the American people."[44] Blair's *Globe,* in fact, became the official organ of both the Jackson administration and its successor, the Van Buren administration. The newspaper enjoyed special access to official political circles as well as financial support from government printing contracts that were distributed by each administration. Its articles were reprinted in pro-Jackson state and local newspapers around the country, fanning the flames of grassroots support for the president and his agenda.[45]

Every Democratic president from Jackson to James Buchanan secured the solid support of at least one important newspaper. The *Globe* and other official organs made clear that they were speaking on behalf of the president. Yet the "administration press" was also a Democratic press, dedicated to the party's program and organization.[46] Thus, a more assertive presidency was bound inextricably to a more aggressive and popular party press.

The "Spoils System"

The printing contacts that abetted the rise of the party press were part of an elaborate patronage system. Jackson implanted a system of rotation into government personnel practices using the president's power of appointment and removal to hire and fire employees for partisan reasons. Until Jackson became president, the prevailing belief was that the government workforce should be stable and, to a large extent, politically neutral. Beginning in 1829, however, Jackson and his successors rejected this principle and either replaced or sanctioned the removal of thousands of subordinates for political reasons. Jackson removed 41 percent of the presidential appointees whom he inherited from his predecessor, a number that rose to 89 percent during fellow Democrat Franklin Pierce's administration. After protesting Jackson's conduct, Whig presidents followed suit – Zachary Taylor and Millard Fillmore removed 68 percent during their combined four years in office, and Abraham Lincoln, a Whig before he became a Republican, removed 96 percent during his presidency.[47]

The credo of the new patronage system among Democratic Party activists was, as New York senator William L. Marcy put it, "to the victor belong the spoils of the enemy."[48] Jackson was hardly insensitive to the partisan advantages of "rotation in office," but he also had a deeper purpose in mind. Unless government jobs changed hands regularly, Jackson believed, the resulting "stasis bred corruption in the executive . . . just as it bred the odious belief that ordinary men lacked the experience necessary to master the mysteries of government service."[49] In truth, Jackson argued, "The duties of all public officers are, or at least admit of being made, so plain and simple that men of intelligence may readily qualify themselves for their performance."[50]

In theory, the new principle of rotation in office (or the "spoils system," as Jackson's opponents lastingly called it) expanded the powers of the executive enormously. As Jackson's dismissal of Duane during the bank controversy illustrated, the president was now in a position to enforce conformity to administration policies within the executive branch. This was in keeping with how Jackson thought constitutional democracy ought to work. In time, however, most federal patronage came to be controlled by local party organizations in a manner that actually circumscribed presidential leadership. When party leaders demanded offices as a reward for rallying voters to the national ticket in congressional and presidential elections, even powerful chief executives were not inclined to refuse them. Moreover, to keep their jobs, many federal officeholders, particularly those who served in the widely scattered land offices, customhouses, and post offices, were required to return part of their salaries to the local party organization, to work for the party at election time, and to "vote right."[51]

The postal system became the primary source of partisan favors. Beginning with Jackson and continuing well into the twentieth century, it was common practice for the president to appoint as postmaster general someone who would serve as the administration's principal patronage officer, representing the interests of the party to the president. Presidents who were insensitive to the demands of partisanship paid a severe political price. James Buchanan was attacked by many Democratic leaders when he removed loyal Democratic officeholders who were appointed by his predecessor, Franklin Pierce.[52]

The powers of the presidency that Jackson brought to life were constrained not only by the party system but also by the fundamental political doctrine that he espoused: to limit the activities of the national government. "General Jackson's power is constantly increasing," Tocqueville wrote, "but that of the president grows less. The federal government is strong in his hands; it will pass to his successor enfeebled."[53]

Martin Van Buren and the Panic of 1837

As Tocqueville prophesied, Jackson's successor, the able and politically shrewd Martin Van Buren, took office in difficult circumstances. Indeed, Van Buren became the first president to have to deal with a nationwide domestic crisis. No sooner was he inaugurated in 1837 than the economy began a steep downward spiral, a decline that was in part the legacy of Jackson's assault on the national bank.

The Panic of 1837, as the crisis was called, was caused in large measure by speculation. A boom in western land and in manufacturing, transportation, banking, and other enterprises, which began in 1825, caused credit to become overextended in the national economy. By removing federal deposits from the financially prudent Second Bank of the United States and placing them in politically favored state banks, the Jackson administration contributed to the rapid expansion of credit. In July 1836, conscious of the problems created by an overextended economy, Jackson issued a Treasury order, the so-called Specie Circular, requiring that gold or silver (specie) be used to pay for all federal lands. This order aroused fears that Jackson and his successor would do all they could to shrink the money supply, causing privately owned banks to call in loans, many of which could not be paid. Financial panic ensued. In early 1837 mercantile houses began to fail, New Yorkers rioted to protest the high cost of flour, and almost every bank in the country suspended specie payments. The state banking system that the Jacksonians had encouraged to replace the national bank collapsed, costing the Treasury some $9 million.

Van Buren was a more pragmatic politician than Jackson, but he was sufficiently wedded to Jacksonian principles to resist government-sponsored solutions to the economic crisis. The new president rejected any proposal to revive the national bank. He also rejected the idea that the Treasury should provide a paper currency to facilitate domestic commerce. Like Jackson, Van Buren believed that the Treasury should attend to its own affairs and let businesses do the same.

Spurning the "constant desire" of the Whigs "to enlarge the power of government," Van Buren's response to the Panic of 1837 was modest. He proposed to establish an independent subtreasury, which would keep federal funds in federal vaults instead of depositing them in state banks. The subtreasury, however, was to have limited powers, leaving state banks free from federal regulation. Van Buren's proposal was not implemented until 1840; it was resisted during most of his term by a coalition of conservative Democrats and Whigs, many of whom wanted the national government to become more active in the economy.[54]

The Jacksonian Presidency Sustained

The presidential election of 1840 took place in the midst of an economic crisis for which many voters held the Democratic Party responsible. The triumph of the Whig candidate, William Henry Harrison, posed a challenge not only to the Jacksonians' domestic program but also to their institutional achievements. The victorious Whig Party was united above all else by opposition to the expansion of executive power that took place during the Jackson administration. Accordingly, Whig leaders such as Henry Clay and Daniel Webster saw the Panic of 1837 as an opportunity to reassert the powers of Congress.

Clay was the obvious candidate to head the Whig ticket in 1840. He was both the architect of the anti-Jackson program and the real founder of the Whig Party. But, believing General Harrison to be more electable, the Whigs nominated the aged (he was sixty-seven years old at the time of the election) hero of the War of 1812's Battle of Tippecanoe. It consoled Clay and his allies to know that the general had proclaimed his support for the Whig assault on the executive in 1838, dedicating himself to a program that would limit the president to one term, free the Treasury from presidential control, and confine the exercise of the veto power to legislation that the president deemed unconstitutional.[55]

Although the 1840 campaign was not distinguished by a serious discussion of the issues, Harrison did pledge publicly to step down after four years. In a speech delivered on September 10, 1840, at Dayton, Ohio, he declared:

> In the Constitution, that glorious charter of our liberties,
> there is a defect, and that defect is, the term of service of the
> President,—not limited. This omission is the source of all the
> evil under which the country is laboring. If the privilege of being

President of the United States had been limited to one term, the incumbent would devote all his time to the public interest, and there would be no cause to misrule the country. . . . *I pledge myself before Heaven and earth, if elected President of the United States, to lay down at the end of the term faithfully that high trust at the feet of the people!*[56]

Harrison's inaugural address, which Webster and Clay helped write, provided further reason to believe that the Whig victory in 1840 might undo Jackson's reconstruction of the presidency. Indeed, when Harrison deemed "preposterous" the idea that the president could "better understand the wants and wishes of the people than their representatives," Jacksonians suspected that designing Whig leaders had persuaded the politically inexperienced general to accept the status of a figurehead, delegating the powers of his office to Congress.[57]

Yet the Jacksonian executive survived the Whig challenge. The importance of the presidency was so firmly established in the popular mind by 1840 that the office no longer could be restored to the weak position it occupied during the latter part of the Jeffersonian era. The Whigs, in fact, unwittingly contributed to the permanent transformation of the presidency by their conduct of the 1840 campaign. Jackson's partisan opponents had looked with disfavor on the popular, even festive campaign tactics that the Democratic Party employed during the three previous presidential elections. But, having lost all of them to Jackson and Van Buren, the Whigs did everything in their power to rouse the people in 1840. They bought newspapers to publish party propaganda, held great rallies, sent popular party leaders on speech-making tours, and worked to mobilize as many voters as possible.

So intent were the Whigs on outdoing the Democrats' campaign in 1840 that they subordinated principles and issues to slogans, songs, and symbols. Not only did "Tippecanoe and Tyler too" catch on (an alliterative catchphrase made possible by the nomination of Virginia's John Tyler for vice president), but a great deal of rabble-rousing occurred that for the first time made the log cabin an important symbol in presidential politics. A Democratic journalist had scornfully said of the rustic Harrison, "Give him a barrel of hard cider and . . . a pension of $2,000, and . . . he will sit the remainder of his days in his log cabin by the side of a . . . fire and study moral philosophy." Clever Whig propagandists pounced on this remark, turning it to their candidate's advantage. In no time, Harrison became "the log cabin and hard-cider candidate," an image that endeared him to many farmers and workers. Log cabin badges, log cabin songs, log cabin newspapers, and cider barrels were seen everywhere.

In the face of such campaigning, Martin Van Buren, whose origins actually were humbler than Harrison's but whose tastes, as displayed in the White House and in his attire, were ostentatious, never stood a chance. Harrison was actually from an established Virginia family, a learned student of classics, and a man who enjoyed luxurious living to the point that he was continually in debt. But the Whig strategy resonated with voters eager to identify with a war hero who shared their down-to-earth values. As the historian William Freehling has observed, the 1840 celebration of "Old Tip" as "One of Us" became "the first true use of political handling, or public image-making," in an American presidential campaign. Even though his administration presided over an economic depression, Van Buren tried to run an issues-driven campaign. Adroitly invoking the Jacksonians' celebration of the "common man," however, Harrison decisively defeated the earnest incumbent president. He received 234 electoral votes to 60 votes for Van Buren.[58]

The log cabin, hard-cider campaign stimulated tremendous interest and enthusiasm around the country. Electoral turnout increased substantially. The 2.4 million voters who cast ballots in 1840 constituted 80.2 percent of the eligible electorate, a percentage that has been surpassed only twice, in 1860 and 1876.[59] Ironically, by accepting and expanding on the Democrats' successful campaign techniques, the Whigs unwittingly ratified the Jacksonian concept of the president as popular leader. The Whig Party's anti-executive doctrine notwithstanding, it was no longer possible for the presidency to be restored to its late Jeffersonian status, however unassuming a particular president might be.[60]

John Tyler and the Problem of Presidential Succession

The consolidation of the Jacksonian presidency became more pronounced when Harrison, who caught pneumonia after delivering a ninety-minute inaugural address in Washington's freezing rain on March 4, 1841, died only a month later. Vice President Tyler quickly took the oath as president and vowed to complete the remaining three years and eleven months of Harrison's term. In doing so, Tyler imposed a solution on the unresolved constitutional problem of the vice president's right to assume the full status of the presidency when the office becomes vacant. Tyler also proved to be a

A HARD ROAD TO HOE!
Or, the White House Turnpike, macadamized by the North Benders.
SOLD BY HUESTIS & Co. 104 NASSAU-ST, N. Y.

This 1840 campaign cartoon shows Andrew Jackson leading Martin Van Buren to the White House for a second term. Van Buren, known as "Old Kinderhook" after his New York home, lost to the "log cabin and hard-cider" candidate, William Henry Harrison. But his partisan rallying cry, "OK," entered the language as an expression of agreement or approval.

Source: Library of Congress.

less enthusiastic proponent of Whig theories of government than Harrison, particularly with regard to the executive. In truth, he agreed with the Democrats more than the Whigs on most issues, having left the Democratic Party only because he objected to Jackson's forceful stance toward South Carolina's threat of nullification. Whig leaders were disappointed to discover that Tyler was no ally in their effort to dismantle either Jackson's policies or his approach to governing.

Tyler's constitutional right to become president was far from certain. The succession clause of Article II was vague, stipulating only that in case of the president's death, resignation, removal, or inability to discharge the powers and duties of the office, "the Same" shall "devolve on the Vice President." Did "the Same" refer to the "Office" or to its "Powers and Duties"? Specifically, did Tyler remain vice president, merely acting as president until a special election could be held, or had he succeeded fully to the office and title of president for the remainder of Harrison's four-year term?

Tyler wasted no time asserting that he was the president in every sense of the word. Soon after hearing that Harrison was dead and despite some rumblings from Congress, he had a judge swear him in and within ten days moved into the executive mansion. Leaving no doubt that he intended to be his own man as president, on April 9, 1841, Tyler went before "the people" and gave an inaugural address to an audience assembled in the Capitol. Tyler's "exposition of the principles" that would govern his administration was a signal to the country that he would not be content to stand in Harrison's shadow. The address was also a warning to Whigs that Tyler did not intend to be a compliant subordinate of Clay and

John Tyler, as the first vice president to succeed to the presidency, faced the constitutional question of whether he succeeded to the office for the rest of the term or only succeeded temporarily to the responsibilities of the office. His decisive actions preempted debate and established a firm precedent for succession to the presidency.

Source: Library of Congress.

other party leaders. By acting boldly and decisively in an uncertain situation, Tyler established, in the absence of clear constitutional guidance, the firm precedent that an "accidental" president enjoys the same status as an elected president.[61] Congress's acquiescence became clear when a motion in the House of Representatives to address him officially in correspondence as "Vice President, on whom, by the death of the late President, the powers and duties of the office of President have devolved" was defeated overwhelmingly.[62] After all, not much was to be gained politically by alienating the person who, whether as president or acting president, wielded "the Powers and Duties of the said Office."

The difficulties that Tyler faced as president went beyond the constitutional doubts shrouding his succession. His elevation also created a political impasse. Tyler, the former Democrat, represented a faction of the Whig Party that dissented from many of the nationalist views preached by its leaders. In accordance with the practice then common in American party politics, his nomination as vice president had stemmed from an effort to balance the Whig ticket as a gesture of reconciliation by the ascendant National Republican wing of the Whig Party to the smaller southern states' rights wing. Yet in this case, ticket balancing backfired. Tyler not only seized the reins of office decisively after Harrison's death but also exercised the powers of the Jacksonian presidency in a way that thwarted the Whigs' efforts to enact Clay's American Plan for government-sponsored economic development.[63] Tyler was, in the apt phrase of political scientists Matthew Crenson and Benjamin Ginsberg, "a lapsed Democrat who relapsed after assuming the responsibilities of the president."[64]

Tyler's opposition to much of the Whig domestic program prompted him to cast more vetoes than any of his predecessors except Jackson. In 1841 Tyler vetoed two successive bills that resembled the old bank legislation Jackson had killed. The outburst of fury against the president after his second veto was extraordinary, expressing the Whigs' frustration at their inability to enact their program even after winning a presidential election. Effigies of Tyler were burned across the country, and the president received hundreds of letters threatening assassination. In Washington, every cabinet member except Secretary of State Daniel Webster resigned. Expressing nostalgia for the era of Democratic-Republican ascendancy, especially for the heir-presumptive role the secretary of state enjoyed during that period, Webster stayed on for another year and a half, trying to work with the new president.[65] Had Webster not resisted pressure from Clay to endorse a Senate scheme to prevent Tyler from appointing a new cabinet, Tyler himself may have had no choice but to resign.

The bank battles were only the beginning of the long struggle between Tyler and his party. Tyler's veto of a tariff measure in 1842 provoked the first attempt in history to impeach a president. His assertive exercise of the veto power was irreconcilable with the Whig theory of executive subordination to Congress. Clay even proposed a constitutional amendment that would permit Congress to override a veto by a simple majority vote.[66] The amendment received majority support, but not the necessary two-thirds majority, in the House.

Tyler, claiming for the president a right to participate in the legislative process that was reminiscent of Jackson, defended his veto of the tariff bill on programmatic rather than constitutional grounds. Responding to Congress's accusation that he had misused the veto power as well as to the talk of impeachment, Tyler issued a strongly worded public message, stating that he represented "the executive authority of the people of the United States" and in "their name" protested "against every attempt to break down the undoubted constitutional power" of the presidency.[67] Like Jackson,

Tyler also argued that when a conflict developed between the president and Congress, it was for the people to decide who was right. When the Whigs were defeated in the congressional elections of 1842, Tyler believed that he had been vindicated. Nothing came of the effort to impeach him, and Clay's proposal for a constitutional amendment to weaken the veto power withered in the face of public indifference.

Although Tyler lost his party's support and with it any chance to be nominated for president in 1844, he prevented a potentially damaging setback to the executive office. As presidential scholar Wilfred E. Binkley wrote, Tyler "prepared the way for the completion of the movement toward executive leadership started by Andrew Jackson."[68]

The Presidency of James K. Polk

Few would have guessed as Tyler's term came to an end in 1845 that his relatively unknown Democratic successor, James K. Polk, would lead a successful administration. Yet Polk strengthened the office, successfully asserting executive responsibilities that were either unsought by his predecessors or denied to them. Polk's achievements did not come easily. He headed a Democratic Party that was beginning to break apart over the slavery issue. He also faced militant Whig minorities in both houses of Congress. Defying the Jacksonians' efforts to mute the Abolitionists, hundreds of petitions with tens of thousands of signatures poured into Congress, pressing for the abolitions of slavery in the nation's capital and asking that neither Florida nor Texas be admitted to the Union as slave states.

In a last, desperate attempt to stifle debate, Democratic leaders proposed a "gag rule" that prohibited the House from discovering or even mentioning the anti-slavery petitions. The gag rule passed in 1835 with Jackson's strong support and was tightened in 1840 during Van Buren's term. This denigration of Jacksonian democracy was turned to the advantage of the anti-slavery forces by Jackson's old political rival, John Quincy Adams, who was first elected to the House in 1834. In January 1842, Adams presented an antislavery petition from a town in his district and ordered the House clerk to read the Declaration of Independence. In doing so Adams exploited the gag rule controversy to remind the country that the basic right of free speech was also under attack. As a result, he was able to enlist support from Americans who, regardless of their views on slavery, believed that the House should remain an open arena of democratic debate. The House repealed the gag rule in 1844.

The First "Dark Horse" Candidate

Former president Van Buren was widely expected to receive the 1844 Democratic nomination. The issue of annexing Texas intervened. Just before the Whig and Democratic nominating conventions, Tyler's secretary of state, John C. Calhoun, concluded an annexation treaty with the Republic of Texas, which had won its independence from Mexico in 1836. As a result, the two major parties' leading presidential aspirants, Van Buren and Clay, were forced to announce their views on the treaty. As the petitions that aroused the gag rule fight made clear, Texas was an issue that aroused serious disagreements between North and South about the desirability of expanding the nation's cotton-growing and slave-holding.

Clay's opposition to annexation caused little controversy in the Whig Party, which increasingly was dominated by northerners. But when Van Buren took the same position, a firestorm erupted among Democrats. They and their hero, Andrew Jackson, had long supported territorial expansion, a cause that was sacred to the emerging plantation interests of the South and frontier interests of the West. To defeat the Whigs, the Democrats needed especially strong support in the South, where states' rights advocates such as Calhoun looked westward to expand slavery. Yet Van Buren, belying his reputation as a pragmatic politician who was willing even to acquiesce to southern views in the gag rule controversy, now chose to follow "the path of duty" and resisted the extension of slavery. His principled decision cost him any chance to return to the office.

Van Buren received a majority of votes in early convention ballots but not the two-thirds that Democratic Party rules required for nomination. The two-thirds rule, adopted in 1832, manifested Calhoun's belief that a "concurrent majority," not just a numerical majority, of all major social interests must agree on a decision before it can take effect. Calhoun's theory never became the law of the land, but it did become the rule of his party for a century. The effect in 1844 was to allow the South to deny Van Buren the Democratic nomination.

With Van Buren's candidacy stymied, former governor of Tennessee and speaker of the House Polk, so close an associate of Jackson that he was known as "Young Hickory," emerged at the deadlocked Democratic convention as a compromise choice between North and South, the first "dark horse" candidate in the history of American presidential elections. Polk did not even receive his first vote for the nomination until New Hampshire was polled on the eighth convention ballot. But New York's support on the ninth ballot started a stampede as delegation after delegation rushed to transfer its votes to Polk and thereby demonstrate its loyalty to the winner.[69] In the election, Polk defeated Clay by 170–105 electoral votes, and the Democrats turned a six-seat deficit in the Senate into a twelve-seat majority.

Reasserting Presidential Power

Through a combination of shrewd political maneuvering and forceful statesmanship, Polk was able to overcome the centrifugal forces that dominated American politics during the mid-1840s. After winning the Democratic nomination, he stole one of the Whigs' main issues by disclaiming any intention to seek a second term. Yet during his four years in office, Polk vigorously and effectively asserted executive functions that for a time reinforced, even expanded, the Jacksonian conception of presidential power. Most significant, he was the first president to exercise close and daily supervision of the executive departments.

Consistent presidential influence was especially absent from previous administrations' relations with the Treasury Department. Presidents had never been granted legal responsibility to oversee the departmental budget estimates submitted annually to Congress. Instead, in the Treasury Act of 1789, Congress assigned to the secretary of the Treasury the duty to prepare and report estimates of government expenditures for the coming year. George Washington's Treasury secretary, Alexander Hamilton, did not even consult the president in this matter. Both Hamilton and Albert Gallatin, who served in the Jefferson and Madison administrations, were distinctive among Treasury secretaries mainly in the initiative they took in budgetary policy making. Their successors in the office simply gathered the departmental estimates and submitted them to Congress in one package. In 1839, for example, Van Buren's secretary of the Treasury, Levi Woodbury, refused to take any responsibility for making a composite budget or for reviewing the estimates that were submitted to him by the other departments.[70]

One of Polk's major achievements was to coordinate the budget. For the first time in history, the president oversaw the formation of a fiscal policy. Not only did Polk review all budget requests, but he also insisted that the department heads revise their planned expenditures downward. Polk was forced to tighten fiscal control after he launched the Mexican–American War in 1846, especially when the government began operating under the reduced revenues of the Walker Tariff, which he considered one of the major accomplishments of his administration.[71] Furthermore, Polk, like his political mentor Jackson, hated public debt and was philosophically committed to limiting government spending. Polk's success in directing the budget was demonstrated by the tight fiscal rein he imposed on the War Department at the end of the Mexican–American War. Polk directed his reluctant secretary of war, William Marcy, to force the department's bureau chiefs to accept a return to the prewar level of expenditures.[72]

The precedents that Polk tried to establish in fiscal policy making were not followed by his nineteenth-century successors. (Abraham Lincoln, another wartime president, was an exception.) But Polk's assertion of the president's right and duty to control personally the activities of the executive departments implanted the Jacksonian concept of the presidency more deeply in the American constitutional order. In the face of belligerent Whig opposition, Polk's last message to Congress proclaimed that "the people, by the Constitution, have commanded the President, as much as they have commanded the legislative branch of government, to execute their will." Indeed, Polk argued, the president occupied a special place as the people's representative because "the President represents in the executive department the whole people of the United States, as each member of the legislative department represents portions of them."[73]

According to historian George Bancroft, who served in the administration as secretary of the navy, Polk succeeded "because he insisted on being its [the administration's] center and in overruling and guiding all his secretaries to act as to produce unity and harmony."[74] To some extent, this unity was the fortunate by-product of Polk's decision to try to hold his ever more fractious party together by excluding from his cabinet nearly every leading Democrat who actively coveted the presidency. "The virus of competing presidential ambitions must not be allowed to infect Polk's inner circle," biographer Robert W. Merry has written. "Hence there would be no offers to Van Buren, [Thomas Hart] Benton, [Lewis] Cass, Old Dick Johnson, or Calhoun." Polk's one exception demonstrated the rule: he named James Buchanan as secretary of state and then spent all four years ruing Buchanan's "self-interested maneuvers."[75]

Unity within the administration also was fostered by Polk's relentless and successful focus on achieving four specific goals: settling with Great Britain which country owned which parts of the Oregon Territory (accomplished by treaty in 1846); reducing tariffs (the Walker Tariff of 1846, the measure named after Polk's secretary of the Treasury, Robert J. Walker); reestablishing an independent national Treasury (a Jacksonian mainstay passed by the Democratic Congress in 1846); and acquiring California from Mexico.

The last of these was the cause of the Mexican–American War. Perhaps Polk's most important contribution to the development of the presidency was his aggressive performance as wartime commander in chief. In his view the war became inevitable after the United States annexed Texas and then admitted it as the twenty-eighth state in early 1845 even though Mexico still claimed Texas and considered the annexation a hostile act. Polk's determination to secure New Mexico and California from Mexico provoked further territorial disputes. Unable to negotiate a purchase, Polk resolved to gain these territories by force. He sent an army led by Gen. Zachary Taylor insultingly close to Mexico. Playing into Polk's hands, Mexican cavalry forces attacked the American troops on May 9, 1846, only four hours after the president and his cabinet decided to ask Congress to declare war. Congress endorsed Polk's request on May 13. The army in New Mexico and the navy on the California coast brought the war to a successful conclusion in eighteen months.

As Leonard D. White has observed, "Polk gave the country its first demonstration of the *administrative* capacities of the presidency as a war agency."[76] To be sure, Polk did not push the executive's power as commander in chief to its limit—that development awaited Lincoln during the Civil War. Unlike Madison in the War of 1812, however, Polk did establish that a president without previous military experience could provide decisive wartime leadership. Polk insisted on being the final authority on all significant military matters. According to White,

> He determined the general strategy of military and naval
> operations; he chose commanding officers; he gave personal
> attention to supply problems; he energized so far as he could
> the General Staff; he controlled the military and naval estimates;
> and he used the Cabinet as a major coordinating agency for
> the conduct of the campaign. He told the Secretaries of War
> and Navy to give their personal attention to all matters, even
> of detail, and to advise him promptly of every important step
> that was to be taken. The President was the center on which all
> else depended; Hamilton's doctrine of the unity of the executive
> power was seldom more truly exemplified.[77]

Polk's efforts as commander in chief were neither mistake free nor wholly nonpartisan. A loyal Democrat, he was disturbed that the war was making a hero of General Taylor, a Whig and potentially a formidable presidential candidate in 1848. In a petty partisan action, Polk refused to sign an order for the troops to fire a salute in honor of Taylor's victory at Buena Vista, a settlement in the northeastern part of Mexico. The president's relationship with the army's top commander, Gen. Winfield Scott, also a Whig, was similarly governed by partisanship. Polk urged Congress to create the post of lieutenant general for a Democratic senator, Thomas Hart Benton, so that a Democrat would supersede Scott as the commanding officer in the field. But Benton's military experience was so limited that the Democratic Senate narrowly rejected the president's recommendation.[78]

Polk's problems with his generals can be traced in part to the close relationship between the Jacksonian presidency and the newly institutionalized party system. Partisan practices that had become embedded in presidential politics during the 1830s and 1840s could not be put aside easily even in wartime. Because Scott and Taylor were regular army officers, Polk could do little about them. But volunteer regiments of state militia, which did much of the soldiering, fought principally under Democratic officers. The decision to call up the militia conformed to the Democratic Party's principled opposition to a large standing army, which it regarded as contrary to the character of free government. But the dependence on volunteers plagued Polk throughout the war. The president eventually was forced to recognize his error and, in December 1846, to ask for an increase in the size of the regular army. Until Congress granted his request in February 1847, critical military operations near Mexico City were halted.[79]

Notwithstanding his partisan practices and doctrine, Polk achieved his main goal as commander in chief during the Mexican–American War by acquiring southwestern territory as far west as California for the United States. Polk thereby became, except for Jefferson, the president who brought the most land into the national domain. By demonstrating that the president could plan and oversee the execution of a wartime strategy, Polk also effectively asserted the principle that the president is ultimately responsible for American military operations.[80]

The Slavery Controversy and the Twilight of the Jacksonian Presidency

Polk was the last president of the Jacksonian era whose administration was not consumed by the slavery question. The annexation of Texas and the Mexican–American War greatly expanded the southwest region of the United States. Most northerners objected strongly to the extension of slavery into the new territories. Meanwhile, southern whites were unwilling to distinguish the North's "free soil" position from outright abolitionism, interpreting every effort to bar slavery from the territories as a threat to slavery where it already existed.

The slavery issue had almost split the Democratic Party in 1844, but it was papered over by the convention's compromise nomination of Polk. The rancorous debate about what to do with the spoils of the Mexican–American War made a similar rapprochement impossible in 1848. Van Buren, the organizational genius who did so much to bring the original Democratic coalition together during the late 1820s, now abandoned his party to run as the Free Soil Party candidate. Although Van Buren received only 10 percent of the popular vote, he drained support from the Democratic candidate, Lewis Cass, thereby helping to elect the Whig nominee, Zachary Taylor.

Taylor, the hero of the Mexican–American War, probably would have won the presidential election in any event. The Whigs, desperate for victory, ran an essentially content-free campaign, adopting no platform at their convention and displaying Taylor in his general's uniform on their banners and posters.[81] But the Free Soil Party drew enough votes to affect the outcome of many state elections, and Van Buren's campaign made it difficult for either major party to ignore the slavery issue any longer. In less than a decade, the party system that dominated the Jacksonian era would collapse, and a new governing coalition would emerge.

The Presidency of Zachary Taylor

Because of its strong base in the South, the Democratic Party survived the slavery controversy and the Civil War, although in a greatly weakened condition. But Taylor's election in 1848 was the last major victory for the Whig Party, which endured for only a few more years. The Whigs stood for national unity, an ideal that was rendered politically marginal by the slavery question. Moreover, the Whigs' opposition to an active presidency was proven unworkable by the last Whig to be elected president. Taylor's inaugural address was replete with Whiggish declarations about the need to limit executive power, but the new president's brief tenure (he died in the cholera epidemic that swept Washington in July 1850, just sixteen months into his term) was hardly true to his promise of political self-restraint.[82] The slavery controversy and Jackson's legacy of presidential leadership had made a hands-off presidency impossible.[83]

More than anything else, Taylor is remembered for his consistent and unyielding opposition to the Compromise of 1850, a congeries of legislative measures designed to preserve a temporary peace on the slavery issue.

Taylor's opposition to the compromise, which imposed no restrictions on slavery in the former Mexican southwest territories and strengthened the federal Fugitive Slave Law, nevertheless angered slaveholders by admitting California to the Union as a free state and ending the slave trade in the District of Columbia. Yet the president stood firm against southern threats of disunion. Although he was a southern slaveholder himself, Taylor told congressional leaders that if necessary, he would personally lead the army into the field to restore the Union and would hang rebels "with as little mercy as he had hanged deserters and spies in Mexico."[84]

The Presidency of Millard Fillmore

Taylor died before the crisis provoked by the Compromise of 1850 matured. His successor, Vice President Millard Fillmore of New York, restated traditional Whig assurances about executive restraint yet proved no more willing than Taylor to leave critical domestic matters to Congress. Fillmore, however, was as determined to see the compromise enacted as his predecessor had been to defeat it. The president's endorsement was politically important: one member of the House reported that between twenty and thirty representatives who before Taylor's death were adamantly opposed to the compromise did a dramatic about-face in response to Fillmore's support.[85] With unwonted confidence, the president exulted in September 1850 that "a final settlement" of the nation's sectional differences had been achieved.[86]

Having seen the Compromise of 1850 through to enactment, Fillmore was determined to enforce the new and stringent Fugitive Slave Act vigorously. When Massachusetts refused to cooperate in the prosecution of citizens who violated the act, Fillmore declared that his administration would admit "no right of nullification North or South." In practice, however, the president was never able to impose compliance with the law on those parts of the country where fugitive slaves were protected by local citizens.[87]

The Presidency of Franklin Pierce

Although Fillmore's tenure demonstrated again that the Jacksonian era had transformed the presidency, even the strengthened executive was no match for the crisis engendered by the slavery question. The last two presidents of the Jacksonian era, Franklin Pierce of New Hampshire and James Buchanan of Pennsylvania, were nominated by the Democrats in part because they were "inoffensive . . . northerners with a high regard for the political sensibilities of southern slaveholders."[88] Each proved to be an irresolute leader who sought vainly to hold the northern and southern wings of the Democratic Party together. In doing so, each tried to defuse, rather than come to terms with, slavery as a political issue. But it was too late for temporizing. The nation's polarization over slavery was only aggravated by the efforts of Pierce and Buchanan to dispel the issue.

The Kansas–Nebraska Act of 1854 was the most telling of Pierce's failures to allay sectional conflict. The brainchild of Stephen A. Douglas, the influential Democratic senator from Illinois, the act tried once again to remove slavery from the national political agenda by resting its status in the territories on the principle of "popular sovereignty." According to this principle, as soon as the people of a territory received Congress's permission to choose a legislature, their elected representatives would decide whether to allow or forbid slavery. Because the act applied popular sovereignty to the Great Plains territories of Kansas and Nebraska, the central ingredient of the Missouri Compromise of 1820, which prohibited slavery north of Missouri's southern boundary line, would be repealed.

The debate on Douglas's popular sovereignty bill dragged on for three months. Pierce used all the powers of his office, including patronage, to help ensure its passage. In the end, party discipline among Democrats prevailed, buttressed by the president's insistence on making support for his bill "an absolute test of loyalty within the Democratic Party."[89] On May 25, 1854, the Kansas–Nebraska Act passed the Senate by a comfortable margin after narrowly passing the House, and Pierce signed it into law. Within six months, however, it became apparent that the repeal of the Missouri Compromise had aggravated, not quelled, the slavery controversy and divided the Democratic Party irrevocably. Perversely, Pierce's forceful leadership of his party hastened its collapse as a governing institution.

The elections of 1856 revealed the emergence of a new national political alignment. The Whigs' demise after their landslide defeat in 1852, along with the northern crusade against slavery in Kansas (Nebraska's vote to become a free territory was never in doubt), prompted a new party to form. Offering a platform that stood squarely against the expansion of slavery beyond its existing borders, the Republican Party nominated John C. Frémont, a celebrated explorer of the American West, for president in 1856. Although the Republicans made a good showing in the election, they received no support in the South and were not yet sufficiently organized in the North to overcome this handicap. Winning Indiana, New Jersey, California, Illinois, his home state of Pennsylvania, and the entire South, the Democratic candidate, James Buchanan, was elected president by an electoral vote majority of 174–114.

The Presidency of James Buchanan

Buchanan, who was just as anxious as Pierce to defuse the slavery controversy, was also determined to avoid the political damage that Pierce suffered by fighting for a legislative solution. In his inaugural address, Buchanan associated himself with an as-yet-unannounced Supreme Court decision, arguing that the proper resolution of the slavery question in the territories belonged to the federal judiciary. Referring to the pending suit by Dred Scott, a sixty-two-year-old slave who claimed that extended residence with his owner on free soil had made him a free man, Buchanan pledged that he would "in common with all good citizens . . . cheerfully submit" to the decision of the Supreme Court "whatever [it] might be."[90]

Such a pledge, Binkley has noted, "was a strange abdication of executive claims by a member of the party of Jackson, who . . . had emphatically denied the right of the judiciary thus to determine public policies through the medium of court opinions."[91] In truth, Buchanan's avowed deference to the Supreme Court was disingenuous. He had already privately urged Justice Robert C. Grier, a fellow Pennsylvanian who held a critical swing vote on the Court, to side with Chief Justice Roger B. Taney and other justices who wanted to deny both Congress and the territorial legislatures the right to prohibit slavery.[92]

Buchanan's attempt to end the agitation over slavery in surreptitious alliance with the Supreme Court failed miserably. Going far beyond the issues needed to decide the case, the Court's decision in *Dred Scott v. Sandford* opened the entire West to slavery, regardless of what the people in the territories might decide.[93] This aggressive foray into the slavery controversy not only severely damaged the prestige of the Court but also opened the floodgates to a new outpouring of sectional strife that further fractured the Democratic Party and catapulted an obscure Illinois Republican, Abraham Lincoln, into the presidency in the election of 1860. Lincoln was among the many Whigs-turned-Republicans who strongly believed that the president should oppose Supreme Court decisions like *Dred Scott* when his own interpretation of the Constitution differed from the justices'. Lincoln did not go quite as far as Jackson in challenging the power of judicial review; he granted that the decision was binding on the parties to the suit. But he and many other Republicans were determined that *Dred Scott* would not determine the future course of slavery policy in America.

Notes

1. Sean Wilentz, *Andrew Jackson* (New York: Times Books, 2005), 8.

2. In April 2016, President Barack Obama's secretary of the Treasury, Jack Lew, announced that Jackson's image on the $20 bill would be replaced by that of the abolitionist Harriet Tubman. But this plan was aborted after the 2016 election by the newly elected president, Donald Trump, a self-proclaimed "populist" and a fan of Jackson. Once ensconced in the White House, Trump hung a portrait of Jackson in the Oval Office; honored the anniversary of Jackson's birth with a visit to the Hermitage, Jackson's cotton plantation in Nashville, Tennessee; and tweeted a photo of himself saluting Jackson's grave. Scott Bixby, "Will Donald Trump Really Replace Andrew Jackson with Harriet Tubman on the $20," *The Daily Beast*, May 1, 2017, https://www.thedailybeast.com/will-donald-trump-really-replace-andrew-jackson-with-harriet-tubman-on-the-dollar20.

3. Robert V. Remini, *Andrew Jackson and the Course of American Democracy, 1833–1845* (New York: Harper and Row, 1984), 7.

4. James D. Richardson, ed., *Messages and Papers of the Presidents*, 20 vols. (New York: Bureau of National Literature, 1897), 4: 1561–1562.

5. Richard R. John. "Affairs of Office: The Executive Departments, the Election of 1828, and the Making of the Democratic Party," in *The Democratic Experiment: New Directions in American Political History*, eds. Meg Jacobs, William J. Novak, and Julian E. Zelizer (Princeton: Princeton University Press, 2003), 67.

6. "America's First Direct Mail Campaign," *Smithsonian's National Postal Museum Blog* (July 2010); and Michael Kent Curtis, *Free Speech, "The People's Darling Privilege"* (Durham, N.C.: Duke University Press, 2000).

7. James Roger Sharp, *The Deadlocked Election of 1800: Jefferson, Burr, and the Union in the Balance* (Lawrence: University Press of Kansas, 2010), 172.

8. As historian Marvin Meyers has written, Jackson's political philosophy called for a return to the principles set forth in Jefferson's first inaugural address:

> [A] wise and frugal government, which shall restrain men from injuring one another, which shall leave them otherwise free to regulate their own pursuits of industry and improvement, and shall not take from the mouth of labor the bread it has earned. This is the sum of good government, and this is necessary to close the circle of our felicities.

As such—and here the bank war was the critical case—the strengthening of the executive office during the Jacksonian period "mobilized the powers of government for what was essentially a dismantling operation." Meyers, *The Jacksonian Persuasion* (Stanford: Stanford University Press, 1957), 20–21.

9. Major L. Wilson, *The Presidency of Martin Van Buren* (Lawrence: University Press of Kansas, 1984), 13.

10. Ibid.

11. Jules Witcover, *The American Vice Presidency: From Irrelevance to Power* (Washington, D.C.: Smithsonian Books, 2014), chap. 7.

12. Richardson, *Messages and Papers of the Presidents*, 3: 1206.

13. Wilson, *Presidency of Martin Van Buren*, 13.

14. John L. O'Sullivan, "An Introductory Statement of the Democratic Principle," *United States Magazine and Democratic Review* (October 1837), in *Social Theories of Jacksonian Democracy: Representative Writings of the Period, 1825–1850,* ed. Joseph L. Blau (New York: Liberal Arts Press, 1954), 22–23.

15. Alexis de Tocqueville, *Democracy in America*, ed. J. P. Mayer (Garden City, N.Y.: Doubleday, 1969), 60. Originally published in 1835 and 1840.

16. Donald B. Cole, *Vindicating Andrew Jackson: The 1828 Election and the Rise of the Two-Party System* (Lawrence: University Press of Kansas, 2009), 4.

17. Wilfred E. Binkley, *President and Congress* (New York: Knopf, 1947), 67.

18. Robert Wiebe, *Self-Rule: A Cultural History of American Democracy* (Chicago: University of Chicago Press, 1996).

19. See "The Tennessee General Assembly's Protest against the Caucus System," in *The Evolving Presidency: Landmark Documents, 1787–2010*, 4th ed., ed. Michael Nelson (Washington, D.C.: CQ Press, 2012), 80–84.

20. Jackson to James Gwin, February 23, 1835, cited in *Niles' Register*, April 4, 1835, 80.

21. Edward S. Corwin, *The President: Office and Powers, 1787–1957*, 4th ed. (New York: New York University Press, 1957), 20–21.

22. Ibid.; see also Leonard D. White, *The Jacksonians: A Study in Administrative History, 1829–1861* (New York: Macmillan, 1954), 24–25.

23. Robert V. Remini, *Andrew Jackson and the Course of American Freedom, 1822–1832* (New York: Harper and Row, 1981), 369.

24. "Andrew Jackson's Veto of the Bank Bill," in Nelson, *Evolving Presidency*, 89–93.

25. Remini, *Andrew Jackson and the Course of American Freedom*, 370.

26. *McCulloch v. Maryland*, 17 U.S. 316 (1819).

27. Quoted in Binkley, *President and Congress*, 72.

28. Richardson, *Messages and Papers of the Presidents*, 3: 1144–1145. On Jackson's view of the courts, see Robert V. Remini, "The Constitution and the Presidencies: The Jackson Era," in *The Constitution and the American Presidency*, eds. Martin Fausold and Alan Shank (Albany: State University of New York Press, 1991), 37–40.

29. Richardson, *Messages and Papers of the Presidents*, 3: 1154; Niles' Register, November 17, 1832, quoted in White, *Jacksonians*, 23; and Remini, *Andrew Jackson and the Course of American Freedom*, 373.

30. Quoted in Binkley, *President and Congress*, 79.

31. Richardson, *Messages and Papers of the Presidents*, 3: 1311 (emphasis in original).

32. H. A. Wise, *Seven Decades of Union* (Philadelphia: Lippincott, 1872), 137.

33. Binkley, *President and Congress*, 82–85; White, *Jacksonians*, 33–44.

34. John F. Marszalek, *The Petticoat Affair: Manners, Mutiny, and Sex in Andrew Jackson's White House* (New York: Free Press, 1997).

35. Ibid., 159.

36. White, *Jacksonians*, 92–95; and Remini, *Andrew Jackson and the Course of American Freedom*, 315–330.

37. Binkley, *President and Congress*, 80.

38. *Worcester v. Georgia*, 31 U.S. 515 (1832).

39. Horace Greeley, *The American Conflict: A History of the Great Rebellion in the United States of America*, vol. 1 (Hartford, Conn.: O. D. Case, 1867), 106 (emphasis in original).

40. Remini, *Andrew Jackson and the Course of American Freedom*, 275–279. Historian Edwin Miles has observed that the decision never reached a point that required enforcement. The Supreme Court merely remanded the case to the Georgia Superior Court for reversal of its earlier decision and then recessed. Therefore, no further action in the matter could take place until the Court's next session in January 1833. By that time, the issue had been resolved. See Miles, "After John Marshall's Decision: *Worcester v. Georgia* and the Nullification Crisis," *Journal of Southern History*, 39 (November 1973): 527.

41. Miles, "After John Marshall's Decision," 533–544.

42. Wilentz, *Andrew Jackson*, 152.

43. Van Buren to Thomas Ritchie, January 13, 1827, Martin Van Buren Papers, Library of Congress, Washington, D.C. For a discussion of Van Buren's concept of political leadership, see James W. Ceaser, *Presidential Selection: Theory and Development* (Princeton: Princeton University Press, 1979), 157–166.

44. Remini, *Andrew Jackson and the Course of American Freedom*, 325.

45. Fred I. Greenstein, *Inventing the Job of President: Leadership Style from George Washington to Andrew Jackson* (Princeton: Princeton University Press, 2009), 94.

46. On the development of the "administration press," see White, *Jacksonians*, chap. 15; and Melvin C. Laracey, *Presidents and the People: The Partisan Story of Going Public* (College Station: Texas A&M University Press, 2002).

47. Cole, *Vindicating Andrew Jackson*, 201–203.

48. Quoted in ibid., 320. On the theory and practice of rotation during the Jacksonian era, see ibid., 33–44 and chaps. 16–17.

49. Sean Wilentz, *The Rise of American Democracy: Jefferson to Lincoln* (New York: Norton, 2005), 325.

50. Michael Nelson, "A Short, Ironic History of American National Bureaucracy," *Journal of Politics*, 44 (August 1982), 747–778.

51. Wilentz, *Rise of American Democracy*, 332–343.

52. Ibid., 313. The deleterious effects of the spoils system have been exaggerated. As Leonard White writes in *Jacksonians*, "The consequences of rotation on the public service were unfortunate as a whole, but they were balanced in part by democratic gains, and because both Whigs and Democrats looked for character and competence among their partisans, and often found these qualities." Moreover, although the number of removals during the Jacksonian era was unprecedented, less than 10 percent of the federal workforce was affected. Wilentz, *Rise of American Democracy*, 308, 343.

53. Tocqueville, *Democracy in America*, 394.

54. On Van Buren's response to the Panic of 1837, see Wilson, *Presidency of Martin Van Buren*, chaps. 3–7; and Donald B. Cole, *Martin Van Buren and the American Political System* (Princeton: Princeton University Press, 1984), chaps. 10 and 11.

55. Gen. William Henry Harrison to Rep. Harmar Denny, December 2, 1838, in *The Growth of Presidential Power: A Documented History*, 3 vols., ed. William M. Goldsmith (New York: Chelsea, 1974), 2: 637–641.

56. In Arthur M. Schlesinger Jr. and Fred I. Israel, eds., *History of American Presidential Elections, 1789–1968*, 4 vols. (New York: Chelsea, 1971), 1: 737–744 (emphasis in original).

57. Binkley, *President and Congress*, 89.

58. William Freehling, "William Harrison: Campaigns and Elections," https://millercenter.org/president/harrison/campaigns-and-elections.

59. Goldsmith, *Growth of Presidential Power*, 2: 647.

60. Binkley, *President and Congress*, 108.

61. Robert J. Morgan, *A Whig Embattled: The Presidency under John Tyler* (Lincoln: University of Nebraska Press, 1954), 16–21.

62. Leonard Dinnerstein, "The Accession of John Tyler to the Presidency," *Virginia Magazine of History and Biography* 70 (October 1962): 447–458; and Stephen W. Stathis, "John Tyler's Presidential Succession: A Reappraisal," *Prologue* 8 (Winter 1976): 223–236.

63. Morgan, *Whig Embattled*, chap. 2; Binkley, *President and Congress*, 92–99.

64. Matthew Crenson and Benjamin Ginsberg, *Presidential Power: Unchecked and Unbalanced* (New York: Norton, 2007), 91.

65. Daniel Walker Howe, *The Political Culture of the American Whigs* (Chicago: University of Chicago Press, 1979), 222–223.

66. Binkley, *President and Congress*, 98.

67. President John Tyler, Protest Message to the House of Representatives, August 30, 1842, in Goldsmith, *Growth of Presidential Power*, 2: 710.

68. Binkley, *President and Congress*, 99.

69. On the nomination of Polk as the first dark horse candidate, see Charles A. McCoy, *Polk and the Presidency* (Austin: University of Texas Press, 1960), chap. 2.

70. McCoy, *Polk and the Presidency*, 74–75; White, *Jacksonians*, 77–79.

71. Polk and the Democrats had long been committed to passing a tariff reform act. As Speaker of the House, Polk had supported presidents Jackson and Van Buren in their attempts to enact low tariffs, and he devoted several pages of his first State of the Union message to a proposal for lowering tariff rates and placing rates on an *ad valorem* basis. Polk's dedication to tariff revision did not falter as war with Mexico approached. Instead, he pressured Congress to pass the Walker Act in 1846. He considered this assault on protectionism his most important domestic accomplishment, a vital measure for codifying the Jacksonian idea of economic justice. "Just as [Jacksonians] interpreted territorial expansion as a way to diminish the threat of industrialization and urbanization," historian Paul H. Bergeron has written, "so they also perceived protective tariffs as beneficial only to manufacturers and therefore detrimental to the working classes and to the vision of an agrarian America." Bergeron, *The Presidency of James K. Polk* (Lawrence: University Press of Kansas, 1987), 185–186. See also McCoy, *Polk and the Presidency*, 148–153.

72. White, *Jacksonians*, 81–82.

73. Quoted in Richardson, *Messages and Papers of the Presidents*, 6: 2514–5.

74. Quoted in Binkley, *President and Congress*, 100–101.

75. Robert W. Merry, *A Country of Vast Designs: James K. Polk, the Mexican War, and the Conquest of the American Continent* (New York: Simon and Schuster, 2009), 114, 135.

76. White, *Jacksonians*, 50 (emphasis in original).

77. Ibid., 51.

78. Ibid., 55–56; McCoy, *Polk and the Presidency*, 103.

79. McCoy, *Polk and the Presidency*, 119–120; White, *Jacksonians*, 66.

80. McCoy, *Polk and the Presidency*, 140.

81. Joel K. Silbey, *Party over Section: The Rough and Ready Presidential Election of 1848* (Lawrence: University Press of Kansas, 2009), 97.

82. Attending a long, hot Fourth of July celebration in Washington, the president consumed large quantities of ice water, chilled milk, and fresh cherries—all items that Washingtonians had been warned away from during the cholera epidemic. The circumstances of Taylor's illness and his death just five days later were unusual, so much so that rumors he had been poisoned endured for more than a century. The rumors were laid to rest only after Taylor's body was exhumed from its Louisville, Kentucky, grave and autopsied in 1991.

83. Binkley, *President and Congress*, 103–105; White, *Jacksonians*, 48.

84. The first seven slaveholding presidents were George Washington, Thomas Jefferson, James Madison, James Monroe, Andrew Jackson, John Tyler, and James K. Polk. Zachary Taylor was the eighth and last.

85. Binkley, *President and Congress*, 106.

86. Quoted in Wilentz, *Rise of American Democracy*, 643.

87. White, *Jacksonians*, 522, 529.

88. Crenson and Ginsberg, *Presidential Power*, 87.

89. Wilentz, *Rise of American Democracy*, 672.

90. Richardson, *Messages and Papers of the Presidents*, 7: 2962.

91. Binkley, *President and Congress*, 107.

92. Elbert B. Smith, *The Presidency of James Buchanan* (Lawrence: University Press of Kansas, 1975), 23–29.

93. *Dred Scott v. Sandford*, 60 U.S. 393 (1857).

6

The Presidency of Abraham Lincoln

Abraham Lincoln was the last nineteenth-century president to make an important contribution to the theory and practice of the executive. Lincoln's accomplishments were born of a national crisis that threatened to destroy the foundations of constitutional government in the United States. The leadership he displayed in navigating the uncharted waters of emancipation and civil war has won him the enduring esteem of Americans as one of the finest presidents. The scholarly community has shared in the celebration of Lincoln's statesmanship. Nearly all recent polls of presidential scholars have rated Lincoln the "greatest" president in history.[1]

Whether Lincoln's talents and achievements strengthened or weakened constitutional government in the course of saving it is a matter of some dispute. Indeed, Lincoln's record as president has led at least a few critics to adjudge him not only a forceful leader but also a dictator, albeit a benevolent one in most accounts.[2] As commander in chief, especially, Lincoln demonstrated the presidency's great potential to assume extraordinary powers during a national emergency. The Civil War began in April 1861, while Congress was in recess, and for nearly four months every act of Union resistance to the seceding states of the South was a presidential act performed without legislative authorization. To be sure, Lincoln considered his early measures to be temporary, emergency actions that would require ratification by Congress to become fully valid. Yet, as the challenges of emancipation and reconstruction emerged later in his presidency, it became clear that Lincoln "believed the rights of war were vested in the President and that as president he had extraordinary legal resources that Congress lacked."[3] Lincoln also acted in ways that preempted normal judicial functions, suspending the writ of habeas corpus over the objections of the chief justice of the United States and declaring martial law in places.[4]

Conceding that Lincoln went far beyond the normal bounds of presidential power during the Civil War, constitutional scholar James Randall nevertheless argued that the president showed notable restraint and leniency in administering his wartime measures, befitting his high regard for individual liberty. By doing so, Lincoln used his extraordinary powers not to subvert democracy but to save it.[5] Lincoln certainly did not regard his presidency as a dictatorship. He defended his conduct by invoking a conception of the Constitution that respected procedural regularity and formal legality but was concerned above all with fulfilling the president's oath to "preserve, protect and defend the Constitution of the United States" and uphold the basic principles of the constitutional order. Lincoln's presidency not only marked a critical moment in political history but also raised anew, under conditions of unprecedented urgency, questions about the appropriate place of executive power in the American system of government.

It is ironic that Lincoln was the president who so forcefully extended the boundaries of executive power. Until 1854, when the Kansas–Nebraska Act was passed to open the western territories to slavery and the Republican Party was founded, Lincoln was a Whig. His early political career was distinguished by his eloquent and forceful expression of the Whig Party's opposition to the Jacksonian Democrats' expansion of presidential power in the 1830s and 1840s. Significantly, Lincoln's first important speech, delivered in January 1838 to the Springfield (Illinois) Young Men's Lyceum, took the form of an allegory against great political ambition. Although the founders were ambitious for fame and influence, he argued, their passion for personal achievement benefited the country because it found outlet in a great and constructive enterprise: writing, ratifying, and implementing the Constitution. But what of succeeding generations?

The twenty-eight-year-old Lincoln warned in his speech that the "perpetuity of our free institutions"—that is, the survival of the Constitution—would be threatened by other leaders of great ambition who would not be content merely to uphold the work of the founding generation. Such men would disdain the well-worn path of constitutional government, Lincoln feared. They were members of the "family of the lion, or the tribe of the eagle" who would seek to use public office to remake politics and government in their own image. Then, in words that could only be understood as an attack on the Jacksonians' aggrandizement of executive power, Lincoln foretold the danger of demagogy, a danger made greater by the rise of the slavery controversy. "It thirsts and burns for distinction," he said of excessive ambition, "and if possible, it will have it, whether at the expense of emancipating the slaves, or enslaving free people."[6] In the peroration of his Lyceum address, Lincoln urged that "a reverence for the constitution and laws" become the civil religion of the nation and thereby serve as a bulwark against immoderate political ambition.[7]

In the mid-1840s Lincoln's devotion to settled, standing law informed his opposition to James K. Polk's assertive leadership in initiating and prosecuting the war with Mexico. As a Whig member of the House of Representatives, Lincoln argued that the Constitution gave the "war making power to Congress," and that "the will of the people should produce its own result without executive influence."[8] Nor did Lincoln give any indication during his rise to political prominence in the Republican Party in the late 1850s that he viewed bold presidential leadership as the appropriate means to resolve the controversy over slavery.

Despite Lincoln's prepresidential commitment to executive restraint, as president he joined the "tribe of the eagle" against which his Lyceum appeal for reverence toward the law had been directed. As Garry Wills has argued, Lincoln imparted a new meaning to the Constitution that allowed little room for states' rights and none for slavery. According to Wills, "Lincoln not only put the Declaration [of Independence] in a new light as a matter of founding *law*, but put its central proposition, equality, in a newly favored position."[9] Still, Lincoln did not transcend the work of the Framers. He was, according to Civil War historian James M. McPherson, a "conservative revolutionary" who wanted to preserve the Union as the nation's revolutionary heritage. For Lincoln, preserving this heritage was the primary purpose of the Civil War. "My paramount object in this struggle," Lincoln wrote in a public letter addressed to New York newspaper editor Horace Greeley in the summer of 1862, "is to save the Union, and is *not* either to save or destroy slavery."[10] Yet Lincoln believed that to save the Union, not just for the moment but enduringly, slavery would have to be placed on the road to extinction in law and policy. Drawing on a verse in the Book of Proverbs—"A Word Fitly Spoken is like apples of gold in pictures of silver"—Lincoln praised the Declaration's principle of "liberty to All" as the essence of American political life. "The assertion of that principle, at that time," he wrote, "was the word 'fitly spoken,' which has proved an 'apple of gold' to us. The Union, and the Constitution, are the pictures of silver subsequently framed around it. The picture was made, not to conceal, or destroy the apple; but to adorn and preserve it."[11]

It took the Civil War to generate the radical momentum that led to a redefinition of politics and government in the United States. But Lincoln's words and actions directed the course of events during the fight for emancipation and union. In this sense, he truly was a conservative revolutionary, committed to preserving, rather than abolishing, the heritage of American constitutional government.

Lincoln and the Slavery Controversy

In the antebellum period Lincoln was no abolitionist. The crisis of the Civil War provided anti-slavery activists with unprecedented opportunities. Lincoln's victory in 1860 brought to the executive office for the first time a president who was hostile to the institution of slavery and dedicated to halting its expansion into new territories. Abolitionists had coveted Lincoln's support since hearing him denounce the Kansas Nebraska Act at Peoria, Illinois, in the fall of 1854. Listening to Lincoln condemn the opening of the Kansas and Nebraska territories to slavery and Stephen Douglas's doctrine of "popular sovereignty" in terms that appeared to embrace the principles of the fledgling Republican Party, leading abolitionists were encouraged. Owen Lovejoy and Ichabod Codding, both instrumental in the grassroots movement to form a Republican organization in Illinois, thought they had found a savvy Whig politician who could make their cause politically effective. Yet Lincoln, assuming a cautious position that typified his relationship with antislavery activists for much of the next decade, declined the invitation of Lovejoy and Codding to join the Illinois Republican central committee. "I suppose my opposition to the principle of slavery is as strong as that of any member of the Republican Party," he wrote Codding, "but I had also supposed that the *extent* to which I feel authorized to carry that opposition, practically, was not all that satisfactory to the party."[12]

Lincoln's famous Peoria address made clear that although he strongly opposed the Kansas–Nebraska Act's repeal of the 1820 Missouri Compromise, which allowed slavery to expand into the northern portion of the Louisiana Territory, he was not yet an abolitionist. The address also confirmed his conservative position on the Constitution, which, he argued, proscribed interference with slavery where it already existed. Tellingly, he did not even condemn the hated fugitive slave law. Despite the speech's soaring rhetoric, which Lovejoy and Codding praised as a "glorious abolition speech," Lincoln's message was a moderate one that sought to command the fragile center in the polarizing struggle over slavery. He was willing to cooperate with but not join the Abolitionist movement or the party that its more moderate wing helped found. Lincoln's rejection of "extremes" on the issue is crystal clear in his address:

> Some men, mostly Whigs, who condemn the repeal of the
> Missouri Compromise, nevertheless hesitate to call for its
> restoration, lest they be thrown in company with the abolitionists.
> Will they allow me as an old Whig to tell them good humoredly,

that I think this is very silly? Stand WITH the abolitionist in restoring the Missouri Compromise; and stand AGAINST him when he attempts to repeal the fugitive slave law. . . . In both cases you oppose the dangerous extremes. In both you stand the middle ground and hold the ship level and steady. In both you are nothing less than national. This is good old Whig ground.[13]

Lincoln did not abandon his conservative Whig principles once he finally joined the Republican Party in 1856. His relative moderation on the slavery issue helped him wrest his party's 1860 presidential nomination away from the avowedly pro-emancipation William H. Seward, the former governor of New York and the most prominent Republican leader.[14] Although Lincoln consistently proclaimed himself "naturally antislavery," he continued to assert that the national government lacked constitutional authority to emancipate the slaves. As he wrote to his closest friend, Kentuckian Joshua A. Speed, in 1855, "I acknowledge *your* rights and my obligations, under the Constitution, in regard to your slaves. I confess I hate to see the poor creatures hunted down, and caught, and carried back to their stripes, and unrewarded toils; but I bite my lip and keep quiet."[15] Well into his presidency, Lincoln's preferred approach to slavery was compensation and colonization. His goals, never achieved, were to persuade slave owners to free their slaves in return for federally funded compensation and then persuade the freed slaves to leave the country and colonize the Caribbean.[16] Much as he hated slavery, Lincoln feared that whites would never treat African Americans as fellow citizens under the law.

At the same time, Lincoln believed that the extension of slavery into new states carved out of the western territories should not be permitted. In his view, extension threatened to perpetuate and expand the vile institution as a "positive good," not a regrettable if constitutionally protected evil. With the enactment of the Kansas–Nebraska Act in 1854, Lincoln could no longer "bite his lip." In opening new land to slaveholders, Congress had violated the Framers' understanding that slavery was a "necessary evil" that must be contained and allowed to die a "natural death." This constitutional impropriety was compounded in 1857 by the *Dred Scott* decision, in which the Supreme Court declared unconstitutional any act by Congress or the territorial legislatures to abolish slavery anywhere.

Lincoln was especially distressed because the Kansas–Nebraska Act and *Dred Scott* decision overturned the Missouri Compromise, which had prohibited slavery in the northern part of the Louisiana Territory. The spirit animating the Missouri Compromise, Lincoln claimed, was true to the principles of the Declaration of Independence as well as to the Constitution. The Declaration's main author, Thomas Jefferson, had first given form to this spirit when he conceived the policy embodied in the Northwest Ordinance of 1787 that banned slavery in the old Northwest Territory, which became the states of Illinois, Indiana, Michigan, Ohio, and Wisconsin. Lincoln wanted to restore the Missouri Compromise for the sake not only of the Union but also of the "sacred right of self government" and the restoration of "the national faith." As he said of the Kansas–Nebraska Act in the Peoria address,

> Our republican robe is soiled, and trailed in the dust. Let us repurify it. Let us turn and wash it white, in the spirit, if not in the blood, of the Revolution. Let us turn slavery from its 'moral rights' back upon its existing legal rights and its argument of 'necessity.' Let us return it to the position our fathers gave it, and there let it rest in peace.[17]

Lincoln's respect for the limits imposed on the national government by the Constitution deterred him from attacking slavery in the southern states, but unlike Stephen Douglas, his Democratic opponent in the 1858 Illinois Senate election and the author of the Kansas–Nebraska Act, Lincoln was unwilling to save the Union at the price of slavery's extension into the territories. To do so would detach the Constitution from its moral foundation in the Declaration. Lincoln argued that the South should join the North in restoring the long-standing national compromise on slavery that was embedded in the Northwest Ordinance and the Missouri Compromise.

The logic of Lincoln's position on slavery could not be satisfied by the political compromise for which he called. In portraying his opposition to slavery as a call to restore the country's basic values, Lincoln shifted the terms of national debate. His plea for a new and explicit connection between the Declaration and the Constitution made a struggle over the existence of slavery all but inevitable. As he said in his speech accepting the Illinois Republican Party's nomination for the Senate in 1858,

> A House divided against itself cannot stand.
>   I believe this government cannot endure, permanently, half *slave* and half *free*.
>   I do not expect the Union to be *dissolved*—I do not expect the House to *fall*—but I do expect it will cease to be divided.
>   It will become *all* one thing, or *all* the other.[18]

The Election of 1860

The 1860 election did not provide Lincoln with a mandate to resolve the moral crisis created by the slavery controversy. He was a minority president who received almost no votes in the South. With the old Whig and Democratic party coalitions supplanted by fiercely sectional politics, the presidential election became a fragmented contest among four candidates. The northern vote was split between Lincoln and Stephen Douglas, the official Democratic nominee. The southern electorate was divided between John C. Breckinridge of Kentucky, the standard-bearer of southern Democrats, and John Bell of Tennessee, who was nominated by the National Constitutional Union, a party formed from the remnant of southern Whiggery. The balloting yielded a decisive Electoral College victory for Lincoln, whose 180 votes easily outnumbered Breckinridge's 72, Bell's 39, and Douglas's 12 combined. Lincoln earned this victory by sweeping every northern state but New Jersey with 54 percent of the North's popular vote. But because he was virtually shut out in the South, his popular vote nationwide was slightly less than 40 percent, the smallest share earned by any successful presidential candidate in history.[19] Lincoln's victory was met throughout the South with threats of secession. In bidding farewell to the citizens of Springfield on the eve of his journey to the nation's capital, Lincoln said, "I now leave, not knowing when, or whether ever, I may return, with a task before me greater than that which rested upon Washington."[20]

Lincoln's likening of his task to the one faced by the first president bespoke not only the troubles he anticipated but also his hope of igniting a renewed faith in freedom and equality. "Washington fought for National Independence and triumphed," Charles Sumner, the militantly anti-slavery Republican senator from Massachusetts, wrote in an 1865 eulogy of Lincoln. "Lincoln drew his reluctant sword to save those great ideas, essential to the character of the Republic, which unhappily the sword of Washington had failed to place beyond the reach of assault."[21]

Lincoln seldom received such fulsome praise from Republican colleagues during his lifetime. Indeed, the troubles he faced on his arrival in Washington were aggravated by the doubtful regard that many of his party's leaders had for him. Seward had led on the first two ballots at the 1860 Republican convention in Chicago. "His claims to the nomination," historian Allan Nevins has written, "on grounds of governmental experience, long service to the free soil cause, and tested ability, seemed to outweigh those of anybody else."[22] But the delegates turned to Lincoln on the

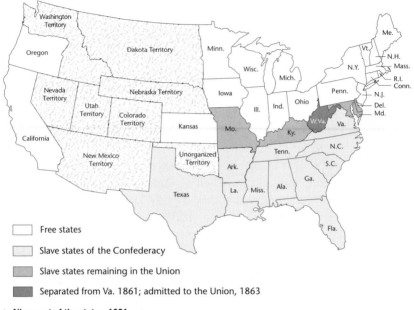

Free states

Slave states of the Confederacy

Slave states remaining in the Union

Separated from Va. 1861; admitted to the Union, 1863

Alignment of the states, 1861.

third ballot, believing that his humble birth, homely wit, skill in debate, and geographical and political centrism would attract votes in Midwestern states, especially Illinois and Indiana, which the Democrats usually won. The Republicans had shown in 1856 that they could count on Seward's Northeast, but they needed to add Lincoln's Midwest to elect a president.

Seward and his allies disdained Lincoln, whose experience in national affairs was limited to one term in the House of Representatives in the mid-1840s and a strong but unsuccessful Senate campaign against Douglas in 1858. "A profound student of the Constitution and the writings of the Founding Fathers," historian David Herbert Donald has observed, "Lincoln had limited acquaintance with the government they had established."[23] Republican leaders in the populous East regarded him as a "prairie law-yer," an upstart who had taken the nomination away from the Republican who was most fit to govern. After the election, Lincoln placated Seward by inviting him to become secretary of state. Indeed, Lincoln constituted his cabinet as a "team of rivals." He drew almost equally from the ranks of former Democrats and former Whigs. In addition to Seward, he appointed Salmon P. Chase of Ohio as secretary of the Treasury and Edward Bates of Missouri as attorney general, each of whom had a political base of his own and thought he was more qualified to be president than Lincoln.[24] In doing so, Lincoln embraced the challenge of persuading the established leaders of his party that the man they had dismissed as a "backwoods president" could rise to the challenge of southern resistance.[25]

Lincoln and Secession

In the face of such dire political circumstances, Lincoln's inaugural address on March 4, 1861, sought to reassure the South that his would be a policy of forbearance, not coercion.[26] He pointed out that despite white southerners' widespread fear that the election of a Republican president threatened "their property and their peace and personal security," there was no "reasonable cause for such apprehension."[27]

Still, Lincoln insisted, as he had since the Peoria address, that this conflict was linked to fundamental principles. The "only substantial dispute" that faced the country, Lincoln said, was over the extension of slavery. "One section of the country believes slavery is *right* and ought to be extended," he said, "while the other believes it is *wrong* and ought not to be extended."[28] This moral dispute was not a matter that could be settled by "legal right," despite the Supreme Court's claim in the *Dred Scott* case that Congress could not prohibit slavery in the territories. More deferential to Courts than Jefferson or Jackson, Lincoln did not "deny that such decisions must be binding in any case upon the parties to a suit as to the object of that suit, while they are also entitled to very high respect and consideration in all parallel cases by all other departments of the Government." Nevertheless, convinced that *Dred Scott* had been wrongly decided on crassly political grounds, he did not regard the decision as settled law. Rather, the new president argued, slavery was an issue to be resolved in the court of public opinion through the regular course of elections. Otherwise, "the people will have ceased to be their own rulers, having to that extent practically resigned their government into the hands of an eminent tribunal."[29]

Lincoln's words fell on deaf southern ears. Ten weeks earlier, on December 20, 1860, South Carolina had become the first state to secede from the Union. Echoing the ordinance of nullification it issued during the 1832 tariff controversy, South Carolina claimed that secession was each state's constitutional right and declared itself restored to a "separate and independent place among nations." By the time of Lincoln's inauguration, six other Deep South states—Alabama, Florida, Georgia, Louisiana, Mississippi, and Texas—also had seceded.[30] Lincoln, following Jackson's example, used his inaugural address to pronounce secession unacceptable:

"I hold that in contemplation of universal law and of the Constitution the behavior
Union of these states is perpetual, . . . that no state upon its own mere
notion can lawfully get out of the Union."[31] The new president declared
that he would enforce federal laws in all the states, as the Constitution
enjoined him to do.

Lincoln's appeal for a peaceful resolution of the slavery controversy was
quickly rejected by secessionist leaders.[32] Southern whites were unwilling
to distinguish his call for compromise from outright abolitionism. They
were at least half right: Lincoln's plea was a thinly veiled expression of
his own moral indignation against slavery. Even the prominent antislavery
activist William Lloyd Garrison, who had harsh words for Republicans,
especially the more moderate wing of the party that Lincoln represented,
was cautiously optimistic that the 1860 election would advance the abolitionist cause. He argued that the Republicans could "create such a moral
and religious sentiment against slavery as shall mould all parties and sects
to effect its overthrow." Despite Lincoln's compromises with America's
peculiar institution, Garrison sensed that his party's ascendance revealed

> a marked division between the political forces of the North
> and the South; and though it relates, ostensibly, solely to the
> question of the further extension of slavery, it really signifies a
> much deeper sentiment in the breasts of the people of the North,
> which, in process of time, must ripen into more decisive action.[33]

Holding firmly to the Republican Party's belief that forced servitude
was bound for ultimate extinction, Lincoln rejected Seward's importun-
ings immediately after the 1860 election that, while still president-elect,
he seek to avert war with a compromise on the extension of slavery into
the territories. When word arrived that Congress was considering a plan
presented by Sen. John J. Crittenden of Kentucky to protect slavery south
of the Missouri Compromise's 36°30′ line and west to the Pacific, Lincoln
intervened to defeat it. To surrender, under threat, what Lincoln defined
as the Republicans' bedrock principle—no expansion of slavery in the
territories—would have been disastrous not only for his party but also
for constitutional democracy. His fellow Republicans in Congress agreed.
Despite Seward's talk of a negotiated settlement, not a single Republican in
Congress voted for the Crittenden Plan.[34]

Lincoln's determination to carry out his party's platform and the
Republicans' rejection of any compromise on their pledge to prohibit
slavery in the territories gave abolitionists hope but reinforced concerns

among white southern leaders that they were engaged in a struggle to preserve slavery from extinction. On March 5, 1861, the day after Lincoln's inauguration, rebel batteries in South Carolina surrounded Fort Sumter in Charleston harbor, making war all but inevitable. As soon as secession became violent and irrevocable, Lincoln believed, his oath to "preserve, protect and defend" the Constitution and his responsibility to "take Care that the Laws be faithfully executed" allowed, even compelled, him to take extraordinary measures to restore the Union, ultimately including emancipating the slaves. As he wrote in an 1864 letter to Albert G. Hodges, a Kentucky newspaper editor, the rebellion imposed on him the obligation to use "every indispensable means" to preserve "the nation, of which the Constitution was the organic law." It was senseless, Lincoln argued, to obey legal niceties while the very foundation of the law was threatened:

> Was it possible to lose the nation and yet preserve the
> Constitution? By general law, life and limb must be protected,
> yet often a limb must be amputated to save a life; but a life
> is never wisely given to save a limb. I felt that measures
> otherwise unconstitutional might become lawful by becoming
> indispensable to the preservation of the nation.[35]

Even more than Lincoln's words, the reaction of the southern states to his election dramatically confirmed the transformation of the presidency that occurred during the Jacksonian era. Although a few southern leaders counseled against secession, arguing that Lincoln's authority over slavery would be limited, such advice meant nothing to people who had witnessed the expansion of executive power since 1829. To be sure, the extent of the president's authority was exaggerated in the popular mind. But the myth that the presidency was the vital organ of the national government was symptomatic of the important precedents that had made the office so powerful.

Lincoln's Wartime Measures

Lincoln did not hesitate to resort to "otherwise unconstitutional" measures after the rebels bombarded Fort Sumter on April 12, 1861. From that day until Congress convened in a special session called by Lincoln on July 4, everything that was done to protect the Union and prosecute the war was done by the president or on his authority.

The early stages of the Civil War marked the clearest instance of a chief executive taking the law into his own hands. To that extent, Lincoln waged a "presidential war."[36] Some of his actions, such as mobilizing seventy-five-thousand-strong state militia, were clearly within the proper bounds of the president's constitutional authority. Yet Lincoln went well beyond these bounds. Hoping to bring the insurrection to a speedy end, he imposed a naval blockade on the southern coast, enlarged the army by twenty-two thousand and the navy by eighteen thousand, and suspended the writ of habeas corpus in northern and border states, where rebellious activity was high. This suspension broadly empowered government officials who were acting under the president's authority. They could make arrests without a warrant, for offenses undefined in the law, without having to answer for their actions before the regular courts.

Several of Lincoln's measures raised grave doubts about the constitutionality of his prosecution of the war. For example, his unauthorized enlargement of the military seemed to disregard blatantly Congress's constitutional power "to raise and support Armies." Indeed, in referring to his executive order of May 3, 1861, which called for enlistments in the regular army far beyond the existing legal limit, Lincoln frankly admitted that he had overstepped his authority. The president's critics also argued that because the power to suspend the writ of habeas corpus during a national emergency appears in Article I of the Constitution, which defines the authority of the legislature, the right to exercise the power belongs to Congress. Lincoln's suspension of habeas corpus was especially controversial because it struck at what constitutional scholar Edward S. Corwin has called "the greatest of all muniments of Anglo-American liberty."[37]

The severity of Lincoln's war measures prompted charges of "military dictatorship," even from some Republicans. The president's decision not to call a special session of Congress in 1861 until Independence Day lent support to these charges. In 1863, the constitutionality of Lincoln's conduct as president became an issue before the Supreme Court in the *Prize Cases*.[38] The Union navy had been capturing ships for violating the president's executive orders of April 19 and 27, 1861, which imposed a blockade along the southern coast. In determining whether it was lawful for the navy to obtain these "prizes," the Court chose to decide the whole issue of the war's legality in its early stages. Shipping interests argued that a war begins only when Congress declares war. No formal declaration of war was passed in support of the president's actions; indeed, Lincoln viewed the Civil War as a domestic rebellion, not a war against another nation. By this logic, the plaintiffs insisted, the actions Lincoln took to suppress the southern insurrection before convening the legislature, including the blockade, were not legally valid.

Considering the urgent circumstances that prevailed in 1863, the Court brushed aside the shipping interests' constitutional claims. That Lincoln had been able to appoint four of the nine justices in 1862 and 1863, outnumbering Chief Justice Roger Taney and his closest allies on the court, made the dismissal of the charges against the president even more likely. The Court upheld the legality of the war from the moment of Lincoln's blockade order, sustaining completely the president's actions while Congress was in recess. In rendering this decision, the Court drew attention to legislation Congress passed on July 13, 1861, to ratify Lincoln's orders. These legislative acts, the majority opinion claimed, although not a formal declaration of war, were enacted to "enable the Government to prosecute the war with vigor and efficiency." Even as the Court emphasized the importance of Congress's action, however, it refused to declare that this legislation was necessary.

The Court's decision in the *Prize Cases* supported Lincoln's claim that his actions were justified by both the threat the southern rebellion posed to the public safety and his expectation that Congress eventually would approve what he had done. As Lincoln said in his Message to Congress in Special Session on July 4, 1861, "These measures, whether strictly legal or not, were ventured upon under what appeared to be a popular demand and a public necessity, trusting then as now, that Congress would readily ratify them. It is believed that nothing has been done beyond the constitutional competency of Congress."[39]

The extraordinary powers that were accorded to Lincoln can be understood only in terms of the extraordinary conditions he faced. It was of considerable legal significance that the Civil War began as an "insurrection," even though it soon became a full-blown war in every meaningful sense of the word.[40] Constitutionally, the president may not declare war but may proclaim the existence of a domestic rebellion, or insurrection. Lincoln believed, and Congress and the Supreme Court generally agreed, that an organized and violent rebellion at home requires quick, unilateral presidential action of a sort that might not be permissible domestically during a formally declared war fought on foreign soil. An internal rebellion, Lincoln proclaimed, may impose a special burden on the legal process because the execution of the laws is "obstructed . . . by combinations too powerful to be suppressed by the ordinary course of judicial proceedings."[41]

Lincoln's conception of the president's responsibility to suppress treasonous activity justified the suspension of habeas corpus and the establishment of martial law in many areas of the country. As such, he claimed sweeping powers to arrest and detain those who were suspected of rebellious activity and then try them before military tribunals. As commander of the American revolutionary army, Gen. George Washington, too, had used military tribunals. These military courts, created to try enemy combatants during wartime, operated outside the rules of evidence and other conventional codes of judicial conduct that apply in civilian courts. Lincoln was the first president to authorize their use.

As the Civil War progressed, Lincoln proclaimed even more comprehensive powers for the military authorities, without any apparent thought of seeking authorization from Congress.[42] On September 24, 1862, he issued an executive order declaring that all rebels and insurgents and all persons who discouraged enlistment in the Union army, resisted the draft, or engaged in any disloyal practice were subject to martial law and to trial by either a court-martial, which observes rules of evidence similar to those in the civilian courts, or a military tribunal.[43] This order provoked sharp controversy in the North. The draft, which was imposed for the first time during the Civil War, was unpopular. As Horace Greeley warned the administration, "The people have been educated to the idea of individual sovereignty and the principle of conscription is repugnant to their feelings and cannot be carried out except at great peril to the free states." Greeley's words proved prophetic. In July 1863 draft riots broke out in New York City, sparking the greatest civil disorder in the nation's history, save for the Civil War itself. Yet resistance to the draft convinced the president that military justice and the suspension of habeas corpus were necessary, not only where the war was being fought but also in certain peaceful regions of the country.[44]

The Supreme Court eventually disapproved Lincoln's more far-reaching martial law measures but not until he was dead and the Civil War was over. In *Ex parte Milligan*, which was decided in 1866, the Court declared illegal the use of military tribunals to try civilians in places that were remote from the fighting.[45] Lambdin P. Milligan had been arrested on October 5, 1864, by order of Gen. Alvin P. Hovey, the Union commander at Indianapolis. Along with certain associates, Milligan was brought before a military tribunal and convicted of conspiracy to free rebel prisoners and smuggle them into Kentucky and Missouri, where they could rejoin the Confederate army. After the tribunal sentenced Milligan to be hanged, the case was brought to the Supreme Court on appeal.

In his opinion for the Court, Justice David Davis, a Lincoln appointee and a close ally, noted the significance of deciding *Milligan* after the war was over. "*Now* that the public safety is assured," Davis wrote, "this question, as well as others, can be discussed and decided without passion or the admixture of any element not required to form a legal judgment."[46] "During the war," Matthew Crenson and Benjamin Ginsberg have noted, "the justices would likely have hesitated to protect a Confederate sympathizer and thwart the president and military authorities."[47] But a year after the Confederate surrender, the Court confidently declared that Milligan's trial and conviction by a military tribunal were illegal, ruling that the constitutional right to a fair trial cannot be swept aside even during a state of insurrection. Instead, conditions had to be so grave as to close the courts and depose the civil administration. Martial law, the Court stated, "could never exist where the Courts are open" but had to be "confined to the locality of actual war."[48]

The *Milligan* case diluted somewhat the legal significance of Lincoln's wartime precedents. But the powers and prerogatives that he assumed during the Civil War demonstrated conclusively, as Corwin has written, "that in meeting the domestic problems that a great war inevitably throws up an indefinite power must be attributed to the president to take emergency measures."[49]

Although Lincoln took extreme measures, neither Congress nor the Court restrained him effectively. Congress did challenge the president's suspension of habeas corpus in an 1863 statute, which directed that prisoners be released unless they were indicted in a civil court. But the law was ineffective. It did not put an end to extralegal imprisonments, nor did it succeed in shifting control over punishment from military to civilian tribunals. Moreover, while the war was still in progress, the Court refused to interfere with a military tribunal in a case that resembled *Milligan*.[50] In legal terms, the Civil War stands out as an exceptional period in American history, "a time when constitutional restraints did not fully operate and the rule of law largely broke down."[51]

The presidential scholar Clinton Rossiter described Lincoln's conduct as a "constitutional dictatorship," an apparent oxymoron that was meant to capture Lincoln's impressive if not fully persuasive argument that constitutional government has an unlimited power of self-preservation and that this power is centered in the president. Although Lincoln's use of power in time of supreme crisis was eminently defensible, Rossiter warned, it might set a damaging precedent, allowing "some future President less democratic and less patriotic . . . to assert the same thing."[52] But other aspects of Lincoln's leadership demonstrated his faithfulness to the purposes for which the Union and the Constitution were ordained.[53] Although the powers that Lincoln claimed were far-reaching, offering ample opportunity for abuse, his exercise of these powers was restrained. In most cases, a short military detention was followed by release or parole. As for martial law, military tribunals almost always were used only to try citizens in military areas for military crimes. Cases like *Milligan* that involved military trials for nonmilitary crimes in peaceful areas were few. Finally, and most remarkably, Lincoln did nothing to obstruct the conduct of free and fair elections during the war.

The Constitution, although stretched severely, was not subverted during the Civil War. It is a "striking fact," as Randall has noted, "that no life was forfeited and no sentence of fine and imprisonment [was] carried out in any judicial prosecution for treason arising out of the 'rebellion.'"[54] Lincoln was driven by circumstances to exercise power more arbitrarily than any other president. He was criticized for leniency as often as for severity.

The Emancipation Proclamation

Lincoln's concern for maintaining the integrity of the Constitution underlay his cautious handling of emancipation.[55] He had argued consistently that to abolish slavery where it existed was beyond the constitutional authority of Congress. Yet, believing that the president's duties as commander in chief allowed him to grasp in war much that lies beyond legal reach in peace, Lincoln issued the Emancipation Proclamation on January 1, 1863.[56] Most presidential proclamations have been ceremonial pronouncements, such as the annual Thanksgiving Proclamation, which was first issued by George Washington.[57] But some proclamations, such as Washington's Neutrality Proclamation of 1793, are hard to distinguish from executive orders of the kind that Lincoln issued after the outbreak of the Civil War because they require the federal government to take an action.

Lincoln's 1863 proclamation added the abolition of slavery to the restoration of the Union as the primary objectives of the Civil War. Even so, the Emancipation Proclamation was a more limited, cautious measure than abolitionists and the so-called Radical Republicans in Congress had hoped it would be. The proclamation did not establish a comprehensive and sweeping policy of emancipation; indeed, Lincoln earlier had declared unauthorized and void the declarations by two of his generals that enslaved people in captured Confederate territory were free. Instead, Lincoln based the proclamation on what he called the "war power" and regarded it as "a fit and necessary war measure for suppressing rebellion."

Building on the precedent established by James K. Polk in the Mexican–American War, Abraham Lincoln not only closely supervised his field commanders but sometimes did so in person.

Source: Library of Congress.

It abolished slavery only in the unconquered parts of the Confederacy.[58] The proclamation also declared that the door was open for African Americans "to be received into the armed services of the United States."

Despite the limited scope of the proclamation's language and spirit, many abolitionists regarded it as a tremendous breakthrough. Confessing that her "gratitude to God" was mixed with "an undertone of sadness that the moral sense of the people was so low that the thing could not be done nobly," Lydia Maria Child acknowledged that she "was truly thankful for the proclamation." Not only was allowing African Americans to fight on the battlefield an important step, but it also helped to persuade Europe, especially Great Britain, which was wavering in its support of the Union, to ally with the northern cause.[59] Joy without reservation was expressed at a New Year's celebration at the Tremont Temple in Boston to honor the proclamation and the new purpose of the war. Speaking to the enthusiastic gathering, Frederick Douglass "thanked God that today he saw a bright light, and if he did not see the abolition of the curse, he saw the beginning of the end." Douglass's sentiment was echoed throughout the North. Horace Greeley hailed the president's order as "the beginning of the new life of the nation," and Garrison described it as "an act of immense historic importance."[60]

Lincoln's executive order declared for the first time that an objective of the struggle to save the Union was to ensure "that all persons held as slaves within any State or designated part of a State shall be then, thenceforward, and forever free." Moreover, as an act of "military necessity," the proclamation had important practical effects. Emancipation struck at the heart of the South's war effort in two ways: by disrupting its labor force and by converting part of that labor force into a northern military asset. Nearly two hundred thousand former slaves stopped bringing in crops on southern plantations, escaped north, and became Union soldiers and sailors. "Some of the commanders of our armies in the field who have given us our most important successes, believe the emancipation policy, and the use of colored troops, constitute the heaviest blow yet dealt to the rebellion," Lincoln wrote to the former mayor of Springfield, James C. Conkling, in August 1863.[61] To be sure, there was grumbling and dissent by some northern soldiers who said they had enlisted to fight for the Union, not for abolition. But most soldiers understood and accepted the policy. As a colonel from Indiana put it, whatever their opinions about slavery and race, his men "desire to destroy everything that gives the rebels strength." Therefore, "this army will sustain the emancipation proclamation and enforce it with the bayonet."[62]

Although emancipation became a critical part of Union war strategy, Lincoln's proclamation neither condemned slavery as immoral nor guaranteed that it would be abolished after the war was over. Lincoln later issued one of his few vetoes against the Wade–Davis Bill of 1864, which included sweeping emancipation and reconstruction measures that he believed the federal government had no constitutional authority to impose on the states. Yet the president realized that to return emancipated African Americans to slavery was unthinkable. When urged to do so by some northern Democrats, who argued that coupling emancipation with restoration of the Union would be an obstacle to peace negotiations with the Confederacy, Lincoln countered that "to announce such a purpose, would ruin the Union cause itself." Why would African American soldiers risk their lives for the Union, he asked, "with the full notice of our purpose to betray them?" The morality of such an act was even more troubling. If he were "to return to slavery the black warriors," Lincoln stated plaintively, "I should be damned in time and eternity for so doing."[63]

Lincoln had long believed that slavery was incompatible with the Union and that the nation was threaded together by a set of principles that required equality before the law. Those who signed the Declaration of Independence "did not mean to assert the obvious untruth, that all were actually enjoying that equality, nor yet, that they were about to confer it immediately upon them," Lincoln had said in criticizing the *Dred Scott* decision. "They meant simply to declare the *right,* so that *enforcement* of it might follow as fast as circumstances should permit."[64] The Civil War created the circumstances. Lincoln's presidential Reconstruction policy, which he announced in December 1863, offered pardon and amnesty to any white southerner who took an oath of allegiance not only to the Union but also to all the administration's wartime policies concerning slavery and emancipation. Reconstructed governments sponsored by Lincoln freed the slaves in the Union-controlled areas of Louisiana, Arkansas, and Tennessee even before the war ended.[65]

1863

Still, Lincoln was too respectful of procedural regularity and formal legality to completely abolish slavery by executive fiat. Instead, he worked to achieve abolition by constitutional amendment. In 1864, joining ranks with abolitionists, Lincoln took the lead in persuading the Republican National Convention to adopt a platform calling for an amendment prohibiting slavery everywhere in the United States. Because slavery was "hostile to the principles of republican government, justice, and national safety," the platform declared, the Republican Party vowed to accomplish its "utter and complete extirpation from the soil of the Republic." Full emancipation became an end as well as a means of Union victory.[66] In 1864 and 1865, lobbying individual members of Congress and thereby "intervening more directly in the legislative process than at any other point in his presidency," Lincoln pushed the Thirteenth Amendment through a reluctant Congress.[67] Ratification of the amendment in 1865 abolished slavery "within the United States or any place subject to their protection."

1864

In sum, Lincoln's disregard for constitutional restrictions on the war power went hand in hand with a deep and abiding commitment to broader constitutional principles and institutions. His ability to reconcile his devotion to the Constitution with his desire to eliminate slavery helped focus the will and resources of the Union on defeating the Confederacy. As historian Phillip Shaw Paludan has written,

> Without Lincoln's unmatched ability to integrate egalitarian ends and constitutional means he could not have enlisted the range of supporters and soldiers necessary for victory. His great accomplishment was to energize and mobilize the nation, affirming its better angels by showing the nation at its best:

engaged in the imperative, life-preserving conversation between structure and purpose, ideal and institution, means and ends.[68]

Lincoln did not become the tyrant he warned against a quarter-century earlier in his speech to the Young Men's Lyceum. Instead, he invested his talent and ambition in strengthening the law by rooting it more firmly in morality. As Lincoln said in his Gettysburg Address, the great purpose of the war was that the American "nation, under God, shall have a new birth of freedom."[69]

The Election of 1864

The free and full party competition that marked the 1864 election further demonstrates that Lincoln did not conduct the war in an unnecessarily dictatorial manner.[70] The stakes were great. Democrats charged that the war was hopeless: the Union army was losing battles, and the Confederacy was persisting in rebellion because Republicans were elevating blacks over whites and the nation over the states. With enthusiastic support from the entire convention, the 1864 Democratic platform declared

> that after four years of failure to restore the Union by the experiment of War, during which under a pretense of a military necessity of war power higher than the Constitution, the Constitution itself has been disregarded in every part, and public liberty and private right alike trodden down, and the material prosperity of the country essentially impaired, justice, humanity, liberty, and the public welfare demand that immediate efforts be made for a cessation of hostilities, with a view of an ultimate convention of the States, or other peaceable means, to the end that, at the earliest practical moment, peace may be restored on the basis of the Federal Union of the states.[71]

Although the Democratic candidate for president, Gen. George B. McClellan, disavowed his party's "peace before reunion" plank, he opposed the Emancipation Proclamation and wanted the Union to continue fighting only until the presecession status quo could be restored. The Republicans held "the reasonable conviction," historian Harold M. Hyman has written, "that a Democratic triumph would mean . . . the perpetuation of slavery, and the further fragmentation of the dis-United States."[72]

Lincoln and most other Republican leaders believed that a Democratic victory was likely in 1864. Not only was there widespread public opposition to Lincoln's conduct of the war, but the custom of the previous three decades was for the president to serve only one term. Since Jackson's victory in 1832, no president had been reelected. Indeed, with the exception of Martin Van Buren in 1840, none was even nominated by his party for a second term. Six days before the Democratic convention in late August, Lincoln was resigned to defeat, hoping only to defuse the rising pressures for an immediate compromise with the Confederacy. "This morning, as for some days past," he wrote privately, "it seems exceedingly probable that the Administration will not be reelected. Then it will be my duty to so cooperate with the President-elect, as to save the Union between the election and inauguration; as he will have secured his election on such ground that he cannot possibly save it afterwards."[73]

In allowing the 1864 elections to take place, historian Herman Belz has argued, Lincoln "accepted a risk and permitted his power to be threatened in a way that no dictator, constitutional or not, would have tolerated."[74] During the campaign, rumors spread that if Lincoln was defeated, he would refuse to accept the verdict of the people and instead try to "ruin the government." Responding to these rumors at a public gathering in October, Lincoln stated that he was "struggling to maintain the government, not overthrow it." He then pledged that whoever was elected in November would be duly installed as president on March 4, 1865. Such a course was "due to the people," Lincoln said, "both on principle and under the Constitution."[75]

Lincoln's commitment to constitutional government cannot be dismissed as empty rhetoric. Throughout the war he supported freedom of speech and freedom of the press. Despite some notable and unfortunate exceptions, anti-Lincoln and anti-Union news organs were left undisturbed.[76] "By all contemporary standards," Hyman has shown, "the 1864 elections were free, and by contemporary standards fair as well."[77] The same was true of the 1862 midterm elections.

Seeing the alternatives, the American people gave Lincoln 55 percent of the popular vote and an overwhelming Electoral College majority of 212–21. Gen. William Tecumseh Sherman's timely capture of Atlanta, Gen. Philip Sheridan's victories in Virginia's Shenandoah Valley, and a spirited and effective Republican campaign, which accused the Democrats of seeking to return to the "hopeless imbecility and rapid progress of national dissolution," turned the tide in the president's favor.

Equally important, perhaps, were two practices that Lincoln followed throughout his presidency to keep him in close touch with the people.

The first, which Lincoln called his "public-opinion baths," were the long hours he spent in the White House listening to any visitor who came to talk with him. "Probably more than any other single agency," historian Richard Carwardine has observed, "they provided the oxygen lacking in the rarified political air of wartime Washington."[78] The second device was the public letter, which usually took the form of a reply to a private letter challenging his leadership. Lincoln caused these exchanges to be widely published in newspapers throughout the country. In keeping with nineteenth-century tradition, he did not campaign. But like earlier presidents, such as James Madison, John Adams, and Thomas Jefferson, Lincoln both observed the convention that proscribed public presidential appeals on behalf of his policies and circumvented it. Just as Jefferson had defended his embargo policy in published correspondence, so Lincoln extended this practice to the presidential campaign, broadcasting his arguments to the American people under the pretense of merely responding courteously to an individual correspondent.[79]

The elections of 1864 were characterized by a remarkably spirited, even strident, campaign in the midst of military hostilities. Some Democrats charged fraud and corruption when the results were tallied, but McClellan himself granted that Lincoln's claim to a second term was untainted. "For my country's sake I deplore the result," he reflected in a private statement, "but the people have decided with their eyes open."[80] After the election, Lincoln granted that partisan discord "add[ed] not a little" to the strain caused by the war. But the election was necessary: "We cannot have free government without elections; and if rebellion could force us to forgo or postpone a national election, it might fairly claim to have already conquered and ruined us." The free and open campaign, Lincoln concluded, "demonstrated that a people's government can sustain a national election in the midst of a great civil war. Until now, it has not been known to the world that this was a possibility."[81]

These were revealing words. The principal task of Lincoln's presidency had been to demonstrate that republican government could endure even in the midst of a violent national struggle that threatened its survival. As he remarked on one occasion, "It has long been a grave question whether any government, not too strong for the liberties of its people, can be strong enough to maintain its existence in great emergencies."[82] Lincoln's conduct of the Civil War seemed to answer this question in the affirmative. As Randall wrote,

> In a legal study of the war the two most significant facts are perhaps these: the wide extent of the war powers; and, in contrast to that, the manner in which the men in authority were nevertheless controlled by the American people's sense of constitutional government.[83]

Lincoln's Legacy

Absent the Civil War, Abraham Lincoln's ability, even his desire to lead the nation would have been severely constrained. The Republican Party he represented in the 1860 presidential election consisted mostly of former Whigs. Like Lincoln, they were dedicated to reversing the executive aggrandizement of the Jacksonians. Indeed, much of what Lincoln accomplished in consolidating presidential power during the Civil War surprised his Republican colleagues in Congress. As described in the next chapter, they acted forcefully to weaken the presidency after he was assassinated in 1865.

Although he was not the main speaker at the dedication of the Union cemetery at Gettysburg, Pennsylvania, on November 19, 1863, Abraham Lincoln's short speech there has become one of the most cherished of the nation.

Source: Library of Congress.

Lincoln never abandoned his political principles. Even in war, he did not forsake entirely the Whig view of executive power that he defended in the 1830s and 1840s. Consistent with this view, Lincoln denied that the president could veto bills merely because he disagreed with them; only legislation that he regarded as unconstitutional was returned to Congress.[84] He deferred almost entirely to Congress on matters unrelated to the war, "contributing little more than his signature" when Republican lawmakers "created a Department of Agriculture, established land-grant colleges, passed the Homestead Act [to encourage western settlement], instituted the income tax, and erected the legislative framework that would lead to the construction of a transcontinental railroad."[85] As Carl Schurz, a postwar Republican reformer, wrote of Lincoln:

> With scrupulous care he endeavored, even under the most trying
> circumstances, to remain strictly within the constitutional limits
> of his authority; and whenever the boundary became indistinct,
> or when the dangers of the situation forced him to cross it, he
> was equally careful to mark his acts as exceptional measures,
> justifiable only by the imperative necessities of the civil war, so

that they might not pass into history as precedents for similar acts in time of peace.[86]

The powers that Lincoln was willing to accumulate as commander in chief during the Civil War freed him to use the executive office energetically. But the end of hostilities led to a counterrevolution of sorts, which showed that Lincoln's stewardship, remarkable as it was, had not expanded presidential power in a way that could survive in peacetime. "By 1875," political scientist Theodore J. Lowi observed, "you would not know there had been a war or a Lincoln."[87] Nevertheless, Lincoln and the Civil War left a lasting imprint on American political life. Lincoln's famous first words in the Gettysburg Address, "Four score and seven years ago," traced America's founding to 1776 (1863 minus 87), not 1787. As such, it elevated the Declaration of Independence—not the Constitution—as the original founding document, the source of "a new nation, conceived in Liberty, and dedicated to the proposition that all men are created equal." Making the most of the November 1863 dedication of the national cemetery at the Gettysburg battlefield, the sort of ceremonial occasion that allowed presidents to speak publicly during the nineteenth century and have their words telegraphed immediately to newspapers across the country, Lincoln invested the national community with a sense of purpose, even sacredness, that transformed the relationship between power and liberty. His indictment of slavery spawned a new, more positive view of liberty, in which government has an affirmative obligation to ensure equality under the law. In the eyes of abolitionists, who relentlessly pushed Lincoln toward emancipation, his slow but steady path to "Canaan" ultimately justified their uneasy partnership with the politically savvy president. "Viewed from genuine abolition ground," Frederick Douglass observed, "Mr. Lincoln seemed tardy, cold, dull, and indifferent; but measuring him by the sentiment of his country, a sentiment he was bound as a statesman to consult, he was swift, zealous, radical, and determined."[88]

Lincoln's celebration of the Declaration was embodied in the Civil War amendments to the Constitution, which not only abolished slavery (the Thirteenth Amendment) but also guaranteed all Americans the "privileges and immunities" of citizenship, "due process," and "equal protection of the law" against encroachment by the states (the Fourteenth Amendment) and promised African Americans the right to vote (the Fifteenth Amendment). These three Civil War amendments changed the course of constitutional development. The first twelve amendments to the Constitution restricted the powers of the national government. Six of the next seven, beginning with these three, expanded its powers.[89]

The immediate consequences of the Civil War amendments were limited. Lincoln's understanding of the equality guaranteed by the Declaration was modest when compared with the economic aspirations of twentieth and twenty-first century presidents such as Theodore Roosevelt, Franklin D. Roosevelt, Lyndon B. Johnson, and Barack Obama. The reforms of the Civil War were tightly bounded, not only by deeply ingrained racial prejudice but also by the nation's long-standing commitment to private property, limited government, and administrative decentralization. Lincoln's contribution was to establish that the national government also had an obligation to ensure equal opportunity. The Union's struggle, he told the special session of Congress in July 1861, was to maintain that

> form and substance of government, whose leading object is, to elevate the condition of men—to lift artificial weights from all shoulders—to clear the paths of laudable pursuit for all—to afford all, an unfettered start, and a fair chance, in the race of life.[90]

Notes

1. See, for example, Robert K. Murray and Tim H. Blessing, "The Presidential Performance Study," *Journal of American History* 70 (December 1983): 535–555; Arthur M. Schlesinger Jr., "Rating the U.S. Presidents: Washington to Clinton," *Political Science Quarterly* 112 (Summer 1997): 179–190; and "C-Span 2009 Historians' Presidential Leadership Survey," http://legacy.c-span.org/PresidentialSurvey/Overall-Ranking.aspx.

2. For a critical examination of the view that Lincoln's presidency was one of "constitutional dictatorship," see Herman Belz, *Lincoln and the Constitution: The Dictatorship Question Reconsidered* (Fort Wayne, Ind.: Louis A. Warren Lincoln Library and Museum, 1984).

3. James G. Randall, *Constitutional Problems under Lincoln*, rev. ed. (Urbana: University of Illinois Press, 1951), 514. See also Edward S. Corwin, *The President: Office and Powers, 1787–1957*, 4th ed. (New York: New York University Press, 1957), 23–24.

4. Acting on his own authority, Chief Justice Roger B. Taney ruled in *Ex Parte Merryman* (17 F. Cas. 144 [1861]) that only Congress could suspend the writ of habeas corpus. Lincoln ignored the order.

5. Randall, *Constitutional Problems under Lincoln*, 30–47; and "Lincoln in the Role of Dictator," *South Atlantic Quarterly* 28 (July 1929): 236–252. See also Belz, *Lincoln and the Constitution*, 5–6.

6. J. B. McClure, ed., *Abraham Lincoln's Speeches* (Chicago: Rhodes and McClure, 1891), 21.

7. Ibid., 22.

8. Corwin, *President: Office and Powers*, 451; Wilfred E. Binkley, *President and Congress* (New York: Knopf, 1947), 110.

9. Garry Wills, *Lincoln at Gettysburg: The Words that Remade America* (New York: Simon and Schuster, 1992), 145 (emphasis in original).

10. James M. McPherson, *Abraham Lincoln and the Second American Revolution* (New York: Oxford University Press, 1991), 41; Lincoln to Horace Greeley, August 22, 1862, in

The Collected Works of Abraham Lincoln, 9 vols., ed. Roy P. Basler (New Brunswick: Rutgers University Press, 1953), 5: 388 (emphasis in original). Lincoln's skillful and persistent efforts to woo Greeley and other prominent newspaper editors are chronicled in Harold Holzer, *Lincoln and the Power of the Press: The War for Public Opinion* (New York: Simon and Schuster, 2014).

11. Undated fragment, written in late 1860 or early 1861, in *New Letters and Papers of Lincoln*, ed. Paul M. Angle (Boston: Houghton Mifflin, 1930), 241–242. Lincoln's reference was to Proverbs 25: 11: "A word fitly spoken is like apples of gold in pictures of silver."

12. Abraham Lincoln to Ichabod Codding, November 27, 1854 (emphasis in original), Roy Basler, ed., *The Collected Works of Abraham Lincoln*, vol. 2, 288, http://quod.lib.umich.edu/l/lincoln/.

13. Lincoln's Speech at Peoria, *The Collected Works of Abraham Lincoln*, vol. 2, 247–283.

14. Allan Nevins, *The Emergence of Lincoln: Prologue to Civil War, 1859–1861* (New York: Scribner's, 1950), 233–239.

15. Lincoln to Joshua A. Speed, August 24, 1855, in *The Political Thought of Abraham Lincoln*, ed. Richard N. Current (Indianapolis, Ind.: Bobbs-Merrill, 1967), 80 (emphasis in original).

16. Eric Foner, *The Fiery Trial: Abraham Lincoln and American Slavery* (New York: Norton, 2010).

17. McClure, *Abraham Lincoln's Speeches,* 127.

18. Current, *Political Thought of Abraham Lincoln*, 95 (emphasis in original).

19. Matthew Crenson and Benjamin Ginsberg point out that most major party presidential candidates who have lost elections have outpolled Lincoln. Crenson and Ginsberg, *Presidential Power: Unchecked and Unbalanced* (New York: Norton, 2007), 99.

20. Basler, *Collected Works of Abraham Lincoln*, 4: 191. Lincoln added, "Trusting in Him who can go with me, and remain with you, and be everywhere for good, let us confidently hope that all will yet be well." This was the first of many public references to God that Lincoln made as president-elect and, especially, as president. See William E. Barton, *The Soul of Abraham Lincoln*, ed. Michael Nelson (Urbana: University of Illinois Press, 2005); originally published in New York by George H. Doran Co. [c. 1920].

21. Charles Sumner, *The Promises of the Declaration of Independence: Eulogy on Abraham Lincoln* (Boston: Ticknor and Fields, 1865), 9.

22. Nevins, *Emergence of Lincoln*, 234.

23. David Herbert Donald, *Lincoln* (London: Jonathan Cape, 1995), 236.

24. Eric McKitrick, "Party Politics and the Union and Confederate War Efforts," in *The American Party System: Stages of Development*, ed. William Nisbet Chambers and Walter Dean Burnham (London: Oxford University Press, 1975), 117–151. See also, Doris Kearns Goodwin, *Team of Rivals: The Political Genius of Abraham Lincoln* (New York: Simon and Schuster, 2005).

25. Stephen B. Oates, *With Malice toward None: The Life of Abraham Lincoln* (New York: Harper and Row, 1977), 224. For an excellent discussion of Lincoln's strained relationship with the more established members of his party, see William Lee Miller, *Lincoln's Virtues* (New York: Knopf, 2002), especially chap. 16, showing how President Lincoln overcame their prejudices and earned their enduring respect.

26. Oates, *With Malice toward None,* 218; Douglas L. Wilson, *Lincoln's Sword: The Presidency and the Power of Words* (New York: Knopf, 2006), chap. 3.

27. James D. Richardson, ed., *Messages and Papers of the Presidents*, 20 vols. (New York: Bureau of National Literature, 1897), 7: 3206.

28. Ibid., 7: 3211 (emphasis in original).

29. Ibid., 7: 3210.

30. At the time, only northern Florida and east Texas, the parts of those states most like the Deep South, were densely settled.

31. Ibid., 7: 3208.

32. For an account of Lincoln's views on slavery and the Constitution, see Robert K. Faulkner, "Lincoln and the Constitution," in *Revival of Constitutionalism*, ed. James Muller (Lincoln: University of Nebraska Press, 1988).

33. Quincy and Garrison quoted in Ford Risely, *Abolition and the Press: The Moral Struggle Against Slavery* (Evanston: Northwestern University Press, 2008), 151.

34. Miller, *Lincoln's Virtues*, 435–440; Phillip Shaw Paludan, *The Presidency of Abraham Lincoln* (Lawrence: University Press of Kansas, 1994), 33.

35. "Abraham Lincoln's Letter to Albert G. Hodges," in *The Evolving Presidency: Landmark Documents, 1787–2010*, 4th ed., ed. Michael Nelson (Washington, D.C.: CQ Press, 2012), 93–94.

36. Randall, *Constitutional Problems under Lincoln*, 51.

37. Corwin, *President: Office and Powers*, 62.

38. *Prize Cases*, 67 U.S. 635 (1863). For a discussion of this case, see Randall, *Constitutional Problems under Lincoln*, 52–59.

39. Richardson, *Messages and Papers of the Presidents*, 7: 3225; Wilson, *Lincoln's Sword*, chap. 4.

40. For a discussion of the importance of the legal distinction between an insurrection and a war against an independent nation, see Randall, *Constitutional Problems under Lincoln*, 59–73.

41. "Proclamation of April 15, 1861," in Richardson, *Messages and Papers of the Presidents*, 7: 3299.

42. Corwin, *President: Office and Powers*, 145–147.

43. Richardson, *Messages and Papers of the Presidents*, 7: 3299.

44. Greeley cited in Mark E. Neely, *The Last Best Hope of Earth: Abraham Lincoln and the Promise of America* (Cambridge: Harvard University Press, 1993), 129.

45. "*Ex parte Milligan*," in Nelson, *Evolving Presidency*, 103–108. For a discussion of this case, see Randall, *Constitutional Problems under Lincoln*, 180–186.

46. "*Ex parte Milligan*," in Nelson, *Evolving Presidency*, 103–108 (emphasis in original).

47. Crenson and Ginsberg, *Presidential Power*, 329.

48. Ibid.

49. Corwin, *President: Office and Powers*, 234.

50. See *Ex parte Vallandigham*, 68 U.S. 243 (1864), which found acceptable the arrest and sentencing of a prominent antiwar agitator who was detained for a speech that he gave in Mount Vernon, Ohio.

51. Randall, *Constitutional Problems under Lincoln*, 521.

52. Clinton L. Rossiter, *Constitutional Dictatorship: Crisis Government in the Modern Democracies* (Princeton: Princeton University Press, 1948), 239.

53. Belz, *Lincoln and the Constitution*, 24.

54. Randall, *Constitutional Problems under Lincoln*, 91.

55. Allen C. Guelzo, *Lincoln's Emancipation Proclamation: The End of Slavery in America* (New York: Simon and Schuster, 2004).

56. For a discussion of Lincoln's policy of emancipation, see Faulkner, "Lincoln and the Constitution."

57. Kenneth R. Mayer, *With the Stroke of a Pen: Executive Orders and Presidential Power* (Princeton: Princeton University Press, 2001), 34–35.

58. Richardson, *Messages and Papers of the Presidents*, 7: 3359.

59. Lydia Child to Mrs. S. B. Shaw, 1863, from *The Letters of Lydia Maria Child* (Boston: Houghton, Mifflin, 1883).

60. "Emancipation Day in Boston," *The Liberator*, January 16, 1863; James McPherson, *Battle Cry of Freedom* (New York: Oxford University Press, 1988), 558; John Hope Franklin, *Emancipation Proclamation* (Washington, DC: National Archives and Records Service, 1994), 61–62.

61. Lincoln to James C. Conkling, August 26, 1863, in Basler, *Collected Works of Abraham Lincoln*, 6: 408–409.

62. Cited in McPherson, *Abraham Lincoln and the Second American Revolution*, 34–35.

63. Lincoln to Charles D. Robinson, August 17, 1864, and Lincoln interview with Alexander W. Randall and Joseph T. Mills, August 19, 1864, in Basler, *Collected Works of Abraham Lincoln*, 7: 499–500 and 7: 506–507, respectively. At the urging of Douglass, Lincoln did not send the letter to Robinson. Douglass objected to the final sentence of the draft letter that added, "If Jefferson Davis wishes . . . to know what I would do if he were to offer peace and reunion, saying nothing about slavery, let him try me." "It would be given a broader meaning than you intend to convey," Douglass warned, and be taken as "a complete surrender of your anti-slavery policy." In the face of continuing pressure to retreat on his position, with the strong support of anti-slavery activists, Lincoln continued to express the moral and practical reasons why he could not go back on the Emancipation Proclamation. See Eric Foner, *The Fiery Trial: Abraham Lincoln and American Slavery* (New York: W.W. Norton, 2010), 305–306.

64. Current, *Political Thought of Abraham Lincoln*, 88–89 (emphasis in original).

65. McPherson, *Abraham Lincoln and the Second American Revolution*, 86.

66. Ibid.

67. Foner, *The Fiery Trial: Abraham Lincoln and American Slavery*, 312. For a dramatic, historically faithful account of Lincoln's campaign for the Thirteenth Amendment, see also the Steven Spielberg film, *Lincoln* (2009).

68. Paludan, *Presidency of Abraham Lincoln*, 319.

69. "The Gettysburg Address," in Nelson, *Evolving Presidency*, 97–99.

70. Belz, *Lincoln and the Constitution*, 15.

71. "Democratic Platform of 1864," in *History of American Presidential Elections*, 4 vols., eds. Arthur M. Schlesinger Jr. and Fred I. Israel (New York: Chelsea, 1971), 2: 1179–1180.

72. Harold M. Hyman, "Election of 1864," in ibid., 2: 1167. See also Lord Charnwood, *Abraham Lincoln* (Garden City, N.Y.: Garden City Publishing, 1917), 414–415.

73. Quoted in Hyman, "Election of 1864," 1170.

74. Belz, *Lincoln and the Constitution*, 16.

75. John G. Nicolay and John Hay, eds., *Complete Works of Abraham Lincoln*, 12 vols. (Harrogate, Tenn.: Lincoln Memorial University, 1894), 10: 244.

76. Randall, *Constitutional Problems under Lincoln*, chap. 9.

77. Hyman, "Election of 1864," 1175. See also Holzer, *Lincoln and the Power of the Press*.

78. Richard Carwardine, *Lincoln: A Life of Purpose and Power* (New York: Knopf, 2006), 197.

79. Mel Laracey, "Dear America: Public Letters as an Early Form of Presidential Mass Communication," paper presented at the Annual Meeting of the American Political Science Association, September 2009, Toronto, Canada.

80. Hyman, "Election of 1864," 1175.

81. Nicolay and Hay, *Complete Works of Abraham Lincoln*, 10: 263–264.

82. Ibid., 10: 263.

83. Randall, *Constitutional Problems under Lincoln*, 522.

84. Belz, *Lincoln and the Constitution*, 12. Lincoln took this position in refusing to veto a bill reducing fees paid to the marshal of the District of Columbia; see Basler, *Collected Works of Abraham Lincoln*, 7: 414–415.

85. Crenson and Ginsberg, *Presidential Power*, 102.

86. Carl Schurz, "Abraham Lincoln," in *Abraham Lincoln*, ed. Carl Schurz (New York: Chautauqua Press, 1891), 72.

87. Lowi is cited in Michael Les Benedict, "The Constitution of the Lincoln Presidency and the Republican Era," in *The Constitution and the American Presidency*, eds. Martin Fausold and Alan Shank (Albany: State University of New York Press, 1991), 45.

88. Philip Foner, ed., *The Life and Writings of Frederick Douglass* (New York: International Publishers, 1955), vol. 4, 316.

89. McPherson, *Abraham Lincoln and the Second American Revolution*, 137–138.

90. Current, *Political Thought of Abraham Lincoln*, 187–188.

The Reaction against Presidential Power

Andrew Johnson to William McKinley

Andrew Johnson, who was elected vice president with Abraham Lincoln in 1864, succeeded to the presidency under extraordinarily difficult circumstances on April 15, 1865, the morning after Lincoln was shot by John Wilkes Booth, a Confederate zealot, at Ford's Theater in Washington. The Civil War established the permanence of the Union and emancipated the slaves, but with the end of hostilities in the spring of 1865 came the enormous problems of Reconstruction. How were the Confederate states to rejoin the Union? What would be the status of the emancipated southern slaves or, for that matter, of northern blacks who had never been enslaved but who still were denied the suffrage and some other basic rights in all but a few states?

Lincoln and a majority of the Republicans in Congress agreed that the major objectives of Reconstruction were to destroy slavery and to strip political power from the erstwhile leaders of the Confederacy. They disagreed, however, about how harsh Reconstruction policies needed to be for freedom to take root in soil tainted by slavery. Lincoln wanted to restore the Union as quickly as possible, without imposing draconian terms for readmission on the rebellious states. The Radicals of his party, however, led by Sen. Charles Sumner of Massachusetts and Rep. Thaddeus Stevens of Pennsylvania, who had close ties to the abolitionist movement, believed that high-ranking Confederates should be punished severely for treason, African Americans should be guaranteed the full rights of citizenship, and southern states should not be granted full membership in the Union until they were thoroughly reconstructed and their loyalty was assured.

The conflict within the Republican Party over Reconstruction remained unresolved as the war drew to an end. In 1863 Lincoln promulgated a program of reunification for the three Confederate states already conquered by the Union army: Arkansas, Louisiana, and Tennessee. According to this program, if even 10 percent of a state's voters took an oath of allegiance to the United States, the state could form a government and elect members of Congress. The Republican-dominated Congress, declaring that Reconstruction was a legislative, not an executive, function, rejected Lincoln's terms as too lenient and refused to seat legislators from any seceding state but Tennessee, which had been the first to fall to Union forces.

Congress's Reconstruction program was the Wade–Davis bill, which disenfranchised all high-ranking Confederates, stipulated that 50 percent of the voters in a rebel state must take a loyalty oath before elections could be held, and made the abolition of slavery a condition for readmission to the Union. Lincoln's pocket veto of this legislation in July 1864, accompanied by a message in which he argued that reunification was an executive function, provoked Republican leaders in Congress to issue the Wade–Davis Manifesto. The manifesto included a bold attack on Lincoln's Reconstruction program and a strong defense of the "paramount" authority of Congress, reminiscent of the Whigs' assaults on Andrew Jackson.[1] Lincoln's landslide reelection in November 1864 took the wind out of the Radical Republicans' sails, but their strength was restored after he was assassinated. As Wilfred E. Binkley has written,

> To those who had applauded the furious blast of the Wade–Davis Manifesto against Lincoln only to see its effect nullified by the triumphant re-election of the President it must have now seemed as if fate, through the assassin's bullet, had at last delivered the government into their hands. Their glee was but ill concealed.[2]

The Radicals initially had confidence in Johnson. Until Lincoln appointed him military governor of Tennessee in early 1862, the post he held when he was nominated as Lincoln's running mate in 1864, then-senator Johnson seemed to be one of them. He served on the Radical-dominated congressional Joint Committee on the Conduct of the War, which criticized Lincoln's wartime initiatives constantly, often charging that the president had usurped the rightful powers of Congress. Although a Democrat until he joined the 1864 "National Union" ticket, Johnson's defiance of secession—he was the only southern senator not to join the rebels—won the esteem of his Republican colleagues. Moreover, his hatred of the southern plantation elite equaled the Radicals' own. Only a few hours after Lincoln died, the Joint Committee paid a visit to the new president. Its chair, Sen. Benjamin Wade, the prominent Radical cosponsor of the Wade–Davis bill and manifesto, declared, "Johnson we have faith in you. By the gods, there will be no trouble now in running the government!"[3]

The Radicals' faith was short-lived. Johnson despised African Americans even more than he reviled the white gentry. His loyalty was to the South's yeomanry from which he, a tailor before entering politics, and Jackson, his political hero and fellow Tennessean, had sprung. He kept Lincoln's cabinet, spurning the Radicals' advice "to get rid of the last vestige of Lincolnism." At war's end, Johnson chose not to call Congress, which as customary had recessed until December, into special session for the purpose of jointly establishing a postwar plan of Reconstruction.[4] Instead, Johnson implemented his own more lenient Reconstruction policies with a series of executive proclamations in the late spring and summer of 1865. These allowed the South's white workers and small farmers to elect new state governments, which promptly enacted "Black Codes" that stripped the freed slaves of much of their freedom. Congressional Republicans were furious but unable to respond.

Johnson's unilateral actions no doubt were influenced by the success that Lincoln repeatedly had in executing major policy decisions while Congress was in recess, leaving the legislature with little choice but to ratify the late president's faits accomplis when it returned to Washington.[5] But Johnson lacked Lincoln's political skill and electoral mandate as well as the latitude that the general sense of wartime urgency allowed him. He also lacked Lincoln's concern for the rights of the emancipated slaves. Congressional Republicans moved to establish control over Reconstruction as soon as Congress, which they dominated in the absence of the South, convened in December 1865.

Reconstruction and the Assault on Executive Authority

Johnson's struggle with Congress was aggravated by the sharp differences of principle that distinguished him from most Republicans. In contrast to Lincoln, who wanted to strengthen the national government's authority to secure legal equality for African Americans, Johnson challenged Reconstruction legislation in the interest of preserving the rights of the states. To be sure, as his refusal to abandon his Senate seat during the secession crisis of 1861–1862 revealed, Johnson was a strong defender of the Union. But in background and belief, he was a Jacksonian Democrat who, like Jackson, believed in an indissoluble union and a strong presidency within a weak national government. Although he surrendered his Democratic affiliation to join Lincoln's National Union campaign in the 1864 election, Johnson was never comfortable in the Republican Party.[6]

The new president's Jacksonian commitment to states' rights put him at odds with nearly all Republicans, not just the Radicals. Moderate lawmakers repeatedly approached Johnson with strategies designed to build a consensus around modified versions of the president's own policies. But Johnson rejected these efforts. In February 1866, he vetoed a bill, sponsored by the moderate Republican senator Lyman Trumbull of Illinois, to continue the Freedman's Bureau. Created in March 1865, the bureau provided food, clothing, and medical care to the hundreds of thousands of freed slaves uprooted by the war and helped them make the difficult transition from bondage to freedom. The head of the bureau, Gen. Oliver O. Howard, was a passionate abolitionist, committed to "the exercise of benevolent functions hitherto always contended against by our leading statesmen."[7] Johnson regarded the bureau as an unconstitutional extension of the national government's authority in peacetime. In vetoing Trumbull's bill, Johnson was challenging not just the Radicals but every Republican in Congress.

The ties between Johnson and the Republican Party were severed irrevocably in March when he vetoed the 1866 Civil Rights Act, which like the Freedman's Bureau enjoyed unanimous support from congressional Republicans. This bill, parts of which later were included in the Fourteenth Amendment, declared African Americans to be citizens and bestowed on all persons born in the United States (except American Indians) an equal right to make and enforce contracts, to sue and be witnesses in the courts, to own land and other property, and to enjoy equal protection of the law.

If Johnson had supported the Civil Rights Act, he would have satisfied the North's desire to protect African Americans in the South. Radical Republicans considered any Reconstruction policy that did not impose some degree of black suffrage on the southern states as tantamount to the perpetuation of "an Oligarchy of the skin." "At this moment," Senator Sumner proclaimed in his eulogy of Lincoln in June 1865, "all turns on the colored suffrage in the rebel states." But even though the late president supported emancipation, he doubted the wisdom of immediately requiring universal male suffrage.[8] Lincoln's position was shared by moderate Republicans, who did not insist on immediate voting rights as long as progress was made toward fulfilling the other rights of African Americans as citizens.

Johnson's veto of the Civil Rights Act united both congressional Republicans and public opinion against him. On April 6, 1866, the Senate voted 33–15 to repass the bill; three days later the House did the same, 122–41. Congress's enactment of the Civil Rights Act over Johnson's veto was a landmark in constitutional development—the first time in history that legislators had overridden a presidential veto on an important issue. The override was equally significant as a political event: Congress, not the president, was now the master of Reconstruction.[9] Soon afterward, when a vacancy occurred on the Supreme Court, Congress voted to abolish the position rather than let Johnson fill it. Anticipating another possible vacancy, it abolished a second position as well, reducing the size of the Court to seven after the next justice died or retired.

Johnson's staunch belief in the inherent racial inferiority of African Americans underlay every aspect of his opposition to a national Reconstruction policy. As a defender of the Union, Johnson supported the abolition of slavery. "This is your country as well as anybody else's," he told a regiment of black soldiers that gathered to pay him tribute in October 1865. "This country is founded upon the principle of equality."[10] Yet the president sometimes displayed a visceral belief in white supremacy. As a member of Congress in 1844, he declared his opposition to one bill because "it would place every splay-footed, bandy-shanked, hump-backed, thick-lipped, flat-nosed, woolly-headed, ebon-colored negro in the country upon an equality with the poor white man."[11] As president, his private secretary recorded in 1868, Johnson "has at times exhibited a morbid distress and feeling against negroes."[12] For example, after meeting with the abolitionist Frederick Douglass, Johnson told his secretary, "I know that damned Douglass; he's just like any nigger, and he would sooner cut a white man's throat than not."[13]

Ideology and politics played an important part in molding Johnson's Reconstruction policies. He was convinced that his views on race relations accorded with those of the vast majority of whites. Any attempt to impose civil rights on the South, he believed, would not only be unconstitutional but also would alienate white southerners and, in all likelihood, most people in the North, where only five states in New England, with minuscule populations of color, allowed African Americans to vote. Johnson calculated that leaving the question of racial equality to the states would satisfy everyone but African Americans, whose disenfranchisement meant they scarcely counted politically, and Radical Republicans, whose principles and politics he abhorred.[14]

The midterm elections of 1866 were widely regarded as a referendum on whether Johnson or Congress should control Reconstruction. Congress had just approved the Fourteenth Amendment, which forbade state governments from abridging the "privileges and immunities" of any citizen, from depriving any person of life, liberty, or property "without due process of law," and from denying anyone the "equal protection of the laws." Desperate to build an alternative to the Republican Party, Johnson focused his campaigning on opposition to ratification by the states. In a speaking tour of the North, which he described as a "Swing around the Circle," the president attacked his congressional opponents and championed a National Union movement made up of those who supported his Reconstruction policies.

That summer, the new Union "party," a loose and fractious coalition of disgruntled Democrats, conservative Republicans, and white southerners, held a convention. Johnson celebrated the delegates' resolutions, which supported his Reconstruction program, as a second Declaration of Independence and Emancipation Proclamation that would free the country from congressional control of Reconstruction. At the same time, the president used his appointment and removal powers to purge the cabinet and the federal work force of those who did not support the Union party and to replace them with conservative Republicans. Of those cabinet members who were sympathetic to a congressional role in Reconstruction, only Secretary of War Edwin Stanton remained.[15] At the same time, Johnson attacked the heart of the patronage system by replacing almost seventeen hundred Republican postmasters with his own loyalists.

In the midterm election, Johnson's efforts to build an alternative, president-centered political organization failed. Radical Republicans won significant victories across the North. Disgusted when all the southern states reconstructed by presidential proclamation rejected the Fourteenth Amendment after enacting racially discriminatory Black Codes, the voters routed the president's followers and gave the Radicals firm control of both houses of Congress. With every southern state except Tennessee still barred by Congress from choosing representatives and senators, all but 53 of the 226 members of the House were Republicans, as were all but 9 of 54 senators. Particularly damaging to Johnson was that he had encouraged the southern states to reject the Fourteenth Amendment.[16]

Spurred by the mandate of the 1866 elections, Congress passed a series of measures in 1867 that deprived Johnson of control over Reconstruction and stripped his office of its authority to conduct the affairs of the executive branch. The Military Reconstruction Act replaced the southern state governments that Johnson had approved with military districts led by military commanders, who were granted almost complete independence from presidential direction.[17] Congress buttressed the commanders' autonomy by tacking riders onto the 1867 army appropriation bill that required the president and the secretary of war to transmit their orders through

General of the Army Ulysses S. Grant and forbade the president to relieve, suspend, or transfer Grant without the Senate's consent. This direct challenge to the president's authority as commander in chief was covertly instigated by Secretary of War Stanton, who along with Grant, cooperated with Republican congressional leaders.

Johnson vetoed the Military Reconstruction Act, charging that it would create an "absolute despotism" in the South.[18] He also protested the riders that Congress attached to the army appropriation bill by claiming that they were "out of place in an appropriation act" and "deprived the President of his constitutional functions as Commander-in-Chief of the Army."[19] Congress ignored the protest and overrode the veto. Then, to prevent Johnson from reasserting presidential control over Reconstruction, Congress arranged to stay in session permanently. This action nullified the president's constitutional privilege to pocket veto legislation that was passed with fewer than ten days remaining in a session of Congress.[20]

Having stripped Johnson of his ability to influence legislation and govern the South, Congress proceeded to divest him of control over the personnel of the executive branch. In March 1867 Congress, overriding Johnson's veto, passed the Tenure of Office Act, which prohibited the president from firing any Senate-confirmed official without first obtaining the Senate's approval. The act reversed the First Congress's decision in 1789 to uphold the president's unilateral authority to remove executive officials. The struggle against Johnson had reached the point that neither settled precedents nor explicit constitutional proscriptions deterred Radical Republicans from undermining the presidency for the sake of punishing the president Congress overrode fifteen of his vetoes, the most of any president in history.

By the spring of 1867 Johnson was helpless to block any legislation that Congress saw fit to pass. His only recourse was to try once again to appeal directly to the American people. Thomas Jefferson and, especially, Andrew Jackson had sought to establish closer ties between the presidency and the people, but they had worked through their party organization to do so. Similarly, Lincoln had relied heavily on the Republican Party to mobilize support for the war and his Reconstruction policies.[21] But Johnson had cut his ties to the Democrats by joining Lincoln's ticket in 1864 and alienated Republicans by his conduct as president. When his effort to build his own political organization failed, the president no longer had a party.

Johnson fancied himself a good orator, but his forceful attacks on Congress were prone to excess, especially when he was fueled by alcohol and goaded by hecklers. On the evening of February 22, 1866, George Washington's birthday, Johnson told a crowd that had marched to the

This illustration of Andrew Johnson's impeachment trial before the Senate appeared on the cover of the March 14, 1868, issue of Harper's Weekly.

Source: Library of Congress.

White House to demonstrate its support for his veto of the Civil Rights Act that new rebels had appeared in the country, this time in the North. These rebels, the Radical Republican leaders in Congress, "had assumed nearly all the powers of government" to prevent the restoration of the Union. Johnson charged Stevens, the Pennsylvania representative who led the Radicals in the House, and Sumner of Massachusetts, the president's main Radical opponent in the Senate, with being just as traitorous as the leaders of the Confederacy. He even claimed that his opponents' "intention was to incite assassination," adding that "when I am beheaded I want the American people to be the witness."[22]

Johnson's rhetoric backfired. The vast majority of northerners were outraged when they read, or read about, his speeches, several of which were as aggressive as his Washington's Birthday harangue. The public resented his attack on Stevens and Sumner who, whatever their faults, were certainly not traitors.[23] Moreover, the purpose of Johnson's speeches—to rouse public opinion against Congress as well as in support of his policies—was generally considered illegitimate conduct during the nineteenth century, a form of demagoguery that was beneath the dignity of the presidency. The use of sharp rhetoric by presidents to sway public opinion would become acceptable, even expected, in the twentieth century, but until then partisan presidential speech making was regarded as a violation of unwritten constitutional norms.[24]

Most of Johnson's speeches were delivered during his 1866 "Swing around the Circle." The press quickly seized on this expression as an object of derision and a subject for political cartoons. As historian David Miller Dewitt described the national reaction,

> His want of dignity, . . . his insensibility to the decorum due to his high office, his eagerness to exchange repartee with any opponent

no matter how low, his slovenly modes of speech and his offenses against good taste, unfairly blazoned as they were before the country, disgusted many persons who were half-inclined to his policy; made many of the judicious among his supporters grow lukewarm; forced his warmest supporters to hang their heads for lack of apology; scattered abroad the ugliest scandals about his personal habits and irretrievably hurt his cause.[25]

The Impeachment of Andrew Johnson

Johnson's politically inappropriate rhetoric strengthened his opponents and served as the basis for one of the eleven articles of impeachment that were brought against him by the House of Representatives on March 2 and 3, 1868. Article X charged that the president had ignored the duties of his office by seeking to impugn Congress. Johnson had delivered "with a loud voice certain intemperate, inflammatory, and scandalous harangues . . . amid cries, jeers, and laughter of the multitude then assembled."[26]

The charge of rhetorical excess was not the main ground for Johnson's impeachment. Many members of Congress doubted that inflammatory speech, however inappropriate, could be construed as an impeachable offense. The *New York Times* echoed these concerns in an editorial, insisting that Johnson's conduct on the stump involved "only questions of taste and opinion—not of law or definable criminality."[27] Yet, because custom placed severe limitations on direct popular leadership by nineteenth-century executives, the charge was not frivolous.[28] In *Federalist* No. 71 Alexander Hamilton had warned that leaders who "flatter the [people's] prejudices to betray their interests" might undermine constitutional norms.[29] "You will find that these denunciations [against Congress] had a deeper meaning than mere opinion," Massachusetts representative Benjamin F. Butler, the leading proponent of Article X, argued during the impeachment trial.

> It may be taken as an axiom in the affairs of nations that no usurper has ever seized upon the legislature of his country until he has familiarized the people with the possibility of so doing by vituperating and decrying it.[30]

Still, the legal controversy regarding Johnson's decision in May 1868 to remove Stanton as secretary of war was the principal issue in the impeachment proceedings. In unilaterally firing Stanton, who despite his position in the cabinet was conspiring regularly with the president's enemies in Congress, Johnson appeared to violate the requirement for Senate approval that was established by the Tenure of Office Act.[31] Although Johnson's intention was to have the courts rule on the constitutionality of the law, the House's strictly partisan 128–47 vote to impeach on February 24, 1868 (no Democrat voted in favor, and no Republican voted against) meant that the constitutional question would be decided by the Senate, not the judiciary.

Johnson's impeachment trial, which lasted six weeks, threatened both his status as president and the constitutional independence of the presidency. The Senate proceedings resembled less a trial to determine if Johnson had committed "high Crimes and Misdemeanors" than a convention of Radical Republicans for the purpose of running Johnson out of office. At the outset of the trial, their chances were good. By author David Stewart's calculation, Johnson could count on receiving only twelve of the nineteen votes he needed to deny his foes the required two-thirds majority for removal: the Senate's nine Democrats plus three Republicans who usually voted with him.[32] He needed to win over at least seven additional Republicans, even as Radical leaders were doing all they could to bring public pressure to bear on them. Moderate Republican senators were threatened in the party press and by voters at home.[33]

If Johnson, however poor a president, had been convicted under these circumstances, the power and prestige of the presidency might have been severely damaged. Seven Republican senators who opposed Johnson's policies and leadership but feared that to remove him would destroy the constitutional system of checks and balances stood up to the pressure of party discipline and public opinion, leaving the Radicals one vote shy of two-thirds. The final tally was 35–19 in favor of removal. They also were motivated in part by their reluctance to replace Johnson as president with Benjamin Wade, the personally controversial and politically radical president pro tempore of the Senate who was, in the absence of a vice president, next in the line of succession under prevailing law. Meanwhile, moderate senator Lyman Trumbull expressed the belief of those who stood with Johnson that to convict the president would open the door for Congress to use the impeachment power cavalierly in the future:

> [N]o future president will be safe who happens to differ with
> a majority of the House and two-thirds of the Senate on any
> measure deemed by them important, particularly if of a political
> character. Blinded by partisan zeal, with such an example before
> them, they will not scruple to remove out of the way any obstacle

to the accomplishment of their purposes, and what then becomes of the checks and balances of the Constitution, so carefully devised and so vital to its perpetuity?[34]

Ulysses S. Grant and the Abdication of Executive Power

The Senate's failure to remove Andrew Johnson did not restore to strength either the president or the presidency. The remainder of Johnson's term was spent in a sullen impasse with Congress. Nor did the election of Ulysses S. Grant in 1868 revive the power of the executive. If the American people, made uneasy by Johnson's subordination to Congress, thought they were electing a forceful political leader in Grant, they were mistaken. Grant's military career justified the belief that he had unusual leadership ability, but his talents did not transfer directly from the battlefield to the White House. Lacking experience in civil administration, Grant had neither the detailed knowledge of the governmental process needed to perform the role of chief executive nor the political experience required to bend other leaders to his purposes.

Grant's shortcomings as a civilian leader were demonstrated almost immediately. The president let it be known after his election that he opposed the Tenure of Office Act and would not make any but cabinet appointments until Congress repealed it. The House soon complied, but the Senate, still controlled by the Radical Republicans, approved a "compromise" amendment that essentially preserved its role in the removal of executive officials. Grant was so popular and respected at the time of his inauguration on March 4, 1869, that if he had asserted himself in favor of repeal, he probably would have prevailed. Instead, not realizing the implications of his decision, Grant capitulated to the Senate, which prompted Republicans in both houses to join ranks and support the amendment. An advocate of repeal, former secretary of the navy Gideon Welles expressed the disappointment of those who hoped Grant would restore the stature of the presidency: "The lawyers duped and cowed him. The poor devil has neither the sagacity and obstinacy for which he has credit, if he assents to this compromise, where the Executive surrenders everything and gets nothing."[35]

Grant's strategic error set the tone for his entire two terms as president. He never recovered the prestige and power that he lost in his first showdown with the Republican leaders.[36] Yet his acquiescence to the Senate on the Tenure of Office Act no doubt was influenced by his concept of the presidency. Grant considered himself to be an administrative officer of the legislature, "disposed to accept without question the work of Congress as the authoritative expression of the will of the American people."[37]

Grant's understanding of executive leadership accorded well with that of the Republican leaders of the Senate, who embraced the old Whig principle of legislative supremacy. In Grant, unlike Lincoln or Johnson, congressional Republicans had a president they could manage. As a result, the Senate was never more powerful than during Grant's tenure. George F. Hoar, a Republican member of the House, described the Senate's attitude toward the president:

> The most eminent Senators . . . would have received as a personal affront a private message from the White House expressing a desire that they should adopt any course in the discharge of their legislative duties that they did not approve. If they visited the White House, it was to give, not to receive advice. [38]

Congress's dominance was apparent in the magnitude of legislative activity. Between 1865 and 1875, an average of forty-eight hundred bills and resolutions were introduced in each two-year Congress, nearly three times as many as during the previous decade. Post–Civil War legislative activity reached its peak when the Forty-Second Congress (1871–1873) enacted 1,012 laws and resolutions.[39]

Grant did not abdicate presidential responsibilities entirely in the face of this legislative onslaught. Unlike Johnson or even Lincoln, Congress trusted Grant not to stretch the bounds of executive power. Soon after he took office, Congress restored the size of the Supreme Court to nine, relying on Grant to fill the vacancies in a way it did not trust his predecessor. Grant also restored to effectiveness the most important power of the nineteenth-century executive:

Despite a highly successful military career that suggested unusual executive ability, Gen. Ulysses S. Grant was unable to transfer that success from the battlefield to the White House.

Source: National Portrait Gallery/Smithsonian Institution.

the veto. Johnson had wielded this weapon aggressively, but most of his vetoes were overturned. Grant vetoed ninety-three bills—more than all of his predecessors combined—and all but four stood.[40] His most important veto killed the 1874 Inflation Bill, which Congress passed in response to the Panic of 1873, a serious recession caused by a wave of bank failures throughout the country. The bill would have increased the amount of paper money ("greenbacks") in circulation in the hope that a more expansive currency would ease the growing debt crisis among the small farmers of the West.

Although Grant was sympathetic to rural hardship (he owned a farm in St. Louis that lost money), he was reluctant to unleash economic forces that might wreck the government's credit and cause a spiral of uncontrolled inflation. Combined with Congress's passage of the Species Resumption Act restoring the gold standard at the president's urging in 1875, historian Frank J. Scaturro has argued, Grant's veto of the Inflation Bill made him "the president most responsible for putting the country on the gold standard."[41] The consequence, according to historian Jean Edward Smith, was that "[b]y the end of the century, the American dollar had become the international symbol of financial stability."[42]

For the most part, however, Grant was uninterested in domestic policy. As a career soldier, he was much more concerned about national security. In particular, Grant cast an expansionist eye on Central America. In his first message to Congress, he called for the construction of a canal linking the Caribbean to the Pacific. The president also believed the navy needed a large natural harbor in the region. He hoped to follow through on plans initiated by the Johnson administration to purchase Santo Domingo (now known as the Dominican Republic), which is the home of Samana Bay, one of the best naval anchorages in the Caribbean. But the scheme ran into a buzz saw of opposition in the Senate. Charles Sumner, the chair of the Senate Foreign Relations Committee, opposed Grant's expansionist policies, considering them an affront to the egalitarian ideals that had given birth to the Republican Party. Sumner bitterly scorned the attempt to annex Santo Domingo, which he thought would threaten the independence of neighboring Haiti, the only independent black republic in the world. "To the African belongs the equatorial belt," Sumner said, "and he should enjoy it undisturbed."[43] The senator's moral indignation was fueled by personal resentment. Sorely disappointed that Grant had not named him secretary of state, Sumner was determined to control American foreign policy through his committee. In this instance he prevailed. In 1870 the Senate rejected Grant's treaty, under which Santo Domingo eventually would have become an American state.[44]

Grant had blundered badly. As Smith has written, "Little effort was made to cultivate public opinion and the Senate was kept in the dark. That was Grant's error."[45] Nevertheless, the president did not take the rejection of his Caribbean policy lightly. He persuaded Republican leaders in the Senate to remove Sumner as chair of the Foreign Relations Committee. This measure of revenge did nothing to advance the president's policy toward Santo Domingo; the treaty was voted down again in 1871. But it did enable Grant to obtain Senate ratification the same year of the Treaty of Washington, which settled the country's lingering disputes with Great Britain. The treaty secured payment to the United States for damages inflicted during the Civil War by the *Alabama* and other British-built Confederate naval vessels. Decrying Great Britain for its hypocrisy (the British had claimed to be antislavery while profiting from the sale of blockade runners to the Confederacy), Sumner had called for an uncompromising stance that would demand compensation for the indirect as well as the direct damages the United States suffered. The ships, he insisted, not only devastated the American merchant fleet but also prolonged the war.

Although Grant shared Sumner's disdain for Great Britain's pose of neutrality during the Civil War, he was anxious to settle the dispute. With Sumner deposed as Foreign Relations Committee chair and Simon Cameron of Pennsylvania, a strong Grant supporter, installed in his place, the treaty committing both nations to submit the issue to arbitration passed the Senate easily. The result was a $15.5 million award to the United States and the establishment of an important precedent in international law. This was the first major quarrel between two world powers to be settled by an international panel of arbitrators.[46] Smith notes that four decades later, "the rules governing maritime neutrality laid out in the Treaty of Washington . . . were formally adopted by all nations at the second Hague Conference in 1907."[47]

Despite his limitations, Grant was a stronger president than most scholars have recognized, especially during his first term. In the face of a white South grown assertive and a northern public grown weary of Reconstruction, he labored vigorously to secure the rights of African Americans, promoting the enactment of the Fifteenth Amendment's bar against racial discrimination in voting and using the army and the Justice Department, newly elevated to cabinet status, to suppress the Ku Klux Klan.[48] He was overwhelmingly reelected in 1872, winning 56 percent of the popular vote, the highest percentage for any presidential candidate in the three-quarters of a century between Andrew Jackson in 1828 and Theodore Roosevelt in 1904. But, according to his biographer Geoffrey Perret, "Grant had no grand vision of his own to guide the country." He was a transitional president in a country that was making its own transition from the Civil War era to the Gilded Age, during which the United States was emerging on the world stage as a commercial and military power. As his stance against the Inflation Bill suggested, Grant tended to view this transition favorably. But he offered no program to oversee its course. Instead, Grant's main concern was to keep "the Republican Party in the White House as long as possible in order to keep the Democrats out: Republicans saved the Union; Democrats had threatened its destruction."[49]

The Grant-led Republicans were practical politicians who depended on the spoils system to maintain the vigor of their party's organization. Out of a misplaced faith in the sanctity of party loyalty, Grant exposed his administration to patronage abuses and outright peculation. The most dramatic and probably the most damaging scandal of his presidency involved the evasion of taxes on distilleries by the so-called Whiskey Ring, a group of distillers and bottlers who routinely bribed revenue agents to avoid paying taxes on their product. The ring included Gen. John A. McDonald, the collector of internal revenue in St. Louis, who colluded with Treasury officials and the president's close friend and secretary, Gen. Orville E. Babcock, to defraud the government of millions of dollars.

One of the most disconcerting aspects of the scandal was Grant's effort to protect Babcock, who was acquitted on the strength of a deposition in his favor from the president. Grant even appointed Babcock as inspector of lighthouses.[50] Still worse, the president repaid Secretary of the Treasury Benjamin H. Bristow's efforts to break the Whiskey Ring and bring its perpetrators, including Babcock, to justice by making clear that Bristow was no longer welcome in the cabinet. Grant, no doubt, was also irritated by Bristow's political ambition. He became convinced that the Treasury secretary had been intriguing against him all along "to ruin his reputation and install Bristow as his successor."[51] Bristow resigned in 1876.

Although Grant's conduct in the Whiskey Ring scandal was unfortunate, he was personally honest and, more important, was concerned about the existing system of public administration. In early 1870 he called for civil service reform, declaring that "the present system [of party patronage] does not secure the best men and often not even fit men, for public place."[52] After receiving the necessary authority from Congress in March, Grant established a board, soon known as the Civil Service Commission, and charged it to devise reformist rules and regulations. George William Curtis, a leader of the national civil service reform movement, was appointed to chair the commission, which also supervised the new competitive examination system for hiring in each department. Ironically, one of the most corrupt presidential administrations in history made the first earnest attempt to reform the civil service.

Despite this promising beginning, most of what happened during Grant's second term thwarted the cause of civil service reform. The patronage system had long been dominated by individual members of Congress, and they liked it that way. Sen. Roscoe Conkling of New York, the leader of the so-called Stalwart wing of the Republican Party, led an assault on the new commission. He was supported not only by the leaders of his own party but by patronage-seeking Democrats as well.

The rise of the Stalwarts reveals much about the political ambiance of the post–Civil War era. Like the Radical Republicans, the Stalwarts initially were committed to the fundamental reconstruction of the South. But as the war and its aftermath gradually faded in political significance, defending patronage and maintaining the party organization became the Stalwarts' paramount concern. They were the product of a new political milieu in which the needs of the party machinery took precedence over principle. As historian Morton Keller noted, the Stalwarts' emergence as the dominant faction in the Republican Party signified the shift from a "politics of ideology to a politics of organization."[53]

Republicans who opposed the Stalwart-led transformation of their party and supported civil service reform turned in the early 1870s to a third party, the Liberal Republicans. But Liberal Republicanism never flourished at the grassroots. After nominating the celebrated New York newspaper editor Horace Greeley to run (unsuccessfully) against Grant in 1872, Liberal Republicans became anathema to the president and therefore were unable to work cooperatively with him to fend off the congressional attack on the Civil Service Commission. Stalwart Republicans and Democrats assailed the commission's rules as unconstitutional, aristocratic, and fatal to the ascendancy of any party.

Instead of defending his civil service reform program, Grant resigned himself to cooperating with the Stalwarts. He then yielded when Congress refused to allocate funds for the Civil Service Commission in 1874. Proclaiming once more his belief that the legislature was the proper branch to make domestic policy, the president announced in his annual message on December 7, 1874, that if Congress did not pass a civil service reform law before adjourning, he would discontinue the system. Congress adjourned without taking action, and on March 9, 1875, Grant ordered that civil service examining boards throughout the country be disbanded.[54]

The Fight to Restore Presidential Power

Grant retired from the presidency in 1877, leaving the office he occupied for eight years at a low ebb. "Grantism" had become synonymous with scandal. Moreover, a severe economic crisis plagued the president's second term. The collapse of the nation's leading bank, Jay Cooke and Company, had triggered an economic depression that lasted from 1873 to 1878. Grant's economic policy, which contracted the money supply, made matters worse for those in debt. In the 1874 midterm elections, a 113-seat Republican majority in the House became a 68-seat deficit, the first time the Democrats had controlled the lower chamber since the mid-1850s.[55] The president's party still controlled the Senate, but the upper chamber, its leaders believed, remained "secure in its mastery over the executive."[56] Yet Grant's successor, Rutherford B. Hayes, was determined to emancipate his office from congressional domination. During the Hayes administration, the powers of the presidency were defended persistently and effectively for the first time since the Civil War.

The Presidency of Rutherford B. Hayes

Although Hayes eventually reversed more than a decade of executive decline, his administration began in the least auspicious of circumstances. After sixteen years of Republican rule, a Democratic victory seemed certain in the elections of 1876. In fact, Democratic candidate Samuel J. Tilden, who as governor of New York exposed the efforts of Boss Tweed's Tammany Hall and other political rings to corrupt the state's canal system, initially appeared to have won the presidential election.[57] Hayes himself told reporters on election night, "Democrats have carried the country and elected Tilden."[58] But the electoral votes of Oregon and the three southern states that still were under military rule—Florida, Louisiana, and South Carolina—were in doubt. Without them, Tilden had only 184 electoral votes. If Hayes carried all of the disputed states, he would have 185 votes and win the election.

The partisan battle began when all four states sent two sets of electoral votes to Washington to be counted. Congress responded by creating a fifteen-member electoral commission to resolve the matter: five Republican members of Congress, five Democratic members, and four Supreme Court justices who were charged to name a fifth from among their ranks. The justices chose a Grant appointee, Joseph Bradley. On March 2, 1877, the electoral commission, by a strict party vote, rejected the Democratic returns from the doubtful states and declared Hayes the winner by a margin of one electoral vote. The Constitution grants the House of Representatives the power to choose the president if the Electoral College does not produce a winner. The partisan machinations that produced the ad hoc commission marked the only time in American history that an extra-constitutional settlement decided a national election.[59]

Still, Congress had to declare the election official before the commission's recommendation could take effect, and the Democratic-controlled House threatened not to meet. According to historian Michael Holt, at this point, a deal—the so-called Compromise of 1877—was struck between Republican and southern Democratic leaders. In return for the Democrats acquiescing to Hayes's election, the Republicans promised to remove the remaining military forces from the South.[60] Both sides kept their end of the bargain. Hayes removed the federal troops, putting an end to virtually all attempts to enforce the Fourteenth Amendment's guarantees of civil rights to every citizen, including former slaves. Nor, thereafter, was any serious effort made to uphold the Fifteenth Amendment, which since 1870 had affirmed the right of citizens to vote regardless of "race, color, or previous condition of servitude."

The negotiations between Democrats and Republicans that led to the 1877 agreement stretched over several months. Prompted by the Democrats regaining control of the House in 1874 and the waning power of the military occupation, Grant maintained a "benevolent neutrality" during the last three months of his administration that enabled the so-called Redeemers of South Carolina and Louisiana to take de facto control of the two remaining southern Republican governments.[61] Meanwhile, Tilden maintained what Morton Keller called an "Olympian (or neurotic)" calm during the 1876 election dispute.[62] He spent one critical month during the crisis compiling a history of past electoral counts. When the issue finally was resolved against him, Tilden said he looked forward to private life "with the consciousness that I shall receive from posterity the credit of having been elected to the highest position in the gift of the people without any cares and responsibilities of the office."[63] As Keller concluded, "The retreat from the purposive, ideological politics of the Civil War could not have been more complete."[64]

It is ironic that such an unsavory political bargain brought to power a president who was uncompromisingly dedicated to reform, in particular of the patronage-dominated civil service. Forgotten amid the fraudulent resolution of the election was that both Hayes and Tilden had promised to institute civil service reform to limit the power of local party organizations by reducing the number of government jobs that could be awarded for services to the party. Hayes had been a reform-oriented governor of Ohio and had written a ringing endorsement of civil service reform in his letter accepting the Republican presidential nomination. The president's appointing power, he declared, too often had passed improperly into the hands of Congress. In his inaugural address, Hayes proclaimed that "the President of the United States of necessity owes his election to the office to the suffrage and zealous labors of a political party . . .; but he should strive to be always mindful of the fact that he serves his party best who serves the country." Civil service reform, he concluded, should be "thorough, radical, and complete."[65]

Congress, for its part, was uninterested in reform. By the end of Grant's second term, the influence of individual senators and, to a lesser extent, representatives on executive appointments had become substantial. Grant lamented, "The president very rarely appoints, he merely registers the appointments of members of Congress."[66] Hayes first offended Republican Senate leaders by making his cabinet nominations without consulting them, thereby disrupting the Stalwarts' plan to dictate the composition of the cabinet. With his nomination of former Confederate David M. Key as postmaster general, Hayes also aroused their patriotic wrath. The major insult that the president perpetrated on the Senate, however, was his choice of the civil service reformer Carl Schurz to head the Department of the Interior, a jobs-laden agency that members of Congress feared Schurz would use to wage war on patronage.

Even though Hayes's cabinet nominees were a broadly qualified group, the offended Senate "oligarchy" took their selection as a challenge. When the president submitted his nominations for confirmation, the entire list was referred to committees for prolonged examination. Hoping that delay would force the president's hand, the Senate did not exempt even Sen. John Sherman, whom Hayes nominated as secretary of the Treasury, from this process, violating the custom that fellow senators, especially those as qualified as Sherman, were confirmed without investigation.

For the Senate to delay the confirmation of an entire cabinet was unprecedented and, it turned out, unpopular. The White House was flooded with telegrams and letters urging Hayes to stand firm. The Senate capitulated to public opinion and, voting almost unanimously, confirmed every cabinet nominee. "For the first time since the Civil War," Wilfred Binkley wrote, "the Senate had been vanquished on a clear-cut issue between it and the President."[67]

Yet a greater battle between Hayes and Congress was still to come. Having installed a cabinet of his own choosing, the president set his sights on the patronage system. "Now for Civil Service Reform," Hayes wrote in his diary on April 22, 1877, seven weeks after taking office.[68] One of his first acts was to appoint independent commissions to investigate the federal custom houses in New York, San Francisco, New Orleans, and several other port cities. These outposts, which were controlled by local party machines, had fallen into outrageous patterns of corruption in the course of collecting federal revenues. Although the commissions' investigations led to reforms in many areas of the country, the custom house in New York, which collected more than two-thirds of all custom revenues and provided the federal government with about half of its income, continued to serve the party machine. The commission that investigated the New York custom house found that employees were expected to contribute a percentage of their salary to the Republican Party.

After receiving the report on the New York custom house, Hayes decided to replace its three highest officials—Collector Chester A. Arthur, Surveyor General George H. Sharpe, and naval officer Alonzo B. Cornell—all of whom were prominent members of New York's Republican organization. The president's intention was impeded, however, when his nominations were referred to the Senate Commerce Committee, chaired by Stalwart Republican leader Roscoe Conkling of New York. Conkling, for whom the custom house was an important base of political power, invoked the Tenure of Office Act, which had been revised in 1869, and the session of Congress ended without the nominations being confirmed. Under the amended terms of the act, the Senate no longer could overturn a presidential removal. But until a majority of senators voted to approve the president's choice of a successor, the suspended official remained in office. When Hayes's nominations, which were greeted in the Senate with derisive laughter, were not confirmed, Arthur, Sharpe, and Cornell kept their posts. More important, Conkling and the New York Republican machine retained control of the custom house.

The stubborn Hayes resolved to continue the fight. On December 12, 1877, he recorded in his diary, "In the language of the press, Senator Conkling has won a great victory over the administration. . . . But the end is not yet. I am right and I shall not give up the contest."[69] The institutional rivalry between the president and the senator was aggravated by personal recrimination. Conkling had opposed Hayes's nomination in 1876 and, after the disputed election, openly mocked him as "Rutherfraud."[70] When Congress adjourned in 1878, Hayes again dismissed the three custom house officials, replaced them temporarily with recess appointments, and in December sent to the Senate his nominations for the positions.

Although Conkling was able to delay Senate action for two months, he finally defeated his own cause by delivering a bitter speech against the president in which he alienated many senators by reading from the private correspondence of cabinet members.[71] The Senate voted to confirm Hayes's nominees on February 3, 1879.

In his letter of congratulation to Gen. E. A. Merritt, who was Arthur's replacement, Hayes established principles for the complete overhaul of the New York custom house's personnel system. Besides insisting that Merritt conduct his office "on strictly business principles," the president required the new collector to confine patronage to the narrowest possible bounds. "Let no man be put out merely because he is a friend of the late collector," he wrote, "and no man be put in merely because he is our friend."[72]

Hayes's victory over Conkling came at great political cost. During the almost eighteen months it took to fire Arthur, Sharpe, and Cornell, the president was virtually powerless as the administrative head of the government. Even though Hayes's triumph restored to the executive some of the powers it had lost since Lincoln's assassination, his administration is remembered mainly for "holding its ground, rather than for developing new frontiers."[73] Still, Hayes was satisfied with the blows he struck against the senatorial group that for so long had directed the government. A year after winning his battle for control of the New York custom house, Hayes wrote in his diary,

> The end I have chiefly aimed at has been to break down
> congressional patronage. The contest has been a bitter one. It has
> exposed me to attack, opposition, misconstruction, and the actual
> hatred of powerful men. But I have had great success. No member
> of either house now attempts even to dictate appointments. My
> sole right to make appointments is now tacitly conceded.[74]

The Presidency of James A. Garfield

Hayes's claim that he restored presidential control of the executive branch was premature. The struggle between the president and Congress for control of the executive branch did not end with Hayes's defeat of Conkling. In fact, the battles over appointments that dominated Hayes's term in office were renewed with unexpected ferocity during the first weeks of James A. Garfield's administration.

By the time of the 1880 election, factionalism had come to dominate American political parties. Garfield, who was nominated by the Republican convention on the thirty-sixth ballot, was chosen as a compromise between Conkling's Stalwarts and the moderate wing of the party (the Half-breeds as they were called), led by Sen. James G. Blaine of Maine.[75] The convention further bandaged party wounds by selecting Chester A. Arthur, Conkling's lieutenant and the deposed head of the New York custom house, as its vice-presidential candidate. The Democrats settled on a compromise presidential nominee of their own, the pallid and unexceptional Civil War general Winfield Scott Hancock of Pennsylvania, in a convention torn by factional disputes. The Democrats' hope was that by nominating a Union general, they could undermine the Republicans' time-tested strategy of "waving the bloody shirt"—that is, branding the Democrats as the party of secession and war. Of the 9,219,467 popular votes cast in the election, Garfield prevailed over Hancock by a razor-thin margin of 9,457. He won the Electoral College by 214–155. As in the 1876 election, the closeness of the contest was not the result of a keen struggle over major issues. Instead, it was the product of two highly organized, competitive national parties, each bringing its supporters to the polls. Voter turnout in the late nineteenth century often exceeded 75 percent.

Garfield seemed well suited to the new game of party politics. Unlike Hayes, he was by nature prone to conciliation and compromise but a champion of civil rights for African Americans, a cause he made clear in his inaugural address. Once in office, he hoped to work cooperatively with both the Stalwart and Half-breed factions of his party. Yet against his will, Garfield was soon caught up in severe factional conflicts. In the heat of these intraparty squabbles, he was forced to continue the assault against overly broad assertions of senatorial courtesy that Hayes had begun.[76] Garfield's attack on the Senate came in response to the Conklingites' attempt to dictate his choice for secretary of the Treasury. Stalwarts demanded that the president appoint Levi P. Morton, a New York banker. Garfield resisted, arguing that Morton's Wall Street connections and extremely conservative economic views made him anathema to western Republicans. His conciliatory offer to name Morton as secretary of the navy and to consider other Stalwart recommendations for the Treasury was scorned. The Stalwarts' answer was unequivocal: Morton must be the Treasury secretary.

Garfield was not so conciliatory as to yield to such an aggressive a challenge to executive authority. After generously recognizing the Conkling wing of the New York Republican Party by placing many of its members in federal positions, he insisted on his own choices for the cabinet, selecting William Windom, a Republican senator from Minnesota, as Treasury secretary. Garfield now realized, as clearly as had Hayes, that the president's constitutional independence "could be preserved only by a bold challenge of the pretensions of the Senate and a duel to the finish with the most militant champion of senatorial courtesy"—the tradition of not appointing anyone to a position in a senator's own state whom the senator found objectionable.[77]

Garfield left no doubt of his intention to challenge the Senate when he nominated William H. Robertson as collector of the port of New York. Robertson was Conkling's political enemy in New York, which made his appointment a more direct challenge to senatorial courtesy than Hayes ever issued. As Garfield wrote to his longtime friend B. A. Hinsdale, the president of Hiram College,

> This [nomination] brings on the contest at once and will settle the question whether the President is registering clerk of the Senate or the Executive of the United States. . . . Summed up in a single sentence this is the question: shall the principal port of entry in which more than ninety percent of all our customs duties are collected be under the control of the administration or under the local control of the factional senator?[78]

Conkling marshaled his political machine in an attempt to compel Garfield to withdraw Robertson's nomination. Vice President Arthur participated fully in these maneuvers, despite stiff criticism from the president's supporters and the press. On the evening of April 14, 1881, Arthur eluded reporters and slipped into the White House for a private conversation with Garfield. He urged the president to withdraw Robertson's nomination on the grounds that it would badly fracture the Republican Party in New York and consign its candidates to certain defeat. Garfield refused to budge. Afterward, he wrote to Whitelaw Reid of the *New-York Tribune,* "Of course I deprecate war, but if it is brought to my door the bringer will find me at home."[79]

When Conkling and his allies in the Senate hatched a plan to outwit the president by confirming all of his nominees except Robertson, Garfield withdrew every other New York appointment. There would be no further nominations, Garfield insisted, until the issue of who controlled the executive branch was settled. The president's bold maneuver left the Senate practically helpless and rallied his supporters. Garfield recorded the triumph in his diary: "The withdrawal of the New York appointments has brought me vigorous responses from many quarters and I think shows that the public do not desire the continuance of boss rule in the Senate."[80]

On May 16, 1881, seeing that Robertson's confirmation was inevitable, Conkling and his fellow New York senator, Thomas C. Platt, resigned, hoping that the state legislature would buttress their political stature in Washington by reelecting them. The legislature refused. After a long struggle, two other men were chosen to represent New York in the Senate.

Garfield's victory was complete. The Senate confirmed Robertson's nomination unanimously, and Conkling never regained public office. The president's triumph ended the long struggle that began with Hayes's attempt to reform the New York custom house and marked a "milestone in the revival of the power and prestige of the White House."[81] Although the influence that senators wield in suggesting candidates for presidential appointments and rejecting objectionable nominees remained substantial, their claim to supersede executive discretion was ended.

Chester A. Arthur and the Enactment of Civil Service Reform

Garfield did not have time to pursue a comprehensive program of civil service reform. On July 2, 1881, in a Washington railroad station, a deranged lawyer named Charles J. Guiteau shot the president in the back. Guiteau, who had convinced himself that he deserved a prominent presidential appointment and resented Garfield's assault on the Conkling machine, exclaimed upon being arrested, "I am a Stalwart and Arthur is president."[82] When Garfield died after lingering until September 19, Vice President Arthur indeed became the president.

Civil service reformers expected little from the New York Stalwart. Former president Hayes predicted that Conkling, Arthur's old patron, would be "the power behind the throne, superior to the throne."[83] But Garfield's assassination inflamed public opinion against the spoils system, and Arthur quickly realized that if he did not support civil service reform, he would jeopardize the precariously superior political position enjoyed by the Republican Party since the Civil War. The new president soon laid to rest the worst fears of those who predicted he would turn the executive mansion "into a larger version of the New York Customhouse."[84] Arthur refused Conkling's "outrageous" demand that he fire Robertson, the Garfield-appointed collector of the New York custom house, and appoint a loyal Stalwart in his place. He felt "morally bound to continue the policy of the former president."[85] Intent on strengthening his political position in the country, Arthur surprised his critics and expressed support for limited civil service reform in his first annual message to Congress.

Arthur's commitment to reform was strengthened by his party's concern about the results of the 1882 midterm elections, in which the Democrats achieved substantial gains in the House of Representatives. In his second annual message, the president called on Congress to pass the Pendleton Act, which was introduced in 1881 by George Hunt Pendleton, a Democratic senator from Ohio. The civil service reform bill contained measures, such as competitive examinations for federal jobs and a ban on political assessments, that Arthur originally had opposed. But when Congress passed the act in early 1883, he signed it. The Pendleton Act was of limited immediate application. Its coverage extended only to employees of the executive branch in Washington and major custom houses and post offices around the country. The vast majority—all but 14,000 of 131,000 federal officeholders, including many postal workers—was not covered. Indeed, control of the rich supply of remaining patronage jobs would be the primary source of conflict between Congress and Arthur's Democratic successor, Grover Cleveland.

Nevertheless, as Leonard D. White has written, the enactment of civil service reform in 1883 "was a fundamental turning point in the history of the federal administrative system."[86] In addition to the foothold it established for merit hiring and the bar it erected against on-the-job solicitations of campaign funds from federal employees, the Pendleton Act established a bipartisan, three-member Civil Service Commission, appointed by the president and confirmed by the Senate. The commission was vested with two important powers: to control hiring examinations and to investigate whether the new civil service rules were being enforced. Finally, the president was authorized to expand the bounds of civil service coverage by executive order. However limited its initial application, the Pendleton Act laid a solid foundation on which to build the civil service in succeeding decades.[87]

Grover Cleveland's First Term

Neither the Republicans' belated support of civil service reform nor their nomination for president of Speaker of the House James G. Blaine, the leader of the moderate, Half-breed faction of the party, could stave off defeat in the 1884 election. The Democratic standard bearer, Gov. Grover Cleveland of New York, won a narrow victory. He was the first Democrat to be elected president in twenty-eight years.

Like all Democrats since the Jacksonian era, Cleveland ran well among the nation's growing population of northern, urban Catholic immigrants and their descendants. Blaine, in an exaggerated version of the Whig and Republican tradition, appealed to native Protestants by raising fears of Catholic influence. He promoted a constitutional amendment—the Blaine Amendment—to prevent public funding of parochial schools and sat quietly at a campaign event at which a Protestant minister labeled Democrats the party of "rum, Romanism and rebellion."

Although his political base in New York, the nation's largest and most politically competitive state at the time, would seem to have positioned Cleveland to enhance his northern constituency, he eschewed local and regional loyalty in favor of national policy positions that aroused factional tensions within the Democratic Party. He was the preeminent "Bourbon Democrat"—that is, he led his party's conservative wing, which closely shared the Republicans' skeptical, even hostile stance toward the growing aspirations of industrial workers and small farmers for wide-ranging social and economic reform. The Bourbons thought of themselves as staunch adherents of traditional Jeffersonian and Jacksonian principles in the face of the tremendous changes that were taking place in the late nineteenth-century American economy. They championed lower tariffs, hard money, and limited government. Although these principles once formed the core of a reform tradition, they had taken on a conservative cast in the Gilded Age. In this new era, large factories and powerful corporations were the real beneficiaries of principles whose original purpose was to protect small farmers, workers, and local business owners. Cleveland strongly endorsed—and with his judicial appointments supported—the Supreme Court's growing emphasis on protecting corporations against state governments' efforts at regulation.

Bourbon Democratic regimes flourished in the South, where politicians representing big business and planters won support from many poor whites by raising the banner of white supremacy. But the Bourbons' Jeffersonian and Jacksonian rhetoric appealed to many northern Democrats as well.[88] Cleveland was especially strong among those Midwestern and northeastern members of the party whose antipathy to centralized power was joined to a pro-business philosophy. Historian Horace Samuel Merrill has described these conservative Democrats as "protectors of the existing, although accelerating, course of the industrial revolution. They jealously guarded this machinery of material progress against threats from restless farmers and wage earners."[89]

Ignoring the recrudescence of terrible racial injustice that followed the Compromise of 1877, as well as the lingering hostility to African Americans in both the North and South, moderates in every section of the country believed that Cleveland's election heralded the true end of the bitter conflicts generated by the Civil War. Cleveland was eager to prove them correct. As the head of the party that received its greatest support from the South, he appointed many white southerners to high office, including two to his cabinet. Republicans, unwilling to stop waving the "bloody shirt" of northern resentment of southern secession, continued to portray the Democrats as unworthy to control the federal government. Cleveland's vetoes of hundreds of private bills granting pensions to Union army veterans and their survivors provided the Republican Party with political ammunition that became even more explosive when the president signed an order returning captured Confederate battle flags to the South.[90]

The Grand Army of the Republic (GAR), a brotherhood of Union veterans formed in 1866 and a powerful constituency within the Republican Party, vehemently protested Cleveland's Confederate flag order. The order was treasonous, the GAR roared, while beseeching God to "palsy the hand" of the president who had signed it. Cleveland backed down, leaving the matter to Congress, which took no action.[91] This angry confrontation was a precursor to the great waves of Confederate monuments built during the 1890s to celebrate the "Lost Cause" and affirm white supremacy.[92]

Yet Cleveland's victory in 1884 was proof that the post–Civil War political order would not be upset by the election of a Democrat as president. The 1884 campaign and its aftermath confirmed that recent elections were more about federal patronage than national issues. The Democratic victory also indicated that the nation was slowly turning its attention from the legacy of the Civil War toward tariffs, currency, and other economic matters.[93]

Not surprisingly, the 1884 election brought no moratorium in the patronage-centered struggle between the president and Congress to control appointments to the federal government. By winning major victories against the Senate, Hayes and Garfield had restored some measure of prestige to the presidency, which had been badly tarnished during the Johnson and Grant years. It fell to Cleveland to fight the battle over appointments that finally secured the repeal of the Tenure of Office Act.

The battle began when Cleveland attempted to appoint loyal Democrats who, after being out of office for a quarter century, were hungry to partake of the spoils of patronage. The president was no mere spoilsman. As mayor of Buffalo and governor of New York, he had earned a reputation for reform. As president, Cleveland enforced the Pendleton Act and devoted an enormous amount of time to scrutinizing the qualifications of candidates for the many federal positions that were not covered by the new merit-based civil service hiring procedures. His approach yielded a number of outstanding appointments and won him praise from civil service reformers.

Still, fashioning himself a Jacksonian Democrat, Cleveland appreciated the benefits of the patronage system. He wanted to place deserving Democrats in jobs that had long been held by Republicans. Operating under the constraints of the amended Tenure of Office Act, however, the president was only able to suspend, not remove, federal employees from their jobs. He could not replace officials unless the Senate was in session and approved his nominees. The Republican-controlled Senate was loath to cooperate. Of the 643 suspensions (and corresponding appointments) that Cleveland made during the early days of his presidency, the Senate, after being in session for three months, considered only 17 and confirmed only 15.

The larger controversy between the president and the Senate was joined in a battle for control of a single office, the U.S. attorney for Alabama. When Cleveland suspended the incumbent, George M. Duskin, and nominated John D. Burnett to replace him, the Republican chair of the Senate Judiciary Committee, George F. Edmunds of Vermont, decided to subject the nomination to intense and protracted scrutiny. He asked Cleveland's attorney general to send to his committee all papers pertaining not just to Burnett's appointment but also to Duskin's dismissal. Cleveland directed the attorney general to comply with the request for information about Burnett. But, determined to establish once and for all the president's right to remove federal officials without interference from Congress, Cleveland refused to release any information about his decision to suspend Duskin.

Cleveland's refusal stung Senate Republicans, who responded with a resolution condemning the administration for its unwillingness to cooperate. The president, in turn, sent a message to the Capitol defending his actions and accusing legislators of infringing on his constitutional responsibility as chief executive. Of the Republicans' demand for information about his suspension of federal officials, Cleveland wrote:

> They assume the right of the Senate to sit in judgment upon the exercise of my exclusive discretion and executive function, for which I am solely responsible to the people from whom I have so lately received the sacred trust of office. My oath to support and defend the Constitution . . . compel[s] me to refuse compliance with these demands.[94]

Cleveland's message to Congress dramatized his conflict with the Senate in a way that attracted national attention. As in other recent battles of this sort, public opinion supported the president. Recognizing that it was beaten, the Senate found a face-saving avenue of retreat. Someone discovered that during the controversy, Duskin's term had expired, which made his suspension by the president no longer necessary. Burnett's appointment as U.S. attorney was readily confirmed.

Cleveland's position on appointments was vindicated a few months later when, with overwhelming support from both parties, Congress voted to repeal the Tenure of Office Act. He signed the legislation on March 3, 1887, twenty years after the statute depriving presidents of the removal power was enacted to punish Andrew Johnson. "Thus," wrote Cleveland many years later, "was an unhappy controversy happily followed by an expurgation of the last pretense of statutory sanction to an encroachment upon constitutional Executive prerogatives, and thus was a time-honored interpretation of the Constitution restored to us."[95]

Congressional Government and the Prelude to a More Active Presidency

During the twelve years that passed between the beginning of the Hayes administration in 1877 and the end of Cleveland's first term in 1889, the post–Civil War decline in the prestige of the presidency came to an end. The Senate's grip on the details of administration, especially the removal power, was loosened by the defeats administered by Hayes, Garfield, and Cleveland. The struggle to rejuvenate executive independence was advanced by the enactment of civil service reform, which began the process of insulating federal appointments from the parochial concerns of party spoilsmen.

These achievements notwithstanding, the presidency remained small in scale and limited in power during the latter decades of the nineteenth century. The president's control of the executive domain was restored, but the domain itself remained highly constricted. Late nineteenth-century presidents had little influence on government expenditures or, apart from appointments, on the policies pursued by the departments and agencies of the executive branch.

In fiscal affairs, the end of the Civil War marked a transition from emergency presidential control of the amounts and purposes of government spending to renewed efforts by Congress to reassert its authority. In response, Hayes and Cleveland exercised the veto aggressively to ward off Congress's most egregious attempts to use spending bills to impose its will on the executive. In 1879 Hayes successfully vetoed an army appropriation bill, which included riders attached by the Democrats that prohibited federal marshals from employing troops or armed civilians in the southern states to keep the peace during congressional elections. In doing so, Hayes established a powerful precedent against appropriation riders that encroach on executive power.[96] Cleveland vetoed twice as many bills by the time his first term ended in 1889 as all of his predecessors combined since George Washington became president in 1789.

Yet the veto was strictly a defensive measure when it came to fiscal policy. Indeed, until the Budget and Accounting Act was passed in 1921, presidential authority for taxing and spending was "almost, if not entirely, lacking."[97] Presidents, at least in peacetime, were never involved when departments and agencies made their annual spending estimates and seldom were consulted when congressional committees reviewed those estimates. The secretary of the Treasury was merely a compiler of budget requests. The absence of executive leadership in fiscal matters fostered irresponsible and disorderly budgets, made worse by Congress's practice of devolving its decision-making authority for spending to the House and Senate appropriations committees.

The president's ability to provide guidance in the legislative process and enlist congressional support for an administration program was also limited during the latter part of the nineteenth century. Indeed, no president of this era advanced a theory of executive power that supported presidential leadership of Congress.

Cleveland fiercely defended executive independence but did not believe that the president's legislative responsibilities went beyond recommending measures for Congress to consider. Even on the tariff issue, which had emerged as the central conflict between Democrats and Republicans in the 1880s, the president made little effort to bend Congress to his will. To be sure, Cleveland opposed protectionism. After the Democrats fared poorly in the 1886 midterm elections, he wrote a forceful message that urged Congress, in conformance with Democratic principles, to reduce tariff rates sharply. According to political scientist Daniel Klinghard, this message marked an important departure in presidential communication with Congress and the public. Traditionally, presidential messages reviewed "the entire public business." Cleveland's innovation was to devote his entire message to a single subject—tariff reform. This break with tradition drew considerable attention. Cleveland, in fact, strategically sought to "grab popular attention, inviting public comment and giving loyal Democratic voters reason to read the message in the privacy of their homes—it was a 'campaign of education' applied to presidential leadership."[98]

Cleveland's innovative message strengthened support within the Democratic Party for the reduction of tariff rates before the newly elected Republican Congress was sworn in. But it did not result in any major policy reform. Constrained by late nineteenth-century practices that proscribed presidential interference in the legislative process, Cleveland did little. As historian John A. Garraty has written, "Like a great lethargic bear, Cleveland had bestirred himself . . . and shaken the political hive, but then he slumped back into querulous inactivity."[99] His tariff policy was rejected overwhelmingly by Congress at considerable cost to his political reputation.

The Presidency of Benjamin A. Harrison

The narrow bounds that constrained presidential leadership in the late nineteenth century led political scientist Woodrow Wilson to declare in 1885, the first year of Cleveland's first term, that "unquestionably, the predominant and controlling force, the center and source of all motive and of all regulative power, is Congress."[100] Cleveland took some important steps to challenge the principle of legislative supremacy. His successor, Benjamin A. Harrison, enthusiastically embraced it.

Harrison, a Republican senator from Indiana, won a close election in 1888, running an innovative, "full-fledged front-porch campaign" in which he greeted about 300,000 visitors to his Indiana hometown with brief remarks. Cleveland abided by the long tradition of staying in Washington, aloof from the campaign.[101] By piling up large majorities in the southern states, where African American Republicans were barred by law or the threat of violence from voting, he actually won the national popular vote, but Harrison narrowly carried the large northern states and therefore the Electoral College. This unusual result (not until 2000 did another discrepancy occur between the popular and the electoral vote outcomes) brought to the presidency a man who understood perfectly Congress's desire to control the conduct of government.

Harrison was one of the Senate leaders who clashed with Cleveland over the president's removal power. A few weeks after the election, he readily accepted the advice of Republican senator John Sherman: "The President should 'touch elbows with Congress.' He should have no policy distinct from his party and that is better represented in Congress than in the Executive." Suggesting that "Cleveland made a cardinal mistake in [seeking to dictate] a tariff policy to Congress," Sherman encouraged the new president to cultivate friendly relations with legislators and to follow rather than try to lead Republicans in the House and Senate.[102]

In spite of Harrison's unquestioned industry and dignified supervision of executive affairs, his tenure marked a retreat in the struggle to revive the status of the presidency. Comparing Harrison with his predecessor, Garraty wrote, "Cleveland had surrendered to the patronage system after a battle; Harrison embraced it from the start. Cleveland squabbled with Congress, and fumbled [in the tariff controversy] toward presidential leadership at least once; Harrison cheerfully submitted to being practically a figurehead."[103] Easing Harrison's stance was his close agreement with congressional Republicans that the federal government should use high tariffs as a way to promote domestic manufacturing.

The absence of presidential leadership and the triumph of congressional supremacy spawned efforts to reorganize the House and the Senate so they could perform their duties more efficiently. Until the 1880s Congress was primarily a deliberative body. By the end of the nineteenth century, it was a complex and well-disciplined institution that was organized to govern.

In the House, especially, lawmaking increasingly came under the control of the leadership—that is, the Speaker and the heads of the major committees. The Republican Speaker during Harrison's tenure, Thomas B. Reed, imposed rules on the House that greatly streamlined its chaotic proceedings. Confronted with the minority Democrats' use of the "disappearing quorum," in which members sat mute during attendance calls to deny the Speaker the quorum needed to conduct business, Reed counted the recalcitrants whether they signified their presence or not. In 1891 the Supreme Court sanctioned the transformation of the House into a more disciplined legislative body by declining to rule unconstitutional this and other "Reed rules," such as a ban on filibusters.[104]

Similar changes occurred in the Senate, so much so that James Bryce, a distinguished English observer of American politics, wrote in 1890 that the upper house was "modern, severe, and practical."[105] Forceful leaders, such as Finance Committee Chair Nelson Aldrich of Rhode Island and Appropriations Committee Chair William B. Allison of Iowa, imposed rules on the Senate that resembled the controls "Czar" Reed established in the House. As a result, Republicans were able to bring a previously unknown degree of partisan and procedural discipline to the Senate during Harrison's tenure as president.

The Harrison administration, then, was one in which Congress and the party organizations reigned supreme, enjoying willing deference from a supportive president. A burst of important legislation during the first two years of Harrison's term, including the protectionist McKinley Tariff Act, the Sherman Anti-Trust Act to reduce the concentration of power in massive corporations, the Sherman Silver Purchase Act to expand the coinage of silver, the Dependent Pensions Act for Union army veterans and their families, and increased spending on internal improvements and the navy marked the rise of party discipline and congressional efficiency.[106] As such, the Harrison years offered a striking example of Whig-style, Congress-centered party government.[107] Indeed, historian Charles Calhoun has observed, "[T]he Fifty-first Congress elected in 1888 set a record for peacetime legislative accomplishment, enacting 531 public laws, a number unequaled until Theodore Roosevelt's second term."[108]

Like the Whigs, and in contrast to conservative Democrats such as Cleveland, the Republicans had long wanted to use the federal government to help achieve their economic objectives. The Republican program originally had been formulated to challenge the slave economy of the South. But this commitment gave way as Republicans lived up to the agreement that had effectively shielded the South from federal protection of African American rights since 1877. They now were dedicated to advancing industrial capitalism. Expressing support for private property with an ardor shared by the radicals of his party, Lincoln said in 1863 that "property is the fruit of labor, . . . a positive good in the world. That some should be rich shows that others may become rich, and hence is just encouragement to industry and enterprise."[109] With the end of Reconstruction, the Republicans' dedication to industrial capitalism became their party's central doctrine, embodied not only in protective tariffs but also in banking policies that provided capital for industrial development. The close identification of the Republican Party with business was, on the whole, politically advantageous because a majority of voters supported protective tariffs and publicly financed internal improvements.[110]

Grover Cleveland, president from 1885 to 1889, lost the 1888 election but regained the White House in the election of 1892. He is the only president to have served two nonconsecutive terms.

Source: Library of Congress.

Yet developments were under way in the country that soon would render the Republican model of party government obsolete. Massive social and economic changes were increasing the scale and complexity of American life, producing jarring economic dislocations and intense political conflicts. In the face of change, pressures mounted for a more expansive national government and more systematic administration of public policy. The limited nineteenth-century polity, which could accommodate decentralized party organizations, political patronage, and a dominant Congress, began to give way to a new style of governance that required consistent and forceful presidential leadership. The rise of intensely ideological political conflict in the 1890s, culminating in the presidential election between Democrat William Jennings Bryan and Republican William McKinley in 1896, as well as the growing role of the United States in world affairs, which accelerated with the Spanish–American War of 1898, set the stage for a significant transformation of the presidency.

Grover Cleveland's Second Term

The effects of the new political order on the presidency first became apparent during the second term of Grover Cleveland, who defeated Harrison in their 1892 rematch. Cleveland owed his political comeback to the pro-business Republicans' failure to assuage rising public concerns about the growth of government and the economic dislocations caused by corporate industrialization. Democrats labeled the activist Republican-controlled Fifty-First Congress the "Billion Dollar Congress" because of its unprecedentedly lavish peacetime spending.[111] In 1890 they swept the House elections by a huge majority—the prelude, as it turned out, to Cleveland's victory two years later. But when Cleveland and the Democrats were themselves blindsided by a severe economic depression in 1893, the Republicans regained control of Congress in the midterm elections of 1894. In the volatile party competition of the era, Republican strength in the House fell from 166 in 1888 to 88 in 1890, then rose to 244 in 1894, giving them a 139-seat majority during Cleveland's final two years as president.

The Democrats' political defeat came soon after Cleveland responded to the Panic of 1893 by wielding the powers of the presidency more vigorously than any president since Lincoln. His call of a special session of Congress to secure repeal of the Sherman Silver Purchase Act represented effective leadership in defense of a gold-based currency. Yet this dramatic departure from the hands-off approach to legislation that Cleveland pursued during his first term cost him the support of his party. He not only alienated inflationist, pro-silver Democrats, such as rural Nebraska representative William Jennings Bryan, but also offended congressional leaders who resented the president's aggressive new posture on domestic policy.

The Democratic Party's repudiation of Cleveland was reinforced by his intervention in the Pullman strike against the railroads in 1894, which paralyzed the western half of the country. Without consulting John P. Altgeld, the Democratic governor of Illinois, Cleveland dispatched troops to Chicago, supposedly to protect federal property and "to remove obstructions to the United States mails" but actually to restore order by ending the strike. This action infuriated Altgeld, who proclaimed in a telegram to Cleveland that

> to absolutely ignore a local government in matters of this
> kind, when the local government is ready to furnish assistance
> needed, and is amply able to enforce the law, not only insults the
> people of this State by imputing to them an inability to govern
> themselves or an unwillingness to enforce the law, but is in
> violation of a basic principle of our institutions.

Unimpressed, Cleveland replied that "in this hour of danger and public distress, discussion may well give way to active efforts on the part of all in authority to restore obedience to law and to protect life and property."[112]

Cleveland's intervention in the Pullman strike elaborated on precedents set by Lincoln during the Civil War by extending the concept of executive emergency powers beyond the bounds of war and domestic insurrection. The president's use of federal troops was all the more significant because he possessed neither explicit statutory authority for his actions nor an invitation to act from state and local officials.[113] Nevertheless, the president's conduct received a strong endorsement from the Supreme Court in the case of *In re Debs*, which upheld the arrest of Eugene V. Debs and other strike leaders for conspiring to obstruct the mail.[114] The Court ruled that the president was authorized to act by the Constitution's charge to "take Care that the Laws be faithfully executed" and therefore employ virtually any measure to protect the peace of the United States.[115]

Although conservative Democrats praised Cleveland, laborers and their supporters turned against the president and his party.[116] The rift between Democrats and industrial workers widened in 1896 when the party's national convention nominated Bryan for president and fought the campaign mainly on the issue of "free silver"—that is, Bryan's proposal to inflate the currency by basing it as fully on silver as on gold. Cleveland was surprised and angered by the convention's repudiation of his leadership. He made no effort to hide his satisfaction when the Republicans won the general election on a platform championing the gold standard. Bryan blamed Cleveland's pro-business policies for his defeat, but his farmers-based campaign had failed to offer a viable alternative.

Cleveland's conservatism, especially during his second term, severely damaged his party's political popularity. But so did city dwellers' suspicion of Bryan.[117] Indeed, the Democrat's campaign framed the 1896 contest as a decisive battle between the industrial North and the rural South and West. As Bryan described the contest in his famous Cross of Gold speech:

> You come to us and tell us that the great cities are in favour of the gold standard. I tell you that the great cities rest upon the broad and fertile prairies. Burn down your cities and leave our farms, and your cities will spring up again as if by magic. But destroy our farms and the grass will grow in the streets of every city in the country.[118]

Ohio governor William McKinley, promising that the gold standard and protective tariffs would bring prosperity and a "full dinner pail," won a solid victory against Bryan by capturing the industrial states of the Northeast and Midwest.[119] Bryan's support came principally from farmers in the South and West. Although the popular vote was close (McKinley garnered 51 percent to Bryan's 47 percent), the Republican won the Electoral College decisively, capturing 271 votes to the Democrat's 176. Because the industrial cities were the fastest-growing part of the country, the heavy losses the Democrats suffered among workers and other urban voters in 1896 precipitated a lasting partisan realignment in favor of the Republicans.[120]

At the same time, the 1896 election marked an important change in presidential campaigning that anticipated a more executive-centered form of politics. Abandoned by many powerful Democrats and yet confident of his oratorical prowess, Bryan broke tradition by touring the country, appealing directly for support from the voters. Blessed with a powerful voice and boundless energy, Bryan visited twenty-seven states and gave more than eight hundred speeches. As historian Gil Troy has described Bryan's groundbreaking campaign, "Consuming up to six meals per day, sleeping in snatches, and taking periodic alcohol rubdowns to preserve his strength—though never imbibing—Bryan sang his silvery song. So many people crowded his train that he simply spoke from the rear platform of the last car, and a campaign tradition was born"—the "whistle-stop" campaign through strings of small-town railway stations.[121]

Although McKinley deliberately offered "a safe, traditional, solidly Midwestern contrast to the fire-breathing Bryan," his approach to campaigning was no less innovative.[122] Building on an approach that Harrison had employed on a smaller scale in 1888, McKinley and his master political strategist, Mark Hanna, mobilized the national Republican Party for a "front porch campaign" in which the candidate greeted delegations of voters at his home in Canton. From mid-June through November, McKinley spoke to more than three hundred crowds totaling 750,000 visitors from thirty states. Although McKinley's front porch speeches were long on platitudes, each event was carefully planned. Shortly before a delegation arrived, a telegram would reach Canton with information about the group's members, political attachments, and hometown. By the time the visitors arrived, McKinley was able to greet some of them by name, mention absent family members, and refer to matters of interest in the visitors' communities.[123]

Like Bryan's whistle-stop tour, McKinley's carefully orchestrated front porch campaign foretold the prominence of candidate-centered rather than party-centered campaigns. Some who visited McKinley's home scavenged souvenirs from Canton, including parts of the famous front porch. Others lavished gifts on the Republican candidate, ranging in size from ink stands to bathtubs. "These gifts," Troy notes, "attested to the increased centrality of the candidate and the desire of individuals to cement their bond with him."[124]

The Presidency of William McKinley

The dramatic Republican triumph in the 1896 election brought an astute and skillful politician to the White House. McKinley's presidency often is regarded as an uneventful prelude to the vigorous and energetic administration of his successor, Theodore Roosevelt. But, continuing the forceful leadership shown by Cleveland in his second term, McKinley inaugurated important changes in the executive during his first four years. To be sure, McKinley's tenure was highly traditional in some respects. He, like Benjamin Harrison, was a Republican professional who came to the presidency after a long political apprenticeship in Congress. Consequently, McKinley believed that good government could come only through a strong party organization. He also carried into office a deep and abiding respect for congressional primacy.

Unlike Harrison, McKinley did not permit the presidency to decline on his watch. But even though McKinley's legislative leadership was active—indeed, he was the first post–Civil War president to take the political initiative in Washington without arousing the resentment of his party in Congress[125]—it did not advance the cause of presidential power in enduring ways. His style of influence in Congress resembled that of Jefferson, who had quietly used the congressional caucus to enact the Democratic-Republican program. Jefferson's successors, including McKinley, were unable to match his legislative influence, thereby demonstrating the limits of behind-the-scenes activity as an instrument for sustained leadership.

McKinley did make an enduring mark on the office as commander in chief and as chief diplomat. The McKinley years coincided with an economic boom that prospered in nearly every sector of American society. Partly as a consequence, his tenure as president was dominated not by legislation but by war and foreign policy. In 1898, a conflict arose with Spain over the desire of its colony, Cuba, to gain independence. McKinley favored a peaceful resolution of the violent revolution, but he ultimately yielded to public opinion, which, inflamed by sensationalistic propaganda in the press, strongly favored war. After setting his course in that direction, McKinley exercised a "day by day, and sometimes . . . hour by hour" supervision of the American military effort that laid the foundation for more intense presidential involvement and greater executive control of foreign policy in the future.[126]

The Spanish-American War was so brief, the American victory so complete, and most important, the acquisition of Spanish territory in the Caribbean and Pacific so considerable that no postwar reaction against executive power occurred, as it had after the Civil War. Indeed, Woodrow Wilson admitted in 1900 that his earlier observations about congressional dominance of the presidency were "hopelessly out of date." As Wilson wrote in the preface to the fifteenth printing of his book *Congressional Government*,

> Much of the most important change to be noticed is the result
> of the war with Spain upon the lodgement and exercise of
> power within our federal system: the greatly increased power
> and opportunity for constructive statesmanship given the
> President, by the plunge into international politics and into the
> administration of distant dependencies, which has been that
> war's most striking and momentous consequence.[127]

In the short term, the "splendid little war," as McKinley's secretary of state, John Hay, famously characterized the brief conquest, greatly benefitted the Republican Party, which gained victories in the 1898 and 1900 elections in campaigns that were framed by the governing party's victory over Spain.[128] At the same time, the acquisition of the Philippines and greater influence over Cuba that accompanied victory broadened the international obligations of the United States in ways that subdued partisan differences. Owning territory in the Pacific also increased the interests of the United States in the Far East. American participation in China during the Boxer uprising of 1900 and the McKinley administration's successful insistence on the Open Door trade policy in Asia reinforced the public's view that the country now occupied a new and prominent position in world affairs.[129] Consequently, the Spanish–American War was a landmark in the constitutional development of the executive.[130] As McKinley said to his secretary, "I can no longer be called the President of a party; I am now the President of the whole people."[131]

McKinley's tenure marked an important transformation of the presidency. To be sure, his administration gave only a hint of what was soon to come in the way of vigorous presidential leadership. Committed to a limited role for the national government in domestic affairs, McKinley did not offer or endorse a program to deal with trusts, labor, the civil service, or race relations. But with respect to certain policies, especially trade and foreign affairs, McKinley did seek to influence public opinion about bills and treaties before Congress. Most notably, in speeches and written messages he strongly defended America's right to seize the Philippines from the defeated Spanish.[132] Following in the tradition of the nineteenth-century executive, McKinley said of American policy toward the Philippines that "the whole subject is now with Congress, and Congress is the voice, the conscience, and the judgment of the American people."[133] Yet, the rhetorical effort he devoted to his party's position on the annexation was another sign that the presidency was undergoing important changes in its relationship to Congress and public opinion.

Significantly, Congress did not enact legislation to determine the civil rights and political status of America's first colony. Instead, the legislative branch authorized the executive to create a military government in the Philippines, which enabled McKinley, a wartime president, to capitalize on a foreign crisis and its aftermath to expand the powers of the presidency beyond the limits that constrained his predecessors.[134]

Notes

1. "The Wade-Davis Manifesto," August 5, 1864, in *History of American Presidential Elections, 1789–1968*, 4 vols., eds. Arthur M. Schlesinger Jr. and Fred L. Israel (New York: Chelsea, 1971), 2: 1195–1196.

2. Wilfred E. Binkley, *President and Congress* (New York: Knopf, 1947), 128. For a discussion of the Reconstruction controversy that Johnson inherited, see Albert Castel, *The Presidency of Andrew Johnson* (Lawrence: University Press of Kansas, 1979), 17–20.

3. Quoted in Castel, *Presidency of Andrew Johnson*, 20.

4. Nicole Mellow and Jeffrey Tulis, "Andrew Johnson and the Politics of Failure," in *Formative Acts: Reckoning with Agency in American Politics*, eds. Stephen Skowronek and Matthew Glassman (Philadelphia: University of Pennsylvania Press, 2007).

5. Castel, *Presidency of Andrew Johnson*, 31.

6. LaWanda Cox, *Lincoln and Black Freedom* (Columbia: University of South Carolina Press, 1981), 38.

7. Howard cited in Morton Keller, *Affairs of State: Public Life in Late Nineteenth Century America* (Cambridge: Harvard University Press, 1977), 208–209.

8. Charles Sumner, *The Promises of the Declaration of Independence: Eulogy on Abraham Lincoln* (Boston: Ticknor and Fields, 1865), 56; Roy P. Basler, ed., *The Collected Works of Abraham Lincoln*, 9 vols. (New Brunswick: Rutgers University Press, 1953), 8: 403–404; and Cox, *Lincoln and Black Freedom*, 38.

9. On the struggle between Johnson and Congress over civil rights legislation, see Castel, *Presidency of Andrew Johnson*, 68–76; and Binkley, *President and Congress*, 134–135.

10. Johnson cited in LaWanda Cox and John H. Cox, *Politics, Principle, and Prejudice: 1865–1866* (New York: Free Press, 1963), 153.

11. Quoted in David O. Stewart, *Impeached: The Trial of President Andrew Johnson and the Fight for Lincoln's Legacy* (New York: Simon and Schuster, 2009), 16.

12. Cox and Cox *Politics, Principle, and Prejudice*, 153.

13. Quoted in Jean Edward Smith, *Grant* (New York: Simon and Schuster, 2001), 426.

14. Castel, *Presidency of Andrew Johnson*, 29–30.

15. Mellow and Tulis, "Andrew Johnson and the Politics of Failure;" see also Keith Whittington, *Constitutional Construction: Divided Powers and Constitutional Meaning* (Cambridge: Harvard University Press, 1999), 114–115, 125.

16. Binkley, *President and Congress*, 136–137.

17. Of this bill, Albert Castel has written,

> This was—and still is—the single most dramatic piece of legislation to emerge from Congress. It placed millions of citizens under military rule in peace time, deprived hundreds of thousands of their political rights, and enfranchised a race which the vast majority of Americans at the time considered unqualified to participate in the government process.

Castel, *Presidency of Andrew Johnson*, 108.

18. James D. Richardson, ed., *Messages and Papers of the Presidents*, 20 vols. (Washington, D.C.: Bureau of National Literature, 1911), 5: 3700.

19. Ibid., 5: 3870.

20. Binkley, *President and Congress*, 138.

21. Eric McKitrick, "Party Politics and the Union and Confederate War Efforts," in *The American Party Systems: Stages of Development*, 2nd ed., eds. William Nisbet Chambers and Walter Dean Burnham (New York: Oxford University Press, 1975); A. James Reichley, *The Life of the Parties: A History of American Political Parties* (New York: Free Press, 1992), 129–134.

22. Castel, *Presidency of Andrew Johnson*, 68–70; and Stewart, *Impeached*, 52.

23. Presidency of Andrew Johnson, 70.

24. For a discussion of how the constitutional and political constraints on popular rhetoric during the nineteenth century contributed to Johnson's problems with Congress, see Jeffrey Tulis, *The Rhetorical Presidency* (Princeton: Princeton University Press, 1987), 87–93.

25. David Miller Dewitt, *The Impeachment and Trial of Andrew Johnson* (Madison: State Historical Society of Wisconsin, 1967), 123–124.

26. "Articles of Impeachment against Andrew Johnson," in *The Evolving Presidency: Landmark Documents, 1787–2010*, 4th ed., ed. Michael Nelson (Washington, D.C.: CQ Press, 2012), 108–118.

27. *New York Times*, March 5, 1868, 4.

28. The improper rhetoric charge had strong support in the House, passing by a vote of 87–41. *New York Times*, March 4, 1868, 1.

29. James Madison, Alexander Hamilton and John Jay, *The Federalist Papers*, with introduction and notes by Charles R. Kessler (New York: Signet, 2003), *Federalist*, 71, 430–431.

30. *New York Times*, March 31, 1868, 8.

31. The act actually provided that department heads hold office "for and during the term of the President by whom they were appointed" unless removed by the president with the Senate's approval. Stanton originally had been appointed by President Lincoln.

32. Stewart, *Impeached*, 164.

33. Dewitt, *Impeachment and Trial of Andrew Johnson*, 517–518.

34. Quoted in ibid., 579.

35. Gideon Welles, *Diary of Gideon Welles*, 3 vols. (Boston: Houghton Mifflin, 1911), 3: 560.

36. William M. Goldsmith, ed., *Growth of Presidential Power: A Documented History*, 3 vols. (New York: Chelsea, 1974), 2: 1102.

37. Binkley, *President and Congress*, 147.

38. George F. Hoar, *Autobiography of Seventy Years*, 2 vols. (New York: Scribner's, 1903), 2: 46.

39. Keller, *Affairs of State*, 108.

40. Frank J. Scaturro, *President Grant Reconsidered* (Lanham, Md.: University Press of America, 1998), 60.

41. Ibid.

42. Jean Edward Smith, *Grant* (New York: Simon and Schuster, 2001), 582.

43. Keller, *Affairs of State*, 95.

44. Geoffrey Perret, *Ulysses S. Grant: Soldier and President* (New York: Random House, 1997), 393–400.

45. Smith, *Grant*, 501.

46. Perret, *Ulysses S. Grant*, 409–410; Keller, *Affairs of State*, 96–97.

47. Smith, *Grant*, 512.

48. Ibid., chap. 18. On the ever more difficult challenges Grant faced in Reconstruction, see Nicholas Lemann, *Redemption: The Last Battle of the Civil War* (New York: Farrar, Straus and Giroux, 2006).

49. Perret, *Ulysses S. Grant*, 416.

50. Leonard D. White, *The Republican Era, 1869–1901: A Study in Administrative History* (New York: Macmillan, 1958), 372–376.

51. Perret, *Ulysses S. Grant*, 44. See also Scaturro, *President Grant Reconsidered*, 36–40.

52. President Ulysses S. Grant, "First Statement to Congress on Civil Service Reform," December 5, 1870, in Goldsmith, *Growth of Presidential Power*, 2: 986.

53. Keller, *Affairs of State*, 266–268.

54. James D. Richardson, ed., *Messages and Papers of the Presidents*, 20 vols. (New York: Bureau of National Literature, 1897), 9: 4254–4255; White, *Republican Era*, 281–287.

55. Michael F. Holt, *By One Vote: The Disputed Presidential Election of 1876* (Lawrence: University Press of Kansas, 2008), 10.

56. Binkley, *President and Congress*, 161.

57. The scandals that afflicted the federal government during the Grant administration were, as historian Samuel Eliot Morison has written, merely "the summit of a pyramid of corruption in the Northern states." In New York City, William Marcy ("Boss") Tweed built a Democratic machine, known as Tammany Hall, that stole an estimated $100 million from the city treasury. A similar ring, which operated at the state level under the auspices of the Republican Party (but included some Democrats as well), perpetrated systematic fraud in canal construction, with estimated losses to the state of nearly $1 million. Morison, *The Oxford History of the American People*, 3 vols. (New York: New American Library, 1972), 3: 36.

58. Richard J. Ellis, *The Development of the American Presidency* (New York: Routledge, 2012), 41.

59. David Mayhew, *Electoral Realignments: An American Genre* (New Haven: Yale University Press, 2002), 56.

60. Holt, *By One Vote*, chap. 10.

61. C. Van Woodward, *Reunion and Reaction* (Boston: Little Brown, 1966), 4, 9–10; Holt, *By One Vote*, 246–247. The Republicans' willingness to end Reconstruction reflected their disillusionment with the program's disorder and corruption. When the Republican governor of Mississippi telegraphed for federal troops to protect black voters from white "rifle clubs" during the state election of 1875, the attorney general rejected his request, declaring that

> the whole public are tired out with these annual outbreaks in the South, and the great majority are now ready to condemn any interference on the part of the government. . . . [P]reserve the peace by the forces in your own state, and let the country see that the citizens of Mississippi, who are largely Republican [i.e., the black majority], have the courage to *fight* for their rights and to destroy the bloody ruffians who murder the innocent and unoffending freedmen.

Edwards Pierrepoint, cited in Richard Nelson Current, *Those Terrible Carpetbaggers* (New York: Oxford University Press, 1988), 321–322 (emphasis in original).

62. Keller, *Affairs of State*, 258.

63. Quoted in ibid.

64. Ibid.

65. Rutherford B. Hayes, "Inaugural Address," March 5, 1877, in Richardson, *Messages and Papers of the Presidents*, 1911 ed., 6: 4396; Hayes's Letter of Acceptance (July 8, 1876), in White, *Republican Era*, 287.

66. Ellis, *The Development of the American Presidency*, 162.

67. Binkley, *President and Congress*, 155.

68. Charles Richard Williams, ed., *Diary and Letters of Rutherford B. Hayes*, 5 vols. (Columbus: Ohio State Archeological and Historical Society, 1924), 3: 430 (April 22, 1877).

69. Ibid., 3: 454 (December 12, 1877).

70. Ari Hoogenboom, *Outlawing the Spoils* (Urbana: University of Illinois Press, 1961), 156.

71. Binkley, *President and Congress*, 157.

72. President Rutherford B. Hayes, "Letter to General E. A. Merritt Defining Criteria for Appointments to the New York Customhouse," February 4, 1879, in Goldsmith, *Growth of Presidential Power*, 2: 1112.

73. Ibid., 2: 1113.

74. Williams, *Diary and Letters of Rutherford B. Hayes*, 3: 612–613 (July 14, 1880).

75. The Stalwarts labeled Blaine's followers "Half-breeds," implying that they were deficient in Republican loyalty. In reality, the partisanship of the Blaine wing, although it paid lip service to civil service reform, was just as strong as that of the Stalwarts.

76. John A. Garraty, *The New Commonwealth, 1877–1890* (New York: Harper and Row, 1968), 268–273.

77. Binkley, *President and Congress*, 158–159, 172; Theodore Clarke Smith, *The Life and Letters of James Abram Garfield*, 2 vols. (New Haven: Yale University Press, 1925), 2: 1103–1104.

78. Quoted in Smith, *Life and Letters*, 2: 1109.

79. Quoted in Thomas C. Reeves, *Gentleman Boss: The Life of Chester Alan Arthur* (New York: Knopf, 1975), 227.

80. Smith, *Life and Letters*, 2: 1127.

81. Garraty, *New Commonwealth*, 273; White, *Republican Era*, 34–35; Binkley, *President and Congress*, 159–160.

82. Kenneth D. Ackerman, *Dark Horse: The Surprising Election and Political Murder of President James A. Garfield* (New York: Carroll and Graf, 2003), 348–380.

83. Williams, *Diary and Letters of Rutherford B. Hayes*, 4: 23.

84. Garraty, *New Commonwealth*, 276.

85. Ackerman, *Dark Horse*, 435.

86. White, *Republican Era*, 346.

87. Ibid., 393; see also 301–302.

88. Keller, *Affairs of State*, 556–558.

89. Horace Samuel Merrill, *Bourbon Democracy of the Middle West, 1865–1896* (Baton Rouge: Louisiana State University Press, 1953), vii–viii. For a view of Cleveland that disputes the characterization of him as a Bourbon Democrat, see Richard E. Welch Jr., *The Presidencies of Grover Cleveland* (Lawrence: University Press of Kansas, 1988).

90. Matthew Crenson and Benjamin Ginsberg, *Presidential Power: Unchecked and Unbalanced* (New York: Norton, 2007).

91. Robert C. Kennedy, "A Memorialized Dream," June 25, 2001, https://archive .nytimes.com/www.nytimes.com/learning/general/onthisday/harp/0625.html. The Confederate flags remained in captivity until the twentieth century.

92. Eric Foner, "Confederate Statues and Our History," *New York Times*, August 20, 2017, https://www.nytimes.com/2017/08/20/opinion/confederate-statues-american-history.html.

93. Garraty, *New Commonwealth*, 287; Keller, *Affairs of State*, 546.

94. President Grover Cleveland, "Message to the Senate on the President's Power of Removal and Suspension," March 1, 1886, in Goldsmith, *Growth of Presidential Power*, 2: 1121.

95. Grover Cleveland, *Presidential Problems* (New York: Century, 1904), 76.

96. White, *Republican Era*, 38.

97. Ibid., 66.

98. Daniel Klinghard, *The Nationalization of American Political Parties, 1880–1896* (New York: Cambridge University Press, 2010), 167. See also Daniel Galvin, "Presidents as Agents of Change," *Presidential Studies Quarterly*, 44 (March 2014): 95–119.

99. Garraty, *New Commonwealth*, 295.

100. Woodrow Wilson, *Congressional Government* (Boston: Houghton Mifflin, 1885; Meridian Books, 1956), 31.

101. Charles W. Calhoun, *Minority Victory: Gilded Age Politics and the Front Porch Campaign of 1888* (Lawrence: University Press of Kansas, 2008), 132–133.

102. John Sherman, *Recollections of Forty Years in the House, Senate and Cabinet* (Chicago: Werner Company, 1895), 2: 1032.

103. Garraty, *New Commonwealth*, 305.

104. Keller, *Affairs of State*, 302–303.

105. James Bryce, *The American Commonwealth*, 2 vols. (London: Macmillan, 1891), 1: 115.

106. Keller, *Affairs of State*, 306.

107. Binkley, *President and Congress*, 182.

108. Calhoun, *Minority Victory*, 185.

109. Lincoln cited in Reichley, *Life of the Parties*, 128.

110. Ibid., 155.

111. R. Hal Williams, *Realigning America: McKinley, Bryan, and the Remarkable Election of 1896* (Lawrence: University Press of Kansas, 2010), 13.

112. Gov. John P. Altgeld, "Telegram to President Grover Cleveland on the Use of Federal Troops in Illinois," July 5, 1894; and President Grover Cleveland, "Telegram to Governor John P. Altgeld on the Use of Federal Troops in Illinois," July 6, 1894, in Goldsmith, *Growth of Presidential Powers*, 2: 1155 and 2: 1157, respectively.

113. Scott C. James, "The Evolution of the Presidency: Between the Promise and the Fear," in *The Executive Branch*, eds. Joel D. Aberbach and Mark Peterson (New York: Oxford University Press, 2005), 16–17.

114. *In re Debs*, 158 U.S. 564 (1895).

115. Edward S. Corwin, *The President: Office and Powers, 1787–1957*, 4th ed. (New York: New York University Press, 1957), 134.

116. J. Rogers Hollingsworth, *The Whirligig of Politics: The Democracy of Cleveland and Bryan* (Chicago: University of Chicago Press, 1963), 24–25.

117. Welch, *Presidencies of Grover Cleveland*, 211–212.

118. William Jennings Bryan, Speech to the 1896 Populist Party Convention, http://historymatters.gmu.edu/d/d5354/.

119. Richard Jensen, *The Winning of the Midwest: A Social Analysis of Midwestern Politics, 1880–1896* (New York: Oxford University Press, 1971), 287.

120. Garraty, *New Commonwealth*, 306.

121. Gil Troy, *See How They Ran: The Changing Role of the Presidential Candidate*, rev. and exp. ed. (Cambridge: Harvard University Press, 1996), 104.

122. Ibid., 105–106.

123. Crenson and Ginsberg, *Presidential Power*.

124. Troy, *See How They Ran*, 106.

125. Binkley, *President and Congress*, 189.

126. Lewis L. Gould, *The Presidency of William McKinley* (Lawrence: University Press of Kansas, 1980), 93.

127. Wilson, *Congressional Government*, 22–23.

128. Robert P. Saldin, *War, the American State, and Politics since 1898* (New York: Cambridge University Press, 2011), chap. 2.

129. The Open Door policy was announced in September 1899 by Secretary of State John Hay. It asked the major powers that had imperialistic designs on Asia—notably, France, Germany, Great Britain, Italy, Japan, and Russia—to agree to support freedom of trade in the region. Great Britain was the only nation to accept Hay's proposals fully; the others agreed but with reservations. Hay, however, chose to interpret their replies as acceptances and announced the Open Door policy to the world.

130. Binkley, *President and Congress*, 191.

131. Quoted in Charles S. Olcott, *William McKinley*, 2 vols. (Boston: Houghton Mifflin, 1916), 2: 296.

132. Mel Laracey, *Presidents and the People: The Partisan Story of Going Public* (College Station: Texas A&M Press, 2002), 134–138.

133. William McKinley speech in Chariton, Iowa, October 13, 1898, McKinley Papers, Library of Congress, Washington, D.C.; see also Tulis, *Rhetorical Presidency*, 87.

134. Lewis L. Gould, *The Modern American Presidency* (Lawrence: University Press of Kansas, 2003), 13.

Progressive Politics and Executive Power

The Presidencies of Theodore Roosevelt, William Howard Taft, and Woodrow Wilson

During the last three decades of the nineteenth century, major changes in American society placed greater burdens on the national government, particularly on the presidency. The population of the United States doubled between 1870 and 1900. Urbanization and immigration increased at extraordinary rates. These changes were accompanied by a shift in business activity from local, small-scale manufacturing and commerce to large-scale factory production and mammoth national corporations. The technological breakthroughs and the frenzied search for new markets and new sources of capital that were associated with rapid industrialization caused unprecedented economic growth. From 1863 to 1899 the index of manufacturing production rose by more than 700 percent. But dynamic growth also generated a wide range of problems that seriously challenged the capacity of the American political system to respond.

For one thing, social and political values were sacrificed in the unchecked pursuit of economic progress and industrial development. The greater concentration of wealth at the turn of the century yielded giant "trusts" that according to reformers constituted uncontrolled and irresponsible bastions of power. These combinations aroused fears that growing corporate influence would jeopardize equality of opportunity for individuals to climb the economic ladder. Moreover, many people believed that the great business interests had captured and corrupted the people and processes of government for their own profit.

The first wave of protest against the financial exploitation and political corruption that industrial growth unleashed was the agrarian Populist revolt, which culminated in William Jennings Bryan's failed campaign for the presidency in 1896. The Progressive era took shape as populism collapsed as a political movement. Yet it was a period of urban and middle-class protest against many of the same forces of expanding industrialization and unrestrained finance capitalism that had vexed the Populists.

Because progressivism represented the fastest-growing segments of the population, it had a major influence on the nation. As Richard Hofstadter noted, the Progressive movement "enlarged and redirected" agrarian discontent, bringing about industrial reforms and changes in government institutions that "affected in a striking way . . . the whole tone of American political life."[1]

One effect of the progressive transformation was a modified understanding of the responsibilities of the national government. American society had long been committed to individualism and limited government. But as Elihu Root, who served in Theodore Roosevelt's cabinet, argued in an address to the New York Bar Association in 1912:

> The relations between the employer and employed, between the owners of aggregated capital and the units of organized labor, between the small producer, the small trader, the consumer, and the great transporting and manufacturing and distributing agencies, all present new questions for the solution of which the old reliance upon the free action of individual wills appears quite inadequate. And in many directions the intervention of that organized control which we call government seems necessary to produce the same result of justice and right conduct which obtained through the attrition of individuals before the conditions arose.[2]

The Progressive movement helped foster important changes in the presidency. Part of this involved a national cultural shift. The success of individual corporate leaders such as John D. Rockefeller, Andrew Carnegie, and Cornelius Vanderbilt seemed to demonstrate to many that all great accomplishments begin with executive power and initiative. The developing "scientific management" school of corporate leadership argued that success was maintained through such leadership as well. Activist governors, including Robert La Follette of Wisconsin and Hiram Johnson of California, were elevating the role of chief executive at the state level.[3]

Although the presidency had developed significantly during the eighteenth and nineteenth centuries in the hands of strong leaders such as George Washington, Thomas Jefferson, Andrew Jackson, and Abraham Lincoln, most of the roles and powers of the president remained tightly restricted until the twentieth century. Congressional government was the prevailing theme of late nineteenth-century politics in America. The presidencies of Grover Cleveland and William McKinley suggested that a more forceful style of presidential leadership might be emerging, but they did not alter fundamentally the long-standing pattern of legislative dominance.

More than anyone else, Theodore Roosevelt changed that pattern. Dedicated to the progressive concept of active, executive-centered government, he advocated and practiced a vigorous form of leadership that broadly extended the reach of presidential influence. In his aggressive pursuit of an activist policy agenda and, especially, in his relentless courting of public opinion, TR (the first president to be known by his initials) recast the presidency in both foreign and domestic affairs, charting the path for future presidents, such as Woodrow Wilson and TR's distant cousin, Franklin D. Roosevelt, to follow.

Theodore Roosevelt and the Expansion of Executive Power

On September 6, 1901, President McKinley was shot by an anarchist while attending the Pan-American Exposition in Buffalo, New York. When McKinley died on September 14, Vice President Roosevelt became president. Soon after, he announced that he would continue McKinley's policies and keep his cabinet, disregarding the warning of friends that by doing so he would seem but a "pale copy" of the late president. "If a man is fit to be President," TR wrote in his autobiography, "he will speedily so impress himself in the office that the policies pursued will be his anyhow, and he will not have to bother as to whether he is changing them or not."[4]

The prospect of Roosevelt impressing himself on the executive office greatly troubled the party politicians who dominated national politics at the beginning of the twentieth century. The conservative leaders of the Republican Party feared that the young president (at forty-two he remains the youngest person ever to assume the office) was not to be trusted. Throughout his political career, including his tenure as governor of New York, Roosevelt had been known as a progressive and impetuous leader who lived uneasily with his party's patronage practices and pro-business policies. During Roosevelt's two terms as governor, he was so troublesome to the state's party regulars that they took pains to remove him from their midst by securing his nomination for vice president in 1900.

"Anything can happen now that that damn cowboy is in the White House," complained Mark Hanna, the chair of the Republican National Committee, when his friend McKinley died. Conservatives now wished that they had heeded the Republican chair who, when presented with the suggestion that Roosevelt be chosen as McKinley's running mate, complained, "Don't you realize that there's only one life between that madman and the White House?"[5]

Roosevelt's plainspoken and unconventional style aside, he was not the "madman" that Hanna feared. TR was no enemy to business or party interests. Like most progressive reformers, he accepted the new industrial order, wanting only to curb its worst excesses through government regulation. Without moderate reform, Roosevelt believed, the connection between citizens and their leaders that was the essence of republican government would be dangerously attenuated. "Sweeping attacks upon all property, upon all men of means, without regard to whether they do well or ill, would sound the death knell of the Republic," he wrote, "and such attacks become inevitable if decent citizens permit rich men whose lives are corrupt and evil to domineer in swollen pride, unchecked and unhindered, over the destinies of the country."[6]

Theodore Roosevelt's Concept of Presidential Power

In both foreign and domestic affairs, Samuel and Dorothy Rosenman have written, "Roosevelt extended executive authority to the furthest limit permitted in peacetime by the Constitution—if not further."[7] Believing that the traditional restraints on presidential power had subjected the American political system to capture by "special interests," Roosevelt proclaimed that the president is "a steward of the people bound actively and affirmatively to do all he could for the people, and not content himself with the negative merit of keeping his talents undamaged in a napkin."[8]

Roosevelt's confidence that the president possessed a special mandate from the people made him a conscious disciple of Andrew Jackson. Unlike Jackson, however, Roosevelt wanted to join popular leadership to a greater sense of national purpose that entailed an unprecedented expansion of the government's responsibility to secure the nation's social and economic welfare. As he explained many years later,

> [M]y belief was that it was not only his [the president's] right but his duty to do anything that the needs of the nation demanded unless action was forbidden by the Constitution or by the laws. Under this interpretation of executive power I did and caused to be done many things not previously done by the President and the heads of the departments. I did not usurp power, but I did greatly broaden the use of executive power. In other words,

I acted for the public welfare, I acted for the common well-being of all our people, wherever and in whatever manner was necessary, unless prevented by direct constitutional or legislative provision.[9]

In important respects, Roosevelt's exposition of executive power drew on the defense of a broad authority for the president that Alexander Hamilton articulated in 1793 under the pen name "Pacificus." "The general doctrine of our Constitution," Hamilton argued, "is that the executive power of the nation is vested in the President; subject only to the exceptions and qualifications which are expressed in the instrument."[10] Jackson and Lincoln had taken an expansive view of the president's authority in moments of national crisis. Roosevelt was the first chief executive to embrace the Hamiltonian position as the proper recipe for the conduct of government in ordinary times.

TR's acceptance of Hamiltonian principles certainly was not complete. Hamilton supported an energetic executive because he thought that it would curb, not abet, popular influence. In contrast, Roosevelt expressed and embodied the Progressives' aspiration to establish the president as an agent of social and economic reform. He looked with favor on the statesmanship of Lincoln, whose uncompromising defense of the Union served the "high purpose" of advancing equality of opportunity. "Men who understand and practice the deep underlying philosophy of the Lincoln school of American political thought," wrote TR, "are necessarily Hamiltonian in their belief in a strong and efficient National Government and Jeffersonian in their belief in the people as the ultimate authority, and in the welfare of the people as the end of government."[11]

Of course, Lincoln's defense of the Union and audacious use of executive power occurred during the stress of a domestic rebellion. His understanding of the national government's powers and of executive prerogative in less dire circumstances was far more circumscribed than Roosevelt's. Moreover, although Roosevelt's belief in executive dominion in ordinary times paved the way for the modern presidency, the program he envisioned did not include a remedy for the so-called Jim Crow laws, enacted in southern states during the 1890s, to subject African Americans to a virulent form of segregation that the Supreme Court sanctified as "separate but equal."[12]

From Theory to Practice: The Beginning of the Rhetorical Presidency

Roosevelt's determination to use the presidency to serve the public interest, as he understood it, brought about a number of significant changes

Theodore Roosevelt, far left on stand, ushered in the "rhetorical presidency"—the use of popular rhetoric as a principal technique of presidential leadership.

in the conduct of the executive office. Arguably, the most important of these changes was to advance the president's role as the leader of public opinion. Roosevelt ushered in the "rhetorical presidency"—that is, the use of popular rhetoric as a principal technique of presidential leadership.[13] TR was an energetic and engaging public speaker and is said to have been the first to describe the presidency as a "bully pulpit."[14]

The rise of the rhetorical presidency signified a dramatic transformation of the founding theory and early history of the presidency. The Framers of the Constitution wanted to proscribe popular presidential leadership. The only two mentions of public presidential communications in the Constitution refer to communications with Congress: vetoing bills "with his Objections" and "giv[ing] to the Congress information of the State of the Union."[15] As Andrew Johnson's ill-fated "Swing around the Circle" confirmed, during the nineteenth century, efforts by the president to rouse the public with oratory to support his leadership or policies were considered illegitimate, a form of demagogy that was beneath the dignity of the office. Strong democratic leaders of the nineteenth century, such as Jefferson, Jackson, and Lincoln, sought to establish closer ties with the people, but they worked through their party organizations and the press to do so.

William McKinley frequently spoke to public audiences on policy matters, but especially in domestic affairs, he took "only small, hesitant steps against the boundaries of the nineteenth century norms and expectations" that discouraged direct popular leadership.[16] Roosevelt's "stewardship" theory of the executive required the president to forge more personal ties with the public. Accordingly, at times TR appealed directly to the people to bring pressure to bear on members of Congress who were reluctant to support his policies.

Much of Roosevelt's legislative program was designed, as TR put it, to "subordinate the big corporation to the public welfare," less by using anti-trust litigation to break up such organizations than by harnessing government regulation to rein in their efforts to suppress competition.[17] But the Republican Party in Congress was led by conservatives—notably Nelson Aldrich of Rhode Island and Eugene Hale of Maine in the Senate and Speaker Joseph Cannon of Illinois in the House—who distrusted anything that smacked of progressivism. Roosevelt sided with the "Old Guard" (they also were called the "stand patters") in their support of the gold standard and recognition of the need, after the Spanish–American War, for a strong American presence in world affairs. Domestic policy was different. As TR later wrote of his relationship with the Republican Old Guard, "Gradually I was forced to abandon the effort to persuade them to come my way, and then I achieved results only by appealing over the heads of the Senate and House leaders to the people, who were the masters of both of us."[18]

Perhaps the most important product of Roosevelt's popular appeals was the Hepburn Act of 1906. The act enhanced the power of the Interstate Commerce Commission (ICC) to regulate railroad shipping rates and enforce its regulations.[19] Previous laws had failed to prevent the largest corporations from receiving better and cheaper rail service than the smaller shippers.[20] Faced with enormous fixed costs—such as the interest they paid on huge bonded debts and the depreciation on their large and expensive equipment—the railroads were able to meet their overhead only by acceding to the demands for price breaks by massive corporations such as the Standard Oil Company, Armour and Company, and the American Sugar Refining Company.

Determined to remedy these conditions, Roosevelt proposed that Congress strengthen the ICC's regulatory power. In his annual message to Congress in December 1904, Roosevelt urged legislators to draft a law that would forbid railroads from providing large shippers with discriminatory rebates and empower the ICC to impose ceilings on railroad rates "to keep the highways of commerce open to all on equal terms."[21]

The president's proposal was received favorably by the House of Representatives, which quickly passed railroad rate legislation in early 1905. But the proposal ran into trouble in the upper house, where the conservative Senate Commerce Committee conducted extensive public hearings, mostly for the purpose of receiving opposing testimony from railroad executives. The committee managed to consume enough time to prevent the Senate from considering the bill before the summer recess.

The railroads' strategy was shrewd. "The House was the only one of the two [congressional] bodies elected directly by the people," one contemporary observer wrote, "and was therefore regarded contemptuously by the railroads and conservatives generally as reflecting the mob; while the Senate, being elected by state legislators, was regarded as a safe city of refuge."[22] Senators were not elected by the people until the Seventeenth Amendment was enacted in 1913.

But Roosevelt was shrewder still. As the Senate hearings proceeded, the president left Washington for a long vacation in the West. Speculation arose that he had given up on rate regulation.[23] In truth, Roosevelt's swing through the Midwest and Southwest in April and May of 1905 turned out to be a campaign trip for the Hepburn bill.

The president fired his first rhetorical blast in Chicago where, speaking before the Iroquois Republican Club on May 10, he called on the federal government to "take an increasing control over corporations." The first step, Roosevelt argued, "should be the adoption of a law conferring upon one executive body the power of increased supervision and regulation of the great corporations engaged primarily in interstate commerce of the railroads." The ICC should have "ironclad" powers to set rates, which could be suspended by the courts only if they proved to be confiscatory.[24] This speech and similar addresses in Dallas, San Antonio, and Denver received extensive and favorable coverage in the press.

Roosevelt's campaign resumed with a speaking tour of the Southwest in the early fall of 1905. The pressure of public opinion eventually overcame Senate resistance to the Hepburn Act. Secretary of War William Howard Taft told his brother that the president of the Rock Island line had admitted to him that senators he had counted on for "allegiance," although privately still opposed to the act, were yielding because the president had so "roused the people that it was impossible for the Senate to stand against the popular demand."[25] After all, the state legislatures that elected the Senate were themselves elected by the people.

When Congress reconvened in 1906, the House once again passed the railroad law quickly, in early February. This time, on May 18 the Senate also passed Roosevelt's bill. Only three senators voted against it.

Theodore Roosevelt and the Press

Roosevelt's remarkable victory in the battle for the Hepburn Act was helped considerably by the press. He was the first president to recognize fully the press's value as a medium to communicate with the people and the first to understand that journalistic support had to be pursued actively and continually. It was TR's good fortune that his presidency coincided with the proliferation of mass-circulation newspapers and popular magazines. At the beginning of the twentieth century, "cheap and rapid manufacture made possible and even necessary a mass market beyond the confines of one faction, party, or following." The age of the "party organ" style of journalism was over.[26]

One group of journalists, including Ida Tarbell, Ray Stannard Baker, Lincoln Steffens, and William Allen White, occupied an especially important place in early twentieth-century politics. They wrote mainly for new and low-priced national magazines such as *McClure's*, a fifteen-cent monthly whose influence on public opinion was almost the equal of Roosevelt's.[27] The president's term for these writers—"muckrakers"—evoked their relentless efforts to expose corruption in the relationship between government and business. According to a writer in the August 1905 issue of the *Atlantic Monthly*,

> They expose in countless pages the sordid and depressing rottenness of our politics; the hopeless apathy of our good citizens; the remorseless corruption of our great financiers and business men, who are bribing our legislatures, swindling the public with fraudulent stock schemes, adulterating our food, speculating with trust funds, combining in great monopolies to oppress and destroy small competitors and raise prices.[28]

Roosevelt's grasp of the political potential of the new media was especially apparent in his use of the mass-circulation magazines. Despite his concern that some magazine journalists were mere scandal mongers who, by fixing their gaze exclusively on the "vile and debasing," neglected the achievements of society's constructive elements, he took advantage of the more serious investigative journalists' success at bringing to light many of the evils he wanted to attack. Partly by inspiring intimates in the press to write articles, and partly through the force of his own personality and ideas, TR "kept the pages of the popular magazines glowing with support" for his crusades.[29]

Roosevelt also made good use of the bully pulpit and press in the struggle over the Pure Food and Drug Act, which made it unlawful to manufacture adulterated or mislabeled food and drugs, and the Meat Inspection Act, a response to the gruesome conditions of the meat-packing houses depicted in Upton Sinclair's sensational novel *The Jungle*. Like the Hepburn Act, these laws were enacted in 1906. TR's triumph in the matters of rate regulation, food and drug marketing, and meat inspection signaled a change in the executive. The president's most important political relationship soon would be with the people rather than with his party or Congress. But Roosevelt also believed that to maintain the constitutional system of government, a balance must exist between presidential initiative and congressional deliberation. Accordingly, even as he insisted that the modern president assume a more prominent place in public affairs than his nineteenth-century predecessors, TR worked assiduously to win support in Congress by cooperating with Republican leaders in the Senate and the House whenever possible.

In fighting for the Hepburn Act, for example, Roosevelt directed his energies not only to the podium but also, more craftily, to the halls of Congress. He feigned interest in a bill to reduce tariffs and then traded his abandonment of that controversial proposal for congressional support of his more important objective, railroad regulation. In late November 1904 the president sent Speaker Cannon, "that arch priest of protection," a draft of a special message to Congress urging tariff revision. Shortly thereafter, in a "concession" to Cannon, Roosevelt delivered his annual message, in which nothing was said of the tariff. As TR wrote to a friend, "On the interstate commerce business, which I regard as a principle, I shall fight. On the tariff, which I regard as a matter of expediency, I shall endeavor to get the best results I can, but I shall not break with my party."[30]

At the other end of Pennsylvania Avenue, Cannon, who was already on record against regulating the railroads, gave the Hepburn Act a clear track. When conservatives rose to fight the bill, Roosevelt revived the tariff issue until they retreated. Old Guard Republicans had always regarded high tariffs as the linchpin of their party's program of industrial development. Ultimately, therefore, they acquiesced to TR's desire for railroad regulation to preserve what they regarded as vital: the hallowed protection of American industry from foreign competition.

Thus in leading Congress, Roosevelt artfully deployed the resources of person and office. He succeeded in part because of his remarkable political gifts and his willingness to compromise to attain his major objectives. But the president's commitment to constitutional government, especially his appreciation of Congress, also was significant. Roosevelt ended his speaking tours before Congress took up the Hepburn bill. He did not speak directly to the people on the eve of crucial votes, nor did he attack members of Congress during the debate. As historian John Morton Blum has written, "Roosevelt's impressive ability to work within the structure of government, like his facility in managing the party, depended less on his arresting manner than on his appreciation of the institutions that shaped American political life."[31]

Roosevelt and Policy Leadership

Roosevelt's ability to get a considerable part of his program enacted in the absence of a national crisis and in spite of the tepid support—and sometimes the outright resistance—of his party indicated that a new era of presidential leadership had arrived. From now on, government action would be much more likely to bear the president's personal stamp than in the past.

Roosevelt called his program the "Square Deal." Its theme was that the proper function of government is to maintain a "just balance" between management and labor, between producer and consumer, and between extremists on both sides of the political divide.[32] What made TR's proclamation of the Square Deal important in the development of the modern presidency was that it invoked principles of fairness as he, rather than his party or Congress, understood them. Several of his successors would define their administrations in similar terms: Woodrow Wilson's New Freedom, Franklin D. Roosevelt's New Deal, Harry S. Truman's Fair Deal, John F. Kennedy's New Frontier, and Lyndon B. Johnson's Great Society. The effort, nonexistent in the nineteenth century but routine after Roosevelt, to attach a catchy phrase to the president's programmatic philosophy was symptomatic of a new style of leadership in which the executive took the lead in formulating public policy.[33]

Significantly, Roosevelt first used the phrase "Square Deal" during the 1904 presidential campaign to describe his vigorous intervention two years before in a nationwide coal strike. Rather than follow the example of Grover Cleveland, who sent troops to break up the Pullman strike of 1894, Roosevelt called representatives of the coal industry and the miners to the White House and asked both sides to agree, in patriotic regard for the health and welfare of the nation, to accept binding arbitration. John Mitchell, the head of the United Mine Workers, appreciated the recognition that Roosevelt conferred on the union by calling the conference and pledged to cooperate fully with the president.

When coal industry leaders balked at Roosevelt's proposal, even lecturing the president about the folly of "negotiating with the fomenters of anarchy," TR prepared to take more drastic action. If he could not persuade management to accept arbitration voluntarily, he would appoint a settlement board without their consent and arrange for the governor of Pennsylvania to request federal assistance to keep the peace. Roosevelt also intended to have federal troops "seize the mines and run them as a receiver for the government."

By previous constitutional interpretation, as recently as the *Debs* decision in 1894, the president clearly had the authority to send soldiers into a state to ensure that the national government could exercise its authorized powers, such as delivering the mail. But nowhere did the Constitution even hint at, much less specify, the president's right to seize and operate private property. As it happened, such an action did not prove necessary: an agreement was reached to end the strike in October 1902, and a five-member commission, appointed by the president, arbitrated the points at issue between the miners and the coal industry. Yet Roosevelt's willingness to act exemplified his style as the "steward of the people."[34] Dedicated to expanding the national government to guarantee a "just balance" between rival claimants in society, Roosevelt became the first president in history to recognize the rights of labor in an industrial dispute.[35] As historian George W. Mowry concluded, "By both his actions and threats Roosevelt had moved the government away from its traditional position of isolation from such economic struggles. The government, by precedent if not by law, had become a third force and partner in major labor disputes."[36]

Roosevelt also expanded the executive's responsibility to manage the nation's natural resources. Although the practice of setting aside nationally owned timberlands began with Benjamin Harrison and was continued by Grover Cleveland, Roosevelt was the first president to adopt a comprehensive conservation program. Hosting the first national conference on conservation, TR lamented the irresponsibility with which Americans had abused the nation's water, forests, and other natural resources. The time had come, he said, to formulate a national philosophy of conservation: "It is the chief material question that confronts us, second only . . . to the great moral questions."[37] Credit for this policy belongs in part to Roosevelt's young Forest Service director, Gifford Pinchot, who inspired the president to make conservation a leading cause of his administration. TR did so with his usual energy. By appealing to public opinion and by setting aside 43 million acres of national forest from excessive commercial exploitation, Roosevelt made conservation a national movement.[38]

By 1908, however, Congress had blocked further progress in the conservation program. Farmers, grazers, and water power interests in the

West, which was home to most woodlands, won legislation to transfer from the president to Congress the authority to establish national forests in several western states. Tensions reached a breaking point when Roosevelt and Pinchot prepared a "midnight forests" proclamation to protect 16 million acres just before the bill went into effect.

Roosevelt's proclamation not only drove a wedge between the executive and legislative branches but also failed to resolve the dispute about the appropriate federal role in managing natural resources. Congress exacted a measure of revenge against the president by killing two important conservation commissions that Roosevelt created in 1908, the National Country Life Commission and the Inland Waterways Commission. Nevertheless, on leaving office TR could claim, with considerable justification, that the movement to protect the nation's natural resources was one of his administration's most important accomplishments.[39]

Roosevelt's use of executive power in the cause of conservation revealed his understanding that the stewardship theory of the presidency empowered him to act without explicit authorization from Congress, or even in the face of legislative opposition, when he deemed such action to be in the public interest. Although Lincoln's executive orders during the Civil War offer the most powerful historical examples of presidential prerogative, TR was the first president to make extensive use of such orders to advance his domestic policy. He issued 1,091 orders during his two terms, rivaling the 1,259 issued by all presidents in the previous 111 years.[40] These orders to executive departments and agencies were issued under the president's legal and constitutional authority, broadly interpreted by Roosevelt himself.

Roosevelt's concept of the president as the "steward of public welfare" resonated widely amid the unsettled conditions of the Progressive era. Yet progressive notions of democracy excluded African Americans and other people of color from the national community. Indeed, as Thomas Dyer has written, Roosevelt's vision of an energetic stewardship presidency "coincided with one of the most violent periods of anti-black activity in American history as lynchings reached an all-time high, southern legislatures completed the legalized exclusion of blacks from meaningful participation in American life, and racial pogroms occurred with alarming frequency."[41] Disappointed by the chaos that followed Reconstruction's failure, Roosevelt made no concerted effort to challenge Jim Crow.

Roosevelt and his political allies could not easily ignore the demand of reformers that Progressivism live up to its promise to provide equal opportunity for the "whole people."[42] He ultimately sought to navigate a middle path between the purveyors of white supremacy and early civil rights activists such as W.E.B. Du Bois, who demonstrated that twentieth-century America's leading injustice was "the problem of the color line."[43] On the one hand, Roosevelt called for "full recognition of the fundamental fact that all men should stand on an equal footing, as regards civic privileges." On the other, he insisted that a commitment to equal rights "in no way interferes with recognition of the further fact that all reflecting men of both races are united in feeling that race purity must be maintained."[44]

Roosevelt's limited conception of racial justice ultimately translated into a call for gradual progress—a plea for forbearance that his successors would echo until the 1960s. TR's middle way was on display on October 16, 1901, when he invited Booker T. Washington, the leader of the Tuskegee Institute who shared the president's measured view of racial progress, to dine with the First Family at the White House—the first time that an African American "broke bread" in the executive mansion. The storm of protest this social courtesy unleashed in the South led to a national controversy over race relations that dramatized the unremitting attention and symbolic importance attached to the modern presidency as well as the intractable prejudice that discouraged the use of executive power to challenge southern conventions.

Roosevelt's actions in the Brownsville, Texas, incident in August 1906 made clear that racial injustice was a national problem. After violence erupted between African American soldiers and local white residents, the president summarily dismissed black troops stationed at nearby Fort Brown who were accused of creating a midnight disturbance that resulted in the murder of a bartender and the shooting of a policeman. He did so even though a local grand jury could not find enough evidence to return an indictment in the episode. Intent on proving that he was as determined to punish black lawlessness as he was to take on white supremacists, Roosevelt ordered the army's inspector general to investigate the matter. The inspector general's report, based on flimsy circumstantial evidence, persuaded the president that dismissing the troops "without honor" was justified. Just as Roosevelt's breaking bread with Washington won acclaim among black leaders and journalists, so did his peremptory actions in Brownsville lead to widespread condemnation from these leaders and the nation's prominent black newspapers. More enduringly, the controversy encouraged the Niagara Movement—the precursor to the National Association for the Advancement of Colored People (NAACP)—led by Du Bois and William Monroe Trotter, which rejected the gradualism that Roosevelt and Washington prescribed.[45]

Roosevelt and Civil Service Reform

Roosevelt sought not only to expand presidential power but also to professionalize administration and thereby prepare the executive branch for its growing responsibilities. He believed that only steady, nonpartisan administration, not the dictates of the courts or the give-and-take of partisan and sectional politics in Congress, could properly direct the development of the United States as an industrial society.[46]

In Roosevelt's view, an orderly system of administrative control required a career civil service. To this end, the president prevailed on Congress early in his tenure to increase the Civil Service Commission's budget so that it could effectively supervise the hiring of federal employees.[47] He also extended the coverage of the merit system for hiring, promotion, and tenure almost to the limit allowed by the Pendleton Act. By the time TR left office, about 60 percent of the civil service was included in the merit system, even as the federal workforce expanded from 275,000 in 1901 to 365,000 in 1909.

Most important, the Roosevelt administration marked the dividing line between the traditional Jacksonian commitment to party patronage and the modern recognition that largely nonpolitical administration is a necessary tool of governance. Americans have never carried the idea that the civil service should be outside politics to the same lengths as the British. But by the end of the Roosevelt presidency, merit had begun to supplant spoils. Presidential leadership, previously dependent on patronage-seeking state and local party machines, now required careful attention to competent administrative management, sometimes to foster economy and efficiency and sometimes to bolster the power of the increasingly active federal government. In the absence of a large, professional White House staff, Roosevelt showed that a president committed to policy innovation could accomplish a great deal by mobilizing the energies of talented civil servants.[48]

The President as World Leader

Roosevelt's innovative and pathbreaking activism in domestic affairs, important as it was, pales by comparison with his conduct of foreign policy. In domestic matters TR led boldly but mostly in the interest of moderate reform. In foreign affairs, he believed that new conditions dictated a more decisive break with the past, without interference from Congress. Although the president's authority to initiate foreign policy and to negotiate treaties had become settled practice during the nineteenth century, Roosevelt also asserted primacy in the execution of such matters, even when congressional support was lacking.

TR's executive theory had a policy purpose. The acquisition of territories from Spain gave the United States a new position in world affairs after 1898. Roosevelt was determined to build on this position and make the United States a global power. "Whether we desire it or not," the president told Congress on December 3, 1901, in his first annual message, "we must henceforth recognize that we have international duties no less than international rights."[49] Just as many Progressives believed that laissez-faire must give way to a greater sense of national purpose in domestic affairs, they also urged that Americans' nineteenth-century preference for international isolation be abandoned in pursuit of the country's "manifest destiny on a global scale." This doctrine proclaimed for the United States a natural right to expand as much as was necessary for freedom and republican government to survive and prosper. Progressives couched these imperialistic doctrine in ethical terms, arguing that to extend American territory and influence was not imperialism but altruism.

Practical considerations also prompted a more active foreign policy. The expansion of American territory in the Pacific and the Caribbean required a new emphasis on the Pacific basin, a dominant military presence in Central and South America, and an isthmus canal so that naval vessels could be maneuvered efficiently between the Atlantic and Pacific Oceans.

The Panama Canal. Roosevelt considered the canal to be especially important. In his first annual message to Congress, he said, "No single great material work which remains to be undertaken on this continent is of such consequence to the American people as the building of a canal across the isthmus connecting North and South America."[50] Panama, the site eventually chosen for this project, belonged to Colombia. But, to Roosevelt's surprise and embarrassment, Colombia was not willing to allow the United States to build the canal on the president's terms. A complicated round of diplomacy and intrigue ensued that revealed some of the most important characteristics of the Roosevelt era in American foreign policy.

On January 22, 1903, Secretary of State John Hay negotiated and signed a treaty with the Colombian minister in Washington, Thomas Herran. Under the Hay–Herran Treaty, the New Panama Canal Company would construct the canal in return for $40 million from the United States, $10 million from Colombia, and an annual subsidy of $250,000. Complete sovereignty in the three-mile canal zone, however, would belong to the United States in perpetuity. These conditions were rejected by the Colombian leader, José Manuel Marroquin, and by the Colombian Senate. The Colombian government proposed several alternative agreements to the

United States, all of which would have provided better financial terms for Colombia and recognized its sovereignty in the canal zone.

Instead of negotiating further, Roosevelt applied direct diplomatic pressure to Colombia by threatening to turn to Nicaragua as an alternative site for the canal. When that tactic failed, Roosevelt took what he wanted by force. He gave tacit support to the efforts of investors in the New Panama Canal Company to foment a secessionist revolution in Panama. He also indicated clearly that if a Panamanian revolution was unsuccessful, he would take possession of the isthmus anyway. Standing on the tenuous legal foundation of an 1846 treaty with Colombia in which both countries agreed to guarantee the right of transit across the isthmus, TR was prepared to recommend to Congress that the United States occupy the canal zone by force.[51] When Mark Hanna, a leading Republican senator, was informed of this plan, he counseled patience. The president's reply typified his preference for action:

> I think it is well worth considering whether we had not better
> warn those cat-rabbits that great though our patience has been,
> it can be exhausted. . . . I feel, that we are certainly justified
> in morals and . . . justified in law, under the treaty of 1846, in
> interfering summarily and saying that the canal is to be built and
> that they shall not stop it.[52]

A successful revolution in Panama made it unnecessary for Roosevelt to attack Colombia, but the president did aid the revolution when it broke out on November 3, 1903. He made sure that an American warship, the U.S.S. *Nashville*, was docked in Colón on the eve of the uprising. During the subsequent fighting, the ship prevented Colombian troops from reinforcing their outnumbered brethren in Panama. On November 6 Panama became an independent nation. The United States granted it diplomatic recognition within ninety minutes. Soon after, the Panamanian government signed a treaty to transfer canal rights to the United States in return for the $10 million Roosevelt originally offered to Colombia.

Roosevelt's course of action in the canal zone controversy applied his stewardship theory of the presidency to foreign policy. He was not reluctant to act quickly and independently, even when congressional support was weak and the legal foundation for his maneuvers was uncertain. Roosevelt treated constitutional criticisms of his policy with disdain. "At different stages of the affair," he wrote, "believers in a do-nothing policy denounced me as having 'usurped authority'—which meant, that when nobody else could or would exercise efficient authority, I exercised it."[53]

Roosevelt built the canal, proclaiming some years later that doing so was "by far the most important action that I took in foreign affairs during the time I was President."[54] Still, Colombia felt cheated and outraged and continued to press its claims for justice. Later, over former president Roosevelt's protest, apologies were extended to Colombia by the Wilson and Harding administrations, along with an indemnity award of $25 million. Even then, as William M. Goldsmith has written, "The wounds inflicted in this incident were never really eradicated."[55]

The Roosevelt Corollary. The taking of the canal zone signified a new policy toward Latin America that entailed greater presidential power in foreign affairs. The basic plan for a new Caribbean and Latin American policy had been worked out by President McKinley and his secretary of state, John Hay. But under Roosevelt, the new policy was greatly extended. It also was given a precision it previously had lacked.[56]

The desire to dominate the Caribbean was buttressed by Roosevelt's concern that many of the independent republics of Central and South America had weak governments with chaotic finances. Venezuela, for example, had borrowed heavily from Europe and then refused to pay its debt. In December 1902 England, Germany, and Italy undertook to blockade Venezuela in an effort to exact payment. Germany threatened to take possession of certain Venezuelan cities or custom houses. Roosevelt persuaded all the parties to submit their cases to the Hague Court, an international tribunal, but not before he increased the strength of the fleet in the Caribbean and described to the Germans how vulnerable they were to American naval power in the western Atlantic.[57]

Later, when a similar problem developed in Santo Domingo, Roosevelt decided to modify significantly the Monroe Doctrine. After a corrupt dictatorship left Santo Domingo bankrupt and unable to pay its debts, a revolution erupted. In the early winter of 1903, France, Germany, and Italy threatened to intervene. By the end of the year, a German naval squadron was rumored to be sailing across the Atlantic to protect German interests in the Caribbean. Roosevelt, facing an election in 1904, responded cautiously at first. Before long, however, he formulated a policy proclaiming that it was the duty of the United States to intervene in the affairs of Latin American countries whose governments the president judged to have acted wrongly or been rendered impotent by their leaders' mismanagement. The president announced this policy in December 1904 in his annual message to Congress. The Roosevelt Corollary to the Monroe Doctrine, as it became known, was a bold statement of future American conduct toward the debt-ridden, unstable governments of Latin America:

If a nation shows that it knows how to act with reasonable efficiency and decency in social and political matters, if it keeps order and pays its obligations, it need fear no interference by the United States. Chronic wrongdoing, or an impotence which results in a general loosening of the ties of civilized society may in America, as elsewhere, ultimately require intervention by some civilized nation, and in the western hemisphere the adherence of the United States to the Monroe Doctrine may force the United States, however reluctantly, in flagrant cases of such wrongdoing or impotence, to the exercise of an international police power.[58]

The Roosevelt Corollary altered the Monroe Doctrine—which had denied to Europeans the right to intervene in the Western Hemisphere—by sanctioning U.S. intervention in Latin American affairs.[59] Less than a month after Roosevelt announced the new policy, worsening conditions in Santo Domingo spurred him to translate words into action. In early 1905, confronted on one side by a nation that faced bankruptcy and on the other by European powers demanding satisfaction for their accounts, Roosevelt imposed a treaty on Santo Domingo to establish an American financial protectorate over the island. The arrangement required the United States to prevent any European interference with the Dominican custom houses and authorized it to collect the custom revenues. Forty-five percent of the revenue was then turned over to the Dominican government, and 55 percent was deposited in a New York account for the benefit of the creditors.

Roosevelt sent the treaty to the Senate, declaring that to ratify it promptly would forestall more drastic action in the future. But the Senate did not share the president's sense of urgency and failed to vote on the agreement. Democrats and some Republicans believed that diplomacy was an inherently misguided approach to commercial matters. Resentment of the president's unilateral development of a new foreign policy also contributed to the Senate's unwillingness to ratify. Roosevelt responded by implementing the Dominican protectorate as an executive agreement, which further antagonized his congressional critics. The executive agreement was two years old before the Senate finally acquiesced and approved the treaty with minor modifications in 1907.

The eventual success of Roosevelt's Caribbean policy strengthened both his personal political position and ultimately, the institutional status of the presidency in foreign affairs. "The Constitution did not explicitly give me power to bring about the necessary agreement with Santo Domingo," Roosevelt crowed in 1913.

But, the Constitution did not forbid my doing what I did. I put the agreement into effect, and I continued its execution for two years before the Senate acted; and I would have continued it until the end of my term, if necessary, without any action by Congress.[60]

The Russo–Japanese War. The extent of Roosevelt's departure from nineteenth-century isolationism was revealed by his bold initiatives in Asia, especially his unprecedented intervention in the conflict between Russia and Japan over China in 1905.

After Russia moved troops into China in 1902—an action that among other things, threatened the United States' Open Door policy of free trade in China—Japan staged a devastating surprise attack on the Russian fleet anchored at Port Arthur.[61] Because Roosevelt considered Russia the greater imperialist threat in Asia, his sympathies lay with Japan. Indeed, the president fortified the Japanese with secret verbal assurances that the United States would support them if any of the European powers supported Russia. This extraordinary commitment also included an agreement by Japan to recognize American jurisdiction in the Philippines in return for Roosevelt's recognition of Japan's claim to Korea.[62] For the first time, a president committed the United States to possible future military action, as well as to the recognition of one nation's claim to another nation's territory and sovereignty, without consulting the Senate.

Roosevelt's audacious diplomacy ended in triumph. Although the president favored Japan as a counterweight to Russia's designs on China, he feared that too great a Japanese victory might endanger the peace of the entire Pacific region. When fighting in the Russo–Japanese War tilted dramatically in Japan's favor, Roosevelt arranged, without the knowledge of the cabinet, Congress, or even most of the State Department, for Russian and Japanese diplomats to meet in a secret peace conference at Portsmouth, New Hampshire. There the president managed, through what historian George Mowry called "patient, tactful and brilliant diplomacy," to bring about the Peace of Portsmouth in September 1905. The agreement achieved a balance of power in Asia that satisfied the interests not just of the warring nations but also, because the Open Door policy was preserved, of the United States.[63] For his efforts, TR became the first American to win the Nobel Peace Prize. Roosevelt's policy advanced further in 1907 when, again without consulting Congress or the cabinet, he sent the American naval battle fleet on a cruise around the world, a daring maneuver that roused public support for an expanded navy and demonstrated to the Japanese the intent and ability of the United States to protect its interests in Asia.[64]

Although Roosevelt's approach to international affairs was singularly successful, he did not complete the task of establishing the United States as a global power. His effort to expand both America's role in the world and the president's responsibility in foreign affairs took place without sustained and serious discussion with either the American people or their representatives in Congress. As Goldsmith has written, "Theodore Roosevelt set the stage for the American President to play a world historical role that in many instances successive Presidents were neither capable of nor inclined to follow, nor were the American people prepared to support it."[65]

The Troubled Presidency of William Howard Taft

Roosevelt was a remarkably popular and influential president. Indeed, had TR decided to seek another term in 1908, he almost certainly would have been renominated and reelected. "Few informed people in the country," Mowry wrote, "seriously doubted the outcome of the election if Roosevelt decided to stand again."[66]

The decision to step down was not easy, but Roosevelt had promised in November 1904 that he would not run four years later. The three-and-a-half years he served after succeeding to the presidency in 1901 constituted his first term, Roosevelt stated on election night, and the term to which he had just been elected would be his second. "The wise custom which limits the president to two terms regards the substance and not the form," Roosevelt declared, "and under no circumstances will I be a candidate for or accept another nomination."[67]

Roosevelt's decision not to go back on his promise in 1908, even though he clearly was tempted to do so, revealed his commitment to the traditions and institutions of constitutional government. TR believed strongly that the powers of the president needed to expand for the benefit, even the survival, of the nation. But he also knew that democracy would be poorly served if too much power were concentrated in one person. "It is not well that the strong executive should be a perpetual executive," he wrote to British historian George Trevelyan.[68] Roosevelt's "act of abnegation," Mowry claimed, "was among his greatest contributions to his country."[69]

Self-denial, however, did not prevent Roosevelt from selecting William Howard Taft, his secretary of war and closest adviser during the second term, as his successor. Confusing amiability and a bottomless willingness to listen to the loquacious president with complete agreement on everything he said and did, Roosevelt was convinced that Taft "and I view public questions exactly alike." When Taft turned out to have a governing philosophy of his own once in office, the exasperated (and still ambitious) TR labeled him "a flubdub with a streak of the second rate and the common in him."[70] Roosevelt's disappointment turned to full-scale rebellion in 1912, when he challenged Taft for the Republican nomination, charging that his friend had betrayed the progressive principles he was elected to uphold. In truth, Taft spent his entire four years as president uncomfortably in the shadow of Theodore Roosevelt.

Taft sincerely intended to carry on the policies of the Roosevelt administration, and he had more success in doing so than Roosevelt gave him credit for. But Taft was disinclined by philosophy and ill-suited by personality to imitate TR's stewardship of the presidency. As historian Paolo E. Coletta has written, "While under the spell of the dynamic Roosevelt, Taft had appeared to be a progressive cut from the full Roosevelt cloth. With Roosevelt gone he would return to his basic conservative self and thereby earn the odium of the progressives as one who had deserted the cause."[71]

In the wake of Roosevelt's presidency, Taft seemed an anachronism. Although never saying so publicly, Taft disapproved of TR's theory that it is the president's duty "to do anything that the needs of the nation demand, unless such action is forbidden by the Constitution or the law." Taft's philosophy of executive power, like the understanding that prevailed during most of the nineteenth century, eschewed a broad interpretation of the president's discretionary authority. As he wrote several years after leaving office,

The true view of the executive function . . . is that the President can exercise no power which cannot be reasonably or fairly traced to some specific grant of power or justly implied or included within such express grant as necessary and proper to its exercise. Such specific grant must be either in the Constitution or in an act of Congress passed in pursuance thereof. There is no undefined residuum of power which he can exercise because it seems to be in the public interest.[72]

Because he construed executive power narrowly, Taft denied that being president required him to exercise either popular or policy leadership. He rejected the notion that he bore a special mandate from the people and refused to make any serious effort to court public opinion or the press. One Taft aide, who also had served with Roosevelt, noted the stark contrast between the two presidents in their relations with reporters and editors:

"Mr. Roosevelt understood the necessity of guiding the press to suit one's ends; President Taft has no conception of the press as an adjunct to his office."[73]

Taft also rejected the kind of speaking tours TR had used to publicize his programs and bring public pressure to bear on Congress. Although Taft and his opponent in the 1908 election, three-time Democratic nominee William Jennings Bryan, campaigned across the country—the first time both major party nominees did so in a presidential contest—Taft happily abandoned the practice once he secured the office. Such rhetorical efforts as Taft made as president came at the urging of his aides and were undertaken with considerable reluctance. A former judge, Taft was used to issuing his judgments from the bench, not repeatedly defending them, and he preferred to follow the same course as president. "After I have made a definite statement," he said, "I have to let it go at that. I am not constituted as Mr. Roosevelt is," Taft added, "in being able to keep the country advised every few days of the continuance of the state of mind in reference to reforms."[74] "The Taft administration," Elmer Cornwell noted, "represented a hiatus in the presidential leadership of opinion, if not actually a retrograde step."[75]

Taft and Congress

Taft dedicated himself to a legislative program that would institutionalize in law the reforms that Roosevelt's vigorous and independent executive actions had begun. "Mr. Roosevelt's function has been to preach a crusade against certain evils. He has aroused the people to demand reform," Taft wrote on February 23, 1909, just before his inauguration. "It becomes my business to put such reform into legal execution by the suggestion of certain amendments of the statute in the governmental machinery."[76]

One important area in which the direction of reform

William Howard Taft, right, who served as Theodore Roosevelt's secretary of war, was elected president in 1908. Although he intended to continue the policies of the Roosevelt administration, he was accused by Progressives of betraying their principles.

Source: Theodore Roosevelt Collection, Harvard College Library.

remained unclear was conservation. Roosevelt aggressively asserted that the president is the steward of the public welfare in protecting the nation's natural resources. But his "midnight forests" proclamation led to a bitter confrontation with Congress. When TR left office, the dispute about the national government's responsibility to manage natural resources was still unresolved.

In an effort to make conservation policy a matter of settled law, Taft prepared a special message in 1909 that asked Congress to pass a bill to codify Roosevelt's executive order. As he wrote to the California conservationist William Kent, "We have a government of limited power under the Constitution, and we have got to work out our problems on the basis of law."[77] But Taft's passive view of presidential leadership shaped his pursuit of the bill in Congress. He had serious misgivings about interfering in the legislative process. "I have no disposition," Taft told Senate majority leader Nelson Aldrich, "to exert any other influence than that which it is my function under the Constitution to exercise."[78]

Although Taft's position on conservation prevailed, his broader policy of forbearance in legislative matters cost him dearly, especially during the early days of his presidency. Indeed, his passivity led people to think that he agreed with the conservative Republican leadership in Congress, which caused an irrevocable split to occur between Taft and the Roosevelt administration alumni whom he had allowed to stay in office. TR's fellow conservationist Gifford Pinchot felt that Taft's unwillingness to act in the absence of explicit authority crippled progressive policies. "It was as though a sharp sword had been succeeded by a roll of paper, legal size," Pinchot later wrote.[79]

Taft's modest definition of executive power governed his relations with Congress even on those policies that were closest to his heart. Of all the campaign promises he made in 1908, Taft was probably the most serious about wanting to reduce tariff rates. Roosevelt had done nothing about tariffs except to use them as a bargaining chip in his fight for the Hepburn Act. Taft considered the Republican Party's long-standing attachment to protectionism unfortunate. Yet he stood by passively in 1910 as Congress watered down his proposal to alter the nation's protectionist trade policies. Senate Republicans added more than eight hundred amendments to the strong tariff reform bill that the House passed. Taft simply signed the version that came out of the House–Senate conference committee, even though it closely resembled the Senate bill.[80]

Faced with a similar challenge, Roosevelt almost certainly would have abandoned his party's congressional leadership, worked to build a bipartisan progressive coalition, and if all else failed, appealed to the people. Taft, however, remained loyal to the Republican organization, even claiming that the Payne–Aldrich tariff, as the final legislation was called, was "really a good bill." Progressive Republicans, most of whom bucked the president and their party's leaders to vote against the measure, disagreed.[81] Taft lost the political initiative and, as Coletta has noted, "the wounds inflicted in the acrid tariff debate never healed."[82]

Public deference to Congress, by itself, did not foreclose the possibility of an impressive legislative record. Jefferson and McKinley had worked quietly within party councils to exercise considerable influence in Congress. But Taft lacked the political skill to provide this kind of leadership. His pre-presidential experience was confined to judicial and administrative offices, leaving him relatively unversed in public and legislative politics.[83] Reflecting on an offer he refused three times from President Roosevelt, Taft lamented to a friend, "If I were now presiding in the Supreme Court of the United States as Chief Justice, I should feel entirely at home, but with the . . . difficulties in respect to the revision of the tariff, I feel just a bit like a fish out of water."[84]

Taft also suffered from changing political conditions. The Republican Party was more divided than ever between its increasingly stubborn conservative, pro-business majority and its large and growing progressive minority, which was bent on reform. The outbreak of virtual civil war in the so-called "Grand Old Party" (GOP) began with a progressive revolt in the House of Representatives. Unwilling to tolerate any longer the conservative policies and arbitrary leadership of Speaker Cannon, Republican insurgents led by Rep. George Norris of Nebraska united with Democrats in March 1910 to strip the speakership of most of its powers. No longer would the Speaker control the members' committee assignments or the strategically important Rules Committee, which set the House's legislative agenda. Even the Speaker's constitutional role as presiding officer was hemmed in by new rules that limited the role's discretionary authority.

The weakening of the party leadership, long a bulwark of congressional government, ultimately hastened the transfer of power from Congress to the White House that had become especially noticeable during Roosevelt's presidency. The same progressive revolt that reduced the Speaker's power in the House also undermined the foundations of party discipline in the Senate, depriving its leaders of their control of legislative deliberations. Power in both houses of Congress devolved to the committees, especially the committee chairs, specialized, nearly autonomous barons of legislation who earned their positions through seniority, not loyalty to their party.

Unable to obtain reform from a fractious Congress, Progressives demanded that the president provide strong leadership in both congressional and party matters. Governor-elect Woodrow Wilson of New Jersey described the situation well when he said on November 5, 1910,

> If I were to sum up all the criticisms that have been made of the gentleman who is now President of the United States, I could express them all in this: The American people are disappointed because he has not led them. . . . They clearly long for someone to put the pressure of the opinion of all the people of the United States upon Congress.[85]

Taft's narrow construction of executive power notwithstanding, he was sensitive to the new public demands. Very late in his term, he suggested that the executive and legislative branches be brought closer by giving cabinet members nonvoting seats in Congress. He also endorsed a presidential commission's call for the president to bind the departments and agencies to a comprehensive budget. Led by a noted authority on public administration, Frederick Cleveland, the Taft-appointed Commission on Economy and Efficiency argued that the absence of presidential leadership in fiscal matters encouraged wasteful and irresponsible spending by the federal government.[86] Leaving budgetary estimates to the departments and agencies also undermined the chief executive's constitutional obligation to oversee the activities of the executive branch. The Cleveland commission argued that the budget "is the only effective means whereby the Executive may get before the country a comprehensive program with respect to which the legislator must assume responsibility either for action or inaction." Embracing the commission's recommendations, Taft submitted the first executive budget in 1913, just before he left office.[87]

Taft's proposals to strengthen the executive were ignored by Congress. But they revealed that even he had come to recognize that Roosevelt's dynamic leadership and the changing character of the country now placed more responsibility in the presidency than during the nineteenth century. Secure in his authority as head of the executive branch, Taft directed the Justice Department to reorient national policy on large trusts from TR's preferred approach of regulating corporations' behavior to one of litigation to break them up. And he instructed his departments to submit a unified presidential budget to Congress along with the traditional compilation of individual departmental requests—whether Congress wanted one or not.[88]

The Election of 1910

Ironically, Taft's most dramatic assertion of presidential leadership proved to be his political undoing. In the 1910 congressional primaries, the president tried to purge several Progressives from the Republican Party. Taft had
criticized Roosevelt for meddling in the legislative process. Yet Taft's intervention in his party's nominating process marked an unprecedented effort by a
president to influence congressional support for his legislative program.

Taft tried first to mediate between the GOP's badly divided factions.
But the Progressives' opposition to the president's legislative program, especially the final version of the Payne–Aldrich tariff, provoked him to join
the conservatives' effort to influence the 1910 primary elections. Although
Taft took no public position in these contests, he distributed government
patronage on the basis of loyalty to his administration's program.

State primary elections to choose parties' nominees for office were a recent
innovation of the Progressive movement. Taft sought to deploy progressive
means to achieve conservative ends, but his aggressive, albeit surreptitious,
intervention in the primaries was manifestly unsuccessful. Not only were
almost all of the progressive Republicans whom he opposed renominated, but
their reformist allies defeated conservative incumbents in several other primaries. In the wake of these reversals came the great disaster of the November
elections. In 1910, for the first time in sixteen years, the Democrats took control of the House of Representatives. Republicans retained a majority in the
Senate, but their control was nominal. Progressive Republican senators now
held the balance of power between the regular Republicans and the Democrats.

Taft's purge campaign revealed not just the limits of his personal influence but also the imposing institutional obstacles to party discipline in
national politics. To be sure, the decline of the party leadership's influence
in Congress required more assertive presidential efforts to bring together
the elected branches of the government. But Taft's approach to this problem, the purge campaign, was undertaken in concert with a Republican
Old Guard that was losing ground throughout the country. Nor were the
American people ready to support an executive assault on their own, locally
elected members of Congress.

Progressive Politics
and the Elections of 1912

After the Republicans lost control of the House in the 1910 elections, it
became apparent that Taft probably would not be reelected. The elections

weakened the Republican Party. Across the country and in Congress, Democratic progressives were elected, most of them unattached to William Jennings Bryan, the fiery rural Populist who led the party to defeat in the 1896, 1900, and 1908 presidential campaigns.

Among the newly elected progressive Democrats was Governor Wilson of New Jersey, a former political science professor and president of Princeton University. Two years later, after a long deadlock, the Democratic National Convention nominated him for president on the forty-sixth ballot. The nomination was secured when Bryan, in a symbolic passing of the torch, threw his full support to Wilson in hopes of thwarting the Democratic Party's conservative eastern business interests. Although James Beauchamp "Champ" Clark, the moderate progressive Speaker of the House, won the votes of a majority of delegates (a sure path to obtaining the required two-thirds at every Democratic convention since 1844) on the tenth ballot, his support from controversial northern party bosses like Tammany Hall's Charles Murphy eventually hurt him. Furious that Clark had joined forces with the "reactionary element of the party," Bryan switched his allegiance from the Speaker to Wilson, a critical turning of the tide that led to Wilson's nomination. After failing for two decades to offer a program that addressed the challenges of the Progressive era, the Democrats suddenly found themselves led by an articulate and forward-looking scholar–politician, the only academician ever to be elected president. Wilson's victory in 1912 was just the third by a Democrat since the Civil War. Enough other Democrats were swept into Congress with him to give the party solid majorities in both houses of Congress for the first time in more than fifty years.[89]

The Democrats' opportunity might not have arisen had the Republicans remained united in 1912. An intraparty progressive revolt against Taft and the Old Guard first gave rise to an insurgent candidacy by Wisconsin senator Robert La Follette, who challenged the president's bid for renomination. When La Follette failed to draw much support outside the Midwest, Republican Progressives turned to Theodore Roosevelt. On February 21, 1912, TR announced, "My hat is in the ring." Bored by four years of political inactivity and persuaded that his candidacy was indispensable to the progressive cause, Roosevelt abandoned his earlier pledge not to run again for president. That he declined a "third cup of coffee" in 1908 did not mean that he never intended to drink coffee again, Roosevelt said.[90]

In 1912, for the first time, presidential primaries contributed significantly to the selection of delegates to the national party conventions. Celebrating the right of voters rather than party bosses to choose presidential candidates, Roosevelt publicly challenged Taft to contest the Republican nomination by means of a direct primary in every state. Taft and most party regulars had no interest in embracing such a radical change in the nominating process. Prior to Roosevelt's campaign, six states had decided to schedule primaries in 1912: North Dakota, California, New Jersey, Wisconsin, Minnesota, and Nebraska. All of the states save New Jersey, which enacted a direct primary law as part of Governor Wilson's reform program, were in the Midwest and West, where progressive reformers were most prevalent. Roosevelt's entry into the race prompted Illinois, Maryland, Massachusetts, Ohio, Pennsylvania, and South Dakota to join the ranks of primary states. With twelve states holding primaries, the result was "a sizeable block of normal Republican states from which a popular referendum could be obtained."[91]

Republican primary voters supported TR in these contests. Of the twelve states that selected convention delegates in primary elections, Roosevelt carried nine, accumulating 276 delegates to Taft's 46 and La Follette's 36. Roosevelt even won Taft's home state of Ohio by an almost three-to-two margin.[92] But two-thirds of the national convention's 1,078 delegates were still selected at gatherings dominated by regular state party leaders, who much preferred Taft's stolidity to Roosevelt's frenetic progressivism. In addition, La Follette's refusal to withdraw from the race denied Roosevelt the votes of some progressive Republican delegates.

When it became clear at the Republican convention that Roosevelt would not be chosen, he and his followers walked out, reconvening in Chicago on August 5 under the banner of the Progressive Party. Announcing that he felt "as strong as a bull moose" (a simile that the new party adopted as its moniker), Roosevelt delivered a stirring "Confession of Faith" in which he called for "strong national regulation" of interstate corporations; social insurance in times of injury, sickness, unemployment, and old age; and constitutional reforms to establish a "pure democracy." TR's vision of democratic government included the universal adoption of the direct primary, government-led industrial planning, an easier method to amend the Constitution, voter initiatives, referenda to restore laws that state courts declared unconstitutional, women's suffrage, and limits on the power of courts to issue labor injunctions.

Since leaving the White House, Roosevelt had moved far beyond the Square Deal to what he called the New Nationalism. He now embraced a vision of government that preserved his original emphasis on regulating rather than breaking up large industrial corporations while adding a plethora of reforms to create a new role for government that in many ways anticipated the welfare state later associated with his cousin Franklin's

New Deal. The national government, Roosevelt wrote, "must inevitably sympathize with the men who have nothing but their wages, with the men who are struggling for a decent life, as opposed to men, however honorable, who are merely fighting for larger profits and autocratic control of big business."[93] TR and his fellow Progressives were certain that voters would put aside their long-standing suspicion of centralized administration if they were convinced they held the reins of power.

Although the Progressive Party was more than a personal vehicle for Roosevelt, his control of it was extraordinary. The Progressive campaign advanced a development initially foretold by the 1896 Bryan–McKinley contest: the coming of presidential elections conducted less by parties than by individual candidates. Roosevelt's speech to the Progressive Party convention was the first in history by a major presidential candidate, and it elicited a fifty-two-minute standing ovation.[94] His closing words—"We stand at Armageddon, and we battle for the Lord"—roused the delegates to an emotional state that could only be subdued by reverential singing of the "Battle Hymn of the Republic."[95] Yet Roosevelt, hoping to crack the Democrats' total dominance of southern politics, accepted "lily-white" delegations and refused to accept Du Bois's passionate appeal to include a civil rights plank in the Progressive Party platform.

Despite the fractious politics that divided the Bull Moose campaign over civil rights and, even more sharply, how to regulate business, the 1912 presidential election marked an important victory for the Progressive movement. But it sent Wilson, not Roosevelt, to the White House. Like Lincoln, Wilson polled much less than a majority of the national popular vote but won the election easily. The final tally awarded 6.3 million popular votes and 435 electoral votes to Wilson, 4.1 million popular votes and 88 electoral votes (the most ever won by a third-party presidential candidate before or since) to Roosevelt, and 3.5 million popular votes and 8 electoral votes to Taft. Eugene V. Debs collected 900,000 popular votes, the highest total ever for a Socialist Party candidate, but no electoral votes. If progressives Wilson and Roosevelt had not been on the ballot, Debs, whose party recently had elected several hundred local officials bearing the Socialist label, undoubtedly would have secured a significantly larger vote.

For all the excitement, active campaigning, and high stakes that marked the 1912 election, turnout continued to decline, from 74 percent of eligible voters in 1900 to 65 percent in 1904 and 1908 and 59 percent in 1912. As historian Lewis L. Gould points out, recent "measures to bar blacks from voting in the South" accounted for part of the reduction. But so did new policies and ideas sparked by the Progressive movement.

These included "techniques to curb voter fraud [and] tighter registration requirements." In addition, argues Gould, "power shifted to government bureaucrats and regulatory agencies" operating outside the electoral system. Perhaps most important, under harsh progressive scrutiny, "political parties no longer seemed the embodiment of democracy" but rather mere "means for unscrupulous leaders to frustrate the democratic will."[96] Roosevelt's crusade championed a direct relationship between candidates and voters that made for good theater but helped undercut the ability of parties to act as agents of mass mobilization.[97]

Above all, the 1912 election was a decisive rejection of the Republican Old Guard. Its candidate, the incumbent Taft, carried only Vermont and Utah. The combined popular vote won by Wilson, Roosevelt, and Debs, each an advocate of progressive policies in one form or another, exceeded 75 percent.[98] The results enabled Wilson to reap the benefits of a reform movement that was cresting just as he entered the White House. The new president seized the opportunity not only to advance progressive social and economic policies but also to extend the restructuring of executive leadership that Roosevelt had begun.

The Democratic Party's platform, expressing a suspicion of presidential power reminiscent of Thomas Jefferson, called for a constitutional amendment to limit presidents to a single term. But Wilson, impressed by the excitement that TR's "Bull Moose" campaign aroused, quickly disavowed this pledge. As he lamented to Rep. A. Mitchell Palmer of Pennsylvania in February 1913, progressive Democrats "are seeking in every way to extend the power of the people, but in the matter of the Presidency, we fear and distrust the people and seek to bind them hand and foot by rigid constitutional provision." Hoping to deflate support for a one-term limit, Wilson resolved to make the executive office more democratic rather than try to diminish its power.[99]

Woodrow Wilson's Theory of Executive Leadership

Wilson had long wanted to reform radically the principles and institutions of American government to ameliorate what he regarded as its disconcerting lack of energy and consistency. In 1879, as a twenty-three-year-old student, Wilson published an article calling for major institutional reforms to establish closer ties between the executive and the legislature. At the time, he believed that this connection could be forged best by enhancing the powers of Congress, the dominant branch of government throughout most of the nineteenth century. Wilson urged the United States to adopt a British-style cabinet system that would concentrate power in an executive board responsible to the legislature. Specifically, he proposed that the Constitution be amended "to give the heads of the Executive departments—the members of the Cabinet—seats in Congress, with the privilege of the initiative in legislation and some part in the unbounded privileges now commanded by the Standing Committees."[100] The president, who in Wilson's view had been rendered virtually useless in the aftermath of the Civil War, would become a figurehead like the British monarch.

Although Wilson never abandoned the idea that checks and balances should be replaced by an American version of parliamentary government, his views about the presidency changed dramatically. In the early 1900s, he argued that the best hope for national leadership now lay in a strong executive.[101] Wilson was influenced by the example of Roosevelt, whose vigorous and independent stewardship demonstrated how powerful even a peacetime president could be. Wilson disagreed strongly with TR about certain institutional and policy matters, but he credited him with charting a new path of presidential leadership. "Whatever else we may think or say of Theodore Roosevelt," Wilson said in 1909, "we must admit he was an aggressive leader. He led Congress—he was not driven by Congress. We may not approve of his methods but we must concede that he made Congress follow him."[102] Roosevelt's success persuaded Wilson that a new theory of constitutional government was needed to justify and make routine the forceful display of presidential leadership. TR had shown that it was not necessary to amend the Constitution to bring about a closer relationship between the elected branches. Instead, the challenge was to exercise the existing powers of the presidency more fully. "His office," Wilson now said of the president, "is anything he has the sagacity and force to make it."[103]

Roosevelt did much to fulfill the promise of the executive, but Wilson believed that he was too inclined to act in defiance of Congress. The radical excesses of Roosevelt's approach to leadership were confirmed for Wilson by the 1912 election, in which TR championed the right of the people to rule without interference by party organizations. For Wilson, responsible democratic government could not be achieved by direct democracy, which risked demagogy. A better strategy, Wilson argued, would be to break down the barriers between the president and Congress by making the president a strong party leader. The components of constitutional government would then work in concert but without violating the principles and institutions that protect the nation from an unhealthy aggrandizement of executive power.[104]

Because the president is uniquely positioned to lead public opinion and his party, Wilson believed that a talented and energetic executive would encourage thoughtful debates in election campaigns and within the councils of government. Unlike members of Congress, who represent states and localities, the president is the only person nominated by an entire party and elected by the entire nation. "The President represents not so much the party's governing efficiency as its controlling ideals and principles," Wilson wrote.

> He is not so much part of its organization as its vital link of connection with the thinking nation. He can dominate his party by being spokesman for the real sentiment and purpose of the country, by giving direction to opinion, by giving the country at once the information and the statements of policy which will enable it to form its judgments alike of parties and men.[105]

Wilson's theory of presidential power required a more comprehensive rethinking of the American constitutional order than did Roosevelt's stewardship model. Although he embraced "pure democracy" as the Progressive Party candidate in 1912, as president TR had accepted the constitutional system of checks and balances, seeking to revive and modify Hamiltonian nationalism so that the government could address the problems of a modern industrial society. Even when he roused the people to bring pressure to bear on Congress, Roosevelt did so in ways meant to preserve the independence of both branches. His deference to traditional constitutional practices was especially clear in domestic matters. TR campaigned for legislation such as the Hepburn Act only as a last resort and always in a manner that showed respect for congressional deliberations.

Wilson agreed with Roosevelt that the president must direct more attention to national problems. But he also believed that executive leadership would be ineffective or even dangerous if not accompanied by a fundamental change in the government's working arrangements. Such a change would unite the constitutionally separated branches of the government.[106] Most significant, the president's role as party leader would be strengthened. Instead of limiting executive power, as it had during much of the nineteenth century, the party system would be modified so that the president could command Congress's support.

Wilson and Party Reform

As president, Wilson tried to perfect TR's methods of popular leadership and apply them in a way that would establish him as the leader of Congress and the Democratic Party. Wilson was not completely successful in this endeavor, but his two terms in office did bring about major changes in the presidency.

Wilson's desire to strengthen the president's position within party councils led him to examine closely the presidential nominating process, especially the convention system, which Roosevelt and the Progressives attacked during the 1912 campaign as boss dominated and unresponsive to the popular will. The advent of the national conventions, which replaced the congressional caucus near the start of the Jacksonian era, had freed the president to some extent from an undue dependence on Congress. But Wilson charged that because the convention system was founded on patronage-based state and local party organizations, it was ill suited to the modern industrial age. Government in the twentieth century required a sense of purpose that could come only from national and programmatic political parties.[107]

Motivated by his understanding of the presidency and the parties, Wilson became a supporter of the presidential primary. In his first annual message to Congress, he urged "the prompt enactment of legislation which will provide for primary elections throughout the country at which the voters of the several parties may choose their nominees for the Presidency without the intervention of nominating conventions."[108] The direct primary, which had been advocated by progressive reformers since the turn of the century and animated Roosevelt's intraparty struggle with Taft, was already being used in many state and local elections. Although Wilson's recommendation to establish a national primary made little headway in Congress, its democratic spirit continued to guide reformers who fought throughout the twentieth century to weaken the grip of traditional party organizations on the presidency.

The Art of Popular Leadership

The national primary proposal was but one manifestation of Wilson's desire to increase the authority of the president and, by doing so, to provide the political system with a greater capacity for change. Wilson also avowed the president's obligation, as the voice of the people, to bring public opinion to bear on Congress. Roosevelt had demonstrated the value of this role but, as Wilson biographer Arthur S. Link wrote, "Wilson used it to its fullest advantage and made it inevitable that any future president would be powerful only in so far as he established communication with the people and spoke effectively for them."[109]

In contrast to TR, who regarded popular rhetoric as a method to be used infrequently and only in defense of specific pieces of legislation, Wilson believed that an ongoing effort to educate and inspire the American people was the main ingredient of presidential leadership. His effective use of oratory set a new rhetorical standard. Henceforth presidents would be expected to articulate a vision of the future and guide the nation toward fulfilling it. As Wilson announced in his first inaugural address,

> We know our task to be no mere task of politics but a task which shall search us through and through, whether we be able to understand our time and the need of our people, whether we be indeed their spokesmen and interpreters, whether we have the pure heart to comprehend and the rectified will to choose our high course of action.[110]

At his best, Wilson was a spellbinding orator. Although some in his audience may not have grasped the full meaning of his carefully crafted sentences, there was no mistaking their moral import or the intelligence and conviction of the man who spoke them. Wilson understood the popular aspirations of his day and was able to translate them into words. In doing so, he explicitly defended and, by example, established the legitimacy of public rhetoric as a principal tool of presidential leadership.

In keeping with his desire to be in close touch with the people, Wilson made enduring innovations in the executive's relationship with the press and with Congress. Unlike Roosevelt, Wilson did not trust reporters and was unwilling to cultivate them personally. He was, however, the first president to have press conferences, which he held frequently during his first two years in office. In a sense, Wilson instituted regular press conferences because he distrusted the Fourth Estate. Less gregarious than Roosevelt, and yet certain that frequent contact with reporters was an essential part of his effort to take the people into his confidence, Wilson found formal press conferences to be an effective forum for his relations with journalists.[111]

Nevertheless, Wilson did not rely solely on the press to communicate his views. The president's preferred devices for public leadership were speeches and formal messages. Wilson began his presidency by reviving the practice—abandoned by Jefferson, who believed it resembled too closely the British monarch's annual speech from the throne—of appearing before Congress to deliver important messages, including the annual State of the Union address.

The White House's announcement that Wilson would speak on the issue of tariff reform to the two houses of Congress on April 8, 1913, shocked some legislators. Especially concerned were Democrats, who revered the Jeffersonian custom. Sen. John Sharp Williams of Mississippi, an original Wilson supporter, led the uprising, arguing that Wilson's speech "would be the only instance of the breach of the perfectly simple, democratic and American custom of messages in writing which Thomas Jefferson instituted."[112] Williams's hope was in vain. Wilson addressed Congress in person frequently, resuming the practice with his first State of the Union address in December 1913. "As he no doubt foresaw," Elmer E. Cornwell Jr. wrote, "this forum would so concentrate public attention as to eliminate the likelihood that the newspapers would either slight or distort his message."[113]

Wilson's Relations with Congress

Appearances before Congress also served Wilson's desire to break down the walls that long had divided the executive from the legislature. Although part of his purpose was to guide public opinion, he found it equally important to establish customs and make symbolic gestures that would strengthen the president's ties to Congress. Wilson began his April 8 tariff address to the somewhat tense legislators by speaking directly to the symbolic purpose of his appearance:

> I am very glad indeed to have this opportunity to address the two houses directly and to verify for myself the impression that the President of the United States is a person, not a mere department of government hailing Congress from some isolated island of jealous power, sending messages, not speaking naturally with his own voice—that he is a human being trying to cooperate with other human beings in a common service. After this pleasant experience I shall feel quite normal in all our dealings with one another.[114]

Wilson's precedent-shattering speech was well received by most members of Congress. It launched the first successful campaign for serious tariff reduction—a core Democratic goal that had gone unfulfilled in the Republican era—since before the Civil War. Some of his other innovations were also significant, such as his practice of visiting Capitol Hill to meet personally with legislators while Congress deliberated on an important bill. Wilson followed his tariff address by appearing the next day in the president's room of the Senate to confer with the Finance Committee, which was responsible for tariff legislation. No president since Ulysses S. Grant had met with members of a congressional committee in the Capitol. Assessing Wilson's revolutionary approach to congressional relations, his close associate Ray Stannard Baker wrote, "These vigorous innovations occasioned an enormous amount of publicity. The country at large was vastly interested, amused, impressed."[115]

Nothing contributed more to Wilson's leadership of Congress than the control he exerted over House and Senate Democrats. The Democratic Party was at least as divided between conservatives and progressives as the GOP. Nevertheless, Wilson decided to work with his party in Congress rather than try to govern through a coalition of progressive Democrats and progressive Republicans, as he might have done. He labored assiduously to formulate a comprehensive legislative program and to establish it as his party's plan. He even persuaded the House Democratic caucus to adopt a rule that bound all of its members to support the administration's policies if at least two-thirds of them agreed. Similar discipline was obtained in the traditionally more individualistic Senate, where the Democratic caucus declared that important pieces of legislation such as the tariff bill were party measures and that it was the duty of every Democrat to support them.[116]

Owing to his effective leadership, Wilson was able to drive through Congress the major policies of his 1912 campaign platform, which he heralded as the "New Freedom." The catchphrase expressed Wilson's belief that progressivism, properly understood, was deeply rooted in the traditions of the Democratic Party.

Roosevelt's New Nationalism had accepted the evolution of great corporations as both inevitable and, with strict public regulation of corporate activities by a powerful national government, desirable. In contrast, Wilson wanted to free business competition from monopoly and special privilege, making unnecessary the correspondingly dangerous centralization of regulatory power in Washington. "As to monopolies, which Mr. Roosevelt proposes to legalize and welcome," Wilson remarked during the 1912 campaign, "I know that they are so many cars of juggernaut, and I do not look forward with pleasure to the time when the juggernauts are licensed and driven by commissioners of the United States."[117] As the leader of the

Democratic Party, Wilson promised not just tariff reform but also an overhaul of the banking and currency system and a vigorous antitrust program that would "disentangle" the "colossal community of interest" and restore fair competition to the economy.[118]

To the astonishment of Wilson's friends and enemies alike, Congress approved most elements of the New Freedom agenda in 1913 and 1914. The Underwood Tariff Act became law in October 1913. The Federal Reserve Act, which created the Federal Reserve Board and over time reconstructed the nation's banking and currency system, followed in late December. Finally, two statutes were passed in 1914, the Clayton Anti-Trust Act and the Federal Trade Commission Act, to strengthen the government's authority to prevent unfair business competition.

Taken as a whole, Wilson's legislative achievements were remarkable. In contrast with TR, Wilson turned his fractious party into a disciplined body that provided near-unanimous support for each of his most important measures. In doing so, he enacted programs that many Progressives had been demanding for two decades. The president used the occasion of his 1914 State of the Union address to report proudly to Congress, "Our program of legislation with regard to regulation of business is now virtually complete."[119]

But the New Freedom program was soon compromised by Wilson's own administrative practices, which undermined the implementation of the new laws. Before becoming president, Wilson often had declared his support for the merit system of hiring, promoting, and firing federal employees. At the time of his election he was a vice president of the National Civil Service Reform League. As president-elect, Wilson promised to nominate "progressives—and only progressives" to federal jobs. But to the dismay of the president's reformist supporters, old-style patronage practices dominated his appointments.[120] "The pity is," Secretary of the Navy Josephus Daniels wrote many years later, "that Wilson appointed some who wouldn't recognize a Progressive principle if he met it in the road."[121]

Wilson's approach to appointments was governed by his belief, reluctantly arrived at, that to assault the patronage system would be to undermine party unity and ensure the defeat of his legislative program. The pressure from within his party to employ traditional partisan practices was great. The Democrats had been without federal patronage for sixteen years, ever since Grover Cleveland left office in 1897. The problem was brought to the president's attention by Postmaster General Albert S. Burleson, who largely owed his place in the cabinet to his strong ties with Congress. When Wilson told Burleson at the beginning of his presidency that appointments were to be made without the advice of the "professional politicians," the postmaster general urged otherwise:

> Mr. President, if you pursue this policy it means that your administration is going to be a failure. It means the defeat of measures of reform that you have next to your heart. These little offices don't amount to anything. They are inconsequential.
> It doesn't amount to a damn who is Postmaster at Paducah, Kentucky. But these little offices mean a great deal to senators and representatives in Congress. If it goes out that the President has turned down Representative So-and-so, and Senator So-and-so, it means that member has great trouble at home.[122]

Wilson was persuaded. His decision to work through the party marked "one of the early decisive turning points in Wilson's presidential career."[123] It underlay his nearly absolute mastery of the Democratic Party, especially its membership in Congress. But Wilson's political approach to appointments weakened the administrative effectiveness of the reform programs he persuaded Congress to enact. Spoilsmen were less able and often less willing to implement the president's New Freedom legislation than officials chosen for their competence and commitment to progressive principles would have been.

Wilson's New Freedom program also failed to address the problem of racial discrimination. Although deeply estranged by what they condemned as the rank hypocrisy of the Progressive movement, which presumed to embody a national program of reform but was silent on the plight of African Americans, Du Bois and many other civil rights activists supported Wilson in 1912. Yet Wilson, who promised blacks "fair dealing" during the campaign, betrayed their leaders' faith in him. Indeed, the Democratic victory in 1912 brought into the executive branch white southerners who strengthened the grip of Jim Crow laws on southern blacks. "The South," a reporter for *Harper's Weekly* observed, "is in the Saddle."[124] As a native Virginian, Wilson supported cabinet members such as Treasury Secretary William McAdoo and Postmaster General Burleson, who solidified racial segregation in the federal workforce. To be sure, neither Roosevelt nor Taft had been champions of racial justice. But Wilson and the Democratic Party actively pursued a policy of segregation in the departments and agencies of the federal government.

Although his commitment to reform was limited by his prejudice and his party, Wilson did transform the presidency substantially. The office that only two decades before had seemed so unimpressive to Wilson the political scientist was elevated by Wilson the president to a position of unrivaled influence in the American political system. As the *New Republic* proclaimed in December 1914,

> Under Mr. Wilson the prestige of the presidency has been fully restored. He has not only expressly acknowledged and acted on this obligation of leadership, as did Mr. Roosevelt, but he has sought to embody it in constitutional form . . . [by] establishing regular forms of cooperation and a better understanding between the Presidency and Congress.[125]

Wilson as World Leader

Wilson's most formative progressive ideas were tested in foreign affairs.[126] From 1901 to 1909 Roosevelt expanded the president's influence and reduced the effectiveness of Congress in these matters. Having run in 1912 on a domestic policy-centered agenda, Wilson observed on the eve of his inauguration, "It would be the irony of fate if my administration had to deal chiefly with foreign affairs."[127] But he did not shirk his office's new global responsibilities. In a lecture at Columbia University in 1907, Professor Wilson expressed the understanding of the executive's obligations in foreign affairs that was to govern President Wilson's conduct in office:

> The president can never again be the mere domestic figure he has been throughout so large a part of our history. The nation has risen to the first rank in power and resources. . . . Our president must always, henceforth, be one of the great powers of the world, whether he act greatly or wisely or not. . . . We have but begun to see the presidential office in this light; but it is the light which will more and more beat upon it, and more and more determine its character and its effect upon the politics of the nation.[128]

Wilson's approach to foreign affairs was just as ambitious as Roosevelt's and somewhat more idealistic. TR's diplomatic initiatives were rooted in a mixture of progressive philosophy and realpolitik which sustained his administration's vigorous pursuit of American strategic and economic interests. Wilson and his first secretary of state, William Jennings Bryan, charted a more high-minded course. They assumed somewhat naively, Link wrote, "that moral force controlled the relations of peace, that reason would prevail over ignorance and passion in the formation of public opinion, and that men and nations everywhere were automatically progressing toward an orderly and righteous international society."[129] Wilson was determined to pursue an energetic foreign policy. But he resolved to base it more on altruism and less on narrow considerations of the national interest than Roosevelt's foreign policy had been.

Conflict with Mexico

Wilson's noble intentions did not prevent, and probably contributed to, his clumsy intervention in Mexico soon after becoming president. The incident was precipitated by his refusal to recognize the government of Victoriano Huerta, who in February 1913 overthrew and arranged the murder of the Mexican reformist president Francisco I. Madero. The Taft administration delayed granting diplomatic recognition to the Huerta government in hopes of obtaining concessions for American business interests in Mexico. Wilson, however, detested "Dollar Diplomacy," as critics called Taft's approach, and sought instead to impose political reforms on Mexico as the price of recognition. "I shall be asked to explain your Mexican policy. Can you tell me what it is?" Sir William Tyrell of the British Foreign Office, who was returning to England in November 1913, asked Wilson. The president replied in his most decisive manner, "I am going to teach the South American Republics to elect good men!" As historian Burton J. Hendrick has noted, "In its attitude, its phrasing, [this statement] held the key to much Wilson history."[130]

Determined to teach nations how to govern themselves, Wilson repudiated the historic presidential practice of recognizing all foreign governments and improvised for Mexico a radical new test for diplomatic recognition: "constitutional legitimacy." In other words, was the Mexican government adhering to its own constitution, and beyond that, was it motivated by a sincere desire to eliminate despotism or merely by self-interest and ambition?[131] To Wilson, the test seemed reasonable and honorable. To the Latin Americans, it was meddling.

Wilson achieved a diplomatic victory when he persuaded Great Britain and other European powers to withhold military and economic support from the Huerta regime. But, still not satisfied, he took measures, such as seizing the port of Veracruz in April 1914, to support a counterrevolution instigated by the "constitutionalist" Venustiano Carranza. Then, when the triumphant Carranza chose to brook no advice from the American president, Wilson threw his support to Gen. Francisco "Pancho" Villa, an erstwhile Carranza ally whose defection prolonged Mexico's civil war for an additional three years. Mexicans deeply resented Wilson's clumsy interventions.

The Mexican situation became especially dangerous after another shift in Wilson's diplomatic position. Villa, who proved no more amenable than Carranza or his predecessor to U.S. control, began to extort ever-increasing financial contributions from American-owned companies in Mexico. In Washington, support for Villa gave way to diplomatic recognition of Carranza, provoking Villa to lead raids into Texas. On March 15, 1916, Wilson sent a punitive expedition in pursuit of Villa under the command of Brig. Gen. John J. Pershing. Carranza, greatly alarmed by the size of the American force in Mexico, even though it was hunting his enemy, demanded that Pershing withdraw. Eventually, after military skirmishes and an exchange of ultimatums, Carranza and Wilson worked out an agreement. The president ordered Pershing to return his troops to Texas on January 26, 1917. Carranza, whose stout resistance to the American government made him a hero to the Mexican people, was elected president on March 11. The United States recognized his government two days later.

The conflict with Mexico demonstrated that Wilson was determined to play a constructive role in world affairs. But his intervention, however well intentioned, did little to undo, and in fact aggravated, the resentment that Roosevelt's less idealistic policies in Central and South America had caused. According to Link, although Wilson helped pave the way for the independence of the Mexican people, he "interfered in the wrong way so often that he embittered Mexican–American relations for many years to come."[132] Wilson's severest tests in foreign affairs lay ahead, during and after World War I when, for the first time, the president was required to exercise executive power in conditions of global conflict. In many respects, Wilson's conduct of the war was exemplary. Yet the same stubbornness and idealism that he displayed toward Mexico eventually led to a tragic defeat in his pursuit of a postwar program of lasting peace.

World War I: The Presidency and Total War

Wilson was narrowly reelected in 1916, the first Democrat to win two consecutive terms since Andrew Jackson more than eighty years earlier. His party's slogan was "He kept us out of war," referring both to war with Mexico and the "Great War" that had been raging in Europe since 1914. On April 6, 1917, five weeks after his second inauguration and in response to a long series of German submarine attacks on American ships, Wilson signed a proclamation that a state of war existed with Germany. Congress voted to declare war four days after hearing the president's moving and eloquent appeal, in which he called on the United States to end its traditional position of neutrality in European conflicts. "It is a fearful thing to lead this great peaceful people into war, into the most terrible and disastrous of all wars," said Wilson. "But, the right is more precious than peace, and we shall fight for . . . a universal dominion of right by such a concert of free peoples as shall bring peace and safety to all nations and make the world itself at last free."[133]

The war to "make the world safe for democracy," as Wilson called it, placed new demands on the powers of the president. Waging a modern "total war" that mobilized not just armies but entire societies required the mass production of complex weapons.[134] It also entailed the mobilization and, at a great distance from the United States, the deployment of troops on a grand scale. The president became responsible for organizing and

Woodrow Wilson was more successful promoting his foreign policy agenda during his European tour of December 1918 than he was during his September 1919 tour of the increasingly isolationist United States.

Source: Library of Congress.

controlling the industrial economy and for coordinating the transportation and communication industries so they could meet the requirements of the military commitment.[135] All this was in addition to the traditional duties of the commander in chief.

The need to impose wartime economic and social controls on American society strained the settled procedures of constitutional government to an extent not seen even during the Civil War. Perhaps conscious of the reaction against presidential authority after that conflict, Wilson sought explicit delegations of authority from Congress whenever possible. But he did not rely on statutory permission for everything. When Congress failed to authorize him to arm merchant vessels, for example, Wilson armed them anyway, realizing that he already had the constitutional right to do so as commander in chief. Yet from the start of his presidency Wilson believed that the full flowering of presidential authority required legislative support even in wartime

Of the many delegations of power to the president that followed Congress's declaration of war, the most striking was the Lever Food and Fuel Control Act of 1917. The Lever Act granted Wilson authority "to regulate by license the importation, manufacture, storage, mining or distribution of necessaries"—in effect, to regulate almost the entire national economy. Because such an expansive grant was without precedent, the Lever Act was assailed by critics as the precursor to dictatorship. To allay such concerns, the Senate added a provision that created a bipartisan committee to oversee the conduct of the war.

Wilson attacked the Senate amendment vehemently. Hoping to kill it in the House–Senate conference committee, he fired off a letter to the bill's House sponsor, Democrat A. F. Lever of South Carolina, protesting that the proposed oversight committee would "amount to nothing less than an assumption on the part of the legislative body of the executive work of the administration." Wilson invoked the "ominous precedent" of the Joint Committee on the Conduct of the War, which Congress had constituted during the Lincoln administration. That committee, he argued, "was the cause of constant and distressing harassment and rendered [Lincoln's] task all but impossible."[136] By standing firm and convincing congressional leaders like Lever to do the same, Wilson managed to have the amendment removed. The president signed the Lever Act on August 10, 1917, confirming once more his claim to legislative leadership.

The emergency powers that Wilson accrued during World War I were extraordinary. As Edward S. Corwin has noted, the difference between Wilson's and Lincoln's versions of wartime "dictatorship" was of "method," not of "tenderness for customary constitutional restraints."[137] Once Wilson obtained his extraordinary authority from Congress, he stopped accommodating his party's desire for patronage and instead appointed competent managers to handle the details of administration. The ranks of accomplished wartime administrators included Bernard Baruch, who chaired the powerful War Industries Board; Herbert C. Hoover, who served as food administrator; and Secretary of the Treasury William Gibbs McAdoo, who managed the railroads. Similarly, Wilson left the management of military affairs to his European commander, General Pershing. The president intervened only when important political and diplomatic considerations were involved.[138]

Wilson's style of delegating detailed tasks to trusted members of his administration while continuing to chart the overall direction of the war effort suited his approach to government. It was also an understandable adaptation of presidential leadership to the exigencies of modern warfare. By the twentieth century, war had become too massive and complex an undertaking for the president to supervise closely, as Polk and Lincoln had done in the mid-nineteenth century. It was by providing moral leadership to rally the public and administrative appointments to sustain the country's engagement in total war that Wilson contributed to the development of the president's role as commander in chief.[139]

As historian John Milton Cooper Jr. observes, Wilson also used war-related moral suasion in a progressive domestic cause. Appearing before the Senate on September 30, 1918, with nearly the entire cabinet in tow, Wilson urged senators to add their approval to the women's suffrage amendment to the Constitution already approved by the House. Wilson had been slow to support the right of women to vote, but gradually he came to see the merit of suffragist Carrie Chapman Catt's argument that disenfranchisement "aroused in patriotic women a just suspicion that man and women are not co-workers for world freedom."[140] "We have made partners of women in this war," Wilson told Congress; "shall we admit them only to a partnership of suffering and sacrifice and not to a partnership of privilege and right?" Although the Senate fell two votes short of the required two-thirds when it voted the next day, it approved the amendment the following June.[141] It was ratified by three-fourths of the states fourteen months later, in August 1920.

Wilson never squared his pledge to make the world safe for democracy with support for civil rights activists' struggle for the right to vote. At the urging of the NAACP, however, he published a strong statement condemning lynching. In this "Statement to the American People," Wilson declared:

There have been many lynchings, and every one of them has
been a blow at the heart of law and humane justice. . . . Germany
has outlawed herself among the nations because she has
disregarded the sacred obligations of law and has made lynchers
of her armies. Lynchers emulate her disgraceful example. I, for
my part, am anxious to see every community in America rise
above that level.[142]

Wilson's address was headline-making news, reprinted in its entirety
in many newspapers.[143] Although it represented a small victory for civil
rights, it kindled a ray of hope in the African American community, especially among the black soldiers fighting in Europe. As the African American
newspaper the *Chicago Defender* rejoiced: "The coming of this message
from President Wilson, a Democrat, was like a bolt out of a clear sky, a bolt
intended to strike our enemies a stinging blow; a bolt intended to bring
these wreckers of order and law to a realization of the fact that they are
deserving of the same consideration from true American citizens as that
shown for the Huns, who are endeavoring to kill democracy."[144]

The Defeat of the League of Nations

Ironically, Wilson met defeat in his effort to accomplish the task for
which he believed his influence and talents were best suited: building a
lasting structure of peace among nations. One reason Wilson was cautious
in asserting his powers as commander in chief during the war was that
he did not want to jeopardize the opportunity to take charge at the peace
table. As historian Ernest R. May has argued, "From the first day of the
war to the last, all that Wilson sought was a peace that could be secured
by the League of Nations, a peace that would make the world safe for
democracy."[145]

Wilson's plan for an international peacekeeping organization was
the most controversial of the Fourteen Points, the program of peace that
he formulated in early 1918. Wilson hoped to persuade the Allies and the
Senate to accept this program, which also included lenient terms for the
defeated German nation. The president had to compromise on some of
his points in the postwar peace negotiations, particularly those pertaining
to the conditions to be imposed on Germany, which the European allies
insisted be much more severe than Wilson preferred. But the League of
Nations was included in the Treaty of Versailles. All of the major powers
signed it in June 1919.

Wilson began the battle for Senate ratification of the treaty with little doubt that he would prevail. He had displayed throughout his presidency an almost unsurpassed ability to enlist public support for the causes he championed. Yet in the fight for the league he disdained the methods that succeeded so well in passing his New Freedom program. In domestic affairs Wilson collaborated closely with the House and Senate Democratic leadership, but in foreign affairs he felt constitutionally justified in acting "without any restriction." Wilson's views on foreign policy making, no less than Roosevelt's, resembled those expressed by Alexander Hamilton in the 1793 Pacificus letters. Like Hamilton, Wilson believed in the superiority of the executive in matters of diplomacy, claiming "virtually the power to control them absolutely."[146]

The conflict between Wilson and the Senate over the League of Nations was greatly exacerbated by his expansive understanding of the president's foreign policy prerogatives. The limits of Wilson's political influence first became evident in the 1918 midterm elections, long before the Versailles treaty was signed. No sooner had the Fourteen Points been pronounced and peace negotiations begun than Congress, tiring of Wilson's independent course, began to challenge his conduct of foreign affairs. Former president Roosevelt abetted the opposition by urging the Senate to repudiate the Fourteen Points. On October 24, 1918, TR sent a telegram encouraging Republican leaders to "dictate peace by hammering guns and not chat about peace to the accompaniment of the clicking typewriters."[147]

Flustered by the Republicans' efforts to discredit him on the eve of the midterm elections, Wilson tried to rally the nation in support of his war policy. On the day after Roosevelt's telegram was released, the president made an unusual appeal to the voters: "If you have approved of my leadership and wish me to be your unembarrassed spokesman in affairs at home and abroad, I earnestly beg that you will express yourself unmistakably to that effect by returning a Democratic majority to both the Senate and the House of Representatives."[148]

Wilson's conflation of partisanship with patriotism was a serious political error. He was loudly criticized for suggesting that the Democrats had a monopoly on loyalty. During the war, many Republicans supported the president, and many Democrats opposed him. In fact, Wilson began his effort to secure a sympathetic Congress in the 1918 elections by intervening in the primaries of his own party in the hope of defeating antiadministration Democratic incumbents in five southern states.[149] Although he was successful in Georgia, Mississippi, South Carolina, and Texas, the intraparty purge campaign cast doubt on the president's claim during the general election that he could not prosecute the war successfully without a Democratic majority in both houses of Congress.[150]

Wilson's unwillingness to tolerate opposition reached beyond the halls of Congress. The president established the Committee on Public Information (CPI), led by the muckraking journalist George Creel, which enlisted seventy-five thousand speakers to persuade the American people that the war was a crusade for freedom and democracy against the Germans, a barbaric people bent on world domination. The campaign to arouse patriotism met with mixed success. Both during and after the war Wilson faced a doubtful public. The fighting resulted in more than three hundred thousand American casualties, more than a third of them deaths. Yet it never was entirely clear to many people why the United States was involved, for the first time in its history, in a war among European nations. Unlike previous wars, the World War was not waged in North America and did not involve the acquisition of new territory or the defense of existing American soil. Many, perhaps most voters supported the war. But the significant minority who opposed it included many German and Irish Americans, whose ethnic ties disposed them to doubt the Allied cause, as well as progressive activists such as the prominent social worker Jane Addams, who feared that American democracy would be corrupted by the necessities and cruelties of total war. The CPI and several self-styled patriotic groups sought to discourage and sometimes repress dissent. People who refused to buy war bonds were often ridiculed, and some were even assaulted. People with German names, scorned as "hyphenate Americans," were prosecuted indiscriminately. Some school boards outlawed the teaching of the German language.

Wilson's progressive principles did not deter this wave of oppression. To the contrary, his view that the war was a moral crusade actually inspired intolerance toward those who disagreed. The president signed the Espionage Act of 1917, which imposed fines of up to $10,000 and jail sentences ranging to twenty years for persons convicted of aiding the enemy or obstructing the recruitment of soldiers. Deciding the following year that the act did not forbid enough forms of dissent, Congress passed and Wilson signed the Sedition Act. Invoking its authority, he authorized the postmaster general to ban from the mails material that seemed treasonable or seditious. The Sedition Act also made "saying anything" to discourage the purchase of war bonds a crime and declared illegal efforts to "utter, print, write, or publish any disloyal, profane, scurrilous, or abusive language" about the government, the Constitution, or the uniforms worn by soldiers and sailors.

In the midst of White House efforts to squelch opposition to the war, Wilson's appeal to partisan loyalty in the 1918 elections fell on deaf ears. Indeed, his administration's intolerance of dissent denigrated the democratic principles he championed as the foundation of a "new world order." When the Republicans won control of both houses of Congress for the first time during Wilson's presidency, the *New Republic* scolded him for having discouraged public debate on foreign affairs. Americans had "voted in the dark," the editors argued, and remained "wholly unprepared to deal with the new responsibilities to which [the nation] is committed as the consequence of its own acts and the convulsions of the world."[151] Roosevelt declared soon after the election that "our allies and our enemies and Mr. Wilson himself should all understand that Mr. Wilson has no authority whatever to speak for the American people at this time. His leadership has just been emphatically repudiated by them."[152]

The 1918 elections diminished the president's prestige at home and abroad, adding to the difficulties he encountered at the postwar peace conference and, especially, with Congress. Although Wilson managed to salvage parts of his program at Versailles, he failed completely in Washington. Senate opposition to the treaty, especially to its provision for the league, was led by an implacable foe, Massachusetts Republican Henry Cabot Lodge. As a result of the midterm elections, Lodge became chair of the Senate Foreign Relations Committee. Rejecting compromise with the senator, Wilson left Washington on September 3, 1919, on a month-long speaking tour of the western states. He hoped to revive his long-neglected role as public educator and in doing so to create, as he had in the past, a popular groundswell that would force the Senate to ratify the treaty.[153]

After Woodrow Wilson fell gravely ill in September 1919 while conducting a speaking tour of the country to gain support for the League of Nations, his wife, Edith, shielded him from the daily responsibilities of the presidency. She screened all papers, business, and visitors while he recovered. The full extent of the power she wielded at this time has never been conclusively determined.

Source: Library of Congress.

Instead, Wilson's speaking tour further reduced his influence. It is possible, but not likely, that the campaign would have succeeded had he not suffered a stroke toward the end of the grueling trip that paralyzed his left side, threw him into an emotionally volatile and cognitively uneven state, and severely weakened him for the remainder of his presidency. Months went by in which no one from either the executive or legislative branches government saw or spoke with him. Instead cabinet members and senators conveyed their messages and documents to and from the president through his young wife, Edith Galt Wilson, whom he had married in the White House two years after his first wife died. When the senior member of the cabinet, Secretary of State Robert Lansing, convened a cabinet meeting, he was chastised by the other two people with whom Wilson spent all his time: his chief aide, Joseph Tumulty, and his doctor, Cary Grayson. Grayson interrupted the meeting to say that Wilson wanted to know why the cabinet was meeting without his permission. Vice President Thomas Marshall, whom some urged to take over, instead maintained a nervous silence, fearful of rebuke for usurping power.[154] Based on what he knew of Wilson's condition, Marshall told his wife, "I could throw this country into civil war, but I won't."[155]

Wilson's disability aside, the tide of public opinion had been moving against the president for some time, as evidenced by the 1918 elections.[156] His unsuccessful campaign for the League of Nations, which the Senate repeatedly failed to approve during the long months that Wilson was disabled, offered dramatic confirmation that although the presidency had attained considerable prominence since the turn of the century, the office was still constrained by a powerful, if no longer dominant, Congress and by the vagaries of popular opinion. Because of TR and Wilson, Americans no longer considered it inappropriate for the president to try to rouse public support with rhetorical appeals. But nothing guaranteed that every campaign of persuasion would succeed. The 1920 presidential election, which Warren G. Harding, the conservative, anti-league Republican senator from Ohio, won in a landslide, was a major setback for progressivism and for Wilson's theory of presidential power. So, too, soon after election day, was the final Senate defeat of the League of Nations treaty.

Notes

1. Richard Hofstadter, *The Age of Reform: From Bryan to FDR* (New York: Knopf, 1956), 5.

2. Quoted in Samuel Eliot Morison, *The Oxford History of the American People*, 3 vols. (New York: New American Library, 1972), 3: 130–131.

3. Erwin C. Hargrove and Michael Nelson, *Presidents, Politics, and Policy* (Baltimore: Johns Hopkins University Press, 1984), 49–50; and Richard J. Ellis, *The Development of the American Presidency* (New York: Routledge, 2012), 168–169.

4. Theodore Roosevelt, *The Works of Theodore Roosevelt*, 20 vols. (New York: Scribner's, 1926), 20: 340.

5. Hanna is quoted in Samuel and Dorothy Rosenman, *Presidential Style: Some Giants and a Pygmy in the White House* (New York: Harper and Row, 1976), 1.

6. Roosevelt, *Works*, 20: 450.

7. Rosenman and Rosenman, *Presidential Style*, 123.

8. Roosevelt, *Works*, 20: 347.

9. Ibid., 20: 347.

10. See "The Pacificus–Helvidius Letters," in *The Evolving Presidency: Landmark Documents, 1787–2010*, 4th ed., ed. Michael Nelson (Washington, D.C.: CQ Press, 2011), 50–58.

11. Roosevelt, *Works*, 20: 414.

12. *Plessy v. Ferguson*, 163 U.S. 537.

13. Elmer E. Cornwell Jr., *Presidential Leadership of Public Opinion* (Bloomington: Indiana University Press, 1965), 9. See also Jeffrey Tulis, *The Rhetorical Presidency* (Princeton: Princeton University Press, 1987), 97–116; and Gerald Gamm and Renée M. Smith, "Presidents, Parties, and the Public: Evolving Patterns of Interaction, 1877–1929," in *Speaking to the People: The Rhetorical Presidency in Historical Perspective*, ed. Richard J. Ellis (Amherst: University of Massachusetts Press, 1998).

14. There is no direct evidence that Roosevelt ever spoke or wrote this term. In fact, the comment "I have got such a bully pulpit" did not become identified with TR until his friend and political ally Lyman Abbott quoted these words in an article he published toward the end of Roosevelt's presidency. See Abbott, "A Review of President Roosevelt's Administration: IV—Its Influence on Patriotism and Public Service," *Outlook*, February 27, 1909, 430. In a 1919 eulogy to Roosevelt at the Century Club in New York City, the publisher George Haven Putnam also recalled the former president speaking these words.

15. Ellis, *The Development of the American Presidency*, 76.

16. Gerald Gamm and Renée M. Smith, "Presidents, Parties, and the Public: Evolving Patterns of Interaction, 1877–1929), in Ellis, ed., *Speaking to the People*, 97.

17. Roosevelt, *Works*, 20: 416.

18. Ibid., 20: 342.

19. For a discussion of Roosevelt's campaign on behalf of the Hepburn Act, see Tulis, *Rhetorical Presidency*, 97–116; and Cornwell, *Presidential Leadership of Public Opinion*, 24–26.

20. John Morton Blum, *The Republican Roosevelt* (Cambridge: Harvard University Press, 1954), 74–75.

21. Roosevelt, *Works*, 15: 225.

22. Mark Sullivan, *Our Times, 1900–1925* (New York: Scribner's, 1939), 3: 226.

23. George W. Mowry, *The Era of Theodore Roosevelt, 1900–1912* (New York: Harper, 1958), 201.

24. "Address delivered before the Iroquois Club, at a banquet in Chicago, May 10, 1905," in *The Roosevelt Policy*, 3 vols., ed. William Griffith (New York: Current Literature, 1919), 1: 266–273. See also Mowry, *Era of Theodore Roosevelt*, 201.

25. Quoted in Mowry, *Era of Theodore Roosevelt*, 203.

26. Cornwell, *Presidential Leadership of Public Opinion*, 10.

27. Doris Kearns Goodwin, *The Bully Pulpit: Theodore Roosevelt, William Howard Taft, and the Golden Age of Journalism* (New York: Simon and Schuster, 2013).

28. George W. Alger, "The Literature of Exposure," *Atlantic Monthly*, August 1905, 210. Roosevelt derived the term *muckraker* from the description in John Bunyan's *Pilgrim's*

Progress of the "Man with the Muck-Rake." "Now it is very necessary that we should not flinch from seeing what is vile and debasing," TR said of some journalists who practiced the literature of exposure:

> There is filth on the floor, and it must be scraped up with the muck-rake; and there are times and places where this service is the most needed of all the services that can be performed. But the man who never does anything else, who never speaks or thinks or writes save of his feats with the muck-rake, speedily becomes, not a help to society, not an incitement to good, but one of the most potent forces for evil.

Address at the laying of the cornerstone of the office building of the House of Representatives, Washington, D.C., April 14, 1906, found in Willis Fletcher Johnson, ed., *Theodore Roosevelt: Addresses and Papers* (New York: Sun Dial Classics, 1908), 311.

29. Sullivan, *Our Times*, 3: 83–84.

30. Roosevelt quoted in Blum, *Republican Roosevelt*, 81.

31. Ibid., 87. Political scientist Jeffrey Tulis has noted, "Roosevelt abandoned nineteenth century practice, to be sure, but he did so in a way that retained nineteenth century objectives and accommodated that 'nineteenth century' institution, the Senate." Tulis, *Rhetorical Presidency*, 106–107.

32. Roosevelt, *Works*, 20: 482; Rosenman and Rosenman, *Presidential Style*, 47.

33. Tulis, *Rhetorical Presidency*, 96.

34. A full account of Roosevelt's activities during the strike appears in a letter he wrote to Gov. Winthrop Murray Crane of Massachusetts, who was a concerned and apprehensive observer. See Roosevelt to Crane, October 22, 1902, in *Letters of Theodore Roosevelt*, 8 vols., ed. Elting Morrison (Cambridge: Harvard University Press, 1951), 3: 359–360. In March 1903 the commission granted the miners a 10 percent wage increase and a nine-hour workday. It also recommended a 10 percent increase in the price of coal, more than enough to compensate the industry for the wage increase. The companies were not required to recognize the United Mine Workers, and formal recognition was not granted for ten years. But the union won an important victory in the court of public opinion, as did the president. For an account of the coal strike settlement, see Edmund Morris, *Theodore Rex* (New York: Random House, 2001), 130–137, 150–169.

35. Mowry, *Era of Theodore Roosevelt*, 138; Rosenman and Rosenman, *Presidential Style*, 73.

36. Mowry, *Era of Theodore Roosevelt*, 140.

37. TR cited in ibid., 516. The conference, held in May 1908, included the nation's governors, the cabinet, all nine justices of the Supreme Court, many members of Congress, representatives of sixty-eight professional societies, social activists, and editors and reporters from both technical and popular publications.

38. Douglas Brinkley, *The Wilderness Warrior: Theodore Roosevelt and the Crusade for America* (New York: Harper, 2009).

39. Clayton S. Ellsworth, "Theodore Roosevelt's Country Life Commission," *Agricultural History*, 34 (October 1960): 155–172; Theodore Roosevelt to Sydney Brooks, December 28, 1908, in Morrison, *Letters of Theodore Roosevelt*, 6: 1444–1445, 1446.

40. Kenneth R. Mayer, *With the Stroke of a Pen: Executive Orders and Presidential Power* (Princeton: Princeton University Press, 2001), 51–52, 75.

41. Thomas Dyer, *Theodore Roosevelt and the Idea of Race* (Baton Rouge: Louisiana State University Press, 1980), 102.

42. Eldon Eisenach, *The Lost Promise of Progressivism* (Lawrence: University Press of Kansas, 1994), 42–43.

43. W.E.B. Du Bois, *The Souls of Black Folk* (Chicago: A.C. McClurg, 1909); first published in 1903.

44. "The Negro Problem," Address at the Lincoln dinner of the Republican Club of the City of New York, February 13, 1905, in Roosevelt, *The Works of Theodore Roosevelt*, 26 vols. (New York: Charles Scribner's Sons, 1926), 16: 348.

45. Sidney Milkis and Daniel Tichenor, *Rivalry and Reform: Presidents, Social Movements, and the Transformation of American Politics* (Chicago: University of Chicago Press, 2018), chap 3.

46. Blum, *Republican Roosevelt*, 105.

47. William H. Harbaugh, "The Constitution of the Theodore Roosevelt Presidency and the Progressive Era," in *The Constitution and the American Presidency*, eds. Martin Fausold and Alan Shank (Albany: State University of New York Press, 1991), 73–76.

48. Peri E. Arnold, *Remaking the Presidency: Roosevelt, Taft, and Wilson, 1901–1916* (Lawrence: University Press of Kansas, 2009), chap. 3.

49. Roosevelt, *Works*, 15: 117.

50. Ibid., 15: 114.

51. Ibid., 20: 510, 549–550.

52. Roosevelt to Marcus Alonzo Hanna, October 5, 1903, in Morrison, *Letters of Theodore Roosevelt*, 3: 625.

53. Roosevelt, *Works*, 20: 501.

54. Ibid.

55. William M. Goldsmith, ed., *The Growth of Presidential Power: A Documented History*, 3 vols. (New York: Chelsea, 1974), 2: 1233.

56. Mowry, *Era of Theodore Roosevelt*, 155.

57. Goldsmith, *Growth of Presidential Power*, 2: 1233–1234.

58. Roosevelt, *Works*, 15: 256–257.

59. Mowry, *Era of Theodore Roosevelt*, 159.

60. Roosevelt, *Works*, 20: 490.

61. When Russia violated the Open Door policy by expanding into Manchuria after 1902, Roosevelt wanted to take action, but he did not think that the American people would support a military intervention in Asia. Therefore, he welcomed Japan's attack on the Russian fleet in Port Arthur.

62. This agreement is described in a confidential memo to Roosevelt from Secretary of War William Howard Taft, July 29, 1905, in Goldsmith, *Growth of Presidential Power*, 2: 1246–1247. TR responded almost immediately, indicating that the agreement Taft had worked out with the Japanese prime minister, Count Taro Katsura, was "absolutely correct in every respect" and that he confirmed "every word you have said" (telegram from Roosevelt to Taft, July 31, 1905, in Morrison, *Letters of Theodore Roosevelt*, 4: 1293). See also Henry F. Pringle, *The Life and Times of William Howard Taft*, 2 vols. (New York: Farrar and Rinehart, 1939), 1: 297–299.

63. Mowry, *Era of Theodore Roosevelt*, 185.

64. Roosevelt describes his decision to send the naval fleet around the world in his autobiography. See *Works*, 20: 535–546.

65. Goldsmith, *Growth of Presidential Power*, 2: 1269.

66. Mowry, *Era of Theodore Roosevelt*, 226.

67. Ibid., 180; Roosevelt, *Works*, 20: 378.

68. Roosevelt to Trevelyan, June 19, 1908, Theodore Roosevelt papers, Manuscript Division, Library of Congress, Washington, D.C.

69. Mowry, *Era of Theodore Roosevelt*, 227.

70. Lewis L. Gould, *Four Hats in the Ring: The 1912 Election and the Birth of Modern American Politics* (Lawrence: University Press, of Kansas, 2008), 2, 49.

71. Paolo E. Coletta, *The Presidency of William Howard Taft* (Lawrence: University Press of Kansas, 1973), 48.

72. William Howard Taft, *Our Chief Magistrate and His Powers* (New York: Columbia University Press, 1916), 139–140.

73. Archie Butt, *Taft and Roosevelt: The Intimate Letters of Archie Butt* (Garden City, N.Y.: Doubleday, Doran, 1930), 1: 30.

74. Goodwin, *The Bully Pulpit*, 589.

75. Cornwell, *Presidential Leadership of Public Opinion*, 27.

76. Taft to W. R. Nelson, February 23, 1909, cited in Coletta, *Presidency of William Howard Taft*, 45–46.

77. Cited in William Henry Harbaugh, *Power and Responsibility: The Life and Times of Theodore Roosevelt* (New York: Farrar Straus and Cudahy, 1961), 384.

78. Cited in Mowry, *Era of Theodore Roosevelt*, 245.

79. Quoted in Harbaugh, *Power and Responsibility*, 384.

80. Mowry, *Era of Theodore Roosevelt*, 246.

81. Ibid., 246.

82. Coletta, *Presidency of William Howard Taft*, 71.

83. Wilfred E. Binkley, *President and Congress* (New York: Knopf, 1947), 200. The only office that Taft ever ran for, except the presidency, was justice of the State Superior Court in Ohio.

84. Goodwin, *The Bully Pulpit*, 15. Taft's wish to be chief justice was granted more than a decade later by President Warren G. Harding.

85. Quoted in Ray Stannard Baker, *Woodrow Wilson: Life and Times*, 8 vols. (Garden City, N.Y.: Doubleday, Doran, 1931), 3: 181.

86. Leonard D. White has written of James K. Polk's earlier coordination of budget appropriations: "The precedent established by Polk disappeared from view, and a new start had to be made many decades later on this aspect of presidential power." White, *The Jacksonians: A Study in Administrative History, 1829–1861* (New York: Macmillan, 1956), 82.

87. Peri E. Arnold, *Making the Managerial Presidency: Comprehensive Reorganization Planning, 1905–1980* (Princeton: Princeton University Press, 1986), 44–45. On Taft's budget proposals, see Goldsmith, *Growth of Presidential Power*, 3: 1471–1478.

88. Gould, *Four Hats in the Ring*, 41; and Ellis, *The Development of the American Presidency*, 273.

89. In the new Congress, Democrats outnumbered Republicans by 51 to 44 in the Senate and 290 to 127 in the House.

90. Quoted in Edward S. Corwin, *The President: Office and Powers, 1787–1957*, 4th ed. (New York: New York University Press, 1957), 36.

91. George W. Mowry, *Theodore Roosevelt and the Progressive Movement* (Madison: University of Wisconsin Press, 1946), 228.

92. George W. Mowry, "The Election of 1912," in *History of American Presidential Elections, 1789–1968*, 4 vols., eds. Arthur M. Schlesinger Jr. and Fred L. Israel (New York: Chelsea, 1971), 3: 2146. The total popular vote in the primaries was Roosevelt, 1,164,765; Taft, 768,202; and La Follette, 327,357. Gould, *Four Hats in the Ring*, 65.

93. Roosevelt, *Works*, 20: 471. On the significance of the 1912 election, see Sidney M. Milkis, *Theodore Roosevelt, the Progressive Party, and the Transformation of American Democracy* (Lawrence: University Press of Kansas, 2009).

94. In accepting the Progressive Party's nomination in person, Roosevelt followed the example of previous third-party candidates who scorned the traditions of the two major parties. Soon after being nominated by the Populist Party in 1892, James B. Weaver was summoned to address the convention. Weaver did not formally accept the nomination until a month later, however. Fred Emory Haynes, *James Baird Weaver* (Iowa City: State Historical Society of Iowa, 1919), 310–343. Socialist nominee Eugene Debs went a step further. He attended his party's convention in 1904 and proclaimed his acceptance before the delegates. Bernard J. Brommel, *Eugene V. Debs: Spokesman for Labor and Socialism* (Chicago: Charles H. Kerr Publishing, 1978), 79–80; H. Wayne Morgan, *Eugene V. Debs: Socialist for President* (Syracuse: Syracuse University Press, 1962), 67–68. Roosevelt's stature made his acceptance

of the Progressive Party convention's 1912 nomination all the more dramatic. "Marking a new departure in the proceedings of national conventions," reported the *San Francisco Examiner*, "the two candidates [Roosevelt and his running mate, California governor Hiram Johnson] were notified of their nominations, and in the midst of deafening cheers they appeared before the delegates to voice their acceptance and to pledge their best efforts in the coming campaign." *San Francisco Examiner*, August 8, 1912, 1. See also John Allen Gable, *The Bull Moose Years: Theodore Roosevelt and the Progressive Party* (Port Washington, N.Y.: Kennikat Press, 1978), 108.

95. Roosevelt, *Works*, 17: 219; and Proceedings of the First National Convention of the Progressive Party, August 5, 6, and 7, 1912, Progressive Party Archives, Theodore Roosevelt Collection, Houghton Library, Harvard University. See also Mowry, "Election of 1912," 3: 2151–2153, 2164. On the Progressive Party and its legacy, see Sidney M. Milkis and Daniel J. Tichenor, "'Direct Democracy' and Social Justice: The Progressive Party Campaign of 1912," *Studies in American Political Development*, 8 (Fall 1994): 282–340; and Milkis, *Theodore Roosevelt, the Progressive Party, and the Transformation of American Democracy*.

96. Gould, *Four Hats in the Ring*, 181, 182.

97. Mark Lawrence Kornbluh, *Why America Stopped Voting: The Decline of Participatory Democracy and the Emergence of Modern American Politics* (New York: New York University Press, 2000), chap. 5.

98. Goldsmith, *Growth of Presidential Power*, 3: 1343; Mowry, "Election of 1912," 3: 2163–2165.

99. Woodrow Wilson to Alexander Mitchell Palmer, February 5, 1913, in *The Papers of Woodrow Wilson*, 69 vols., ed. Arthur S. Link (Princeton: Princeton University Press, 1974), 27: 98–102. Palmer, who worked closely with Wilson in his 1912 campaign, was appointed attorney general in 1919.

100. Woodrow Wilson, "Cabinet Government in the United States," *International Review*, 7 (August 1879): 146–163.

101. As noted in Chapter 7, Wilson's revised views on presidential power were first expressed in 1900 in the preface to the fifteenth printing of *Congressional Government*. The growing role of the United States in world affairs and other developments, he came to believe, was likely to place the president at the center of national politics and government. See Woodrow Wilson, *Congressional Government* (Boston: Houghton Mifflin, 1885; New York: Meridian Books, 1956), 19–23. Subsequently, TR's dynamic leadership convinced Wilson that this likelihood had become a reality. Wilson's mature views on presidential leadership and constitutional change are expressed in Woodrow Wilson, *Constitutional Government in the United States* (New York: Columbia University Press, 1908).

102. Quoted in David Lawrence, *The True Story of Woodrow Wilson* (New York: Doran, 1924), 39.

103. Wilson, *Constitutional Government in the United States*, 68–69.

104. Ibid., 71–72.

105. Ibid., 68.

106. Ibid., 68–69. For a comprehensive treatment of Wilson's understanding of constitutional government, see Daniel D. Stid, *The President as Statesman: Woodrow Wilson and the Constitution* (Lawrence: University Press of Kansas, 1998).

107. James Ceaser, *Presidential Selection: Theory and Development* (Princeton: Princeton University Press, 1979), 173.

108. Woodrow Wilson, "First Annual Message," December 2, 1913, in *The State of the Union Messages of the Presidents*, ed. Fred L. Israel (New York: Chelsea, 1966), 2548.

109. Arthur S. Link, *Wilson and the New Freedom* (Princeton: Princeton University Press, 1956), 149.

110. Link, *Papers of Woodrow Wilson*, 27: 151. Wilson's contribution to popular leadership in the United States is assessed in Jeffrey Tulis, *The Rhetorical Presidency* (Princeton:

Princeton University Press, 1987), 117–144. For an alternative view of Wilson that portrays him as a reluctant reformer, see Terri Bimes and Stephen Skowronek, "Woodrow Wilson's Critique of Popular Leadership: Reassessing the Modern-Traditional Divide in Presidential History," in Ellis, ed., *Speaking to the People*.

111. Elmer E. Cornwell Jr., *Presidential Leadership of Public Opinion* (Bloomington: Indiana University Press, 1965), 32–44.

112. *New York Times*, April 8, 1913, 1.

113. Cornwell, *Presidential Leadership of Public Opinion*, 46.

114. American Presidency Project, "Woodrow Wilson, Address to a Joint Session of Congress on Tariff Reform, April 8th, 1913," http://www.presidency.ucsb.edu/ws/index.php?pid=65368.

115. Ray Stannard Baker, *Woodrow Wilson: Life and Letters*, 8 vols. (London: Heinemann, 1932), 4: 109.

116. Arthur S. Link, *Woodrow Wilson and the Progressive Era, 1910–1917* (New York: Harper and Row, 1954), 35.

117. Quoted in ibid., 21.

118. Woodrow Wilson, "Monopoly or Opportunity," in Goldsmith, *Growth of Presidential Power*, 3: 1334–1342.

119. Link, *Papers of Woodrow Wilson*, 31: 415.

120. Paul Van Riper, *History of the United States Civil Service* (Evanston, Ill.: Row, Peterson, 1958), 230; William Dudley Foulke, *Fighting the Spoilsmen* (New York: Putnam's, 1919; New York: Arno Press, 1974), 226–259.

121. Daniels to Franklin D. Roosevelt, December 15, 1932, Ray Stannard Baker Collection, Franklin D. Roosevelt File, Firestone Library, Princeton University.

122. Quoted in Baker, *Woodrow Wilson: Life and Letters*, 4: 45.

123. Link, *Wilson and the New Freedom*, 159.

124. Maurice Low, "The South in the Saddle," *Harper's Weekly*, February 8, 1913, 20; Lewis L. Gould, *The Modern American Presidency* (Lawrence: University Press of Kansas, 2003), 48.

125. *New Republic*, December 5, 1914, 11–12.

126. Stephen Skowronek, "The Reassociation of Ideas and Purposes: Racism, Liberalism, and the American Political Tradition, *American Political Science Review*, vol. 100 (August 2006): 385–401.

127. H. W. Brands, "Woodrow Wilson and the Irony of Fate," *Diplomatic History*, 28 (September 2004): 503–512.

128. Wilson, *Constitutional Government in the United States*, 78.

129. Link, *Wilson and the New Freedom*, 277.

130. Burton J. Hendrick, *The Life and Letters of Walter J. Page*, 3 vols. (New York: Doubleday, 1922), 1: 204–205.

131. Link, *Wilson and the New Freedom*, 350; Sidney Warren, *The President as World Leader* (Philadelphia: Lippincott, 1964), 81.

132. Link, *Woodrow Wilson and the Progressive Era*, 144.

133. Link, *Papers of Woodrow Wilson*, 41: 526.

134. The concept of "total war" applied in part to the Civil War. The assault on slavery and the military tactics of Gen. William Tecumseh Sherman, who used armed force against the civilian population of the rebel states, demonstrated the effectiveness of a plan of action that would destroy the enemy's economic system and demoralize the civilian population. See John Bennett Walters, "General William T. Sherman and Total War," *Journal of Southern History*, 14 (1948): 447–480. In the twentieth century, however, the concept of total war took on a new, more expansive meaning. With the development of the modern state, war became an instrument of national policy that mobilized the society's entire population and resources for a prolonged conflict. Edward S. Corwin defined total war as "the politically

ordered participation in the war effort of all personal and social forces, the scientific, the mechanical, the commercial, the economic, the moral, the literary, the artistic, and the psychological." Corwin, *Total War and the Constitution* (New York: Knopf, 1947), 24.

135. For a discussion of Wilson's leadership during World War I, see Goldsmith, *Growth of Presidential Power*, 3: 1699–1733.

136. Quoted in Baker, *Woodrow Wilson: Life and Letters*, 7: 185–186.

137. Corwin, *President: Office and Powers*, 237.

138. Goldsmith, *Growth of Presidential Power*, 3: 1705, 1711.

139. Ibid., 3: 1706.

140. Carrie Chapman Catt to Woodrow Wilson, September 29, 1918, as cited in Daniel J. Tichenor, "Leaders, Citizenship Movements, and the Politics Rivals Make," in *Formative Acts: American Politics in the Making*, eds. Stephen Skowronek and Matthew Glassman (Philadelphia: University of Pennsylvania Press, 2007), 261.

141. John Milton Cooper Jr., *Woodrow Wilson: A Biography* (New York: Knopf, 2009), 411–414.

142. John Shillady to Wilson, July 25, 1918, Link, *The Papers of Woodrow Wilson*, vol. 49, 88–89; Wilson, "A Statement to the American People," Ibid, 97–98.

143. "President Wilson's Proclamation Denouncing Lynching," *Afro-American*, August 2, 1918, 1.

144. "Our President Has Spoken," *Chicago Defender*, August 3, 1918, 16.

145. Ernest R. May, "Wilson (1917–1918)," in *The Ultimate Decision: The President as Commander in Chief*, ed. Ernest R. May (New York: Braziller, 1960), 131.

146. Wilson, *Constitutional Government in the United States*, 77–79. On Wilson's dual conception of the presidency, see Daniel Stid, "Rhetorical Leadership and 'Common Counsel' in the Presidency of Woodrow Wilson," in Ellis, ed., *Speaking to the People*.

147. Warren, *President as World Leader*, 107.

148. Link, *Papers of Woodrow Wilson*, 51: 381.

149. *New York Times*, August 12, 1918, sec. 3, 1. Sidney M. Milkis, "Presidents and Party Purges: With Special Emphasis on the Lessons of 1938," in *Presidents and Their Parties: Leadership or Neglect?* ed. Robert Harmel (New York: Praeger, 1984), 154–157.

150. Cooper judges Wilson's intervention in these 1918 Democratic primaries "the only successful party purge by a president in American history." *Woodrow Wilson*, 437.

151. *New Republic*, November 9, 1918, cited in Thomas J. Knock, *To End All Wars: Woodrow Wilson and the Quest for a New World Order* (New York: Oxford University Press, 1992), 186.

152. Quoted in Warren, *President as World Leader*, 108. The Republicans outnumbered the Democrats in the Sixty-sixth Congress by 237 to 191 in the House and 48 to 47 in the Senate.

153. Knock, *To End All Wars*, 260.

154. A. Scott Berg, *Wilson* (New York: G. P. Putnam's Sons, 2013), chap. 16.

155. Quoted in Jules Witcover, *The American Vice Presidency: From Irrelevance to Power* (Washington, D.C.: Smithsonian Books, 2014), 264.

156. Nevertheless, the failure of Wilson's campaign for the League of Nations was hardly a foregone conclusion. Indeed, before his health failed, Wilson was attracting large, enthusiastic crowds, and the opponents of the treaty were sufficiently concerned about his influence to send out Senators William E. Borah of Idaho and Hiram Johnson of California to give the other side of the argument. See Kendrick A. Clements, *The Presidency of Woodrow Wilson* (Lawrence: University Press of Kansas, 1992), 196.

CHAPTER

9

The Triumph of Conservative Republicanism

The election of Warren G. Harding by a huge majority in 1920 marked the end of the Progressive era. Harding won 60 percent of the national popular vote against the Democratic nominee, Ohio governor James M. Cox, who received just 34 percent. The Socialist Party candidate, Eugene V. Debs, won 3.4 percent of the vote, even though he was in jail for urging resistance to the draft in violation of the 1918 wartime Sedition Act. Harding also swept the Electoral College, winning 404 votes to Cox's 127. Harding carried every state outside the South, and he managed to win 40 percent of the popular vote below the Mason–Dixon Line. His victory in Tennessee marked the first time since the end of Reconstruction that one of the eleven states of the Confederacy voted for a Republican for president. The only bright spot for the Democrats in 1920 was the impression made by their thirty-eight-year-old vice-presidential candidate, Franklin D. Roosevelt, a distant cousin of TR and the assistant secretary of the navy under President Woodrow Wilson. Roosevelt's energetic campaign earned him a prominent national reputation and launched a political career that led to his election as governor of New York in 1928 and president in 1932, despite his battle with polio, which began in 1921 and lasted until he died in 1945.

The landslide election that brought Harding to office was fought on the issues of World War I and the League of Nations.[1] But in rejecting the league, so closely identified with Wilson and his aspirations for national and international reform, voters were expressing their general desire for quieter times after two decades of far-reaching and fundamental political change. The return to isolation from world affairs, which the repudiation of the league inaugurated, was accompanied at home by a return to a laissez-faire approach to governing—that is, a partial restoration of the wall that had largely separated government from the economy before the advent of progressivism.

Harding's election could be explained in no small part by his identification with the nation's longing for a moratorium on change. In May 1920 he told the Home Market Club in Boston, "America's present need is not heroics, but healing; not nostrums but normalcy; not revolution but restoration . . . not surgery but serenity."[2]

The word *normalcy*, in particular, attracted immediate and lasting attention, and a "return to normalcy" became the theme of the 1920 Republican presidential campaign.[3] Normalcy captured the temper of the times as it related not just to public policy but to the presidency as well. Harding capitalized on the popular reaction against what the Republicans called "executive autocracy." Meanwhile, a stricken President Wilson played into the Republicans' hands. Before Congress adjourned in the summer of 1920, it passed an act to repeal sixty wartime laws that conferred extraordinary powers on the executive. The Repeal Act was approved by the House of Representatives in a 343–3 vote and by the Senate unanimously. Nevertheless, after Congress adjourned, Wilson pocket-vetoed the act, thereby retaining his war powers until Congress met again in December 1920. Historian William Starr Myers has noted that in doing so, "President Wilson . . . took one more step which decisively alienated the average American citizen."[4]

The Republicans resumed power in March 1921, militant in their determination to restore Congress and the party organization to their former stature. As the leader of the committee that officially notified Harding of his nomination by the 1920 Republican convention, Sen. Henry Cabot Lodge presented the candidate with something of an ultimatum. Alluding to the transfer of power from Congress to the presidency during the Wilson administration, Lodge reminded Harding that "the makers of the Constitution intended to coordinate the three great elements of government and strove to guard against either usurpation or trespass by one branch at the expense of the other." "In that spirit," the senator added, "*we all know well*, you will enter upon your great responsibility."[5]

Neither Harding nor his two Republican successors, Calvin Coolidge and Herbert C. Hoover, took exception to the sentiment that Lodge expressed. Their understanding of executive power owed more to William Howard Taft than to Theodore Roosevelt. In fact, the twelve-year tenure of these three presidents is generally regarded as the nadir of presidential power in the twentieth century.

There was, however, no restoration of congressional government during the 1920s. Transformed social and economic conditions, as well as the precedents that TR and Wilson established, did not allow for a complete return to the old order. As Elmer E. Cornwell Jr. observed, "The stature of the [executive] office in the eyes of the public, which had been growing since 1900, and was given powerful impetus during the Wilson years, at least held its own if it did not actually continue to grow after 1920."[6] Even Harding's concept of "normalcy" did not entail turning back the clock entirely. As he wrote during the campaign,

President Woodrow Wilson rides with President-elect Warren G. Harding to Harding's inauguration on March 4, 1921. Harding promised a "return to normalcy" after the Progressive era and the tumultuous war years.

Source: Library of Congress.

The common people—the people of whom Lincoln said that God must have loved them, because he made so many of them—have seen themselves lifted to a new level in the social and economic scheme of the world; and our problems of the future will be to maintain them there.[7]

The Harding Era

In his acceptance speech for the Republican presidential nomination, Harding tried to reassure Lodge and his Senate colleagues that he would resist the lure of executive aggrandizement. The nominee pledged that if elected, he would restore "party government as distinguished from personal government, individual, dictatorial, autocratic, or what not."[8] True to his promise as a candidate, President Harding made little effort to lead Congress. His expressed intention was to reign rather than rule. The president would announce his legislative program, which the Constitution directed him to do, but after that, lawmaking would be the work of Congress. On those rare occasions when Harding did take an interest in legislative matters, his actions almost always showed great deference to Congress. Harding's model was William McKinley, whose influence on Capitol Hill was exercised through consultation and compromise with his party's leadership.[9]

But McKinley-style legislative leadership was no longer possible in the 1920s. The congressional revolt of 1910, which dethroned the Speaker, weakened the bonds of party in the House. Gone were the days when the president and the Speaker could bring together the executive and legislative branches of the government through quiet conversation. The Senate, too, was affected by an insurgent revolt against strong party leadership. Moreover, the enactment in 1913 of the Seventeenth Amendment, which provided that voters, not the state legislatures, would elect senators, further undermined party discipline in the upper house. The typical senator, one observer wrote in 1922, "came to think more in terms of himself and his reelection, nearly always an impelling motive, and less in terms of party."[10] Wilson's bold methods of party leadership had forged, at least for a time, new connections between the president and Congress. Harding's passivity guaranteed deadlock and confusion.

One consequence of the new president's forbearance was that his program to address the problems of the postwar economy through higher tariffs and lower taxes made little headway in the legislature. Instead, Congress became bogged down in its own disagreements about what to do. Harding's relations with legislators were aggravated by a battle over bonus payments to World War I veterans. Although most Republicans in Congress, pressured by the American Legion of Ex-Servicemen, supported cash compensation for war veterans, Harding and Treasury Secretary Andrew Mellon feared that the high cost of these payments threatened their plan for substantial tax cuts prior to the 1922 election.[11] An old friend of the president, Malcolm Jennings, wrote him in the late summer of 1921 that effective "congressional action can only follow the establishment of dominant leadership upon your part."[12] Harding began to regret his pledge to defer to Congress. As his policies foundered on Capitol Hill, he replied to Jennings, "I find that I can not carry out my pre-election ideals of an Executive keeping himself aloof from Congress."[13]

Yet regret was unaccompanied by reform. Even when, to the astonishment of many, Harding went before Congress on July 12, 1921, to chide the House and, especially, the Senate for inaction on his economic program, he did not follow through with the sort of forceful and painstaking efforts at public or personal persuasion that might have moved his fractious party to action. Harding did not bow down to Congress, but neither did he have the desire or the ability to lead it.[14]

Fresh from its defeat of the League of Nations, Congress was determined to influence foreign affairs during Harding's term. Most significant, the Senate took the initiative to curb the naval arms race that had preoccupied the major powers since the beginning of World War I. The rejection of the Versailles treaty ensured that the nation's naval buildup would continue after the war. Many public officials, including Harding, believed that attaining naval supremacy was the only alternative to joining the league. Yet an arms race would be expensive, especially because Great Britain and Japan were determined to match the American deployments.

Responding to this dilemma, progressive Republican senator William E. Borah of Idaho attached an amendment to the 1921 naval appropriation bill that called on the president to invite Great Britain and Japan to a naval disarmament conference. Although Harding tried to replace the rider with a weaker resolution, it passed. Harding was not opposed to having a conference, but he thought it would be prudent to build up the American fleet first.

Still, Harding was not one to engage Congress in a bitter and protracted struggle. Bowing to the legislative will, he convened an international disarmament conference in Washington in late 1921 and early 1922. The Washington Naval Disarmament Conference successfully worked out an agreement not only on naval armaments but also on relations between the major Pacific powers. Partly to avoid the mistakes of his predecessor in the League of Nations fight, Harding allowed Secretary of State Charles Evans Hughes to take the lead in the disarmament treaty negotiations. The president also appointed Henry Cabot Lodge and Oscar W. Underwood, the ranking members of the Senate Foreign Relations Committee, to the American delegation. Harding then gave Lodge and Underwood full responsibility for steering the treaties negotiated at the conference through the Senate.[15] Characteristic of Harding's presidency, however, his outstanding foreign policy accomplishment was the result of a Senate initiative, an indication of "how great had been the reaction against the Wilsonian type of executive."[16]

The Harding Scandals

Harding's presidency began slowly and ended disastrously. By 1923 it was clear that the country was paying a heavy price for his passive leadership and fawning deference to his party's apparatus. The president's pledge to restore normalcy included a revived enthusiasm for patronage appointments. The steady extension of the merit civil service that began with passage of the Pendleton Act in 1883 and continued afterward, especially during Theodore Roosevelt's presidency, went no further in the Harding administration. Wilson had been willing to manipulate the civil service when party patronage proved useful in getting his program through Congress. But Harding was the only twentieth-century president to embrace the spoils system as worthy in its own right. According to Paul Van Riper, "By the middle of the summer of 1921 the spoils efforts of the Republicans began to assume the proportions of a sizable if not full-scale raid."[17]

Nor was Harding himself reluctant to manipulate the remaining unclassified service, which now constituted only around one-fourth of the federal workforce. Some of Harding's appointments were excellent, especially his selection of Hoover as secretary of commerce and Hughes as secretary of state. Many others, however, were reminiscent of the Grant era. Collectively, Harding's appointees produced the worst corruption of any administration since the advent of civil service reform.

The first disturbing situation to come to light involved Charles Forbes, the director of the Veterans Bureau. In March 1923 Harding was told that Forbes was selling items from the government's medical supply base in Perryville, Maryland, to private contractors at suspiciously low prices. He also was making undercover deals for hospital building contracts and site selections. Forbes was forced to resign, and his principal legal adviser, Charles F. Cramer, committed suicide.[18]

When the Veterans Bureau scandal was quickly followed by another in the attorney general's office, Harding became convinced that his administration was deeply tainted with corruption. Fearing for his reputation and for the fortunes of his party, the president reportedly lamented to journalist William Allen White, "My God, this is a hell of a job! I have no trouble with my enemies. I can take care of my enemies all right. But my damn friends, my god-damn friends, White, they're the ones that keep me walking the floor nights."[19]

Despondent and in poor health, Harding decided to escape Washington on a cross-country speaking tour that would culminate in Alaska. In the course of his return trip, he fell ill with ptomaine poisoning, then pneumonia, and died of an embolism in San Francisco on August 2, 1923. Vice President Calvin Coolidge, the former governor of Massachusetts, became president.

Mercifully for Harding, he died a few months before the uncovering of the Teapot Dome scandal, a complicated and subtle plot to defraud the government that was hatched and executed during his presidency. Teapot Dome, one of the most notorious political scandals in American history, originated with the administration's effort to modify, and in some cases reverse, the conservation policies of Roosevelt, Taft, and Wilson.[20] The prime mover in the affair was Harding's secretary of the interior, Albert

B. Fall, who wanted to prevent the navy from continuing to withdraw petroleum-rich lands from private development, a practice devised to provide a reliable supply of oil in future naval emergencies. In 1921 Fall, who was a strong advocate of private development, persuaded Secretary of the Navy Edwin Denby to turn over management of the petroleum reserves to the Interior Department. Fall then rapidly implemented a new program to lease the reserves to certain oil companies, which favored him in turn with personal loans and gifts.

Fall probably did not require payoffs to pursue most of his policies; the leasing program meshed with his ideas about resource development.[21] But the secretary's greed got the better of him, thereby exposing his policies to attack from conservationists and their allies in the Senate. An exhaustive Senate investigation chaired by Montana senator Thomas J. Walsh disclosed that Fall had entered into a corrupt bargain with the oil companies of Edward L. Doheny and Harry F. Sinclair, granting them access to some valuable petroleum deposits that President Wilson had reserved for the navy. The Elk Hill, California, oil reserve was leased to Doheny and the Teapot Dome oil reserve in Wyoming to Sinclair. In return for the leases, Doheny and Sinclair built some pipelines and storage facilities for the navy on the West Coast and at Pearl Harbor in Hawaii. But Fall personally received at least $100,000 from Doheny and $300,000 from Sinclair.

Armed with these facts and other damaging revelations unearthed by the Senate committee, a special commission appointed by President Coolidge initiated criminal prosecutions in early June 1924. Sinclair, Doheny, and Fall, who resigned as secretary of the interior before the scandal broke, were charged with conspiracy to defraud the government. The trials and legal maneuvering lasted almost six years, after which Fall was sentenced to a year in jail and a $100,000 fine. Sinclair received a six-month sentence. But Doheny was acquitted, a ridiculous verdict considering that Fall was convicted of taking a bribe from him. The acquittal provoked George W. Norris, the progressive Republican senator from Nebraska, to remark that it is "very difficult, if not impossible to convict one hundred million dollars."[22]

Budget and Accounting Act of 1921

Harding's public reputation, which remained high while he was alive, suffered tremendously from the scandalous revelations that rocked Washington after he died. But the Harding administration was not without its achievements. During his tenure, the first national budget system was created, enhancing significantly the president's authority to oversee the expenditures of the executive departments and agencies. The Budget and Accounting Act of 1921 carried into effect the major recommendations of the 1913 Commission on Economy and Efficiency created by President Taft.

The budget act required the president to compile an annual, comprehensive executive budget based on estimates of both the government's financial needs and its revenues for the coming fiscal year. The act also established the Bureau of the Budget to help the president exercise the new budget authority. Although formally part of the Treasury Department, the Bureau of the Budget was meant to serve as a presidential staff agency. Its director was a presidential assistant and did not require Senate confirmation. Finally, the act created the General Accounting Office as an auditing arm of Congress.

With the passage of the budget act, the president finally obtained legal authority to oversee the allocation of expenditures in the executive branch (in the past each department had sent its annual budget request straight to Congress). In exercising this authority, the president still had to contend with the powerful fiscal committees in Congress, especially the House Ways and Means Committee, the Senate Finance Committee, and the Appropriations Committees of both chambers, as well as with the executive agency heads, who for so long had dealt directly with legislators. But the president certainly was able to exert greater authority in budgetary matters with the new act than without it. Indeed, Herbert Emmerich, a scholar and civil servant, has judged the budget act to be "the greatest landmark of our administrative history except for the Constitution itself."[23]

Harding was not the first president to advocate a national budget system. Not just Taft but also Wilson supported measures to strengthen the president's authority in fiscal affairs. Indeed, the Republican Congress passed such a measure in 1920, but Wilson vetoed the bill because it restricted the president's power to remove the comptroller general, who is the head of the General Accounting Office. With a Republican administration in office in 1921, Congress passed the bill again, and President Harding, more willing than Wilson to share this power with Congress, signed it.[24] Harding and the first director of the budget bureau, the capable Charles G. Dawes, made effective use of the authority that the new law placed in the president's hands. Harding's 1920 call for a return to normalcy had included a pledge to reduce government spending. Dedicated to fulfilling this pledge, Harding, who gradually become aware of the need to exercise more purposeful leadership of his party, held his cabinet to a stern fiscal program that in 1923 achieved almost $2 billion in savings—a nearly 40 percent reduction in federal spending that produced annual budget surpluses for the remainder of the decade.[25]

Expansion of the President's Removal Power

Harding also made an indirect contribution to the president's control of administrative affairs by appointing William Howard Taft as chief justice of the United States in 1921. Taft's majority opinion in *Myers v. United States* (1926) gave constitutional sanction to a sweeping interpretation of the president's removal power.[26] Although repeal of the Tenure of Office Act in 1887 eliminated one obstacle to presidential removal, nothing prevented Congress from deciding to enact a similar statute in the future. Indeed, as the budget act's restriction on the president's power to remove the comptroller general illustrates, Congress continued to limit the president's ability to create new federal offices and establish the procedures for filling them.

The 1876 statute that was at issue in the *Myers* case required the president to obtain the advice and consent of the Senate before removing a first-class postmaster from office. On January 20, 1920, President Wilson requested the resignation of postmaster Frank S. Myers for "autocratic" behavior in his Portland, Oregon, post office. When Myers refused the request, Wilson removed him by order of the postmaster general.

Surprisingly, the legality of Wilson's action was upheld by a Supreme Court, whose chief justice had endorsed, while serving as president, a narrow theory of executive power. But, properly understood, Taft's opinion expressed his position, demonstrated in efforts toward the end of his tenure in the White House to strengthen the president's authority over fiscal policy, that constitutionally the chief executive may govern energetically within his branch of government.[27] The chief justice ruled that Wilson's order was valid because the law restricting the president's authority to remove postmasters was unconstitutional. Arguing that the removal power was inherently executive, Taft insisted that the president must be able to control all executive officeholders, not just highly placed ones. He declared both the 1876 statute and the 1867 Tenure of Office Act unconstitutional, even though the latter had long ago been repealed. "The imperative reasons requiring an unrestricted power to remove the most important of his subordinates in their most important duties," the chief justice explained, "must . . . control the interpretation of the Constitution as to all appointed by him."[28]

The *Myers* decision was the Court's first foray into the long struggle between the president and Congress for possession of the removal power.

Issued by a conservative chief justice appointed by a conservative president, *Myers* offered a telling constitutional endorsement of the expanding boundaries of executive authority. The Supreme Court eventually restricted somewhat the application of Taft's ruling.[29] But the *Myers* decision, on the heels of the Budget and Accounting Act, was additional evidence that regardless of who was president, the presidency was unlikely to return to its more modest nineteenth-century status.

Public Relations in the Harding Era

Although neither Harding nor his successor, the taciturn Coolidge, aspired to be a lawgiver or a steward of the people in the manner embraced by Roosevelt and Wilson, each found that he could not advance the laissez-faire economic policies he preferred without taking a strong hand in the administration of the executive departments and agencies. Certainly, Harding's promise of economy in government could not have been fulfilled without the expanded fiscal powers granted to the president by the Budget and Accounting Act. Nor could the national government's involvement in domestic affairs have been reduced without public support. In the wake of TR and Wilson, public relations had become a critical ingredient of successful presidential leadership.[30]

Despite its disastrous end, Harding's presidency did manage to add to the arsenal of presidential techniques for leading public opinion. Having served as the editor and publisher of the *Marion Star* in Ohio before entering politics, Harding had a good sense of how the press worked. He developed an intimacy with journalists that greatly benefited both his 1920 presidential campaign and, until the scandals began to break in 1923, his image as president.

Harding fostered good relations with the press through personal courtesies and institutional innovations. During the 1920 campaign, he had a three-room cottage built near his home in Marion to accommodate the press. There, Harding would meet with reporters daily to discuss political developments in frank, off-the-record sessions. He continued to cultivate the journalistic fraternity during the postelection transition period as he waited to be inaugurated. He was the first president to recognize that the press could be courted in casual as well as formal encounters, even to the extent of playing golf with certain correspondents.[31]

As president, Harding revived the practice of holding regular press conferences, which Wilson had begun but then allowed to taper off after 1915. It was under Harding that the "White House spokesman" ruse came into being to convey information from the administration to the public without directly attributing it to the president. Harding recognized that this veil between himself and newspaper readers gave him room to maneuver. Finally, Harding was the first president to benefit from "photo opportunities." His administration issued identification cards to members of the newly formed White House News Photographers' Association that granted them access to all public and some private events at which the president appeared. Harding himself posed willingly for photographers several times a week.

Harding's innovations in press relations helped amplify the effects of his warm and engaging personality and win support for his administration's policies. He also decided to retain Wilson's practice of delivering the annual State of the Union message to Congress in person. Outside of Washington, Harding immensely enjoyed speechmaking tours. The mounting burden of the rhetorical presidency led him to appoint the first presidential speechwriter, journalist Judson Welliver. Although earlier presidents had sometimes relied on friends and political allies to help them prepare speeches, most had written their own. By 1921, however, the growing importance of the executive office and the expanding newspaper coverage of the president were fueling a greater demand for presidential rhetoric. Harding turned to Welliver to compose brief remarks for ceremonial events as well as the final drafts of major addresses. Yet for all the practical advantages, using a speechwriter distanced the president from the words he spoke. Presidents "relinquished some part of the mental discipline of thinking through an issue for themselves and deciding how best to make a case for a particular policy in exchange for the convenience of having packaged speeches readily available."[32] For this reason they were loath to admit that their words were not their own. Harding disguised Welliver's true function in the White House by hiring him with the title "chief clerk."

Harding died on August 2, 1923, well before the American people realized his shortcomings. Dedicated to a concept of party politics and congressional supremacy that no longer seemed practicable, Harding had always found the White House an uncomfortable place. Sensitive to attacks on his leadership, Harding "maintained the unusual and time-consuming habit of writing personal responses to dozens of letters from ordinary citizens, a habit which increased his workload significantly and eventually contributed to undermining his health."[33] Poring over an immense stack of correspondence, Harding reportedly lamented to an aide, "I am not fit for this office and should never have been here."[34]

Harding served barely two years in office, and scholars have numbered him among the least successful presidents. But Harding's death caused an extraordinary outpouring of national emotion.[35] The crowds that came out to view the train carrying his body to Washington were immense. As historian Robert K. Murray has written, "Every town, every city, every hamlet turned out mourning people, standing silently or kneeling by the tracks and on the station platforms."[36]

The public's reaction reflected the growing prominence of the presidency. Because of the relentless journalistic coverage of the president's activities that began during Harding's administration, the stature of the office did not shrink but, to a surprising degree, continued to expand during his brief tenure. As Cornwell wrote, "More than ever before, thanks to the media and the use made of them on the President's behalf, the presidency was destined to blow up the man to heroic proportions and project this image constantly on the nation's screen."[37]

The "Silent" Politics of Calvin Coolidge

At first glance, Calvin Coolidge was an unlikely heir to the increasingly public presidency. Plain in appearance and so sparing with words that he was dubbed "Silent Cal," Coolidge's public persona was ordinary at a time when the executive office seemed to require persons of heroic demeanor. Yet in spite of his limitations, and perhaps in part because of them, Coolidge was one of the most popular presidents in history.

Coolidge raised inactivity to an art. When it came to exerting his will on matters of public policy, Coolidge felt even less responsibility to act than had Harding. He made little effort to join with Republican leaders in Congress to advance a legislative program. "I have never felt it was my duty," Coolidge wrote in his autobiography,

> to attempt to coerce Senators or Representatives, or to take
> reprisals. The people sent them to Washington. I felt I discharged
> my duty when I had done the best that I could with them. In
> this way I avoided almost entirely a personal opposition, which
> I think was of more value to the country than the attempt to
> prevail through arousing personal fear.[38]

Restraint in legislative relations comported with Coolidge's general disdain for programmatic initiatives. "The key to an understanding of the presidential career of Calvin Coolidge is to be found in the fact that he had a distaste for legislation," Wilfred Binkley wrote.[39] Even more than

Harding, Coolidge believed that there were too many federal programs and that the president's energies should be spent administering the government economically and efficiently. One of the few legislative measures that Coolidge promoted vigorously was the Mellon tax reduction plan of 1923, which took its name from Andrew Mellon, the Pittsburgh banker and committed tax cutter who served as Treasury secretary during the Harding and Coolidge administrations. From 1924 to 1926, the president and Mellon joined forces to reduce the 70 percent tax rate on the wealthiest Americans that was instituted during World War I down to 25 percent. The core of Mellon's program, popularly known as "scientific taxation," was the belief that cutting the top tax rates would lead the most prosperous to invest their savings and thereby spur productivity to the benefit of all. As Coolidge stated in his 1925 Inaugural Address,

> The method of raising revenue ought not to impede the transaction of business; it ought to encourage it. I am opposed to extremely high rates, because they produce little or no revenue, because they are bad for the country, and, finally, because they are wrong. We cannot finance the country, we cannot improve social conditions, through any system of injustice, even if we inflict it upon the rich. . . . The wise and correct course to follow in taxation and all other economic legislation is not to destroy those who have already secured success but to create conditions under which everyone will have a better chance to be successful.[40]

Aside from bills such as the tax cut that reduced the national government's involvement in the economy, Coolidge maintained a public silence about legislation that would have befitted a nineteenth-century president. Even in the matter of the protocol of the World Court, a treaty that Coolidge sent to the Senate for ratification, he gave neither encouragement nor direction to Republican senators. Instead, the president spoke barely a word as his supporters fought a valiant but, in the face of the isolationist mood that gripped the nation after World War I, a losing battle.

Despite Coolidge's lack of success with Congress, he forged a strong bond with the American people. "No other president in our day and time," one commentator observed after Coolidge left office, "has had such close, such continuous and such successful relations with the electorate as Calvin Coolidge had."[41] To some degree, Coolidge had the virtue of his defects. His stern Yankee demeanor and businesslike administrative style offered a welcome respite from the scandals of the Harding administration.

He also benefited from the postwar economic boom. The Harding–Coolidge economic program, with its emphasis on tax cuts, unregulated domestic markets, and protection from foreign competition, put "business in the saddle."[42] For a time, business seemed up to the task. As the acerbic journalist H. L. Mencken marveled, "[T]he successful businessman . . . enjoys the public respect and adulation that elsewhere bathe only bishops and generals."[43] Throughout the spring of 1924, revelations about the Harding administration's scandals competed for attention on the front pages with news of rising dividends, profits, and sales.[44] Good times seemed to call for a president who was content to sit tight.[45]

Coolidge's enormous popularity was grounded not just in his commitment to business but also in his ability to express that commitment in words that exalted the governing principles of the era. Just as Lincoln had viewed the Declaration of Independence as the guiding star for resolving the slavery crisis, so Coolidge sought refuge in its universal principles to refine the "pagan materialism" that tainted the Roaring '20s. Expressing the civic pride cultivated by his New England upbringing (no doubt reinforced by his Fourth of July birthday), Coolidge sermonized on the 150th anniversary of the signing of the Declaration that the individual rights proclaimed in 1776 had "their source in the roots of religious convictions."

Coolidge's version of "idealism in its most practical form" was severely tested by the surge of nativism aroused by the explosion of immigration since the 1890s and the revival of the Ku Klux Klan, whose members regarded the arrival of Jews and Catholics from eastern and southern Europe as a new threat to their commitment to preserving "America for Americans."[46] Coolidge appeared to acquiesce to this virulent isolationism by signing the Immigration Act of 1924, the most restrictive immigration legislation in American history. Under the new law, which Coolidge promised would uphold the maxim that "America must remain American," immigration remained open only to those with a college education or special skills. Entry was denied to Mexicans and disproportionately reduced for eastern and southern Europeans and Japanese. At the same time, the act allowed more immigration from northern European nations such as Great Britain, Ireland, and Scandinavian countries. It set a quota that limited immigration to 2 percent of any nation's residents already in the United States as of 1890, a provision designed to maintain America's largely northern European ethnic composition.

Although he signed legislation that restricted the flow of immigrants, Coolidge publicly avowed that he did not intend to deny immigration's importance to the American creed or justify discrimination against them.

He designated the Statue of Liberty as a national monument a few months later and pleaded for tolerance, which he defined as "respect for different kinds of good," in a well-received address to the American Legion in October 1925.[47] Coolidge's speech did not resolve the nativist and racial tensions that roiled the country. It was generally well received, however, by those who suffered most from intolerance, including African Americans. Some black leaders berated Coolidge for not speaking more strongly against intolerance during the 1924 election campaign, but the American Legion address was generally recognized as a clear rejection of the Ku Klux Klan. As the *Baltimore Afro-American* noted in a supportive editorial, "Two years [after the presidential campaign] and without apparent new cause, he whales the Ku Klux Klan between the eyes."[48]

Coolidge sought to speak for a nation undergoing unsettling social and economic changes. Yet his popularity was sealed by his mastery of public relations. Extraordinarily faithful in discharging what he felt were his obligations to reporters, Coolidge held 520 press conferences during his five years in office, more per month than any other president, even the gregarious Franklin D. Roosevelt. Under Coolidge, the press conference became a Washington institution that future presidents could not easily abandon.[49] Moreover, efforts to provide for the comfort and convenience of White House correspondents reached new heights during his administration.[50] Not surprisingly, Coolidge's concern for the press corps won him a considerable measure of goodwill in the press.

On rare occasion, the president used his exceedingly cordial relations with reporters to exert legislative leadership. For example, in ten press conferences between December 1923 and June 1924, Coolidge urged Congress to enact the Mellon tax reduction plan. But much of Coolidge's public relations effort was designed to sell himself rather than his policies.

Characteristically, while Republican senators, without an encouraging word from the president, fought a losing battle for the World Court treaty, Coolidge used a White House lunch with prominent writers and editors to display the most benign facets of his personality. "Instead of trying to guide Congress and impress his views on party leaders," a Washington correspondent wrote in 1926, "Mr. Coolidge devotes himself to playing the sort of politics he knows how to play, doing the sort of thing he can do—and in which he is far more interested than in the World Court proposal, which was from the start more or less an annoyance to him."[51]

The politics Coolidge "knows how to play" was a politics of personality that embodied his keen understanding of the public's interest in the human side of the presidency. Convinced that news about his personal activities would pave the way for popular acceptance of his more serious pronouncements, the shy Coolidge threw open his private life to unprecedented press scrutiny. One contemporary reporter suggested that

> he was probably the most photographed man who ever occupied the White House. It was a joke among photographers that Mr. Coolidge would don any attire or assume any pose that would produce an interesting picture. He was never too busy to be photographed; nor is it recorded that he ever resented any revelation as to his personal habits.[52]

Coolidge also benefited from the rise of the film industry and the rapid increase in movie attendance during the 1920s to about half the population every week. The addition of newsreels to the evening theater programs allowed Americans to see their president in motion on a regular basis.

Important as the newspapers and newsreels were to Coolidge, his most significant contribution to the development of White House communications was his use of the radio. Lacking the "barnstorming ability" of his recent predecessors, Coolidge was blessed with a new mass medium, which he used effectively to enhance his image. I am very fortunate I came in with the radio," he told Sen. James E. Watson of Indiana. "I can't make an engaging, rousing, or oratorical speech to a crowd . . . but I have a good radio voice, and now I can get my messages across to them without acquainting them with my lack of oratorical ability.[53]

Eugene McDonald, the president of the National Association of Broadcasters, told Coolidge that his talent for radio broadcasts would outdo the rhetorical innovations of his progressive predecessors: "Radio will draw close to the American fireside," he wrote in words that anticipated FDR's fireside chats, "for you will be speaking to the people as they sit in their living room . . . and talk in terms of that home's interest and prosperity."[54] In the same way he courted reporters, Coolidge used the radio less to rouse public support for his policies than to enhance his popularity. If he had not formed a bond with the voters in this way, Coolidge might have failed to be nominated by his party for a full term in 1924.

Coolidge's first significant public appearance as president was his 1923 State of the Union address, which he delivered at the Capitol on December 6. His speech was also the first presidential message to Congress to be broadcast. Coolidge's clear, incisive diction and the appealing content of his message apparently made a profound impression on the national radio audience.[55] From then until the Republican

National Convention in June 1924, Coolidge made certain to speak to the American people at least once each month in carefully prepared radio addresses. The Coolidge administration also arranged for radio stations to broadcast the GOP convention, marking the first time voters could listen to the proceedings of the quadrennial party gathering. The president's speech accepting his party's nomination, which as was the custom until the 1930s, he made several weeks after the convention, was carried live on radio as well.[56] His 1925 inaugural address reached a radio audience of about 20 million, more than had heard all previous presidential speeches combined.

Coolidge's overwhelming first-ballot nomination marked an important advance, as Coolidge himself recognized, in the emergence of the president as "the sole repository of party responsibility."[57] The conservative Republican senators who had controlled the GOP since 1912 had little regard for Coolidge. Unlike former senator Harding, Coolidge was not one of them—his background was in state politics. Yet they had little choice but to support the president's bid for a full term in 1924. As William Allen White wrote in 1925, "The reason why the senatorial group ceased hoping to defeat Coolidge for the Republican nomination was the obvious fact that Coolidge was getting stronger and stronger with the American people."[58] Noting that the radio had in no small measure made this possible, Cornwell wrote:

> Here was the first President in history whom more than a tiny fraction of the populace could actually listen to, and whose voice they could come to know at first hand. Small wonder that the man developed a tangible meaning for millions—more so perhaps than any of his predecessors.[59]

Coolidge's hold on the voters was demonstrated in the general election when he defeated the Democratic nominee, John W. Davis, by a three-to-one majority in the Electoral College and by nearly two to one in the national popular vote.

Herbert C. Hoover and the Great Depression

Coolidge demonstrated that the growing power and prominence of the executive office could be used as effectively by a president who wanted only to preside as by one who, like TR and Wilson, wanted to lead.[60]

Calvin Coolidge, fourth from the right, skillfully cultivated the press and generated favorable public opinion with photo sessions such as this March 1925 meeting with members of the Sioux Indian Republican Club.

Source: Library of Congress.

Coolidge was not simply a throwback to the era of Benjamin Harrison and Rutherford B. Hayes. Instead, his tenure suggested that a president with a shrewd sense of politics and public relations could thrive in the new political conditions of the twentieth century, even a president who was philosophically opposed to expanding government programs and executive power.

When Herbert Hoover, capitalizing on Coolidge's popularity, handily defeated New York Democratic governor Al Smith in the 1928 election, many expected that Hoover would be an able, even a brilliant national leader. The "Great Engineer," as he was called, brought to the White House a tremendous reputation for accomplishment and public service from his tenure as food administrator during the Wilson administration and secretary of commerce under Harding and Coolidge. Hoover was dedicated to his Republican predecessors' pro-business policies, which he celebrated as "rugged individualism" during the campaign. He also was confident that knowledgeable and efficient administration in Washington could build a strong foundation for national prosperity. Hoover seemed perfectly qualified to consolidate the gains of the postwar economic recovery.

Yet the same president who entered office amid such great expectations left four years later as the object of scorn and derision. This startling political reversal was caused in part by the Great Depression, the worst economic crisis in the nation's history. The depression struck with full force when the stock market crashed in October 1929, less than seven months after Hoover was inaugurated. But the Hoover administration was in trouble even before the crash.

Much of Hoover's difficulty as president stemmed from the contrast between his desire to bring about important changes in American society and his unwillingness or inability to undertake the tasks of leadership that could have made these changes possible. Like Harding and Coolidge, Hoover subscribed to a political philosophy that confined the national government to the few activities for which it had clear constitutional authority. But Hoover's fear of big government coexisted with his TR- and Wilson-style faith, born of the Progressive era, in the government's ability to improve social and economic conditions.[61]

Early in his presidency, Hoover called a special session of Congress to recommend a significant legislative program. "No president in a hundred years, excepting Woodrow Wilson, had moved his administration so quickly and so extensively into domestic reform," historian Martin L. Fausold has argued.[62] Hoover called for major changes in tariffs, taxes, conservation, and government organization. He urged Congress to develop programs to deal with the nation's already long-standing depression in agriculture.

Hoover believed that his administration should mobilize industrial and civic organizations to facilitate better economic coordination and enhanced economic opportunities through voluntary action. He was particularly concerned about several flaws in the nation's recent prosperity: the imbalance between high production and low consumption; the weak agricultural sector; the feverish financial speculation, fueled by unsound monetary and lending policies; the poor organization of labor; and inefficient practices in the industrial sector. The solutions to these problems, Hoover was convinced, lay not in expanding the national government but in using the presidency and the rest of the executive branch to encourage private institutions to develop more equitable and rational economic arrangements.

Hoover's faith in the private sector's willingness and ability, in cooperation with government, to act in the public interest was grounded in experience. As President Wilson's food administrator during World War I, Hoover eschewed government rationing. Instead, historian Donald Ritchie has written, "Hoover's skillful use of slogans and mass-marketing techniques encouraged voluntary compliance."[63] As secretary of commerce under Coolidge, Hoover dealt with the massive Mississippi River flood of 1927, which washed out millions of acres of farms and displaced 600,000 people, by securing contributions from the Red Cross and the railroads to provide relief. Now, as president, he hoped to expand these activities. "By his position," Hoover told the Gridiron Club on December 14, 1929, the president "must, within his capacities, give leadership to the development of moral, social, and economic forces outside of government which make for the betterment of our country."[64]

Hoover's philosophy and personality rendered him sadly incapable of providing the brand of leadership he advocated, especially after the stock market crash in October 1929 accelerated the economy's rapid descent into depression. Sharing Coolidge's respect for the autonomy of the legislature, he did little to lead the special session of Congress that he called in 1929. After leaving office, Hoover explained his reticence: "The weakening of the legislative arm leads to encroachment by the executive upon the legislative and judicial functions, and inevitably that encroachment is upon individual liberty."[65]

Despite the president's lack of assertiveness, his farm bill, at least, was enacted. The Agricultural Marketing Act of 1929 created the Federal Farm Board to administer loans so that agricultural cooperatives could help farmers produce and market their crops. Before a bill that was acceptable to Hoover could pass, however, Republican leaders in the Senate had to quell a revolt by party insurgents. Against the president's wishes, western progressives moved to subsidize farmers who were exporting commodities at prices lower than the domestic rates. After weeks of deadlock, Congress approved the president's version of the agriculture measure but with little help from Hoover. "There is some very bad leadership from the bottom of 16th Street," complained former secretary of agriculture William M. Jardine, referring to the White House.[66]

The Republican-controlled Congress was not so accommodating when the issue was tariffs. The president favored a limited revision of the tariff schedules that would aid only stricken farmers. But a Senate resolution to confine tariff revision to the agricultural schedule was defeated by a single vote. Hoover, who in all likelihood could have swung the vote he needed in order to prevail, refused even to try.[67] He then remained silent as Congress, particularly the Senate, proceeded to increase tariffs on nonfarm as well as farm commodities, eventually passing a bill that raised tariffs to their highest levels in history. Bowing to his party's ongoing commitment to high tariffs, Hoover signed the protectionist Smoot–Hawley Act, which he privately characterized as "vicious, extortionate, and obnoxious," in the face of ardent pleas from all parts of the country to veto it.[68] What Hoover realized and his party did not was that high tariffs, however useful they may have been at fostering domestic manufacturing in the nineteenth century, had become dysfunctional in the newly integrated international economy. America's trading partners responded to Smoot–Hawley by raising their own tariffs, and trade ground to a standstill. Hoover saw this coming, but as the renowned columnist Walter Lippmann wrote, "The prospect of a controversy with his own party silenced him, and as far as one can judge by his public acts he abdicated all claims to leadership in the tariff battle."[69]

Hoover's refusal to lead the special session of Congress he called in 1929 tempered the widespread enthusiasm that greeted his election. Coolidge's reticence had frustrated some people, but it was in keeping with his indifference to programmatic activism. Hoover's passivity, however, seemed inappropriate to his ambitions for the nation. As Fausold has observed, "No activist president in this century has kept his distance from Congress as did Hoover."[70] By the fall of 1929, even Republican congressional leaders were criticizing Hoover's nonpolitical approach to the presidency. The press, not yet willing to dismiss Hoover as a weak executive, was mystified. Assessing the president's aloofness from the special session, one commentator concluded that "a strange paralysis seemed to rest upon Mr. Hoover during the first year after Congress met."[71]

Hoover's "strange paralysis," which caused only concern and confusion during the early days of his presidency, provoked bitter jests and withering scorn after the onslaught of the depression. Dignified silence in the face of congressional interference with his program was one thing, but for the president to remain above the fray when unemployment soared from 3 percent of the workforce in 1929 to 15 percent in 1931 and 24 percent in 1932 seemed heartless. Yet Hoover resisted growing public demands that he assume the mantle of legislative leader and prod Congress to produce a body of law that would authorize the executive departments and agencies to assume more responsibility for economic coordination and social services. Instead, White House conferences proliferated. Hoover convened a series of economic stabilization conferences in the cabinet room, inviting the leaders of major industries and labor unions to participate. The main purpose of these conferences was to urge industries and workers to act voluntarily to ameliorate the economic crisis. "We could no more legislate ourselves out of a worldwide depression," Hoover insisted, than we could "exorcise a Caribbean hurricane by statutory law."[72]

The president's remote stance became especially disabling after the Republicans suffered significant losses in the 1930 midterm elections, in which the GOP barely hung onto a majority in the Senate while losing control of the House. When congressional Democrats refused to cooperate with him, Hoover chose to suffer in silence, bewailing their intransigence in the privacy of his White House study but declining to go over their heads to the people. As he later wrote in his memoirs, "I had felt deeply that no President should undermine the independence of the legislative and judicial branches by seeking to discredit them. The constitutional division of powers is the bastion of our liberties and was not designed as a battle-ground to display the prowess of presidents."[73]

The struggling president's constitutional principles were reinforced by personal qualities that ill suited him for the tasks of legislative, party, and popular leadership. Like Ulysses S. Grant and William Howard Taft, Hoover came to the presidency with no background in elected office. His experience was as a builder and manager of organizations, not as a politician working to forge legislative coalitions or a popular following. He was comfortable dealing with data, which he could marshal to support a course of action.[74] But, as Lippmann wrote, Hoover was "diffident in the presence of the normal irrationality of democracy."[75]

Uncomfortable with politics and politicians, Hoover also proved unable to form close relationships with reporters or build on Coolidge's pioneering efforts in radio broadcasting. In the history of presidential communications, Hoover's presidency was important mainly in a negative sense. He abandoned the practice resuscitated by Wilson of presidents appearing in person to deliver major speeches before Congress. He fought losing battles to keep both his private life and his behind-the-scenes efforts to influence policy out of the public's view. His administration "served to make painfully plain," Cornwell observed, "that no future President could hope to emerge from his White House ordeal unless he was prepared in talent and temperament to cope with and master the demands of an age of mass communications."[76]

That said, Herbert Hoover was hardly the do-nothing president that Franklin Roosevelt and the Democrats made him out to be in the 1932 election. He repeatedly encouraged efforts by various sectors of the economy to pursue more rational and just business practices. With the onset of the depression, he tried even harder to supply the leadership that the public was demanding.

But Hoover was willing to go only so far. Although he called for programs such as the Reconstruction Finance Corporation (RFC), which provided federal loans to banks, railroads, and agricultural organizations, he did little to rally popular support for them or ensure their effective operation. New York representative Fiorello LaGuardia denounced the RFC as "a millionaire's dole." But LaGuardia and others soon recognized the critical precedent it represented. If Hoover granted federal relief to the banks, then how could he continue to refuse support for the unemployed? "Hoover had given up the ground of high principle," historian David M. Kennedy has written. "He now stood ideologically shorn before a storm of demands for unemployment relief."[77]

Hoover grimly resisted these demands, lecturing Congress and the country about preserving the nation's rugged individualism and the integrity of the federal budget. Characteristically, he marshaled the entire executive branch to encourage private and local groups to provide the needy with relief from the depression but refused to offer direct federal aid. Seeking to come to terms with the great drought of 1930 and 1931, Hoover admonished the Red Cross to feed people, as it had after the Mississippi flood, rather than have the federal government do it. When the Red Cross balked at the magnitude of the task and Congress demanded that the government act, Hoover still demurred, stating that direct federal assistance to people in the beleaguered "Dust Bowl" was unconstitutional.

By the end of 1931, Hoover was more willing to relax his stalwart defense of rugged individualism. Excoriating budget deficits and the dangers of the dole, he vetoed the Garner–Wagner relief bill on July 11, 1932. Ten days later, however, the president reluctantly accepted a compromise measure, the Relief and Reconstruction Act, which he signed on July 21, a few weeks after Franklin Roosevelt accepted the Democratic nomination for president. The act authorized the RFC to finance $1.5 billion in "self-liquidating" public works and to loan $300 million to the states for relief. But this concession was too little and came too late, "especially and woefully so," Kennedy notes, "in the politically crucial area of relief."[78]

Hoover put traditional, nineteenth-century American political practices and principles to their greatest test. But his unalterable commitment to preserve these traditions even in the face of national calamity served only to discredit them. In this way, Hoover unwittingly laid the groundwork for a fundamental break with the politics and policies of the past.

The Twentieth Amendment

On February 6, 1933, less than a month before the end of Hoover's term, the Twentieth Amendment became part of the Constitution. It had cleared Congress in March 1932 and was ratified less than two months later by all the states, the first constitutional amendment in history to win unanimous ratification when initially considered.[79] The amendment was written mainly to shorten the time between the election of the president, vice president, and members of Congress and their entry into office. The hiatus for newly elected representatives and senators (unless the president called Congress into special session, as Hoover did in 1929) had been thirteen months: from election day in November until the first Monday in December of the following year, the date established by Article I of the Constitution as the initial meeting time for each new Congress. The delay for presidents and vice presidents was about four months, from election day until March 4, the inauguration date enshrined in a law passed by Congress in 1792.

Sen. George Norris, the main author of the Twentieth Amendment, sought to remedy three major flaws in the traditional arrangement, which he regarded as suited to the age when travel was difficult and time-consuming and the business of the federal government was relatively minor. The first flaw was the biennial lame-duck session of Congress, which typically lasted from the December after the election until the following March and included many outgoing members of the defeated party. Second, by not having Congress begin its term before the president, existing procedures authorized the lame-duck Congress, not the newly elected one, to choose the president in the event of a deadlock in the Electoral College, as had happened in 1801 and 1825. Third, Norris regarded four months as too long a time for the nation to have, in effect, two presidents: an outgoing incumbent and an incoming president-elect.

To remedy the lame-duck and two-presidents problem, section 1 of the Twentieth Amendment set noon on January 20 as the beginning of the president's and vice president's four-year term and noon on January 3 as the start of the term for members of Congress. Norris used section 3 of the amendment to address two other potential problems in the presidential and vice-presidential selection process. It provided that if a president-elect were to die before the start of the term, the vice president-elect would be inaugurated as president. Section 3 also stated that if by inauguration day no presidential candidate had received either a majority of electoral votes or the support of a majority of state delegations in the House, the vice president-elect, chosen by a simple majority vote of the Senate, would act as president until a president was chosen. (The same would be true if a president-elect were found to be unqualified by virtue of age, citizenship, or residency.) Other provisions of the amendment dealt with equally real but remote possibilities: for example, that a vice president-elect might not be chosen or that either a winning presidential or vice-presidential candidate might die before receiving "elect" status when Congress counted the electoral votes in early January.

As unlikely as some of the situations contemplated by the Twentieth Amendment are, two events that occurred near the time of the amendment's passage testified to its value. From November 1932 to March 1933, in the last of the four-month transitions, the nation endured a long and awkward interregnum between Hoover, the discredited and defeated incumbent president, and Franklin Roosevelt, his successor—all this in the midst of the Great Depression. And on February 15, 1933, nine days after the amendment entered the Constitution, President-elect Roosevelt narrowly escaped an assassination attempt in Miami, Florida.

Notes

1. Robert P. Saldin, "World War I and the 'System of 1896,'" *The Journal of Politics*, 72, no. 3 (July 2010): 825–836.

2. Harding quoted in Robert K. Murray, *The Harding Era: Warren G. Harding and His Administration* (Minneapolis: University of Minnesota Press, 1969), 70.

3. Confusion still exists about how the word *normalcy* originated. The best guess is that Harding meant *normality* but said *normalcy*.

4. William Starr Myers, *The Republican Party: A History* (New York: Century, 1928), 441.

5. Lodge quoted in Andrew Sinclair, *The Available Man: The Life Behind the Masks of Warren Gamaliel Harding* (New York: Macmillan, 1965), 152 (emphasis in original).

6. Elmer E. Cornwell Jr., *Presidential Leadership of Public Opinion* (Bloomington: Indiana University Press, 1965), 60.

7. Warren Harding, "We Need a Newly Consecrated Americanism," *Independent*, October 1920, in *History of American Presidential Elections, 1789–1968*, 4 vols., eds. Arthur M. Schlesinger Jr. and Fred L. Israel (New York: Chelsea, 1971), 3: 2437–2439. See also *New York Times*, July 21, 1920, 7.

8. Quoted in Wilfred E. Binkley, *President and Congress* (New York: Knopf, 1947), 217.

9. Ibid.

10. George Rothwell Brown, *The Leadership of Congress* (Indianapolis, Ind.: Bobbs-Merrill, 1922; New York: Arno Press, 1974), 258.

11. Harding vetoed the World War Adjusted Compensation Act in September 1922. Although the House voted to override his rejection of the bonus bill, the Senate, after a bitter struggle, failed to do so by four votes. Historian Niall Palmer argues that this confrontation shattered Harding's hope that the White House and Congress could return to a cooperative working relationship. See Palmer, "The Veterans' Bonus and the Evolving Presidency of Warren G. Harding, *Presidential Studies Quarterly*, 38, no. 1 (March 2008): 39–60.

12. Jennings quoted in Murray, *Harding Era*, 314.

13. Ibid., 128.

14. Ibid.

15. Robert F. Martin, "Warren Gamaliel Harding," in *The American Presidents*, ed. Melvin I. Urofsky (New York and London: Garland, 2000), 309–310.

16. Binkley, *President and Congress,* 221. For a discussion of the events that led up to the Washington Naval Disarmament Conference, see Murray, *Harding Era*, 140–166;

and Lindsay Rogers, "American Government and Politics: The Second, Third, and Fourth Sessions of the Sixty-Seventh Congress," *American Political Science Review*, 18 (February 1924): 91–93.

17. Paul Van Riper, *History of the United States Civil Service* (Evanston, Ill.: Row, Peterson, 1958), 287.

18. Murray, *Harding Era*, 430.

19. William Allen White, *The Autobiography of William Allen White* (New York: Macmillan, 1946), 619.

20. On the events leading up to the Teapot Dome scandal, see J. Leonard Bates, *The Origins of Teapot Dome: Progressives, Parties, and Petroleum, 1909–1921* (Urbana: University of Illinois, 1963), esp. chaps. 13 and 14; and Burt Noggle, "The Origins of the Teapot Dome Investigation," *Mississippi Valley Historical Review*, 64 (September 1957): 237–266. See also "The Teapot Dome Resolution," in *The Evolving Presidency: Landmark Documents, 1787–2010*, 4th ed., ed. Michael Nelson (Washington, D.C.: CQ Press, 2012), 135–137.

21. Fall could not be dismissed as merely one of the "grafters" who attached themselves to the Harding administration. He was able to defend his belief that the public domain should be opened to private development. As he once told a critic, "Every generation from Adam and Eve down has lived better than the generation before. I don't know how they'll do it—maybe they'll use the energy of the sun or the sea waves—but . . . [they] will live better than we do. I stand for opening up every resource." Quoted in Bates, *Origins of Teapot Dome*, 227–228.

22. George W. Norris, *Fighting Liberal: The Autobiography of George W. Norris* (New York: Macmillan, 1945), 233.

23. Herbert Emmerich, *Federal Organization and Administrative Management* (Tuscaloosa: University of Alabama Press, 1971), 40–41. For a discussion of the enactment and early history of the Budget and Accounting Act, see William M. Goldsmith, ed., *The Growth of Presidential Power: A Documented History*, 3 vols. (New York and London: Chelsea, 1974), 3: 1478–95; and Peri E. Arnold, *Making the Managerial Presidency: Comprehensive Reorganization Planning, 1905–1980* (Princeton: Princeton University Press, 1986), 53–55.

24. Lindsay Rogers, "American Government and Politics," *American Political Science Review*, 14 (November 1920): 659–671. The comptroller general is appointed by the president, with the advice and consent of the Senate, for a fifteen-year nonrenewable term. The president selects a nominee from a list of at least three individuals recommended by an eight-member bipartisan, bicameral commission of congressional leaders. The comptroller general may not be removed by the president but only by Congress through impeachment or a joint resolution passed by both houses of Congress. Since 1921, there have been only eight comptrollers general, and no formal attempt has ever been made to remove one.

25. Murray, *Harding Era*, 178.

26. *Myers v. United States*, 272 U.S. 53 (1926).

27. Sidney M. Milkis, "William Howard Taft and the Struggle for the Soul of the Constitution," in *Toward an American Conservatism: Constitutional Conservatism during the Progressive Era*, eds. Joseph W. Postell and Johnathan O'Neill (New York: Palgrave MacMillan, 2013).

28. Ibid., at 134.

29. See "*Humphrey's Executor v. United States*," in Nelson, *Evolving Presidency*, 151–157. See also chap. 10 in this volume.

30. Cornwell, *Presidential Leadership of Public Opinion*, 62. Much of the following discussion draws on Cornwell's interesting chapter on public relations in the Harding and Coolidge administrations.

31. Ibid., 63.

32. Lewis L. Gould, *The Modern American Presidency* (Lawrence: University Press of Kansas, 2003), 63. Welliver gained some posthumous fame after the creation of the Judson Welliver Society, an organization of former White House speechwriters, which was founded

by William Safire, a speechwriter for Richard Nixon. On the origins and development of presidential speechwriting, see Robert Schlesinger. *White House Ghosts: Presidents and Their Speechwriters* (Simon and Schuster, 2008); and Michael Nelson, "Speeches, Speechwriting, and the American Presidency," in *The President's Words: Speeches and Speechwriting in the Modern White House*, eds. Michael Nelson and Russell L. Riley (Lawrence: University Press of Kansas, 2010), 1–26.

33. Palmer, "The Veterans' Bonus and the Evolving Presidency of Warren G. Harding," 54.

34. Quoted in Murray, *Harding Era*, 418.

35. Scholars have consistently ranked Harding, along with James Buchanan, Ulysses S. Grant, and Franklin Pierce among America's worst presidents. See Jill L. Curry and Irwin L. Morris, "Explaining Presidential Greatness: The Roles of Peace and Prosperity?" *Presidential Studies Quarterly*, 40, no. 3 (September 2010): 515–530 (516–517).

36. Murray, *Harding Era*, 452.

37. Cornwell, *Presidential Leadership of Public Opinion*, 73.

38. Calvin Coolidge, *The Autobiography of Calvin Coolidge* (New York: Cosmopolitan, 1929), 232.

39. Binkley, *President and Congress*, 223.

40. Calvin Coolidge, Inaugural Address, March 4, 1925, https://millercenter.org/the-presidency/presidential-speeches/march-4-1925-inaugural-address.

41. William Allen White, *A Puritan in Babylon* (New York: Macmillan, 1938), v.

42. Edward S. Martin, "Shall Business Run the World?" *Harper's Magazine*, February 1925, 381.

43. David Greenberg, *Calvin Coolidge* (New York: Times Books, 2006), 73.

44. Murray, *Harding Era*, 505.

45. In sitting tight, however, Coolidge failed to address certain ominous economic signs, such as underconsumption and feverish stock speculation, that foreshadowed the Great Depression. See Robert H. Ferrell, *The Presidency of Calvin Coolidge* (Lawrence: University Press of Kansas, 1998), 186–189.

46. "Speech on the 150 Anniversary of the Declaration of Independence," July 5, 1926, http://teachingamericanhistory.org/library/document/speech-on-the-occasion-of-the-one-hundred-and-fiftieth-anniversary-of-the-declaration-of-independence/ and "The Destiny of America," delivered at Memorial Day services, Northampton, Mass., May 30, 1923, in Calvin Coolidge, *The Price of Freedom: Speeches and Addresses* (New York: Scribner's, 1924), 342; and Calvin Coolidge, "Inaugural Address," March 4, 1925, in *Calvin Coolidge, 1872–1933*, ed. Philip R. Moran (Dobbs Ferry, N.Y.: Oceana, 1970), 65.

47. "Address Before the American Legion Convention" at Omaha, Nebraska, October 6, 1925, http://www.presidency.ucsb.edu/ws/?pid=438.

48. Greenberg, *Calvin Coolidge*, 158.

49. Gould, *Modern American Presidency*, 68.

50. Cornwell, *Presidential Leadership of Public Opinion*, 74–75.

51. T. R. B., "Washington Notes," *New Republic*, February 10, 1926, 326.

52. The reporter quoted is Jay C. Hayden of the *Detroit News*, who covered the White House for sixteen years. Hayden considered Coolidge to be as masterful as Theodore Roosevelt at the "human interest" game, although "the Coolidge process was more subtle." *Literary Digest*, July 25, 1931, 8.

53. Quoted in Cornwell, *Presidential Leadership of Public Opinion*, 90.

54. Greenberg, *Calvin Coolidge*, 100.

55. Ibid., 323.

56. Gould, *Modern American Presidency*, 70.

57. Coolidge, *Autobiography*, 231.

58. William Allen White, *Calvin Coolidge: The Man Who Is President* (New York: Macmillan, 1925), 137.

59. Cornwell, *Presidential Leadership of Public Opinion*, 92.

60. Ibid., 97.

61. Ellis Hawley, "The Constitution of the Hoover and F. Roosevelt Presidency during the Depression Era, 1900–1939," in *The Constitution and the American Presidency*, eds. Martin L. Fausold and Alan Shank (Albany: State University of New York Press, 1991), 89–91.

62. Martin L. Fausold, *The Presidency of Herbert C. Hoover* (Lawrence: University Press of Kansas, 1985), 56.

63. Donald A. Ritchie, *Electing FDR: The New Deal Campaign of 1932* (Lawrence: University Press of Kansas, 2007), 20, 24.

64. *Public Papers of the Presidents: Herbert Hoover, March 4 to December 31, 1929* (Washington, D.C.: Government Printing Office, 1974), 472.

65. Herbert Hoover, *The Challenge to Liberty* (New York: Scribner's, 1934), 125–126.

66. Quoted in Fausold, *Presidency of Herbert C. Hoover*, 51.

67. Arthur W. MacMahan, "American Government and Politics: First Session of the Seventy-First Congress," *American Political Science Review*, 24 (February 1930): 50–56; Binkley, *President and Congress*, 229–230.

68. Robert Allen and Drew Pearson, *Washington Merry-Go-Round* (New York: Horace Liveright, 1931), 66.

69. Walter Lippmann, "The Peculiar Weakness of Mr. Hoover," *Harper's Magazine*, June 1930, 5.

70. Fausold, *Presidency of Herbert C. Hoover*, 49.

71. Quoted in Binkley, *President and Congress*, 229.

72. Hoover quoted in Matthew Crenson and Benjamin Ginsberg, *Presidential Power, Unchecked and Unbalanced* (New York: Norton, 2007), 149.

73. Herbert Hoover, *The Memoirs of Herbert Hoover: The Great Depression, 1929–1941*, 3 vols. (New York: Macmillan, 1952), 3: 104.

74. Binkley, *President and Congress*, 227–228.

75. Lippmann, "Peculiar Weakness of Mr. Hoover," 5.

76. Cornwell, *Presidential Leadership of Public Opinion*, 113.

77. David M. Kennedy, *Freedom from Fear: The American People in Depression and War, 1929–1945* (New York: Oxford University Press, 1999), 85.

78. Ibid., 93.

79. David E. Kyvig, *Explicit and Authentic Acts: Amending the U.S. Constitution, 1776–1995* (Lawrence: University Press of Kansas, 1996), 274.

10 The Consolidation of the Modern Presidency

Franklin D. Roosevelt to Dwight D. Eisenhower

The 1932 elections marked the beginning of a new political era. The Democratic candidate, Franklin Delano Roosevelt, became the first member of his party since Franklin Pierce in 1852 to be elected president with a majority of the national popular vote. In the Electoral College, Roosevelt scored a 472–59 landslide, carrying forty-two states to six for the incumbent, Herbert C. Hoover. In the new Congress, Democrats outnumbered Republicans by 60 to 35 in the Senate and 310 to 117 in the House. FDR's victory indicated, in the opinion of progressive Republican journalist William Allen White, "a firm desire on the part of the American people to use government as an agency for human welfare."[1]

Roosevelt did not disappoint this desire. He embraced the progressive reformers' commitment to regulate business in the public interest. But he also believed that it was the federal government's responsibility to guarantee the economic security of its people. The new president brought the welfare state to the United States, years after it became a fixture in other Western nations.

The emergence of the welfare state was closely associated with a redefinition of the public's understanding of rights. In the new version of the American social contract offered by FDR, the national government would assume responsibility for providing an adequate standard of living for families and individuals. In his Commonwealth Club address, which he delivered during the 1932 campaign, Roosevelt declared that the task of modern government was "to assist the development of an economic declaration of rights, an economic constitutional order." He argued that the traditional American emphasis on individual self-reliance must give way to a new understanding of individualism in which the government acts as a regulating and sustaining agency, guaranteeing to each person protection from the worst uncertainties of the marketplace.[2]

Roosevelt's commitment to build a welfare state required a stronger presidency. As he put it, "The day of enlightened administration has come."[3]

This concept of presidential responsibility informed his extraordinary leadership in expanding the federal government to address the demands of a severe domestic crisis, the Great Depression, and then an international one, World War II. The modern presidency became an enduring fixture of the American political system during Roosevelt's long tenure in the White House.

What is the modern presidency?[4] Many of the most important characteristics of the executive date from the Constitutional Convention and the earliest days of the Republic. During the nineteenth century, too, significant presidential patterns and practices took shape. What marked the twentieth-century transformation of the executive was the emergence of the president, rather than Congress or political parties, as the leading instrument of popular rule, "the steward of the public welfare."

Acting on this modern concept of presidential power, Theodore Roosevelt and Woodrow Wilson inaugurated the practices that strengthened the president as a popular and legislative leader, closely associated with the rise of rhetorical leadership. TR and Wilson also took the first steps to construct an administrative presidency, which gave the president more control of the executive departments and agencies and more power to carry out policies with formal congressional authorization.[5] It then fell to Franklin Roosevelt to consolidate, or institutionalize, the changes in the executive office that were initiated during the Progressive era by establishing rhetoric and administration as the pillars of a reconstituted presidency. After Roosevelt's long tenure, this new understanding of executive responsibilities led even conservative Republican presidents to wield the powers of the office in the manner of their liberal forebears.

Franklin D. Roosevelt and the Modern Presidency

So great an impression did Franklin Roosevelt make on the American political system that surveys of historians nearly always rank him alongside Abraham Lincoln and George Washington as one of the three greatest presidents in history.[6] In large measure, FDR's high rating owes to his efforts to lead the American people through the Great Depression and World War II. Roosevelt came to office in the fourth year of a world economic crisis whose persistence raised grave doubts about the viability of republican government. British historian Arnold J. Toynbee observed that 1931 was distinguished from previous years by one outstanding feature: "In 1931, men and women all over the world were seriously contemplating and frankly discussing the possibility that the Western system of society might break down and cease to exist."[7]

Americans had reason to share these doubts. As Roosevelt prepared to take the oath of office on March 4, 1933, the ranks of the unemployed numbered 15 million, about one-third of the workforce. In thirty-two states, every bank had been closed by state government edict. On the morning of FDR's inauguration, the New York Stock Exchange closed its doors. Merle Thorpe, the editor of *Nation's Business*, wrote ominously, "Fear, bordering on panic, loss of faith in everything, our fellowman, our institutions, private and government. Worst of all, no faith in ourselves, or the future."[8]

Other thoughtful commentators looked toward the apparent social stability and recent economic revival of Nazi Germany under Adolf Hitler, Fascist Italy under Benito Mussolini, and among those on the political left, the Communist Soviet Union under Joseph Stalin, and argued that democracy may have had its day. Nicholas Murray Butler, the president of Columbia University, told students that dictatorships such as these were producing "men of far greater intelligence, far stronger character and far more courage than the system of elections." One month before Roosevelt's inauguration, the respected columnist Walter Lippman told the president-elect, "You may have no alternative but to assume dictatorial powers." Such views were not unusual. According to political scientist Ira Katznelson, "Parliamentary democracies were widely thought to be weak and incapable compared to the assertive regimes" led by the new dictators. "This problem seemed especially acute in the United States, whose government reflected the most radical separation of powers between the executive and legislative branches of government in the world."[9]

In this atmosphere of national doubt and despair, Roosevelt's arrival in Washington was greeted with hope. Everyone who watched and waited, wrote *New York Times* columnist Arthur Krock, was "ready to be enthusiastic over any display of leadership" and eager to be convinced that the new president would exhibit the kind of bold and energetic initiative that the American people had demanded but not received from Hoover.[10]

Unlike his predecessor, Roosevelt was admirably suited to lead by virtue of personality and background. Hoover was aloof and uncomfortable with the demands of the modern presidency, but FDR believed that he belonged in the office. "The essence of Roosevelt's Presidency," political scientist Clinton Rossiter has written, "was his airy eagerness to meet the age head on" with confidence and resolution.[11] His confidence stemmed from the combination of a privileged, albeit challenging, upbringing in Hyde Park, New York, and an admirable political education as state senator, assistant secretary of the navy in the Wilson administration, vice-presidential candidate in 1920, and two-term governor of New York, then the largest state in the Union. His resolution owed in no small part to his determination, after losing the use of his legs to poliomyelitis in 1921, not to let disability stand in the way. Roosevelt, who was thirty-nine when stricken by the disease, spent much of the next decade developing techniques to divert people's attention from his inability to walk or stand unsupported. Like a magician using misdirection to foster an illusion, FDR drew audiences' attention to his strong upper body, not his withered legs, and to his jaunty, upward-tilted chin and expressive eyes. He even learned to "walk" by leaning heavily on the arm of an aide while swinging each leg forward with his hips.[12] News photographers helped preserve Roosevelt's personal dignity and public image by never showing him in a wheelchair or being carried.

Roosevelt's faith in his own abilities was accompanied by a willingness to experiment, which he displayed throughout his presidency. The nation became aware of FDR's innovating spirit when, shattering precedent, he hired a small plane to take him to the 1932 Democratic National Convention in Chicago to accept his party's nomination for president. In the past, major party nominees stayed away from the convention, waiting for official notification that they had been nominated.[13] But Roosevelt wanted to demonstrate dramatically that his physical disability would not hinder him as a candidate or as the president. "The convention rose enthusiastically to the voyageur of the skies" marveled one reporter, "and accepted his method of travel and the fact that he endured its rigors so well as a proof of his venturesome spirit and fine physical equipment for the office of the President of the United States."[14]

Roosevelt also wanted to show his party and the nation that he would not hesitate to break traditions if they stood in the way of his vision of progress. "I have started out on the tasks that lie ahead by breaking the absurd traditions that the candidate should remain in professed ignorance of what has happened for weeks until he is formally notified of that event many weeks later," Roosevelt told the convention on July 2, 1932. "Let it also be symbolic that in so doing I broke traditions. Let it be from now on the task of our party to break foolish traditions."[15]

The Critical Early Days

On inauguration day, March 4, 1933, the cheers that greeted Roosevelt as the car carrying President Hoover and the president-elect approached the Capitol seemed to convey "a tone of understanding," the *New York Times* reported,

> that the motor bore not only two men, not only a Democrat elected to succeed a Republican whom he had defeated, but two antagonistic philosophies of government. . . . In the greeting there appeared to be a note of jubilation that the day had come when the new philosophy was to replace the rejected theories of the old.[16]

No such jubilation was evident in Roosevelt's demeanor that day. The president delivered a solemn, compelling inaugural address that spelled out in clear and uncompromising language both his disdain for the age-old practices he thought should be abandoned and his intention to act boldly to deal with the crisis at hand. Laying the blame for the depression squarely on the laissez-faire economic doctrines and halting leadership of his conservative Republican predecessors, Roosevelt summoned the nation to a higher purpose: "The money changers have fled from their high seats in the temple of our civilization. We may now restore that temple to ancient truths. The measure of that restoration lies in the extent to which we apply social values more noble than mere monetary profit."[17]

Just as boldly, making clear that he rejected Lippman's advice that he become a dictator, the new president stated his determination to lead the nation and its government in ways that might bend but would never break the proper bounds of constitutional government:

> It is to be hoped that the normal balance of Executive and legislative authority may be wholly adequate to meet the unprecedented task before us. . . . But in the event that Congress shall fail to take [action] . . . and in the event that the national emergency is still critical, I shall not evade the clear course of duty that will then confront me. I shall ask the Congress for one remaining instrument to meet the crisis—broad executive power to wage a war against the emergency, as great as the power that would be given to me if we were in fact invaded by a foreign foe.[18]

Roosevelt lost no time translating intentions into action. On March 5, one day after taking the oath of office, he issued the Bank Holiday Proclamation, which suspended "the heavy and unwarranted withdrawals of gold and currency from our banking institutions" in the states where banks remained open. The bank edict, an unprecedented exercise of executive power in peacetime, declared that from March 6 to March 9, banks in the United States must suspend all transactions.[19]

During the final days of the Hoover administration, Secretary of Commerce Ogden Mills urged the outgoing president to call a bank holiday, arguing that legal authority to do so could be found in the Trading with the Enemy Act of 1917. But Hoover was reluctant to act on his own initiative, especially after his attorney general questioned whether a wartime measure could be applied to a peacetime situation, no matter how grave. Hoover might have been willing to close the banks if the president-elect had offered public support, but Roosevelt refused to assume responsibility for any action before becoming president.

Once sworn in, FDR did not hesitate to use the full powers of his office to address the national emergency. He felt no reluctance about attacking the banking crisis with a World War I measure. On the same day that he declared the bank holiday, Roosevelt issued another executive order calling Congress into special session. Four days later, on March 9, he introduced the Emergency Banking Bill, which marshaled the full resources of the Federal Reserve Board to support the faltering banks and thereby restore the people's confidence in the banking system. The bill was the first to be passed during the extraordinary One Hundred Days (from noon on March 9 to 1:00 a.m. on June 15, 1933), when Congress passed a relentless succession of Roosevelt-sponsored laws. Remarkably, the bank bill was enacted in less than eight hours. Forty-five minutes later, with photographers recording the scene, Roosevelt signed it into law.

FDR promptly announced that he would speak directly to the people on Sunday evening, March 12, to explain in a radio address what he had done about the banks and why he had done it. This was the first of his "fireside chats," which were a revolutionary advance in presidential use of the mass media.[20] Calvin Coolidge and, less successfully, Hoover had spoken on the radio but only to broadcast fixed, formal pronouncements. Although no less scripted, FDR's chats sounded relaxed, creating the illusion that the president was dropping by his listeners' homes to tell them what he was doing in Washington and why he was doing it. The purpose was less to pronounce policy or rouse citizens to action than to develop an intimate bond with the people and shape their opinions.

Of all the fireside chats that Roosevelt gave (he delivered two or three each year), none was more successful than the first. Both FDR's comfortable radio style and the phrasing of his message were ideally suited to his purpose of reassurance. "We had a bad banking situation," he said. "Some of our bankers had shown themselves either incompetent or dishonest in handling people's funds." Yet most bankers worked hard and well, Roosevelt pointed out, and besides, the task at hand was not to lay blame for the crisis but to end it:

> It was the government's job to straighten out the situation and do it as quickly as possible. And the job is being performed. . . . Confidence and courage are the essentials of success in carrying out our plan. You people must have faith; you must not be stampeded by rumors or guesses. Let us unite in banishing fear. We have provided the machinery to restore our financial system; it is up to you to support it and make it work.[21]

The bank bill and the fireside chat ended the banking crisis. There were no runs on the banks when they reopened on Monday morning, March 13. On the contrary, deposits far exceeded withdrawals as hoarded currency poured back into the vaults. A few days later, the New York Stock Exchange, closed since March 4, opened with the greatest single-day rise in memory. "Capitalism was saved in eight days," Roosevelt's aide Raymond Moley declared dramatically.[22] Similar adulation was expressed not just by FDR's friends but also by some opponents. An "incredible change has come over the face of things here in the United States in a single week," editorialized the business-friendly *Wall Street Journal*, because "the new administration in Washington has superbly risen to the occasion." To be sure, the *Journal* warned, only "a good beginning had been made" and "incalculable tasks" remained. But "there are times when a beginning is nearly everything."[23]

The first two weeks of Roosevelt's presidency lifted the spirit of the country. Clearly, the new president had forged a vital link between the government and the people. White House clerks who were accustomed to opening a thousand pieces of mail per day during peak periods found themselves snowed under by the 460,000 letters that greeted FDR's inauguration. As William Hopkins, who worked in the White House correspondence section, remembered, "The mail started coming in by the truckloads. They couldn't even get the envelopes open."[24]

The New Deal

The early days of the Roosevelt administration brought the presidency into its own as the nation's primary source of popular and legislative leadership. A close bond developed between most Americans and their president during the struggle to end the depression. The advent of the welfare state, which entailed a massive transfer of the burden to help those in need from the states and the private sector to the national government, created new responsibilities for the president. Roosevelt initiated this transfer, carefully preparing the nation for the revolutionary departures in public policy that took place during the 1930s.

The centerpiece of Roosevelt's program was the Social Security Act, which created a comprehensive federal system of old age and unemployment insurance. Selling social security to Congress and the country was no easy task. On June 19, 1934, remarking on the unusual American commitment to individual self-reliance, Sen. Hugo Black of Alabama wrote to a member of the Roosevelt administration: "The public in our country has little conception of the possibilities of social insurance. . . . [T]here are few people in this country who realize such systems of social insurance have been adopted in most of the civilized countries in the world."[25]

Fourteen months after Black's letter, the Social Security Act of 1935 sailed through Congress and was ceremoniously signed into law by the president. In the interim, FDR had nurtured public opinion carefully. He saw his task as one of civic education, teaching the American people that social insurance was consistent with, not alien to, their values. The president was confident that if he taught the people well, they would pass the lessons on to their representatives in Congress.

In performing his role as teacher, Roosevelt argued that the development of a national industrial society made it impossible for most individuals to achieve financial security within the familiar bonds of family and neighborhood. Instead, the complexities of great cities and organized industry required that the federal government help people secure their welfare in time of need. To bring this lesson home, in a fireside chat on June 28, 1934, Roosevelt included a folksy yet effective illustration: the remodeling of the White House's West Wing, which he likened to the adoption of social security. After describing the wiring and plumbing and the modern means of keeping offices cool that were being installed during the hot Washington summer, Roosevelt noted, "It is this combination of the old and new that marks orderly peaceful progress, not only in building buildings, but in building government itself. . . . All that we do seeks to fulfill the historic traditions of the American people."[26]

Roosevelt's leadership on this issue involved, as one presidential scholar has written, "a careful process of grafting social security onto the stalk of traditional American values."[27] By the end of the process, the president had moved the nation beyond the traditional idea that rights embody only guarantees against government oppression to a new understanding, first articulated in his Commonwealth Club address, that government must also ensure the right to economic security. He credited Abraham Lincoln for transfusing "with new meaning the concepts of our constitutional fathers" and for assuring "a Government having for its broad purpose the promotion of life, liberty, and happiness of all the people."[28] Lincoln had praised the Declaration of Independence for giving birth to a positive understanding of liberty, in which government's "leading object" was "to afford all, an unfettered start, and a fair chance in the race of life." Roosevelt now argued that the time had come to adopt, at least in spirit, a new Declaration, a new idea of rights that acknowledged that "necessitous men are not free men."[29] It was just such an understanding that Roosevelt had in mind when, at the 1932 Democratic convention, he pledged to offer "a new deal for the American people."[30]

The 1935 Social Security Act included old age insurance, unemployment insurance, and Aid to Dependent Children (ADC), popularly known as welfare. By European standards, the social security program was quite limited. Because old age insurance did not cover domestic and hotel workers, farm laborers, teachers, and nurses, it excluded most African Americans and women from its benefits. Furthermore, it did not include any support for health care, and its levels of welfare spending were low. The welfare and unemployment provisions also left considerable discretion and funding responsibility to the states, which dealt out payments unevenly. Nevertheless, social security marked a watershed in the national government's assumption of the responsibility to protect individuals from the uncertainties of the market. Its components, especially old age pensions, grew over the years so that social security became the largest of all federal programs.

Significantly, the need for voters to ratify the New Deal agenda, with its embodiment of a new individualism, was the principal message of Roosevelt's first reelection bid in 1936. The Democratic Party's platform for that campaign, drafted by the president, was written in the cadence of the Declaration of Independence. The platform claimed with respect to the Social Security Act, "We hold this truth to be self-evident—that the test of representative government is its ability to promote the safety and happiness of the people. . . . On the foundation of the Social Security Act we are determined to erect a structure of economic security for all our people."[31] The New Deal was a series of legislative acts, executive orders, and presidential proclamations that sought to remedy the broader economic problems that underlay the Great Depression as well as to secure individual security. During Roosevelt's tenure as president, not only was social security established to aid the aged, the unemployed, the disabled, and widows with dependent children, but work projects were financed by the greatest peacetime appropriation in history. In addition, for the first time the national government fostered unionization. When Roosevelt became president, almost no factory workers belonged to a labor union. Within a few years, industrial unionism was firmly established, largely because of the National Labor Relations Act (the Wagner Act) of 1935, which empowered the government to enter factories and conduct elections so that workers could freely decide whether to join a union.

Finally, Roosevelt demanded that business recognize the superior authority of the federal government. Like his cousin Theodore, he fashioned himself a conservative reformer who sought not to oppose private enterprise but to strengthen it by curbing business's most abusive practices and by ameliorating the most extreme conditions of economic hardship. FDR was opposed in this effort by a segment of the American business community, which denied to the federal government any right to regulate commercial activity. As the president complained in a letter to Harvard law professor Felix Frankfurter in February 1937, "It is the same old story of those who have property to fail to realize that I am the best friend the profit system ever had, even though I add my denunciation of unconscionable profits."[32]

Roosevelt's resentment of his critics in business was intense. "These economic royalists complain that we seek to overthrow the institutions of America," he told a roaring crowd at the 1936 Democratic convention. "What they really complain of is that we seek to take away their power." The time had come, Roosevelt insisted, "to overthrow this kind of power." The New Deal regulatory program greatly extended the responsibility of the federal government, especially the president, to guarantee "equal opportunity in the market place" to the average citizen.[33] Describing a range of Roosevelt-sponsored regulatory laws, such as the Securities and Exchange Act and the Public Utility Holding Company Act, historian William E. Leuchtenburg wrote: "Although the New Deal always operated within a capitalist framework, Roosevelt insisted that there was a national interest that it was the duty of the President to represent and, when the situation called for it, to impose."[34]

Not every major innovation in public policy during the 1930s originated in the White House. Some New Deal programs, such as the Tennessee Valley Authority, had long been on the public agenda, lacking only the impetus of a national crisis and a presidential endorsement.[35] Other parts of what Roosevelt called the new "economic constitutional order," such as the Wagner Act and a new program of federal insurance of bank deposits, redounded to the president's political benefit even though he accepted them only haltingly. That FDR was hailed for the efforts of New York senator Robert F. Wagner and others signified the American people's growing tendency to think of the president as the government.

The 1936 election ensured that the important political changes of Roosevelt's first term would endure. In 1932 his victory was more a rejection of Hoover than an endorsement of FDR and his party. The 1936 election, however, was a sweeping confirmation of his leadership and of the New Deal. The Republican campaign sought to resuscitate Hoover's idea of "rugged individualism." The GOP candidate, Kansas governor Alf Landon, argued in a September speech in Milwaukee, Wisconsin, that the Social Security Act

> assumes Americans are irresponsible. It assumes that old-age pensions are necessary because Americans lack the foresight to provide for their old age. I refuse to accept any such judgment of my fellow citizens. . . . To get a workable old-age pension plan we must repeal the present compulsory plan. The Republican Party is pledged to do this.

Landon echoed Hoover's blistering attack on New Deal principles and policies. The Republican Party, Hoover insisted during the 1932 campaign, with its historical commitment to protecting natural rights and private property, was the "true liberal party." The New Deal, he said, was a "false liberalism" that regimented people and extended bureaucracy.[36]

In the teeth of the Great Depression, FDR got the better of the debate about New Deal principles and policies. He won 60 percent of the popular vote—the largest majority yet obtained by a presidential candidate—and carried every state but Maine and Vermont.[37] The election also strengthened the Democrats' hold on Congress, marking their emergence as the nation's new majority party.

Institutionalization of the Modern Presidency

As Americans' regard for the presidency as the government's preeminent source of moral leadership, legislative guidance, and policy innovation grew, pressures mounted to increase the size and professionalism of the president's staff. A modest office since the time of its creation, the presidency developed after the 1930s into a full-blown institution.

Roosevelt hastened this development when he named three of the country's foremost scholars of public administration—Louis Brownlow,

Charles E. Merriam, and Luther Gulick—to the newly formed President's Committee on Administrative Management. Concluding that "the President needs help," the Brownlow Committee, as it came to be called, proposed the creation of the Executive Office of the President (EOP). The EOP included the Bureau of the Budget, which had been housed in the Treasury Department since its birth in 1921, and a new White House Office, to be staffed by loyal and energetic presidential aides whose importance would be constrained by their "passion for anonymity." In contrast to the cabinet departments and independent agencies, which were extensively influenced by Congress, the EOP was designed as a presidential institution, responsible for tasks closely linked to the president's priorities and staffed by individuals who shared the president's political and policy objectives.[38] Most of those named by the president to fill important positions in the EOP did not require Senate confirmation.

The Brownlow Committee also sought to enhance the president's control of the expanding activities of the executive branch. During his first term Roosevelt insisted that virtually every new program be administered by a new agency created for that purpose, lest they get buried in the bureaucratic routines of the existing departments. The resulting "alphabet soup" of dozens of new agencies—NRA (National Recovery Administration), WPA (Works Progress Administration), PWA (Public Works Administration), CCC (Civilian Conservation Corps), and so on—did an excellent job of putting hundreds of thousands of people to work quickly. But by 1937 the president confronted a bewildering array of new and sometimes autonomous government agencies whose number and independence had come to offend his vision of a unified and energetic executive. Roosevelt, in fact, remarked shortly after the 1936 election that administrative management was the least successful aspect of his first term and professed relief that the Republicans did not concentrate their fire on this weakness during the campaign.[39] The Brownlow Committee called for an overhaul of the executive branch, recommending that all of the more than one hundred agencies then in existence be integrated into twelve major departments, each controlled by the president. Thus would "the national will be expressed not merely in a brief, exultant moment of electoral decision, but in a persistent, determined, competent day-by-day administration of what the nation has decided to do."[40]

Not surprisingly, Roosevelt wholeheartedly supported the Brownlow Committee's recommendations. Congress, for its part, had little quarrel with the new EOP. But the proposal embedded in the 1937 executive reorganization bill to overhaul the departments and agencies sparked one of the most intense controversies of FDR's presidency. His two-year battle for comprehensive administrative reform wrote a new chapter in the long-standing struggle between the president and Congress for control of administration.

What gave the battle special intensity was that it occurred just as the administration of government programs was becoming an important arena of public policy. As Gulick reported approvingly, the expansion of welfare and regulatory programs during the New Deal meant that the complex responsibilities of government increasingly were set forth in loosely written statutes, each little more than "a declaration of war [on a problem], so that the essence of the program is in reality in the gradual unfolding of the plan in actual administration."[41] The struggle between the president and Congress for control of the departments and agencies was no longer a simple squabble over patronage and power. The right to shape the direction and character of American society was also at stake.

When Congress finally did enact the Executive Reorganization Act of 1939, it granted the president some but not all of the administrative powers that he wanted. It placed a two-year limit on FDR's authority to reorganize the bureaucracy and exempted twenty-one important government agencies. Nevertheless, Roosevelt's implementation of the 1939 statute by Executive Order 8248 effected many of the Brownlow Committee's recommendations. The order created the EOP and moved several existing agencies under its umbrella. In addition to the White House Office and the refurbished and strengthened Bureau of the Budget, the new EOP included the National Resources Planning Board, a long-term planning agency. The transplanted Budget Bureau began to acquire much greater power, eventually assuming responsibility to oversee the formation of the president's domestic program. By the end of Roosevelt's tenure as president, the bureau had grown from fewer than fifty employees to more than five hundred.

Because the creation of the EOP enhanced the president's capacity to manage the expanding activities of the executive branch, it was an "epoch making event in the history of American institutions," wrote Gulick, and "perhaps the most important single step in the institutionalization of the presidency."[42] Most significant, the 1939 reforms hastened the development of the "administrative presidency," in which domestic policy is shaped on the president's behalf through executive orders, rule making by executive departments and agencies, and policy implementation.[43] To be sure, the absence of detail in Article II of the Constitution had always left the door open for independent presidential action, and Theodore Roosevelt and Woodrow Wilson significantly tested the boundaries of the rule of law. But the institutionalization of the presidency established an organizational apparatus that presidents and their appointees could use to short-circuit the separation of powers, accelerating the transfer of authority from Congress to the executive.

Constitutional Crisis

The New Deal provoked a serious constitutional crisis toward the end of FDR's first term. Roosevelt argued that the modern presidency, like the welfare state, was consistent with sound constitutional principles. "The only thing that has been happening," he told the nation in a fireside chat on May 7, 1933, "has been to designate the President as the agency to carry out certain of the purposes of Congress. This was constitutional and in keeping with past American traditions."[44] Opponents of the New Deal strenuously disagreed. "As they saw it," historian Ellis Hawley has written, "the balance and separation of powers established by the Constitution were being destroyed by a power-seeking presidency gathering into itself the power that should be exercised by Congress and the states."[45]

The ranks of New Deal critics included not just Roosevelt's enemies in Congress and business but also a majority of the Supreme Court. In 1935 and 1936 the Court struck down several important pieces of New Deal legislation, and many legal commentators expected that the Social Security Act and Wagner Act would be the next to fall. Roosevelt, whose second-term inauguration was the first to be held on January 20 under the new Twentieth Amendment, responded on February 5, 1937, with the most controversial action of his presidency, the "Court-packing" bill. The bill provided that for every justice who failed to retire within six months of reaching the age of seventy, the president must appoint a new justice. Six of the nine justices were already seventy or older, which meant that Roosevelt would be able to enlarge the Court from nine to fifteen members by making new appointments. Presumably, these new justices would overcome the Court's resistance to the New Deal.

Although some earlier strong presidents—notably Thomas Jefferson, Andrew Jackson, and Abraham Lincoln—had fought with the Supreme Court, the intensity of the response to FDR's Court plan was unprecedented. Day after day for the next several months, stories about the Court-packing conflict rated banner headlines in the nation's newspapers. The controversy sparked debates in every corner of the country. In Beaumont, Texas, a movie audience cheered rival arguments about the Court bill when they were shown on the screen.[46]

Roosevelt's plan sought to eliminate the final constitutional barrier to a vast expansion of government activity, thereby ratifying the president's power to direct the affairs of state. Significantly, the two Supreme Court decisions that enraged FDR the most were *Humphrey's Executor v. United States* and *Schechter Poultry Corp. v. United States*, both of which imposed constraints on the president's personal authority.[47] The decisions were handed down on May 27, 1935, soon known to New Dealers as "Black Monday." In different ways, both decisions threatened to derail the institutional changes that Roosevelt believed were necessary to solve the underlying problems of the depression.

The Court's ruling in *Humphrey's Executor* denied the president the right to remove appointees from the independent regulatory commissions, a legal power that Roosevelt and his advisers thought had been established by tradition and affirmed by precedent in *Myers v. United States* nine years earlier.[48] The *Schechter* ruling was a direct challenge to the modern administrative state. It declared that the discretionary authority Congress had granted at Roosevelt's request to the NRA, the leading economic agency of the early New Deal, was an unconstitutional delegation of legislative power to the executive.

Although the Court-packing bill failed in Congress, Roosevelt claimed that in losing the battle, he won the war. Beginning in March 1937, Justice Owen Roberts switched from the conservative to the liberal wing of the Court, and in rapid succession the justices approved a minimum wage law in Washington state, which was similar to a New York statute they found unconstitutional just a year earlier and, more significantly, upheld both the National Labor Relations Act and the Social Security Act. The "constitutional revolution of 1937" was cemented after a wave of deaths and retirements allowed Roosevelt to appoint a majority of justices by the end of his second term.[49] The Court never again struck down a New Deal law. In fact, since 1937 the Supreme Court has not invalidated any significant federal statute to regulate the economy, nor has the Court judged any law (with the exception of the Line Item Veto Act of 1996) to be an unconstitutional delegation of congressional authority to the president.[50] Most of the judicial barriers to presidential power have fallen.

But the bitter fight over Court packing cost the president dearly. Although the 1936 election had given the Democrats roughly three-fourths majorities in both the House and the Senate, the Court issue effectively brought Roosevelt's mastery of Congress and his party to an end. Moreover, it served as a lightning rod for the New Deal's opponents, spurring a resurgence of congressional independence and the formation of a bipartisan "conservative coalition." The new alliance of Republican and southern Democratic legislators blocked nearly every presidential domestic reform initiative from 1937 until the mid-1960s.

The Democratic Party had long been an unruly alliance between southern whites and European immigrants and their descendants in the North, held together in coalition by the economically marginal status that these groups shared. Desperate for infusions of federal money into the impoverished southern states and northern cities, both wings of the party enthusiastically supported FDR's legislative initiatives during his first term. Because of their seniority-based control of the congressional committees, southern Democrats were especially influential in promoting and helping pass virtually every New Deal program. But their support came with a condition: nothing must interfere with the superior status of whites in the South. As a result, provisions written into worker-protection laws such as the Fair Labor Standards Act and the Social Security Act excluded two-thirds of southern blacks, who worked as maids or labored on farms or in food-processing facilities.

As part of their loyalty to Roosevelt, congressional southerners even supported the Wagner Act, not anticipating how many northern workers would unionize and how politically liberal those racially integrated unions would become on issues of civil rights. Nor did they expect that jobs-seeking blacks would move north in such numbers, gaining the vote and, in gratitude for the benefits they derived from even racially discriminatory New Deal programs, converting from the GOP to the Democratic Party. For fear of alienating the white South, Roosevelt responded mildly to these new political pressures. He never did promote antilynching legislation or any other civil rights bill. Nevertheless, anticipating the worst, during FDR's second term southern members of Congress began voting with the Republicans on domestic issues while remaining Democrats.[51]

Roosevelt's first response to the ideological fissure in Congress was to try to unseat entrenched conservative Democrats in the 1938 midterm elections. He intervened in one gubernatorial primary and several congressional primaries in a bold effort to replace recalcitrant Democrats with candidates who were "100 percent New Dealers." Although William Howard Taft and Woodrow Wilson also tried to rid their parties of uncooperative members, Roosevelt's campaign was conducted on an unprecedented scale and, unlike the previous efforts, it bypassed the regular party organization. The extent to which his action was regarded as a shocking departure from the norm was indicated by the label—"the purge"—that the press gave it. The term evoked Hitler's attempt to weed out dissenters from the German Nazi Party and Stalin's elimination of suspected opponents from the Soviet Communist Party.

The purge campaign failed. All but two of the incumbent Democrats whom Roosevelt opposed were renominated. Widely condemned as an assault on the constitutional system of checks and balances, the president's actions galvanized the political opposition, contributing to the heavy losses the Democrats sustained in the 1938 midterm elections. Indeed, the purge campaign, like the Court bill, strengthened the anti-New Deal conservative coalition. Peter Gerry, a conservative Democratic senator from Rhode Island, wrote to North Carolina senator Josiah Bailey, a fellow conservative Democrat, in September 1938: "The victories of [conservative Democrats] have had even a greater effect than I had hoped for. They show that Roosevelt cannot control Senators for he does not have the weight with voters in his party that the New Dealers thought he possessed."[52] Since FDR's unhappy experience in 1938, most presidents have shied away from open intervention in House and Senate primaries.[53] Nevertheless, even though the purge failed, it further advanced changes in the Democratic coalition that shifted the center of power to the party's northern urban wing.

The first dramatic example of how Roosevelt transformed liberalism was his response to the 1941 March on Washington movement, spearheaded by the civil rights leader A. Phillip Randolph. As president of the Brotherhood of Sleeping Car Porters and head of the National Negro Congress, Randolph challenged the president to use the expanded power of the executive to strike a blow against the sort of forced segregation that tainted not only the South but also the federal government. For months, the Roosevelt administration gave vague assurances that it would do something about discrimination against black Americans in the defense industries that were mobilized in response to the outbreak of war in Europe and Asia. Weary of inaction, Randolph organized support throughout the country for a march of 100,000 supporters on the nation's capital. The most important objective was to "cause President Roosevelt to Issue an Executive Order Abolishing Discrimination in All Government Departments, Army, Navy, Air Corps, and National Defense Jobs."[54]

Wary of fracturing the Democratic Party, Roosevelt initially tried to resist Randolph's demands. Yet when faced with a large demonstration that might prove embarrassing to the White House and risk violence in the capital, the president relented and issued Executive Order 8802, which forbade discrimination by defense industries or government. To enforce this action, FDR established the Fair Employment Practices Committee. Although the prohibition on discrimination in the "arsenal of democracy," as Roosevelt called it, never fulfilled Randolph's expectations, it marked a major step forward in the long struggle for African American rights.

Foreign Policy

As the March on Washington movement revealed, the economic crisis that dominated Roosevelt's first two terms was displaced in the late 1930s by the approach and then the outbreak of World War II. Even before the United States declared war one day after the Japanese attack on Pearl Harbor on December 7, 1941, the growing American involvement in the conflicts intensified the concentration of power in the national government, its administrative apparatus, and the president. Significantly, it was the international crisis that allowed Roosevelt to stand for reelection in 1940, arguing that dangerous and uncertain times required continuity in leadership. His victory made him the only president in history to break the two-term tradition. FDR was elected a third time and, in 1944 during the latter stages of the war, a fourth. Only his death in April 1945 cut short his protracted reign.[55]

In 1937 Roosevelt began to confront the isolationist mood that had dominated the country since the end of World War I.[56] Speaking in Chicago, he strongly attacked the aggression of Germany and Japan, whose armies

Franklin Roosevelt, center, made several trips overseas to confer with Allied leaders about military strategy and the post–World War II world. In February 1945 Roosevelt conferred at Yalta with Winston Churchill, left, and Joseph Stalin, right.

Source: National Archives.

had recently invaded the demilitarized Rhineland and China, respectively. "The peace, the freedom and the security of ninety percent of the population of the world is being jeopardized by the remaining ten percent who are threatening a breakdown of all international order and law," said Roosevelt. "Surely the ninety percent who want to live in peace under law and in accordance with moral standards that have received almost universal acceptance through the centuries, can and must find some way to make their will prevail."[57]

Although the immediate reaction to the president's speech was favorable, a severe backlash soon set in, demonstrating clearly that neither Congress nor the American people were prepared to intervene in Europe or Asia. To some extent, the clash between interventionists and isolationists became a clash between the president and Congress over which branch would control foreign policy, just as it had in the final months of the Wilson administration. But Roosevelt was more willing than Wilson to act on his own, often with little warrant in statute or precedent. Ironically, his efforts were fortified by the same Court that had been such an obstacle to his domestic program.

On December 21, 1936, in *United States v. Curtiss-Wright Export Corp.*, the Supreme Court upheld a 1934 law that authorized the president to place an embargo on the sale of American-made weapons to countries engaged in armed conflict. The law was passed with the so-called Chaco war between Bolivia and Paraguay in mind, and Roosevelt quickly forbade the sale of arms to both countries. Weapons merchants challenged the measure as an unlawful delegation of legislative authority to the president. A federal district court agreed. But in a somewhat surprising opinion written by conservative justice George Sutherland, a near-unanimous Supreme Court laid down a sweeping doctrine of presidential supremacy in foreign policy.

The Court held that the president's constitutional powers in domestic and foreign affairs are fundamentally different. "The broad statement that the federal government can exercise no power except those specifically stated in the Constitution, and such implied powers as are necessary and proper to carry into effect the enumerated powers," Justice Sutherland wrote, "is categorically true only in respect to internal affairs." In foreign affairs, the actions of the president as the government's "sole organ" in international relations depend neither on a specific grant of power from the Constitution nor on authorization from Congress. Because executive authority in foreign policy is "plenary and exclusive," the president enjoys a freedom from statutory restriction that "would not be admissible were domestic affairs alone involved."[58]

The *Curtiss-Wright* case established as constitutional doctrine the sweeping defense of the president's authority in foreign affairs that Alexander Hamilton, writing as "Pacificus," offered in 1793 to defend President Washington's Neutrality Proclamation. Along with *United States v. Belmont* (1937), which justified the president's right to circumvent the treaty process by negotiating binding executive agreements with the leaders of other countries, *Curtiss-Wright* made it virtually impossible to challenge Roosevelt's increasingly internationalist policies on constitutional grounds.[59]

Relying on his broad, Court-sanctioned understanding of presidential authority, Roosevelt concluded a controversial agreement with Great Britain in 1940. The deal, which paved the way for the United States to send fifty naval destroyers to help Great Britain in its desperate battle with Nazi Germany, marked a departure from the official American policy of neutrality. In contrast, Roosevelt's Lend Lease program to aid Great Britain required congressional action because it involved an initial appropriation of about $7 billion. The debate over Lend Lease and its eventual enactment by Congress produced the sort of broad, albeit rough, consensus within the government that Roosevelt had not been able to achieve through unilateral executive action. Before Lend Lease, "the most Americans would commit themselves to was aid to the democracies short of war," historian David M. Kennedy has written. Now Roosevelt "edged them closer to a commitment to aid the democracies even at the risk of war."[60]

This fragile consensus was severely challenged by the rise of the American First Committee, the isolationist and anti-Semitic national organization that sought to pressure the United States to appease Adolf Hitler. Seeking to exploit the powerful isolationist strain and nativism that roiled the politics of the 1920s, the growing organization soon included powerful men like Col. Robert McCormick of the *Chicago Tribune*; Minnesota meatpacker Jay Hormel; Sterling Morton, the president of Morton Salt Company; and Lessing Rosenwald, the former chairman of Sears. Several hundred chapters formed with almost a million members, two-thirds of whom resided in the Midwest. Charles Lindbergh, the celebrated pilot of the first transatlantic flight, joined the American First Committee in April 1941, serving as principal spokesman and chief drawing card at its rallies. But the committee's virulent anti-Semitism prevented it from becoming a mainstream organization. Moreover, southern Democrats who had broken with the president on domestic issues were his strongest supporters against those who wanted nothing to do with another European war. Ethnically, Katznelson has pointed out, nearly all southern whites were of English or Scotch–Irish extraction. More important, southern agriculture found its major markets in the British Isles and the other Allied nations.[61]

Once under way, World War II greatly accelerated the flow of power from Congress and the courts to the president, allowing Roosevelt to assert an inherent executive prerogative more boldly than he could have before Japan's attack on Pearl Harbor and Germany's declaration of war against the United States. Under conditions of total war, Roosevelt believed, the president is authorized not only to direct military operations abroad but also to manage economic and social affairs at home. In a bold—critics said brazen—expression of his theory of presidential power, Roosevelt insisted that an effective program of wage and price controls be created. "I ask the Congress," FDR said in his Labor Day message of September 7, 1942, "to take . . . action by the first of October. Inaction on your part by that date will leave me with an inescapable responsibility to the people of this country to see to it that the war effort is no longer imperiled by threat of economic chaos." If Congress did not act, Roosevelt warned, "I shall accept the responsibility and I will act."[62] Congress enacted the controls on the economy that the president demanded, and Roosevelt never had to follow through on his threat.

The Supreme Court's acquiescence to presidential power also peaked during World War II.[63] In *Yakus v. United States* (1944) the justices upheld the wage and price controls that Roosevelt issued to implement the authority he secured from Congress in 1942. In justifying regulatory controls that relied on the vaguest of legislative standards, the Court all but abandoned the nondelegation principle announced in its 1935 *Schechter* decision.[64] In *Ex parte Quirin*, the Court sanctioned Roosevelt's use of a military tribunal to try eight Germans who came to America to commit acts of sabotage. After the Germans were captured in June 1942, Roosevelt convened a secret tribunal on July 2, which sentenced the eight men to death. The president later commuted the death sentences of the two prisoners who confessed and assisted in capturing the others. The remaining six were executed on August 8 in Washington.

The Court issued the *Quirin* decision on July 31, 1942, but did not release its full opinion until October 29. Writing for the Court, Chief Justice Harlan Fiske Stone distinguished *Quirin* from the Civil War–era case of *Ex parte Milligan* because Milligan, the defendant in that case, was not "part of or associated with the armed forces of the enemy." Moreover, Stone wrote, the conditions of modern warfare made more likely and insidious the acts of sabotage on American soil that justified military commissions:

> Modern warfare is directed at the destruction of enemy
> war supplies and the implements of their production and
> transportation, quite as much as at the armed forces. . . . The

law of war cannot rightly treat those agents of enemy armies who enter our territory, armed with explosives intended for the destruction of war industries and supplies, as any the less belligerent enemies than are agents similarly entering for the purpose of destroying fortified places or our Armed Forces.[65]

Although the public strongly supported the Roosevelt administration's treatment of Nazi saboteurs, a large part of the academic and legal community argued that *Quirin* set a dangerous precedent. Indeed, because of the harsh criticism leveled at Roosevelt's military tribunals order, the White House modified it when a second set of saboteurs was captured in 1944.

The Court's most controversial decision during World War II was *Korematsu v. United States* (1944), in which a majority of justices condoned the Roosevelt administration's use of a racial classification to imprison many Japanese Americans.[66] Even as the March on Washington movement and Roosevelt's executive order proscribing racial discrimination in the defense industry gave a foretaste of how the modern presidency might be deployed to advance civil rights, the internment of Japanese Americans testified dramatically to the dangers executive power could pose to racial justice. On February 8, 1942, Roosevelt signed an executive order authorizing the removal of more than one hundred thousand American citizens of Japanese descent from their homes on the West Coast to isolated, desolate relocation camps. These citizens had committed no crimes. Although FDR justified his order on grounds of "military necessity," he offered no real evidence to demonstrate that they posed a security risk. Indeed, to prove their patriotism, many of the young men who were sent to the camps enlisted in the American armed forces and served with distinction.

This affront to American ideals of justice was not FDR's idea. It originated with California politicians, most notably state attorney general Earl Warren, who later served as chief justice of the United States. The politicians were reacting to the widespread fears that arose in the wake of Japan's sneak attack on Pearl Harbor and the racism that falsely equated Japanese Americans with Japanese nationals. Some members of the administration opposed the internment order, but like FDR, they were preoccupied with winning the war and unwilling to go out of their way to help such politically vulnerable victims. One such victim, Fred Korematsu, was a twenty-three-year-old American-born citizen who had a good job, an Italian American fiancée, and no wish to leave either one. After his arrest for violating the military's evacuation order, Korematsu authorized the American Civil Liberties Union to use his case as a test of the internment policy.

Clearly uneasy about the *Korematsu* case, the Court acknowledged that "all legal restrictions which curtail the civil rights of a single racial group are immediately suspect." Nevertheless, Justice Hugo Black's majority opinion concluded that military necessity provided sufficient grounds to believe that the internment of Japanese American citizens was justified. "[W]hen under conditions of modern warfare our shores are threatened by hostile forces," Black wrote, "the power to protect must be commensurate with the threatened danger." In dissent, Justice Robert Jackson argued that such extreme judicial deference to executive power in wartime posed a dire threat to constitutional rights:

> [O]nce a judicial opinion rationalizes . . . an order to show that it conforms to the Constitution, or rather rationalizes the Constitution to show that the Constitution sanctions such an order, the Court for all time has validated the principle of racial discrimination in criminal procedure and of transplanting American citizens. The principle then lies about like a loaded weapon ready for the hand of any authority that can bring forward a plausible claim of an urgent need.[67]

In the decades since *Korematsu*, no racially restrictive law has ever passed the constitutional test of military necessity endorsed by the Supreme Court in that case. In truth, soon after the war ended in 1945 the Court's ruling came to be regarded as a judicial travesty. In 1948 Congress provided $37 million in reparations for the victims of Japanese internment. In another burst of conscience forty years later, Congress awarded $20,000 to each surviving detainee. In 1998 President Bill Clinton awarded the nation's highest civilian honor, the Presidential Medal of Freedom, to Fred Korematsu.[68] Yet these official acts of atonement never completely erased the deeply troubling failure of Congress and the Supreme Court to strike a constitutional balance that gave the president enough authority to make the nation safe while preventing serious abuses of individual freedom.

Yalta and the Cold War

The national security state continued to grow when World War II gave way to a new international struggle, which became known as the Cold War. The historic summit in February 1945 at Yalta, a Soviet port on the Crimean Peninsula, set the stage for this struggle. The leaders of the "Big Three" wartime allies—Joseph Stalin of the Soviet Union, Winston Churchill of Great

Britain, and Roosevelt—came to the conference hoping not just to develop a strategy to end World War II but also to reach an agreement on the shape of the postwar world.

Roosevelt's principal objective at Yalta was to create the sort of structure for cooperation among the major powers that the victorious nations had failed to achieve after World War I. He attached special significance to the voting procedures and membership rules that would govern the United Nations (UN), the new international organization approved in outline form at Dumbarton Oaks, in Washington, in the fall of 1944. Stalin, fearing that the United States and Great Britain would combine to relegate the Soviet Union to permanent minority status, held out for a single-nation veto in the UN Security Council, the body charged with principal responsibility for maintaining international peace. Roosevelt and Churchill acceded to Stalin's demand, ensuring that no action could be taken without every major power's consent.[69]

The UN agreement was forged in the midst of intense wrangling about the future of eastern Europe, especially Poland. The Red Army had already overrun Bulgaria, Hungary, and Romania and advanced through eastern Germany to within miles of Berlin. Stalin was determined to translate his hard-won military advantage into permanent political gain. Anxious to involve Stalin in the war against Japan, Roosevelt had neither the will nor a way to challenge Soviet domination of eastern Europe. But, joined by Churchill, he wanted political cover for his acquiescence to Russian hegemony. The result at Yalta was the Declaration on Liberated Europe. The declaration pledged the signatories "to arrange and conduct free elections" in the liberated nations of eastern Europe to create governments that were "broadly representative of all elements." But this pledge proved hollow. As Roosevelt's chief of staff, Adm. William Leahy, said when he saw the draft, "Mr. President, this is so elastic that the Russians can stretch it all the way from Yalta to Washington without ever technically breaking it."[70]

After Yalta, instead of implementing the agreed-on procedure to form a democratic government in Poland, the Russians installed a pro-Soviet regime. Churchill advocated a forceful response, but Roosevelt urged the British prime minister to "minimize the general Soviet problem as much as possible." FDR agreed with Churchill that the United States and Great Britain "must be firm," but he remained committed to diplomacy. In the president's view, the prospects for peace depended on the success of the UN in fostering cooperation among the victors. Although the single-veto voting procedure established for the UN Security Council threatened to hamstring the new organization, Roosevelt hoped that Yalta had at least established a framework for continued negotiation.[71]

Because the Yalta agreements were purely executive, the president did not send them to Congress for debate and ratification. They proved to be highly controversial. Critics alleged that Roosevelt, sick and mentally enfeebled, had conceded too much to Stalin, betraying Poland and delivering eastern Europe into Soviet hands. These charges, David Kennedy has concluded, are "vastly overdrawn."[72] Roosevelt was unquestionably ill. But he conceded little at Yalta that he had not signaled his willingness to yield at an earlier conference in Tehran, when he was in full command of his faculties. Arguments that Roosevelt was too soft in accepting Stalin's demands ignore the military situation on the ground, which gave the president few options. Even as the Soviets were completing their victorious drive in eastern Europe, the Americans and British were still recovering from the terrible Battle of the Bulge in which they had fought to regain lost ground against a massive German counterattack in Belgium and France. Roosevelt's military advisers also were pushing him to secure a firm Soviet commitment to enter the war against Japan as soon as possible, and the president had no reason to count on the atomic bomb being ready in time.[73] "I didn't say the result was good," Roosevelt conceded to an associate. "I said it was the best I could do."[74]

The Modern Presidency Sustained: Harry S. Truman and Dwight D. Eisenhower

Franklin Roosevelt dominated American political life for more than twelve years. His long tenure raised serious concerns about the dangers of concentrating too much power in the executive. After he died in 1945, conservative political leaders stood poised to modify the constitutional and political changes that had greatly enhanced presidential power since 1933. But FDR, building on the changes in the office wrought by Theodore Roosevelt and Woodrow Wilson, had transformed politics in the United States permanently. Under his tutelage, Americans expected the federal government to remain active in domestic and global affairs and presidents to take the lead within the constitutional framework of government. The presidency's place in the larger political system was therefore settled but uneasy.

Truman and the Roosevelt Inheritance

When the Senate adjourned at about five o'clock on April 12, 1945, Vice President Harry S. Truman made his way to the office of House Speaker Sam Rayburn to join his friends for an afternoon round of bourbon and water. No sooner had his drink been poured than the vice president received a telephone call from White House press secretary Steve Early, who told him to come to the White House as soon as possible. When Truman arrived, Eleanor Roosevelt put her arm around his shoulders and said softly, "Harry, the president is dead." After a moment of shock, Truman recovered sufficiently to ask, "Is there anything I can do for you?" She replied, "Is there anything we can do for you? For you're the one in trouble now."[75]

Eleanor Roosevelt was not the only one who felt that Truman was in trouble. With the country still at war, it seemed incomprehensible that anyone, let alone this "little man" from Missouri, as some of Truman's contemporaries disdainfully called him, could take Roosevelt's place as president of the United States. "For a time he walked," journalist William S. White wrote, "as completely as the smallest laborer who had been a 'Roosevelt man,' in the long shadow of the dead President."[76]

Truman eventually was able to emerge from FDR's shadow but not because he had much ability to rouse the public. In this respect, the contrast between Truman and Roosevelt was striking. "Truman possessed little or no charisma, struggled with an ego more fragile than most observers have understood, and had extreme distaste for the need to manipulate others," historian Alonzo L. Hamby has written.[77] A poor speaker who was awkward in the presence of reporters and microphones, Truman suffered persistently low popularity. His public approval rating was less than 50 percent during most of his tenure, including his final three years as president.[78]

In other respects, however, Truman was a solid successor to Roosevelt. He believed deeply in the changes the New Deal had brought about in American society. Well aware of his personal limitations, he also recognized that the legacy of FDR called for active and ongoing presidential leadership. Indeed, Truman likened being president to "riding a tiger. You have to keep on riding or be swallowed."[79]

The Fair Deal. When Truman assumed the presidency, some predicted that this supremely practical politician, who was placed on the ticket as the Democratic nominee for vice president in 1944 mainly to appease the party's southern and big-city leaders, would readily adapt to the more conservative mood that befell the country during the twilight of the war. A close Roosevelt associate, Samuel Rosenman, informed the new president that his "conservative friends," particularly some of his former colleagues on Capitol Hill, believed that Truman was "going to be quite a shock to those who followed Roosevelt—that the New Deal [was] as good as dead."[80]

Truman's twenty-one-point message to Congress on September 6, 1945, made clear that he would not be to Roosevelt what Harding was to Wilson. The message, which introduced the president's Fair Deal agenda, marked the moment when Truman felt he finally assumed the executive office in his own right. "This legislative program," he wrote in his memoirs, "was a reminder to the Democratic Party, to the country, and to the Congress that progress in government lies along the road to sound reform in our private enterprise system and that progressive democracy has to continue to keep pace with changing conditions."[81]

The Fair Deal was Truman's attempt to codify Roosevelt's vision of a postwar economic order. "We have accepted," Roosevelt proclaimed in his 1944 State of the Union address, "a Second Bill of Rights under which a new basis of security and prosperity can be established for all—regardless of station, race, or creed."[82] To fulfill Roosevelt's vision, Truman argued, the federal government must guarantee everyone a useful and remunerative job, adequate medical care, a decent home, and a good education.

The program that Truman presented to Congress in 1945 was an appeal, as he put it, "to make the attainment of those rights the essence of post-war economic life."[83] He called for the extension of social security to more workers, a higher minimum wage, national health insurance, urban development, and full employment. But Congress approved few of Truman's twenty-one points, and the results of the 1946 congressional elections appeared to represent the public's dramatic rejection of the Fair Deal. The Republicans campaigned on the theme that the country had "had enough" of Roosevelt–Truman-style liberalism. For the first time in sixteen years, the Democrats lost control of Congress.

Truman marshaled all of the resources accrued by his office during Roosevelt's tenure in an effort to prove otherwise. In the aftermath of the 1946 elections, he fought every attempt by the Republican Eightieth Congress to dismantle the New Deal. Truman cast more than two hundred vetoes during his presidency, mostly on matters of tax and labor policy. The conservative coalition of Republicans and southern Democrats, the same alliance that plagued FDR during his second term, often overrode these vetoes. But as political scientist Fred I. Greenstein has noted, Truman's forceful defiance in the face of overwhelming legislative opposition "accustomed all but the most conservative national political actors to look at the president as the main framer of the agenda for political debate—even when much of the debate involved castigation of his proposals."[84]

Truman's most significant veto was of the Taft–Hartley Act, which was widely regarded as an attack on labor unions.[85] On June 20, 1947, Truman sent a stinging veto message to Congress asserting that the bill "would reverse the basic direction of our national labor policy." That evening he went on the radio to declare, "We do not need—and we do not want— legislation which will take fundamental rights away from our working people."[86] Although Truman's Taft–Hartley veto was overridden by Congress, organized labor lined up solidly behind him. The veto also earned him praise from middle-class liberals, most of whom supported the unions. Truman "has given American liberalism the fighting chance that it seemed to have lost with the death of Roosevelt," the *Nation* editorialized.[87]

Shrewdly taking the political initiative, Truman turned the 1948 presidential election into a referendum on the New Deal. When he surprised nearly everyone by winning a come-from-behind victory against his Republican opponent, Gov. Thomas E. Dewey of New York, Truman stepped at least partially out of FDR's shadow. The president had saved the New Deal and revived enough of the New Deal Democratic coalition to prevail. Beyond that, the assertiveness he displayed in his battles with Congress confirmed the preeminence of the modern executive in legislative affairs.

Although Truman never was able to shatter the stalemate in domestic policy that endured throughout his presidency, he could claim some successes. His social security, minimum wage, and public housing proposals were enacted during the Eighty-First Congress, which as a result of the 1948 elections was again controlled by the Democrats. More important, the Truman administration was remarkably successful in assembling a bipartisan congressional coalition to support the president's policy toward the Soviet Union. In the weeks preceding his death, FDR had begun to take a more jaundiced view of Stalin. But it was left to Truman to formulate the American response to Soviet aggression in Europe.

Appearing before a joint session of Congress on March 12, 1947, Truman requested military aid for the endangered governments of Greece and Turkey. Unlike his most recent Democratic predecessors, Wilson and FDR, Truman was not responding to an obvious military threat, such as Germany's unrestricted submarine warfare in 1917 or the Nazi conquest of western Europe in 1940. Both of these events had led to war, which the president desperately wanted to avoid in the era of nuclear weaponry, inaugurated by his decision to drop atomic bombs on Japan to force its surrender in 1945. Instead, Truman articulated a policy of containment, promising to keep the Soviet empire from extending its borders.[88] Although maintaining a strong nuclear arsenal, stationing American troops in Europe and Asia, and supplying arms to vulnerable regimes would help to deter Soviet imperialism, Truman argued, the most effective way to assist threatened nations was with economic and financial aid. "The seeds of totalitarianism," he said, "are nurtured by misery and want." Proclaiming a policy that reporters quickly dubbed the Truman Doctrine, the president declared "that it must be the policy of the United States to support free peoples who are resisting attempted subjugation by armed minorities or by outside pressures."[89]

To win support for his containment policy, Truman had to overcome resistance in both political parties. The most vociferous opposition came from liberal Democrats led by FDR's third term vice president, Henry Wallace. Speaking at enthusiastic rallies around the country, Wallace appealed to those on the left who continued to think of the Soviet Union as an ally rather than a hostile power. In 1948 he challenged Truman's election as the nominee of the third-party Progressives. Republican opponents of the Truman Doctrine were led by Ohio senator Robert A. Taft, whose staunch defense of isolationism and fiscal restraint earned him the title of "Mr. Republican." Seizing the political center, the strategic high ground of American politics, Truman eventually prevailed over the forces of appeasement and isolation.[90] Internationalist Republicans and Democrats in Congress united to authorize the Truman Doctrine to contain communist expansion, the Marshall Plan to rebuild Europe economically, and the North Atlantic Treaty Organization (NATO) to defend the West against Soviet aggression.

The Marshall Plan. The creation of the Marshall Plan was especially remarkable: it was enacted in 1948 by a Republican-controlled Congress, at the behest of a Democratic president, during an election year.[91] In part, Truman owed his success in implementing the plan to the escalating threat posed by the Soviet Union. In February 1948 Soviet-backed communists seized power in Czechoslovakia, eliminating the last independent democracy in eastern Europe and consolidating Soviet control of the region.

Equally important, however, was Truman's deft statesmanship. Recognizing the enormous prestige of Secretary of State George C. Marshall, who had served with distinction as the army's chief of staff during World War II, Truman dismissed White House aide Clark M. Clifford's suggestion that the plan bear the president's name. Marshall's commencement address at Harvard University in June 1947 had given prominence to the idea of helping rebuild Europe, and Truman knew that the widely venerated general would do a much better job of selling the measure than he could.[92] Assisted by Marshall, the president adroitly cultivated bipartisan support, working effectively with Senate Foreign Relations Committee chair Arthur H. Vandenberg of Michigan, who assumed the critical and delicate role of mediator between the administration and congressional Republicans.

Vandenberg expected advance consultation from the administration, and received it in frequent meetings with the president and secretary of state. In addition, when Vandenberg requested that a "nonpartisan" business leader, Studebaker Corporation president Paul Hoffman, head the agency created to direct the Marshall Plan, Truman appointed Hoffman despite his initial preference for someone else.[93]

Civil Rights. Frustrated by his limited success with Congress in domestic matters, Truman resolved to stake out a substantial sphere for independent presidential action concerning civil rights. In doing so, he became the first president to enlist the powers of the modern office in the cause of racial justice. On December 5, 1946, Truman established by executive order the President's Committee on Civil Rights (PCCR), which was authorized "to determine whether and in what respect current law enforcement measures and the authority and means possessed by Federal, State, and local governments may be strengthened and improved to safeguard the civil rights of the people."[94]

Truman was a Missouri politician with close ties to southern legislators and strong sympathy for the region they represented. But more than most elected officials of his day, he was determined to do something about racial segregation. This determination stemmed from the president's own commitment to equal rights as well as the influence of northern liberals and African Americans in the Democratic Party. But foreign policy also helped inspire Truman's civil rights program. Jim Crow-style southern segregation threatened to undermine the American claim in its burgeoning rivalry with the Soviet Union that the United States was "the leader of a free world." Discrimination against Americans of color damaged the United States as it vied for influence in Africa, Asia, and Latin America. Indeed, new groups like the Committee against Jim Crow in Military Service and Training threatened to organize protests against the administration, and the National Association for the Advancement of Colored People (NAACP) petitioned the United Nations to pressure the United States "to be just to its people."[95]

Although African Americans first became an important part of the Democratic coalition in 1936, Roosevelt's New Deal, with the important exception of the president's Fair Employment Practices Committee (FEPC), did little to address directly the injustices of southern segregation. But World War II and its aftermath spurred Truman to come to terms with the "Negro Question." During the war, more than a million African Americans migrated to large northern and western states, such as Michigan and California, that were rich in electoral votes. Moreover, Truman believed that the president was obligated to uphold the fundamental rights of all

Americans. Truman found it especially intolerable that outrageous discriminatory acts were inflicted on black men in uniform, to whom he felt the country owed a great debt of gratitude.[96]

The president's bold initiative in launching a national investigation of racial injustice reopened critical issues that generally had been ignored in Washington since the end of Reconstruction. The PCCR's recommendations formed the basis of Truman's message to Congress on February 2, 1948, calling for a ten-point civil rights program that would provide federal protection against lynching, secure the right to vote, prohibit discrimination in interstate transportation facilities, and restore the FEPC, which Congress, ignoring Truman's protest, had eliminated in June of 1946.[97] "No political act since the Compromise of 1877," biographer Taylor Branch has argued, "so profoundly influenced race relations; in a sense it was a repeal of 1877."[98]

Conservative southern Democrats in Congress blocked Truman's civil rights proposals. But when legislators failed to approve the bill he recommended after receiving the PCCR's report, Truman did what he could on his own authority as chief executive. In July 1948, during the presidential campaign, Truman issued two executive orders. One drew on the president's power as commander in chief to decree that "there should be equality of treatment and opportunity in the Armed Services without regard to race, color, religion or national origin." Although the order did not explicitly condemn racial segregation, Truman established a committee headed by Solicitor General Charles Fahey that set the stage for the integration of the armed forces. Truman's other executive order forbade racial and ethnic discrimination in the federal civil service and established a Fair Employment Board to monitor hiring. This order was designed to uproot the discriminatory federal employment practices planted by the Wilson administration.

Truman's civil rights orders risked alienating southern white Democrats—the "Solid South" that constituted his party's traditional bastion of electoral strength. He was already leaking support on his left, but in the end Wallace received only 2 percent of the national popular vote and no electoral votes. After the 1948 Democratic convention adopted a civil rights plank, however, the president faced a more serious challenge from southern Democrats on his right. South Carolina governor Strom Thurmond and his segregationist allies bolted to form a third party that threatened Truman's chances for winning the election. Running as the States' Rights Party, or "Dixiecrat," nominee, Thurmond also won just 2 percent of the popular vote, but because his support was geographically concentrated, he carried the four Deep South states of Alabama, Louisiana, Mississippi, and South Carolina.

Although losing these states cost Truman only thirty-nine electoral votes, his civil rights agenda had opened a fissure in the Democratic Party that later spurred major defections of southern white voters to the GOP.[99] Not wishing to aggravate this cleavage, Truman de-emphasized civil rights after his triumphant 1948 election. But his civil rights initiatives and his use of executive power to advance them had significant consequences for both African Americans and the modern presidency. As historian John Hope Franklin stated in a 1968 address, "The crucial turning point in viewing the problem of race as a national problem occurred when the executive branch of the federal government began actively to assume a major role."[100]

Executive Action and Foreign Affairs. As bold and controversial as his civil rights measures were, Truman's most daring and politically costly independent initiatives came in the realm of international security. These included his 1945 decision to use atomic weapons against Japan to bring an end to World War II and his decision in 1950 to commit American troops to combat in Korea. The Korean intervention, which followed communist North Korea's invasion of South Korea, was another important extension of the president's powers as commander in chief. For the first time, American troops waged a full-scale overseas war without a congressional declaration.

In part, Truman's intervention in Korea was a logical consequence of the postwar emergence of the United States as a superpower, actively and constantly engaged in international affairs as the leader of the Free World. In 1945 the Senate overwhelmingly ratified the charter that established the United Nations. Congress then passed the United Nations Participation Act, which made the United States subject to certain UN decisions. Truman invoked this act as the primary legal justification for his deployment of troops in Korea. Once the UN Security Council decided to help South Korea, the president argued, he had no choice but to respond under Articles 39 and 42 of the UN Charter.

But Truman also defended his actions in Korea by claiming to have a sweeping executive power to deploy the armed forces of the United States without consulting Congress. To be sure, Truman was able to cite precedents from the administrations of earlier commanders in chief. But all of these precedents involved limited interventions to suppress piracy or protect American citizens who were endangered by foreign disorders. Truman's real rationale was that the Cold War against communism and the president's new responsibilities as the leader of the free world greatly diminished Congress's role in foreign policy. As he said in March 1951, "The congressional power to declare war has fallen into abeyance because wars are no longer declared in advance."[101]

The powers of the modern presidency were not completely unrestrained, however, even in foreign policy. Truman paid dearly in the coin of public and congressional criticism as the war in Korea continued for the length of his presidency. Most important, Truman's claim that the Korean conflict endowed the president with emergency economic powers was rebuffed by the Supreme Court after he seized control of the nation's strike-threatened steel mills in 1952. For fear of alienating the unions, Truman refused to apply the Taft–Hartley Act, which authorized the president to impose an eighty-day cooling-off period on labor and management in an industrial dispute in order to postpone a strike. Instead, on April 8 he ordered Secretary of Commerce Charles Sawyer to take control of the steel mills. Truman argued that because steel is the essential ingredient in weapons manufacturing, a "work stoppage would immediately jeopardize and imperil our national defense."

Less than two months later, the Court, in *Youngstown Sheet and Tube Co. v. Sawyer*, disabused the president of his belief that in a national emergency, he could do anything that the Constitution or Congress did not explicitly forbid. Justice Hugo Black declared in his majority opinion that Truman must return the mills to their owners because his seizure order was a de facto statute that preempted Congress's lawmaking power. "The Constitution is neither silent nor equivocal about who shall make laws which the President is to execute," Black wrote.[102]

The Court's decision surprised many people. Truman could cite numerous precedents of presidents intervening militarily in labor disputes. Theodore Roosevelt threatened to seize and run the mines during the anthracite coal strike of 1902 if mediation failed.[103] Franklin Roosevelt seized the North American Aviation Plant at Inglewood, California, on June 9, 1941, six months before Pearl Harbor, arguing that his power to act derived from the "aggregate" of the Constitution and the laws.[104] Not since 1866 had the Supreme Court ruled against a president in the exercise of prerogative power, and in that case, *Ex parte Milligan*, the Court only declared that Lincoln's use of military tribunals during the Civil War was invalid after the war was over.[105] Small wonder, then, that Truman believed his action would be upheld, especially because the Court consisted entirely of his and Roosevelt's appointees.[106]

In truth, the Court's decision did not severely circumscribe the president's powers as commander in chief. Only Justices Black and William O. Douglas questioned whether the president had emergency powers. The opinions of the four other justices in the six-member majority applied strictly to the case at hand, emphasizing that Congress explicitly rejected presidential seizure as a method of settling industrial disputes when it passed the Taft–Hartley Act. Justice Robert Jackson's concurring opinion turned out to be the most influential of all in shaping future constitutional interpretation.

Jackson offered a test for the Court to use when weighing presidential powers against congressional action. Whenever the president acts "pursuant to an express or implied authorization of Congress," Jackson argued, "his authority is at its maximum, for it includes all that he possesses in his own right plus all that Congress can delegate." The most difficult cases involve presidential actions taken "in absence of either a congressional grant or denial of authority." Where the law is silent, Jackson acknowledged, there is "a zone of twilight" in which the president and Congress have "concurrent authority." In this gray area, the test of constitutionality depends on the circumstance—"the imperatives of events and contemporary imponderables rather than on abstract theories of law." Truman's actions in the steel dispute, however, disavowed a law properly passed by Congress, placing him in direct conflict with the legislature's expressed will and clearly exceeding the limits of presidential authority:

> When the president takes measures incompatible with the expressed or implied will of Congress, his power is at its lowest ebb, for then he can rely only upon his own constitutional powers minus any constitutional powers of Congress in the matter. Courts can sustain exclusive Presidential control in such a case only by disabling the Congress from acting upon the subject.[107]

Youngstown was "an important foundation," historian Maeva Marcus has written, "for the reaffirmation of the proposition that the President is not above the law."[108] Truman's defeat in the steel crisis meant that he and his successors would have to exercise the expanded powers of the presidency more carefully. But the Court did not strike a crippling blow to the president's powers as commander in chief. Indeed, the justices might have sustained Truman's seizure of the steel mills if Congress had not passed the Taft–Hartley Act, which provided the president with other ways to keep the mills running.

Truman and the Modern Presidency. Truman's tenure as president affirmed the modern presidency and extended it into the national security arena permanently, not just in times of war. He demonstrated that a president without extraordinary political gifts or popularity could achieve important objectives, define the terms of national political debate, and control at least the main lines of domestic and foreign policy. In part, Truman succeeded because he was operating in the new governing environment that emerged from the Great Depression and World War II. The welfare state at home and international leadership abroad inevitably concentrated major responsibilities in the White House.

But Truman also made an independent contribution to the development of the presidency by formalizing and expanding it as an institution. Although Franklin Roosevelt created the EOP, FDR's own staff was loosely structured, reflecting his penchant for improvised, ad hoc arrangements. Truman, in contrast, was a systematic administrator. During his administration, responsibilities within the White House Office were defined clearly. Truman also used the Bureau of the Budget more extensively than Roosevelt, relying on it heavily in performing his executive and legislative duties. Truman assigned responsibility to the Budget Bureau to clear and coordinate all legislative requests that originated within the federal departments and to draft White House-sponsored legislation and executive orders.[109] As a result, he developed an advisory process in which most policies came to him only for decision, not, as with FDR, for development.

Congress helped Truman to institutionalize the presidency, sometimes unintentionally. Congressionally initiated statutes established the Council of Economic Advisers (CEA) in 1946 and the National Security Council (NSC) in 1947 to help the president formulate fiscal and foreign policy, respectively. Although many legislators hoped that the CEA and NSC would serve as checks on the president's autonomy in economic and security matters by making the president consult with other, Senate-confirmed officials, Truman effectively domesticated the councils—that is, he made them part of the president's team.

In addition to establishing the NSC, the National Security Act created two executive bodies that strengthened the president's capacity to influence world affairs. One was the Central Intelligence Agency (CIA), a powerful new tool of American foreign policy in the Cold War era. Although Truman feared he might be creating a "Gestapo"-style secret police force, unification of the government's previously far-flung intelligence activities appealed to his desire for centralization and clear lines of responsibility.

The other new agency was the Department of Defense, which housed under one roof the previously separate branches of the military. By the end of World War II, most members of Congress were convinced that the antagonistic bureaucracies responsible for national defense needed to be consolidated. Truman, characteristically, favored any effort to make administration more orderly. The 1947 statute created the National Military

Establishment headed by a secretary of defense who was charged with coordinating the operations of the army, navy, marines, and air force. This task proved to be herculean; indeed, it eventually helped drive the first secretary, James Forrestal, to nervous collapse and suicide. In 1949 Congress enacted amendments proposed by Forrestal and Truman to strengthen the authority of the secretary and replace the National Military Establishment with a full-blown Department of Defense. To further centralize military planning, the 1949 amendments also created the position of chairman of the Joint Chiefs of Staff (JCS) to denote the officer who would serve as the principal military adviser to the defense secretary and the president. These changes did not eliminate interservice rivalries, but the new cabinet-level department, along with the NSC and CIA, greatly increased the resources available to the president in directing foreign and military policy.[110]

The creation of a large, powerful, and permanent military establishment was unprecedented in American history. The Framers of the Constitution anticipated and even feared that a "standing army" would extend the power of the executive beyond its proper bounds. In Truman's case, however, the sword proved two-edged and made his ability to engage in an undeclared war burdensome. After a sharp disagreement with Gen. Douglas MacArthur about American strategic aims in Korea and, more importantly, about who was entitled to make those decisions, Truman fired the popular general. He paid a high political price for doing so. Truman suffered further losses of popularity as the war—the president's war—dragged on inconclusively, with heavy loss of life.[111]

Still, Truman's effort to strengthen the institutional presidency was endorsed at every turn by Congress, including the powerful southern Democrats who thwarted many of his domestic initiatives but supported the growth of the military, a mainstay of the region's economy.[112] This collaborative effort to strengthen the institutions of the modern executive also received surprising help from former president Hoover. The Republican-controlled Eightieth Congress appointed Hoover to head the Commission on the Organization of the Executive Branch of the Government. The task of the commission, as Republican leaders understood it, was to lay the groundwork for an assault on New Deal programs and to circumscribe the executive by foreclosing the possibility of another personalized, FDR-style administration. Yet Hoover, who as president had grappled with the problems of running the executive branch, saw the need to fortify the presidency.[113]

After much study, the Hoover Commission submitted a report similar to the one the Brownlow Committee wrote in 1937 to support FDR's program of administrative reform. The president still needs help, the Hoover Commission argued, especially to supervise the far-flung activities of the enlarged executive branch. Its recommendations formed the basis of the 1949 Reorganization Act, which authorized Truman, who enthusiastically embraced the commission's report, to make important changes in many of the departments, agencies, and independent regulatory commissions.

Especially significant was Truman's Reorganization Plan No. 8, which he issued in 1950. Truman included provisions that eroded the regulatory commissions' autonomy from presidential influence and thereby reduced the effect of the Court's ruling in *Humphrey's Executor v. United States* that the president may not fire a commissioner. Under the reorganization plan, the chairs of the regulatory commissions would be "appointed by the president and serve at his pleasure." The chairs, in turn, were granted considerable authority to oversee the daily operation of their commissions and to appoint and supervise commission staff. Consequently, presidents were better able to give direction to regulatory agencies than in the past.[114]

Hoover's endorsement of executive reorganization suggested that a bipartisan consensus had formed in support of the modern presidency. Republicans had "historically been against Presidents," one Truman aide noted, but Hoover's interest in the problems of administrative management offered Republican support for "the kind of Chief Executive office that will have enough authority and the right kind of organization to do the most difficult jobs."[115]

The Twenty-Second Amendment

One of the political aftershocks of the New Deal and Fair Deal was the Twenty-Second Amendment, which was proposed by the Republican-dominated Eightieth Congress in 1947 and ratified by the states in 1951. The amendment prohibits any person from being elected president more than two times. It also limits vice presidents who succeed to the presidency to one elected term if they have served more than half of a departed president's four-year term. If they have served half or less than half of a term, they may be elected twice, for a maximum tenure of ten years.

Although the amendment specifically exempted the incumbent Truman from its coverage, it was a posthumous slap at Franklin Roosevelt, who challenged the two-term tradition by being elected president four times.

The Two-Term Tradition. The source of the two-term tradition was Thomas Jefferson, who was the first president to argue that no one should serve more than eight years as chief executive. Responding on December 10, 1807, to a letter from the Vermont state legislature asking him to run for a third term (six other states sent similar letters), Jefferson replied, "If some termination of the services of the Chief Magistrate be not fixed by the Constitution, or supplied by practice, his office, nominally four years, will in fact become for life, and history shows how easily that degenerates into an inheritance." To strengthen his argument for a two-term limit, Jefferson invoked "the sound precedent set by an illustrious predecessor," George Washington.[116]

Jefferson's invocation of Washington was historically inaccurate. Washington left the presidency after two terms, but as he explained in his Farewell Address, he did so not as a matter of principle but because he thought the country needed to learn that the Constitution would work even if he were not president. More personally, he longed for "the shade of retirement."[117] Even so, Jefferson's defense of a two-term limit took root quickly in presidential politics. Indeed, the Whig Party and many Democrats soon argued for a one-term limit. Of the first thirty presidents (Washington to Hoover), twenty served one term or less, and none served more than two terms.

In the late nineteenth and early twentieth centuries, the issue of a third term arose only occasionally. Ulysses S. Grant (in 1876) and Woodrow Wilson (in 1920) would have liked to serve another four years, but they were too unpopular at the end of their second terms even to be renominated by their parties. In 1908 Theodore Roosevelt declined a certain renomination and, considering his great popularity, a probable reelection, calling the two-term limit a "wise custom." Four years later, however, he ran for president again, first as an unsuccessful contender for the Republican nomination and then as a third-party candidate.

The two-term tradition was broken by Franklin Roosevelt in 1940. In 1937 Roosevelt had declared that his "great ambition on January 20, 1941," was to "turn over this desk and chair in the White House" to a successor. But in 1939 war broke out in Europe, with little prospect that the United States would be able to remain above the fray. Waiting until the Democratic convention in July 1940, Roosevelt finally signaled his willingness to be renominated. The delegates jubilantly approved, knowing that FDR offered the party its best chance for victory.

Public opinion polls showed that voters were deeply divided about the propriety of Roosevelt's candidacy, and Republicans took up the cry "No Third Term!" on behalf of their nominee, business leader Wendell Willkie. Democrats rejoined that in perilous times the country would be foolish to "change horses in midstream." Roosevelt won the election but by a much narrower popular vote margin than in 1936—5 million votes, down from 11 million. In 1944, with the United States and its allies nearing victory in World War II, Roosevelt won another term by 3 million votes. Ill at the time of his fourth election, he died less than three months after the inauguration.

The Amendment Passes. Congress had never been fully satisfied with the original Constitution's provision for unrestricted presidential reeligibility. From 1789 to 1947, 270 resolutions to limit the president's tenure were introduced in the House and Senate.[118] But the Roosevelt years added a partisan dimension to this long-standing concern. In 1932 the Republicans, who had formed the nation's majority party since 1860, were driven from power by Roosevelt's New Deal Democratic coalition. Conservative Democrats, mostly southerners, lost control of their party to liberals and northerners.

In the midterm elections of 1946, Republicans regained a majority of both houses of Congress. On February 6, 1947, less than five weeks after the opening of the Eightieth Congress, the House passed a strict two-term amendment to the Constitution by a vote of 285–121. Republicans supported the amendment unanimously (238–0). Democrats opposed it 47–121, with three-fourths of the Democratic yea votes coming from southerners. Freshman representative John F. Kennedy of Massachusetts, whose father, Ambassador Joseph P. Kennedy, had fallen out with Roosevelt, was one of only two northeastern Democrats to support the amendment. Five weeks later, on March 12, the Senate passed by a vote of 59–23 a slightly different version of the amendment. It allowed a successor president who served one full term and half or less of another to seek an additional term. Republican senators, like their House colleagues, were unanimous in support (46–0); Democrats opposed the amendment by a vote of 13 (9 of them southerners) to 23. The differences between the two houses' versions were ironed out in favor of the Senate. Final congressional passage took place on March 24, 1947.

Debate on the Twenty-Second Amendment painted a highly partisan issue with a thin coat of constitutional philosophy. Republicans contended that a two-term limit would protect Americans against the threat of an overly personalized presidency. Republican representative Karl Mundt of South Dakota less cautiously proclaimed that the amendment "grows directly out of the unfortunate experience we had in this country in 1940 and again in 1944." Democrats such as Rep. Estes Kefauver of Tennessee argued that the people, "by a mere majority vote, have the opportunity of deciding every four years whether they want to terminate the services of the President

Despite numerous precedents for executive intervention in labor disputes, President Harry Truman's seizure of steel mills during the Korean War was widely denounced. The Supreme Court ruled the action illegal.

Source: Library of Congress.

if he stands for reelection."[119] Little, if any, consideration was given to the reasoning behind the Constitutional Convention's carefully considered decision to place no restrictions on presidential reeligibility.

After it was proposed by Congress, the Twenty-Second Amendment received a mixed response from the states. Only one other amendment to the Constitution has taken longer to ratify than the three years, eleven months, required for the two-term limit.[120] Eighteen state legislatures—exactly half the needed number—approved the amendment in 1947, all of them in predominantly Republican states. Afterward, ratification proceeded slowly, with most victories coming in the conservative Democratic South.[121] Approval from the required three-fourths of the states was attained on February 27, 1951. Had the amendment not exempted Truman from its coverage, it might have foundered on the shoals of overt (instead of merely implicit) partisanship.

Dwight D. Eisenhower: The Reluctant Modern President

Like the Hoover Commission, and in contrast to the Twenty-Second Amendment, the presidency of Dwight Eisenhower fostered bipartisan acceptance of the modern presidency.[122] But Eisenhower's contribution was reluctant. Although the first Republican president in twenty years had no intention of trying to dismantle the Roosevelt Revolution, he came to the White House in 1953 with a different understanding of the executive office than Roosevelt as well as with different aspirations for the federal role in American society.

Eisenhower served as Supreme Allied Commander in Europe, a position to which FDR appointed him, and was the most celebrated of the

World War II generals. "Ike," as he was known to the nation and the world, brought to the presidency a soldier's sense of duty. He was determined not to lead the federal government into new and untried activities but instead to restore a sense of national calm after the controversial and frenetic activism of the Roosevelt and Truman years. "Eisenhower has been a sort of Roosevelt in reverse," Richard Neustadt wrote in 1960. "Roosevelt was a politician seeking personal power; Eisenhower . . . came to crown a reputation not make one. He wanted to be arbiter, not master. His love was not for power but for duty."[123]

Eisenhower's concern for duty initially inclined him to accept the argument of some Republicans that balance should be restored to the relationship between the president and Congress. He was not a strong partisan; in fact, some Democrats tried to draft him to run for president in 1948, only to discover that he considered it so much his soldierly duty to remain above politics that he never had voted.[124] But Eisenhower did accept the prevailing Republican doctrine that the proper relationship between Congress and the president had been upset by his immediate Democratic predecessors, FDR and Truman. He even decided not to submit a legislative program to Congress in 1953.

Some Americans regarded Eisenhower's constant professions of respect for Congress as refreshing evidence that the hallowed traditions of legislative government were being restored. Others, however, especially in the press, looked disdainfully on what one observer called Eisenhower's "civic textbook concept of the three branches of the federal government."[125] With FDR's first term in mind, reporters insisted on grading Ike at the end of his first hundred days, and he did not fare well. In an article published in May 1953, Washington correspondent Joseph C. Harsch observed, "The memory of Franklin Roosevelt's voracious seizure and joyous exercise of presidential power twenty years earlier contributes to a companion illusion of a man who slipped into the White House by the back door on January 20, 1953, and hasn't yet found his way to the President's desk."[126]

The Hidden Hand. Appearances to the contrary, Eisenhower did not passively watch history unfold. He exercised power with much more relish and shrewdness than his contemporaries realized. Ike's was a "hidden-hand" presidency, as Fred Greenstein has called it, in which the president exercises power behind the scenes while presenting the public with an image of detachment from Washington's political machinations.[127] Eisenhower's approach to leadership was designed to free him from an inherent difficulty of the modern presidency. On the one hand, the president is expected to be a chief of state who stands above politics, upholds the Constitution, and lends dignity to the national government—a kind of latter-day George Washington. On the other hand, the president must be a chief of government in the style inaugurated by Thomas Jefferson and Andrew Jackson— that is, an engine of change who gets things done by leading his party and Congress in pursuit of a program. Ultimately, Eisenhower believed, the dignity and influence of the office were lost when the president not only led politically but also appeared to lead politically, as he thought Truman had done.

Ike's solution to the dilemma of modern executive leadership was not to abdicate responsibility for policy. Although he was a domestic conservative who had no desire to significantly expand the welfare state, Eisenhower believed that the New Deal was an established part of modern American government. When his conservative brother Edgar criticized him privately for carrying on FDR's liberal policies, the president replied bluntly: "Should any political party attempt to abolish social security, unemployment insurance and eliminate labor laws and farm programs, you should not hear of that party again in our political history."[128] As historian Oscar Handlin wrote soon after Ike left office, "Eisenhower made palatable to most Republicans the social welfare legislation of the preceding two decades. In the 1950s, the New Deal ceased to be an active political issue and became an accepted part of the American past. No other figure could have achieved that transformation."[129]

Two years after his 1952 election Eisenhower worked with Congress to pass an expansion of social security that built on Truman's effort to extend benefits to groups in society, notably African Americans and women, that FDR's compromise bill failed to cover. These included hotel workers, domestic servants, all agricultural workers, and state and local government employees. More telling of the bipartisan commitment to the fledgling national state was the creation of an interstate highway system, first proposed in 1944, which Eisenhower celebrated as "the biggest peacetime construction project ever undertaken by the United States or any other country."[130]

In foreign policy, too, Eisenhower carried on most of the policies of his two Democratic predecessors. Unlike many Republicans, he shared the internationalist perspective of FDR and Truman. He was contemptuous of Republicans—notably Senate leader Robert Taft, his main rival for the party's presidential nomination in 1952—who wanted the United States to withdraw into isolation from world affairs.[131] Eisenhower decided to run for president, some said, not because he enjoyed politics but because he felt a duty to lead the internationalist wing of the Republican Party and to preserve the postwar foreign policy that he as the first NATO commander had helped to create.[132] "Observers sensed," William Leuchtenburg has noted, "that even when Eisenhower did not acknowledge that he was FDR's legatee, he had the same internationalist aspirations."[133]

Eisenhower realized that because of the New Deal legacy and the emergence of the United States as the leader of the Free World, it was no longer possible for the president simply to preside. The task instead, as he understood it, was to lead without seeming to lead, to remain quietly and persistently involved in political affairs while maintaining the public face of the genial national hero.

The most instructive example of Eisenhower's hidden-hand approach to governing was his handling of Sen. Joseph McCarthy. Since 1950 the nation had been traumatized by the Wisconsin Republican. McCarthy had taken a real problem—communist infiltration of the federal government during the 1930s and 1940s—and made it seem much bigger and more frightening than it was through wild exaggeration and reckless slander. Eisenhower refused to publicly attack McCarthy, who chaired the Senate Committee on Government Operations and its subcommittee on investigations, even though he regarded the senator's "red-baiting" as demagogy of the worst sort. The president's critics claimed that by not upbraiding McCarthy, Eisenhower abetted the senator in unjustly ruining many lives and careers. But Eisenhower's public silence did not bespeak timidity or tacit approval. Rather, he feared that to take on McCarthy publicly would undermine the dignity of the presidency and the unity of the Republican Party, thereby jeopardizing his chances of pursuing an internationalist foreign policy. "I will not," Eisenhower told his brother Milton, "get into a pissing contest with that skunk."[134]

Working closely with his press secretary, James Hagerty, the president instead used the media and his congressional allies to undermine McCarthy's political effectiveness.[135] Through Hagerty, Eisenhower helped manage the congressional hearings that culminated in McCarthy's censure by the Senate in December 1954. In addition, Eisenhower and Vice President Richard Nixon condemned in general terms the kinds of actions in which McCarthy engaged without condemning the senator by name. The public would not turn against McCarthy, Ike was convinced, until it was persuaded that the values and institutions the senator was attacking needed to be defended.

Eisenhower's most notable reproof came when McCarthy's adherents around the country purged libraries of politically controversial books and harassed educators. "Don't join the book burners," the president told an audience at Dartmouth College. "Don't think you are going to conceal faults by concealing evidence that they ever existed. . . . How will we defeat communism unless we know what it is?" The right of the people to express ideas, he said, is "unquestioned, or it isn't American."[136] A few months later, Eisenhower proclaimed that teachers were loyal citizens who enjoyed "true freedom of thought, untrammeled by political fashion or expediency."[137] Although the president named no names in his speeches and press conferences, he said in response to a reporter's question that McCarthy's Senate investigations threatened the values it claimed to be defending.[138]

As his handling of McCarthy illustrates, Eisenhower did not reject the modern presidency. Rather, he tried to manage its responsibilities in a way that suited his own strengths and political objectives. Despite criticism in the press, Eisenhower remained extraordinarily popular with the American people. Calvin Coolidge had shown that presidential leadership of public opinion need not be confined to efforts at reform or innovation. Eisenhower's popularity similarly indicated that the public sometimes appreciates quiet leadership to preserve the status quo. "Among the qualities that the American government must exhibit is dignity," Eisenhower wrote in a 1960 letter to Henry Luce, the publisher of *Time* and *Life* magazines. "In turn, the principal governmental spokesman must strive to display it."[139]

Eisenhower's Legacy. Eisenhower was criticized in his time by presidential scholars for the work he left undone. "No president in history," wrote Clinton Rossiter, "was ever more powerfully armed to persuade the minds of men and face up to the inevitable and then failed more poignantly to use his power."[140] To be sure, the foundations of the welfare state and of America's international obligations were sustained during Eisenhower's tenure and, in some instances, were extended. Social security was expanded, the government became more active in fostering economic development, most notably in developing the new highway system, and additional regional security alliances such as the Southeast Asia Treaty Organization (SEATO) were formed with the United States at their center. But to most liberals, Eisenhower, for all his popularity, failed as president by not rousing the country to redress its problems of civil rights and education.

Critics charged, in particular, that Eisenhower's approach to civil rights revealed a troubling deficiency in his understanding of presidential responsibility. In 1954 the Supreme Court decision in *Brown v. Board of Education of Topeka*, a case brought by the distinguished civil rights attorney Thurgood Marshall of the NAACP's Legal Defense Fund, struck down state laws that mandated racially segregated public schools. The Truman administration supported the plaintiffs in this case, submitting a thirty-two-page brief that proved useful to the justices.[141] By uniting the executive and judiciary in the struggle against racial discrimination, the Court's unanimous ruling in *Brown* raised the hopes of civil rights reformers that segregation had finally been routed.[142]

Eisenhower dampened these hopes. In what the historian William Hitchcock calls "a classic expression" of his "inner conviction," Eisenhower signaled that unlike Truman he did not intend to confront the issue of Jim Crow head on. Prejudice, he insisted, would not "succumb to compulsion," and any imposition of federal law on states "would set back the cause of progress in race relations for a long time." Eisenhower reluctantly supported his attorney general, Herbert Brownell, who issued a brief echoing the Truman administration's constitutional arguments against forced segregation. Moreover, in 1953, Eisenhower appointed the formidable governor of California, Earl Warren, to the Supreme Court. A moderate Republican, Warren led his fellow justices to a unanimous decision in the landmark *Brown* decision. Although he boasted in 1955 of his progressive record on civil rights, the cautious Eisenhower was determined not to use federal power to impose dramatic change on the South. He refused to state clearly whether he approved or disapproved of the *Brown* decision. The president's equivocation helped set the stage for an ugly racial incident in Little Rock, Arkansas.[143]

In September 1957 the Democratic governor of Arkansas, Orval Faubus, mobilized his state's National Guard in an effort to thwart a federal court order to begin desegregating Little Rock's all-white Central High School. Eisenhower tried to stay out of the controversy, initially conducting only a single, inconclusive meeting with Faubus at the president's summer home in Newport, Rhode Island, on September 14. Upon returning to Arkansas, Faubus, who believed that Eisenhower was indifferent to the situation in his state, defied the president's private request to instruct the Arkansas National Guard to enforce the court order. Instead, Faubus withdrew the guard from around the school. On September 23, nine African American students were turned away from Central High School by a howling, hate-filled mob of segregationists from Arkansas and other states. Faubus continued to inflame the onrushing crisis with defiant rhetoric.

Eisenhower was still reluctant to interfere in Little Rock, believing that to use federal troops to enforce desegregation might cause the violence to spread. But when neither state nor local authorities dispersed the mob, the president no longer could avoid responsibility. If he failed to act in the face of Faubus's defiance of the court order, Eisenhower would yield to every segregationist governor the right to break the law. The unfortunate consequence of delay was that when Eisenhower did act, he was forced to deploy massive military power domestically. On September 24 a contingent of army paratroopers from the 101st Airborne Division was dispatched to Little Rock. The next day, Americans saw shocking, front-page photographs of troops wielding bayonets in an American city.

"In my career," the former Supreme Allied Commander told Attorney General Brownell, "I have learned that if you have to use force, use overwhelming force and save lives thereby."[144] In doing so Eisenhower established a precedent that made it difficult for future presidents to deny the federal interest in race relations in the nation's schools, which until then had been regarded as essentially state and local matters.[145]

Eisenhower also contributed to the institutionalization of the modern presidency. Drawing on his long experience with military staffs, the president enlarged and formally organized the White House Office. This is not to say that Eisenhower arranged his staff along military lines, as many Washington observers concluded. Instead, the respect for careful organization that Ike developed as an army general predisposed him to take seriously the recommendations of the Brownlow and Hoover Commissions that a clearer and more formal line of command and communications be established between the White House and the executive departments and agencies.[146] The line Eisenhower established ran from the president through his chief of staff to the rest of the president's team and back again. Former New Hampshire governor Sherman Adams, who was the first presidential chief of staff, worked zealously to free the president from the everyday demands of the White House and executive branch.[147]

Eisenhower also created the first White House Office of legislative liaison. The liaison office was headed by Maj. Gen. Wilton B. "Jerry" Persons, a retired army officer who handled Eisenhower's congressional relations when he was the army chief of staff and, after World War II, NATO commander. The task of the liaison office was to promote the president's policies on Capitol Hill as well as to keep him informed about sentiment in Congress.

Although Eisenhower offered no program to Congress during his first year, pressure from several quarters soon forced him to become more involved in legislative matters. Having talked of "restoring the balance" between the branches, Eisenhower quickly realized that even a moderately conservative president who wants mostly to curb policy innovation must ensure that his views are presented effectively to Congress. A presidential program accompanied the State of the Union message in January 1954, and Eisenhower and his legislative liaison office worked to enact it. During his eight years as president, Ike became increasingly involved in legislative issues such as the prodigious effort to create the highway system and, in reaction to the Soviet Union's launch of the Sputnik satellite, to develop a space program. He even managed to work well with a Congress that after the 1954 midterm elections was controlled by the Democrats.

Eisenhower's "special triumph" in congressional relations was to hold down defense spending.[148] The former general wanted to avoid an arms race with the Soviet Union, fearing that a military buildup would trigger uncontrollable inflation and eventually bankrupt the United States without providing additional security. His "New Look" foreign policy was designed to "save money without sacrifice to security by reducing military manpower and relying instead on the threat of nuclear weapons"—a threat that Soviet leaders took seriously.[149] Democrats in Congress, including the Democratic senator from Massachusetts, John Kennedy, criticized the president for putting a balanced budget ahead of the national defense. Confident of his own military judgment, Eisenhower was unmoved. Inheriting a $50 billion annual defense budget from Truman, he reduced it to $40 billion.

The importance of controlling defense spending was the principal theme of Eisenhower's 1961 farewell address, the first of its kind to be delivered on television. During his first term, Eisenhower resisted pressure from several of his own counselors to intervene militarily on behalf of France when it teetered on the verge of defeat in Vietnam or of France and Great Britain when they tried to occupy the Suez Canal in Egypt.[150] Throughout his second term, he ignored congressional Democrats' specious charge that a "missile gap" had opened between the United States and the Soviet Union. In his farewell address, the president did not downplay the threat of communism, which he said "commands our whole attention, absorbs our whole being." At the same time, he warned the country "to guard against the acquisition of unwarranted influence, whether sought or not, by the military-industrial complex." The conjunction of an immense military establishment and a large arms industry held "the potential for the disastrous rise of misplaced power." The task of statesmanship, Eisenhower insisted, was to constrain the national security state through "the proper meshing of the huge industrial and military machinery of defense with our peaceful methods and goals, so that security and liberty may prosper together."[151]

Eisenhower's commitment to constrain the military-industrial complex coincided with his determination to strengthen the constitutional foundation of modern presidential diplomacy. His defense of the twentieth-century executive was never more apparent than in his efforts to defeat the Bricker Amendment, which proposed changing the Constitution to curtail the president's authority to conduct the nation's foreign policy. By the terms of the amendment, executive agreements with other nations would take effect only if they were approved by Congress and did not conflict with state laws. As historian Elmo Richardson has noted, "The idea was, of course, a belated response to Franklin Roosevelt's personal diplomacy."[152] The amendment's author, Republican senator John Bricker of Ohio, and its adherents in Congress endorsed isolationist sentiments that Eisenhower believed would threaten the future of the Republican Party and, ultimately, the United States.

In the Senate, mostly because of the president's personal influence, the Bricker Amendment fell one vote shy of passage. The close division indicated that many Americans still believed that the modern chief executive's power in foreign affairs was excessive. It was the reluctant modern president, "Dwight D. Eisenhower—nobody else," an embittered Senator Bricker claimed, who preserved the executive's right to make international agreements unilaterally.[153]

Notes

1. White quoted in Stefan Lorant, *The Presidency: A Pictorial History of Presidential Elections from Washington to Truman* (New York: Macmillan, 1957), 594. For a full and excellent account of the election, see Donald A. Ritchie, *Electing FDR: The New Deal Campaign of 1932* (Lawrence: University Press of Kansas, 2007).

2. Franklin D. Roosevelt, *Public Papers and Addresses*, 13 vols., ed. Samuel J. Rosenman (New York: Random House, 1938–1950), 1: 751–752.

3. Ibid., 1: 752.

4. Many political scientists, most notably Fred I. Greenstein, consider Franklin Roosevelt to be the first "modern" president. See Greenstein, "Introduction: Toward a Modern Presidency," in *Leadership in the Modern Presidency*, ed. Fred I. Greenstein (Cambridge: Harvard University Press, 1988). As Jeffrey K. Tulis argues, however, many of the characteristics of the executive that Greenstein identifies as distinctly modern, such as legislative leadership, found practical expression in the nineteenth century, if not earlier. Tulis, *The Rhetorical Presidency* (Princeton: Princeton University Press, 1987), esp. chap. 1. Stephen Skowronek provides the most systematic challenge to the traditional–modern divide. He offers a cyclical theory of presidential power that downplays the transformation of the executive office during the twentieth century. Skowronek, *The Politics Presidents Make: Leadership from John Adams to Bill Clinton* (Cambridge: Harvard University Press, 1997).

5. Peri Arnold, *Remaking the Presidency: Roosevelt, Wilson and Taft, 1901–1916* (Lawrence, Kansas: University Press of Kansas, 2009).

6. See, for example, Robert K. Murray and Tim H. Blessing, "The Presidential Performance Study: A Progress Report," *Journal of American History*, 70 (December 1983): 542; and Arthur M. Schlesinger Jr., "Rating the Presidents: Washington to Clinton," *Political Science Quarterly* 112 (Summer 1997): 179–190. These polls ranked FDR as the second-greatest president in history, surpassed only by Abraham Lincoln. A 2005 poll conducted by the *Wall Street Journal*, with James Lindgren of Northwestern Law School and the Federalist Society, in which the editors adjusted the results to give Democratic- and Republican-leaning scholars equal weight, rated Roosevelt third, behind George Washington and Abraham

Lincoln: http://www.opinionjournal.com/extra/?id=110007243. On the consistent rank-
ing of FDR as one of America's greatest presidents, see Jill L. Curry and Irwin L. Morris.
"Explaining Presidential Greatness: The Roles of Peace and Prosperity?" *Presidential Studies
Quarterly*, 40, no. 3 (September, 2010): 515–530.

7. Arnold J. Toynbee, *Survey of International Affairs, 1931* (London: Oxford
University Press, 1932), 1.

8. Thorpe quoted in Robert M. Collins, *The Business Response to Keynes* (New York:
Columbia University Press, 1981), 28.

9. Ira Katznelson, *Fear Itself: The New Deal and the Origins of Our Time* (New York:
Liveright, 2013), 115, 118, 12.

10. *New York Times*, March 3, 1933, 2.

11. Clinton Rossiter, *The American Presidency*, 2nd ed. (New York: Harcourt, Brace
and World, 1960), 145.

12. For a vivid account of how Roosevelt adjusted to polio, see Jonathan Alter,
The Defining Moment: FDR's Hundred Days and the Triumph of Hope (New York: Simon and
Schuster, 2006), chaps. 8–9. Alter identifies several qualities that FDR developed in the
course of dealing with polio that later marked his presidency: "compassion . . . theatrical-
ity . . . distrust of expert opinion . . . and, most inspiring, his implausible but invigorating
hope," 65.

13. After bolting from the Republican Party in 1912, Theodore Roosevelt appeared
before the gathering in Chicago that launched the Bull Moose campaign. FDR was the first
nominee to address a regular national convention.

14. *New York Times*, July 3, 1932, 1.

15. Roosevelt, *Public Papers and Addresses*, 1: 647–648.

16. *New York Times*, March 5, 1933, 3.

17. "Franklin D. Roosevelt's First Inaugural Address," in *The Evolving Presidency:
Landmark Documents, 1787–2010*, 4th ed., ed. Michael Nelson (Washington, D.C.: CQ Press,
2012), 146–151.

18. Ibid.

19. Ibid.

20. The term *fireside chat* was first used by Robert Trout of the Columbia Broadcasting
System's Washington station, who introduced FDR on the occasion of his first radio address.
At ten o'clock on the evening of March 12, 1933, Trout told 60 million people, seated before
20 million radios, that "the President wants to come into your home and sit at your fireside
for a little fireside chat." Kenneth S. Davis, *FDR: The New Deal Years, 1933–1937* (New York:
Random House, 1986), 60.

21. Roosevelt, *Public Papers and Addresses*, 2: 65.

22. Raymond Moley, *After Seven Years* (New York: Harper and Brothers, 1939), 155.

23. *Wall Street Journal,* March 13, 1933, in Frank Freidel, *FDR: Launching the New
Deal* (Boston: Little, Brown, 1973), 236.

24. Hopkins is quoted in Fred I. Greenstein, "Nine Presidents in Search of a Modern
Presidency," in Greenstein, *Leadership in the Modern Presidency*, 299. See also James T.
Patterson, "The Rise of Presidential Power before World War I," *Law and Contemporary
Problems* 40 (Spring 1976): 53–57; and Louis Brownlow, *The President and the Presidency*
(Chicago: Public Administration Service, 1949), 69–71.

25. Black to James Farley, June 19, 1934, box 34, folder "Roosevelt, Franklin D.,
1934," James Farley Papers, Manuscripts Division, Library of Congress, Washington, D.C.

26. Roosevelt, *Public Papers and Addresses*, 3: 317–318.

27. Elmer E. Cornwell Jr., *Presidential Leadership of Public Opinion* (Bloomington:
Indiana University Press, 1965), 131.

28. Franklin D. Roosevelt, "'A Tribute to Abraham Lincoln,' to Be Read on His
Birthday," January 25, 1936, *Public Papers and Addresses*, 5: 68.

29. Ibid., 5: 233.

30. Ibid., 1: 659.

31. "Democratic Platform of 1936," in *National Party Platforms,* ed. Donald Bruce Johnson (Urbana: University of Illinois Press, 1978), 360. Evidence of FDR's dominant role in drafting the platform can be found in the president's secretary file 143, folder "Democratic Platform," Franklin D. Roosevelt Papers, Franklin D. Roosevelt Library, Hyde Park, N.Y.

32. Roosevelt to Frankfurter, February 9, 1937, Felix Frankfurter Papers, microfilm reel 60, Manuscripts Department, Library of Congress, Washington, D.C.

33. Roosevelt, *Public Papers and Addresses,* 5: 234.

34. William E. Leuchtenburg, "Franklin D. Roosevelt: The First Modern President," in Greenstein, *Leadership in the Modern Presidency,* 27.

35. Greenstein, "Nine Presidents," 299. Congress created the Tennessee Valley Authority (TVA) in May 1933. The agency was authorized to sell electric power to states, counties, and municipalities; it also was empowered to construct dams on the Tennessee River. The TVA is widely regarded as one of the most successful New Deal programs, contributing greatly to flood control and to the dissemination of electric power throughout the southeastern United States.

36. "Landon Hits Social Security Act as Cruel Hoax in Milwaukee Speech," *The Day,* September 28, 1936. http://news.google.com/newspapers?nid=1915&dat=19360928& id=XqktAAAAIBAJ&sjid=Z3EFAAAAIBAJ&pg=999,2342658; Hoover is quoted in Ronald Rotunda, "The Liberal Label: Roosevelt's Capture of a Symbol," in *Public Policy,* eds. John D. Montgomery and Albert O. Hirschman (Cambridge: Harvard University Press, vol. 17, 1968), 399.

37. The magnitude of FDR's popular vote victory has been exceeded only by Lyndon B. Johnson's triumph over Barry Goldwater in 1964.

38. Matthew Dickinson, "The Executive Office of the President: The Paradox of Politicization," in *The Executive Branch,* eds. Joel D. Aberbach and Mark A. Peterson (New York: Oxford University Press, 2005).

39. Louis Brownlow, *A Passion for Anonymity* (Chicago: University of Chicago Press, 1958), 392.

40. *Report of the President's Committee on Administrative Management* (Washington, D.C.: Government Printing Office, 1937), 53. See also "Report of the Brownlow Committee," in Nelson, *Evolving Presidency,* 168–173.

41. Luther Gulick, "Politics, Administration, and the New Deal," *Annals* 169 (September 1933): 64.

42. Gulick quoted in Rossiter, *American Presidency,* 129.

43. The term *administrative presidency* is drawn from Richard Nathan's book on the use of administrative strategies by modern presidents to pursue their policy objectives. See Richard Nathan, *The Administrative Presidency* (New York: Wiley, 1983).

44. Roosevelt, *Public Papers and Addresses,* 2: 161.

45. Ellis Hawley, "The Constitution of the Hoover and F. Roosevelt Presidency during the Depression Era, 1900–1939," in *The Constitution and the American Presidency,* eds. Martin L. Fausold and Alan Shank (Albany: State University of New York Press, 1991), 94.

46. William E. Leuchtenburg, "Franklin D. Roosevelt's Supreme Court 'Packing' Plan," in *Essays on the New Deal,* eds. Harold M. Hollingsworth and William F. Holmes (Austin: University of Texas Press, 1969), 76–77. See also Michael Nelson, "The President and the Court: Reinterpreting the Court-Packing Episode of 1937," *Political Science Quarterly,* 103 (Summer 1988): 267–293; and Jeff Shesol, *Supreme Power: Franklin Roosevelt vs. the Supreme Court* (New York: Norton, 2010).

47. *Humphrey's Executor v. United States,* 295 U.S. 602 (1935); *Schechter Poultry Corp. v. United States,* 295 U.S. 495 (1935).

48. See the discussion of *Myers* in Chapter 8 in this volume.

49. William Leuchtenburg, *The Supreme Court Reborn: Constitutional Revolution in the Age of Roosevelt* (New York: Oxford University Press, 1996).

50. Leuchtenburg, "Franklin D. Roosevelt's Supreme Court 'Packing' Plan," 115. On the line-item veto, see "*Clinton v. City of New York*," in Nelson, *Evolving Presidency*, 273–278.

51. Katznelson, *Fear Itself*.

52. Gerry to Bailey, n.d., Josiah William Bailey Papers, Senatorial Series, Political National Papers, box 476, folder "September to October, 1938," Manuscripts Division, William R. Perkins Library, Duke University, Durham, N.C.

53. For a detailed account of the 1938 purge campaign, see Sidney M. Milkis, "Presidents and Party Purges: With Special Emphasis on the Lessons of 1938," in *Presidents and Their Parties: Leadership or Neglect?* ed. Robert Harmel (New York: Praeger, 1984).

54. The Papers of Eleanor Roosevelt, 1933–1945" (ed. Susan Ware and William Chafe), housed jointly by the Library of Congress (Washington, D.C.) and the Franklin D. Roosevelt Presidential Library (Hyde Park, NY).

55. Because no other Democrat seemed capable of carrying forward the New Deal principles, many Progressives began working for Roosevelt's renomination at the end of 1938. It was the foreign policy crisis, however, that finally persuaded Roosevelt to stand for reelection in 1940.

56. Hawley, "Constitution of the Hoover and F. Roosevelt Presidency," 99–100.

57. Roosevelt, *Public Papers and Addresses*, 6: 410.

58. *United States v. Curtiss-Wright Export Corp.*, 299 U.S. 304 (1936).

59. *United States v. Belmont*, 301 U.S. 324 (1937). On Hamilton, see Chapter 3 in this volume.

60. David M. Kennedy, *Freedom from Fear: The American People in Depression and War, 1929–1945* (New York: Oxford University Press, 1999), 474.

61. Katznelson, *Fear Itself*, 287–289.

62. *Congressional Record*, 77th Cong., 2nd sess., 1942, 7044.

63. R. Shep Melnick, "The Courts, Jurisprudence, and the Executive Branch," in Aberbach and Peterson, *Executive Branch*, 458.

64. *Yakus v. United States*, 321 U.S. 414 (1944).

65. *Ex parte Quirin*, 317 U.S. 1 (1942).

66. *Korematsu v. United States*, 323 U.S. 214 (1944).

67. Ibid. at 245–246.

68. Kennedy, *Freedom from Fear*, 756–759.

69. George McJimsey, *The Presidency of Franklin Delano Roosevelt* (Lawrence: University Press of Kansas, 2000), 277–278. The five nations that could veto any proposal before the Security Council were the United States, Soviet Union, Great Britain, France, and China.

70. Leahy quoted in Kennedy, *Freedom from Fear*, 802. The discussion of Yalta owes much to Kennedy's examination of this conference. See especially chap. 22.

71. McJimsey, *Presidency of Franklin Delano Roosevelt*, 281–282.

72. Kennedy, *Freedom from Fear*, 807. For an incisive critique of Roosevelt's foreign policy, see Seyom Brown, "Idealism, Realpolitik, or Domestic Politics," in *The New Deal and the Triumph of Liberalism*, eds. Sidney M. Milkis and Jerome Mileur (Amherst: University of Massachusetts Press, 2002).

73. Brown, "Idealism, Realpolitik, or Domestic Politics," 306–307.

74. Roosevelt quoted in Kennedy, *Freedom from Fear*, 807.

75. Harry Truman, *Memoirs*, 2 vols. (Garden City, N.Y.: Doubleday, 1955), 1: 4–5; William E. Leuchtenburg, *In the Shadow of FDR: From Harry Truman to Ronald Reagan*, rev. ed. (Ithaca: Cornell University Press, 1985), 1.

76. William S. White, "The Memoirs of Harry S. Truman," *New Republic*, November 7, 1955, 16.

77. Alonzo L. Hamby, "Harry S. Truman: Insecurity and Responsibility," in Greenstein, *Leadership in the Modern Presidency*, 42.

78. Ibid., 42–43.

79. Quoted in Larry Berman, *The New American Presidency* (Boston: Little, Brown, 1987), 212.

80. Truman, *Memoirs*, 1: 483.

81. Ibid., 1: 485–486.

82. Roosevelt, *Public Papers and Addresses*, 13: 41.

83. Harry S. Truman, *Public Papers of the Presidents of the United States: Harry S. Truman*, 14 vols. (Washington, D.C.: Government Printing Office, 1961–1966), 1: 279.

84. Greenstein, "Nine Presidents," 306.

85. The Taft–Hartley Act outlawed the closed shop, made unions liable for damages caused by breaches of contract, enabled the president to declare an eighty-day cooling-off period before a strike, forbade unions to make political contributions or to exact excessive dues, and required elected union officials to take an oath that they were not communists.

86. Truman, *Public Papers of the Presidents*, 3: 289, 299.

87. *Nation*, June 28, 1947, 755.

88. Alonzo L. Hamby, *Man of the People: A Life of Harry S. Truman* (New York: Oxford University Press, 1995), 387.

89. Truman, *Public Papers of the President*, 3: 178–179.

90. Hamby, *Man of the People*, 393.

91. Richard Neustadt, *Presidential Power and the Modern Presidents: The Politics of Leadership from Roosevelt to Reagan*, 4th ed. (New York: Free Press, 1990), 40. The first edition of this book was published in 1960 by Wiley.

92. Hamby, *Man of the People*, 395.

93. Neustadt, *Presidential Power and the Modern Presidents*, 45.

94. President Harry S. Truman, "Executive Order 9308 Establishing the President's Committee on Civil Rights," December 5, 1946, in *Growth of Presidential Power: A Documented History*, 3 vols., ed. William M. Goldsmith (New York: Chelsea, 1974), 3: 1568–1569.

95. Dunn, *Roosevelt's Purge*, 241–42. Sidney M. Milkis and Daniel J. Tichenor, *Rivalry and Reform: Presidents, Social Movements and the Transformation of American Politics* (Chicago: University of Chicago Press, 2018), chap. 4.

96. William E. Leuchtenburg, *The White House Looks South: Franklin Roosevelt, Harry S. Truman, and Lyndon B. Johnson* (Baton Rouge: Louisiana State University Press, 2005), 147–225.

97. President Harry Truman, "Special Message to Congress on Civil Rights, February 2, 1948, in Goldsmith, ed., *The Growth of Presidential Power*, 3: 1586–1592.

98. Branch quoted in Leuchtenburg, *The White House Looks South*, 367.

99. Andrew E. Busch, *Truman's Triumphs: The 1948 Election and the Making of Postwar America* (Lawrence: University Press of Kansas, 2012).

100. John Hope Franklin, "Civil Rights and the Truman Administration," Public Address at the University of Chicago, April 5, 1968, in *Conference of Scholars on the Truman Administration and Human Rights*, eds. Donald McCoy, Richard T. Reutten, and J. R. Fuchs (Independence, Mo.: Harry S Truman Library Institute, 1968), 134. On the presidents' use of executive orders to promote civil rights, see Kenneth R. Mayer, *With the Stroke of a Pen: Executive Orders and Presidential Power* (Princeton: Princeton University Press, 2001), chap. 6.

101. Truman, *Public Papers of the President*, 11: 176.

102. *Youngstown Sheet and Tube Co. v. Sawyer*, 343 U.S. 579 (1952).

103. See Chapter 8 in this volume.

104. Richard M. Pious, *The American Presidency* (New York: Basic Books, 1979), 66; and Edward S. Corwin, *The President: Office and Powers, 1787–1957*, 4th ed. (New York: New York University Press, 1957), 408–410.

105. Pious, *American Presidency*, 67; see also Chapter 6 in this volume.

106. On Roosevelt's Court appointees, see Noah Feldman, *Scorpions: The Battles and Triumphs of FDR's Great Supreme Court Justices* (New York: Twelve, 2010).

107. *Youngstown Sheet and Tube Co. v. Sawyer*, 637; Pious, *American Presidency*, 64–69.

108. Maeva Marcus, *Truman and the Steel Seizure Case: The Limits of Presidential Power* (New York: Columbia University Press, 1977), 248.

109. Greenstein, "Nine Presidents," 304.

110. Hamby, *Man of the People*, 309–311. With the enactment of the Goldwater–Nichols Act in 1986, the president's authority over the military was further strengthened. It authorized the president rather than the Joint Chiefs of Staff to select the JCS chair.

111. Michael D. Pearlman, *Truman and MacArthur: Policy, Politics, and the Hunger for Honor and Renown* (Bloomington: Indiana University Press, 2008).

112. Katznelson, *Fear Itself*, 427.

113. Peri E. Arnold, *Making the Managerial Presidency: Comprehensive Reorganization Planning, 1905–1980* (Princeton: Princeton University Press, 1986), 127.

114. Martha Derthick and Paul J. Quirk, *The Politics of Deregulation* (Washington, D.C.: Brookings, 1985), 61–74.

115. Truman's budget director James Webb, as quoted in Arnold, *Making the Managerial Presidency*, 142.

116. "Thomas Jefferson's Letter to the Vermont Legislature," in Nelson, *Evolving Presidency*, 73–75.

117. Indeed, Washington wrote in a 1788 letter that "I differ widely myself from Mr. Jefferson . . . as to the expediency of rotation in that department [the presidency]." Corwin, *President*, 333.

118. Paul G. Willis and George L. Willis, "The Politics of the Twenty-Second Amendment," *Western Political Quarterly* 5 (September 1952): 469.

119. Ibid., 470.

120. The Twenty-Seventh Amendment, which restricts Congress's ability to raise its members' salaries, was ratified in 1992, a record 203 years after Congress proposed it in 1789.

121. Every Truman-sponsored civil rights initiative prompted a few more southern legislatures to ratify. David E. Kyvig, *Explicit and Authentic Acts: Amending the U.S. Constitution, 1776–1995* (Lawrence: University Press of Kansas, 1996), 332–333.

122. The second Hoover Commission was created by Congress in 1953. Republican leaders in the House and Senate hoped that this time the commission would not be sidetracked from its mission to reduce the size of the government. These hopes were realized. Although the first Hoover Commission was interested primarily in improving the administrative management of the executive branch, the second concentrated on issues of policy and function. At the heart of the second commission's recommendations was the idea that many of the Roosevelt-era programs and agencies were counterproductive. But the commission's conservative ideological approach guaranteed that it would have little influence on the Eisenhower administration, which accepted most of the changes brought by the New Deal. See Arnold, *Making the Managerial Presidency*, 166–227.

123. Neustadt, *Presidential Power and the Modern Presidents*, 139.

124. Gallup and Roper polls indicated that Eisenhower was Republican voters' first choice for their party's nomination and Democratic voters' first choice for theirs. Jean Edward Smith, *Eisenhower in War and Peace* (New York: Random House, 2012), 470.

125. Marquis Childs, *Eisenhower: Captive Hero* (New York: Harcourt, Brace, 1958), 179.

126. Joseph C. Harsch, "Eisenhower's First Hundred Days," *Reporter*, May 12, 1953, 9.

127. Fred I. Greenstein, *The Hidden-Hand Presidency: Eisenhower as Leader* (New York: Basic Books, 1982).

128. Dwight David Eisenhower to Edgar Newton Eisenhower, November 8, 1954, http://zfacts.com/metaPage/lib/Eisenhower-1954-not-abolish-social-security.pdf.

129. Oscar Handlin, "The Eisenhower Administration: A Self-Portrait," *Atlantic Monthly*, November 1963, 68.

130. Moynihan quoted in David Mayhew, "The Long 1950s as a Policy Era," in Jeffery A. Jenkins and Sidney M. Milkis, ed. *The Politics of Major Policy Reform in Postwar America* (New York: Cambridge University Press, 2004), 35. Ibid, 35.

131. Elmo Richardson, *The Presidency of Dwight D. Eisenhower* (Lawrence: University Press of Kansas, 1979), 14.

132. Erwin C. Hargrove, *The Power of the Modern Presidency* (Philadelphia: Temple University Press, 1974), 60.

133. Leuchtenburg, *In the Shadow of FDR*, 48.

134. Eisenhower quoted in Stephen E. Ambrose, "The Eisenhower Revival," in *Rethinking the Presidency*, ed. Thomas E. Cronin (Boston: Little, Brown, 1982), 107.

135. Greenstein, *Hidden-Hand Presidency*, chap. 5.

136. "Remarks at Dartmouth College Commencement Exercises," Hanover, N.H., June 14, 1953, *Public Papers of the Presidents of the United States: Dwight D. Eisenhower, 1953* (Washington, D.C.: Government Printing Office, 1960), 415.

137. "Address at the Sixth National Assembly of the United Church of Women," Atlantic City, October 6, 1953, *Public Papers of the Presidents of the United States: Dwight D. Eisenhower, 1953*, 639.

138. Richardson, *Presidency of Dwight D. Eisenhower*, 55.

139. Quoted in Fred I. Greenstein, "Dwight D. Eisenhower: Leadership Theorist in the White House," in Greenstein, *Leadership in the Modern Presidency*, 104–105.

140. Rossiter, *American Presidency*, 163.

141. Leuchtenburg, *White House Looks South*, 219.

142. *Brown v. Board of Education of Topeka*, 347 U.S. 483 (1954).

143. William Hitchcock, *The Age of Eisenhower: America and the World in the 1950s* (New York: Simon and Schuster, 2018), chap. 9.

144. Smith, *Eisenhower in War and Peace*, 721.

145. Goldsmith, Growth of Presidential Power, 3: 1619. See also "Dwight D. Eisenhower's Little Rock Executive Order," in Nelson, *Evolving Presidency*, 183–186.

146. Philip G. Henderson, *Managing the Presidency: The Eisenhower Legacy—From Kennedy to Reagan* (Boulder: Westview Press, 1988), 17–24.

147. Greenstein, "Nine Presidents," 307–311.

148. Ambrose, "Eisenhower Revival," 108.

149. Jim Newton, *Eisenhower: The White House Years* (New York: Doubleday, 2011), 129.

150. David A. Nichols, *Eisenhower 1956: The President's Year of Crisis—Suez and the Brink of War* (New York: Simon and Schuster, 2011).

151. Eisenhower, *Public Papers of the Presidents, 1960–1961*, 1038–1039. See also James Ledbetter, *Unwarranted Influence: Dwight D. Eisenhower and the Military-Industrial Complex* (New Haven: Yale University Press, 2011).

152. Richardson, *Presidency of Dwight D. Eisenhower*, 51.

153. Bricker quoted in Gary W. Reichard, *The Reaffirmation of Republicanism: Eisenhower and the Eighty-Third Congress* (Knoxville: University of Tennessee Press, 1975), 67.

CHAPTER 11

Personalizing the Presidency

John F. Kennedy to Jimmy Carter

In his influential book *Presidential Power*, first published in 1960, political scientist Richard E. Neustadt, a former aide in the Truman White House, declared that "the same conditions that promote [the modern president's] leadership in form preclude a guarantee of leadership in fact."[1] Neustadt's study reaffirmed Woodrow Wilson's argument at the beginning of the twentieth century that the president is responsible for leading the United States to a higher level of political discourse and national action. But Neustadt cautioned that at mid-century, this obligation fell upon the president with no assurance of "an influence commensurate with services performed." In fact, the modern president could count only on being a "clerk" whose help would be demanded by others but not always reciprocated by them.[2]

Neustadt's solution to the dilemma of the modern presidency was for each president to struggle to overcome the political obstacles that fetter the office. It was the president's job to resurrect the aggressive and skillful style of leadership that Franklin D. Roosevelt displayed so that congressional leaders, cabinet officers, party officials, and others would "feel obliged" to do what the president "wants done."[3] Neustadt regarded the relatively restrained approach to the office that Dwight D. Eisenhower took as a sure path to political stagnation.

John F. Kennedy read Neustadt's book—indeed, some pundits believed at the time that it was the blueprint for the vigorous style of leadership that animated his presidency. But, as Fred Greenstein has noted, *Presidential Power* mostly clarified and defended the theory of good presidential leadership that already was current—namely, "that of an informal, Rooseveltian conduct of the presidency that contrasted with current perceptions of Eisenhower's operating manner."[4] Not surprisingly, then, the effort to expand the powers of the modern executive characterized not only the Kennedy administration but also the administrations of his two successors, Lyndon B. Johnson and Richard Nixon.

In the early 1970s serious doubts arose about how compatible unrestrained executive power was with the public interest. Developments during the Johnson and, especially, the Nixon era kindled the belief that a return to the traditional separation of powers was needed to restore constitutional government to its proper moorings. Nixon's successors, Gerald R. Ford and Jimmy Carter, inherited a much-tarnished and somewhat diminished office.

John F. Kennedy and the Rise of the "Personal Presidency"

Kennedy was elected president in 1960 to "get this country moving again" by lifting the United States out of the complacency that seemed to settle on it during the Eisenhower years.[5] The combination of a sluggish economy, a simmering civil rights movement, and the Soviet threat had created doubts about the nation's future that led a slim plurality of voters back to the Democratic Party. In addition, the still-popular Eisenhower, who disapproved of the Twenty-Second Amendment, was forbidden to run again—an ironic consequence of the Republican-inspired two-term constitutional limit.[6]

Running against Vice President Richard Nixon, Kennedy campaigned on a theme of change, tying that theme to the presidency itself. The United States, he declared, could no longer afford a president "who is praised primarily for what he did not do, the disasters he prevented, the bills he vetoed—a President wishing his subordinates would produce more missiles or build more schools." Instead, the nation

> needs a Chief Executive who is the vital center of action in our whole scheme of government. The president must be willing and able to summon his national constituency to its finest hour— to alert the people to our dangers and our opportunities—to demand of them the sacrifices that will be necessary.[7]

On November 22, 1963, less than three years after he took the oath as president, Kennedy was assassinated by Lee Harvey Oswald in Dallas, Texas. His death traumatized the nation. All of the presidents who died in office had been deeply mourned, but only Abraham Lincoln's death evoked as profound a sense of unfulfilled promise as Kennedy's. Forty-three years old at the time of his inauguration, Kennedy was the youngest person ever elected as president. The striking down of a vital, attractive leader in the prime of life, leaving behind his stoic young widow and two small children, left Americans with an extraordinary sense of personal loss.[8] Yet despite his truncated term, or perhaps because of it, Kennedy enjoys a lasting place in American culture. Much like the warrior Achilles in ancient Greece, Kennedy is "part not of history but of myth."[9]

Long after his assassination, national surveys continued to show that Americans regarded Kennedy as the finest of the modern presidents. In 2013, a half-century after he was murdered, Kennedy had a higher approval rating than any of his successors: 90 percent.[10] Kennedy's popularity persisted not only because of his tragic death but also because of certain qualities that he displayed as president. "Beyond question," historian Carl M. Brauer has written, "Kennedy was inspirational in a way that few presidents have been."[11]

Franklin Roosevelt's great achievement as a moral leader was to bring the United States through the dark days of the Great Depression and World War II. In a like manner, Kennedy sought to inspire the nation to meet the challenges of the postwar era. Roosevelt's New Deal, Kennedy said in his acceptance speech at the 1960 Democratic convention, "promised security and succor to those in need." But more prosperous times called for a New Frontier that was "not a set of promises" but "a set of challenges." The New Frontier "sums up not what I intend to offer the American people, but what I intend to ask of them," he declared. "It appeals to their pride, not their pocketbook—it holds out the promise of more sacrifice instead of security."[12]

Kennedy's inaugural address placed this challenge before the nation. Uplifting and optimistic in tone, it articulated a vision that greatly augmented the fragile basis of support he received from the extremely close election (Kennedy's margin of victory was only 120,000 popular votes out of the nearly 69 million cast). Both liberals and conservatives found something to applaud in the new president's celebration of sacrifice and mission. The best-remembered passage from the address emphasized these themes: "ask not what your country can do for you—ask what you can do for your country."[13]

Kennedy's call for personal sacrifice and national glory resonated with the historical experience of postwar America. The giftedness, or charisma, of the young president matched America's feeling that it could solve the world's problems and break through the ancient barriers that previously limited humankind—even, as Kennedy pledged, "landing a man on the moon and returning him safely to the Earth . . . in this decade."[14]

The First Television President

It was not just Kennedy's words that stirred the public but also the vibrant and reassuring image he conveyed when delivering them. His administration marked a revolutionary advance in the use of television in politics. Although Eisenhower was the first president to appear on television regularly, "it was under and because of Kennedy that television became an essential determinant—probably the essential determinant—of a president's ability to lead the nation."[15] As political scientist Bruce Miroff has written, throughout his presidency Kennedy and other members of his administration staged widely publicized "spectacles," or message-laden symbolic displays, that "projected youth, vigor, and novelty, that recast the [presidency] itself as a headquarters for intelligence and masterful will."[16]

Kennedy's televised speeches were but one element of his strategy of public communication. After his inauguration, the president went before the cameras only nine times to deliver prepared addresses. Convinced that viewers would tire quickly of formal speech making, he relied instead on press conferences as his principal forum for reaching the public. Kennedy was the first president to allow press conferences to be televised without restriction, recognizing that live broadcasts of his give-and-take with reporters would display his wit, intellectual sure-footedness, and physical attractiveness to best effect. Eisenhower's press conferences had been televised, but they were taped, and the White House retained the right to edit them for broadcast. Ike's press secretary, James C. Hagerty, believed that live television was dangerous because the president might misspeak on a sensitive matter, jeopardizing national security. Kennedy, who had benefited greatly from his televised debates with Nixon in 1960, regarded television as an ally.

Previous presidents, especially FDR, used press conferences to encourage reporters to convey their messages to the American people. But the live, televised press conference relegated reporters to the role of supporting actors. Under Kennedy's auspices, the press conference became the functional equivalent of the fireside chat. It gave the president a relatively informal and personal way to reach the public directly, over the heads of Congress and the proprietors of the media.

The public saw and heard more of Kennedy through press conferences than in any other way. Yet he held only sixty-four of them, fewer per month than Roosevelt, Truman, or Eisenhower. "He realized the dangers as well as the possibilities of television," historian James N. Giglio has written. "Overexposure became his major concern."[17]

Kennedy's adept and well-timed television appearances made a positive impression on the American people. Opinion surveys revealed a 91 percent public approval rating of his performance in press conferences. The keys to his success were careful preparation and an ability to appear relaxed and in command before the cameras.[18] Kennedy's pleasing personality, quick wit, and impressive knowledge of government set a standard that his successors have struggled to meet.[19]

The Personal Presidency

Woodrow Wilson believed that the "extraordinary isolation" of the presidency, if used effectively, allowed the president both to inspire and to benefit from public opinion. Wilson himself, and later FDR, did much to advance the president's relationship with the people. But with Kennedy and the advent of television, what political scientist Theodore Lowi called the "personal presidency" came into its own.[20]

All of Kennedy's campaigns for office, including his run for the presidency, were highly personal undertakings. Indeed, they were managed by members of his family, usually his brother Robert. The success of Kennedy's organization, the "Kennedy Machine" as it was called, diminished the importance of the regular party organization. In winning the Democratic nomination for president in 1960, Kennedy outmaneuvered most of the established leaders of the party, whose initial attitude toward his candidacy was skeptical, if not hostile, mostly because no Roman Catholic had ever been elected president. To thwart them, he went outside normal party channels, using political amateurs to round up votes in the state primaries and, after succeeding in that arena, virtually forcing the convention to accept him as its nominee. Kennedy's triumph changed presidential politics. Henceforth, campaigns for president would be directed by the candidates' personal advisers and strategists. Coordination and liaison with the party apparatus would be of secondary importance.[21]

The Kennedy organization also made its mark on the government. Kennedy appointed most members of his campaign staff to similar positions in the White House Office, which further contributed to the personalization of the presidency. To reinforce this development, Kennedy concentrated more responsibility for policy making in the White House than was the practice in past administrations. The once-anonymous staff, now highly visible in the media and assigned to oversee the activities of the departments and agencies, began to develop into a government unto itself. For example, Kennedy's assistant for national security, McGeorge Bundy, carried out many duties traditionally reserved for the secretary of state.[22] According to Robert F. Kennedy, JFK "felt at the end that the ten or twelve people in the White House who worked under his direction with Mac Bundy . . . really performed all the functions of the State Department."[23] Operations that were too big to be run out of the White House Office, such as the Peace Corps, were housed in independent agencies, where they would be free of standard bureaucratic routine. As political scientists Matthew Crenson and Benjamin Ginsberg have written, "[T]he Kennedy administration foreshadowed a new anti-bureaucratic consensus" that would enable each president to more readily put his or her stamp on the executive branch but at the risk of sacrificing valuable political experience and policy expertise.[24]

Kennedy hoped to reduce this risk by embedding politically loyal policy experts within the White House Office. In an effort to extend the New Deal ideal of "enlightened administration" to economic policy, he entrusted Walter Heller, the director of the Council of Economic Advisors, with a central role in formulating the Public Works Acceleration Act, which was designed to buttress the economy with government spending. Franklin Roosevelt had imbued the Democratic Party with a commitment to government management of the economy. Kennedy sought to complete the "fiscal revolution" by equipping the modern presidency with the power to transform economic issues into a nonpartisan science. Hoping to draw a contrast with Republicans, Kennedy wanted to distinguish Democrats as the modern, expert-driven party that confidently embraced unbalanced budgets in the service of prosperity while subordinating partisanship to administration.[25] Addressing a White House Conference on National Economic Issues in May 1962, Kennedy declared:

> Most of us are conditioned for many years to have a political
> viewpoint—Republican or Democratic—liberal, conservative,
> moderate. The fact of the matter is that most of the problems
> or at least many of them that we now face are *administrative
> problems*. They are very sophisticated judgments which do not
> lend themselves to the great sort of "passionate movements"
> which have stirred the country so often in the past.[26]

Like many of Kennedy's ideals, his vision of an end of ideology collided with the formidable obstacles facing policy planning of any kind in a complex system of constitutional checks and balances that was modified but not transcended during the 1960s. Nor did Kennedy foresee that a powerful civil rights movement, a woman's liberation movement, and anti-war activists would soon pressure presidents to abandon his model of pragmatic reform. It was Lyndon Johnson's Great Society that envisioned the modern presidency as the steward of a "qualitative" rather than a prosperity-based "quantitative" liberalism that would fight for individual dignity and identity in a mass society.

The Kennedy Legacy

Although Kennedy was popular during his brief stay in the White House, many aspects of his presidency were unsuccessful. His administration was responsible for the disastrous invasion of Cuba on April 17, 1961, by a brigade of fourteen hundred exiles from the communist regime of Fidel Castro. The rebels were crushed three days after landing in Zapata Swamp at Cuba's Bay of Pigs. Their failure to overthrow Castro was a humiliating defeat for Kennedy, who had been in office less than one hundred days.

The Bay of Pigs was not Kennedy's final attempt to overthrow Castro. The president's militant anticommunism and strong animus against Cuba's ruler led to a series of failed plots to assassinate him. "Although the defenders of the president have asserted that these schemes went forward without his knowledge," historian Lewis L. Gould has written, "it is clear that John and Robert Kennedy created a climate in the White House where such covert ventures received implicit sanction at the highest levels." Moreover, reliance on covert action advanced the dangerous creed that on matters of national security, presidents may work outside the law to accomplish their foreign policy objectives.[27]

Kennedy also can be faulted for accelerating the deployment of nuclear missiles to fulfill a campaign promise to close the "missile gap" with the Soviet Union. The nuclear buildup was carried out even though an intelligence analysis conducted soon after Kennedy took office revealed that the missile gap was a myth. In truth, Soviet missile development lagged far behind that of the United States. Yet once the Soviets responded to Kennedy's buildup with a buildup of their own, the United States was forced into a spiraling nuclear arms race.[28]

Finally, the Kennedy administration extended the ill-fated American involvement in Vietnam. Intense pressure to intervene in southeast Asia had been brought to bear on President Eisenhower by the military when the French colonial government collapsed in July 1954. But, other than providing economic aid and military equipment, Eisenhower decided to stay out of the region, certain that victory on the battlefield was impossible. Kennedy also doubted the wisdom of direct involvement in Vietnam, but he sent more than sixteen thousand military advisers to assist the South Vietnamese army in counterinsurgency warfare. He later encouraged a military coup against the government of Ngo Dinh Diem in Saigon. Diem's resulting death profoundly destabilized South Vietnam. In the view of Kennedy's successor, Lyndon Johnson, it also obligated the United States to support any subsequent regime. "Though [Kennedy] privately thought the United States 'overcommitted' in Southeast Asia," Arthur M. Schlesinger Jr., a historian who served on Kennedy's staff, wrote, "he permitted the commitment to grow. It was the fatal error of his presidency."[29]

Yet Kennedy did not lack for significant accomplishments as president. During the Cuban missile crisis, in particular, he led brilliantly under the most difficult circumstances. For several days in October 1962 after the United States discovered Soviet missiles in Cuba, the world was poised on the brink of a nuclear war. Kennedy and Soviet premier Nikita Khrushchev engaged in what Secretary of State Dean Rusk later called an "eyeball to eyeball" confrontation. The impasse was resolved only when, in response to an American naval quarantine of Cuba, the Soviets agreed to dismantle their newly installed missiles. In return, the United States pledged not to attack Cuba. Kennedy also assured Khrushchev privately that he would remove American nuclear missiles from Turkey, which shared a border with the Soviet Union. Throughout the crisis, Kennedy combined firmness with restraint, a course that allowed Khrushchev to yield to the president's demands without being publicly humiliated. As Carl Brauer has written of Kennedy's conduct, "He looked at things from the Soviet side, compromised on secondary issues, did not play politics, and when he succeeded in getting the missiles removed, did not gloat or boast."[30]

Kennedy's triumph in the missile crisis demonstrated that he matured considerably after the Bay of Pigs fiasco. His growth in office also was apparent when he took steps to make another such crisis less likely. Speaking at American University on June 10, 1963, Kennedy called for a nuclear test ban treaty that would reduce tensions with the Soviets. Both the United States and the Soviet Union, he argued, had a mutual interest in halting the arms race and seeking an eventual end to the Cold War:

> For in the final analysis, our most basic common link is that we all inhabit this small planet. We all breathe the same air. We all cherish our children's future. And we are all mortal. . . . Let us reexamine our attitude toward the cold war, remembering that we are not engaged in a debate, seeking to pile up debating points.[31]

On August 5, 1963, the United States and the Soviet Union signed a nuclear test ban treaty, their first bilateral arms control agreement.

The treaty was only a small step forward—for example, it did not ban underground tests. But it did lay the groundwork for more substantial progress in the future.

For supporters of the president, the missile crisis and the test ban treaty were signs of developing greatness. But Kennedy's destiny, as journalist Theodore H. White observed, was to be "cut off at the promise, not after the performance."[32] One of the most frequent criticisms of Kennedy, both when he was president and after his death, was that he pledged much more in the way of domestic reform than he delivered. In particular, JFK was faulted for his failures as a legislative leader. His New Frontier program embodied the high expectations he articulated in his inaugural address. In advocating medical insurance for the elderly (Medicare) and federal aid to education, Kennedy sought to extend the accomplishments of Roosevelt and Truman, his most recent Democratic predecessors. In other ways, however, he sought to reshape his party's liberal tradition by offering initiatives, notably the Peace Corps, that reflected the theme of national service he injected into the 1960 presidential campaign. Some of Kennedy's legislative initiatives, including the Peace Corps, became law. But most of his important bills were spurned by Congress.[33]

Kennedy's relations with legislators were extraordinarily difficult throughout his abbreviated presidency. The Democrats had a 65–35 majority in the Senate and a 263–174 advantage in the House. But twenty-one of the Democratic senators and ninety-nine of the Democratic representatives were southerners, and most of them voted with the Republicans against Kennedy's liberal agenda.

Kennedy's precarious position in Congress was revealed within days of his becoming president. The administration, with Speaker Sam Rayburn's support, moved to take control of the House Rules Committee, the conservative coalition's principal legislative stronghold. In the previous Congress the Rules Committee, which had the power to prevent legislation from reaching the floor for debate, had eight Democratic and four Republican members. But two of the Democrats were southern conservatives who joined with Republicans to block reform legislation. At the outset of the Kennedy administration, Rayburn proposed adding three new members, two of them administration loyalists, which would provide an 8–7 majority for most of Kennedy's bills. Yet even with the new president's open and active support and with Rayburn drawing on his considerable store of influence and goodwill, the administration won the House vote to expand the committee by only a narrow majority, 217–212. As Kennedy told one of his aides, the outcome was not so much a show of strength as a measure of "what we are up against."[34]

Not wanting to alienate the southern wing of his party any more than was necessary, Kennedy approached the issue of civil rights warily. He and his brother, Attorney General Robert Kennedy, did their best for more than two years to shun serious action. But the president was finally goaded to act by a persistent campaign and an immediate event.

The persistent campaign was the cresting civil rights movement, which under the leadership of Rev. Martin Luther King Jr. and others had been staging a series of real-life morality plays throughout the South. In Birmingham and elsewhere, nonviolent, hymn-singing demonstrators stood up for justice against virulently segregationist southern sheriffs who ruthlessly deployed overwhelming force. What the Kennedys hated most about these spectacles were the images of whites beating blacks that appeared in newspapers all over the world—particularly in the dozens of newly independent African and Asian nations that had become the main Cold War battleground between the United States and the Soviet Union. Communists offered these scenes as living disproof of America's claim to stand for the principle that all individuals are created equal.

The event that spurred Kennedy to take a stronger stand against racial injustice occurred on June 11, 1963, when Alabama governor George C. Wallace, surrounded by network television cameras, theatrically defied and then yielded to federal officials who came to Tuscaloosa to enroll two black students in the previously all-white University of Alabama. That night, a fed-up Kennedy delivered a stirring prime-time address in which he told the nation that he would ask Congress "to make a commitment it has not fully made in [the twentieth] century to the proposition that race has no place in American life or law." Eight days later he sent a civil rights bill to Capitol Hill, triggering vows by southern Democratic senators to wage a filibuster against it.[35]

Kennedy's troubles in persuading Congress to enact his domestic program were not just a matter of stubborn legislative resistance to change. Although he was superb at planning and running a presidential campaign, Kennedy was just as bored and impatient with congressional politics during his presidency as he had been while serving in the House for six years and the Senate for eight years. "The very qualities of appearance, style and cast of mind that won [Kennedy] the admiration of the intellectual and diplomatic worlds somehow marked him as an outsider in his dealings with the Congress," noted columnist James Reston.[36]

Kennedy was far from indifferent to the legislative process, however. The one area where he expanded on the staff organization of the Eisenhower administration was in congressional relations. Under Lawrence O'Brien, the Office of Congressional Relations was joined to a network of legislative liaison specialists in the executive agencies and departments that greatly increased the administration's visibility and effectiveness on Capitol Hill. Yet some members of Congress complained that Kennedy's congressional relations staff lacked respect for the legislative process. By late 1963 the president's program was in deep trouble.[37] Several measures that Kennedy sought, particularly Medicare, federal aid to education, and civil rights, remained in legislative limbo at the time of his death.

Before he went to Dallas on November 22, 1963, JFK was looking forward to the 1964 election, which he hoped would bring enough new liberal Democrats into Congress to move the New Frontier forward. It is impossible to know whether Kennedy would have accomplished his domestic goals and avoided the travail of Vietnam if he had lived, but a yawning gap between expectations and achievements has been a recurring problem of the modern presidency.

Partly because of Kennedy, the evolution of the executive gave rise to a more powerful, prominent, and yet politically isolated presidency. The modern office was transformed into an elaborate and far-reaching institution with considerable autonomous power. At the same time, however, most recent presidents have distanced themselves from their party and Congress, making it more difficult to satisfy public demands by enacting lasting reforms. Kennedy did not create most of these conditions. But his legacy to his successors was a significant personalization of the presidency that greatly accentuated its separation from the other centers of political power in the United States.

During Kennedy's one thousand days in office, the great promise of the personal presidency was widely celebrated. But developments within a few years of his death—the escalation of the Vietnam War and the divisions it opened in American society, the growing tendency of both liberals and conservatives to distrust government, and the popular disillusionment with presidential power—revealed the less desirable consequences of the Kennedy administration's innovations.

Lyndon B. Johnson and Presidential Government

The tragedy in Dallas placed the presidency in the hands of Lyndon Johnson, a Texan whom Kennedy selected as his vice-presidential running mate in 1960 to balance the ticket geographically. LBJ's effective campaigning in the South, especially in Texas and Louisiana, was crucial to the Democrats' narrow victory against Nixon. Before becoming vice president, Johnson was known as a consummate political operator in the Senate, where as majority leader he exercised enormous influence during the Eisenhower years.[38] It remained to be seen, however, whether the quintessential legislative insider could adapt successfully to the requirements of the presidency.

Johnson's challenges as a successor president were compounded by the bitterness that many liberals felt about a southern power broker taking the place of their fallen leader. Johnson himself observed that African Americans, whose hopes for equality and justice had been raised by Kennedy, were disconcerted to awake "one morning to discover that their future was in the hands of a President born in the South."[39] After all, it was southern Democrats in Congress who blocked Kennedy's civil rights legislation. From the moment Johnson became president, the press stressed that he was the first southerner in a century to occupy the White House—"the first since another southerner named [Andrew] Johnson had taken power, also as the result of an assassination."[40]

Despite these obstacles, Johnson quickly grasped the reins of power. Indeed, he did more than reassure the nation and build confidence in his leadership. "In the wake of Kennedy's assassination," Jeffrey K. Tulis has written, "Lyndon Johnson was able to turn the country's grief into a commitment to a moral crusade."[41] Johnson's crusade extended beyond completing the New Frontier. As William E. Leuchtenburg has observed, "He aimed instead to be 'the greatest of them all, the whole bunch of them.' And to be the greatest president in history, he needed not to match Roosevelt's performance but to surpass it."[42]

In many ways, Johnson was inadequate to the demands of the modern presidency, especially as a public educator. Unlike other twentieth- and twenty-first-century presidents who wanted to remake the nation, LBJ was not adept at using the bully pulpit. Yet Johnson was determined to make his own mark on the office. He viewed civil rights and an alliance with civil rights leaders as critical to the success of his ambitious reform program. The enactment of the 1964 and 1965 civil rights laws formed the core of a profoundly important record of achievement. Regrettably, his failings, most evident in the national tragedy of the Vietnam War, brought into serious question, for the first time since the 1930s, the widespread assumption that the national interest is served whenever the president dominates the affairs of state.

On November 22, 1963, Lyndon Johnson took the presidential oath of office aboard Air Force One from federal district judge Sarah T. Hughes. Jacqueline Kennedy is on Johnson's left.

Source: Cecil Stoughton/The Lyndon Baines Johnson Presidential Library.

The Great Society

Johnson defined as his first task the enactment of Kennedy's New Frontier, including civil rights, a tax cut, and Medicare. He succeeded: Congress passed all of these controversial measures in short order. Especially noteworthy was the Civil Rights Act of 1964. When Kennedy died, the bill was bogged down in the Senate. But, invoking the memory of the slain president and bringing to bear his own extraordinary skill and experience in legislative politics, Johnson prevailed.

As vice president, Johnson urged JFK to go after Jim Crow aggressively, telling Kennedy aide Theodore Sorenson that "the Negroes are tired of this patient stuff and tired of this piecemeal stuff and what they want more than anything else is not an executive order or legislation, they want a moral commitment that he's behind them." Recalling FDR's 1938 purge campaign that targeted southern Democrats, LBJ believed that Kennedy should make an appeal to conscience.

> I'd say, "Now we have a problem here." . . . A hundred years ago in the Lincoln-Douglas debate, Lincoln said, "No Nation can long endure half slave and half free." Now no world can long endure half slave and half free and we've got to do something about it in our country.[43]

To a remarkable degree, during the early days of his presidency, Johnson practiced what he preached. He delivered a widely praised speech to Georgia Democratic officials in May 1964, declaring unequivocally that the time had come for "justice among the races." Johnson insisted that he would never feel that he had fulfilled his "high office" so long as old hatreds continued to rend the country. "Georgians helped write the Constitution. Georgians have fought and Georgians had died to protect that Constitution," he calmly but firmly declared. "Because the Constitution requires it, because justice demands it, we must protect the constitutional rights of all of our citizens, regardless of race, religion, or the color of their skin."[44]

Johnson's widely praised trip to Georgia strengthened his resolve to see civil rights legislation enacted that would dismantle the Jim Crow system. Martin Luther King Jr., who had met LBJ during his tenure as vice president, quickly sized him up as a "man of careful practicality," a valuable ally who recognized the importance of the president's early and earnest advocacy of civil rights:

> [Johnson's] emotional and intellectual involvement was genuine and devoid of adornment. . . . [I]t was Vice President Johnson I had in mind when I wrote in *The Nation* that the white South was splitting, and that progress could be furthered by driving a wedge between the rigid segregationists and the new white elements whose love of their land was stronger than the grip of old habits and customs.[45]

For a time, LBJ's "careful practicality" and moral leadership made him an indispensable ally of the movement. The new president's greatest strength as majority leader of the Senate had been personal persuasion, a talent he now used to convince the Senate Republican leader, Everett Dirksen, to endorse the bill and enlist moderate Republicans in the cause. But this support came with a price. Dirksen insisted on legislative compromises that limited the power of the new Equal Employment Opportunity

Commission (EEOC) and authorized the Justice Department to bring suits only against businesses that had a clear "pattern and practice" of discrimination.[46] These compromises assuaged moderate Republicans' distaste for overlapping bureaucracies and excessive litigation as well as their desire to protect northern and western businesses from intrusive federal agencies. Still, the principal objective of the civil rights bill—eliminating entrenched segregation in the South—was preserved.

The bipartisan alliance forged by Johnson and Dirksen sounded the death knell for the conservative coalition against civil rights. For the first time, the Senate voted cloture against a southern filibuster designed to thwart a civil rights bill and did so by a substantial 71–29 majority. Once the filibuster was ended, Congress passed the bill quickly, and Johnson signed it on July 2, 1964.[47] The passage of the Civil Rights Act of 1964 signaled a dramatic reinvigoration of the president's preeminence as a legislative leader. Even more important, the act enlisted the president and several executive agencies in the ongoing effort to ban racial discrimination. It empowered the federal bureaucracy—especially the Department of Justice, the Department of Health, Education and Welfare, and the newly formed EEOC—to assist the courts by creating parallel enforcement mechanisms for civil rights. These mechanisms proved to be effective. In four years the Johnson administration accomplished more desegregation in southern schools than the courts had in the previous fourteen, after the Supreme Court's decision in *Brown v. Board of Education*.[48]

Johnson's successful battle for civil rights dazzled the liberals in his party. Presidential scholar and self-professed Kennedy loyalist James MacGregor Burns wrote, "What will baffle the historian . . . will be how the complete Senate man moved so surely into the presidency and began to employ from the start the levers of presidential influence."[49] But the civil rights bill was only the beginning. "Many people felt we should rest after the victory of the 1964 Civil Rights Act, take it easy on Congress, and leave some breathing space for the bureaucracy and nation," wrote Johnson in his memoir. "But, there was no time to rest."[50]

Johnson's desire to move beyond Kennedy's New Frontier agenda toward what he called the "Great Society" made him impatient to push on. The 1964 elections, in which he and the Democrats won a resounding victory over the Republicans, and their candidate, the archconservative senator Barry Goldwater of Arizona, provided the opportunity to do so. The election gave LBJ the most convincing popular mandate in history—more decisive, even, than FDR's triumph in 1936. Johnson won more than 60 percent of the national popular vote, and the Democrats gained thirty-seven seats in the House and one in the Senate, which secured two-thirds majorities for them in both houses of Congress. The coalition of conservative Republicans and southern Democrats no longer had the votes to obstruct the president's liberal agenda.

Johnson gave the signature speech of his presidency on May 22, 1964, in a commencement address at the University of Michigan. His bold vision treated the reform aspirations of the past only as a point of departure:

> The Great Society rests on abundance and liberty for all. It
> demands an end of poverty and racial justice, to which we are
> totally committed in our time. But this is just the beginning. . . .
> The Great Society is a place where every child can find knowledge
> to enrich his mind and to enlarge his talents. It is a place where
> leisure is a welcome chance to build and reflect, not a feared
> cause of boredom and restlessness. It is a place where the city of
> man serves not only the needs of the body and the demands of
> commerce but the desire for beauty and the hunger of community.[51]

Johnson's vision gave rise to a legislative program of extraordinary breadth, which he placed before the Eighty-Ninth Congress when it convened in January 1965. Congress responded enthusiastically. "No [Congress] since Reconstruction," Theodore White observed, "or perhaps since Roosevelt's seventy-third Congress of 1933–34, did more to reorder the nation."[52] In 1965 alone, Congress passed eighty of Johnson's legislative proposals, denying him only three. The new laws included important policy departures such as Medicare and Medicaid, the Voting Rights Act, the Older Americans Act, the Elementary and Secondary Education Act, the Equal Opportunity Act, the Air Pollution Control Act, and legislation to create the Department of Transportation and the Department of Housing and Urban Development.

The enactment of the 1965 Voting Rights Act was an especially noteworthy achievement. After his landslide victory in the 1964 election, Johnson was determined to live up to a promise he made at the Democratic convention, after imposing a highly controversial compromise on the Mississippi Freedom Democratic Party. The MFDP had challenged its state's "Lily White" delegation. One year later, Johnson pledged to fight for the voting rights legislation that ultimately enfranchised millions of African Americans.[53] To the surprise of Martin Luther King, who was skeptical that LBJ would move quickly on voting rights, the president urged the civil rights leader and his grassroots organization to put pressure on Congress. Looking for another episode like the one in Birmingham in 1963 to "create a crisis" that would compel federal action, King launched the "Alabama Project" against voting rights violations with a powerful sermon at the Brown Chapel African Methodist Episcopal Church. Echoing his condemnation of forced segregation in Birmingham, King condemned Selma, Alabama, for its "bitter-end resistance to the Civil Rights movement in the Deep South."

When King sought the president's public endorsement of the Selma campaign, Johnson took up the demonstrators' cause despite the efforts of White House aides to shield him from public involvement. On March 15, 1965, for the first time in nineteen years, a president appeared before a joint session of Congress to present a legislative message. Seizing the opportunity presented by the civil rights demonstrators, Johnson spoke with unusual feeling about the Voting Rights Act. He argued that enacting the voting rights bill was but one front in a larger war that must include not just federal laws to throw open the "gates of opportunity" but also affirmative action against ignorance, ill-health, and poverty so men and women could "walk through those gates":

> What happened in Selma is part of a far larger movement which reaches into every section and State of America. It is the effort of American Negroes to secure for themselves the full blessings of American life. Their cause must be our cause too. Because it is not just Negroes, but really it is all of us, who must overcome the crippling legacy of bigotry and injustice.

For effect, the president's next line—his invocation of a civil rights anthem—was expressed with dramatic flair, with distinctive emphasis on every word: "And we shall overcome."[54]

LBJ's nationally televised address, with its strong embrace of the movement's cause, did not win over southern congressmen, most of whom slumped in their seats as the joint session erupted in applause. Yet he triumphed where FDR failed—and without embroiling himself in an enervating purge campaign against conservative Democrats. The *Chicago Daily Defender* rejoiced that an American president "swung the full weight of the federal government behind the drive to make good the promise of equality—unkept for a century—given the American Negro."[55]

Johnson and the Institution of the Presidency

Johnson's domination of the political process had enduring effects on the presidency, some of which extended developments that began with Kennedy. Acting on his legislative ambitions, Kennedy had designed a freewheeling process of policy innovation that departed from the existing practice of letting domestic proposals move methodically through the departments and agencies and then undergo screening and clarification in the Bureau of the Budget. Under Johnson more and more policies began to be invented by the White House staff, which was committed to moving quickly on the president's agenda. Career officials in the departments and agencies and professional policy analysts in the Bureau of the Budget became less influential.

Joseph Califano, the chief White House aide for domestic affairs, supervised the creation of dozens of task forces composed of government officials and prominent academics. These task forces were charged with formulating innovative proposals in virtually every area of domestic policy, including poverty, environmental quality, urban planning, and aid to education. The Johnson administration took great care to immunize the task forces against political pressure, even keeping their proceedings secret. Moreover, task force members were told not to worry about whether their recommendations would be acceptable to Congress or party leaders.[56]

Several task force proposals became law; indeed, they formed the heart of the Great Society agenda. Almost as important, however, was the revolutionary character of the process itself. By placing policy development under White House supervision, free from traditional institutional restraints, the task force approach avoided what Johnson and his advisers regarded as the bureaucratic timidity and conservatism of the existing departments and agencies. Califano's small staff was the precursor of the Domestic Council, which was established by Johnson's successor, Richard Nixon, and of the domestic policy staffs that have been a part of every subsequent administration.[57]

The early years of the Johnson administration marked the historical height of "presidential government." The White House office and the rest of the Executive Office of the President (EOP) had been increasingly active in formulating programs since the administration of Franklin Roosevelt. Under Johnson, however, political and policy responsibility was concentrated in the presidency to an unprecedented extent. Major domestic policy innovations were conceived in the White House, hastened through Congress by the extraordinary legislative skill of the president and his congressional liaison team, and administered by new or refurbished executive agencies designed to respond to the president's directives. Finally, Johnson established a personal governing coalition that reached beyond his party. As columnist David Broder wrote in 1966, LBJ's leadership and program depended "for its success largely on the skill, negotiating ability, and maneuvering of the president."[58]

Soon, however, Johnson overextended himself. Ironically, the personalization of his presidency contributed to its undoing. Although LBJ was a gifted Washington insider, he could not rouse the American people in the ways required by the office he helped to re-create. As his aide Harry MacPherson noted, Johnson was incapable of "rising above the dirt of 'political governing,' so that he could inspire the nation."[59] His best words and teachings were laws and policies, but he was unable to cultivate the broad, stable base of popular support that his domestic agenda required to be implemented effectively. Even Johnson realized that his most serious weakness as president was "a general inability to stimulate, inspire, and unite all the public in the country."[60] The presence of television cameras seemed to intimidate this gregarious, consummate operator in political backrooms. Wanting to appear dignified on television, Johnson shrank his naturally outsized personality in a way that seemed inauthentic to viewers because it was.

Lack of charisma was not the sole source of Johnson's problems. His difficulties also were attributable to the personal presidency's creation of expectations that no president could satisfy. Since its inception under Theodore Roosevelt and Woodrow Wilson, the modern presidency has been grounded in a theory of executive power that enjoins the president to be both the shaper and the instrument of the popular will. Johnson, however, was inclined to ignore the normal tasks of public leadership in his pursuit of policies and programs that he hoped would serve the nation's long-term interests. Moreover, LBJ's "gargantuan aspirations" magnified the burdens of the personal executive. His obvious domination of the political agenda and legislative process ensured that he, not Congress, would be blamed if Great Society programs failed. And fail many of them did, the victims of hasty packaging and unrealistic goals.[61]

The Fall of Lyndon Johnson

The war in Vietnam clearly demonstrated both Johnson's shortcomings and the more troubling aspects of presidential government. In 1965 the president concluded that only by committing a large contingent of American forces to combat could he prevent a communist takeover in South Vietnam. Johnson's extraordinary ability to build a governing coalition in Washington helped sustain the Americanization of the war.[62] With little resistance from either Congress or, in the beginning, the public, the troop commitment rose from 23,000 at the end of 1964 to 181,000 a year later, 389,000 a year after that, and more than 500,000 by the end of 1967.

The war in southeast Asia became, in an unprecedented way, the president's war. Harry S. Truman had at least been able to claim that the United States was "carrying out an obligation for the United Nations" when he sent troops to fight in Korea. But in Vietnam, Richard M. Pious has noted, "no treaty obligations or other commitments required the United States to intervene."[63] Nor did Congress declare war. It passed only the Gulf of Tonkin Resolution, which was rushed through both houses at Johnson's request on August 7, 1964, after the communists allegedly attacked two American naval destroyers off the coast of North Vietnam. The resolution stated that Congress "approves and supports the determination of the President, as Commander-in-Chief, to take all necessary measures to repel any armed attack against the forces of the United States and to prevent further aggression."[64] Johnson, who believed that Truman erred politically by not asking Congress to support the Korean War, was anxious to have a legislative endorsement.

But the Gulf of Tonkin Resolution was hardly "the functional equivalent of a declaration of war," as Under Secretary of State Nicholas Katzenbach claimed at a Senate hearing in 1967.[65] Johnson believed that the resolution could help protect his political flank but that he already had all the constitutional authority he needed to deploy troops to Vietnam. In March 1966 the State Department's legal adviser wrote, "There can be no question in present circumstances of the President's authority to commit U.S. forces to the defense of South Vietnam. The grant of authority to the President in Article 2 of the Constitution extends to the actions of the United States currently undertaken in Vietnam." Johnson embraced this position at a news conference on August 18, 1967. Speaking of the Gulf of Tonkin Resolution, he said,

> We stated then and we repeat now, we did not think the
> resolution was necessary to do what we did and what we're
> doing. But we thought it was desirable and we thought if we
> were going to ask them [Congress] to stay the whole route and
> if we expected them to be there on the landing we ought to ask
> them to be there on the take off.[66]

By early 1968, the military situation in Vietnam had deteriorated so severely that Johnson's political consensus at home crumbled. The last president not to seek reelection after only five years in office was Calvin Coolidge.

On March 31 Johnson astonished the nation and the world by announcing, "I shall not seek, and I will not accept, the nomination of my party for another term as your President." But Johnson never lost his faith in the extraordinary powers of the presidency. Nor, even under the stress of war, as his alliance with civil rights leaders and other liberal constituencies imploded, did he ever give up his dream of the Great Society. Indeed, Johnson's insistence on trying to have "guns and butter"—the Vietnam War and the Great Society—subjected the economy to inflationary strains that were aggravated by his reluctance to ask Congress to enact a tax increase.

The Twenty-Fifth Amendment

One enduring legacy of the Kennedy–Johnson years was the Twenty-Fifth Amendment, proposed by Congress in 1965 and ratified by the states in 1967. The main purpose of the amendment was to provide for two separate but related situations: presidential disabilities and vacancies in the vice presidency.

The need for a reform like the Twenty-Fifth Amendment had long been apparent. As with the death, resignation, or impeachment of the president, the original Constitution stated in Article II, section 1: "[I]n Case of the . . . Inability [of the president] to discharge the Powers and Duties of the said Office, the Same shall devolve on the Vice President." The Constitution gave no guidance about what a disability was, how the vice president was to step in should the need arise, or even whether the vice president was to become president or merely assume the powers and duties of the office until the president recovered (did "the Same" refer to "the Powers and Duties" or to "the said Office"?).[67] During the long disabilities of Presidents James A. Garfield and Woodrow Wilson, the problems raised by the Constitution's vagueness became obvious.[68]

Vice-presidential vacancies were another frequent historical occurrence. The vice presidency becomes vacant when the president dies, resigns, or is impeached and removed, or when the vice president dies, resigns, or is impeached and removed. Such circumstances left the nation without a vice president on sixteen occasions between 1789 and 1963: seven times because the vice president died, eight times because the president died, and once because the vice president resigned.[69] By the merest chance, a double vacancy in the presidency and vice presidency never occurred.

Public and congressional disquiet about the problems of presidential disability and vice-presidential vacancy was minor and episodic through most of American history. Concern usually rose for a brief period while a president was disabled and then waned when the crisis passed. From 1945 to 1963, however, a combination of events placed these problems high on the nation's constitutional agenda.

The invention and spread of nuclear weapons after 1945 heightened public desire that an able president always be available to wield the powers of the office in the event of a sudden Soviet attack. Then, in rapid succession, President Eisenhower suffered a series of temporarily disabling illnesses—a heart attack in 1955, an ileitis attack and operation in 1956, and a stroke in 1957. Kennedy's assassination in 1963 left the nation with a president, Lyndon Johnson, who had a history of heart trouble and whose legally designated successors under the Presidential Succession Act of 1947 were an old and ailing Speaker of the House, John W. McCormack, and, as Senate president pro tempore, an even older and frailer Carl Hayden.

In December 1963, less than a month after Kennedy was assassinated, Birch Bayh, a Democratic senator from Indiana and the chair of the Senate Judiciary Committee's Subcommittee on Constitutional Amendments, announced that he would hold hearings in early 1964 to consider constitutional remedies to the disability and vacancy problems. Coordinating his efforts with those of a special committee of the American Bar Association, Bayh drafted the proposal that, with minor modifications, soon entered the Constitution as the Twenty-Fifth Amendment.

The Senate approved the amendment on September 29, 1964, by a vote of 65–0. The House did not act in 1964, possibly because to propose an amendment to fill vice-presidential vacancies would be perceived as a slap at Speaker McCormack, who was still first in line to succeed President Johnson. In 1965, however, just months after the election of Hubert H. Humphrey as Johnson's vice president, the House joined the Senate, which reaffirmed its support of the amendment by a 72–0 vote on February 19, and on April 13 voted its approval, 368–29.

Presidential Disabilities

From the beginning, most congressional interest in the Twenty-Fifth Amendment involved its disability provisions. As drafted by Bayh and enacted by Congress, three situations were covered by sections 3 and 4 of the amendment. In the first, the president is "unable to discharge the powers and duties of his office" and recognizes this condition—say, before or after undergoing surgery. A simple letter from the president to the Speaker of the House and the president pro tempore of the Senate is all it takes to make the vice president the acting president. A subsequent presidential letter declaring that the disability is ended restores the president's powers.

In the second situation, the president is disabled but, perhaps having suddenly lost consciousness, is unable to say so. Should this happen, either the vice president or the head of an executive department may call a meeting of the vice president and cabinet to discuss the situation. If both the vice president and a majority of the department heads declare the president disabled, the vice president becomes acting president—again, until the president writes to the leaders of Congress to announce an end to the disability.

The third situation covered by the disability portions of the amendment is the most troubling. It involves instances, such as questionable mental health or severe physical impairment, in which the president's ability to fulfill the office is in doubt—the president claims to be able, but the vice president and the cabinet disagree. The amendment provides that if this happens, the vice president becomes acting president until Congress can resolve the matter. Congress would have a maximum of three weeks to decide whether the president is disabled, with a two-thirds vote of both the House and the Senate needed to overturn the president's judgment. But because the Twenty-Fifth Amendment only transfers power to the vice president for as long as the presidential disability lasts, a subsequent claim of restored health by the president would set the whole process in motion again.

Some critics of the Bayh proposal argued that it vested too much power in the executive branch to make disability determinations. An alternative proposal was to create a disability commission that included members of all three branches, perhaps joined by some physicians. Bayh defended his proposal by saying that any move to strip power from the president by officials outside the administration risked violating the constitutional separation of powers. In the end, both to satisfy the critics and to preclude the possibility that a president might fire some or all department heads to forestall a disability declaration, the amendment authorized Congress, at its discretion, to substitute another body for the cabinet.

Although the Twenty-Fifth Amendment created an elaborate set of procedures for disability determinations, it included no definition of *disability*. It is clear from the congressional debate that disability is not to be equated with incompetence, laziness, unpopularity, or impeachable conduct. As to what disability is, Congress thought that any definition it might write into the Constitution in 1965 would be rendered obsolete by changes in medical science.

Vice-Presidential Vacancies

By the mid-1960s members of Congress generally agreed that the vice president should be replaced when the office becomes vacant, both to increase the likelihood of a smooth succession to the presidency, if needed, by a member of the president's party and to ensure that the presidential disability provisions of the amendment will always have a vice president on hand to execute them. Bayh proposed that the president nominate a new vice president when a vacancy occurs and that a majority of both houses of Congress, voting separately, decide whether to confirm the nomination. His proposal prevailed and became section 2 of the Twenty-Fifth Amendment but not before consideration was given to having Congress or the Electoral College from the previous election choose the vice president. Additional proposals to impose a time limit on Congress to either vote on a president's nominee for vice president or forfeit its right to reject the nomination were also considered and rejected.

No serious opposition to the Twenty-Fifth Amendment arose during the ratification process. The required approval of thirty-eight states was attained on February 10, 1967, barely a year and a half after Congress proposed the amendment. Little did any of those involved in its passage realize that during the next seven years, an extraordinary series of events would cause the vice presidency to become vacant twice.

The Presidency of Richard Nixon

The legacy of the Johnson years for the presidency was mixed: more governing authority but less political influence. Soon after LBJ left the White House, one of his closest assistants, George E. Reedy, wrote, "We may well be witnessing the first lengthening shadows that will become the twilight of the presidency."[70] The failure in Vietnam fostered cynicism about the merits of presidential policies, opposition to the unilateral use of presidential power, and a greater inclination in the news media to challenge the wisdom of presidential proposals and the veracity of presidential statements.[71] Yet the personal presidency endured: much was still demanded of presidents. They remained at the center of citizens' ever-growing expectations of government.

The 1968 Election: Party Reform and Divided Government

Nineteen sixty-eight was marked by a series of alarming events: in January, North Vietnam's Tet offensive against South Vietnam, which severely undermined public confidence in Johnson's conduct of the war; in March, the challenges to LBJ's renomination by anti-war senators Eugene McCarthy of Minnesota and Robert Kennedy of New York, which triggered the president's withdrawal from the election; in April, the assassination of civil rights leader Martin Luther King Jr. and the scores of race riots that erupted in its wake; in June, the assassination of Senator Kennedy on the night of his victory in the California primary; in August, the rioting surrounding the Democratic National Convention; and all year long, the simmering anger that attended the third-party candidacy of former Alabama governor George C. Wallace.

The 1968 elections dramatically displayed the political disarray in which Johnson left the country.[72] Vice President Humphrey, the Democratic nominee for president, led a bitterly divided party. Its convention in Chicago was ravaged by controversy, both within the hall and in the streets, where anti-war demonstrators clashed violently with the Chicago police. Without contesting a single primary, Humphrey was nominated with support from his party's state and local leaders, who still controlled a majority of the delegates and who preferred him to Senator McCarthy, whose early challenge to Johnson's renomination had helped trigger the president's withdrawal. The assassination of Humphrey's more powerful opponent, Senator Kennedy, made his nomination certain.

Politically, Humphrey was damaged goods. As Johnson's loyal, even submissive vice president, he found it difficult to distance himself from "Johnson's war." Unwilling to embrace the war, yet unable to make a clean break, he looked weak. Humphrey was rejected not only by the anti-war wing of his party but also by conservative Democratic voters, many of whom looked with favor on Wallace's third-party candidacy.

Humphrey's controversial nomination and the failure of his general election campaign against the Republican candidate, former vice president Richard Nixon, gave rise to important institutional reforms. The rules of the Democratic Party were revised in 1971 by the party-appointed McGovern–Fraser Commission in an effort to make presidential nominating conventions more representative of the party's rank and file.[73] In response to the new rules, states shifted from selecting delegates in closed councils of party regulars to electing them in direct primaries or open caucuses. Although the Democrats initiated these changes, many were codified in state laws that affected the Republican Party almost as much.

The declining influence of the traditional party organizations was apparent not only in the new nominating rules but also in the perceptions and habits of voters. Beginning with the 1968 election, voters began to express strong ambivalence about entrusting either the Democratic or Republican Party with complete control of the government.

The chief result of public alienation from the two-party system was divided government, in which the president's party does not control Congress. Divided government was the exception during the first two-thirds of the twentieth century. Starting in 1968 it became the norm. This not only had a profound effect on the course of the Nixon administration but also exacerbated the problems of modern presidential governance that became apparent during the Johnson years. Despite the Democratic disarray in 1968, Nixon did not win a decisive mandate to govern. The Democrats retained clear control of both houses of Congress, making Nixon the first new president since Zachary Taylor in 1848 to be elected without a majority for his party in either the House or the Senate.

Congress was not the only rival for power that Nixon faced. Because the country had elected only one other Republican president since 1932, the departments and agencies of the executive branch included a large preponderance of Democrats. Most of them were protected by civil service procedures, which had been extended "upward, outward and downward" since the New Deal to encompass almost the entire federal workforce. Moreover, as Paul Van Riper observed, because patronage since the 1930s had been "a sort of intellectual and ideological patronage rather than the more traditional partisan type," the domestic and diplomatic bureaucracies were infused with a strong liberal bias.[74] Eisenhower faced pockets of bureaucratic resistance, but the magnitude of the opposition was much more threatening to a more conservative Republican president whose party did not control either house of Congress.

In his memoirs, Nixon explained in colorful terms that one of his administration's most important tasks was to place its stamp on the federal bureaucracy as rapidly as possible:

> I urged the new Cabinet members to move quickly to replace holdover bureaucrats with people who believed in what we were trying to do. I warned that, if we did not act quickly, they would become captives of the bureaucracy they were trying to change. . . . "If we don't get rid of those people, they will either sabotage us from within, or they'll just sit back on their well-paid asses and wait for the next election to bring back their old bosses."[75]

All the more galling to the Nixon White House was the ease with which the president's own appointees to head the departments and agencies were co-opted by civil servants who managed to enlist them as allies against many of the administration's policies. Nixon's White House domestic policy adviser, John Ehrlichman, remarked at a press briefing in late 1972 that after administration officials were appointed and had their pictures taken with the president, "we only see them at the annual White House Christmas Party; they go off and marry the natives."[76]

The New Federalism

The first Republican president of the New Deal era, Dwight Eisenhower, often spoke of "restoring the balance" between the branches by returning authority from the president to Congress. Eisenhower eventually accepted the responsibilities of the modern executive, especially as he came to realize that even politically moderate presidents have to exert strong leadership if they want to limit the expansion of the federal government's activities. But Eisenhower was a reluctant modern president. His "hidden-hand" approach emphasized both flexible accommodation to the New Deal and respect for the other institutions of American government.

Nixon, in contrast, aggressively sought to expand presidential power. At the time he took office, aspects of the New Deal approach to the modern welfare state were being seriously questioned, even by liberals. Social problems such as poverty, crime, and family disintegration that once had seemed solvable with sufficient will and wallet had proven stubbornly resistant to Great Society-style programmatic solutions. The new intellectual and political climate seemed to present an opportunity to change domestic policy significantly. Moreover, unlike Eisenhower, who was cautious almost to a fault, Nixon was a self-described "chance taker."[77] His entire political career was punctuated by personal crises and bold responses. "It is therefore not surprising," historian Joan Hoff-Wilson has written, "that as president he rationalized many of his foreign and domestic initiatives as crises (or at least intolerable impasses) that could be resolved only by dramatic and sometimes drastic measures."[78]

Nixon made a more determined effort than Eisenhower to use the presidency as a lever for a broadly conservative domestic policy. Indeed, he was the first Republican president since Theodore Roosevelt to embrace an expansive understanding of executive authority. But in contrast to TR, who was also the first chief executive of either party to regard the president as the steward of the public welfare, Nixon sought to recast the office as the agent of the growing skepticism about social reform.

Nixon was not rigidly opposed to the welfare state, however.[79] The main purpose of his major domestic policy initiative, the New Federalism, was to sort out the responsibilities of governance so that national problems would be handled by the national government, and problems more amenable to decentralized solutions would be handled by state and local authorities. Welfare, which Nixon believed required a national set of standards, was an example of the former. Job training, which he thought would benefit from a more flexible approach, typified the latter.

Nixon also pursued a liberal civil rights program that made affirmative action—the practice of granting preferences in employment, contracting, and education on the basis of race or gender—a national policy. Johnson had issued Executive Order 11246, which authorized the secretary of labor to require compliance reports on hiring practices from government contractors and mandated that these contractors make serious efforts to recruit minority applicants. The order also created the Office of Federal Contract Compliance to oversee administration of the new policy. Under Nixon, the potential power of Executive Order 11246 was fully exploited. Nixon's labor secretary, George Shultz, issued a directive called the Philadelphia Plan, which required local construction companies and unions to adopt "specific goals and timetables" for hiring minorities. A second implementing order extended the first one to federal contractors of all kinds and stipulated that they had to recruit workforces that reflected the racial makeup of the applicant pools in their local areas. The Nixon administration aggressively pursued affirmative action, even to the point of preferential treatment, not only in contract compliance but also, through Executive Order 11478, in hiring for the federal civil service. In doing so, political scientist Kenneth R. Mayer has written, Nixon created "the modern structure of affirmative action that has repeatedly been upheld [by the courts] as a valid exercise of the president's executive authority."[80]

Nixon's New Federalism was conservative mainly in its challenge to the New Deal presumption that social problems are always addressed most effectively at the national level. This challenge was enough, however, to provoke powerful opposition in the Democratic Congress and, especially, in the departments and agencies of the executive branch, which stood to lose power to the states and localities if the New Federalism was enacted.[81]

Nixon's commitment to selective decentralization in the federal system went hand in hand with his paramount desire to centralize power in the White House. Like Andrew Jackson, he was convinced that the federal government and its special interests had grown so powerful that only a strong president could "reverse the flow of power and resources from the states and communities to Washington."[82] Leonard Garment, a member of the president's legal staff, observed that "the central paradox of the Nixon administration was that in order to reduce federal power, it was first necessary to increase presidential power." Or, as Nixon himself said, "Bringing power to the White House was necessary to dish it out."[83]

Nixon and Vietnam

Nixon took office knowing it was in his political interest to end the war in Vietnam as soon as possible. "I am not going to end up like LBJ," he said, "holed up in the White House afraid to show my face on the street. I'm going to stop that war. Fast."[84]

But Nixon was no more successful than Johnson in obtaining what he called "peace with honor"—that is, a way to bring American troops home without losing South Vietnam to the communists.[85] The "honor" component of this goal was of primary importance to Nixon. He and his national security adviser, Henry Kissinger, believed that unless they could extricate the United States from the war in a manner that demonstrated resoluteness of purpose and certainty of action, they would lose respect abroad from friends and foes alike. "Ending the war honorably," Kissinger argued, "is essential for the peace of the world. Any other solution may unloose forces that would complicate the prospects of international order."[86]

Vietnam consumed much of Nixon's first term, from January 20, 1969, until the war was concluded, at least formally, on January 27, 1973. Seeking to navigate a polarized political environment rent by bitter recriminations between "Hawks" and "Doves," he asked the "great silent majority" of Americans to support a policy that would gradually turn the burden of ground combat over to the South Vietnamese.[87] During these four years, however, Nixon actually escalated the American involvement by publicly bombing North Korea and secretly bombing its military enclaves in Cambodia, a neighboring neutral country. When bombing failed to do the latter job, Nixon told the nation on April 30, 1970, that he was sending troops to attack the North Vietnamese bases in Cambodia. The venture was militarily futile and provoked massive anti-war demonstrations around the country as well as an uncommonly hostile reaction from Congress.

Nixon's policies in Vietnam not only reinforced his aggressive use of presidential power but also made it even more controversial. Like Truman and Johnson, Nixon believed that in time of war the president may assume extraordinary powers. But he found, as Truman and Johnson did, that public acceptance of a claim of sweeping executive power does not redound automatically to a president who prosecutes an unpopular, undeclared war.

Nixon's determination to expand the boundaries of presidential power in the face of growing political resistance encouraged him to pursue his domestic and foreign policies by executive fiat. In doing so, he effected significant changes in the organization and conduct of the personal presidency nurtured by Kennedy and Johnson. But he also planted the seeds of his own disgrace and resignation in 1974.[88]

Nixon and the Administrative Presidency

Nixon's "administrative presidency" was born of his inability to persuade Congress to enact the New Federalism. Although Nixon took a legislative approach to reform during his first two years as president, most of his proposals bogged down in the Democratic House and Senate. In response, he shifted to a strategy to achieve his objectives through administrative action. As scholar–practitioner Richard P. Nathan has noted, "Nixon came to the conclusion sometime in 1971 that in many areas of government, particularly domestic affairs, *operations is policy.* Many day-to-day management tasks for domestic programs—for example, regulation writing, grant approval, and budget apportionment—are substantive and therefore involve policy."[89]

The first phase of Nixon's administrative strategy was to expand and reorganize the EOP so that it could preempt the traditional responsibilities of the departments and agencies. Nixon doubled the staff of the White House Office from 292 under Johnson to 583 by the end of his first term. With size came power. Nixon loyalists in the White House and in the other agencies of the EOP not only formulated policy, as in the Johnson administration, but also tried to carry out policy.

In international affairs, Kissinger created the first completely White House–dominated system of foreign policy making. Starting with Kennedy, the president's national security adviser had assumed a greater share of the responsibilities of the State Department. But Nixon and Kissinger built a foreign policy staff of unprecedented scale and influence. So marginal was the State Department that Secretary William Rogers was not even told in advance of the administration's most important diplomatic initiative, the opening to China. Nixon visited China in February 1972 after nearly a quarter-century of fierce hostility between the United States and the communist Chinese government that took power in 1949.[90]

The staff of the newly formed Domestic Council, headed by Ehrlichman, took charge of domestic policy making. In addition, Nixon reorganized and expanded the Bureau of the Budget to strengthen the president's influence in domestic affairs. On July 1, 1970, by executive order, the Budget Bureau became the Office of Management and Budget (OMB), with a new supervisory layer of presidentially appointed assistant directors for policy inserted between the OMB director and the office's senior civil servants. Consequently, the budget office not only assumed additional responsibility for administrative management but also became more responsive to the president.

By itself, the swelling of the EOP, both the president's own White House–based office staff and the OMB, did not bring about full presidential control of public policy. Recalcitrant bureaucrats and their allies in Congress were still able to resist many of Nixon's efforts to seize the levers of administrative power. Two weeks before the 1968 election, former president Eisenhower wrote that he hoped for a victory so sweeping that it would give Nixon "a strong, clear mandate" and a Republican Congress. Eisenhower noted that such a victory would help Nixon "change the ingrained power structure of the federal government (the heritage of the years of Democratic rule), placing more responsibility at state and local levels."[91] Not only did Nixon's razor-thin victory in 1968 fail to bring in a Republican Congress but, befitting his four-year-long emphasis on an autonomous presidency, even his landslide reelection in 1972 did little to help his party. The Republicans failed to make meaningful inroads in the House, the Senate, or the state legislatures.

Still lacking the support he needed from Congress to become an effective legislative leader, Nixon resolved to carry the administrative presidency a step further during his second term. In 1973 he undertook an extensive reorganization plan designed to re-create the bureaucracy in his own image. The president moved proven loyalists into the management ranks of the departments and agencies and then consolidated leadership of the bureaucracy in a "supercabinet" of five secretaries whose job was to implement all of the administration's policies. One of these "supersecretaries" was Kissinger, who became secretary of state while retaining his position as the assistant to the president for national security affairs. As such, Kissinger became responsible, in a formal as well as an informal sense, for foreign policy, second only to Nixon. The president consolidated domestic power in the hands of Secretary of Agriculture Earl Butz, who was made responsible for all policies related to natural resources; Casper Weinberger, the secretary of Health, Education and Welfare, whose portfolio included all programs related to human resources; James Lynn, head of the Housing and Urban Development department, who assumed responsibility for all public commitments that fell under the broad rubric of community development; and George Shultz, the director of the newly formed OMB, who took over all matters pertaining to economic policy. Strongly resisted by the departments and by Congress, Nixon's experiment did not survive his administration.

An Imperial Presidency?

Nixon's attempt to extend the bounds of presidential authority and, by so doing, to achieve his political and policy objectives unilaterally has been widely regarded as an unprecedented usurpation of power and, ultimately, the cause of the Watergate scandal, which forced him to resign from office in 1974. It was, to be sure, both the improprieties of the president's personal reelection organization, the Committee to Re-Elect the President (CREEP to its critics)—particularly its attempt to bug telephones in the offices of the Democratic National Committee—and the subsequent efforts by the president and his aides to cover up the planning of the break-in that brought down the Nixon administration.

But Nixon's version of the administrative presidency was not entirely new. In important respects, it was a logical extension of the evolving institution, one that presumed to bestow bipartisan acceptance on the personalization of the executive office. The reelection committee's complete autonomy from the regular Republican organization during Nixon's campaign for a second term was merely the culmination of the recent history of presidential preemption of the traditional responsibilities of the national party committees. As for the post-reelection phase of Nixon's administrative reform strategy, in which he concentrated managerial authority in the hands of a few White House aides and cabinet secretaries, it simply extended recent presidents' practice of weakening bureaucratic constraints on the presidency. The irony is that the strategy of pursuing presidential policy goals through administrative action, which was invented mainly by Roosevelt, Johnson, and other Democrats, was considered especially suitable by a Republican president who faced a Congress and a bureaucracy that were determined to preserve those Democratic presidents' programs.

After witnessing the indiscretions of the Johnson and Nixon years, historian Arthur M. Schlesinger Jr., until then an eloquent defender of strong presidential leadership, wrote in 1973, "In the last years presidential primacy, so indispensable to the political order, has turned into presidential supremacy. The constitutional presidency—as events so apparently disparate as the Indochina War and the Watergate affair showed—has become the imperial presidency and threatens to be the revolutionary presidency."[92]

Several of Nixon's innovations in presidential leadership of the executive branch endured. Nearly all of his successors have, in some cases reluctantly, appointed a strong chief of staff to centralize control of the White House Office. Each has preserved the Domestic Council, although sometimes under a different name, such as the Office of Policy Development.

Each has made use of the more politicized OMB to control spending and agency operations. And each has stressed personal loyalty when making appointments to the departments and agencies.[93]

But, as Nixon learned to his regret, the rest of the federal government could not be remade by executive fiat. The modern presidency was never truly imperial. Its power depended on agreement by Congress, the bureaucracy, and the courts that responsibilities should be delegated to the executive. By the time Johnson left office, the political environment was less supportive of strong presidential leadership. Nixon strengthened opposition to the unilateral use of executive power by further attenuating the bonds that tied the president to Congress and the party system.

More than anything else, perhaps, Nixon's bitter relations with Congress were the source of his downfall. His early inability to win support on Capitol Hill for most of his New Federalism proposals and his conduct of the war led him to construe the powers of his office much too broadly, which only aggravated the relationship. Nixon's use of his power as commander in chief to bomb Cambodia in 1969 and invade it in 1970 provoked a major public and legislative protest. So too did his sweeping application of the president's traditional right to impound—that is, not spend—funds appropriated by Congress. Nixon defended his challenge to Congress's power of the purse as inherent in his own authority as chief executive. Although Caspar Weinberger, Nixon's deputy budget director at the time, conceded in a 1971 appearance before a Senate panel that Congress had the power to appropriate, he insisted that it "did not follow from this . . . that the *expenditure* of government funds involved an exclusively legislative function." A law passed by Congress to appropriate funds, Weinberger asserted, was "permissive and not mandatory in nature."[94]

Unlike several of his predecessors, Nixon did not impound funds to achieve economy and efficiency. Instead, he was attempting to contravene the policies of the Democratic Congress by undoing the legislative process. His assault on the Office of Economic Opportunity (OEO), the agency responsible for leading the War on Poverty and a symbol of the Great Society, was undertaken to challenge Congress for the right to govern. Congress appropriated funds to continue the OEO, but Nixon had the agency's acting director, Howard Phillips, issue orders to dismantle it. Nixon also refused to nominate Phillips as the permanent OEO director because he knew the nomination would be rejected by the Senate.[95] Former vice president Humphrey, who was elected to the Senate in 1970, charged that the Nixon administration's assault on the OEO amounted to a "policy impoundment"—that is, the modification or even elimination of a program authorized by Congress.[96]

These institutional confrontations strongly suggest that, Watergate or no Watergate, a war still would have occurred between Nixon and Congress. Both sides geared up for a constitutional struggle before anything was known about the Watergate affair. Indeed, Congress's willingness to take the extraordinary step of removing the president in 1974 was in part a response to Nixon's repeated efforts to circumvent the legislative process.[97]

Watergate and Its Legacy

The unsavory events that forced Nixon to resign as president on August 9, 1974, created a political atmosphere so sour with disgust and disillusionment that it threatened the civility and public trust on which any government depends.[98] The break-in at the Democratic National Committee was carried out by five members of a secret White House investigating unit (the so-called plumbers), which originally was formed to plug the leaks to reporters that compromised the Nixon administration's policy in Vietnam. In 1972, however, the plumbers' activities were extended to "campaign intelligence" relating to Nixon's bid for reelection. On June 17, the five men who were trying to bug the Democrats' telephones were caught and arrested in the party's national headquarters at the Watergate Hotel in Washington.

"At its simplest, most tangible level," political scientist A. James Reichley has observed, "Watergate was nothing more than dirty politics. A gang of officeholders, unsure of their chances of winning the next election, set out through illegal means to shift the odds in their favor."[99] Such behavior, however deplorable, was hardly unprecedented.

What made the Watergate scandal more than a "third-rate burglary"— the characterization offered by Nixon's press secretary, Ron Ziegler—was its close association with the modern presidency. The malicious activities sanctioned by Nixon and some of his associates accentuated one of the ill effects that followed from the personalization of the modern executive office: presidential isolation. For years, presidents had been encouraged to try to run the government from the White House and to vest their political fortunes in a small circle of loyalists.

As James Madison warned in his Pacificus-Helvidius debate with Alexander Hamilton over the president's foreign policy, personal power was amplified and rendered more dangerous by war, "the true nurse of executive aggrandizement." The planning of the break-in and other acts of political sabotage, in which Attorney General John Mitchell and several White House aides participated, and the efforts by the president and others to interfere with the Federal Bureau of Investigation's (FBI's) investigation and the Justice Department's prosecution of the case after the Watergate burglars were arrested, involved a logical, although perverse, extension of the national security state. Many of these powers originated in wartime, and not surprisingly, one of the Nixon administration's first lines of defense was to avow its concern for national security in a perilous world. Nixon even justified his decision to fire Archibald Cox, the special Watergate prosecutor who issued a subpoena to force the president to release certain secret White House tape recordings, by arguing that to acquiesce to Cox's aggressive investigation would make the president appear weak in the eyes of Soviet Communist Party chief Leonid Brezhnev and other foreign leaders.[100]

The president invoked an absolute executive privilege—that is, a claim that the president's confidential discussions and papers are exempt from examination by the other branches of government—in carrying out the "Saturday night massacre," as the firing of Cox on October 20, 1973, came to be called. Nixon also claimed executive privilege in response to the demands of a Senate select investigating committee, the Watergate grand jury, and the House Judiciary Committee. To be sure, presidents had always invoked executive privilege. Historically, such assertions had been constitutionally less controversial than, for example, the extent of the president's removal power. But Nixon was the first president to argue that executive privilege has no limit. In doing so, he conflated legitimate national security interests with his own political interest in staying in power.

The firing of Cox aroused a firestorm of protest, forcing Nixon to appoint a new special prosecutor, Leon Jaworski, and to give him the same powers that Cox had wielded, including specific authorization to go to court to contest the president's effort to withhold any evidence that the prosecutor sought. On April 16, 1974, Jaworski asked that Nixon be subpoenaed to produce tapes and documents relating to sixty-four White House conversations, which the special prosecutor believed he needed in order to try seven associates of the president who were indicted by the Watergate grand jury for conspiracy to defraud the United States and obstruct justice. Jaworski also expected that the White House tapes would establish whether Nixon was part of the original Watergate conspiracy, the post-break-in cover-up, or both.

The controversy that was created by Jaworski's motion and Nixon's refusal to comply was ultimately settled by the Supreme Court. In *United States v. Nixon*, the Court rejected Nixon's claim to an absolute executive privilege and, specifically, to the exclusive right to determine when the privilege was properly invoked. The Court's unanimous decision, issued on July 24, 1974, and written by Chief Justice Warren Burger, a Nixon appointee, stated that "to read the Art[icle] II powers of the President as providing an absolute privilege as against a subpoena essential to enforcement of criminal statutes . . . would upset the constitutional balance of 'a workable government.'"[101]

The Court agreed with Nixon that some form of executive privilege is "fundamental to the operation of government and inextricably rooted in the separation of powers under the Constitution."[102] As such, the decision was the first in which the justices formally upheld any version of the privilege. But the Court brushed aside Nixon's argument that executive privilege may be invoked even in criminal proceedings that involve no issues of national security. It endorsed, instead, Justice Robert Jackson's argument in *Youngstown Sheet and Tube Company v. Sawyer* (1952) that presidential claims must be balanced against the powers and duties of Congress and the courts. The *Youngstown* precedent led Chief Justice Burger to conclude that

> when the ground for asserting privilege as to subpoenaed
> materials sought for use in a criminal trial is based only on the
> generalized interest in confidentiality, it cannot prevail over
> the fundamental demands of due process of law in the fair
> administration of criminal justice. The generalized assertion
> of privilege must yield to the demonstrated specific need for
> evidence in a pending criminal trial.[103]

Nixon's presidency came to an end shortly after the House Judiciary Committee, acting on the heels of the Court's decision in the tapes case, voted on August 4 to impeach him. The president's chances of surviving a Senate trial were dealt a further blow when he admitted that among the tapes he was ordered to surrender were some that clearly implicated him in the Watergate cover-up.[104] Even the president's Republican supporters on the Judiciary Committee conceded that he had virtually confessed to obstruction of justice.[105] All of them announced that they would vote for impeachment on the House floor.

On August 8, in a speech to the nation, Nixon announced his decision to resign the next day, saying, "[I]t has become evident to me that I no longer have a strong enough political base in the Congress."[106] Thus, as Alonzo L. Hamby has written, Nixon's ongoing effort to forge a conservative modern executive "ended in personal disaster. Worse, he left the presidency itself an object of suspicion and scorn, awaiting a new Roosevelt or Eisenhower to restore its standing and provide a demoralized public with a sense of movement and purpose that could come only from the occupant of the White House."[107]

The Watergate scandal provoked Congress to pass a multitude of new laws to curb the powers of the presidency. More significant, Watergate shattered the recent consensus in American politics—already undermined by the controversies of the Johnson administration and Nixon's earlier claims to unilateral executive authority—that strong presidential leadership embodies the public interest. When asked in 1959 whether the president or Congress should have "the most say in government," a representative sample of Americans favored the president by 61 percent to 17 percent. A similar survey in 1977 indicated a striking reversal: 58 percent believed that Congress should have the most say. Only 26 percent supported presidential primacy.[108]

One important law that Congress passed to restrict the unilateral exercise of presidential power was the Congressional Budget and Impoundment Control Act of 1974, which required the president to obtain Congress's approval before impounding any funds. The act also established budget committees in the House and the Senate to coordinate and strengthen the legislature's involvement in fiscal policy making. It created the Congressional Budget Office, a legislative staff agency that would make available to Congress the same sort of fiscal expertise that the OMB provided to the executive branch. In a separate bill, Congress modified the OMB. After fifty-three years as a purely presidential agency, the OMB's director and deputy directors were made subject to Senate confirmation.[109]

Congress reasserted its influence in foreign affairs, as well. The Case Act, which it passed in 1972 to curb the growing presidential tendency to engage in personal diplomacy, required that all executive agreements with foreign governments be reported to Congress. The War Powers Resolution, which Congress enacted over Nixon's veto in 1973, was intended to prevent another Vietnam—that is, any prolonged period of presidential war making without formal authorization from Congress. The resolution required the president to consult with Congress "in every possible instance" before committing troops to combat and to submit a report to the legislature within forty-eight hours of doing so. After sixty days, the troops were to be removed unless Congress voted either to declare war or to authorize their continued deployment.[110]

In and of themselves, these laws did not restrict the modern presidency severely. For example, presidents consistently refused to acknowledge the constitutionality of the War Powers Resolution and seldom observed it. But their enactment expressed Congress's determination to reestablish itself as an equal, if not the dominant, partner in governing the nation. Congressional procedures were reformed to produce a more aggressive legislature. Decentralized since its rebellion against Speaker Joseph Cannon in the early twentieth century, Congress became even more so. Some of the power of the standing committees devolved to the subcommittees, whose numbers, staff, and autonomy grew rapidly. The rise of subcommittee government posed a severe challenge to the modern president's preeminence in legislative and administrative affairs. As political scientist R. Shep Melnick has written,

> Using subcommittee resources, members initiated new programs and revised old ones, challenging the president for the title of "Chief Legislator." No longer would Congress respond to calls for action by passing vague legislation telling the executive to do something. Now Congress was writing detailed statutes which not infrequently deviated from the president's program. Subcommittees were also using oversight hearings to make sure that administrators paid heed not just to the letter of legislation, but to its spirit as well.[111]

Gerald R. Ford and the Post-Watergate Era

Vice President Gerald Ford succeeded to the presidency on August 9, 1974. He inherited some of the most difficult circumstances faced by any president. Ford had never run for national or even statewide office. His electoral experience was confined to Michigan's Fifth Congressional District. He was representing this district in the House, which he served as Republican leader, when on October 10, 1973, Vice President Spiro T. Agnew was forced to resign in response to the revelation that he had taken bribes ever since he was the county executive of Baltimore County, Maryland.[112] Invoking the recently enacted Twenty-Fifth Amendment, Nixon nominated Ford to replace Agnew.[113] The new vice president took office on December 6, after being confirmed by both houses of Congress. When the Watergate scandal forced Nixon to resign, Ford became the first, and so far the only, president never to have been elected either president or vice president.

Ford was a unique president in one other respect. Never before had a vice president succeeded to the presidency because his predecessor resigned. That Nixon left office in disgrace made the start of Ford's tenure especially inauspicious. Not only did Ford lack an electoral mandate, but he became president when the country was still deeply scarred and divided by the Vietnam War, when respect for the presidency was greatly

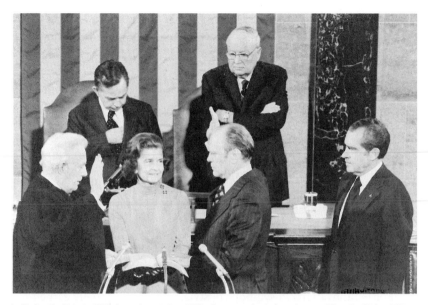

Under the Twenty-Fifth Amendment, Gerald Ford was nominated as vice president by Richard Nixon after the resignation of Spiro T. Agnew. A year later Ford became the first president to succeed to the presidency because his predecessor resigned and the first never to have been elected to the office of president or vice president.

Source: The Gerald Ford Presidential Library.

diminished, and when the nation's economy and foreign relations were in disarray, with inflation and unemployment rising sharply and the Soviet Union aggressively supporting communist advances in third-world nations such as Angola. Reflecting on this period, Kissinger later recalled, "The Presidency was in shambles."[114]

Combining symbolic actions with changes in public policy and leadership style, Ford made an earnest effort to restore integrity to the presidency and to purge the nation of its preoccupation with Watergate.[115] One of his first decisions was to nominate Nelson A. Rockefeller, the long-respected former governor of New York, for vice president. He also removed many of the trappings of the so-called imperial presidency. Within weeks Ford reduced the White House staff by 10 percent, from 540 to 485. On a lighter note, on certain occasions the Marine band was instructed to replace "Hail to the Chief" with the University of Michigan's fight song. The living quarters in the White House became officially "the residence" rather than "the mansion."

Symbolic changes were accompanied by new policies and a new presidential style. After three days in office, Ford accepted the Senate's recommendation that he convene a White House "summit" on the economy. The Conference on Inflation, which included business and labor leaders and a bipartisan group of economists, and other events, such as numerous meetings between the new president and groups of governors, mayors, and county officials, were all part of Ford's attempt to open the doors of the White House.

Perhaps Ford's most dramatic gesture to heal the nation's wounds was his plan of amnesty for the fifty thousand draft evaders and deserters from the Vietnam War. The president offered not an unconditional pardon but a program in which those who wanted amnesty could earn it. Ford announced the program on August 19, 1974, the eleventh day of his presidency, before the most challenging of audiences, the annual convention of the Veterans of Foreign Wars in Chicago. "This decision," a Ford aide has written, "was not preceded by full or elaborate deliberations. His decision appears to have been driven not only by compassion but also by its symbolic value in helping to put the recent past behind the nation."[116]

Ford's innovations in symbolism, style, and policy initially earned his administration considerable goodwill. His self-effacing manner seemed less to diminish the presidency than to endow it with an endearing folksiness. The press responded with favorable accounts and images of the new president toasting his own English muffin in the morning and taking a healthy swim at the end of the day. During his first week in office, Ford received a 71 percent approval rating in the Gallup poll. Only 3 percent of Americans disapproved of his performance.[117]

Almost overnight, however, Ford's standing with the public and the press crumbled. On September 8, barely four weeks after he became president, Ford announced that he was granting "a full, free and absolute pardon unto Richard Nixon for all offenses against the United States which he, Richard Nixon, has committed or may have committed" as president."[118] As with the Vietnam amnesty program, Ford wanted to lay to rest the nation's recent unhappy past. Instead, sprung as it was on an unprepared public that wanted to see Nixon indicted and convicted, if not jailed, before clemency was considered, the pardon turned Ford into Watergate's final victim. As political scientist Roger Porter, a member of the Ford administration, has noted, "For many Americans, this single act overwhelmed the aura of openness, accessibility, and candor that he had so successfully begun to establish."[119] By the end of September, Ford's approval rating had dropped to 50 percent.[120] The press's early celebration of his unpretentious personal style gave way to ridicule. The president was now caricatured as a clumsy, slow-witted bumbler at best and, at worst, a craven politician who had secretly traded the promise of a pardon for Nixon's resignation.

Few joined the most cynical of Ford's critics in challenging his personal integrity. Despite the outcry over the Nixon pardon, the new president's plain, forthright manner did much, as his successor Jimmy Carter said in his 1977 inaugural address, "to heal our land."[121] But Ford was unable to restore the power of the modern presidency. The limits of his influence were revealed most clearly by his failure to work his will with an aggressive and sometimes hostile Democratic Congress. The 1974 congressional elections, which swelled the already substantial Democratic majority by fifty-two seats in the House and four in the Senate, made the task of legislative leadership still more difficult.

Ford did not wilt in the face of partisan opposition. He even had some success with Congress in reducing corporate regulations and cutting taxes. But, for the most part, Ford's influence was greatest when it was negative. He cast sixty-six vetoes, mostly against spending bills, during his twenty-nine months in office and was overridden only twelve times. Indeed, more often than not, the mere threat of a veto spurred congressional Democrats to modify legislation to make it less unpalatable to the president. As such, the Ford administration was more like the late nineteenth-century executive than the modern presidency. "The strength of Congress consists in the right to pass statutes; the strength of the President in his right to veto them," British scholar James Bryce observed in 1890.[122]

Ford's difficulties with Congress did not stop at the water's edge. As in domestic policy, Congress was unwilling to let the Ford administration have its way in foreign affairs, the area in which presidents traditionally operate from their strongest legal and political position. Ford was determined not to diminish the foreign policy powers of his office despite the Vietnam legacy and the War Powers Resolution. He did not consult Congress in May 1975 when he sent troops to recover the merchant ship *Mayaguez* and its crew after they were seized by Cambodia. But Congress refused to respond to some of Ford's most urgent proposals, including his request for emergency assistance for the disintegrating government of South Vietnam (the bitter denouement of Nixon's "Vietnamization" policy), his plea to lift an embargo on American aid to Turkey, and his plan to help the anti-Marxist guerrillas in Angola. More than anything, the lack of congressional support in foreign affairs caused Ford to complain in March 1976 that "there had been a swing of the 'historic pendulum' toward Congress, raising the possibility of a disruptive erosion of the president's ability to govern."[123]

Ford's ability to govern was also weakened by the reformed presidential nominating process. He had barely settled into office when his administration was forced to shift its attention from the politics of governing to the politics of election. Although Ford hoped to win his party's nomination for president in 1976 by staying on the job in Washington, he had to campaign furiously to stave off defeat. The new primaries-based, media-driven nominating process enabled Ronald Reagan, the conservative former governor of California, to mount a strong challenge to the incumbent president within his own party. Reagan did not defeat Ford, but he came close, earning nearly half the votes at the Republican National Convention and complicating the president's task of winning the fall election.[124] Ford's victory at the convention was Pyrrhic. Incumbent presidents who face tough fights for their party's nomination almost always lose the general election.

Ford was no exception. When he lost to former Georgia governor Jimmy Carter, a man whom he viewed as "an outsider with little more going for him than a winning smile," Ford felt he had every reason to believe that the presidency was slipping into receivership.[125] Carter's four years as president did little to convince observers that he was wrong.

A President Named Jimmy

James Earl Carter—he preferred "Jimmy"—embodied the extremes of promise and disappointment to which the contemporary executive office is prone. His elevation to the White House was a remarkable personal triumph, as was his initial popularity as president. Yet so far did Carter fall politically that, as Fred Greenstein has noted, "at the time he left office his reputation had nowhere to go but up."[126]

A one-term governor who was virtually unknown outside of Georgia before he ran for president, Carter won the 1976 Democratic nomination with little support from his party's leaders. His campaign demonstrated how readily, under the new rules that governed the nominating process, a political outsider could win a presidential nomination by parlaying early primary victories in a few small states into a national convention majority. After the election, hoping to solidify his personal relationship with the people, Carter went further than Ford in trying to eliminate imperial trappings from the presidency, sometimes carrying his own luggage as a candidate and as president. At his inauguration, the new president and his family stepped from their black limousine and walked the mile from the Capitol to the White House.

Yet Carter's informality, which appealed to many voters during the campaign, worked to his detriment once he became president. As with Ford, it did not take long for the White House press corps to begin treating the president's unpretentious manner as evidence of his modest talents. Carter's early attempt to deliver the televised equivalent of a fireside chat, for example, was remarked less for its content (it was about energy policy) than for his appearance in a cardigan sweater. In part, this reaction indicated, as House Speaker Thomas P. "Tip" O'Neill observed, "that most people prefer a little pomp in their presidents."[127] More fundamentally, it reinforced the suspicion that Carter lacked what it takes to lead the Washington community.

As most presidents since George Washington had recognized, presidential authority requires a certain measure of ceremony. Carter eventually came to understand this, albeit too late. "In reducing the imperial presidency," he wrote in his memoirs,

> I overreacted at first. We began to receive many complaints that I had gone too far in cutting back the pomp and ceremony, so after a few months I authorized the band to play 'Hail to the Chief' on special occasions. I found it to be impressive and enjoyed it.[128]

But Carter's problems went beyond style and symbolism. Before the end of his first year as president, it became obvious that he was having a terrible time with Congress. Nixon and Ford had experienced similar problems, but they confronted a legislature that was controlled by the opposition party. As a result of the post-Watergate midterm election in 1974, Carter's Congress was two-thirds Democratic. His presidency revealed that the tensions between the White House and Congress were not simply an artifact of divided government. Presidents and legislators had become, in effect, independent political entrepreneurs, each establishing their own constituencies. As a result, the two branches were even less likely than in the past to regard each other as partners in the shared endeavor of promoting the party program. "I learned the hard way," Carter wrote, "that there was no party loyalty or discipline when a complicated or controversial issue was at stake—none. Each legislator had to be wooed and won individually. It was every member for himself, and the devil take the hindmost!"[129]

Arguably, Carter contributed to the disarray he protested. He ran for president by building a personal electoral coalition. Having won, he saw no need to court either his party's leaders in Congress or, in the newly decentralized legislature, its rank and file. As political scientist Larry Berman has written, "Carter believed that as an outsider his greatest advantage was that he could 'dance with the lady he came to the dance with.' He believed that the mere threat of going to the people would make Speaker Tip O'Neill or Senate Finance Committee Chairman Russell Long quiver."[130]

Carter's failures with Congress also may be attributed in part to the inexperience of his staff, which consisted mainly of "the provincial veterans of his campaign team."[131] But the Georgia loyalists' lack of schooling in the ways of Washington was less problematic than their arrogance toward Congress as an institution. Assessing Carter's ineffective legislative liaison office, O'Neill complained,

> Frank Moore, a former public relations man from Georgia, was the [director of] congressional liaison, but he didn't know beans about Congress. On the other hand you don't have to be a legislative genius to figure out that Pennsylvania Avenue is a two-way street, and that members of Congress are entitled to certain basic courtesies. As Speaker, I didn't always have time to return my phone calls, either. But at least I made sure that somebody on my staff got back to the callers.[132]

Carter learned from his mistakes, and after his first year in office, he established better relations with Congress. The president's record with the Ninety-Fifth Congress was, in fact, quite respectable. In 1978, at Carter's urging, the Senate ratified the controversial Panama Canal treaties, which gradually turned over control of the canal to Panama. Congress enacted airline deregulation, civil service reform, and natural gas pricing legislation. It even eliminated some of the most egregious pork barrel public works projects from the budget.

Carter's improved performance as chief legislator benefited from his effective Office of Public Liaison (OPL). Nixon created the OPL in 1970 as an organizational home within the White House staff for the growing number of aides assigned to cultivate support from constituency groups. Carter expanded and formalized the OPL's activities. By the time he left office in 1981, specific staff members were assigned not only to traditional constituencies such as African Americans, labor, and business but also to consumers, women, the elderly, Jews, Latinos, white ethnic Catholics, Vietnam veterans, and gays.[133] Headed by Anne Wexler, Carter's OPL represented a significant contribution to the institutional presidency, making it possible for presidents who lack great rhetorical ability to form linkages with the public. As political scientist Erwin C. Hargrove has written, "The Wexler office compensated for Carter's limitations as a presidential persuader by institutionalizing the persuasion function . . . by bringing groups of citizens to the White House for briefings by the president and others on current legislative issues."[134]

In addition to his occasional legislative achievements, Carter scored a personal diplomatic triumph with the September 17, 1978, signing of the Camp David Accords by Egyptian president Anwar Sadat and Israeli prime minister Menachem Begin. Frustrated with the difficulty of persuading Begin and Sadat to negotiate solutions to the conflicts that made their countries enemies, Carter boldly invited both leaders to the presidential retreat at Camp David. His unwavering determination to reach an agreement and keen mind for detail, which he displayed throughout the thirteen days of diplomacy between the two Middle Eastern leaders, were crucial in bringing about the first rapprochement between Israel and an Arab nation.[135] But, despite the accomplishments of his last three years in office, Carter never recovered fully from the confusion and ineptness of his early days as president. His poor start colored his relations with the press and public for the rest of his term.

In important respects, the Carter administration was a reckoning with the personal presidency. Much of his problem was that his outsider's approach to the office required the kind of effective popular leadership that would enable him to appeal to the people over the heads of legislators and lobbyists. Yet rousing the American people was not Carter's strong suit.[136] He was an effective campaigner in 1976, presenting himself to the voters as a moral, trustworthy leader and a competent manager at a time of widespread disillusionment with dishonesty and inefficiency in Washington. But, in addition to his modest speaking abilities, Carter lacked a unifying vision that would enable him to lead the nation in a particular direction. Having offered, during his first few months in office, a bewildering array of legislative proposals on energy, welfare, education, urban decay, and much more, Carter failed to provide any integrating themes that the public or his party could use to make sense of these measures. "I came to think," wrote his speechwriter James Fallows, "that Carter believes fifty things, but no one thing."[137]

The incoherence of Carter's early domestic program embodied the indecisive approach to politics and policy that permeated his entire presidency. Politically, Carter wanted to move the Democratic Party to the center so that it could compete more effectively in an era when New Deal and Great Society liberalism was losing support among the voters. He said often and earnestly that he intended to reduce government waste, run the bureaucracy efficiently, and balance the budget. In practice, however, Carter's approach to his party was usually aloof, occasionally accommodating, but seldom purposeful.

In matters of public policy, the White House staff embodied the president's desire to be fiercely independent and a scourge to traditional Democratic approaches. But when it came to the cabinet, most of his appointees were liberal Washington insiders, such as Joseph Califano (Health, Education and Welfare), Cyrus Vance (State), and Patricia Roberts Harris (Housing and Urban Development). Carter also appointed aggressive liberal advocates to many regulatory agencies, including Michael Pertschuk (Federal Trade Commission) and Joan Claybrook (National Highway Traffic Safety Administration). Not surprisingly, they proceeded to convert their strong commitment to social and economic regulation into government policy. Carter's appointments gave the collective impression that he was an irresolute leader who was eager to accommodate the loudest factions of his party.

Even when some of Carter's proposals were enacted, the public seldom believed he deserved the credit. Yet, perversely, during the latter part of Carter's presidency, when he was overcome by two setbacks that really were beyond his control, he was roundly blamed. One was the sharp increase in oil prices generated by the Organization of Petroleum Exporting Countries (OPEC), which led to spiraling inflation and interest rates and severe shortages at the gas pump. The other was the seizure by Iranian revolutionaries of more than fifty American diplomats as hostages. Any president, no matter how gifted, would have had trouble dealing with these problems. But Carter's style of leadership brought down on him the full brunt of adversity. His tendency to personalize problems of state was especially damaging during the hostage crisis, which lasted 444 days, from November 4, 1979, until the final day of his presidency, January 20, 1981, when the hostages were at last released. "As the problem failed to go away," Hargrove has noted, "Carter became a prisoner in the White House, and the initial public favor that he had received by personalizing the issue turned sour."[138]

Jimmy Carter brought together Egyptian president Anwar Sadat and Israeli prime minister Menachem Begin at Camp David in September 1978. Their signing of the Camp David Accords was a historic moment in the arduous process of bringing peace to the Middle East.

Source: Bill Fitz-Patrick—The White House.

The consuming crises of Carter's presidency did not prevent him from fending off a serious challenge from Massachusetts senator Edward M. Kennedy for the 1980 Democratic nomination. Indeed, during the crucial early primaries of January and February, Carter benefited from the surge in popularity that any president receives at the onset of a foreign policy crisis. But Carter entered the fall campaign burdened, as Ford was in 1976, by a divided party as well as by a public image as a weak and indecisive leader that only grew as the hostage crisis dragged on inconclusively. He was trounced by Ronald Reagan in the general election, the first time that a president had been defeated for reelection since Herbert Hoover lost to Franklin Roosevelt in 1932.

Notes

1. Richard E. Neustadt, *Presidential Power and the Modern Presidents: The Politics of Leadership from Roosevelt to Reagan*, 4th ed. (New York: Free Press, 1990), 8. For an appreciative assessment of *Presidential Power*, see Michael Nelson, "Neustadt's 'Presidential Power' at 50," *Chronicle of Higher Education*, April 2, 2010, B6–8.

2. Neustadt, *Presidential Power*, 8.

3. Ibid., 9.

4. Fred I. Greenstein, "Nine Presidents in Search of a Modern Presidency," in *Leadership in the Modern Presidency*, ed. Fred I. Greenstein (Cambridge: Harvard University Press, 1988), 314.

5. For an excellent account of the 1960 election, see W. J. Rorabaugh, *The Real Making of the President: Kennedy, Nixon, and the 1960 Election* (Lawrence: University Press of Kansas, 2009). Rorabaugh's book challenges and supplants the original classic work, Theodore H. White, *The Making of the President 1960* (New York: Viking, 1961). Kennedy's hard-won, razor-thin victory, Rorabaugh argues, was attributable less to his legendary charisma and New Frontier idealism, emphasized by White, than to his massive campaign treasury, effective campaign organization, and television image making, all of which were especially important at a time when candidate-centered politics was transforming the electoral process.

6. John Eisenhower, the president's son and deputy chief of staff, reported that Eisenhower would have run again. Michael R. Beschloss, *Mayday: Eisenhower, Khrushchev, and the U-2 Affair* (New York: Harper and Row, 1986), 3.

7. John F. Kennedy, speech to the National Press Club, Washington, D.C., January 14, 1960, in *"Let the Word Go Forth": The Speeches, Statements and Writings of John F. Kennedy*, ed. Theodore C. Sorensen (New York: Delacorte, 1988), 17–23.

8. Jacqueline Kennedy planted in the public mind the Camelot mythology that has grown up around her husband's legend. Summoning the highly regarded journalist Theodore White to Hyannis Port a few days after JFK's funeral, the grieving widow said that she did not want her husband's enemies to shape the history of his short administration. Instead, she did some shaping of her own, relating how she and the president had enjoyed listening to the music from the popular Broadway show *Camelot* in the evenings before they went to sleep. Jack's favorite line, she told White, defined his tragic presidency: "Don't let it be forgot, that once there was a spot, for one brief shining moment that was known as Camelot." Barbara A. Perry, "John Fitzgerald Kennedy," in *The American Presidents*, ed. Melvin I. Urofsky (New York: Garland, 2000), 395.

9. William E. Leuchtenburg, *In the Shadow of FDR: From Harry Truman to Ronald Reagan*, rev. ed. (Ithaca: Cornell University Press, 1985), 119. See also Michael Nelson, "Kennedy and Achilles: A Classical Approach to Political Science," *PS: Political Science and Politics* 29 (September 1996): 505–510.

10. "CNN Poll: JFK Tops Presidential Ranking for Last 50 Years," November 22, 2013. http://politicalticker.blogs.cnn.com/2013/11/22/cnn-poll-jfk-tops-presidential-rankings-for-last-50-years/.

11. Carl M. Brauer, "John F. Kennedy: The Endurance of Inspirational Leadership," in Greenstein, *Leadership in the Modern Presidency,* 109.

12. John F. Kennedy, "Acceptance of Presidential Nomination," Democratic National Convention, Los Angeles, California, July 15, 1960, in Sorensen, *"Let the Word Go Forth,"* 101.

13. "John F. Kennedy's Inaugural Address," in *The Evolving Presidency:* Landmark *Documents, 1787–2010,* 4th ed., ed. Michael Nelson (Washington, D.C.: CQ Press, 2012), 187–191. See also James N. Giglio, *The Presidency of John F. Kennedy* (Lawrence: University Press of Kansas, 1991), 2728.

14. For a more complete discussion of the Kennedy myth in popular culture, see Nelson, "Kennedy and Achilles."

15. Brauer, "John F. Kennedy," 119.

16. Bruce Miroff, "The Presidency and the Public: Leadership as Spectacle," in *The Presidency and the Political System*, 5th ed., ed. Michael Nelson (Washington, D.C.: CQ Press, 1998), 305.

17. Giglio, *Presidency of John F. Kennedy*, 261.

18. Kennedy's preparation for press conferences involved his press secretary, Pierre Salinger, and cabinet members, who anticipated the questions that reporters would ask, gathered background information, and prepped the president in briefing sessions. Salinger occasionally prompted friendly reporters to ask certain questions, hinting that the president would have something important to say in response. On Kennedy's relationship with the press, see ibid., 255–275.

19. Brauer, "John F. Kennedy," 118.

20. Theodore J. Lowi, *The Personal President: Power Invested, Promise Unfulfilled* (Ithaca: Cornell University Press, 1985).

21. Ibid., 75–76; Harold F. Bass, "The President and the National Party Organization," in *Presidents and Their Parties: Leadership or Neglect?* ed. Robert Harmel (New York: Praeger, 1984), 62; David Broder, *The Party's Over: The Failure of Politics in America* (New York: Harper and Row, 1972), 18–26.

22. Greenstein, "Nine Presidents," 325–326.

23. Quoted in Brauer, "John F. Kennedy," 131.

24. Matthew Crenson and Benjamin Ginsberg, *Presidential Power: Unchecked and Unbalanced* (New York: Norton, 2007), 188.

25. Nicholas F. Jacobs and James D. Savage, "Kennedy's Keynesian Budget Politics and the 1962 Public Works Acceleration Act," *Journal of Policy History*, 30, no. 3 (July 2018): 522–551.

26. Kennedy 1962 (emphasis added).

27. Lewis L. Gould, *The Modern American Presidency* (Lawrence: University Press of Kansas, 2003), 133.

28. Desmond Ball, *Politics and Force Levels: The Strategic Missile Program of the Kennedy Administration* (Berkeley: University of California Press, 1980), esp. chap. 11.

29. Arthur M. Schlesinger Jr., *The Cycles of American History* (Boston: Houghton Mifflin, 1986), 414.

30. Brauer, "John F. Kennedy," 132. Recent findings, based on tapes of the president's meetings with the Executive Committee of the National Security Council (ExComm), the group he convened to manage the Cuban missile crisis, support the proposition that this was Kennedy's finest hour. See Ernest R. May and Philip D. Zelikow, eds., *The Kennedy Tapes:*

Inside the White House during the Cuban Missile Crisis (Cambridge: Harvard University Press, 1997), 663–701.

31. *Public Papers of the Presidents of the United States: John F. Kennedy, 1963* (Washington, D.C.: Government Printing Office, 1964), 462.

32. Theodore H. White, *In Search of History: A Personal Adventure* (New York: Harper and Row, 1978), 518.

33. On Kennedy's New Frontier program, see Giglio, *Presidency of John F. Kennedy*, 97–121.

34. Broder, *Party's Over*, 31; James L. Sundquist, *The Decline and Resurgence of Congress* (Washington, D.C.: Brookings, 1981), 373–374.

35. John F. Kennedy, Address on Civil Rights, June 11, 1963, http://millercenter.org/president/kennedy/speeches/speech-3375; and Michael Nelson, "Triumph and Tragedy," *Claremont Review of Books*, 14 (Summer 2014): 81–87.

36. Reston, "What Was Killed," 126.

37. Crenson and Ginsberg, *Presidential Power*, 189–190.

38. Robert A. Caro, *Master of the Senate: The Years of Lyndon Johnson* (New York: Random House, 2002); Rowland Evans and Robert Novak, *Lyndon B. Johnson: The Exercise of Power* (New York: New American Library, 1966).

39. Lyndon Baines Johnson, *The Vantage Point: Perspectives on the Presidency, 1963–1969* (New York: Holt, Rinehart, and Winston, 1971), 18.

40. William E. Leuchtenburg, *The White House Looks South: Franklin D. Roosevelt, Harry S. Truman, and Lyndon B. Johnson* (Baton Rouge: Louisiana State University Press, 2005), 297.

41. Jeffrey K. Tulis, *The Rhetorical Presidency* (Princeton: Princeton University Press, 1987), 162.

42. Leuchtenburg, *In the Shadow of FDR*, 142.

43. Telephone conversation between Lyndon Johnson and Ted Sorensen, June 3, 1963, *George Reedy Office Files*, Johnson Library.

44. Lyndon Johnson, "Remarks at a Breakfast of the Georgia Legislature," in *Public Papers of the Presidents: Lyndon B. Johnson, 1963–1964* (Washington, D.C.: Government Printing Office) I: 645–651.

45. Martin Luther King, *The Autobiography of Martin Luther King, Jr. and the Laws that Changed America* (New York: Warner Books, 1998), 242–243.

46. At Dirksen's insistence, the EEOC, which was charged in the administration's bill with preventing racial and sexual discriminatory practices in employment, was stripped of its authority to file suit in the courts. The commission had the power to recommend litigation, but only the Justice Department had the power to initiate a suit. The Justice Department, in turn, could file suits only under conditions in which obvious discriminatory practices, notably Jim Crow laws in the South, prevailed. On Dirksen's relationship with Johnson and the role that the Republican Senate leader played in enacting civil rights legislation, see Byron C. Hulsey, *Everett C. Dirksen and His Presidents: How a Senate Giant Shaped American Politics* (Lawrence: University Press of Kansas, 2000), 183–204.

47. LBJ describes the legislative maneuvering that led to the enactment of the 1964 civil rights bill in his memoirs; see Johnson, *Vantage Point*, 159–160.

48. R. Shep Melnick, "The Courts, Congress, and Programmatic Rights," in *Remaking American Politics*, eds. Richard A. Harris and Sidney M. Milkis (Boulder: Westview Press, 1989), 192–195. In 1954 in *Brown v. Board of Education of Topeka*, the Supreme Court had declared segregated public schools to be unconstitutional.

49. James MacGregor Burns, "Confessions of a Kennedy Man," in *To Heal and to Build: The Programs of President Lyndon B. Johnson*, ed. James MacGregor Burns (New York: McGraw Hill, 1968), 417.

50. Johnson, *Vantage Point*, 160.

51. "Lyndon B. Johnson's Great Society Speech," in Nelson, *Evolving Presidency*, 199–203.

52. Theodore White, *America in Search of Itself: The Making of the President, 1956–1980* (New York: Harper and Row, 1982), 124.

53. The forced compromise included three key parts: seating the regular Mississippi delegation if its members signed a pledge to support the presidential ticket; the symbolic gesture of making Mississippi Freedom Democratic Party (MFDP) delegates honored guests at the convention, with two of its members seated as special delegates at large; and a prohibition of racial discrimination in delegate selection at the 1968 convention. For a full discussion of the fraught Democratic Convention, see Sidney Milkis and Daniel Tichenor, *Rivalry and Reform: Presidents, Social Movements, and the Transformation of American Politics* (Chicago: University of Chicago Press, 2018), chap. 4.

54. Lyndon Johnson, "Special Message to Congress, The American Promise," March 15, 1965, http://millercenter.org/president/lbjohnson/speeches/speech-3386.

55. "LBJ Puts U.S. Might Behind Voting Rights," *Chicago Daily Defender*, "March 17, 1965.

56. William E. Leuchtenburg, "The Genesis of the Great Society," *Reporter*, April 21, 1966, 38.

57. Greenstein, "Nine Presidents," 329. See also Michael Nelson, "Domestic Policy, Domestic Policy Advisers, and the American Presidency," in *Governing at Home: The White House and Domestic Policy Making*, eds. Michael Nelson and Russell L. Riley (Lawrence: University Press of Kansas, 2011), 1–23.

58. David Broder, "Consensus Politics: End of an Experiment," *Atlantic Monthly*, October 1966, 62.

59. Sidney M. Milkis, interview with Harry MacPherson, July 30, 1985.

60. *CBS Cronkite Interview with Lyndon Johnson*, no. 1, December 27, 1969, "Why I Chose Not to Run," 5, Lyndon Baines Johnson Library, Austin, Texas.

61. Tulis, *Rhetorical Presidency*, 172.

62. Fredrik Logevall, *Choosing War: The Last Chance for Peace and the Escalation of War in Vietnam* (Berkeley: University of California Press, 2001).

63. Richard M. Pious, *The American Presidency* (New York: Basic Books, 1979), 399.

64. "Lyndon B. Johnson's Gulf of Tonkin Message," in Nelson, *Evolving Presidency*, 203–207.

65. Senate Foreign Relations Committee, "National Commitments," Senate Report 797, 90th Cong., 1st sess., 1967, 19–22.

66. Quoted in ibid., 21–22.

67. The right of the vice president to succeed to the office, not just assume the powers, of the presidency also is treated in the amendment. In 1841 John Tyler had asserted the vice president's right to full succession when he succeeded William Henry Harrison, which set the precedent for future successions. Section 1 of the Twenty-Fifth Amendment simply wrote this precedent into the Constitution: "In case of the removal of the President from office or of his death or resignation, the Vice President shall become President."

68. Garfield lay dying for eighty days after he was shot in 1881. His cabinet met to discuss the situation but concluded that if Vice President Chester A. Arthur were to invoke paragraph 6, he would legally become president, thus barring Garfield from resuming the office should he recover. Woodrow Wilson's cabinet and many members of Congress were more disposed to transfer power temporarily to Vice President Thomas R. Marshall during Wilson's long disability in 1919 and 1920, but the Constitution's lack of guidance stayed their hands. When Secretary of State Robert Lansing raised the possibility with Joseph Tumulty, Wilson's secretary, Tumulty replied, "You may rest assured that while Woodrow Wilson is lying in the White House on the broad of his back I will not be a party to ousting him." Marshall confided to his secretary, "I am not going to seize the place and then have Wilson—

recovered—come around and say, 'Get off, you usurper." John D. Feerick, *The Twenty-Fifth Amendment* (New York: Fordham University Press, 1976), 9; Irving G. Williams, *The Rise of the Vice Presidency* (Washington, D.C.: Public Affairs Press, 1956), 112–114. Although Garfield's and Wilson's disabilities were unusual for their length, nearly one in three presidents has been disabled for at least a brief period of his term. In addition to Garfield and Wilson, James Madison, William Henry Harrison, Chester A. Arthur, Grover Cleveland, William McKinley, Warren G. Harding, Franklin D. Roosevelt, Dwight D. Eisenhower, John F. Kennedy, and Ronald Reagan were temporarily disabled. Feerick, *Twenty-Fifth Amendment*, chap. 1. Historian Robert Dallek argues that the problem of presidential fitness is so serious that the provisions of the Twenty-Fifth Amendment provide inadequate protection against it. He proposes that a panel of independent experts be established to advise the public on whether a candidate is healthy enough to serve as president. If the public does not follow the panel's lead, but the experts prove to be more foresighted than the public, the people should be able to remove a president. Dallek prescribes a constitutional amendment allowing voters to remove a president in a referendum. Robert Dallek, "Presidential Fitness and Presidential Lies: The Historical Record and a Proposal for Reform," *Presidential Studies Quarterly*, 40, no. 1 (March 2010), 14: 9–22.

69. The seven vice presidents who died in office were George Clinton, Elbridge Gerry, William R. King, Henry Wilson, Thomas A. Hendricks, Garret A. Hobart, and James S. Sherman. The eight presidents who died in office were William Henry Harrison, Zachary Taylor, Abraham Lincoln, James A. Garfield, William L. McKinley, Warren G. Harding, Franklin D. Roosevelt, and John F. Kennedy. The vice president who resigned was John C. Calhoun.

70. George E. Reedy, *The Twilight of the Presidency* (New York: New American Library, 1970), xv.

71. Greenstein, "Nine Presidents," 330.

72. See Michael Nelson, *Resilient America: Electing Nixon in 1968, Channeling Dissent, and Dividing Government* (Lawrence: University Press of Kansas, 2014).

73. "The McGovern-Fraser Commission Report," in Nelson, *Evolving Presidency*, 210–216.

74. Paul Van Riper, *History of the United States Civil Service* (Evanston, Ill.: Row, Peterson, 1958), 327.

75. Richard Nixon, *RN: The Memoirs of Richard Nixon* (New York: Grosset and Dunlap, 1978), 352.

76. Quoted in Richard P. Nathan, *The Administrative Presidency* (New York: Wiley, 1983), 30.

77. Stewart Alsop, "Mystery of Richard Nixon," *Saturday Evening Post*, July 12, 1958, 28.

78. Joan Hoff-Wilson, "Richard M. Nixon: The Corporate Presidency," in Greenstein, *Leadership in the Modern Presidency*, 165.

79. Michael Nelson, "The President as Potentate," *American Prospect*, November 5, 2001, 42–46.

80. Kenneth R. Mayer, *With the Stroke of a Pen: Executive Orders and Presidential Power* (Princeton: Princeton University Press, 2001), 204.

81. Nathan, *Administrative Presidency*, 27.

82. "Annual Message to Congress on the State of the Union," January 22, 1971, *Public Papers of the Presidents of the United States: Richard Nixon, 1971* (Washington, D.C.: Government Printing Office, 1972), 53. See also A. James Reichley, *Conservatives in an Age of Change: The Nixon and Ford Administrations* (Washington, D.C.: Brookings, 1985), 257–259.

83. Garment quoted in Reichley, *Conservatives in an Age of Change*, 259. Nixon quoted in Hoff-Wilson, "Richard M. Nixon," 177.

84. Quoted in George C. Herring, *America's Longest War: The United States and Vietnam* (New York: Wiley, 1979), 219.

85. Larry Berman, *No Peace, No Honor: Nixon, Kissinger, and Betrayal in Vietnam* (New York: Free Press, 2001).

86. Henry A. Kissinger, "The Viet Nam Negotiations," *Foreign Affairs* 47 (January 1969): 234. For a dissenting view on the need to secure "peace with honor" lest the international standing of the United States be diminished, see Robert Dallek, *Nixon and Kissinger: Partners in Power* (New York: HarperCollins, 2007).

87. Address to the Nation on the War in Vietnam, November 3, 1969, http://www.presidency.ucsb.edu/ws/?pid=2303.

88. Hoff-Wilson, "Richard M. Nixon," 165.

89. Nathan, *Administrative Presidency*, 45 (emphasis in original).

90. Greenstein, "Nine Presidents," 332; "Richard Nixon's China Trip Announcement," in Nelson, *Evolving Presidency*, 207–210. For a balanced account of Nixon's "administrative presidency," see Nathan, *Administrative Presidency*, 43–56; on Kissinger's NSC, see John D. Leecacos, "Kissinger's Apparat," *Foreign Policy*, 5 (Winter 1971–1972): 3–27; on the China trip, see Margaret Macmillan, *Nixon and Mao: The Week that Changed the World* (New York: Random House, 2007).

91. Eisenhower quoted in Stephen E. Ambrose, *Eisenhower: The President* (New York: Simon and Schuster, 1984), 673.

92. Arthur M. Schlesinger Jr., *The Imperial Presidency* (New York: Popular Library, 1973), 10.

93. Richard J. Ellis, *The Development of the American Presidency* (New York: Routledge, 2012), 288.

94. Weinberger cited in Andrew Rudalevige, *The New Imperial Presidency* (Ann Arbor: University of Michigan Press, 2005), 89 (emphasis in original).

95. Berman, *New American Presidency*, 263.

96. Humphrey cited in Rudalevige, *New Imperial Presidency*, 90.

97. Greenstein, "Nine Presidents," 334; Stephen E. Ambrose, *Nixon: Ruin and Recovery, 1973–1990*, 3 (New York: Simon and Schuster, 1991), 59–80.

98. This section draws on the insights of Reichley, *Conservatives in an Age of Change*, 250–261.

99. Ibid., 250.

100. Ibid., 259.

101. *United States v. Nixon*, 418 U.S. 683 (1974), at 707, 712.

102. Id. at 708.

103. Id. at 713.

104. Recently released tape recordings suggest that one of the motivations for the cover-up may have been to prevent exposure of the so-called Chennault Affair. Concerned that President Lyndon Johnson's plans to halt the bombing of North Vietnam in an effort to revive peace negotiations during the later stages of the 1968 campaign was a ploy to assist his opponent Vice President Hubert H. Humphrey, who trailed in the polls, Nixon's law partner (and later attorney general) John N. Mitchell spoke to Anna Chennault, a Chinese-born Republican activist, about using her contacts in South Vietnam to stall peace negotiations. She in turn spoke to Bui Diem, South Vietnam's ambassador to the United States, urging him to persuade South Vietnamese president Nguyen Van Thieu to reject LBJ's initiative, promising a better deal once Nixon was elected. This action may have violated the Logan Act, which bars private citizens from freelancing in foreign policy. See Ken Hughes, *Chasing Shadows: The Nixon Tapes, the Chennault Affair and the Origins of Watergate* (Charlottesville: University of Virginia Press, 2014).

105. William M. Goldsmith, ed., *The Growth of Presidential Power: A Documented History*, 3 vols. (New York: Chelsea, 1974), 3: 2274; Pious, *American Presidency*, 75–78. See also "The 'Smoking Gun' Watergate Tapes," in *The Evolving Presidency: Addresses, Cases,*

Essays, Letters, Reports, Resolutions, Transcripts, and Other Landmark Documents, 1787–2004, 2nd ed., ed. Michael Nelson (Washington, D.C.: CQ Press, 2004), 201–207.

106. Richard M. Nixon, "Resignation Address," August 8, 1974, in Goldsmith, *Growth of Presidential Power*, 3: 2275.

107. Alonzo L. Hamby, *Liberalism and Its Challengers: From FDR to Bush*, 2nd ed. (New York: Oxford University Press, 1992), 338.

108. These surveys are discussed in James MacGregor Burns, J. W. Peltason, and Thomas Cronin, *Government by the People*, 11th ed. (Englewood Cliffs, N.J.: Prentice Hall, 1981), 359.

109. Greenstein, "Nine Presidents," 335.

110. "The War Powers Resolution," in Nelson, *Evolving Presidency*, 4th ed., 216–222.

111. R. Shep Melnick, "The Politics of Partnership," *Public Administration Review* 45 (November 1985): 655.

112. Jules Witcover, *Very Strange Bedfellows: The Short and Unhappy Marriage of Richard Nixon and Spiro Agnew* (New York: Public Affairs, 2007).

113. In the absence of the Twenty-Fifth Amendment, Agnew's resignation would have left Carl W. Albert, the Democratic Speaker of the House, next in the line of succession, immensely complicating the Nixon removal process.

114. Kissinger quoted in Roger Porter, "Gerald Ford: A Healing Presidency," in Greenstein, *Leadership in the Modern Presidency*, 199.

115. These changes are discussed in ibid., 206–213.

116. Ibid., 208.

117. Berman, *New American Presidency*, 293–294.

118. "Gerald Ford's Pardon of Richard Nixon," in Nelson, *Evolving Presidency*, 4th ed., 234–238.

119. Porter, "Gerald Ford," 208–209.

120. Michael Nelson, ed., *Congressional Quarterly's Guide to the Presidency*, 2nd ed. (Washington, D.C.: Congressional Quarterly, 1996), 2: 1757.

121. "Inaugural Address of President Jimmy Carter," January 20, 1977, *Public Papers of the Presidents of the United States: Jimmy Carter, 1977* (Washington, D.C.: Government Printing Office, 1977), 1: 1.

122. James Bryce, *The American Commonwealth*, 2 vols. (London: Macmillan, 1891), 1: 221.

123. Ford quoted in Philip Shabecoff, "Presidency Is Found Weaker under Ford," *New York Times*, March 28, 1976, 1.

124. For a lively account of the nominating contest and surrounding event, see Rick Perlstein, *The Invisible Bridge: The Fall of Nixon and the Rise of Reagan* (New York: Simon and Schuster, 2014).

125. Gerald R. Ford, *A Time to Heal* (New York: Harper and Row, 1979), 378.

126. Greenstein, "Nine Presidents," 340.

127. Tip O'Neill, with William Novak, *Man of the House* (New York: St. Martin's Press, 1987), 376.

128. Jimmy Carter, *Keeping Faith: Memoirs of a President* (New York: Bantam Books, 1982), 27.

129. Ibid., 80.

130. Berman, *New American Presidency*, 315.

131. Greenstein, "Nine Presidents," 339.

132. O'Neill, *Man of the House,* 369. See also John A. Farrell, *Tip O'Neill and the Democratic Century* (Boston: Little, Brown, 2001).

133. John P. Burke, "The Institutional Presidency," in Nelson, *Presidency and the Political System*, 419.

134. Erwin C. Hargrove, "Jimmy Carter: The Politics of Public Goods," in Greenstein, *Leadership in the Modern Presidency*, 251.

135. William B. Quandt, *Camp David: Peacemaking and Politics* (Washington, D.C.: Brookings, 1986); and Lawrence Wright, *Thirteen Days in September: Carter, Begin, and Sadat at Camp David* (New York: Alfred A. Knopf, 2014)

136. Hargrove, "Jimmy Carter," 233.

137. James Fallows, "The Passionless Presidency," *Atlantic Monthly*, May 1979, 42.

138. Hargrove, "Jimmy Carter," 254.

CHAPTER 12

A Restoration of Presidential Power?

Ronald Reagan and George Bush

In 1980 Richard E. Neustadt wrote, "Watching President Carter in early 1979 sparked the question, is the Presidency possible?"[1] It seemed during the final days of the Carter administration that the presidency no longer worked, that presidents had become frustrated beyond the possibility of success by a weakened party system, hostile news media, a congeries of powerful special interest groups, an intransigent bureaucracy, an aggressive Congress, assertive courts, and a demoralized public. The "personal presidency," which began with John F. Kennedy's "Camelot," now seemed trapped in a political time warp marked by clamorous demands and deep distrust of authority. Of the five presidents who held office from 1961 to 1980, none completed two terms.

"Among the consequences of [Ronald] Reagan's election to the presidency," Jeffrey K. Tulis wrote in 1987, "was the rewriting of textbooks on American government." No longer could one claim that fragmented and demoralized political conditions inevitably "would frustrate the efforts of any president to accomplish substantial policy objectives, to maintain popularity, and to avoid blame for activities beyond his control."[2] In contrast to Gerald R. Ford and Jimmy Carter, Reagan successfully advanced an ambitious legislative program in 1981 and 1982. He was renominated by his party without opposition and reelected handily in 1984. From the beginning of his first term until the damaging revelations of the Iran–Contra affair in 1986, Reagan and his associates convinced most Americans that a strong, effective, popular leader had restored the presidency to preeminence in the political system. Rebounding from Iran–Contra, he retired from the presidency as the most popular president since John F. Kennedy. Indeed, many pundits and scholars viewed Reagan as the "Roosevelt of the Right." His two terms advanced a conservative movement that renewed partisan conflict, albeit in a more national and programmatic form than the traditional party politics that dominated the nineteenth century, and posed the first fundamental challenge to the national state that arose from the New Deal and Great Society.

The Reagan Revolution

Reagan's political success prompted considerable speculation that the 1980 election, like the election of 1932, launched a partisan realignment in American politics. Although the New Deal Democratic coalition had been unraveling since the 1960s, Reagan was the first president since William McKinley in 1896 to envision an enduring conservative Republican majority. Richard Nixon, Ford, and Carter were relatively conservative presidents, and each of them challenged certain policies of the New Deal and the Great Society. But they generally accommodated themselves to liberalism, seeking mainly to curb its excesses and administer its programs more economically. Reagan, in contrast, had been outspoken in his conservatism for many years, prompting some pundits to dub his landslide victory in 1980 the "Reagan Revolution."[3]

In truth, Reagan's victory was somewhat ambiguous. In the three-way race with Carter and a former Republican running as an independent, Rep. John Anderson of Illinois, Reagan won by a landslide in the Electoral College, sweeping forty-four states with 489 electoral votes. Yet his 51 percent of the popular vote was only a three-percentage-point increase over Ford's tally as the Republican nominee in 1976. The results of the congressional elections were more impressive. For the first time since 1952, the Republicans won a majority in the Senate, where several prominent liberal Democrats were defeated. The ranks of House Republicans rose by thirty-three seats, although the Democrats retained their majority in the lower chamber.

Reagan's ability to transform his and his party's electoral victory into concrete legislative achievements testified in part to his considerable rhetorical gifts. Critics dismissed his ability to communicate effectively as a former actor's trick of the trade—the talent to learn and deliver his lines on camera. But Reagan's supporters maintained that there was logic and substance to his message. In their view he was not the "Great Communicator" but the "Great Rhetorician" who, like Woodrow Wilson, the two Roosevelts, and Kennedy before him, articulated a vision that inspired the nation.[4]

Reagan's message as candidate and as president was but a variation on the theme that he had been enunciating ever since he gave a nationally televised address on behalf of the Republican Party on October 27, 1964. "The Speech," as conservative admirers called it, had a single theme: centrally administered government weakens a free people. A strong national state had so perverted the concept of liberty in the United States, Reagan argued, that "natural unalienable rights" had come to be regarded as a "dispensation of government," stripping the people of their self-reliance and capacity for self-rule. "The real destroyer of the liberties of the people," Reagan warned, "is he who spreads among them bounties, donations, and benefits."[5] Seventeen years later, in his inaugural address—the first by a president in more than fifty years to appeal for limited government—Reagan sounded the same theme:

> In this present crisis, government is not the solution to our problem; government is the problem. From time to time we've been tempted to believe that society has become too complex to be managed by self-rule, that government by an elite group is superior to government for, by, and of the people. Well, if no one among us is capable of governing himself, then who among us has the capacity to govern someone else? All of us together—in and out of government—must bear the burden.[6]

Reagan's rhetoric challenged the fundamental principles of the New Deal. Its most important quality, political scientist Hugh Heclo argued, was not that Reagan "said anything fundamentally new" but rather that in the political context created by the New Deal and Great Society, "Reagan continued to uphold something old."[7] Yet Reagan issued his challenge to the welfare state in terms that paid homage to Franklin Roosevelt. Indeed, Reagan made an extraordinary effort to associate himself with the New Deal president. In 1980 he referred to FDR so frequently in his acceptance speech to the Republican National Convention that the *New York Times* titled its lead editorial the next day "Franklin Delano Reagan."[8]

Quoting Roosevelt did not mean that Reagan had "moved toward the center," as the *Times* editorial claimed. Instead, William E. Leuchtenburg has observed, Reagan "exploited Roosevelt for conservative ends." He concluded his speech by calling on the delegates to fulfill the promise that FDR made in his own acceptance speech to the Democratic convention in July 1932: "to eliminate unnecessary functions of government." Reagan's invocation of Roosevelt, then, was designed in part to dramatize the failures and false promises of the New Deal and to highlight what Reagan had been proclaiming for two decades: government had become too big and too remote from the people.[9]

But Reagan's identification with Roosevelt also reflected his desire to lead as FDR had led, fully exploiting the powers of the modern presidency to move the United States toward a new "rendezvous with destiny." Nixon had seen the possibility of using his office to guide the country away from the New Deal but not as clearly as Reagan saw it. As for public policy, Reagan's agenda was less reminiscent of Nixon than of an earlier defender of limited government—Calvin Coolidge. Reagan's public addresses, like Coolidge's, conveyed the president's commitment to limited government in moral terms, as a righteous cause that served humankind at home and abroad.[10]

In truth, Reagan did not envision a return to Coolidge-era limited government. He stood for a religiously inspired, if not messianic, foreign policy that would restore the ideal—diminished amid the recriminations of the 1960s—of America as a "City on a Hill," an example to the entire world. Significantly, Reagan's inclination to state his governing philosophy in exalted language shone forth most clearly in his March 8, 1983, speech to the National Association of Evangelicals, a gathering of Christian conservatives. After expressing disdain for the Soviet Union's "evil empire" as another "sad, bizarre, chapter in human history," Reagan concluded,

> I believe . . . the source of our strength in the quest for human freedom is not material, but spiritual. And because it knows no limitation, it must terrify and ultimately triumph over those who would enslave their fellow man. For in the words of Isaiah: "He giveth power to the faint; and to them that have no might He increased strength. . . . But they that wait upon the Lord shall renew their strength; they shall mount up with wings as eagles; they shall run, and not be weary. . . ."
>
> Yes, change your world. One of our Founding Fathers, Thomas Paine, said, "We have it within our power to begin the world over again." We can do it, doing together what no one church could do by itself.[11]

Reagan's privately stated approach to the Cold War with the Soviet Union was simple: "We win. They lose."[12] Diplomatic historian John Lewis Gaddis has argued that far from being naïve, Reagan "could see beyond complexity to simplicity." According to Gaddis, although "theorists of international relations insisted that . . . Soviet-American bipolarity would last as far into the future as anyone could see," Reagan saw something different: an economically backward Soviet Union that would topple if pushed. He dramatically accelerated the arms race, straining the Soviet economy to the breaking point, and then delivered the coup de grâce by vowing to develop the Strategic Defense Initiative, his dream of a high-tech anti-missile shield over the United States. "The reaction, in the Kremlin, approached panic" because the Soviets knew they lacked both the money and the computer technology to keep up.[13] Driven past their economic breaking point, the Soviet empire and then the Soviet Union itself dissolved shortly after Reagan left office.

Reagan's political opponents, who were far less optimistic about his policies than he was, found the president's rhetoric to be merely bright packaging on a harshly conservative public philosophy. But Reagan's words and the political vision they expressed stirred many

Although critics accused former actor Ronald Reagan of making insubstantial speeches that glossed over the issues, others called him the "Great Rhetorician," pointing to his ability to inspire the nation with his ideas.

Source: Pete Souza—The White House.

Americans' deeply rooted and widely shared political values. The religiosity of his message, the dignity of his public demeanor, even his limited faith in government, captivated the popular imagination.

Reagan and Congress

Drawing on his experience as the two-term governor of California, Reagan matched his rhetoric with skill as a legislative leader. Unlike the Carter administration, one scholar has observed, the Reagan administration "hit the ground running." Reagan's aides carefully studied Carter's errors and crafted a first-year strategy that would succeed in just those ways that Carter failed. In contrast to Carter's lengthy array of early and unrelated legislative proposals, Reagan concentrated on two themes: shrinking the welfare state and expanding the military.[14] His administration embodied these themes in the three bold proposals on which he had based his election campaign: a large income-tax cut, a significant reduction in domestic spending, and an enormous increase in spending on national defense.

Reagan's clear sense of direction was not his only point of contrast with Carter. Like Carter, another former governor, Reagan campaigned for president by running against the ills of Washington. But, once elected, Reagan recognized that it no longer made sense to continue attacking the Washington community. He lavished attention on members of Congress, frequently visiting Capitol Hill for meetings or telephoning members of the House and Senate on the eve of important votes. "We had to lasso him to keep him off the Hill," one close aide recalled about the president's first year.[15]

Reagan's personal relations with Congress were buttressed by a strong Executive Office of the President (EOP). In contrast to Carter, who had relied on the parochial veterans of his presidential campaign to organize and operate his staff, Reagan's White House Office and the Office of Management and Budget (the two main units of the EOP) included not just personal loyalists but also skilled veterans from earlier Republican administrations. Reagan's able and experienced staff compensated for the president's own lack of interest in the details of public policy. Even his political opponents were impressed. "All in all, the Reagan team in 1981 was probably the best run political operation unit I've ever seen," Speaker of the House Thomas P. "Tip" O'Neill, a Democrat, noted in his memoirs. "I didn't like their mean-spirited philosophy, but they knew where they were going and they knew how to get there."[16]

The president's enormous popular appeal, his willingness to lobby Congress for his programs, and the political skill of his staff enabled the Reagan administration to mount a legislative campaign in 1981 that rivaled the early breakthroughs of Woodrow Wilson's New Freedom, FDR's New Deal, and LBJ's Great Society. Reagan persuaded Congress to approve a dramatic departure in fiscal policy: more than $35 billion in domestic program reductions; a multiyear package of nearly $750 billion in tax cuts; and a three-year, 27 percent increase in defense spending. "In slightly more than six months," journalist Hedrick Smith wrote in 1982, Reagan "achieved more than political Washington had dreamed possible on the day of his inauguration."[17]

Reagan's first year as president seemed to restore the executive's pre-eminence as chief legislator. Both by courting members of Congress assiduously and by going over their heads to the people when necessary, Reagan worked his will on the legislative process, despite the Democratic majority in the House. In doing so, he actually turned the Congressional Budget and Impoundment Control Act, which Congress had enacted in 1974 to strengthen its own hand in fiscal policy making, on its head.

Reagan's OMB director, David Stockman, discovered a way that the administration could use one provision of the budget act—the "reconciliation" process, which Congress created to coordinate its budget-making activities more effectively—to bind the legislature to the president's program.

Reconciliation authorized the House and Senate budget committees to bring together every proposed change in the budget in a single bill. The House Appropriations Committee belatedly described in a 1982 report how this approach played into the hands of the president:

> It is much easier for the Executive Branch to gain support for its program when it is packaged in one bill rather than pursuing each and every authorization and appropriation measure to insure compliance with the Executive's program. This device tends to aid the Executive Branch in gaining additional control over budget matters and to circumvent the will of Congress.[18]

After a televised speech to Congress on April 28, 1981, made all the more dramatic by his rapid recovery from a would-be assassin's near-fatal gunshot on March 30, Reagan won a substantial legislative victory on a comprehensive budget resolution. The resolution incorporated every element of his economic policy: greater spending on defense, less spending on domestic programs, and a huge tax cut. The president's appearance on Capitol Hill produced what House Republican leader Robert Michel described as "the kind of reception that makes a few of the waverers feel, 'Gosh, how can I buck that?'"[19] Yet Reagan directed his speech beyond the mostly Democratic Congress to the television audience at home. The House majority leader, Jim Wright of Texas, was among those who lamented Reagan's budget victory as a dramatic setback in Congress's post-Watergate struggle to regain its independence. He complained bitterly that the administration was trying to "dictate every last scintilla, every last phrase" of legislation.[20] Even worse from Wright's standpoint, the president succeeded.

But Reagan's economic package suffered from some of the same defects as the Great Society. As Tulis has written, "Like Johnson's, this public policy was prepared hastily in the executive branch, and like the War on Poverty, the nation's legislature played no substantive role in planning the program."[21] The substantial tax cuts and large increases in defense spending exceeded by far the reductions in domestic spending. Conservatives such as New York representative Jack Kemp argued that the tax cut would not increase the budget deficit. They were persuaded by supply-side economists such as Arthur Laffer and Paul Craig Roberts that a large tax cut would stimulate productivity so much that rising tax revenues would balance the budget by 1984. Inflation would fall, the supply-siders maintained, along with interest rates. Private savings, in turn, would increase because investors' fears of inflation would be allayed.[22] Yet, as OMB director Stockman privately admitted at the time, "None of us really understand what's going on with all these numbers."[23] Some of the supply-siders' predictions came true: the economy eventually boomed, and with strong support from Federal Reserve Board chair Paul Volcker, inflation dropped steeply. Other predictions proved inaccurate. In particular, tax receipts did not grow enough to prevent the Reagan administration from running the largest annual budget deficits in history. The national debt grew from $1 trillion in 1981 to $3 trillion in 1989, when Reagan left office.

Yet the unintended consequences of Reagan's fiscal program did not affect the president's standing with the public. Even when he faced political adversity, as he did during the severe economic recession of 1982, Reagan remained confident, vowing to "stay the course." Unlike Johnson, he seldom agonized over his own or his office's legitimacy. As Fred Greenstein has written, "Several of the modern presidents bore their responsibilities like crosses. Others, including Reagan for most of his presidency, were able to maintain control of the national political agenda, in part by concrete accomplishments but also by exuding confidence and self-assurance."[24]

Reagan as Party Leader

Reagan's hopes that his principles would animate a national political realignment never flagged, even after the Democrats increased their House majority in the 1982 congressional elections. His own reelection in 1984, in which he won 59 percent of the popular vote and all but thirteen electoral votes, convinced the president that events were moving his way. In a speech to the National Conservative Political Action Conference in March 1985, Reagan claimed that the triumphs of 1980 and 1984 laid the foundation for a new conservative political orthodoxy that would endure well beyond his administration: "The tide of history is moving irresistibly in our direction. Why? Because the other side is virtually bankrupt of ideas. It has nothing more to say, nothing to add to the debate. It has spent its intellectual capital—such as it was—and it did its deeds."[25]

Reagan's efforts to inaugurate a new political era benefited from, and in turn helped galvanize, a renewal of party politics. The nearly century-long development of the modern presidency had helped foster a serious decline in the traditional, decentralized, patronage-based political parties. Yet during the late 1970s and 1980s, a new form of party politics began to emerge. The erosion of old-style partisan organizations allowed a more national and issues-oriented party system to take shape, forging new bonds between presidents and their parties.

The Republican Party, in particular, developed a strong institutional apparatus, which displayed unprecedented strength at the national level during the 1980s.[26] Because the reconstituted party system was associated less with political patronage than with issues, ideology, and sophisticated fund-raising techniques, it did not pose as much of an obstacle to the personal and programmatic ambitions of presidents as the traditional system had. Indeed, by 1984 the Republicans had become a solidly conservative party, made over in Reagan's image. In laying out his policy in Vietnam during his first year in office, Nixon appealed to a "silent majority" of Americans who felt shut out of the political agenda that the civil rights and anti-war movements had advanced. Reagan gave voice to these muted Americans with more principled and purposeful leadership than Nixon. He summoned a scattered but potentially powerful coalition composed of business interests; white Southerners, who continued the exodus from the Democratic Party that began with Harry Truman's commitment to civil rights; blue-collar workers from the North (the so-called Reagan Democrats), who also were deeply opposed to the anti-war movement and the extension of civil rights policies, especially new-style remedies such as affirmative action and busing; an emergent Christian Right that Reagan courted in the 1980 election with an appeal to "traditional values"; and "Neoconservatives," a foreign policy elite who scorned what they perceived as the Democrats' rejection of the idea that America has a special role to play in the world.

The South's political realignment from Democratic to Republican was the most important element in Reagan's reconstruction of American politics. Although Nixon and political aides like Patrick Buchanan conceived and began to implement a "Southern Strategy," it was Reagan who realized the potential of the GOP incursion into the South. Carter, a native son, interrupted the political transformation of his region in 1976, winning every southern state but Virginia, but Reagan's election with the support of every southern state but Carter's Georgia marked a crossing of the Rubicon. In the wake of the Reagan presidency, the South would become the territorial bulwark of a conservative Republican Party.

As Reagan became the patron saint of a revitalized Republican Party, the modern presidency was pulled into the vortex of partisan politics. Significantly, it was Reagan who broke with the practice of the modern presidency and identified closely with his party. The president worked hard to strengthen the Republicans' organizational and popular base, surprising his own White House political director with his "total readiness" to raise funds and make speeches for the party and its candidates.[27] Even after the 1984 election, in which the Reagan campaign generally went its own way, Sen. Robert J. Dole said, "Nixon thought he could build a conservative majority that was above party, and Ford tried to strengthen the traditional Republican Party. Reagan is trying to expand the Republican Party to include a majority."[28]

Although the renewal of partisanship risked political gridlock, Reagan's experience suggested that the relationship between modern presidents and the modern parties could be mutually beneficial in ameliorating the political isolation and institutional estrangement of the contemporary executive office. Republican support solidified Reagan's personal popularity and laid the political foundation for his program in Congress. In turn, the president served his fellow Republicans by strengthening their fund-raising efforts and encouraging voters to extend their loyalties not just to him but to his party. Surveys taken after the 1984 election revealed that the Republicans had attained virtual parity with the Democrats among voters for the first time since the 1940s.[29]

The 1980s marked a watershed of renewed and strengthened ties between presidents and the party system. Unwilling to fall permanently behind the Republicans, the Democrats also became a more centralized and programmatic party, with an ideological center that was decidedly liberal. The combined effect of the New Deal, the Great Society, and the conservative Republican response was to sharply reduce the presence of traditional southern Democrats in Congress. In the Seventy-Fifth Congress (1937–1939), which balked at Franklin Roosevelt's "Court-packing" plan, the thirteen southern states (the Old Confederacy plus Kentucky and Oklahoma) held 120 House seats, of which 117 were in Democratic hands. In the 100th Congress, near the end of the Reagan era, those same states had 124 seats in the House. But only 85 of them were Democratic. Nearly a third had migrated to the Republican side of the aisle. Meanwhile, the 1965 Voting Rights Act had substantially increased the number of African American voters in the South, transforming the behavior of southern Democrats in Congress in a liberal direction. "It was the sign of the times in 1983," journalist Alan Ehrenhalt wrote in 1987, "when Southern Democrats [in Congress] voted 78–12 in favor of the holiday honoring the Rev. Martin Luther King."[30]

Reagan and the Administrative Presidency

Despite the transformation of the party system, the Reagan Revolution was hardly the dawn of a new era of collective partisan responsibility. Reagan never converted his personal popularity into Republican control of Congress. In fact, the Reagan administration seldom presented its programs in strongly partisan terms that would give the voters a compelling reason to endorse a Republican realignment. Because Reagan's successful campaign in 1984 relied on fuzzy, feel-good themes such as "It's morning again in America" rather than on sharply defined issues that would clarify the voters' choice between Democratic and Republican views of the future, the Democrats had no trouble maintaining their strong majority in the House of Representatives. Two years later, they recaptured the Senate. The White House worked closely with the Republican National Committee and Republican candidates, but it avoided issuing a forthright partisan message. As Rep. Vin Weber, a Minnesota Republican, complained in 1986, "The focus was on . . . the same feel good empty rhetoric that dominated the 1984 race."[31]

The failure to bring about a Republican realignment circumscribed the achievements of the Reagan administration. Nevertheless, Reagan accomplished a great deal as president. Although his 1981 tax and budget victories did not dismantle the welfare state, they did set the stage for a significant reordering of priorities in Washington. The enormous budget deficits that the tax cuts and defense buildup created limited the Democratic Congress's ability to enact new spending programs. In fact, during Reagan's first six years as president, Congress did not create a single major program. In 1986 the Reagan-sponsored Tax Reform Act further reduced congressional hopes of raising more revenue by lowering income-tax rates and eliminating many of the exemptions, deductions, and preferences that traditionally made it politically possible to increase those rates.

The budget deficit and the overhaul of the tax system placed the Democratic Party in a serious bind. As former vice president Walter F. Mondale, the Democratic presidential nominee in 1984, lamented,

> Reagan has practiced the politics of subtraction. He knows the public wants to spend money on the old folks, protecting the environment and aiding education. And he's figured out the only way to stop it is to deny the revenues. No matter how powerful the argument the Democrats make for the use of government to serve some purpose, the answer must be no.[32]

Conservatives gleefully called this strategy "starving the beast."

Foreign Policy

The Reagan administration was more than willing to spend money on conservative objectives. Indeed, it oversaw the largest peacetime military buildup in history. The president also demonstrated that it was politically possible, despite the lingering trauma of Vietnam, to deploy troops abroad. In 1983, disregarding the War Powers Resolution, Reagan reasserted the president's powers as commander in chief by invading the Caribbean island of Grenada and deposing its communist government. In 1986 he ordered that Libya be bombed in retaliation for a terrorist attack in West Berlin that took the lives of two American soldiers. In both of these episodes, the duration of the military involvement was brief, casualties were few, and victory was assured. Consequently, public and congressional support for the president was high.

Still, Reagan suffered reversals on some important matters. After 1982 Congress refused to cut domestic spending any further. It also required the administration to slow the pace of its rearmament program and restricted the president's ability to aid the anti-Marxist contra rebels in Nicaragua.

In the face of mounting legislative opposition, the Reagan White House resorted to some of the same tactics of "institutional combat" against Congress that Nixon and his staff employed.[33] The renewal of such combat, however, was animated by a fervent anti-communism, which Nixon, Ford, and Henry Kissinger, in their pursuit of détente, had proscribed. To support the Nicaraguan contras, aides in the Reagan White House secretly built an alternative intelligence network within the staff of the National Security Council (NSC). This covert network conducted operations that Congress either had forbidden (such as continued military aid to the contras) or almost certainly would not have countenanced if Reagan had ever asked it to (such as the sale of weapons to Iran). Its efforts exposed the administration to severe political risks and, eventually, to a damaging scandal, the Iran–Contra affair. In November 1986 the nation learned that with Reagan's approval, the United States sold weapons to Iran and that, with or without the president's knowledge, some of the proceeds were used by Marine colonel Oliver North and other NSC staff members to assist the contras.

Public reaction to the Iran–Contra affair in November 1986 was swift and dramatic. Reagan's approval rating fell from 67 percent to 46 percent in one month. The Iranian arms sales, which apparently were undertaken to secure the release of seven Americans who were being held hostage by terrorists in Beirut, Lebanon, were not illegal. But they ran directly counter to the administration's hard-line antiterrorism policies. The diversion of funds to the Nicaraguan rebels clearly violated the Boland Amendment, a 1985 congressional ban on aid to the contras.

Responding to strong political pressure from Congress, the news media, and the American people, the president appointed former Texas

Republican senator John Tower to chair a bipartisan review board. The Tower Commission roundly criticized Reagan's management style in its 1987 report, even suggesting that the president was blithely out of touch with his own administration, a figurehead who reigned while his staff ruled. But the Iran–Contra affair was not simply a matter of the president being asleep on his watch. It also revealed the Reagan administration's determination to carry out its foreign policy without interference from Congress or anyone else.

Although the president may not have known about the diversion of funds to the contras, the news should not have surprised him. The so-called Reagan Doctrine committed the United States to support insurrections throughout the world against third-world Marxist states, such as Nicaragua, Angola, and Afghanistan. Reagan also made it clear to his national security adviser, Robert C. McFarlane, and to McFarlane's successor, John M. Poindexter, that he wanted them to keep the contra resistance alive "body and soul."[34] As the minority (that is, the Republican-written) report of the congressional committee that investigated the Iran–Contra affair concluded,

> President Reagan gave his subordinates strong, clear and
> consistent guidance about the basic thrust of the policies he
> wanted them to pursue toward Nicaragua. There is some
> question and dispute about *precisely* the level at which he chose
> to follow the operational details. There is no doubt, however . . .
> [that] the President set the U.S. policy toward Nicaragua, with
> few if any ambiguities, and then left subordinates more or less
> free to implement it.[35]

Many, if not most, of the Republican senators and representatives who signed the minority report supported Reagan's efforts to aid the contras: "Our *only* regret is that the administration was not open enough with Congress about what it was doing." Reagan's long-term efforts to build support for his policies would have been enhanced, they argued, if he had confronted Congress directly by vetoing the Boland Amendment and taking his case to the American people.[36]

The Reagan administration's strategy of circumventing rather than publicly confronting Congress testified to both the continuing limits on presidential party leadership and the ineffectiveness of the statutory restraints that Congress had imposed on the presidency in foreign affairs since the Vietnam War and the Watergate scandal. The prospects for a new spirit of cooperation and discipline within a revamped party system dissolved in Reagan's reliance on the "administrative presidency." According to Richard M. Pious, "Iran–Contra was not due to a weak and uninvolved president mismanaging the national-security decision-making process," as the Tower Commission claimed. Rather, it was symptomatic of the restoration of presidential prerogative in foreign policy—the excesses of what Pious called the "National Security Constitution."[37]

Domestic Policy

Reagan's use of the administrative presidency in foreign policy was hardly an aberration. As a matter of course, when the president and his advisers confronted legislative resistance on any issue, foreign or domestic, they chose administrative avenues to advance their goals unilaterally. Indeed, often they did not even try to modify the statutory basis of a liberal program, turning instead to executive discretion as a first resort.

Of the modern presidents who preceded him, Reagan was the most administratively ambitious. Policy making was concentrated in the White House staff and other units of the EOP, and care was taken to plant Reagan loyalists in the departments and agencies to ride herd on civil servants and carry forth the president's policies. As political scientist Bert A. Rockman has noted, "It was the Nixon Presidency, particularly in its aborted second term, that became celebrated for its deployment [of the administrative presidency], but the Reagan Presidency intended to perfect the strategy and to do that from the beginning."[38]

Reagan's most controversial administrative action targeted Social Security.[39] Without consulting even Republican members of Congress, in May 1981 the president proposed deep and immediate cuts in benefits for early retirees—that is, persons between the ages of sixty-two and sixty-four who chose to retire with reduced benefits rather than wait for full benefits at the normal retirement age of sixty-five. The attempt to cut Social Security payments sparked a furious reaction in Congress. Members of both parties repudiated the administration overwhelmingly, with the Senate voting 96–0 against any reduction in early retirement benefits and the House voting 405–13 against the proposal to eliminate the guarantee of minimum benefits. Although Congress's opposition was bipartisan, Speaker O'Neill turned the Reagan administration's mistake into a campaign issue that Democrats successfully exploited in the 1982 midterm elections and for years to come. O'Neill famously called Social Security the "third rail" of American politics because, as in the New York City subway system, to touch it was to die.[40]

OMB director Stockman, the leading proponent of the president's Social Security proposals, conceded that the punishing defeat in Congress marked the end of the Reagan administration's effort to arrest the growth of Social Security. "The centerpiece of the American welfare state had now been overwhelmingly ratified and affirmed in the white heat of political confrontation," he wrote after leaving office.[41] Nevertheless, the defeat did not discourage Reagan appointees in the Social Security Administration (SSA) from trying to cut Social Security through administrative action. Claiming authority from a 1980 law that mandated a review of the disability program, they engaged in a large-scale effort to purge the rolls of those whom they considered ineligible. Between 1981 and 1984 the SSA informed nearly a half-million people that they no longer qualified for disability benefits.

Congressional Democrats maintained that the Reagan administration's action violated the intent of the 1980 act by reviewing cases with budget savings, not administrative reform, as the real goal. Federal courts overturned the agency's rulings against more than two hundred thousand claimants and interpreted the disability statute to require the SSA to prove that a recipient's medical condition had improved before cutting off benefits. The SSA, under Reagan's appointees, refused to accept this ruling, arguing that the statute itself made no mention of a "medical improvement standard." After a two-year struggle to resolve the dispute, Congress passed the Disability Benefits Reform Act of 1984, which enshrined the medical improvement standard in law. The protracted battle over disability insurance testified dramatically to the Reagan administration's fervent commitment to challenge the social welfare policies of the past, with or without authorization from Congress or the courts.[42]

The political battle over disability benefits epitomized one of the Reagan administration's principal objectives: to remake the executive branch in the president's own conservative image. A year before his election in 1980, a member of the campaign staff, Pendleton James, was assigned to identify "committed Reaganites" to serve in the administration, an assignment he continued after the inauguration as director of the White House Office of Presidential Personnel. James developed a deep talent pool not just for the cabinet and subcabinet but also for the roughly 700 noncareer managerial positions in the Senior Executive Service, which was a Carter administration innovation, and the nearly 1,300 Schedule C positions in the departments that provide support for higher-level presidential appointees. One consequence of this systematic effort to remake the departments and agencies was that Reagan's White House staff did not have to micromanage the activities of the far-flung bureaucracy to ensure its conformity to the president's policies. Another, less fortunate consequence was that individuals appointed for their loyalty did not always have the competence to do their jobs effectively.

The strengths and weaknesses of Reagan's administrative strategy were demonstrated dramatically in the area of social and economic regulation, including environmental, consumer, and civil rights enforcement. Reagan's Executive Orders 12291 and 12498 mandated a comprehensive review of proposed agency regulations by the OMB. The regulatory review process was carried out by a new agency, the Office of Information and Regulatory Affairs (OIRA), which was established within OMB by the 1980 Paperwork Reduction Act. Stockman and the first OIRA director, James C. Miller, launched an aggressive effort to review all new federal regulations proposed by the executive departments and agencies. Within a few years, about three in ten proposed regulations were being rejected or revised by OIRA. Getting the message, departments began writing regulations that conformed to administration policy in order to avoid rejection. Reagan also appointed a Task Force on Regulatory Relief, headed by Vice President George Bush, to apply cost-benefit analysis to existing rules. The task force's review included a reconsideration of the "midnight rules" issued in the last days of the Carter administration. On January 29, 1981, Reagan imposed a sixty-day freeze on these regulations and ultimately rejected many of them.[43]

In sum, Reagan advanced the development of the administrative presidency by resuming the decades-long trend toward concentrating power in the White House that was suspended briefly in the aftermath of the Vietnam War and Watergate scandal. He also confirmed for conservatives that centralizing power in the presidency was essential to carrying out their objectives. As Greenstein has written, "Nixon and Reagan had the courage to act on what once were the convictions of liberals, taking it for granted that the president should use whatever power he can muster, including power to administer programs, to shape policy."[44]

Except for the Iran–Contra affair, reliance on blunt partisan administration did not appear to affect Reagan's strong ties to the broader public. After the televised Iran–Contra congressional hearings concluded in the summer of 1987, Reagan recaptured a large measure of public approval. By the end of the year, with the signing in Washington of the Intermediate-Range Nuclear Forces (INF) Treaty with the Soviet Union, Reagan had reclaimed fully the political high ground. During his first term, the president endured unrelenting criticism from liberals for his decision to deploy Pershing missiles in West Germany as a deterrent to the Soviet nuclear presence.

The INF Treaty, which eliminated both American and Soviet intermediate-range nuclear missiles from Europe, vindicated Reagan's hard-line stance against his critics at home and the Soviets abroad, enshrining him as a peacemaker on the great stage of East–West relations.[45] Throughout 1988 Reagan's approval rating improved steadily, eventually reaching 63 percent.

Underlying Reagan's political resilience was his ability to make his program the new foundation of national political discourse. As political scientist Walter Dean Burnham wrote in 1989, "Ronald Reagan was the most ideological President, and the leader of the most ideological administration, in modern American history."[46] To a remarkable extent, Reagan demonstrated that a firm ideological purpose could substitute for long hours, exhaustive attention to detail, and a dominant political party. Lacking a firm ideological purpose, Nixon's version of the administrative presidency was little more than a strategy to make the government dance to his tune. For Reagan, Rockman has noted, "the administrative presidency was a mechanism to ensure responsiveness to a political agenda that Reagan, and certainly his followers, hoped would outlast his own tenure in office."[47] Reagan's rhetoric defined the agenda of his presidency. His reconstruction of the executive branch was a principal instrument through which his rhetoric gained force.

Yet for all of his popularity, and despite his policy successes at home and abroad, Reagan did not become the Roosevelt of the Right. "The one goal that consistently eluded him, and the one that Roosevelt achieved," Alonzo L. Hamby has written, "was that of an enduring political realignment."[48] The importance of presidential politics and administration in the Reagan presidency may actually have reduced the prospects for a Republican realignment. As journalist Sidney Blumenthal has argued, Reagan "did not reinvent the Republican Party so much as transcend it. His primary political instrument was the conservative movement, which inhabited the party out of convenience."[49] To be sure, Reagan's commitment to strengthening the GOP was sincere and, in many respects, effective. Nevertheless, his administration's devotion to certain tenets of conservative ideology led it to rely on unilateral executive action in ways that sometimes subordinated his party's identity as a broad-based organization with a past and future to the political and programmatic ambitions of the president. "Too many of those around [the president] seem to have a sense of party that begins and ends in the Oval Office," Secretary of Labor William Brock lamented in 1987. "Too many really don't understand what it means to link the White House to a party in a way that creates an alliance between the presidency, the House, and the Senate, or between the national party and officials at the state and local level."[50] Brock's criticism was echoed by many Republican officials as the Reagan years drew to a close.

To some extent, Republican leaders were justified in blaming Reagan's personalistic style of leadership for his failure to convert his good intentions and personal popularity into Republican control of the entire government. From a broader historical perspective, however, Reagan's emphasis on presidential politics was a logical response to the New Deal and its consolidation of the modern presidency. Although Roosevelt's leadership was the principal ingredient in a full-scale Democratic realignment, it aimed to establish the president rather than the party as the steward of the public welfare. The New Deal, like its successor in the 1960s, the Great Society, was less a partisan program than an exercise in expanding the president's power. It was not surprising, then, that the challenge to liberal policies that culminated in the elevation of Reagan to the White House in 1980 produced a conservative administrative presidency, which gave rise to an executive-centered partisanship that, paradoxically, weakened party organizations.[51]

A Reagan Court?

Reagan's effect on the federal judiciary is perhaps the best example of both the force and the limitations of the Reagan Revolution. During the 1960s and 1970s, the courts joined with liberal members of Congress and interest groups to broaden legal rules and procedures in ways that served the interests of African Americans, feminists, environmentalists, and other Democratic constituencies. The Reagan administration worked hard to disrupt this alliance.[52] In a break with previous practice, candidates for district and appeals court judgeships underwent all-day interviews with officials in the Justice Department to assure their conservative approach to jurisprudence. By the end of Reagan's second term, he had appointed enough conservative judges to move the federal courts considerably to the right.

Many of those whom Reagan appointed to the bench were associated with the Federalist Society, an increasingly important conservative legal organization founded in the early 1970s. "What they shared," political scientist David M. O'Brien has written, was "a sense of being in the vanguard of a new conservative legal movement—a movement that went beyond opposition to . . . 'liberal jurisprudence' and also sought to define an activist conservative judicial position on economic and social issues."[53] In keeping with this dedication to transform the terms of national political discourse, the Reagan administration "hoped to foster an intellectual revolution on the bench and enhance the influence of conservative principles on American jurisprudence."[54] Prominent conservative legal scholars, such as Ralph K. Winter and Robert H. Bork of Yale University and Richard Posner of the University of Chicago, were appointed to the federal appeals courts. In 1986, when Chief Justice Warren Burger announced his retirement from the Supreme Court, Reagan promoted Justice William H. Rehnquist to chief justice and replaced him with Judge Antonin Scalia, who joined Reagan's earlier appointee, Sandra Day O'Connor, the first woman justice in history. Rehnquist and Scalia strongly supported the administration's legal agenda; indeed, they had indirectly helped shape it. The administration based many of its positions concerning separation of powers, federalism, and the competing claims of majority rule and minority rights on Rehnquist's and Scalia's legal writings and judicial opinions.[55]

Reagan's campaign to reconstitute the federal judiciary reached its limit in 1987, when he nominated Judge Bork to the Supreme Court. Bork was perhaps the most prominent conservative legal scholar in the country, a brilliant and outspoken critic of the liberals' recent procedural and programmatic judicial innovations. Because he would have replaced the retiring moderate conservative Lewis Powell, Bork's appointment almost certainly would have tilted a closely divided Court decisively to the right on controversial issues such as abortion, affirmative action, and the death penalty.[56]

The controversy that greeted Bork's nomination was extraordinary. The public debate was without parallel in the history of judicial nominations for its partisanship and vitriol. The debate was stoked in part by extensive media and direct-mail campaigns by liberal and conservative advocacy groups. Equally incendiary were the Senate confirmation hearings, which were broadcast on national television. In five days of questioning before the Judiciary Committee, which after the 1986 midterm elections was controlled by the Democrats, Bork abandoned the practice of previous controversial nominees of letting their records speak for them. Instead, O'Brien has noted, "Bork sought to explain, clarify, and amend his twenty-five year record as a Yale Law School professor, as a solicitor general, and as a judge. That broke with tradition and gave the appearance of a public relations campaign."[57]

In a resounding defeat for the Reagan administration, Bork became the twenty-eighth Supreme Court nominee in American history—but only the fourth in the twentieth century—to fail to be confirmed by the Senate. No previous nominee was battered as badly as Bork during his nearly thirty hours of testimony before the Judiciary Committee. The vote to reject him was 58–42, the widest margin of disapproval in the history of Supreme Court nominations.

In part, Bork's rejection testified to the widespread public resistance to the Reagan administration's social agenda. Although most voters supported cutting taxes and strengthening the nation's defenses, the administration's plan to restore "traditional" American values by retreating from liberal policies on civil rights, abortion, and prayer in the public schools was as controversial among Democrats and independents as it was appealing to the emerging conservative base. The breadth of the opposition to Reagan's social agenda was apparent in the vote against Bork, which included thirteen southern Democratic senators and six moderate Republicans.

Bork's rejection also testified to the heightened level of conflict over judicial nominations that have marked the era of divided government, which was ushered in by the elections of 1968. From 1900 to 1968, a period in which the same party usually controlled both the presidency and the Senate, the president's nominees were almost always confirmed; the approval rate was forty-two of forty-five, or 93 percent. Since then, however, institutional combat and the expanding policy activism of the judiciary have combined to overtly politicize the judicial appointment process.[58]

Still, the eight years of judicial appointments by Reagan left an important and enduring legacy. A minor, although highly publicized, postscript to the Bork nomination was Reagan's next nominee, federal appeals court judge Douglas H. Ginsburg. A young protégé of Bork, Ginsburg was forced to withdraw amid revelations that he had smoked marijuana not only as a student but also as a law professor. Eventually, the administration nominated a moderate conservative jurist who was acceptable to the entire Senate, Judge Anthony M. Kennedy.

Because Reagan was the first two-term president since Dwight D. Eisenhower, he was able to select 78 appeals court judges and 290 district court judges, nearly one-half of the entire federal judiciary. In making these appointments, Reagan successfully modified the tradition that lower-court judgeships are mostly a matter of senatorial patronage. He strengthened the president's control over judicial selection by requiring prospective nominees to demonstrate their conservative credentials. In doing so, Reagan ensured that the federal courts, although not prepared to roll back the national government's responsibilities or reverse the civil rights revolution of the 1960s and 1970s, would issue more conservative rulings than in the past.[59]

Immigration and Naturalization Service v. Chadha

The most important Supreme Court decision affecting the institutional power of the presidency during the Reagan years was *Immigration and*

Naturalization Service v. Chadha, also known as the legislative veto case. In the half-century since FDR's New Deal expanded the scope of federal activity, Congress increasingly dealt with complex problems of public policy by writing laws in broad language and granting the executive branch wide discretion in how to implement them. To prevent federal agencies or even the president from exercising this discretion in ways that legislators disapproved, Congress also included in many laws a provision that enabled it to pass judgment on what the executive did. This provision, known as the legislative veto, permitted Congress to overturn an executive regulation or action within a prescribed length of time, often ninety days. The veto requirement ranged in difficulty from a concurrent resolution of both the House and the Senate to an objection by a single designated committee in either house. In all cases, legislative vetoes were final: the president, who can veto ordinary bills passed by Congress, had no power to overturn a legislative veto. From 1932 to 1982 the legislative veto was written into more than 250 laws, including the War Powers Resolution.

On June 23, 1983, the Supreme Court ruled 7–2 that the legislative veto was unconstitutional. The case originated in 1974 when Jagdish Rai Chadha, a Kenyan student who overstayed his visa, received permission from the Immigration and Naturalization Service (INS) to remain in the United States. Relying on the legislative veto provision of the Immigration and Naturalization Act of 1952, the House voted in 1975 to deport Chadha. He then sued, challenging the constitutional basis of the House action.

Writing for a majority of justices, Chief Justice Burger argued that the legislative veto violated the Constitution's separation of powers, in particular the "presentment clause" of Article I, section 7, which says that binding actions by Congress must be presented to the president for signature or veto in toto. "The Constitution sought to divide the delegated powers of the new federal government into three defined categories, legislative, executive, and judicial," Burger wrote, "to assure, as nearly as possible, that each Branch of government would confine itself to its assigned responsibility." In a blistering dissent, Justice Byron R. White complained that after allowing the legislature to delegate substantial authority to the executive ever since the legal controversy over the New Deal, the Court was foolish to deny Congress its best tool for overseeing how that authority was exercised.[60]

The *Chadha* decision turned out to be a less decisive victory for the presidency than it seemed at the time. After the Court's ruling, Congress continued to pass laws that contained legislative veto provisions, most of which require the executive to obtain the approval of the House and Senate appropriations committees. Indeed, more legislative vetoes were enacted after the *Chadha* decision than before it. Furthermore, de facto legislative vetoes have been implemented through informal agreements between Congress and the executive.[61]

The 1988 Election and the Continuation of Divided Government

Reagan did not transform either Washington or national politics completely. But he did strengthen the Republican beachhead in the federal government, solidifying his party's recent dominance of the presidency and providing more and better opportunities for conservatives to attain positions of influence. At the same time, Reagan's two terms witnessed an intensification of the struggle between the executive and the legislature.

The era of divided government that began in 1968 has been marked not just by differences between the president and Congress about public policy but also by each branch's harsh assaults on the other. Efforts by the party that controlled the White House to enhance the unilateral powers of the executive and to circumvent legislative restrictions on presidential

After two popular terms as president, Ronald Reagan passed leadership of the Reagan Revolution to the newly inaugurated President George Bush.

Source: Donald Valdez—The White House.

conduct have been matched by the other party's attempts to burden the executive with smothering oversight by congressional committees and statutory limits on presidential power.

A major, if not the main, forum for partisan conflict during the Reagan years was a series of investigations in which the Democrats and the Republicans sought to discredit one another. From the early 1970s to the mid-1980s, the number of indictments brought by federal prosecutors against national, state, and local officials increased tenfold. These indictments involved more than a dozen members of Congress, several federal judges, and a substantial number of high-ranking executive officials. As political scientist Morris P. Fiorina has noted, "Divided government encourages a full airing of any and all misdeeds, real and imagined."[62]

To be sure, the heightened legal scrutiny of public officials was in part a response to the Watergate scandal. To prevent another Nixon-style "Saturday night massacre" of a special prosecutor, Congress passed the Ethics in Government Act of 1978, which provided for the appointment of independent counsels to investigate allegations of criminal activity by executive officials. Not surprisingly, divided government encouraged the exploitation of the act for partisan purposes. In the 1980s congressional Democrats found themselves in a position to demand criminal investigations and possible jail sentences for their Republican opponents in the executive branch. When Bill Clinton became president in 1993, congressional Republicans turned the tables with a vengeance. As partisan disagreements were transformed into criminal charges, disgrace and imprisonment joined electoral defeat as risks of political combat.[63] Moreover, investigations under the new ethics statute tended to deflect attention from legitimate constitutional and policy debates and to focus the attention of Congress, the news media, and citizens on scandals.

Institutional polarization and divided government did not end with Reagan's retirement in 1989. On November 8, 1988, when the voters elected a Republican president, George Bush, and a Democratic Congress, it was the fifth time in the previous six presidential elections that they divided control of the government between the parties. In contrast, when Eisenhower took the oath of office for the second time in 1957, he was the first president since Grover Cleveland in 1885 to begin a term with even one house of Congress controlled by the opposition party.

Vice President Bush's easy victory over his Democratic opponent, Massachusetts governor Michael Dukakis, was in one sense a triumph for Reagan. Bush won the support of almost 80 percent of the voters, who said they approved of Reagan's performance as president.[64] Like Andrew

Jackson, who in 1836 aided Martin Van Buren, the last incumbent vice president to be elected president, Reagan proved to be unusually helpful to his vice president, both in his popularity and in his active support during the campaign.[65]

Yet Bush's triumph was limited. Never before had a new president—elected by a 426–111 electoral vote landslide, no less—had to endure the other party gaining ground on election day in the House, the Senate, the state governorships, and the state legislatures.[66] Never before had the voters given a newly elected president fewer fellow partisans in Congress than they gave Bush. Never had the constitutional system of "separated institutions sharing powers" been characterized by such clear partisan segmentation.

Divided government was nothing new at the time Bush became president. Of his four most recent predecessors, only Carter served with a Congress controlled by the president's party. But the intensity of the division between the parties had grown, aggravating the estrangement between the branches. When Nixon and Ford were in the White House, the majority of Democrats in Congress were liberals, but a significant minority were southern conservatives who often supported the Republican president. Similarly, although most congressional Republicans in this era were conservatives, several were northeastern or Pacific Coast liberals who often voted with the Democrats. By the time Bush became president, southern voters had replaced most conservative Democrats in Congress with Republicans, and northeastern voters had replaced the vast majority of liberal Republicans with Democrats.[67] Starting with Bush's election, divided government has meant that Congress is controlled not just by the opposite party from the president but by an ideologically united opposition party as well.

The Bush Presidency

The story of the Bush presidency is briefly, if oversimply, told: triumph in foreign affairs and failure in domestic policy.[68] Unfortunately for Bush, in November 1992 the voters cared more about the latter than they did about the former. In his bid for reelection, the president was soundly defeated by Bill Clinton, the Democratic governor of Arkansas.

Foreign Affairs

By experience and interest, George Bush was strongly oriented toward foreign policy. Although international affairs was not a prominent theme of his election campaign in 1988, it was in a sense the theme of his career. Before becoming president, Bush served as the American ambassador to the United Nations, the emissary to China, and the director of the Central Intelligence Agency. In the diplomatic arena, Bush was the most widely traveled vice president in history. Through these positions, he cultivated a vast personal acquaintance with world leaders. As president, Bush spent hours at a time touching base with his fellow presidents and prime ministers by telephone. He also chose strong foreign policy advisers: former Reagan chief of staff and secretary of the Treasury James A. Baker III as secretary of state, former Ford chief of staff Richard B. Cheney as secretary of defense, former air force general Brent Scowcroft as national security adviser (a position he also held in the Ford administration), and former Reagan national security adviser and army general Colin Powell as chairman of the Joint Chiefs of Staff.[69] Once they were selected, Bush forged his advisers into a cohesive team.

Bush's accomplishments in foreign policy nearly spanned the globe. He inherited two simmering problems in Latin America from the Reagan administration: one in Nicaragua and the other in Panama. In 1989 Bush was able to work out an agreement with Democratic congressional leaders on Nicaragua, the most acrimonious issue that divided Reagan from Congress. Although Bush and Secretary of State Baker were contra supporters, they understood that Congress could not be persuaded to approve new military assistance to the anticommunist Nicaraguan rebels. Determined to find a bipartisan solution that would end the long and enervating interbranch conflict over contra aid, Baker and congressional leaders struck a deal to provide $4.5 million a month in nonlethal assistance to the contras for a limited period. The administration then roused sufficient pressure from Europe, the Soviet Union, Latin America, and Democratic members of Congress to persuade the Marxist Sandinista government of Nicaragua to conduct a fair election in February 1990. To Bush's delight, the Sandinistas lost.

Bush acted militarily rather than diplomatically to accomplish his main objective in Panama, which was to remove from power the anti-American dictator, Gen. Manuel Noriega. In Bush's view, Noriega's offenses were legion: election fraud, money laundering, clandestine arms trading, and drug trafficking. (The Panamanian leader was indicted on the latter charge by a U.S. federal grand jury in 1988.) Matters came to a head when Noriega annulled the results of a presidential election. On December 15, 1989, the Panamanian legislature accorded him "maximum leader" status in a self-declared "state of war" with the United States. Five days later, Bush responded by sending twelve thousand troops to the Canal Zone to join the twelve thousand already stationed there. He directed them to capture Noriega and return him to American soil to stand trial. Guillermo Endara, the winner of the annulled election, was sworn in as president. Operation Just Cause, as Bush named the Panama invasion, was not only the largest American military effort since Vietnam but was also considerably more successful.

In Europe, Bush oversaw the collapse of the Soviet empire and, soon after, of the Soviet Union itself—a dream of presidents since Truman that no one foresaw would come true. Bush was encouraging but not intrusive in 1989 and 1990 when first Poland, then East Germany, and then the other Soviet-dominated governments of eastern Europe dissolved, followed in 1991 by the dissolution of the Soviet Union. Critics variously charged that the president was either too reticent in publicly celebrating communism's fall or too willing to interfere in other countries' affairs. In truth, Bush adroitly avoided both extremes. A more assertive policy may well have provoked a defensive, even military, response from the Soviets. A less supportive one could have turned the newly free and democratic governments of eastern Europe against the United States. Meanwhile, under pressure from the Democratic Congress, Bush responded to the fall of communism with substantial but not draconian reductions in defense spending.

Although the four-decades-long Cold War with the Soviet Union was over, it was far from clear what international politics would be like without it. Bush hoped to create a "new world order" in which the United States, as the only remaining superpower, would foster free trade and peaceful relations among the nations. But Bush did not view the end of the Cold War as marking the end of American ambition. He envisioned a new international regime, historian Jeffrey A. Engel has written, that was "newly bonded across Cold War lines, that would unite against aggression."[70] In the Middle East, Bush's ambition faced—and passed—its first test.

The test came on August 1, 1990, when Iraq and its brutal leader, Saddam Hussein, invaded and occupied Kuwait, a neighboring oil-rich state. Bush quickly assembled a large and diverse multinational coalition to support and finance his Operation Desert Shield campaign. Working the phone, he rallied the leaders of China, Japan, Europe, several Arab nations, and even the crumbling Soviet Union to support his strategy of diplomatic, economic, and military pressure on Iraq. He also dispatched nearly half a million American soldiers to Saudi Arabia and persuaded the other members of the coalition to pay $54 billion of the operation's $61 billion final cost.

When Hussein remained adamant in his refusal to withdraw from Kuwait, Bush won strong approval from the United Nations on November

29, 1990, and narrow approval from Congress on January 12, 1991, to drive Iraq from Kuwait if it did not leave voluntarily by January 15. After the deadline came and went, Operation Desert Shield became Operation Desert Storm. On January 16 American and other allied bombers began a thirty-eight-day air campaign to cripple Iraq's military and communications infrastructure. On February 23 the ground invasion was launched, and in four days the allies' military offensive drove the Iraqi forces out of Kuwait and severely weakened Saddam Hussein's capacity to threaten neighboring nations and dominate the world's petroleum market. Nevertheless, Hussein remained in power, much to Bush's surprise and disappointment. The president had expected that military defeat would lead to Hussein's overthrow by the Iraqis themselves.

Substantively and politically, the victory over Iraq was the high point of the Bush presidency—it was all downhill from there. The patriotic fervor aroused by the Gulf War served only to conceal fundamental differences about foreign policy between the president and Congress that foreshadowed a renewal of interbranch conflict. The January 1991 vote that authorized Bush to use troops against Iraq revealed a legislature deeply divided along partisan lines. Not since the War of 1812 had Congress so narrowly approved the use of military force. Although Republicans lined up solidly in favor of the president (42–2 in the Senate and 165–3 in the House), Democrats voted against authorizing military action by large margins: 45–10 in the Senate and 179–86 in the House. After the vote, the Bush administration issued a statement denying that the president needed legislative approval to implement the UN resolution authorizing force against Iraq.

Although he was not able to transcend partisan differences over foreign policy, Bush displayed a deft and steady hand in this arena throughout his four years as president. After losing the 1992 election, he was the most active lame-duck president in history. In December 1992 and January 1993 Bush dispatched twenty-five thousand American troops to restore order and bring humanitarian relief to the starvation-plagued, warlord-dominated African nation of Somalia. He signed the North American Free Trade Agreement (NAFTA) with Canada and Mexico and reached an agreement with Boris Yeltsin, the president of the newly independent nation of Russia, on a second Strategic Arms Reduction Treaty (START II) that promised to reduce the number of nuclear warheads in the American and former Soviet arsenals from nearly twenty-four thousand to no more than sixty-five hundred. Finally, Bush outraged congressional Democrats by pardoning former secretary of defense Caspar Weinberger and five other high

Reagan administration officials for any crimes they may have committed during the Iran–Contra affair.

Bush's pardons represented a Republican protest against the independent counsel law. The president and his advisers were furious that Iran–Contra special prosecutor Lawrence Walsh handed down his indictment of Weinberger and the other officials just four days before the 1992 election. Moreover, Walsh's announcement charged not only that Weinberger lied when he denied taking extensive notes during Reagan administration meetings about ransoming hostages from Lebanon but also that Bush, as Reagan's vice president, was involved in at least one of those meetings. Bush had claimed that he was not "in the loop" when the arms-for-hostages deal was discussed.[71] The president and his supporters cried foul, charging that Walsh had engaged in improper politicking.

Bush offered no defense of his role in the Iran–Contra affair. But in his postelection announcement of the pardon, he criticized the Ethics in Government Act, especially its independent counsel provisions, for "a profoundly troubling development in the political and legal climate of our country: the criminalization of policy differences." Reflecting on nearly two decades of institutional combat, the president proposed that these differences be "addressed in the political arena, without the Damocles sword of criminality hanging over the heads of some combatants. . . . [T]he proper forum is the voting booth, not the courtroom."[72]

Although congressional Democrats and the press attacked Bush for pardoning the Reagan administration officials and criticizing the Ethics in Government Act, Bush had offered the first effective defense by a president against independent prosecutions. "Walsh had become the issue by the end" of the controversy, political scientist Katy Harriger has observed, "in large measure . . . through the effective creation of doubt by his targets about his methods and motives." Most important, the Iran–Contra investigation precipitated a raging debate about the Ethics in Government Act. As Harriger concluded, "The real question is whether something designed to promote public confidence is in fact undermining it."[73] This question would become all the more important during the presidency of Bush's successor, Bill Clinton.

Domestic Affairs

In his 1988 presidential campaign, Bush portrayed himself as the true heir to Reagan in domestic policy, albeit a "kinder and gentler" version of the conservative president, as he put it in his acceptance speech to the

In November 1990 President Bush and Gen. Norman Schwarzkopf reviewed U.S. troops stationed in the Persian Gulf region. Three months later the United States led a coalition of twenty-eight nations to victory over Iraq in Kuwait.

Source: Bush Presidential Materials Project.

Republican National Convention. Bush's "Read my lips: no new taxes" campaign pledge was joined to a promise to be the "education president" and the "environmental president." Bush carried the theme of consolidation past the election. His inaugural address not only thanked Reagan "for the wonderful things that you have done for America" but also was laden with repeated invocations of words such as *continuity, continuance,* and *continuum.* In April 1989 Bush reaffirmed his status as Reagan's heir by telling reporters, "We didn't come in here throwing the rascals out." His chief of staff, former New Hampshire governor John Sununu, described the Bush administration as a "friendly takeover" of its predecessor.[74]

In contrast to Reagan, however, Bush gave almost all of his attention as president to his constitutional roles as chief diplomat and commander in chief. International triumphs and crises aside, domestic policy, not foreign policy, usually drives the electoral process.[75] National security and foreign policy were Republican strong suits in recent elections and helped attract some erstwhile opponents—most notably, the Reagan Democrats—to the party. By 1992, however, the collapse of the Soviet empire had removed the threat of communism and greatly lessened concerns about national security and foreign policy.[76] On election day only 8 percent of the voters said that foreign policy was an important consideration in their choice of a presidential candidate. Eighty-seven percent of this small group voted for Bush, but many more voters resented what they regarded as his concentration on the world's problems at the expense of their own, especially the economic recession that began in 1990.[77]

Bush could have done things differently. Riding high politically after the triumph of Operation Desert Storm in March 1991 (his approval rating reached 89 percent, a record for any president), Bush enjoyed a rare opportunity to try to mobilize Congress in support of a domestic legislative agenda. But he had no such agenda. As Sununu told a conservative audience in November 1990, "There's not a single piece of legislation that needs to be passed in the next two years for this president. In fact, if Congress wants to come together, adjourn, and leave, it's all right with us."[78]

To the extent that Bush did deal with domestic affairs, he was generally unsuccessful. His main challenge, coming after Reagan, was to smooth out the rough edges of his predecessor's economic policies, especially the huge budget deficits. But Bush failed in this effort. In September 1990 he abandoned his "no new taxes" pledge in return for congressional Democrats' agreement to reduce federal spending over a five-year period and to enact a budgetary reform, dubbed PAYGO, that required all increases in direct spending or decreases in revenue to be offset by other spending decreases or revenue increases. Announcing the budget deal at the White House, Bush proclaimed, "It is balanced, it is fair, and in my view, it is what the United States of America needs." A month later, inundated by criticism from conservative, antitax Republicans and from voters who were outraged that he violated his main campaign promise, Bush told reporters that the agreement made him "gag."[79] Although he maintained this sentiment through the end of the 1992 election campaign, the most conservative elements of his party never forgave him. In 1992 Bush faced a challenge for his party's nomination from right-wing columnist Pat Buchanan. As with Ford in 1976 and Carter in 1980, this challenge seriously wounded the reelection-seeking president.

Although Buchanan's insurgency proved most damaging to Bush in domestic politics, his campaign harked back to the blend of isolationism and nativism that roiled the nation during the 1920s. Embracing an America First slogan, Buchanan warned that the United States was losing its stature as the first among nations amid challenges to American economic dominance, a softening of national identity and a growing fondness for multinational institutions. "We must not trade in our sovereignty for a cushioned seat at the head table of anyone's new world order," he warned. Buchanan questioned whether America should keep paying for its allies' defense and, more generally, railed against the effects of globalization He called for "a new patriotism, where Americans begin to put the needs of Americans first."

Despite the relatively halcyon global climate of the early 1990s, Bush never could gain command of the deficit-ridden economy he inherited from Reagan. Even after paying a high political price to achieve the budget agreement, the deficit continued to rise. The accumulated shortfalls of Bush's four years as president added another trillion dollars to the national debt, raising it to $4 trillion. The reason for the growing deficits was that although inflation remained low and the Federal Reserve Board pushed down interest rates, the economy was suffering in other ways that had strong budgetary side effects. Real economic growth averaged about 1 percent per year during the Bush administration, the lowest rate in any four-year period since the Great Depression. In response, Americans' real per-capita income fell, unemployment rose to 7.8 percent, and more businesses failed than during any administration since Hoover's. Because of the weak economy, tax revenues decreased even as government expenditures increased to meet the rising demand for unemployment insurance, food stamps, and other forms of public assistance. With gradual improvements in the economy and the budget agreement, the deficits eventually improved but too late to do Bush any good.

Bush's record was at best mixed in his other domestic challenge: to soften the hard edges of Reagan's conservative approach to the environment and civil rights, which was unpopular even when Reagan was president.[80] Bush acted to remedy this neglect by signing the Clean Air Act of 1990 and the Civil Rights Act of 1991. But in each case his commitment to reform was less than total. The Civil Rights Act became law only after a long and acrimonious battle with Congress over the issue of racial quotas. The Clean Air Act was soon undermined by the Council on Competitiveness, a regulatory review board chaired by Vice President Dan Quayle that served as business's court of last resort in the Bush administration.

Bush's failures in domestic policy were of purpose and interest, not of political skill. The president wooed members of Congress and reporters with an endless series of White House visits, games of golf and horseshoes, personal notes, and other favors and courtesies. Such encounters, along with scores of formal and informal news conferences, helped Bush, who was a poor speechmaker, to get his message out to the American people. Partly as a result of these efforts, he was able to persuade Congress to sustain all but one of his forty-six vetoes. Bush's 98 percent success rate was unprecedentedly high for a president facing a Congress controlled by the other party.[81]

Bush also shepherded two Supreme Court nominations through the Democratic Senate without losing any, something Reagan was unable to do. This was no easy task. New Hampshire judge David Souter's nomination in 1990 was controversial because of his alleged lack of appropriate experience, and in 1991 federal appeals court judge Clarence Thomas, a black conservative, was charged with sexual harassment by a former employee, Anita Hill, in a series of televised public hearings. In addition, Bush named 37 federal appeals court judges and 148 federal district court judges during his presidency. All of them won Senate approval.

Although the White House boasted of securing a conservative majority on the Supreme Court, Souter turned out to be much more liberal than Bush expected, and the fierce battle waged over the Thomas nomination left the nation uneasy. The Senate confirmed Thomas by a margin of 52–48, the closest Supreme Court vote in more than a century and one that reflected the same sort of bitter partisan division that characterized the Bork hearings. Thomas was spared Bork's fate by the votes he received from eleven Democratic senators, most of them southerners, whose support was encouraged by the strong endorsement that the judge, a Georgia native, won from southern blacks.

The heightened level of conflict over the judiciary in the era of divided government extended to legislative battles about court rulings, such as the one that led Congress to pass the 1991 Civil Rights Act. The act, championed by congressional Democrats, nullified nine previous Supreme Court decisions in order to shift the burden of proof in antidiscrimination lawsuits from employees to employers. Bush had vetoed a similar bill in 1990, arguing that it would lead to hiring quotas for minorities and women. But in the wake of the explosive Thomas hearings, he decided to sign the modified version of the bill that Congress passed in 1991. At the same time, Bush issued a "signing statement"—that is, a written statement by the president interpreting the law being signed—that offered a narrower construction of the act than Democratic members of Congress intended when they passed it.[82]

Bush's signing statement for the Civil Rights Act of 1991 was the most controversial use of a tactic that he sometimes employed during his presidency to shape legislation. As Bush described this practice in an address delivered at Princeton University, "[On] many occasions during my presidency, I have stated that statutory provisions violating the Constitution have no binding legal force."[83] Such signing statements declared certain features of congressional statutes null and void by executive fiat. Previous presidents had used signing statements, and the Reagan administration was the first to deploy these actions as part of a comprehensive plan to strengthen the administrative presidency.[84] But Bush issued more of them, and with greater consequences, than his predecessors. In doing so, he significantly expanded a method by which the president could avoid directly confronting Congress with a veto and yet still pursue his legislative objectives. "Taken overall," a former general counsel of the House of Representatives has written, "the 1989–1992 outpouring of signing statements that purposed to strike down or revise new laws staked a major presidential claim to personal power."[85]

It soon became clear that institutional conflict between Bush and the Democratic Congress would not be confined to legislation and nominations. As the 1992 elections approached near the end of a serious recession, the Bush administration turned its attention to "liberating the economy" from new government regulations spawned by legislation on the environment, consumer protection, and discrimination against the disabled.[86] The Council on Competitiveness assumed increasing importance in executive deliberations, putting regulatory agencies on notice that the administration expected them to justify the cost to business and consumers of existing and proposed regulations. One liberal interest group complained that the president was "waging war" on his own agencies.[87]

Bush ran against the Democratic Congress as well as Clinton in 1992. In the end, however, the Democrats not only captured the presidency but also retained control of both houses of Congress, temporarily ending twelve years of divided government. In his 1989 inaugural address, Bush had urged that harsh ideological and partisan conflict give way to a new spirit of cooperation. Yet serious disagreements between the president and Congress defied Bush's efforts to make "the old bipartisanship new again." Some political analysts regarded divided partisan control of the presidency and Congress as the healthy consequence of the voters' desire to mute the ideological polarization that characterizes modern party politics. But the Bush years dramatically revealed how thoroughly divided government obscures political responsibility and mires the president and Congress in petty, virulent clashes that undermine respect for the nation's political institutions. Clinton's victory represented more than a rejection of the incumbent president. It also expressed the voters' hope that the institutional combat they had witnessed during the era of divided government would abate.

Notes

1. Richard E. Neustadt, *Presidential Power and the Modern Presidents: The Politics of Leadership from Roosevelt to Reagan*, 4th ed. (New York: Free Press, 1990), 230.

2. Jeffrey K. Tulis, *The Rhetorical Presidency* (Princeton: Princeton University Press, 1987), 189.

3. The best account of the 1980 election is Andrew E. Busch, *Reagan's Victory: The Presidential Election of 1980 and the Rise of the Right* (Lawrence: University Press of Kansas, 2005).

4. On Reagan's use of rhetoric, see William Ker Muir Jr., *The Bully Pulpit: The Presidential Leadership of Ronald Reagan* (San Francisco: Institute for Contemporary Studies, 1992); and Hugh Heclo, "Ronald Reagan and the American Public Philosophy," in *The Reagan Presidency: Pragmatic Conservatism and Its Legacies*, eds. Elliot Brownlee and Hugh Davis Graham (Lawrence: University Press of Kansas, 2003). Heclo argued that Reagan "is among that handful of American politicians, and a much smaller group of Presidents, who have conducted their careers primarily as a struggle about ideas" (18).

5. Ronald Reagan, "A Time for Choosing," October 27, 1964, in *Ronald Reagan Talks to America*, ed. Richard M. Scaife (Old Greenwich, Conn.: Devin Adair, 1983), 4–5. See also Muir, *Bully Pulpit*, 175–176.

6. "Ronald Reagan's First Inaugural Address," in *The Evolving Presidency: Landmark Documents, 1787–2010*, ed. Michael Nelson (Washington, D.C.: CQ Press, 2012), 253–259.

7. Heclo, "Ronald Reagan and the American Public Philosophy," 23.

8. *New York Times*, July 20, 1980, E20.

9. William E. Leuchtenburg, *In the Shadow of FDR: From Harry Truman to Ronald Reagan*, rev. ed. (Ithaca: Cornell University Press, 1985), 210. See also Alonzo L. Hamby, Liberalism and Its Challengers: From F. D. R. to Bush, 2nd ed. (New York: Oxford University Press, 1992), chap. 8.

10. One of Reagan's speechwriters claimed that Calvin Coolidge—not FDR—was the president who most affected Reagan during both his early years and his presidency. In crafting Reagan's addresses, speechwriters often studied those of Coolidge. Rep. Dana Rohrabacher, R–Calif., former speechwriter to President Reagan, interview by Sidney M. Milkis, July 31, 1989.

11. *Public Papers of the Presidents of the United States: Ronald Reagan, 1983* (Washington, D.C.: Government Printing Office, 1984), 1: 364. See also Muir, *Bully Pulpit*, 74–78.

12. Richard Reeves, *President Reagan: The Triumph of Imagination* (New York: Simon and Schuster, 2006), xiv.

13. John Lewis Gaddis, *The Cold War: A New History* (New York: Penguin, 2006), 217, 196.

14. Marc Landy and Martin A. Levin, "The Hedgehog and the Fox," *Brandeis Review*, 7 (Fall 1987): 17–19.

15. Charles O. Jones, "Ronald Reagan and the U.S. Congress," in *The Reagan Legacy*, ed. Charles O. Jones (Chatham, N.J.: Chatham House, 1988), 37.

16. Tip O'Neill, with William Novak, *Man of the House* (New York: St. Martin's Press, 1987), 410, 413.

17. Hedrick Smith, "The President as Coalition Builder: Reagan's First Year," in *Rethinking the Presidency*, eds. Thomas E. Cronin (Boston: Little, Brown, 1982), 274.

18. House of Representatives, Committee on Appropriations, *Views and Estimates on the Budget Proposed for Fiscal Year 1983*, 97th Cong., 2nd sess., 1982, 12.

19. Quoted in Smith, "President as Coalition Builder," 278.

20. Quoted in Samuel Kernell, *Going Public: New Strategies of Presidential Leadership* (Washington, D.C.: CQ Press, 1986), 118.

21. Tulis, *Rhetorical Presidency*, 197.

22. James P. Pfiffner, *The President and Economic Policy* (Philadelphia: Institute for the Study of Human Issues, 1986), 122.

23. Quoted in William Greider, *The Education of David Stockman and Other Americans* (New York: Dutton, 1982), 33. See also David Stockman, *The Triumph of Politics: Why the Reagan Revolution Failed* (New York: Harper and Row, 1986), 79–99.

24. Fred I. Greenstein, "Nine Presidents in Search of a Modern Presidency," in *Leadership in the Modern Presidency*, ed. Fred I. Greenstein (Cambridge: Harvard University Press, 1988), 345.

25. "Remarks of the President to the 12th Annual Conservative Political Action Conference," Sheraton-Washington Hotel, Washington, D.C., March 1, 1985 (mimeographed copy provided to the authors by the White House).

26. On the transformation of party politics, see A. James Reichley, "The Rise of National Parties," in *The New Direction in American Politics*, eds. John E. Chubb and Paul E. Peterson (Washington, D.C.: Brookings, 1985). By the end of the 1980s, Reichley was much less hopeful that the emerging national parties were well suited to perform the historic partisan function of mobilizing public support for political values and governmental policies. See his richly detailed study, *The Life of the Parties: A History of American Political Parties* (New York: Free Press, 1992), esp. chaps. 18–21.

27. David S. Broder, "A Party Leader Who Works at It," *Boston Globe*, October 21, 1985, 14; Mitchell Daniels, assistant to the president for political and governmental affairs, interview by Sidney M. Milkis, June 5, 1986.

28. Dole quoted in Reichley, "Rise of National Parties," 176.

29. Earl Black and Merle Black, *Divided America: The Ferocious Power Struggle in American Politics* (New York: Simon and Schuster, 2007).

30. Alan Ehrenhalt, "Changing South Perils Conservative Coalition," *Congressional Quarterly Weekly Report*, August 1, 1987, 1704.

31. Vin Weber, interview by Sidney M. Milkis, July 28, 1987.

32. James M. Perry and David Shribman, "Reagan Era Restored Faith in Government until Recent Slippage," *Wall Street Journal*, November 30, 1987, 1, 13. See also William Schneider, "The Political Legacy of the Reagan Years," in *The Reagan Legacy*, eds. Sidney Blumenthal and Thomas Byrne Edsall (New York: Pantheon Books, 1988); and Walter Dean Burnham, "The Reagan Heritage," in *The Election of 1988: Report and Interpretations*, ed. Gerald M. Pomper (Chatham, N.J.: Chatham House, 1989).

33. Benjamin Ginsberg and Martin Shefter, *Politics by Other Means: Politicians, Prosecutors, and the Press from Watergate to Whitewater*, rev. and updated ed. (New York: Norton, 1999), esp. chap. 5.

34. *Final Report of the Independent Counsel for Iran/Contra Matters, vol. 1: Investigations and Prosecutions*, Lawrence E. Walsh, Independent Counsel, Washington, D.C., August 4, 1993, esp. chap. 27.

35. *Report of the Congressional Committees Investigating the Iran–Contra Affair*, with supplemental minority and additional views, H. Doc. 100–433, S. Doc. 100–216, 100th Cong., 1st sess., November 13, 1987, 501 (emphasis in original). See also Lou Cannon's biography of Reagan, which covers the Iran–Contra episode in great detail. Cannon reports that

> Reagan, who knew little about how any federal program operated and was largely uninterested in matters of process, may not have known specifically that proceeds from the Iran arms sales were being placed into accounts for the contras. . . . But what Reagan certainly knew and consistently conveyed to his subordinates was that the contras needed far more help than Congress was willing to give them. Because of this knowledge and belief, Reagan encouraged Americans and friendly foreign leaders to help the contra cause. Oliver North may have gone beyond his instructions, but he was carrying out missions that Reagan wanted accomplished,

both in his efforts to free the hostages and to help the Nicaraguan rebels. It is no wonder that Reagan considered North a national hero.

Cannon, *President Reagan: The Role of a Lifetime* (New York: Simon and Schuster, 1991), 718.

36. *Report of the Congressional Committees Investigating the Iran–Contra Affair*, 515 (emphasis in original). The division among those who served on the House and Senate select committees was highly partisan but not completely so. Three Republican senators signed the majority document, which was far more condemning of the administration's actions: Warren Rudman of New Hampshire; William Cohen of Maine; and Paul Tribble of Virginia. The House committee divided strictly along party lines.

37. Richard M. Pious, "Prerogative Power and the Reagan Presidency: A Review Essay," *Political Science Quarterly*, 106 (Fall 1991): 499–510.

38. Bert A. Rockman, "The Style and Organization of the Reagan Presidency," in Jones, *Reagan Legacy*, 10.

39. On the Reagan administration's efforts to reform Social Security, see Martha Derthick and Steven M. Teles, "Riding the Third Rail: Social Security," in Brownlee and Graham, *The Reagan Presidency*.

40. Ibid, 184.

41. Stockman, *Triumph of Politics*, 193.

42. Pamela Fessler, "Disability Measure Wins Unanimous Approval," *Congressional Quarterly Weekly Report*, September 22, 1984, 2332–4. For a comprehensive discussion of the running battle between the Reagan administration and the federal courts over statutory interpretation, see R. Shep Melnick, *Between the Lines: Interpreting Welfare Rights* (Washington, D.C.: Brookings, 1994).

43. Richard A. Harris and Sidney M. Milkis, *The Politics of Regulatory Change: A Tale of Two Agencies*, 2nd ed. (New York: Oxford University Press, 1996). The "midnight rules" were issued by the Carter administration between December 29, 1980, and January 23, 1981. The strong disagreement in regulatory philosophy between Carter's appointees and the incoming conservative Republican administration intensified the traditional last-minute attempt by departing officials to push through favored policies. Carter's regulators essentially cleared their desks of all rules pending at the end of 1980, producing more than two hundred new regulations in both proposed and final form. The rules, which represented a wide range of social causes for which Reagan and his regulatory task force had little sympathy, fell largely within the purview of the Environmental Protection Agency and the Occupational Safety and Health Administration. See Edward Paul Fuchs, *Presidents, Management, and Regulation* (Englewood Cliffs, N.J.: Prentice Hall, 1988), 85–90.

44. Greenstein, "Nine Presidents," 345.

45. I. M. Destler, "Reagan and the World: An Awesome Stubbornness," in Jones, *Reagan Legacy*, 249–253.

46. Burnham, "Reagan Heritage," 1.

47. Rockman, "Style and Organization of the Reagan Presidency," 11.

48. Hamby, *Liberalism and Its Challengers*, 385.

49. Sidney Blumenthal, *The Rise of the Counterestablishment: From Conservative Ideology to Political Power* (New York: Times Books, 1986), 9.

50. William Brock, secretary, Department of Labor, interview by Sidney M. Milkis, August 12, 1987.

51. On the New Deal and its legacy for the presidency and party system, see Sidney M. Milkis, *The President and the Parties: The Transformation of the American Party System since the New Deal* (New York: Oxford University Press, 1993).

52. R. Shep Melnick, "The Courts, Congress, and Programmatic Rights," in *Remaking American Politics*, eds. Richard A. Harris and Sidney M. Milkis (Boulder: Westview

Press, 1989). See also Mark Silverstein and Benjamin Ginsberg, "The Supreme Court and the New Politics of Judicial Power," *Political Science Quarterly*, 102 (Fall 1987): 371–388.

53. David O'Brien, "Federal Judgeships in Retrospect," in Brownlee and Graham, *The Reagan Presidency*, 331. For a comprehensive treatment of the conservative legal movement, see Stephen Teles, *The Rise of the Conservative Legal Movement: The Battle for the Control of the Law* (Princeton: Princeton University Press, 2010).

54. Ginsberg and Shefter, *Politics by Other Means*, 154–156.

55. David M. O'Brien, "The Reagan Judges: His Most Enduring Legacy?" in Jones, *Reagan Legacy*, 86–87.

56. Ibid., 90.

57. Ibid., 91.

58. For a discussion of the politics of judicial appointments under the conditions of divided rule, see Michael Nelson, "Constitutional Aspects of the Elections," in *The Elections of 1988*, ed. Michael Nelson (Washington, D.C.: CQ Press, 1989), 201–205.

59. David A. Yalof, "The Presidency and the Judiciary," in *The Presidency and the Political System*, 8th ed., ed. Michael Nelson (Washington, D.C.: CQ Press, 2006), 481–507.

60. "Immigration and Naturalization Service v. Chadha," in Nelson, *Evolving Presidency*, 259–269.

61. The 1996 Contract with America Advancement Act, which restricted the payment of public benefits to substance abusers, included a "report and wait" provision that requires an executive agency to submit a report to each house of Congress on any significant rule it issues. For these "major rules," the statute grants Congress a minimum of sixty days to review the measure, during which time it may pass a joint disapproval resolution rejecting it. Although some critics have argued that the availability of "report and wait" provisions and other devices that allow Congress to scrutinize executive action has rendered *Chadha* largely irrelevant, congressional oversight has decreased significantly since the mid-1970s. Any congressional vote to reject an executive rule under the Contract with America Advancement Act must be signed by the president to take effect.

62. Morris P. Fiorina, *Congress: Keystone of the Washington Establishment*, 2nd ed. (New Haven: Yale University Press, 1989), 164, no. 27; Ginsberg and Shefter, *Politics by Other Means*, 23–46; Nelson, "Constitutional Aspects of the Elections," 201. For an excellent account of the cultural and institutional bases of scandal in U.S. politics, see Suzanne Garment, *Scandal: The Culture of Mistrust in American Politics* (New York: Random House, 1991).

63. Linda Greenhouse, "Ethics in Government: The Price of Good Intentions," *New York Times*, February 1, 1998, sec. 1, 5; Cass Sunstein, "Unchecked, Unbalanced: The Independent Counsel Act," *American Prospect* (May–June 1998): 20–27.

64. Nelson, "Constitutional Aspects of the Elections," 192.

65. Ibid., 191–192.

66. The Democrats gained two seats in the House, one in the Senate, one governorship, and more than a dozen seats in the state legislatures.

67. Keith T. Poole and Howard Rosenthal, *Congress: A Political History of Roll Call Voting* (New York: Oxford University Press, 1997).

68. For a thorough account of Bush's political career and presidency, see *41: Inside the Presidency of George H. W. Bush*, eds. Michael Nelson and Barbara A. Perry (Ithaca: Cornell University Press, 2014).

69. Cheney was not Bush's first choice as secretary of defense; it was former Texas Republican senator John Tower. But in a partisan display characteristic of the divided government era, the Senate rejected Tower's nomination, the first time in history that a newly elected president's cabinet nominee had not been confirmed. Ironically, the Senate rejected Tower on the recommendation of the committee he formerly had headed—Armed Services.

70. Jeffrey A. Engel, "When George Bush Believed the Cold War Ended," in Nelson and Perry, *41: Inside the Presidency of George H.W. Bush*, 119.

71. Irvin Molotsky, "Bush Aides Urging Weinberger Pardon in Iran–Arms Affair," *New York Times*, November 7, 1992, 1; "Prosecutor in Iran–Contra Rebukes Dole," *New York Times*, November 11, 1992, D2; "Inquiry into Iran–Contra Prosecutor Is Asked," New York Times, November 12, 1992, A21.

72. "Text of President Bush's Statement on the Pardon of Weinberger and Others," *New York Times*, December 25, 1992, A22.

73. Harriger quoted in Greenhouse, "Ethics in Government: The Price of Good Intentions."

74. Quoted in Michael Duffy and Dan Goodgame, *Marching in Place: The Status Quo Presidency of George Bush* (New York: Simon and Schuster, 1992), 19.

75. Stephen Hess and Michael Nelson, "Foreign Policy: Dominance and Decisiveness in Presidential Elections," in *The Elections of 1984*, ed. Michael Nelson (Washington, D.C.: CQ Press, 1985), 129–154.

76. James Ceaser and Andrew Busch, *Upside Down and Inside Out: The 1992 Elections and American Politics* (Lanham, Md.: Rowman and Littlefield, 1993), 15.

77. Laurence I. Barrett, "A New Coalition for the 1990s," *Time*, November 16, 1992, 47–48.

78. Duffy and Goodgame, *Marching in Place*, 70–71, 283.

79. Ibid., 83, 285.

80. Erwin C. Hargrove and Michael Nelson, "The Presidency: Reagan and the Cycle of Politics and Policy," in Nelson, *Elections of 1984*, 201–202.

81. Congress's one successful veto override came on October 5, 1992, on a bill to reregulate cable television.

82. The Civil Rights Act of 1991 restored the legal standard established by the Supreme Court's ruling in *Griggs v. Duke Power Company*, 401 U.S. 424 (1971), which held employers responsible for justifying employment practices that were avowedly race- and gender-neutral but in practice had an "adverse impact" on women and minorities. The 1989 ruling in *Wards Cove Packing Co. v. Atonio*, 490 U.S. 642 (1989) had shifted the burden, declaring that workers had to show that companies had no legitimate need for the challenged practices. The new legislation instructed the courts to follow the standard of *Griggs* and eight related rulings prior to *Ward's Cove*. Bush agreed to sign the 1991 act, but he proclaimed in his signing statement that documents introduced by Senate Republican leader Robert Dole, which offered a narrow interpretation of the statute, would "be treated as authoritative guidance by all officials in the executive branch with respect to the law of disparate impact as well as other matters covered in the document." Joan Biskupic, "Bush Signs Anti-Job Bias Bill amid Furor over Preferences," *Congressional Quarterly Weekly Report*, November 23, 1991, 3463.

83. Bush quoted in Charles Tiefer, *The Semi-Sovereign Presidency: The Bush Administration's Strategy for Governing without Congress* (Boulder, Col.: Westview Press, 1994), 3.

84. Christopher S. Kelley, "A Matter of Direction: the Reagan Administration, the Signing Statement, and the 1986 Westlaw Decision," *William and Mary Bill of Rights Journal*, 16, no. 1 (2007): 283–306.

85. Tiefer, *The Semi-Sovereign Presidency*, 3.

86. Jonathan Rauch, "The Regulatory President," *National Journal*, November 30, 1991, 2902–2906.

87. OMB Watch, "President Bush's Regulatory Moratorium," *OMB Watch Alert*, January 24, 1992.

13 Bill Clinton and the Modern Presidency

From the beginning, Bill Clinton's presidency was marked by an unusual number of "firsts." With his electoral victory in 1992, he became the first Democrat to be elected president in sixteen years, the start of a twenty-year period in which his party won four of six presidential elections, reversing the pattern of Republican dominance of the White House that had endured since 1968. Reelection in 1996 made him the first Democrat to win a second term since Franklin D. Roosevelt. The 1996 presidential election was also the first in history in which a Democratic candidate was able to surmount a Republican victory in the accompanying congressional elections. In policy terms, Clinton became the first president to balance the federal budget since fiscal year 1969.

The Clinton presidency was also marked by some less-desirable firsts, at least from the standpoint of the president and his supporters. Clinton was the first two-term president since Woodrow Wilson to win with less than a majority of the popular vote in both of his elections and the only twentieth-century president to gain the office twice with fewer than four hundred electoral votes. More important, he was the first Democratic president to serve more than two years with a Republican Congress. Divided government remained the normal governing situation in Washington, as it had been since 1968.

From January 1998, when the president's sexual relationship with White House intern Monica Lewinsky was revealed, until February 1999, when the Senate voted to acquit him of impeachment charges, Clinton navigated uncharted political waters. He was plagued all year by press and prosecutorial investigations into his relationship with Lewinsky and his efforts to conceal that relationship from the courts. In December 1998 Clinton became the first elected president in history to be impeached by the House of Representatives (Andrew Johnson, the only other impeached president, succeeded to the office when Abraham Lincoln died). Yet in the

November midterm elections, for the first time since 1822, the party of a second-term president gained seats in Congress.

President Clinton's dramatic ups and downs can be attributed both to his qualities as a leader and to the political times in which he served. In some ways, volatility was the story of Clinton's political life. As governor of Arkansas and later as president, Clinton's first two years in office were politically unsuccessful. In other ways, the fluctuations of Clinton's fortunes mirrored the instability of American politics in an era of divided government, strong partisan loyalties in Congress and among Republican and Democratic activists, and widespread public distrust of the political process. Even as he was criticized by ardent liberals and militant conservatives for failing to provide a compelling vision for the future, Clinton's extraordinary dexterity often served him well at a time when most Americans tended to resist the programmatic and ideological ambitions of both major parties.

The Election of 1992

The 1992 presidential election that brought Clinton to power was no ordinary affair. Perhaps the most remarkable feature of the campaign was the precipitous decline in President George Bush's political fortunes throughout the year. So formidable was Bush's standing in the polls in 1991 that his reelection, and a fourth consecutive Republican victory, appeared all but inevitable. The president's post–Gulf War popularity, however, masked the country's profound uneasiness about his seeming indifference to domestic affairs.

Bush's experience was a painful reminder of the modern executive's extraordinary isolation.[1] Over the years, the presidency was freed from the constraints of party only to be subjected instead to a volatile political environment. The twentieth-century evolution of the office taught Americans that the president was to serve as their tribune, the embodiment of the popular will. Yet Bush was ill suited to the tasks of public leadership. His 38 percent of the national popular vote in 1992 was the lowest received by an incumbent president since William Howard Taft finished third in 1912. Like Taft, whose bid for reelection was plagued by the presence in the race of Theodore Roosevelt, the former Republican president, Bush was beset by a strong independent candidate, the self-made Texas billionaire H. Ross Perot. In fact, for a time Perot's 19 percent of the popular vote appeared to pose the most serious electoral challenge to the two-party system since Roosevelt's Progressive Party campaign.

The comparison between TR and Perot is instructive. Roosevelt's candidacy foretold not only the emergence of an active and expansive national government but also presidential elections conducted less by party organizations than by candidates and their personal advisers. Roosevelt and his Democratic rival in the 1912 election, Woodrow Wilson, offered a new concept of political leadership that regarded the president, rather than the party or Congress, as the leading agent of representative government in the United States. The public's acceptance of that concept triggered a new dynamic, later enhanced by Franklin D. Roosevelt's approach to leadership and by the emergence of the broadcast media, that subordinated the collective responsibility of the political party to the president's leadership of public opinion. Ronald Reagan's presidency revealed that even conservative chief executives now considered it legitimate, even essential, to rouse the public in support of their programs.

The Perot campaign underscored just how much presidential politics had been emancipated from the constraints of the party organizations. Perot had never held public office of any kind, and his campaign, dominated by thirty-minute "infomercials" and hour-long appearances on television talk shows, set a new standard for direct, plebiscitary appeals to the voters without even the pretense of a party campaign. (He added the pretense four years later, running in 1996 as the nominee of the Reform Party, his own short-lived creation.) Turning aside pleas to form a genuine third party from those who were interested in renewing the party system, Perot held no primary elections or nominating convention to launch his candidacy. Instead, he called his supporters to arms on the popular CNN talk show *Larry King Live*.[2] To be sure, Perot's success as an independent candidate was not based merely on a personal following. His campaign aroused supporters who strongly identified with his commitment to fiscal responsibility, campaign finance reform, economic nationalism, and a restrained foreign policy. Nevertheless, the plebiscitary style of Perot's leadership raised serious questions about how his personal standing and issue positions could ever become enduring features of American politics.

A change in the structure of the media during the 1980s abetted Perot's circumvention of party politics in 1992. With the advent of cable television and the proliferation of political talk shows, candidates had unprecedented opportunities to address the voters directly. These shows served as Perot's early primaries and caucuses. His ratings victories in cable appearances sparked invitations to appear on *Good Morning America* and *Today*, which in one instance gave him two hours to answer viewers' questions.[3] In the end, however, the American people invested their hopes for constructive change more cautiously, in the possibility that Clinton represented a new form of Democratic politics that would cure the ills brought on by the ideological and institutional conflicts that had plagued the party since the late 1960s.

Like Perot, Clinton took advantage of cable television and the growing importance of talk shows. Perot used the new media to portray an iconoclastic businessman seeking to save the country from crippling budgets. Clinton and his political strategists were anxious to refute the perception revealed by focus group-based research that "he was a rich kid whose family were big shots in Arkansas and who had bought his way into government . . . Yale, Georgetown, Oxford . . . [when really he was] the son of a single mother who worked as a nurse anesthetist." According to campaign pollster Stanley Greenberg, this finding meant our "main task was biography," and so "we went to popular culture shows" such as *The Arsenio Hall Show*, *Good Morning America*, and MTV "because we could talk about biography, which is hard to do in newsrooms."[4]

Clinton dedicated his campaign to principles and politics that he claimed "transcended" the left-right debate that immobilized the nation during the previous quarter century. For the central themes of his presidential campaign, Clinton drew on ideas developed by the Democratic Leadership Council (DLC), a centrist group within the Democratic Party. (He served as the group's leader in the late 1980s.) As Clinton declared frequently during the 1992 campaign, these ideas heralded a "New Covenant" that in the name of "opportunity, responsibility, and community" would seek to constrain the public demands for economic entitlements that had been unleashed by the New Deal.[5]

The essence of Clinton's message was that the long-standing liberal commitment to guarantee economic welfare through entitlement programs such as Social Security, Medicare, Medicaid, and Aid to Families with Dependent Children had gone too far. The main objective of the New Covenant was to correct the tendency of Americans to celebrate individual rights and government entitlements unreservedly, without acknowledging the responsibilities citizens have to each other and to their country. An admirer of John F. Kennedy, Clinton based his philosophy of government on Kennedy's call for a renewed dedication to national community and service, as exemplified by the Peace Corps.

Clinton's New Democratic message appeared to work. To be sure, his 43 percent share of the popular vote was hardly a mandate. Indeed, it was roughly the same percentage that losing Democratic candidates received in the previous three elections. But his margin of victory over Bush was more impressive. Clinton won a 370–168 Electoral College majority by sweeping thirty-two states, many of which had not voted for a Democrat since 1964. In the congressional elections, the Democrats preserved their majorities in both the House and Senate. Most victorious Democrats, however, ran in safe constituencies and had no incentive to depart from their party's traditional liberalism in favor of Clinton's New Covenant-style centrism. Virtually all won a larger share of the vote than Clinton, providing them with further confirmation that the Democratic party did not have to be remade. The ranks of Democratic women and ethnic and racial minorities in Congress rose substantially, moving the Democratic caucus several degrees to the left. These developments, added to the President's lack of a popular vote majority, initially made it difficult for Clinton to resist pressure from conventionally liberal Democratic leaders to abandon his campaign pledge to forge a "third way." [6]

The First Year of the Clinton Presidency

Clinton's first one hundred days as president "diminished public expectations," the *Washington Post* reported, "that he—or anyone else—can do much to turn around a country that seven out of ten voters think is going

In a bid to reach younger voters, presidential candidate Bill Clinton plays the saxophone on the June 3, 1992, edition of The Arsenio Hall Show.

Source: AP Photo/Reed Saxon.

in the wrong direction."[7] Hoping to be a dominating president in the tradition of FDR, LBJ, and Ronald Reagan, Clinton was targeted with the same sort of ridicule that had plagued his most recent Democratic predecessor, Jimmy Carter. Like Carter, Clinton was a former governor of a southern state whom many believed was in over his head. As Walter Dean Burnham observed during the summer of 1993, "There has been no successful transition yet from the very small and parochial world of Little Rock to Big Time Washington."[8]

The White House press corps, the most hostile faced by any president since Richard Nixon, amplified Clinton's weaknesses. Because the proliferation of television talk shows and local news programs allowed the new president to speak directly to the American people, Washington correspondents often felt left out of the picture. Indeed, Clinton held only one White House press conference during his first three months as president.[9] Frustrated by their diminishing influence, White House correspondents eagerly pounced on the administration's gaffes. News accounts of lapses in presidential judgment, ranging from a much-maligned $200 onboard haircut as *Air Force One* was parked at the Los Angeles airport to the trashing of Clinton's first two choices for attorney general, Zoë Baird and Kimba Wood, for employing undocumented immigrants as nannies, left the country incredulous.[10]

The transition from governor to president became rocky when Clinton assembled a White House staff headed by close associates from Arkansas such as Chief of Staff Thomas F. "Mack" McClarty, who appeared unprepared for the complexity and toughness of Washington politics. Clinton did name some impressive figures to the cabinet, including Sen. Lloyd Bentsen of Texas as secretary of the Treasury, Wisconsin representative Les Aspin as secretary of defense, and former Arizona governor Bruce Babbitt as secretary of the interior. But he was limited in his choices by the scarcity of Democrats with executive experience in Washington. Shut out of the White House since 1981, the party had been in no position to groom skilled administrators. Even Aspin and Bentsen, accomplished lawmakers, were not fully prepared for the challenges of running a major executive department.[11] The larger problem, however, was Clinton's governing style. He centered political and policy decisions in the White House staff. The staff, in turn, manifested the virtues and flaws of the president, who, to a much greater extent than his recent Republican predecessors, assumed the daily burden of detailed decision-making.[12]

Indeed, most of Clinton's early political difficulties originated with the president himself. Clinton seemed desperate to please all sides, a leadership flaw that was magnified by a Democratic Party fashioned from a demanding constellation of sometimes competing interest groups.[13] During the 1992 campaign, Clinton had professed to be a New Democrat who would challenge these groups and ignore their demands for more entitlement programs. But the president's commitment to controlling government spending and recasting the welfare state was obscured during the first hundred days by his traditional liberal actions. For example, no sooner was Clinton inaugurated than he announced his intention to issue an executive order to lift the long-standing ban on gays and lesbians in the military. This policy could be carried out instantly—"with the stroke of a pen," Clinton believed—leaving him free, as he had promised during his quest for the presidency, to focus "like a laser" on the economy.

In the social climate that prevailed in the early 1990s, however, it was unrealistic to expect that such a divisive issue could be resolved by executive order. To be sure, the development of the administrative presidency had given presidents more power to conduct domestic policy by executive fiat. But, as Reagan and Bush had discovered, the use of this power often provoked powerful opposition from Congress, interest groups, and the bureaucracy. Intense resistance by the respected head of the Joint Chiefs of Staff, Gen. Colin Powell, and the influential Democratic chair of the Senate Armed Services Committee, Sam Nunn of Georgia, forced Clinton to defer his executive order on gays and lesbians for six months, while he sought a compromise solution. The president's retreat then aroused the ire of gay and lesbian activists, who had given him strong financial and organizational support in the election.[14] In the end, Clinton and the Congress settled on a compromise—the "Don't Ask, Don't Tell" policy passed into law in 1993—that banned gays from serving openly in the military.

In his frustration, the president announced that he was "frankly appalled" at how much time he was spending on enervating social issues. Even more distressing, his plan to invest new federal funds in the economy foundered on the rock of the budget deficit. Citing the $350 billion shortfall for Fiscal Year 1993 that he inherited from the Bush administration, Clinton withdrew his campaign promise of a middle-class tax cut. He proposed instead to cut $500 billion from the deficit in five years through additional taxes and a shift away from the spending priorities pursued during the Reagan and Bush years. In his first budget, Clinton proposed to transfer funds from the Defense Department to an array of traditional Democratic social programs. He called for a large expansion of federal tax credits for low-income working families with children, at a cost to the Treasury of $27 billion; an extra $13.8 billion for the Head Start program; and $3.6 billion for the Supplemental Food Program for Women, Infants, and Children.

Clinton's plan, even though it promised to reduce the deficit, did not clearly distinguish him from conventional "tax-and-spend" Democrats, a charge that congressional Republicans leveled at the president with alacrity. Meanwhile, the Republicans marched in lockstep opposition to Clinton's economic program, especially his $16 billion short-term stimulus package, which he offered as a hedge against the economic contraction that might result from shrinking the budget deficit.

The White House's situation was made more untenable by harsh partisan acrimony. The Republican leader in the Senate, Robert J. Dole, regularly resorted to the filibuster as a tool of partisan opposition.[15] His army of forty-three Republican senators was too small to enact legislation, but it was more than adequate to thwart Clinton on the stimulus bill and most other measures. Except in budgetary matters, imposing cloture on a Senate filibuster required sixty votes.

The Republican strategy was unprecedented. Historically, the filibuster was employed by Senate mavericks or regional minorities.[16] That the Republican leadership orchestrated filibusters to ensnare the president testified to the bitter partisanship that lingered from the Reagan–Bush era as well as to Clinton's failure during the early days of his presidency to move the country beyond the interbranch conflicts spawned by divided government. Moderate Democrats, including Clinton's allies in the DLC, argued that the president would have been less vulnerable to the Republicans' obstructionist tactics if he had governed more clearly as a New Democrat. Instead, the tax increases and liberal social policies that Clinton supported enabled Republicans to tar him as a conventional liberal whose commitment to reform expired at the end of his presidential campaign.[17]

Because his electoral mandate was modest, Clinton's acquiescence to traditional liberal causes was in some ways understandable. It was a logical response to the modern institutional separation between presidents and their parties. The centrist wing of the Democratic Party that Clinton represented was a minority wing. The majority of Democratic activists and members of Congress still preferred entitlements to opportunities and regulation to responsibility.[18] Only the decline of political support for some traditional liberal groups and the modern emphasis on candidate-centered presidential campaigns made Clinton's nomination and election possible. The media-driven caucuses and primaries that determine party nominations enabled him, like Carter in 1976, to seize the Democratic mantle as a political outsider. But they offered the new president no means to transform his party when he took office. To bring about the centrist agenda he advocated during the election, Clinton would have had to risk a brutal confrontation with the major powers in the Democratic Party. Such a battle might have left him no less isolated than Carter.

Although the early Clinton presidency was a period of profound political frustration, the president won some important victories. Most important, in June 1993 the Senate and House narrowly passed modified versions of his $500 billion deficit reduction plan. In August Clinton deployed the reconciliation process that the Reagan administration found so useful in the enactment of the 1981 economic package to forge a budget agreement in a congressional conference committee. He did so without any support from Republican legislators, who voted unanimously against the plan. The House adopted the conference report by 218–216, and the Senate approved it 50–50, with Vice President Al Gore casting the deciding vote. Clinton won this narrow, bruising victory only after promising moderate Democrats that he would offer another package of spending cuts in the fall.[19]

In November 1993 Clinton achieved a second important first-year victory, winning the battle to pass the North American Free Trade Agreement (NAFTA) with Canada and Mexico, which President Bush had negotiated. This time he knew that a partisan approach would not work. Indeed, Democrats' support for free trade was so weak that Clinton had to rely on winning more Republican than Democratic votes in Congress. Reviving his identity as a political outsider, the president launched a successful campaign for the treaty by reaching beyond Congress to the American people. The turning point in the struggle came when the administration challenged Perot, the leading opponent of NAFTA, to debate Gore on *Larry King Live*. Gore's forceful and optimistic defense of open markets went down well with the large television audience, securing enough popular support to persuade Congress to approve the trade agreement.[20] The fight over NAFTA, with labor unions, an important constituency of the Democratic Party since the New Deal, strongly opposed was bitter. But in this battle for the soul of the party, Clinton's defense of global free enterprise gave his "New Democrat" allies hope that he had finally begun the task of moving Democrats toward the principles and policies he championed during the 1992 campaign.

NAFTA was one of the few foreign policy issues in which Clinton initially took much interest. "No president in the last fifty years has tried to do what Bill Clinton has done in foreign policy," observed presidential historian Michael Bechloss, "which is essentially to keep it away from the Oval Office as much as possible."[21] Nevertheless, when Clinton took office, he found the international arena brimming with actual and potential crises that demanded his attention. Among other things, he faced a challenge from Saddam Hussein, whose assassination plot against former president-

Bush provoked Clinton in June 1993 to order air strikes against an Iraqi intelligence installation. Saber rattling by the Iraqi leader would be a recurring irritant throughout the Clinton presidency.

The administration faced its most troubling foreign policy predicament in Somalia, where Clinton allowed American troops deployed for humanitarian purposes at the end of Bush's tenure to become part of a dangerous and controversial United Nations peacekeeping mission. Operating under the authority of Security Council resolutions that ordered the capture of warlord Mohammed Aidid, the mostly American UN forces became the target of attacks in which soldiers were wounded, captured, or killed. In October, despite strong pressure from Congress to withdraw from Somalia, Clinton sent reinforcements. Finally, with Congress threatening to cut off funding by February 1, 1994, two months earlier than the president intended, the Clinton administration agreed to limit the mission to protecting American forces and securing supply lines for relief aid.[22] The Somalia intervention appeared to underscore both increased congressional willingness to thwart presidential initiatives in the aftermath of the Cold War and Clinton's lack of sure-footedness in international affairs.

The 1994 Elections and the Restoration of Divided Government

After the successful fight for NAFTA in November 1993, hopes rose among Democratic moderates that Clinton would tackle the fraught issue of welfare reform, which besides national service, was the signature New Democrat issue of his 1992 campaign. As he put it at the party's 1992 Convention, "We will say to those on welfare: You will have, and you deserve, the opportunity, through training and education, through childcare and medical coverage, to liberate yourself. But then, when you can, you must work, because welfare should be a second chance, not a way of life."[23] The president managed to provide economic support for the working poor by inserting an expanded Earned Income Tax Credit (EITC) into the 1993 budget reconciliation. But welfare reform, dedicated to placing the most economically disadvantaged Americans in jobs, was the president's most popular antipoverty program. As White House aide Bruce Reed notes, "Welfare was the best example of what Clinton would prove to be a master of, of taking an issue that Republicans had demagogued for years and turning it into an affirmative, political, and substantive agenda for Democrats. It was not without controversy."[24]

The challenge of taking on a divisive but long-standing Democratic commitment played large in Clinton's decision to delay the overhaul of welfare in favor of an ambitious health care program, which promised to "guarantee all Americans a comprehensive package of benefits over the course of an entire lifetime." For dramatic effect, Clinton brandished a red, white, and blue "health security card" in his September 1993 speech to Congress on health care reform, a symbol of his ambition to carry out the most important extension of social policy since the enactment of Social Security in 1935. To White House stewards of New Democratic principles, this was an unfortunate strategic choice. But health care reform became the major initiative of the first lady Hillary Rodham Clinton, who as political scientist Barbara Perry has written, "established her unprecedented role in the White House from the day her husband took the presidential oath." She "became the first presidential spouse to have an office for herself and an extensive staff in the West Wing, as well as the customary suite in the East Wing." Moreover, "Hillaryland," as the president's secretary Betty Currie dubbed the first lady's staff, became a critical beachhead in the Clinton administration for the advancement of progressive causes favored by liberal advocacy groups and the Democratic congressional caucus.[25] Just as welfare reform divided the party, so did health care reform—the holy grail of progressives since the New Deal—promise to unify it. "Every Democrat had a different idea how to do it," Reed recalls, "but they all wanted to do it."

Hillary Clinton sought to elide these disparate reform ambitions by creating a highly insulated policy process, which seemed to violate New Democratic administrative principles and practices. The New Democrats' remedy for bureaucratic torpor was the administration's Reinventing Government (REGO) program, which Vice President Gore was assigned to direct. Originally championed by journalist David Osborne and former city manager Ted Gable, this initiative promised "a new customer service contract with the American people, a new guarantee of effective, efficient and responsive government." REGO, announced with much fanfare in September 1993, was not, as many of its critics charged, merely hollow rhetoric. As political scientist Donald Kettle has written, "It energized employees, . . . attracted citizens, . . . drew media attention to government management, . . . and made the point that management matters."[26] Curiously, however, REGO-style lessons about how to recast administration were disregarded in the development of the health care program. Indeed, the formulation of this program appeared to mark the apotheosis of New Deal administrative politics. It was designed "behind closed doors" by the Health Care Task Force, which was headed by the first lady and the president's longtime friend, Ira Magaziner. Moreover, the health care proposal sought to create a new government entitlement program and an administrative apparatus that would signal the revitalization rather than the reform of traditional social welfare policy.[27]

White House aides warned Clinton that he had campaigned in 1992 for national service and welfare reform, not health care. "It was clear by the fall of 1994," Galston lamented, "that the American people had decided that the Clinton campaign of '92 had been a bait-and-switch operation, and they didn't like it."[28] In truth, the Clinton administration's health care proposal offered an alternative to more liberal as well as more conservative plans. But the president's "third way," which purported both to guarantee universal coverage and to contain costs, resulted in a Rube Goldberg contraption that appeared to require an intolerable expansion of the federal bureaucracy. With its complexity (the bill was 1,342 pages long) and obtrusive bureaucratic framework, the Clinton proposal was an easy target for Republicans.[29]

Although the administration offered conciliatory overtures to the plan's opponents, hoping to forge bipartisan cooperation on Capitol Hill and a broad consensus among the general public, the possibilities for comprehensive reform hinged on settling differences about the appropriate role of government that had long divided the parties. This task proved impossible. Health care reform died in 1994 when a compromise measure, negotiated by Senate Democratic leader George Mitchell of Maine and Republican senator John Chafee of Rhode Island, failed to win enough Republican support to break a threatened filibuster.[30] In the end, Clinton enraged conservatives by proposing an ambitious program and dismayed liberals by failing to enact it. Most significant, the defeat of the president's health care program created the overwhelming impression that he had not lived up to his campaign promise to transcend the bitter philosophical and partisan battles of the Reagan and Bush years.

Clinton and his party paid dearly in the 1994 midterm elections, not just for the failure of health care reform but also for the success of his 1993 deficit reduction plan. As political scientist Gary C. Jacobson has shown, the public's long-standing desire for a balanced budget has always been tempered by its opposition to the reductions in government spending on specific programs and the increases in federal taxes that balancing the budget usually requires.[31]

The Republicans gained fifty-two seats in the House and eight in the Senate, taking control of Congress for the first time in forty-two years. They achieved their victory in a campaign that was unusually ideological and partisan. The charged atmosphere of the election owed much to the efforts of House Republican leader Newt Gingrich of Georgia. Gingrich persuaded more than three hundred of his party's House candidates to sign a Republican "Contract with America," which promised to restore limited government by eliminating federal programs, reducing regulatory burdens, and cutting taxes. Clinton's attack on the Republican program during the campaign seemed to backfire, serving only to abet the GOP in its effort to highlight the president's failure to fulfill his promise to "reinvent government."

Disenchantment with Clinton was especially strong in the South, where Republicans registered some of their greatest gains. White southerners had begun rebelling against the Democratic Party in presidential elections with the Dixiecrat revolt of 1948. More recently, Reagan had expanded the Republicans' appeal by taking conservative positions on taxes, national defense, and social issues. In 1980 Reagan won ten of the eleven former Confederate states against Jimmy Carter, a Georgian. Clinton managed to win only four in 1992.

What distinguished the 1994 elections is that a large majority of southern whites supported Republican candidates in congressional and state contests. Previously, southern Democrats were able to insulate themselves from those aspects of the national party that whites found unappealing. But Clinton's first two years as president eroded that insulation. "Clinton had earned praise as one of the brightest, most agile governors in his region," journalists Dan Balz and Ronald Brownstein wrote after the 1994 elections, "but, as President his policies, from his advocacy of ending discrimination against homosexuals in the military to his economic and health care programs that stressed big government activism, often seemed like a stick in the eye of his native South."[32] Starting with the 1994 elections, southern Republicans commanded a majority of the region's governorships, a majority of seats in the Senate, and a majority of seats in the House.

The dramatic Republican triumph in 1994 led political pundits to suggest that Clinton was, for all intents and purposes, a lame-duck president. Indeed, as Gingrich seized the legislative initiative during the early months of the 104th Congress, Clinton was left to assert plaintively in April, "The president is relevant here." Clinton's battle with the Republican-controlled Congress was made all the more difficult by the sweeping changes that the new Speaker and his allies made in the House's rules. House Republicans strengthened the power of the party leaders to control committees (weakening seniority's status even more than did the 1970s reforms), reduced the number of standing committees and their staffs, limited the tenure of committee chairs, and prohibited closed-door hearings and unrecorded votes. These reforms made the House a more partisan, less professional institution, thereby equipping it to do battle with the beleaguered Democratic president. Although the rule changes affected the House more than the Senate, the upper chamber, which already had adopted tough partisan tactics under Dole, was also affected by the Gingrich "revolution." As political scientist Sean Theriault has documented, many House members who began their careers during the heady days of Gingrich's rise to prominence were elected to the Senate and went on to transform the Senate into a similarly partisan institution.[33]

The Comeback President

The seeds of Clinton's reelection in 1996 were sown in the disastrous elections of 1994. This was an ironic but not altogether surprising result: in 1946, 1954, and 1986 the party that took away control of one or both houses of Congress from the president's party proceeded to overreach politically and open the door for a presidential comeback. Clinton's initial response to the conservative Republican triumph in 1994 was conciliatory, even contrite. "I think what [the voters] told us was, 'Look, two years ago we made one change, now we made another change.'"[34] Hoping to revive the impression created during the 1992 campaign that he represented a fresh approach to government, Clinton resurrected his New Covenant message of "opportunity, responsibility, and community." In translating this message into action, Clinton embraced campaign adviser Dick Morris's goals of "triangulation" in policy and, in presidential style, a more dignified, statesmanlike demeanor.

Triangulation, or the "Third Way"

Morris persuaded Clinton that it was important not only to stake out a position in the political center but also to find new issues that would allow him to rise above the conventional left-right political spectrum and offer a "third way." The baseline of the new political triangle would be occupied at opposite ends by liberal Democrats and conservative Republicans, with Clinton hovering at a point above and between them. As Morris urged Clinton to embrace, and thereby neutralize, Republican issues such as crime, taxes, welfare, and the budget, the president displayed a renewed commitment to middle-class concerns. "I had discovered the middle class in [my] presidential campaign," Clinton said, "and forsaken them as president."[35]

Clinton's adoption of the triangulation strategy clearly accounts for his approach to the defining controversy of his third year as president: the battle with the 104th Congress over the fiscal year 1996 budget. Fresh from their triumph in the midterm elections, the Gingrich-led Republicans went beyond the promises of the Contract with America by committing themselves to cut taxes and domestic spending dramatically. Congressional Democrats opposed them on both counts, aiming most of their fire at the proposed spending reductions. In mid-1995 Clinton angered these Democrats by boldly embracing the Republicans' goal of a balanced budget. But he also infuriated the Republicans by insisting that Democratic programs such as Medicare, Medicaid, educational funding, and environmental enforcement be left substantially unaltered. The public, roused by the millions of dollars in pro-administration television ads financed by the Democratic National Committee, supported the president. When the Republicans tried to impose their own budget on Clinton, he refused to yield. The president then persuaded the voters that Gingrich, Dole, and the Republican Congress were responsible for the two federal government shutdowns that began in late 1995 in the absence of a budget agreement.

When Congress returned to Washington in January 1996 for the second session of the 104th Congress, the president, having outmaneuvered the Republicans the previous year, now co-opted their most popular theme.

Fresh from the triumph of his budget battle with the Republican Congress, President Bill Clinton, center, enters the House chamber to deliver his 1996 State of the Union address.

Source: Scott Ferrell—Congressional Quarterly.

In the State of the Union address, Clinton declared that "the era of big government is over."[36] He withstood furious criticism from liberal members of his party and in August signed the Welfare Reform Act of 1996, which replaced a sixty-year-old entitlement to cash payments for low-income mothers and their dependent children with temporary assistance and a strict work requirement.[37] Clinton conceded that the act was flawed, cutting too deeply into nutritional programs for the working poor and unfairly denying support to legal immigrants. Nevertheless, by forcing welfare recipients to take jobs, the new act advanced a fundamental principle that Clinton championed in the 1992 campaign: "recreating the Nation's social bargain with the poor" to require responsibility in return for benefits.[38] Clinton's embrace of "middle-class values" was not limited to rolling back government. In September, concerned that he not be caught again on the politically unpopular side of a controversial social issue, Clinton signed the bipartisan Defense of Marriage Act, which defined marriage as between a man and a woman and authorized states to withhold recognition of same-sex marriages that had been legally performed in other states.

Acting Presidential

Hoping to strengthen his credentials as an effective, independent executive, Clinton began to present himself to the voters as statesmanlike rather than partisan or political. After the April 19, 1995, bombing of the Oklahoma City federal building by domestic terrorist Timothy McVeigh, the president had his first opportunity since the 1994 elections to do so. His effort was successful. As one observer recorded, in the aftermath of the traumatic bombing Clinton "exhibited the take-charge determination as well as the on-key rhetoric that Americans expect of their president in times of trouble."[39]

Clinton's presidential sure-footedness after Oklahoma City was not an isolated event. Political scientist Paul Light has pointed out that presidents typically undergo a "cycle of increasing effectiveness" that comes with experience in office.[40] Adhering to the pattern of his long tenure as governor of Arkansas, Clinton put his on-the-job training to good use. The White House staff, hastily thrown together late in the transition period that followed the 1992 election and equally chaotic during the first two years of his presidency, began to function more effectively after he appointed longtime Washington insiders Leon Panetta as chief of staff and Michael McCurry as press secretary while keeping the most effective of the Arkansans, notably deputy White House counsel Bruce Lindsey.[41] Meanwhile, Clinton learned how to deal with a highly partisan Republican Congress after many years of working with the part-time, Democrat-dominated legislature of his state. His deportment mirrored his growth. Out went his much-photographed (and much-ridiculed) jogging shorts, public confession of his preference for "boxers" over "briefs," and diffident salutes on formal military occasions. In came (after sessions spent studying videotapes of Reagan) a straight, shoulders-back posture, dignified attire, and with some coaching, crisp salutes.

In foreign policy, the president gained confidence as commander in chief when he discovered during the final two years of his first term that the American people respected him for having the courage to make the unpopular decisions that extended American assistance to Bosnia, Haiti, and Mexico in times of crisis. In November 1995, after Clinton overruled public opinion and strong congressional opposition by sending twenty thousand troops to a peacekeeping mission in Bosnia, the voters' approval of his handling of foreign policy went up. Privately, he likened the phenomenon to "telling your children to go to the dentist—they don't want to go, but they know you're right."[42]

Clinton initially was reluctant to intervene in the Balkans, but the plight of the Bosnian Muslims, who were being victimized by Serbian leader Slobodan Milosevic's "ethnic cleansing" exile and extermination schemes, and pressure from America's European allies eventually persuaded the president to deploy military force to the region. His resolve to uphold American responsibilities in the world, coming on the heels of his confrontation with Congress over the budget, appeared to belie his reputation as an irresolute amateur who lacked a clear set of principles. The president really was, as Clinton had insisted in the aftermath of the 1994 elections, "relevant."

The Elections of 1996

Clinton's strategy of triangulation and acting presidential was clearly evident in his 1996 general election campaign. The president held firmly to the centrist ground he staked out after the 1994 midterm elections, campaigning on the same New Democratic themes that served him well in 1992. In dozens of appearances around the country, Clinton argued that he and Gore represented a proven, moderate alternative to the extremism of Gingrich and the 104th Congress. He pointed with pride to the economic progress that had flowed from the initially unpopular tax increases and spending reductions of his first term: four consecutive years of low inflation, a sharp drop in the unemployment rate, steady economic growth, and a reduction in the annual budget deficit from $290 billion the year he became president to $106 billion in the fourth year of his term. He celebrated the first-term enactment of laws such as welfare reform and the service-based AmeriCorps program, along with his successful defense of "Medicare, Medicaid, education, and the environment" against alleged assaults by Republican budget cutters. Finally, to buttress his stature as a unifying rather than a partisan leader, Clinton struck appealing presidential poses for the television cameras, signing environmental legislation at the Grand Canyon, and presiding over an emergency Arab–Israeli summit conference at the White House.

Still, Clinton's discussion of the future during the campaign was hardly the stuff of which mandates are made. To the dismay of New Democratic advisors such as Reed and Galston, the triangulation strategy subordinated substantive third way objectives such as national service and welfare reform to empty rhetoric and imagery. Standing under banners that proclaimed "Building America's Bridge to the 21st Century," Clinton repeatedly offered vague "bridge" rhetoric to the voters in lieu of discussing his plans for a second term. In addition, even when his lead in the polls stretched to fifteen points, Clinton resisted tying his campaign to the fortunes of congressional Democrats.

The president's remarkable political comeback in 1995 had been fueled by "soft money" donations supposedly designated for party-building activities and therefore not limited by existing federal campaign finance laws.[43] But these donations were used instead to mount television advertising campaigns, such as the media blast at Congress during the 1995 budget battle, that championed the president's independence from partisan squabbles. Determined to win a clear majority of the national popular vote and wary of alienating voters who might resist giving him too cooperative a Congress, Clinton seldom championed the election of a Democratic House and Senate. He did not raise money for his party's congressional candidates until late in the campaign. Media exposure during the election's final days of the administration's legally questionable fund-raising methods helped push Clinton's share of the popular vote below 50 percent as well as undermining the Democrats' effort to retake the House.[44]

Bland as it was, Clinton's campaign was visionary when compared with that of his Republican opponent, Robert Dole.[45] The seventy-three-year-old Senate veteran, who in three previous runs for national office had never displayed strong gifts as a campaigner, showed little improvement in 1996. Only Ross Perot could claim the mantle of outsider in 1996, but his quirky personality did not wear well the second time around. "When we ask people to use one word to describe him," reported the pollster Andrew Kohut, "the words are just awful—'rich,' 'crazy,' 'idiot,' 'egotistical.'"[46] Nevertheless, Perot's campaign drew a respectable 8 percent of the national popular vote, demonstrating once again the vulnerability of the ideologically polarized two-party system to a centrist attack, however eccentric.

In some ways, Clinton openly imitated Perot's personalistic politics. Triangulation was conceived as a campaign strategy that portrayed the president as an outsider who disdained the petty and mean-spirited skirmishes that had entangled both major parties since the late 1960s. On election day, Clinton won 49 percent of the popular vote to Dole's 41 percent and 379 electoral votes to Dole's 159. Although the president's reelection strategy, supported by a strong economy, was effective, the candidate-centered campaign that Clinton conducted denied him any chance to win a mandate based on a change-oriented policy agenda and long congressional coattails. In fact, the Democrats lost two seats in the Senate, which nearly outweighed their modest gain of nine seats in the House.

Balanced Budgets, Impeachment Politics, and the Limits of the Third Way

Clinton staked his success as president on forging a third way between Republican conservatism and Democratic liberalism.[47] His willingness to

President Bill Clinton, left, is emphatic in denying he had an affair with White House intern Monica Lewinsky. His main adversary, independent counsel Kenneth Starr, right, regarded the president's lies about the Lewinsky affair as impeachable conduct.

Source: (both) Reuters.

compromise in the face of continued Republican control of Congress was displayed in May 1997, when he and Republican congressional leaders agreed on a plan to balance the budget by 2002. Arguably, this deal was struck on Republican terms. The most dramatic measures in the budget—the first tax cut in sixteen years, the largest Medicare savings ever enacted into law, and five-year constraints on discretionary spending—shifted national priorities in a decidedly conservative direction.[48]

Nevertheless, Clinton exacted some important concessions from the Republicans, enough to enable him to persuade a majority of Democrats in Congress to support the plan. Most significant, the 1997 Balanced Budget Act smoothed the rough edges of the Welfare Reform Act of 1996. It provided substantial additional funding for immigrant benefits and food stamps. It also included $16 billion for the new federally funded State Children's Health Insurance Program (CHIP) for low-income, working families who were not eligible for Medicaid.[49] These concessions, along with the earlier increases Clinton won in the earned income tax credit for the working poor, allowed him to claim that he had fulfilled his promise to negotiate a new social contract with people who were trying hard to work their way out of poverty.[50]

To be sure, the budget agreement between the White House and the Republican-controlled Congress was possible only because of a revenue windfall caused by the robust economy, which enabled Clinton and Republican leaders to avoid the kinds of hard choices over program cuts and taxes that animated the bitter struggles of the Bush presidency and Clinton's first term.[51] Most economists attributed the economic boom of the 1990s more to the spread of technological innovations such as the personal computer and the Internet than to the federal government's fiscal policies. Even so, the rapprochement between the Democratic president and Republican Congress, which in fiscal year 1998 brought about the first balanced budget in three decades, testified to the possibility of the modern executive advancing principles and pursuing policies that defy the sharp cleavages of the national party system.

The Clinton administration and Republicans in Congress also collaborated to enact the 1999 Gramm–Leach–Bliley Act, which repealed the Glass–Steagall Act, a law passed during the early days of the New Deal to establish a wall between banking and speculation. Gramm–Leach–Bliley removed this barrier by allowing banks to merge with insurance companies and investment houses. The restraint on banks' financial activity had come to be viewed as an impediment to economic growth since the 1980s, and there were several attempts to remove it during the Reagan and Bush presidencies. The view shared by Clinton and his secretary of the Treasury,

Lawrence Summers, that New Democrat principles called for a "modernization" of financial markets appealed to a Republican-controlled Congress anxious to foster free enterprise. The act passed with overwhelming bipartisan support and was signed by the president in December 1999.

Bipartisan agreements between Clinton and the Republicans were the exception. Polarized partisan politics remained the rule. Just as Reagan and Bush were plagued by independent counsels who investigated alleged abuses in their administrations, so too were Clinton and members of his cabinet subjected to intense legal scrutiny. Republicans had long opposed reauthorization of the 1978 Ethics in Government Act, which provided for the appointment of independent counsels to investigate and prosecute alleged wrongdoing by government officials. But their resistance to Democratic efforts to reauthorize the statute came to an end in 1993, when the president and first lady were accused of shady financial dealings in an Arkansas real estate investment known as Whitewater while he was governor during the 1980s. Before Clinton became president, the activities pursued by a chief executive prior to taking office were rarely the subject of controversy or even serious inquiry. But partisan rancor in Washington fueled Republicans' eagerness to repay the Democrats for their attacks on the Reagan and Bush presidencies by subjecting the Clintons to unprecedented congressional and legal scrutiny.

Although no clear evidence of impropriety was found in the Whitewater investigation, in January 1998 independent counsel Kenneth W. Starr was authorized to expand the scope of the Whitewater inquiry to pursue allegations that the president lied under oath about an affair with a twenty-one-year-old White House intern, Monica Lewinsky, and that Clinton and his friend Vernon Jordan encouraged her to do the same. The Clinton administration's response was to accuse Starr, a prominent Republican, and his supporters in Congress of constituting, in Hillary Clinton's phrase, a "vast right wing conspiracy" to bring down the president. The Clintons' rapid counterattack proved effective in the court of public opinion. The president's approval rating remained high as voters continued to focus on his record of "peace, prosperity, and moderation."[52]

But reluctant to cooperate with Starr's investigation, Clinton made broad claims of executive privilege that were, as the *New York Times* observed, "freighted with echoes of Watergate and President Nixon's efforts to keep his White House tapes secret."[53] The president's assertion of an executive privilege to keep aides Sidney Blumenthal and Bruce Lindsey, as well as Secret Service agents, from testifying before the grand jury convened by Starr was rebuffed by a federal district court judge.

Congressional Democrats were slow to rally to Clinton's defense. Most Democratic legislators, still smarting from the president's seeming indifference to their programmatic commitments and desire to regain control of Congress, initially were silent as the Republicans sought to exploit his peccadilloes.[54] Clinton's uneasy relationship with his party in Congress also threatened his legislative program. For example, the great majority of House Democrats, who had opposed NAFTA during his first term, refused to give the president fast-track authority to negotiate international trade agreements, a power that previous Democratic Congresses had readily conferred on Republican presidents Ford, Reagan, and Bush.

Democrats also challenged the line-item veto, a power that the Republican Congress granted to the president in a 1996 act in the hope that a Republican would be wielding it after the election. The new law was passed with Clinton's strong support over widespread Democratic opposition. It empowered the president to cancel any new spending projects, narrowly targeted tax breaks, and entitlement programs within five days of signing a money bill, subject to override by a two-thirds vote of both the House and the Senate. Clinton used the line-item veto to cancel twenty-eight provisions in eleven laws, ranging from $15,000 for a new police training center in Arab, Alabama, to $30 million for an air force program to intercept an asteroid in space.

Within days of the Line Item Veto Act of 1996 taking effect, Sen. Robert Byrd of West Virginia and several other congressional Democrats sued to overturn it as a violation of the constitutional provision that allows the president to veto only a "bill," not part of a bill. The Supreme Court dismissed their case in 1997, ruling that Byrd and his colleagues lacked standing to sue because they had not suffered any direct injury from the line-item veto. On June 25, 1998, however, in *Clinton v. City of New York*, a six-justice majority declared the act unconstitutional in response to lawsuits filed by New York City, which objected to Clinton's veto of a tax break tied to the Medicaid program, and by the Snake River (Idaho) Potato Growers, who lost a capital gains tax advantage for farmers' cooperatives. Relying on the presentment clause of Article I, section 7 (every bill "shall be presented to the President of the United States" for either approval or veto), Justice John Paul Stevens wrote that line-item vetoes are "the functional equivalent of partial repeal of acts of Congress" even though "there is no provision in the Constitution that authorizes the president to enact, amend, or to repeal statutes."[55] Fifteen years earlier, the Court relied heavily on the same constitutional clause in *Immigration and Naturalization Service v. Chadha*, when it declared unconstitutional Congress's long-standing use of the legislative veto to second-guess the executive branch after delegating it authority to make discretionary decisions about how laws should be implemented.

With the decline of Clinton's personal stature and the historical pattern of substantial losses for second-term presidents' party at midterm, nearly every political expert predicted that the Republicans would emerge from the 1998 elections with a tighter grip on Congress and, consequently, on the president's political fate.[56] But the Republicans were preoccupied by the Lewinsky scandal for the entire year and lacked an appealing campaign message. They were unable to increase their 55–45 margin in the Senate and lost five seats in the House, leaving them with a slim 223–211 majority. Clinton, the first Democrat since FDR to be reelected to a second term, also became the first president since Roosevelt to see his party gain seats in a midterm election. Severely disappointed by the results, the Republicans fell into soul-searching and recriminations. Ironically, it was the hero of their 1994 ascent to power, Speaker Gingrich, whose political fate was sealed by the elections. Soon after the results were tallied, Gingrich announced that he was resigning not only his leadership position but also his seat in Congress. Clinton's supporters felt it was poetic justice that Gingrich's fall from grace was abetted by his admission during the impeachment hearings that he, too, had engaged in an extramarital affair.

The 1998 elections seemed likely to take the steam out of the House impeachment inquiry. But as the president gathered with friends and aides to celebrate what appeared to be another remarkable political comeback, the Republicans prepared to move forward with impeachment. A centrist, poll-sensitive politician, Clinton underestimated the willingness of congressional Republicans to defy the survey-tested will of the people.[57] In truth, the hands of Republican legislators were tied. Their core constituencies—the GOP primary voters and, especially, the conservative party activists who control congressional nominations—strongly favored impeachment.[58]

In December 1998, after nearly a year of dramatic and tawdry politics, Clinton was impeached on separate counts of perjury and obstruction of justice by a sharply divided House of Representatives. The House voted virtually along party lines to recommend that the Senate remove the president from office. Article I, the perjury count, was approved by a vote of 226–206, with Republicans providing all but five of the aye votes and Democrats providing all but five of the nays. The 221–212 vote in favor of Article II, which charged Clinton with obstruction of justice, was almost as partisan. Only five Democrats voted for the article, and only thirteen Republicans voted against it.[59]

But even impeachment did not undermine Clinton's popular support. After a five-week Senate trial, the president's accusers failed to gain a simple majority, much less the constitutionally mandated two-thirds, to support either charge against him. On February 12, 1999, the Senate rejected the perjury article, 55–45, with ten Republicans joining all forty-five Democrats to vote against conviction. Just six minutes later, with five Republicans breaking ranks, the Senate split 50–50 on the article accusing the president of obstruction of justice. Clinton's job was safe.

The most obvious casualty of the impeachment controversy was the Ethics in Government Act, which Congress did not reauthorize when it lapsed in the summer of 1999. Less obvious was the effect of the impeachment debacle on the modern presidency. To be an effective deterrent of executive abuse, Alexander Hamilton wrote in *Federalist* No. 65, impeachment should be used only to investigate a serious "violation of some public trust." Although sharp partisanship was evident in the impeachment inquiries concerning Andrew Johnson and Richard Nixon, both of these cases involved contests over important constitutional questions. In contrast, the Clinton impeachment failed to rise above raw and disruptive partisan combat.

Although he was acquitted by the Senate and remained popular with the public, Clinton's problems with the Republican Congress continued. Virtually every item on his legislative agenda—each of them politically appealing in its own right—failed to be enacted, including campaign finance reform, tobacco regulation, school construction, a minimum wage increase, and a patient's bill of rights. But the perception that Clinton was an enfeebled president, thwarted at every turn by fierce Republican opposition and unsteady Democratic support, was belied by his aggressive use of the administrative presidency during all six years that the Republicans controlled Congress. Beginning in 1995 the president issued a blizzard of executive orders, regulations, proclamations, and other decrees on matters such as tobacco regulation and environmental protection to achieve his goals, with or without the blessing of Congress.[60]

Clinton also upheld Lyndon Johnson's Executive Order 11246, which mandates affirmative action targets for federal contractors, against a frontal assault by the courts. In *Adarand Constructors, Inc. v. Pena* (1995) the Supreme Court overturned a program that paid contractors a bonus of up to 10 percent for each subcontract awarded to "socially or economically disadvantaged"—that is, minority-owned—firms.[61] Ruling that all racial preferences are constitutionally suspect, this opinion was the first in which the Court rejected a contracting set-aside program. In the face of judicial scrutiny and mounting political opposition to Executive Order 11246, the

Clinton administration eliminated seventeen set-aside programs but preserved the affirmative action employment practices it had imposed on government contractors. In May 1998 Clinton issued Executive Order 13087, which for the first time prohibited federal agencies from discriminating in employment on the basis of sexual orientation. Although Republican legislators and conservative religious groups denounced Clinton for creating a new protected class of people eligible for affirmative action benefits, Congress did not act. As it had throughout the twentieth century, Congress proved unable, or unwilling, to reverse executive orders through legislation.[62]

Late in his second term, Clinton also defied congressional opposition to the use of military force in the Balkans. This time it was in Kosovo, a province of Serbia, where Slobodan Milosevic's ruthless and repressive domination of the majority Muslim population revived the terrible specter of ethnic genocide. Although the House defeated a resolution in May 1999 endorsing the administration's bombing campaign in Kosovo, Clinton's persistence eventually forced Milosevic to accept a peace settlement. Once criticized for his lack of experience and interest in military affairs, Clinton now readily embraced the president's authority as commander in chief.[63]

Still, any moral authority Clinton may have had at the beginning of his administration to establish a "new covenant" of rights and responsibilities between citizens and their government was severely undermined by the public's distaste for his personal conduct. The virulent partisanship that characterized the impeachment process forced Clinton to seek refuge once again among his fellow Democrats in Congress, thereby short-circuiting his plans to pursue entitlement reform as the capstone of his presidency.[64] In the wake of the impeachment debacle, Clinton positioned himself as the champion of the status quo when it came to Social Security and Medicare, urging Congress to invest a significant share of the mounting budget surplus in these traditional liberal programs.[65]

Meanwhile, Clinton's efforts to avoid litigation and impeachment led to a series of court decisions that weakened the authority of the presidency. On May 27, 1997, in *Clinton v. Jones*, the Supreme Court unanimously rejected the president's claim of immunity against a sexual harassment lawsuit brought by Paula Corbin Jones, a former Arkansas state employee.[66] The ruling established that even sitting presidents are subject to civil suits. It also set the stage for the sworn depositions by Lewinsky and Clinton in Jones's case that provoked the House, guided by the independent counsel, to charge the president with perjury and obstruction of justice. Moreover, Starr's investigation established legal precedents by securing court rulings declaring that neither the president's Secret Service agents nor the government lawyers he consulted could refuse to testify in a criminal investigation by invoking executive privilege.[67] The main effect of Clinton's efforts to forestall investigations of his conduct as governor and president was to corrode the constitutional safeguards of presidential immunity and executive privilege.

Even without these protections, the rise of a plebiscitary form of presidential leadership made presidents politically less accountable than in the past. As with the "third way," Clinton's president-centric alternative not just to the opposition party but also to his own made it more likely that contemporary presidents would encourage citizens to invest their support in an individual leader for a time, subject to quick abandonment if they become dissatisfied with the president's style or performance.

Yet Clinton's presidency-focused politics could not withstand the rising tide of partisanship that arose in the 1980s and continued after Ronald Reagan left the White House. The 1994 congressional elections widened the ideological divide between the Republican and Democratic parties and eventually pulled Clinton into the vortex of partisan combat, with significant institutional and constitutional consequences. The final five years of his administration suggested that presidents harried by the prospects of governing in a sharply divided party system might choose to retreat to the realm of administration in pursuit of both personal and policy objectives. Instead, Clinton became the victim of partisan rancor that resulted in his becoming the first elected president ever tried for impeachment. His administration thus raised troubling questions about how partisan warfare might tempt even a political moderate—one seemingly determined to pioneer a synthesis of liberalism and conservatism—to circumvent constitutional principles and institutional arrangements. Such concerns only intensified during the George W. Bush presidency, which transformed Republican policy objectives into a governing creed—the "unitary executive"—that dramatically expanded unilateral presidential power, especially in foreign affairs.

Notes

1. The term *extraordinary isolation* is Woodrow Wilson's. See Wilson, *Constitutional Government in the United States* (New York: Columbia University Press, 1908), 69.

2. See, for example, Theodore J. Lowi, "The Party Crasher," *New York Times Magazine*, August 23, 1992, 28, 33.

3. James Ceaser and Andrew Busch, *Upside Down and Inside Out: The 1992 Elections and American Politics* (Lanham, Md.: Rowman and Littlefield, 1993), 105. See also Philip Meyer, "The Media Reformation: Giving the Agenda Back to the People," in *The Elections of 1992*, ed. Michael Nelson (Washington, D.C.: CQ Press, 1993), 89–98.

4. Greenberg cited in Michael Nelson, "Redividing Government: National Elections in the Clinton Years and Beyond," in *Inside the Presidency of Bill Clinton*, eds. Michael Nelson, Barbara Perry, and Russell Riley (Ithaca, Cornell University Press, 2016), 35.

5. William Clinton, "The New Covenant: Responsibility and Rebuilding the American Community" (speech delivered at Georgetown University, Washington, D.C., October 23, 1991).

6. Nelson, "Redividing Government," 38.

7. Dan Balz and David Broder, "President Clinton's First One Hundred Days," *Washington Post*, April 29, 1993, A1. The first one hundred days of an administration are an early benchmark of presidential performance that Franklin Roosevelt inadvertently bequeathed to his successors.

8. Walter Dean Burnham, "On the Shoals, Nearing the Rocks," *American Prospect*, 14 (Summer 1993): 10–11.

9. Sidney Blumenthal, "The Syndicated Presidency," *New Yorker*, April 5, 1993, 42–47.

10. Kimba Wood was never actually nominated as attorney general. Burned once by his hasty pick of Zoë Baird, Clinton awaited the results of a full background check before announcing his near-certain choice of Wood, a New York federal judge. When it was disclosed that Wood, like Baird, had hired an undocumented immigrant to babysit her children, a jittery White House pushed her to withdraw.

11. Lewis L. Gould, *The Modern American Presidency* (Lawrence: University Press of Kansas, 2003), 218.

12. "From what one can tell," presidential scholar Joel D. Aberbach has written, "real responsibility for most [of the early political and policy difficulties] lies primarily in the White House [and White House staff] . . . not in the agencies or their appointed or career personnel." Aberbach, "The Federal Executive under Clinton," in *The Clinton Presidency: First Appraisals*, eds. Colin Campbell and Bert A. Rockman (Chatham, N.J.: Chatham House, 1996), 176. See also Burt Solomon, "A One-Man Band," *National Journal*, April 24, 1993, 970–974.

13. James W. Cicconi, a former member of the Reagan and Bush White Houses, cited in Burt Solomon, "Musical Chairs in the West Wing May Bring Order from Cacophony," *National Journal*, June 26, 1993, 1661.

14. Thomas L. Friedman, "Ready or Not, Clinton Is Rattling the Country," *New York Times*, January 31, 1993, sec. 4, 1.

15. George Hager and David S. McCloud, "Test for Divided Democrats: Forge a Budget Battle," *Congressional Quarterly Weekly Report*, June 26, 1993, 1631–1635.

16. Alan Brinkley, "The 43% President," *New York Times Magazine*, July 4, 1993, 22.

17. Will Marshall, president, Progressive Policy Institute, interview by Sidney M. Milkis, May 20, 1997. See also Sidney Blumenthal, "Bob Dole's First Strike," *New Yorker*, May 3, 1993, 40–46.

18. As an official of the Democratic National Committee acknowledged, there were serious "institutional" difficulties in reconciling Clinton's New Democratic principles with the "base" of the party. The leading financial contributors and core voters of the party were more liberal than the president, making it difficult for the administration to provide clear moral leadership. Personal interview, not for attribution, by Sidney M. Milkis, July 11, 1997.

19. Douglas Jehl, "Rejoicing Is Muted for the President in Budget Victory," *New York Times*, August 8, 1993, 1, 23; David Shribman, "Budget Win a Hollow Win for President," *Boston Globe*, August 8, 1993. See also Paul J. Quirk and Joseph Hinchcliffe, "Domestic Policy: The Trials of a Centrist Democrat," in Campbell and Rockman, *Clinton Presidency*, 272–274.

20. David Shribman, "A New Brand of D.C. Politics," *Boston Globe*, November 18, 1993, 15; Gwen Ifill, "56 Long Days of Coordinated Persuasion," *New York Times*, November

19, 1993, A27. See also Barbara Sinclair, "Trying to Govern in a Negative Era," in Campbell and Rockman, *Clinton Presidency*, 109–111.

21. CNN transcripts, July 5, 1993.

22. Clifford Krause, "White House Reaches a Deal with Byrd on Role in Somalia," *New York Times*, October 15, 1993, A12.

23. William J. Clinton, Address Accepting the Presidential Nomination at the Democratic Convention in New York, July 16, 1992, http://www.presidency.ucsb.edu/ws/?pid=25958.

24. The William J. Clinton Presidential History Project, Bruce Reed, Domestic Policy Advisor, February 2004, https://millercenter.org/the-presidency/presidential-oral-histories/bruce-reed-oral-history-february-2004-domestic-policy.

25. Barbara A. Perry, "Hillary Rodham Clinton: Recasting the Role of First Lady," in Barbara A. Perry and Russell Riley, *42: Inside the Presidency of Bill Clinton* (Ithaca and London: Cornell University Press), 182.

26. Donald F. Kettle, *Reinventing Government? Appraising the National Performance Review* (Washington, D.C.: Brookings, 1994), IX.

27. Address to Congress on Health Care Plan, printed in *Congressional Quarterly Weekly Report*, September 25, 1993, 2582–2586; Robin Toner, "Alliance to Buy Health Care: Bureaucrat or Public Servant," *New York Times*, December 5, 1993, 1, 38.

28. Clinton Presidential History Project, William Galston, deputy assistant to the president for domestic Policy, April 2004, https://millercenter.org/the-presidency/presidential-oral-histories/william-galston-oral-history-deputy-assistant-president.

29. For a fuller account of the health care reform battle, see Haynes Johnson and David S. Broder, *The System: The American Way of Politics at the Breaking Point* (Boston: Little, Brown, 1996); and Theda Skocpol, *Boomerang: Clinton's Health Security Effort and the Turn against Government* (New York: W.W. Norton, 1996).

30. Adam Clymer, "National Health Program, President's Greatest Goal, Declared Dead in Congress," *New York Times*, September 27, 1994, A1, B10. For a sound and interesting case study of the Clinton health care program, see Cathie Jo Martin, "Mandating Social Change within Corporate America" (paper presented at the annual meeting of the American Political Science Association, New York, September 1–4, 1994). Martin's study shows that health care reform became the victim of a battle between "radically different world views about the state and corporation in modern society."

31. Gary C. Jacobson, "Deficit Cutting Politics and Congressional Elections," *Political Science Quarterly*, 108 (Fall 1993): 375–402; Jacobson, "The 1994 House Elections in Perspective," in *Midterm: The Elections of 1994 in Context*, ed. Philip A. Klinkner (Boulder: Westview Press, 1996), 1–20.

32. Dan Balz and Ronald Brownstein, *Storming the Gates: Protest Politics and the Republican Revival* (New York: Little Brown, 1996), 207.

33. Sean M. Theriault, Patrick T. Hickey and Megan Miller, "Compromise and Confrontation: Clinton's Evolving Relationship with Congress," in Nelson, Perry, and Riley, *42: Inside the Presidency of Bill Clinton*.

34. Bob Woodward, *The Choice* (New York: Simon and Schuster, 1996), 23.

35. Ibid., 25.

36. "Bill Clinton's Third State of the Union Address," in *The Evolving Presidency: Landmark Documents, 1787–2010*, 4th ed., ed. Michael Nelson (Washington, D.C.: CQ Press, 2012), 269–273.

37. The replaced program was Aid to Families with Dependent Children (AFDC). In reality AFDC never existed as an entitlement program in the sense that Social Security and Medicare did. The program only guaranteed federal matching funds to states that established AFDC programs. R. Shep Melnick, "The Unexplained Resilience of Means-Tested Programs" (paper delivered at the annual meeting of the American Political Science Association, Boston, Massachusetts, September 3–6, 1998).

38. William Jefferson Clinton, "Remarks on Signing the Personal Responsibility and Opportunity Reconciliation Act," *Weekly Compilation of Presidential Documents*, August 22, 1996, 1484–1489. Political scientists Joe Soss and Sanford Schram argue that welfare reform did not change the public's negative view of "welfare"; nor did it redound to the benefit of the Democratic Party. See Soss and Schram, "A Public Transformed: Welfare Reform as Policy Feedback," *American Political Science Review*, 101, no. 1 (February 2007): 111–127.

39. "Victory March," *Newsweek*, November 18, 1996, 48.

40. Paul Light, *The President's Agenda: Domestic Policy Choice from Kennedy to Reagan* (Baltimore: Johns Hopkins University Press, 1991), 37.

41. Howard Kurtz, *Spin Cycle: Inside the Clinton Propaganda Machine* (New York: Free Press, 1998).

42. Woodward, *Choice*, 368.

43. Anthony Corrado, "Financing the 1996 Elections," in *The Election of 1996*, ed. Gerald Pomper (Chatham, N.J.: Chatham House, 1997). "Soft money" had its home in the 1979 amendments to the campaign finance legislation of 1974 as part of a broader effort to strengthen national party organizations. By 1992 both Democrats and Republicans had come to depend on it to finance the expensive media campaigns that dominated national elections. As such, the parties violated the spirit of the 1979 amendments, which were meant to increase party spending on traditional grassroots boosterism and get-out-the-vote drives rather than mass-media campaigns. More to the point, the institutional separation between the president and the parties allowed, even encouraged, the exploitation of these funds by presidential candidates. See Beth Donovan, "Much-Maligned 'Soft Money' Is Precious to Both Parties," *National Journal*, May 15, 1993, 1195–1200. The Bipartisan Campaign Finance Reform Act of 2002 prohibited national parties from raising and spending "soft money."

44. Michael Nelson, "The Election: Turbulence and Tranquility in Contemporary American Politics," in *The Elections of 1996*, ed. Michael Nelson (Washington, D.C.: CQ Press, 1997), 52; Gary C. Jacobson, "The 105th Congress: Unprecedented and Unsurprising," in Nelson, *The Elections of 1996*, 161.

45. Almost one in five voters identified a "vision for the future" as the most important quality driving their presidential vote; Clinton received 77 percent of their votes. See James W. Ceaser and Andrew E. Busch, *Losing to Win: The 1996 Elections and American Politics* (Lanham, Md.: Rowman and Littlefield, 1997), 166.

46. "The Third Dimension," transcript of segment on *The NewsHour with Jim Lehrer*, August 19, 1996.

47. Clinton's "third way" politics is placed in historical perspective and carefully analyzed in Stephen Skowronek, *The Politics Presidents Make: Leadership from John Adams to Bill Clinton* (Cambridge: Harvard University Press, 1999), 447–464.

48. Daniel J. Palazzolo, *Done Deal? The Politics of the 1997 Budget Agreement* (Chatham, N.J.: Chatham House, 1999), 189.

49. States are given flexibility in designing CHIP eligibility requirements and policies within broad federal guidelines.

50. R. Kent Weaver, "Ending Welfare as We Know It," in *The Social Divide: Political Parties and the Future of Activist Government*, ed. Margaret Weir (Washington, D.C.: Brookings, 1998), 397.

51. Richard Stevenson, "After Year of Wrangling, Accord Is Reached on Plan to Balance the Budget by 2002," *New York Times*, May 3, 1997, 1.

52. John R. Zaller, "Monica Lewinsky's Contribution to Political Science," *PS: Political Science and Politics*, 31 (June 1998): 182–189.

53. John M. Broder, "In Aide's Claim, Echoes of Watergate," *New York Times*, May 12, 1998.

54. Adam Clymer, "Under Attack, Clinton Gets No Cover from His Party," *New York Times*, March 16, 1997, 1; Jeffrey L. Katz and Dan Carney, "Clinton's Latest, Worst Troubles

Put His Whole Agenda on Hold," *Congressional Quarterly Weekly Report*, January 24, 1998, 164–165; Richard L. Berke, "Republicans End Silence on Troubles of President," *New York Times*, March 1, 1998, 20; Peter Baker, *The Breach: Inside the Impeachment and Trial of William Jefferson Clinton* (New York: Scribner's, 2000).

55. *"Clinton v. City of New York,"* in Nelson, *Evolving Presidency*, 273–278.

56. Janny Scott, "Talking Heads Post-Mortem: All Wrong, All the Time," *New York Times*, November 8, 1998, A22.

57. Richard L. Berke, John M. Broder, and Don Van Natta Jr., "How Republican Determination Upset Clinton's Backing at the Polls," *New York Times*, December 28, 1998.

58. Gary C. Jacobson, *The Politics of Congressional Elections*, 5th ed. (New York: Longman, 2000), 258–259.

59. Two other proposed articles were defeated in the House: one dealing with perjury by 205–229 and the other dealing with abuse of power by 148–285. Only the latter vote, which included eighty-one Republican nays, was anything close to bipartisan.

60. Robert Pear, "The Presidential Pen Is Still Mighty," *New York Times*, June 28, 1998.

61. *Adarand Constructors, Inc. v. Pena*, 515 U.S. 200 (1995).

62. Kenneth R. Mayer, *With the Stroke of a Pen: Executive Orders and Presidential Power* (Princeton: Princeton University Press, 2001), 210–215.

63. Emily O. Goldman and Larry Berman, "Engaging the World: First Impressions of the Clinton Foreign Policy Legacy," in Campbell and Rockman, *Clinton Legacy*, 246–249; Paul Starobin, "The Liberal Hawk Soars," *National Journal*, May 14, 1999.

64. Will Marshall, president, Progressive Policy Institute, interview by Sidney M. Milkis, June 14, 1999.

65. David E. Rosenbaum, "Surplus a Salve for Clinton and Congress," *New York Times*, June 29, 1999.

66. *Clinton v. Jones*, 520 U.S. 681 (1997).

67. See *In re: Sealed Case*, No. 98-3069 (United States Court of Appeals), July 7, 1998; and *In re: Bruce Lindsey (Grand Jury Testimony)*, No. 98-3060 (United States Court of Appeals), July 27, 1998. On how Clinton's legal battles set precedents that limited the institutional prerogatives of the presidency, see David M. O'Brien, "Judicial Legacies: The Clinton Presidency and the Courts," in Campbell and Rockman, *Clinton Legacy*.

CHAPTER 14

George W. Bush and Unilateral Presidential Power

By the close of the Clinton era, the Republicans controlled both houses of Congress and occupied the governorships of nine of the ten largest states, all except California. Realizing that to defeat Vice President Al Gore, the Democratic nominee for president in 2000, they would have to find a moderate conservative candidate, the large-state Republican governors united behind a colleague, Gov. George W. Bush of Texas. The governors' display of solidarity was evidence that even though candidate-centered politics had supplanted party-centered politics since the waning of the New Deal, it was still possible to put the party's political well-being first. The governors rallied behind Bush in part because he came from the largest Republican state and shared his father's name. In securing the nomination, Bush also benefited from being close to the leaders of the GOP's strongly conservative congressional wing, especially House leaders Richard K. Armey and Tom DeLay, both Texans.

Neither Bush's prepresidential experience nor the themes he stressed in his campaign gave any hint that he would be able to deal with a foreign policy crisis if one should arise. Like three of his four most recent predecessors—Jimmy Carter, Ronald Reagan, and Bill Clinton—Bush was a governor with no experience in Washington. Like them, too, he was elected on an almost purely domestic platform. Unlike Carter, Reagan, and Clinton, however, Bush assembled an experienced team of foreign policy professionals to staff his administration. The senior Bush's secretary of defense, Richard B. Cheney, became George W. Bush's vice president. Colin Powell, who had served as Reagan's national security adviser and then as chair of the Joint Chiefs of Staff, returned to government as secretary of state. Condoleezza Rice, previously a National Security Council staff member, became the president's national security adviser. For secretary of defense, Bush chose Donald H. Rumsfeld, who had held the same position under Gerald R. Ford.

After terrorists attacked the World Trade Center and the Pentagon on September 11, 2001, Bush declared, "This is what my presidency is about."[1] To be sure, his presidency was about other things as well, some of them significant as policy and some as politics. In the end, however, the fate of the Bush presidency hinged less on his decision to launch the war on terrorism against the al Qaeda network and the Taliban regime in Afghanistan that protected it than on his subsequent decision to extend the war to an additional front. The controversial extension of the "War on Terror" to Iraq transformed homeland security—a new federal responsibility—into a highly charged partisan issue.

Bush's resolute leadership in the wake of the September 11 attacks advanced the executive-centered partisanship that roiled the Reagan and Clinton presidencies. Bush's party leadership initially earned him and the Republican Party considerable political success, culminating in a narrow but decisive reelection victory in 2004. By 2006, however, the growing unpopularity of the war in Iraq and other policy failures had thrown the Bush administration into political free fall. In 2008 Bush was a political albatross around the neck of the Republican candidate bidding to succeed him, Sen. John McCain of Arizona.

The Democrats' strong comeback in the 2006 midterm elections, in which they regained control of Congress for the first time in twelve years, and the victory of their presidential nominee in 2008, Sen. Barack Obama of Illinois, badly compromised Bush's first-term political achievements. More broadly, the successes and failures of the Bush presidency raised once again a familiar dilemma: how can the country maintain an executive that is strong enough to meet imposing challenges at home and abroad but not so strong as to defy accountability to Congress and the public? Although this dilemma is as old as the Republic, Bush's joining of partisanship to the unilateral powers of the presidency, some of them widely disputed, raised it in an especially extreme form.[2]

The 2000 Election

At the September 2000 meeting of the American Political Science Association, seven renowned scholars forecast the outcome of the November presidential election using models that incorporated measures of economic growth and public approval of the incumbent president. They unanimously predicted that Gore would defeat Bush by a margin of 6 percent to 20 percent in the national popular vote.[3] For four years the economy had grown at an annual rate of at least 4 percent, and President Clinton's job approval rating had stayed above 60 percent, the most consistently high ratings for a second-term president in the history of polling. In addition, unemployment fell during every year of Clinton's two-term presidency, eventually dropping below 4 percent; the average annual rate of inflation during the Clinton years was the lowest since the early 1960s; and the enormous budget deficits that Clinton inherited from his predecessor became substantial budget surpluses.

The political scientists' predictions were wrong: the election was extremely close and in the end Gore lost. Telling the voters in his acceptance speech at the Democratic National Convention that "I stand here tonight as my own man" was a politically appropriate response to the candidate-centered nature of modern presidential politics, which places a premium on distinguishing oneself from one's party and predecessors.[4] But rejecting Clinton's repeated offers to campaign for him, which party leaders pleaded with Gore to accept, was not.[5] Even worse, instead of emphasizing the national prosperity that marked the Clinton–Gore years, Gore ran a populist-style, "people, not the powerful" campaign, better suited for a candidate challenging an incumbent in economic hard times than for a vice president seeking to extend his party's control of the presidency in good times. In the three nationally televised debates with Bush, Gore never mentioned Clinton. "We might have blown it," a Gore aide said near the end of the campaign. "We didn't remind people of how well off they are."[6]

Third-party politics also worked to Gore's disadvantage. The Reform Party, formed by Ross Perot in 1996, seemed likely to draw voters from the Republican nominee, but it self-destructed in 2000 after conservative political commentator Pat Buchanan captured its nomination. Buchanan shared some core Reform positions, especially strong opposition to free trade. But reviving the culture war that animated his challenge to George Bush in the 1992 Republican primaries, he spoke more frequently about issues that divided the party such as abortion, affirmative action, and gay rights. Buchanan's nomination at the Reform convention provoked Perot to endorse Bush. On election day, Buchanan received less than 1 percent of the national popular vote.

Ralph Nader, the longtime consumer activist and Green Party nominee, ran a much stronger campaign than Buchanan, winning 3 percent. Because many of Nader's votes came at Gore's expense, Gore had to campaign harder to carry northern progressive states such as Minnesota and Oregon than he would have had Nader not been on the ballot. In Florida, Nader received 97,419 votes, many more than Gore needed to win the state, its twenty-five electoral votes, and the presidency. Nationally, the exit poll indicated that Nader supporters preferred Gore to Bush by 47 percent to 21 percent.[7]

In the end, both Bush and Gore presented themselves to the voters as pragmatic centrists. For all Gore's efforts to separate himself from Clinton by adopting a populist theme, the actual policy positions he took during the campaign gave no indication that he contemplated a significant departure from Clinton's "third way" Democratic course. Bush fashioned an appeal based on "compassionate conservatism." Instead of being reflexively antigovernment in the Reagan tradition, he emphasized the need for a federal role both in ameliorating poverty by involving faith-based organizations in the administration of social services and in improving education by holding schools accountable for how well they served their most disadvantaged students.[8]

The 2000 election ended in a virtual tie, with the deadlock ultimately resolved by the Supreme Court. In the end, the Bush-versus-Gore election campaign was less decisive than the *Bush v. Gore* Supreme Court case. In many of its features, the protracted, bitter legal dispute that lasted for five weeks after the voters cast their ballots resembled the partisan clashes between the White House and Congress that prevailed during the final third of the twentieth century, culminating in the Clinton impeachment. These clashes raised doubts about whether a nation that historically resolved most of its political conflicts through the electoral process had grown accustomed to institutional combat instead.[9]

Bush v. Gore

The "postelection election" of 2000 began in the predawn hours of Wednesday, November 8, when the television networks, which earlier had declared Bush the winner on the basis of his victory in Florida, decided that Florida was actually too close to call. Gore dispatched a team of lawyers to Tallahassee to investigate charges by local Democrats that they had been cheated out of their votes. Claiming that voting machines failed to count all of his ballots and therefore thwarted the will of the people, Gore called for a hand count in four counties that voted strongly Democratic and were controlled by Democratic election commissions. The core of Gore's legal challenge, which was supported by Florida's Democrat-dominated supreme court, was that a hand count would show the true intent of the voters and, in all likelihood, overcome Bush's minuscule lead, which had shrunk from a reported 1,784 votes on election night to 327 votes (out of nearly 6 million cast) after a statewide machine recount was conducted a few days later.

Bush's lawyers appealed to the U.S. Supreme Court to stop the hand count ordered by the state supreme court in the four disputed counties. They argued that the Florida court's decision violated both the Constitution's provision that the state legislature must determine how a state's electors will be chosen and the 1887 Electoral Count Act's requirement, passed in the wake of the disputed 1876 Hayes–Tilden election, that electors must be chosen according to state laws enacted in advance of the election. Bush's lawyers also claimed that the recount violated the equal protection clause of the Fourteenth Amendment because no uniform standard would govern the counting of votes in the state's different counties.

Even as the lawyers from both sides chased each other from courtroom to courtroom, Bush pressed advantages that he alone enjoyed. Florida secretary of state Katherine Harris, who under state law was charged to certify the results of the election and oversee any recounts that took place, had cochaired the state's Bush campaign. The state legislature, which arguably had the power under the Electoral Count Act to appoint a slate of electors if all other approaches failed, was heavily Republican. The governor of Florida was Bush's brother. As governor, Jeb Bush was charged by the Electoral Count Act to notify the National Archives in Washington which slate of electors his state had chosen.[10] Republican presidents had appointed seven of the nine justices of the U.S. Supreme Court, which on December 9 agreed to the Bush legal team's request to resolve the controversy. Bush also benefited from the simple passage of time. Because the Electoral Count Act required that states decide by December 12 which candidate's slate of electors had been chosen, any recounts presumably would have to be completed by then.

Discerning the intent of voters who imperfectly marked their ballots was the subject of the Supreme Court decision in the case of *Bush v. Gore*. A seven-justice majority decreed that the counting process ordered by the Florida Supreme Court, which required a manual count of every "undervote" (that is, every ballot for which a machine did not register a vote for president), was unconstitutional. By failing to establish a uniform standard that every county in the state would use to judge the voters' intention, the Florida court had violated the Fourteenth Amendment's requirement that states safeguard the right of individuals to the "equal protection of the laws."

The Court divided more closely and bitterly in the second part of its ruling. In a 5–4 vote, the Court found that the Florida court also violated the Constitution by overruling the state legislature, which had indicated its intention to take advantage of an Electoral Count Act provision that insulates a state's electors from challenge as long as they are certified by December 12. Because any recount would frustrate the constitutional prerogative of the state legislature to determine how electors are chosen, the Court decreed, "[W]e reverse the judgment of the Supreme Court of Florida ordering the recount to proceed."[11] The Supreme Court issued its decision on the evening of December 12, leaving Florida no time to recount the votes even if identical procedures for doing so could be implemented in every county.

Florida's twenty-five electoral votes raised Bush's total to 271, one more than he needed to be elected. Gore conceded defeat the next day. But his surrender did not take place without considerable protest. Democratic activists were emboldened by Justice John Paul Stevens's dissenting opinion, in which he decried the Court's majority for emphasizing Florida's need to certify its electoral votes by December 12 rather than enforcing the state's obligation to determine the intention of its voters. "Although we may never know with complete certainty the identity of the winner of this year's Presidential election," Stevens wrote, "the identity of the loser is perfectly clear. It is the Nation's confidence in the judge as an impartial guardian of the rule of law."[12] Although the Court's verdict was accepted by most of the American people, it left a bitter taste in the mouth of Democratic partisans, diminishing the prospects for a bipartisan consensus to form behind Bush's pledge to govern as a compassionate conservative.

The Early Months of the Bush Presidency

Bush began his presidency in 2001 with the Republicans in control of Congress, although by the narrowest of margins. The Republican majority in the House was 222–211, the same as before the election. A four-seat Democratic gain in the Senate elections created a 50–50 division between the parties, with Vice President Cheney able to break any ties in the Republicans' favor. Like Clinton at the beginning of his administration, Bush initially chose to cooperate with his party's strongly ideological leaders in Congress. His decision to emphasize traditional conservative issues such as tax cuts, regulatory relief, energy production, and missile defense risked alienating moderate Republicans, a small but pivotal group in the closely divided House and Senate.

Bush reaped both the benefits and the costs of this early strategy of partisan conservatism. The president persuaded Congress to enact the leading conservative proposal of his 2000 campaign, a $1.3 trillion tax cut. But the Republicans lost control of the Senate in May 2001 when Sen. James M. Jeffords of Vermont announced that he was changing his allegiance from the Republican to the Democratic caucus.[13] Within days, every Senate committee and subcommittee chair was transferred to Democratic hands.

Facing the prospect of ongoing partisan obstruction in the Senate, the Bush administration intensified its efforts to consolidate authority within the White House. The president assigned his political adviser, Karl Rove, to take the lead in recruiting candidates and devising Republican campaign strategies for the 2002 state and congressional elections. In doing so, Bush undercut the authority of the Republican National Committee chair, Gov. James S. Gilmore III of Virginia. Politics was joined to policy when, midway through 2001, Rove began repositioning the president as a centrist, nontraditional Republican. By the end of his first summer in office, Bush had begun to stress educational reform and faith-based social services, not taxes and national defense.[14]

After being sworn in as the forty-third president of the United States, George W. Bush sings the national anthem with former president Bill Clinton and former vice president Al Gore on inauguration day, January 20, 2001.

Source: Reuters.

Bush's revival of his campaign theme of compassionate conservatism, White House aides argued, embodied conservative values but not conservative opposition to an active federal government.[15] "The invisible hand works many miracles," Bush had said of market capitalism in July 1999. "But it cannot touch the human heart. . . . We are a nation of rugged individuals. But we are also the country of the second chance—tied together by bonds of friendship and community and solidarity."[16]

In part, Bush proposed to fulfill the moral commitment he endorsed with policies that supported nonprofit groups working outside of government. In doing so, he called for changes in federal and state regulations that would allow churches and other faith-based organizations to play a larger role in providing government-funded social services to the poor, the addicted, the illiterate, and others in need of help. But Bush also wanted the federal government to take an important part in securing the general welfare. Although conservatives previously had sought to eliminate the Department of Education, Bush proposed the No Child Left Behind Act, which charged the department to make public schools more accountable by linking federal aid to national standards and measurements of student learning.

For as long as the president continued to emphasize it, compassionate conservatism promised to soften the often harsh antigovernment edge of the Republican Party. It also gave the president a platform from which to act independently of his party. Because programs such as faith-based initiatives and educational reform were not major priorities within Republican councils, Bush advanced several of his objectives through bipartisan cooperation. The No Child Left Behind Act in particular seemed less a use of government to secure Republican principles than an uneasy compromise between liberals' demand for more spending and conservatives' insistence on standards.[17] Bush trumpeted his alliance with the Democratic Party's leading liberal icon, Sen. Edward M. Kennedy of Massachusetts, when signing the bill in January 2002. One year later, Bush persuaded both parties in Congress to adopt PEPFAR—the President's Emergency Plan for AIDS Relief—a five-year, $15 billion plan to combat AIDS in Africa.[18]

On occasions when Congress refused to cooperate, the president often turned to executive orders. On January 29, 2001, Bush created a faith-based office in the White House and charged it to "eliminate unnecessary legislative, regulatory, and other bureaucratic barriers that impede faith-based and other community efforts to solve social problems." He also ordered the Departments of Labor, Education, Health and Human Services, Housing and Urban Development, and Justice to establish Centers for Faith-Based and Community Initiatives within their departments. These centers were to perform internal audits, identifying barriers to the participation of faith-based organizations in providing social services, and to devise plans to remove these barriers.[19]

No less than Clinton's third way, Bush's compassionate conservatism promised to transcend the long-standing contest in American politics between rights-based claims to entitlement programs and the virtues of individual responsibility. His first prime-time address to the nation on a specific issue, stem cell research, represented another effort to satisfy both sides. Many religious conservatives viewed stem cell research using human embryos as a form of abortion that violates the rights of the unborn. But most Americans opposed closing the door to stem cell research, valuing its promise of scientific progress toward curing diseases.

Bush's August 9, 2001, address tried but failed to bridge the two sides of the debate. In a solution that the president characterized as "careful and prayerful," but which detractors dismissed as clumsy and calculating, the president announced that federal grants could be used to conduct studies on stem cells that already had been harvested from embryos left over at fertility clinics. But he prohibited the national government from supporting research that involved the creation or destruction of new embryos.

Bush's attempt to resolve the stem cell controversy highlighted the tension between the modern presidency and constitutional democracy. The president's policy came in the form of an executive order, which granted authority to oversee stem cell research to the newly created President's Council on Bioethics. But the controversy could not be ended by fiat. It resurfaced in the 2004 presidential election and again in Congress's decision in 2006 to pass a bill lifting the restrictions that Bush placed on federally funded embryonic stem cell research. Bush's veto of this bill, the first veto of his presidency, ended the legislative challenge at the expense of fueling the political one. Democrats kept the issue alive in the 2006 midterm elections, in which they took control of both houses of Congress from the Republicans. If public debate over stem cells was truly required, Democrats argued, why should the issue be resolved by appointed experts rather than by elected officials in Congress? By delegating the issue to an administrative board, Bush had confirmed an important legacy of the modern presidency: a more active and better-equipped national government but one that often eschews legislative deliberation.[20] The fragility of this approach was revealed in February 2009, when the Democratic Congress overturned Bush's executive order by passing a bill to broadly fund stem cell research, and Barack Obama, the newly elected Democratic president, signed it into law.

September 11 and the War on Terrorism

Bush's agenda changed dramatically when the United States was struck by terrorists from the al Qaeda network on September 11, 2001. In the aftermath of the first attack on the American continent since the War of 1812, and the deadliest in the nation's history, the country rallied behind the president. Polls showed a remarkable and almost immediate jump in public support for Bush, from 51 percent approval of the job he was doing as president to 90 percent approval within days of the attacks. A strong public and congressional consensus quickly formed in support of his initial military response against al Qaeda and the Taliban regime in Afghanistan that harbored the terrorist network's leaders.[21]

Hardly a critical word was heard when the Bush administration created the White House Office of Homeland Security, imposed tighter restrictions on airport security, and embraced deficit spending to help the economy and fight the war in Afghanistan. Bush justified the war on terrorism in words reminiscent of Franklin D. Roosevelt's promise of greater security and Winston Churchill's call for resoluteness in the face of an evil foe. "Freedom and fear are at war," Bush told a joint session of Congress in a televised address on September 20. "The advance of human freedom—the great achievement of our time and great hope of every time—now depends on us. . . . We will not tire, we will not falter, and we will not fail."[22]

Bush's response to the September 11 attacks was both a continuation of and a departure from the progressive internationalist tradition that has dominated the modern presidency since Theodore Roosevelt and Woodrow Wilson. Like a true progressive, Bush emphasized that the war on terrorism was both an effort to protect American lives and property and a crusade to advance liberty and democracy. But he also made clear that the United States would set its own course, welcoming consultation and assistance from other nations but refusing to be deterred by the misgivings of even its closest allies. Wilson trumpeted the need for a League of Nations to enforce a lasting peace. FDR invested considerable diplomatic and political capital in working with the wartime allies to found the United Nations. Bush's father gathered a broad international coalition to prosecute the Persian Gulf War of 1991. But Bush did not wait for a massive allied force to form before invading Afghanistan in October 2001. The war was fought and the Taliban overthrown by American special forces and Central Intelligence Agency (CIA) operatives working in close coordination with Afghanistan's Northern Alliance, a rebel force that opposed the Taliban.

The war on terrorism created a political dilemma for the Democrats. Although Bush's public approval ratings declined from their 90 percent peak, the decline was gradual, and his conduct of the presidency was still supported by 68 percent of Americans in November 2002, the month of the midterm election.[23] For as long as Bush remained popular, Democratic officeholders could not oppose his policies without risk of appearing unpatriotic. But they were most in tune with Wilsonian progressivism on the very matter that Bush was least so: international cooperation. Democrats treasured close ties with the West European allies and were strongly committed to respecting and working through international bodies, especially the United Nations.

President George W. Bush addresses a crowd of firefighters, rescue workers, and volunteers at Ground Zero—the sixteen-acre plot where the 110-story World Trade Center towers once stood—three days after two hijacked planes struck the buildings on September 11, 2001.

Source: Reuters.

The heightened fears of additional terrorist attacks on American soil enabled the Bush presidency to frame the nation's challenge as a battle between good and evil. Drawn to the rhetoric of the Reagan administration, Bush embraced a narrative "in which evil is real, but courage and decency triumph." But Reagan's moral clarity and employment of power during the cold war was tempered by careful calculations of national interest, which encouraged him to respond eagerly to the diplomatic overtures of Mikhail Gorbachev. In contrast, the Bush administration's invasion of Iraq, historian Melvyn Leffler has argued, manifested a "recalibration of the relationship between ideals and interests" that portended an "ominous assertion of American power."[24]

An Expanded Presidency

As Bush prepared the nation for new responsibilities at home and abroad, presidential scholars and public officials revived warnings, dormant since the Nixon years, about what political scientist Andrew Rudalevige has called "the new imperial presidency."[25] Already executive-centered in its approach to politics and policy, the Bush White House became even more insulated from Congress and the Republican Party as it planned and fought the multifront war on terrorism. Democratic and Republican legislators complained when White House Homeland Security director Tom Ridge refused to testify before Congress. The administration claimed that Ridge's office was a presidential agency whose director and staff were thereby exempt from congressional grilling.

Similarly, bipartisan criticism of Attorney General John Ashcroft emerged when the administration unilaterally instituted measures to crack down on terrorism at home, including military tribunals to try suspected foreign terrorists.[26] According to an executive order issued by President Bush on November 13, 2001, "unlawful enemy combatants"—that is, those not wearing the uniform of an enemy nation's military—would be brought to trial not in a civil court but in a military tribunal with no right of appeal. Although some American citizens were later designated as enemy combatants, the order targeted noncitizens whom the president determined to be present or former members of al Qaeda; to have "engaged in, aided or abetted, or conspired to commit acts of international terrorism or acts in preparation thereof" that would have "adverse effects" on the United States; or to have "knowingly harbored" someone who had done so. The executive order defended the president's power to establish military tribunals without congressional authorization by invoking Franklin Roosevelt's 1942 proclamation concerning the German *Quirin* saboteurs. But, as critics pointed out, FDR's order was drafted retrospectively to apply to a specific case, not prospectively to apply to any individuals the president might decide were enemies of the United States.[27]

For a time, these complaints paled against the aura of political invincibility that Bush enjoyed after September 11. But the roots of Congress's resentment of executive slights ran deep and agitated its relationship with the White House for the rest of Bush's presidency. Beginning in spring 2002, Bush administration officials openly pursued the possibility of a war in Iraq aimed at removing Iraqi dictator Saddam Hussein from power. In October 2002, at the president's request, Congress passed a resolution authorizing him to use military force against Iraq "as he determines to be necessary." In doing so, legislators sustained Bush's revival of the Cold War-era belief that any overriding cause—the containment of communism then, the war against terrorism now—justifies the expansive use of presidential power around the globe. Nearly every congressional Republican voted for the use of force resolution, as did 40 percent of House Democrats and 58 percent of Senate Democrats, including all six Democratic senators who were seriously contemplating a presidential candidacy in 2004 or 2008.[28]

The Bush administration's decision to seek a congressional endorsement of its policy toward Iraq was an exception to its general rule of unilateral executive action but only a partial one. Bush made clear that he would not be bound by an adverse vote. The president's broader determination to fight the war on terrorism outside the bounds of conventional legal constraints was a constant source of tension between the White House and Congress. Indeed, congressional resistance became bipartisan during Bush's second term. By late 2005, buttressed by revelations that the administration used the highly secret National Security Agency to monitor suspicious domestic communications without judicial review or consultation with Congress, legislators began to fight back. In addition to their concern about the president's policy of creating military tribunals to try enemy combatants and his use of surveillance to monitor overseas phone calls, they objected to the administration's broad rules permitting harsh interrogations of suspected terrorists.

In particular, a series of memos from the CIA's general counsel and the Justice Department's Office of Legal Counsel claimed for the agency wide powers of imprisonment and interrogation that in some cases overrode the Geneva Conventions, the international code that has governed the treatment of prisoners and civilians during wartime and postwar occupations for more than half a century. Because terrorists were not fighting on behalf of an established state or in uniform, the Bush administration argued, they were not covered by the international law of war. The president approved a permissive set of rules governing interrogations, which allowed the CIA to establish detention centers in secret overseas locations. Suspected terrorists were subjected to severe interrogation techniques, including "waterboarding," in which a bound prisoner is brought to the brink of drowning.

In the face of vigorous White House opposition, Congress, led by Senator McCain, himself a victim of torture as a prisoner of war in Vietnam, passed the Detainee Treatment Act of 2005. Bush signed the bill, which prohibited interrogation techniques that involve "cruel, inhuman, or degrading treatment or punishment." But the president appended a statement to his signature, objecting to some of the new law's provisions and explicitly reserving the right to interpret them "in a manner consistent with the constitutional authority of the President to supervise the unitary executive branch and as Commander in Chief." The phrase "unitary executive branch" referred to the Bush administration's theory, popular in certain conservative legal circles, that neither Congress nor the courts may restrict the president's authority to command employees and agencies of the executive branch.[29] Following, indeed wildly exceeding the practice of his three most recent predecessors—Reagan, Bush, and Clinton—Bush used signing statements to declare that he would not enforce about twelve hundred provisions of laws as he signed them, about twice as many as all previous presidents combined.[30] In each case, Bush's purpose was to insulate executive power from legislative and judicial direction, especially in matters pertaining to national and homeland security.[31]

The president's defense of a largely unchecked unitary executive branch was challenged in the Supreme Court. On June 29, 2006, the Court's ruling in *Hamdan v. Rumsfeld* strongly limited the president's power to create military tribunals for and employ aggressive interrogation techniques against suspected terrorists imprisoned at the American naval base in Guantánamo Bay, Cuba.[32] Brushing aside the administration's pleas not to second-guess the commander in chief during wartime, a five-justice majority ruled that the tribunals were not justified by military necessity and that they violated both the Geneva Conventions and the congressionally enacted Uniform Code of Military Justice (UCMJ). Consequently, the Court ordered, no military tribunal could try either Salam Ahmed Hamdan, a former personal aide to al Qaeda leader Osama bin Laden, or anyone else unless the president did one of two things that he had steadfastly refused to do: operate the tribunals in accordance with the UCMJ, which required regular military courts martial, or ask Congress for specific permission to proceed differently.

Responding to *Hamdan*, Bush had little choice but to press for legislation endorsing his approach to terrorists. His efforts to persuade Congress to narrowly define American obligations under the Geneva Conventions met strong resistance in the Senate. Three respected Republicans—McCain, Lindsay Graham of South Carolina, and John Warner of Virginia, the chair of the Armed Services Committee—rejected the administration's approach not only as unbefitting a free nation but also as an invitation to other countries to abuse any American soldiers they might hold as prisoners. Anxious to resolve this dispute before the 2006 elections, Bush and the dissident Republicans reached a compromise in September 2006. The White House yielded its desire to secure congressional approval for a constricted interpretation of Article 3 of the Geneva Conventions, which requires humane treatment of detainees and prohibits "violence to life and person," including "outrages upon personal dignity." In return, Congress delegated to the president the dominant role in deciding which interrogation methods are permitted by Article 3. The Military Commissions Act, which Bush signed into law on October 18, 2006, also authorized the use of military tribunals and eliminated habeas corpus jurisdiction for any "enemy combatant" held in American custody. Although the Supreme Court ruled two years later in *Boumediene v. Bush* that enemy combatants have a constitutional right to file petitions for habeas corpus in civilian federal courts, it left intact the remainder of the Military Commissions Act.[33]

The war on terrorism affirmed the preeminence of the modern presidency in other ways as well. The new responsibilities that the war thrust on the executive led Bush, at the urging of many members of Congress, to pursue major institutional reforms of the executive branch. In June 2002 he called for the creation of a Department of Homeland Security, outlining the most ambitious reorganization of the national government since the 1940s. Likening his plan to the 1947 National Security Act, which authorized President Harry S. Truman to create the National Security Council, the Central Intelligence Agency, and the Department of Defense, Bush asked Congress to create "a single, permanent department with an overriding and urgent mission: securing the homeland of America, and protecting the American people."[34]

Bush had initially resisted forming another government department.[35] The small Office of Homeland Security that he created by executive order in the frantic days after September 11 was part of the White House Office and was headed by Ridge, who enjoyed a close personal relationship with the president. The administration changed course, however, when faced with criticism about whether it had done everything possible to prevent the September 11 attacks and taken adequate measures to forestall similar acts in the future. Ridge's office, critics claimed, lacked authority over the budgets and activities of the many executive agencies whose actions he was responsible for coordinating.

Once Bush was persuaded to transform the homeland security office into a full-scale homeland security department, he urged Congress to enact legislation moving twenty-two executive agencies and 170,000 federal employees, including the Customs Service, Secret Service, Immigration and Naturalization Service, and Federal Emergency Management Agency, into the new department.[36] Congressional Democrats and Republicans looked favorably on Bush's proposal, in part because Congress has more authority over a department than over the White House Office. The president's plan promised to end the protracted struggle about whether Ridge was obligated to testify before Congress concerning his budget and programs. As the head of a department, he clearly was accountable to the legislature.

At the same time, the creation of the department signified that homeland security had become an ongoing responsibility of the national government. "Before 9–11," political scientists Jennifer Morolla and Paul Pulido have argued, "no one had even conceived of the notion of 'homeland security,' but the term rapidly became ubiquitous and the publicized focus on intelligence failure and the need for vigilance made sacrifices for the sake of security more palatable." An important institutional consequence followed: the blurring of the boundary between executive prerogatives in foreign affairs and the more limited authority the White House exercised in domestic matters.[37]

Bush and the Republican Party

For much of the history of the modern presidency, executive power has undermined the major political parties. The forging of direct ties between the White House and the public, combined with aggressive executive administration, has tended to subordinate party loyalty to the personal and programmatic ambitions of the president. Building on the merging of partisanship and executive prerogative during Reagan's two terms in office, Bush further advanced a presidency-centered party system. After winning the 2000 election, Bush and political adviser Karl Rove became strongly committed to making the Republican Party an enduring governing majority. As such, the Bush presidency surpassed the Reagan administration in showing how a strongly partisan president can use the expanded powers of the office for party-building purposes.

With steadfast support from Republican leaders in Congress, Bush exploited his party's ideology and organization to advance a conservative, executive-centered administrative state. A similar effort occurred during the Reagan administration, but Bush trumped Reagan in his commitment to "big government conservatism."[38] The most dramatic example of this approach was Bush's foreign policy, especially the controversial Bush Doctrine of preventive war against terrorist states or states that harbor terrorists. "If we wait for threats to materialize," the president declared in a June 1, 2002, graduation address at the United States Military Academy at West Point, "we will have waited too long." Because "the war on terrorism will not be won on the defensive," he added, "we must take the battle to the enemy, disrupt his plans, and confront the worst threats before they emerge." Referring to "unbalanced dictators with weapons of mass destruction," Bush left little doubt that he intended to use his new prevention doctrine to justify a war against Saddam Hussein's regime in Iraq.[39]

Bush-style conservatism extended to domestic policy as well. Rather than try to curtail New Deal and Great Society entitlement programs, as

Reagan and the Gingrich-led 104th Congress tried to do, Bush sought to recast these programs in conservative form. His goal was to cement ties between the Republican Party and groups that embraced generally conservative values but whose members relied on government help. Bush's faith-based social services initiative was, in part, a response to religious organizations' belief that they were unfairly disadvantaged in obtaining federal funds to help the poor, uneducated, and addicted. With his commitment to the No Child Left Behind education reform, Bush sought to mobilize conservatives in support of a federal program to make public schools better by making them more accountable. Finally, in an effort to win support from senior citizens, in 2003 Bush secured congressional enactment of a costly prescription drug program as a new part of Medicare.

Even Bush's most spectacular domestic policy failure, his doomed effort at the start of the second term to reform Social Security, reflected his commitment to deploy the federal government for conservative objectives. Unlike Reagan, Bush proposed not to cut Social Security benefits but to privatize them by allowing workers to divert some of their Social Security payroll taxes into personal retirement accounts. This reform, the president claimed, would yield beneficiaries a better rate of return on their contributions and would recast the core New Deal entitlement program so that individuals would assume greater responsibility to plan for their own retirements. But the federal government would still force people to save, restrict the investment choices they could make, and regulate the pace at which they could withdraw their money in retirement.[40] Bush campaigned strenuously around the country for his plan, but it went nowhere in Congress. Like Clinton's equally sweeping proposal to reform health care in 1993 and 1994, Social Security reform foundered on the shoals of partisan opposition and the public's reluctance to change a system that most felt worked reasonably well. Bush's national speaking tour on behalf of his proposal produced no increase in public support.

The Bush administration's party-building activities complemented its agenda of big government conservatism, with greater success. The president's active recruitment of Republican candidates and diligent fund-raising considerably strengthened the national party organization. His public displays of religious faith and use of strong moral language solidified the Republican loyalties of religious conservatives. Large tax cuts in 2001 and 2003 were equally appealing to the party's economic conservatives, who bitterly recalled George Bush's abandonment of his "no new taxes" pledge. During his son George W. Bush's first term, these efforts yielded handsome political returns.

Risking the bipartisan support he accrued in the aftermath of September 11, Bush threw himself into the 2002 midterm elections earlier and more energetically than any president in history. Bush and Rove recruited strong Republican challengers to face incumbent Democratic senators, even to the point of intervening in state party politics to do so. The president spoke at sixty-seven fund-raising events that raised a record $141 million in campaign contributions for the GOP and its candidates. Throughout the fall, he campaigned ardently for his party's nominees. The Democrats' maladroit handling of legislation establishing the Department of Homeland Security, which saw them delay passage of the bill until after the election in a failed effort to extend full union protections to the new department's civil servants, gave Bush and Republican congressional candidates an issue that they exploited effectively in several close Senate elections. Most controversially, Bush made this issue a cause célèbre in championing Saxby Chambliss's successful challenge to Georgia Democrat Max Cleland, who lost both legs and an arm in Vietnam. The attack on Cleland for "voting against the president's vital homeland security efforts" featured a campaign ad that mixed footage of Osama bin Laden and Saddam Hussein with an unflattering picture of the Democratic incumbent. The commercial infuriated Cleland's partisan brethren in Washington.[41]

This harsh partisanship would eventually engulf Bush's presidency, but the results of the elections appeared to vindicate his decision to become actively involved in the campaign. The Republicans gained two seats in the Senate in 2002, moving them from minority to majority status, while also increasing their majority in the House of Representatives. Political analysts were quick to describe the historic nature of the Republican victory. It marked the first time in more than a century that the president's party regained control of the Senate in a midterm election. It was the first election since 1934—and the first ever for a Republican president—in which the president's party gained seats in both houses of Congress midway through the first term.

Yet Bush and Rove could not take all the credit for the Republican gains. Since the late 1970s the Republican Party had been developing into a formidable national organization in which the Republican National Committee, rather than the state and local organizations, was the principal sponsor of party-building activities. For a time, this top-down approach risked becoming too centralized and too dependent on television advertising to perform the parties' traditional role of mobilizing voters. Convinced that it had been out-organized on the ground by the Democrats in 2000, Republicans developed a massive grassroots voter mobilization operation for Bush's reelection campaign in 2004. Unlike the Democrats, who since the New Deal had relied on auxiliary groups such as labor unions to get out the vote, the GOP created its own national organization to mobilize supporters.[42] Indeed, one could argue that the Republicans built the first national party machine in American history—an elaborate network of campaign volunteers concentrated in the sixteen most competitive states. The Republican organization was crucial to Bush's narrow but decisive victory against the Democratic nominee, Sen. John Kerry of Massachusetts: 51 percent to 48 percent in the popular vote and 286 to 251 in the Electoral College.[43]

Testifying to his attention to party building, Bush also became the first incumbent since Franklin Roosevelt to win a second term while his party was gaining seats in the House and Senate. Bush's four most recently reelected predecessors—Dwight D. Eisenhower in 1956, Richard Nixon in 1972, Ronald Reagan in 1984, and Bill Clinton in 1996—won by much larger margins than he did. But theirs were "lonely landslides" in which the president did exceptionally well but his party suffered in the congressional elections.[44]

The 2004 campaign may have marked a milestone in the development of united, ideologically distinctive political parties. The new party system had already strengthened partisan discipline in Congress, and it was a valuable source of campaign funds and other services for candidates. But it had failed to stir the passions and allegiance of the American people, as attested by declining voter turnout from the 1960s to 2000. In contrast, the 2004 campaign was passionate, polarized, and participatory. Significantly, both the Republicans' grassroots organizations and the get-out-the-vote campaign of Americans Coming Together (ACT), the group that assumed principal responsibility for Kerry's voter mobilization effort, were organized outside the regular state and local party organizations.[45] Both campaigns sought to recruit new grassroots activists to serve as local leaders in a national party offensive. Voter turnout rose from 51 percent in 2000 to 55 percent in 2004, allowing Bush to win 11.5 million more popular votes in 2004 than he had in his first victory, the largest increase ever for a president from one election to the next.[46] Beyond its immediate effectiveness in securing Bush's reelection, then, the Republicans' White House-inspired mobilization effort in 2004 provided a plausible blueprint for a revitalized party politics that could draw more people into the political process and renew the linkages between citizens and their elected officials.

Although Bush's leadership of the GOP marked the most systematic effort by a modern president to create a strong national party, the prospect of parties holding the modern presidency accountable still was not great.

As Rove has argued, the executive-centered parties that have emerged since the 1980s are "of great importance in the tactical and mechanical aspects of electing a president." But they are "less important in developing a political and policy strategy for the White House." In effect, parties serve as a critical "means to the president's end."[47]

Not surprisingly, the Bush reelection campaign sought to frame the voters' choice in 2004 as between two individuals, not between the Republican and Democratic platforms. Voters were urged to focus on the candidates' character and temperament. In the lingering aftermath of the September 11 attacks, Republicans wanted Americans to ask themselves which candidate would do a better job of waging the war on terrorism. As Matthew Dowd, the Bush campaign's top strategist, suggested, "People want someone they can count on in tough times, and [after September 11] Bush filled this paternalistic role."[48] The Kerry campaign, for its part, emphasized the senator's intelligence and strength of character. A central theme of the 2004 Democratic National Convention was Kerry's military service in Vietnam. He accepted the nomination with a crisp salute and an emphatic announcement that he was "reporting for duty!" The convention focused on presenting Kerry as the candidate who displayed the "strength required of a leader in post-9–11 America."[49]

Kerry's electoral chances suffered when Republicans characterized his erratic support for the war in Iraq as "flip-flopping," which appeared to defy his campaign's emphasis on the candidate's strength of character. Like many Democrats in Congress, Kerry justified his vote for the Iraq war resolution in 2002 by claiming that he was merely voting to authorize the president to decide whether to go to war. Kerry maintained throughout the campaign that he would have cast the same vote even after seeing how frustrating the situation became in Iraq. After all, he said, "I believe it's the right authority for the president to have."[50] Kerry's acceptance of executive aggrandizement badly hamstrung his effort to challenge Bush on the central issue of the 2004 election. Ultimately, as Dowd acknowledged, "both parties' organizing force focused on President Bush—the Republicans in defense of his leadership; the Democrats in opposition—hostility—to it."[51]

The 2006 midterm elections confirmed this tendency toward president-centered partisan voting, even in a nonpresidential year. The Democrats based their victorious campaign on opposition to a president who, although increasingly unpopular because of the violent aftermath of the war in Iraq, the failed Social Security reform effort, and the administration's initially ineffective response to the devastation wrought in New Orleans by Hurricane Katrina in August 2005, would not be on the ballot in 2008.[52] Even after

Early in his second term, President George W. Bush appointed two justices to the Supreme Court. Bush looks on as his first appointee, Chief Justice John Roberts, administers the oath of office to his second appointee, Justice Samuel Alito.

Source: AP Photo/Charles Dharapak.

the election, attitudes toward Bush and the parties remained closely interwoven, both in Congress and the country. An April 2007 *New York Times/CBS News* poll found that Bush's approval rating among all voters was 32 percent, but among Republicans it was more than twice as high—66 percent.[53] That same month, in a crucial vote on funding for the Iraq war, House and Senate Republicans voted 195–2 and 45–2, respectively, against a bill to tie the appropriation to a schedule for military withdrawal. House and Senate Democrats voted 216–13 and 49–0, respectively, in favor of the bill.[54] When Bush vetoed the legislation, Republican loyalists in Congress united to prevent the Democrats from attaining the two-thirds majority needed to override the veto.

Courts and Parties

Despite his severe decline in popularity, Bush did make an enduring contribution to the Republican Party: the appointment of two Supreme Court justices with impeccable conservative credentials. Since the end of the

Lyndon Johnson administration, presidents and the Senate had engaged in acrimonious battles over nominations to the Supreme Court and appellate judgeships. But partisan rancor reached new heights during the Bush presidency. In the wake of the Republicans' victory in 2004, Senate majority leader Bill Frist of Tennessee, with encouragement from Bush, considered employing what came to be called the "nuclear option"—that is, having Vice President Cheney rule filibusters against judicial nominations out of order so that judges could be voted on and confirmed by a simple majority of senators. The polarizing struggle over the filibuster was resolved in May 2005 when a bipartisan group of Senate moderates—dubbed the Gang of 14—agreed to oppose both the nuclear option and filibusters except under "extraordinary circumstances."

Just how long this uneasy truce would last remained uncertain. The retirement of Justice Sandra Day O'Connor and the death of Chief Justice William H. Rehnquist in the fall of 2005 gave Bush the opportunity to move the Supreme Court in a conservative direction.[55] The White House, the Senate, and activists on both the left and right immediately prepared to renew their partisan combat over judicial nominations.

Ironically, the main conflict that ensued was not between Democrats and Republicans but between the president and conservatives in his own party. Bush's first nominee, appellate court judge John G. Roberts Jr., did not generate much opposition. Roberts had a conservative record as a member of the Reagan administration's Justice Department, and as a federal judge he had not left a long enough paper trail for liberals to attack. Equally important, Roberts was nominated to replace the conservative Rehnquist. The prospect of appointing one conservative, especially someone who showed great poise and charm during his Senate confirmation hearings, in place of another did not arouse fierce partisan fervor.

Bush's choice to replace Justice O'Connor, who for a decade cast the swing vote between liberals and conservatives in many critical cases, drew much greater scrutiny. When the president announced that he was nominating his White House counsel, Harriet Miers, to the seat, conservative Republicans responded angrily. Miers had been a respected lawyer in Texas, the president's personal attorney, and a legal adviser during Bush's two gubernatorial campaigns—but not much else. Republican activists were outraged that the president passed over proven conservative judges in favor of a nominee with no record as a constitutional jurist. Bush, for his part, assumed that the Republican base he had cultivated so assiduously for five years would support anyone he chose. He assured Senate Republicans and conservative activists that Miers was an evangelical Christian who as a justice would uphold traditional family values. But judicial politics had become too polarized for conservatives to accept an unknown quantity on anyone's say-so, even the president's. After weeks of acrimony, Bush withdrew Miers's nomination and substituted Samuel A. Alito, who like Roberts had been a proven conservative in the Reagan administration and was an appellate judge.

The epic battle many pundits predicted over the Alito nomination never materialized. Memos that Alito had written in the 1980s expressing conservative positions on abortion and affirmative action did arouse liberal ire when they came to light. But Alito's modest demeanor before the Senate Judiciary Committee, his strong professional reputation as a judge, and his pledge to uphold the law rather than promote conservative doctrine made it difficult for Senate Democrats to portray him as extreme enough to justify a filibuster. Alito's confirmation was ensured when the Gang of 14 met shortly before the Senate vote and unanimously decided that the "extraordinary circumstances" stipulation of their 2005 agreement did not apply in this case. Absent a filibuster, Alito was confirmed on a nearly straight party-line vote of 58–42.

As Republicans celebrated and Democrats lamented the consolidation of a narrow conservative majority on the Supreme Court, liberals conceded that their only hope of influencing judicial politics was to start winning congressional and presidential elections. The first of these hopes was realized in 2006. The Democrats' aggressive and well-organized national campaign secured a congressional majority capable of blocking any conservative judicial nominations Bush might make during his final two years in office. No additional Supreme Court vacancies occurred while Bush was president, and his remaining appellate court nominees were either judicial moderates or, in many cases, remained unconfirmed by the Senate. In addition, in 2007 congressional Democrats went after Attorney General Alberto Gonzales with a vengeance when the Bush administration fired eight U.S. attorneys for being insufficiently partisan. Although the ninety-three U.S. attorneys (one for each federal judicial district) serve four-year terms "at the pleasure of the president," their role in the judicial process gave Democrats reason to argue that the Bush administration was subverting the nonpartisan enforcement of the law.

For a brief period before the Democrats took control of Congress in January 2007, Bush was able not just to fire attorneys but to replace them without securing Senate confirmation. In the immediate aftermath of September 11, the president had persuaded Congress to pass with little debate the USA Patriot Act, an antiterrorism measure that enhanced the powers of the executive in matters of detention and surveillance, in part by breaking down the existing wall between domestic law enforcement and foreign intelligence activities. When Congress renewed the act in March 2006, a provision was slipped in that replaced federal judges with the attorney general as the appointing authority when an unexpected vacancy occurred in a U.S. attorney position. The newly appointed attorneys served in an interim capacity (thus removing the need for Senate confirmation) but would remain in office until the end of Bush's second term. This allowed Gonzales, spurred on by Rove, to replace every attorney who was fired with a Bush loyalist. The Democratic Congress's retaliation for this unprecedented politicization of the appointment power consisted not just of embarrassing public investigations but also the passage of a new law that once again reined in the attorney general's interim appointment power.[56]

Partisanship and Unilateralism at the Twilight of the Bush Presidency

As unpopular as Bush was in early 2007, his reliance on executive authority left him far from powerless. That Democrats won the midterm elections by promising to end the war in Iraq meant nothing to a president whose willingness to resort to unilateral executive action characterized his entire administration. The day after the election Bush fired Secretary of Defense Rumsfeld, signaling his desire for a new strategy for success in the war. He found such a strategy in the counterinsurgency approach championed by Gen. David Petraeus, who argued that American forces could bring stability to Iraq only by protecting the Iraqi people in the neighborhoods where they lived. Far from requiring fewer troops, this new strategy required more. Relying on his authority as commander in chief, Bush sent an additional twenty thousand soldiers to Iraq—the so-called surge. Congressional Democrats sputtered but acquiesced, pinning their hopes on the election of a new Democratic president in 2008 who they hoped would use his or her own unilateral authority to bring the American involvement in Iraq to a speedy conclusion.

Bush's final exercise of power required the full involvement of Congress, the Treasury Department, the Federal Reserve Board, and other independent financial agencies. In September 2008 several of the nation's largest banks, insurance conglomerates, and investment firms teetered on the verge of bankruptcy, the result of rampant speculation and loose lending in the home mortgage market facilitated by the passage of the Gramm–Leach–Bliley Act and other financial deregulatory measures in the 1990s. Although Bush did not know how to remedy what appeared to be a looming depression, he relied on those who did, notably Secretary of the Treasury Henry Paulson and Federal Reserve chair Ben Bernanke. They came up with an unprecedentedly large bailout program, the Troubled Asset Relief Program (TARP), with a budget of $700 billion. Democrats in Congress were reluctant to pass the bill because it came from the lame-duck Republican president, and congressional Republicans blanched at any massive market intervention by the federal government. On September 29 the House voted down the measure, and the Dow Jones Industrial Average immediately fell 777 points, the largest single-day drop in history. The Senate passed the bill on October 1, the chastened House followed suit on October 3, and the president signed it into law later that day.[57] TARP stopped the bleeding and stabilized the financial system. But the dampening effects of the financial crisis on the nation's economy persisted, there to await the winner of the 2008 election.

Notes

1. Bob Woodward, *Bush at War* (New York: Simon and Schuster, 2002), 102.

2. Starting with Richard Nixon, Republican success in presidential elections fostered an embrace of presidential power among conservatives, who during the Democratic administrations of Franklin D. Roosevelt and Harry S. Truman had been harshly critical. Liberal Democrats followed a reverse trajectory. See Julian E. Zelizer, "How Conservatives Learned to Stop Worrying and Love Presidential Power," in *The Presidency of George W. Bush*, ed. Julian Zelizer (Princeton: Princeton University Press, 2010), chap. 2; and Stephen Skowronek, "The Conservative Insurgency and Presidential Power: A Developmental Perspective on the Unitary Executive," *Harvard Law Review*, 122, no. 8 (June 2009): 2074–2103.

3. Robert G. Kaiser, "Academics Say It's Elementary: Gore Wins," *Washington Post*, August 31, 2000. "It's not even going to be close," said Michael Lewis-Beck of the University of Iowa as early as May. Robert G. Kaiser, "Is This Any Way to Pick a Winner?" *Washington Post*, May 26, 2000.

4. Thomas M. DeFrank, "I'm My Own Man, Says Al," *New York Daily News*, August 18, 2000.

5. David S. Broder, "Gore's Clinton Problem," *Washington Post National Weekly Edition*, October 30, 2000, 4.

6. "What a Long, Strange Trip," *Newsweek*, November 20, 2000, 126.

7. Thirty percent said they would not have voted at all. Peter Slevin, "A Defiant Nader Stands Up to Criticism," *Washington Post*, November 9, 2000.

8. James W. Ceaser and Andrew Busch, *The Perfect Tie: The True Story of the Presidential Election* (Lanham, Md.: Rowman and Littlefield, 2001), 37–46. See also Wilson Carey McWilliams, "The Meaning of the Election," in *The Election of 2000*, ed. Gerald Pomper (New York: Chatham House, 2000), 179–185.

9. Michael Nelson, "The Postelection Election: Politics by Other Means," in Nelson, *Elections of 2000*, ed. Michael Nelson (Washington, D.C.: CQ Press, 2001), 211–224.

10. Ibid., 220–221.

11. "*Bush v. Gore*," in *The Evolving Presidency: Landmark Documents, 1787–2010*, 4th ed., ed. Michael Nelson (Washington, D.C.: CQ Press, 2012), 283–290.

12. Ibid., Justice Stevens, with whom Justice Ginsberg and Justice Breyer join as dissenting judges, 290.

13. Tish Durkin, "The Scene: The Jeffords Defection and the Risk of Snap Judgments," *National Journal*, May 26, 2001.

14. Fred Barnes, "The Impresario: Karl Rove, Orchestrator of the Bush White House," *Weekly Standard*, August 20, 2001; Carl M. Cannon and Alexis Simendinger, "The Evolution of Karl Rove," *National Journal*, April 27, 2002, 1210–1216.

15. Karl Rove, interview by Sidney M. Milkis, November 15, 2001. Michael Gerson, Bush's principal speechwriter, noted that the president's rhetoric did not try to "split the difference" between liberalism and conservatism. Rather, Bush's speeches sought to convey how "activist government could be used for conservative ends." Michael Gerson, interview by Sidney M. Milkis, November 15, 2001.

16. George W. Bush, "Duty of Hope Speech," Indianapolis, Indiana, July 22, 1999.

17. David S. Broder, "Long Road to Reform: Negotiators Force Education Legislation," *Washington Post*, December 17, 2001.

18. For a thoughtful treatment of compassionate conservatism in the Bush presidency, see Kevin M. Kruse, "Compassionate Conservatism: Religion in the Age of George W. Bush," in Zelizer, *Presidency of George W. Bush*, chap. 10.

19. Executive Order 13198, Agency Responsibilities with Respect to Faith-Based and Community Initiatives, January 29, 2001, http://www.gpo.gov/fdsys/pkg/FR-2001-01-31/pdf/01-2851.pdf.

20. "President Names Members of Bioethics Council, Statement by the Press Secretary," January 16, 2002, http://georgewbush-whitehouse.archives.gov/news/releases/2002/01/20020116-9.html.

21. Richard Morin, "He Has the Public's Approval," *Washington Post National Weekly Edition*, September 24–30, 2001, 8. See also Marc J. Hetherington and Michael Nelson, "Anatomy of a Rally Effect: George W. Bush and the War on Terrorism," *PS: Political Science and Politics*, 36 (January 2003): 37–42.

22. "George W. Bush's War on Terrorism Address," in Nelson, *Evolving Presidency*, 290–298.

23. Hetherington and Nelson, "Anatomy of a Rally Effect."

24. Melvyn L. Leffler, "9/11 and American Foreign Policy," *Diplomatic History*, 29, no. 3 (June 2005), 413: 395–413.

25. Andrew Rudalevige, *The New Imperial Presidency: Renewing Presidential Power after Watergate* (Ann Arbor: University of Michigan Press, 2005). See also Matthew Crenson and Benjamin Ginsberg, *Presidential Power: Unchecked and Unbalanced* (New York: Norton, 2007).

26. David Nather and Jill Barshay, "Hill Warning: Respect Level from White House Too Low," *CQ Weekly*, March 9, 2002.

27. Rudalevige, *New Imperial Presidency*, 229–231.

28. The six Democratic senators were Christopher Dodd (Conn.), John Edwards (N.C.), Hillary Clinton (N.Y.), John Kerry (Mass.), Joseph Lieberman (Conn.), and Joseph Biden (Del.).

29. For a discussion of the unitary executive that places it in historical perspective, see Skowronek, "Conservative Insurgency: A Developmental Perspective on the Unitary Executive."

30. "George W. Bush's Signing Statement for the Defense Supplemental Appropriations Act," in Nelson, *Evolving Presidency*, 304–308. See also Crenson and Ginsberg, *Presidential Power*, 190–202. Reagan used signing statements to challenge 71 provisions of new laws, and Clinton did so 105 times. Each president served eight years.

31. Thomas Mann and Norman Ornstein, "The Threat of Bush's Signing Statements," *San Diego Union–Tribune*, July 7, 2006.

32. *Hamdan v. Rumsfeld*, 548 U.S. 557 (2006).

33. Michael A. Fletcher, "Bush Signs Terrorism Measure," *Washington Post*, October 18, 2006; *Boumediene v. Bush*, 553 U.S. 723 (2008).

34. George W. Bush, "Address to the Nation," June 6, 2002, http://georgewbush-white house.archives.gov/news/releases/2002/06/20020606-8.html.

35. Michael Nelson, "George W. Bush and Congress: The Electoral Connection," in *Considering the Bush Presidency*, eds. Gary L. Gregg II and Mark J. Rozell (New York: Oxford University Press, 2004), 141–159.

36. Mike Allen and Bill Miller, "Bush Seeks Security Department; Cabinet-Level Agency Would Coordinate Anti-Terrorism Effort," *Washington Post*, June 6, 2002.

37. Jennifer L. Merolla and Paul Pulido, "Follow the Leader: Major Changes to Homeland Security and Terrorism Policy," in Jeffery A. Jenkins and Sidney M. Milkis, *The Politics of Major Policy Reform in Postwar America* (New York: Cambridge University Press, 2014), 257–258: 253–281; Aaron Wildavsky, "The Two Presidencies," *Society*, January/February 1998, 24–31 (first published in 1966).

38. Michael Nelson, "Ronald Reagan, George W. Bush, and GOPtimism," *Chronicle Review*, March 17, 2006, B13–15.

39. "The Bush Doctrine," in Nelson, *Evolving Presidency*, 298–304.

40. Stephen Mufson, "FDR's Deal in Bush's Terms," *Washington Post*, February 20, 2005.

41. George W. Bush, *A Divider, Not a Uniter: George W. Bush and the American People*, 2nd ed. (New York: Pearson, 2010), 70.

42. The Democratic strategy was increasingly less effective, however, as union membership declined from about 40 percent of the workforce in 1950 to about 20 percent in 1980 and 13 percent in 2004. Michael Nelson, "George W. Bush, Majority President," in *The Elections of 2004*, ed. Michael Nelson (Washington D.C.: CQ Press, 2005), 1–17.

43. Matthew Dowd, political strategist for the Bush–Cheney campaign, interview by Sidney M. Milkis, July 8, 2004. See also Matt Bai, "The Multilevel Marketing of the President," *New York Times Magazine*, April 25, 2004, 43.

44. Nelson, "George W. Bush, Majority President."

45. The tendency of the Democratic Party to rely on auxiliary organizations such as labor unions was reinforced by the enactment of the Bipartisan Campaign Finance Reform Act in 2002, which proscribed party organizations, but not independent issue groups, from raising and spending "soft" money. The "527 groups," named for the section of the tax code that regulates them, were formed outside of the regular party organization in part to circumvent campaign finance regulations. No less important, however, was the view of some leaders of the 527 organizations that the Democratic National Committee and state parties were not capable of mobilizing the base support of liberal causes. Personal interview with ACT official, not for attribution, by Sidney M. Milkis, August 19, 2005. These groups formed an alliance to build an impressive media and ground campaign to match the efforts of the Republican Party.

46. Paul R. Abramson, John H. Aldrich, and David W. Rohde, *Change and Continuity in the 2004 and 2006 Elections* (Washington, D.C.: CQ Press, 2007), 85.

47. Karl Rove, interview by Sidney M. Milkis, November 15, 2001.

48. Matthew Dowd, interview by Sidney M. Milkis, July 20, 2005.

49. Tad Devine, political strategist, John Kerry–John Edwards 2004, interview by Sidney M. Milkis, July 2004.

50. Comment by John Kerry on CNN's *Inside Politics*, August 9, 2004.

51. Matthew Dowd, interview by Sidney M. Milkis, July 26, 2004.

52. The 2006 elections are discussed in Abramson, Aldrich, and Rohde, *Change and Continuity*, and in Larry J. Sabato, *The Sixth Year Itch: The Rise and Fall of the George W. Bush Presidency* (New York: Longman, 2007).

53. Janet Elder, "For Most Bush Voters, No Regrets after 2 Years," *New York Times*, May 2, 2007.

54. CNN.com, "Senate Passes Iraq Withdrawal Bill; Veto Threat Looms," April 26, 2007, http://www.cnn.com/2007/POLITICS/04/26/congress.iraq/index.html.

55. See Jan Crawford Greenburg, *Supreme Conflict: The Inside Story of the Struggle for Control of the United States Supreme Court* (New York: Penguin Press, 2007).

56. Richard J. Ellis, *The Development of the American Presidency* (New York: Routledge, 2012), 340–343. According to a 1986 statute, the attorney general was authorized to select an interim replacement who could serve for 120 days. If after those 120 days the president had not appointed and the Senate had not confirmed a permanent replacement, then a federal judge was empowered to fill the vacancy on an interim basis. The reauthorization of the Patriot Act gave the Justice Department the opportunity to remove the 120-day limit on the president's interim appointments, which was anathema to the Bush administration's idea of a unitary executive. The new law passed by Congress in the wake of the U.S. attorney scandal restored the 1986 law that limited the attorney general's interim appointments to 120 days.

57. Peter Baker, *Days of Fire: Bush and Cheney in the White House* (New York: Doubleday, 2013), chap. 35.

CHAPTER 15

Barack Obama and Presidential Leadership in Polarized Times

Democratic senator Barack Obama of Illinois offered voters "Change We Can Believe In" during the 2008 presidential campaign. But his two-year quest for the White House left unclear what kind of change he proposed. In substantial part, Obama ran an idealistic campaign that sought to recover the Progressive era vision of a modern executive who represents the "whole people." An African American who promised to bridge the country's seemingly intractable racial divide, Obama further pledged to overcome the raw partisanship that polarized the Washington community during the Clinton and Bush administrations.

The hopes Obama raised for a "post-partisan era" disguised the partisan practices animating his quest for the White House, which employed some of the same tactics that already had redefined twenty-first-century American politics.[1] Launching his campaign in early 2007, with George W. Bush's political fortunes in free fall, Obama naturally sought to distinguish himself from the incumbent. If Bush was "a divider, not a uniter,"[2] Obama would seek to bridge the partisan divisions in the name of national unity. Yet the lessons of Bush's first term, in which the president racked up numerous impressive victories by taking a strongly partisan approach to campaigning and governing, could not be easily dismissed. Because of the gains the Democrats made in the 2006 and 2008 elections, Obama enjoyed large—and largely supportive—congressional majorities when he became president in January 2009. Regional realignments since the 1960s greatly reduced the influence of conservative southerners—the "ball and chain that had hobbled liberalism's forward march"—within the Democratic Party.[3] Consequently, Democrats were no longer ideologically fragmented, as they had been in 1977 when Carter assumed office, or even in 1993 when Bill Clinton became president. Rather, they were a cohesive left-of-center party that was responsive to Obama's legislative program.[4]

Many of Obama's campaign promises—such as major government investments in health care, education, the environment, and alternative energy—were long-standing Democratic commitments. Furthermore, Obama and his advisers found inspiration in the national party politics that Bush practiced; indeed, the Obama campaign's organizational efforts in 2008 were modeled on techniques that Republicans pioneered in 2004. Eschewing the Democrats' traditional reliance on organized labor and other constituency groups to mobilize the party faithful, Obama built a powerful, centralized, grassroots organization linked to the national party. His victory in the election thus advanced an executive-centered party system that relied on the president to pronounce party doctrine, raise campaign funds, mobilize grassroots support, recruit candidates, campaign on behalf of the party's other candidates, and advance party programs.

After becoming president, Obama continued to walk the fine line between the post-partisan approach that appealed to many of his young, idealistic followers and the partisan politics practiced by his Republican predecessor and favored by many Democratic activists. The president's legislative strategy tacked between bipartisan efforts to reach out to Republican members of Congress and partisan appeals designed to shore up support from Democrats. At the organizational level, Obama established his grassroots campaign machine as an essential, but partially independent, component of the Democratic National Committee (DNC), modifying its name after the election from Obama for America to Organizing for America (OFA). The president exhibited both a willingness to work collaboratively on legislative issues with Congress, especially Democratic leaders in the House of Representatives and Senate, and an enthusiasm for the independence afforded by the modern administrative presidency. In attempting this difficult balancing act, however, Obama risked looking weak or indecisive. The results of the 2010 and 2014 midterm elections, in which the Republicans regained control first of the House and then of the Senate, cast serious doubt on his ability to effectively strike a balance between sharp partisanship and nonpartisan administration.

In truth, Obama became a more decisive partisan leader in the run-up to his bitterly contested reelection victory over former Massachusetts governor Mitt Romney in 2012. This victory was achieved through OFA's effective ground game and unilateral actions that tied the president directly to a scattered but potentially powerful coalition of ethnic and racial minorities, youth, the LBGTQ community, and educated white voters, especially unmarried women.[5] But the momentum Obama achieved during his reelection campaign was lost during the first two years of his second term. Although the frustrations he and his supporters experienced owed in large part to the fiercely divided polity, their response to this bitter factionalism—in particular, a growing tendency for the president to try to manage the nation's problems through unilateral action—revealed that the progressive vision of the president as a unifying national figure spearheading programmatic advances in the public interest might no longer be attainable.

The 2008 Elections

From the beginning, 2008 promised to be one of the most wide-open presidential contests in all of American history. For the first time since 1952, the ballot listed neither a president seeking reelection nor a vice president seeking to become president. Moreover, the two leading candidates for the Democratic nomination were an African American and a woman, Sen. Hillary Rodham Clinton of New York, the former first lady. Never before had a major political party nominated anyone other than a white male for president. Adding to the stakes of the election were the critical international and domestic challenges the country faced: wars in Iraq and Afghanistan and a severe recession at home, the worst economic crisis since the Great Depression.

That the 2008 campaign aroused such interest and participation can also be attributed to Obama's insurgent campaign, which combined Internet-based recruitment of volunteers, the use of data files to target potential supporters, and old-fashioned door-to-door canvassing to upset the heavily favored Clinton in the nomination contest and then defeat the highly respected Republican nominee, Sen. John McCain of Arizona, in the general election. Obama's campaign strategy elaborated on the grassroots organizational tactics that worked for Bush and the Republicans in 2002 and, especially, in 2004. The remarkable effectiveness of Obama's fund-raising operation, which drew heavily on Internet-solicited donations, further reflected lessons learned from the Bush campaign. Especially adept at raising large sums through small contributions, Obama became the first major party candidate for president to refuse public funds for the general election.

Obama's experience as a young community organizer in Chicago, which many Republicans mocked, helped him appreciate the importance of being present in local communities. His impressive grassroots organization was the institutional manifestation of his transformational message. In contrast, Clinton and McCain offered the voters experience in a year when they were looking for change. In 2002 Obama, then an Illinois state senator, had criticized the Iraq war, while Clinton was voting for the congressional resolution to authorize military action. Clinton hoped to deflect attention from this controversial part of her record by arguing that she was the more qualified candidate to assume the burdens of office in a dangerous, uncertain world. But basing her campaign on experience rather than her bid to become the first woman president weakened Clinton's claim to be a transformational leader.[6]

Similarly, the general election pitted the youthful Obama, now a U.S. senator, against a seventy-two-year-old Republican who would have been the oldest person ever to assume the presidency. McCain's steadfast support for the Iraq war, joined to his comment during the height of the fall 2008 financial crisis that "the fundamentals of our economy are strong," inclined independent voters to associate his candidacy with the unpopular policies of the Bush administration. Seeking to add excitement to his campaign, McCain tapped the relatively unknown governor of Alaska, Sarah Palin, as his running mate, the first time a woman had been placed on a Republican presidential ticket. Palin's conservative positions, especially her fossil-fuel – promoting mantra—"Drill, baby, drill"—energized the GOP's base. But her inexperience and ignorance about national issues led to frequent gaffes on the campaign trail that compromised her ability to infuse the desultory McCain campaign with partisan fervor.

Obama's victory was hardly inevitable: many pundits doubted that an African American could ever be elected president, let alone a candidate of such limited experience in government who bore such an exotic-sounding name. Yet Obama and his more conventional choice for vice president, Sen. Joseph Biden of Delaware, triumphed. Winning 53 percent of the national popular vote, Obama became the first Democrat since Lyndon B. Johnson in 1964 to win a decisive majority from the electorate. In securing more than two-thirds of the electoral votes (365 to McCain's 173), Obama held all twenty states won by John Kerry in 2004 and added nine states that Bush had captured, including three in the South: Florida, North Carolina, and Virginia. Like the formidable Bush–Cheney machine in 2004, the Obama–Biden organization relied in part on the regular party apparatus. Howard Dean, chair of the DNC, had decided in 2006 to strengthen Democratic organizations throughout the country, an approach that state and local party leaders credited with abetting the party's impressive victories in that year's midterm elections and in 2008.[7] While Obama was winning the presidency, Democrats won twenty-one additional seats in the House and eight in the Senate. These victories, coming on top of major Democratic gains in 2006, appeared to have "effectively reversed the verdict of 1994, leaving the partisan balance in Congress as solidly Democratic as it was before that year's Republican takeover."[8]

The New Foundation and Partisan Rancor

The historic nature of Obama's victory in 2008 prompted speculation that he might become a transformational president like George Washington, Thomas Jefferson, Andrew Jackson, Abraham Lincoln, Theodore Roosevelt, Woodrow Wilson, Franklin D. Roosevelt, Lyndon B,. Johnson, and Ronald Reagan. Obama's considerable political gifts and ambition further encouraged analogies to America's most consequential presidents. Obama claimed a particular kinship with Lincoln. He launched his campaign in Springfield, Illinois; took the oath of office with his hand on the same Bible that Lincoln used in 1861; and in Lincoln-like fashion, celebrated the Declaration of Independence as the lodestar of equality.

But Obama's style of governing and the programs he advanced during his first two years in office revealed that his ambition more closely resembled that of the most important progressive leaders of the twentieth century—Theodore Roosevelt, Wilson, and especially, FDR—who celebrated a new understanding of liberty that relied less on natural rights and individual self-reliance than on a more expansive, collective sense of freedom at home and abroad. FDR and his New Deal political allies committed themselves, rhetorically and programmatically, to two new freedoms—freedom from want, embodied by the welfare state, and freedom from fear, embedded in the national security state—to supplement the traditional First Amendment freedoms of speech and religion. This new understanding went hand in hand with the development of the modern executive establishment, which gave form to the federal government's new commitments. TR memorably described the modern president as the "steward of the public welfare." This role, which FDR embraced, was what most appealed to Obama.[9]

From the start of his administration, Obama channeled FDR and the New Deal. He asked scholars to prepare memos on Roosevelt's first hundred days; pursued "bold, persistent experimentation" during the early days of his administration in the form of an $814 billion economic stimulus package; and trumpeted an ambitious long-term program of structural reform, which he dubbed the "New Foundation" (an attempt at branding that never caught on). First announced in an address at Georgetown University on April 14, 2009, and echoed in subsequent speeches, Obama's New Foundation proposed to build a new regulatory framework for the economy; to substantially enhance access to higher education; to harness renewable energy to reduce climate change and create jobs; and most important, to achieve major health care reform, the signature program of Obama's first term.[10]

Steeped in the progressive tradition, Obama tended to reject in principle partisan solutions to domestic and international problems. But the tension between his post-partisan rhetoric and his commitment to traditional Democratic priorities became more jarring when he confronted the realities of governing. The artful joining of pragmatism and partisanship gave way to awkward vacillation amid fierce battles over the major issues that dominated his first year in office: economic stimulus, financial regulation, and health care reform. True to his promise to transcend partisan divisions, Obama repeatedly sought to attract support for his initiatives from Republican legislators, thereby frustrating liberal Democrats who feared that he was conceding too much.[11] But Obama's fundamentally Democratic policies were anathema to all but a few members of the staunchly conservative Republican caucus. From the start, GOP leaders resisted what they viewed as a liberal agenda garbed in the cloak of post-partisanship. Consequently, even as Obama scored major legislative victories, his simultaneous efforts to transcend party and rally the Democratic base led many independent voters to question his leadership, bringing about a steady decline in his public approval ratings from the high sixties to the mid-forties.

The limits of Obama's pragmatism were first exposed in his attempt to respond to the worsening economic crisis. He regarded his stimulus package as an extension of the Bush administration's Troubled Asset Relief Program (TARP), which was impressively bipartisan. Indeed, candidate Obama had joined the deliberations on the financial industry bailout during Bush's final days in office and lent critical support to the effort to persuade a reluctant Democratic Congress to pass it. Yet as president, Obama failed to set the terms of his party's response to the economic emergency or to invest it with bipartisan legitimacy.[12] Democrats and many liberal activists urged him to support a massive economic stimulus bill that would spend more than a trillion dollars to create jobs and rebuild the nation's infrastructure. Although the president's plan was large in scope and relied on "traditionally liberal notions of using government spending to spur growth," it was not as large as many liberals had hoped and included $300 billion in tax breaks designed to appeal to Republican legislators.[13] This approach dismayed many Democrats without eliciting enthusiasm from Republicans.[14] The stimulus bill, formally titled the American Recovery and Reinvestment Act, passed without a single Republican vote in the House.[15] In the Senate, Democratic leaders cut a deal with moderate Republican senators to reduce the bill's price tag by $82 billion, but only three Republicans voted for it.[16]

The epic battle over reform of the nation's health care system brought the tension between post-partisanship and partisanship into sharp relief.

Health care for all Americans had been the Democrats' holy grail since the Roosevelt administration, and Obama's determination to be the "last president" to have to address the issue spoke to liberal Democrats' hopes for a fundamental break from the patchwork, employment-based system of insurance that left millions of Americans uncovered. Liberals saw Obama's support for a government-administered "public option" that would compete with private providers as the emblem of his commitment to sweeping reform. Appealing to deficit hawks in both parties, however, Obama vowed to promote only those proposals that did not add to the national debt. From the start, the president walked a tightrope between satisfying his party's liberal base and reaching out to centrist Democrats, independents, and moderate Republicans.

As health care legislation wended its way through Congress, Obama continued to tack between conciliatory and partisan leadership strategies. He shifted position to support a proposal offered by McCain during the 2008 campaign but opposed by many liberal Democrats and union members that would help pay for reform by limiting the tax exemption for employer-provided health benefits.[17] The issue of whether federal funds should support health plans that paid for abortion found Obama siding with centrists over liberals. In the end, he agreed to issue an executive order blocking federal funding for abortions.[18] Most important, as resistance to reform among Republicans and centrist Democrats intensified in the waning months of 2009, Obama gradually retreated from the public option in a bid to consolidate support among moderates in both parties.[19] These moves—especially the president's abandonment of the public option—enraged many Democratic activists. Howard Dean urged congressional Democrats to kill the legislation.[20]

Even as he tacked to the center on some provisions, however, Obama used partisan strategies to help move the legislative process forward, especially when it became apparent that virtually every congressional Republican intended to oppose health reform legislation. As early as April 2009, Obama pressed Democrats not to foreswear use of the budget reconciliation process to secure victory in the Senate. Bundling health care reform with budget reconciliation would allow passage with fifty-one votes instead of the sixty needed to overcome a filibuster.[21] This decision proved important when Sen. Edward Kennedy, a longtime advocate of health care reform, died of brain cancer in January 2010 and his seat was won by Republican Scott Brown, reducing the Democrats' sixty-vote filibuster proof majority to fifty-nine. The president also made numerous appearances at rallies and town hall meetings to whip up support among Democratic voters, and he leveraged OFA, his grassroots organization, to pressure members of Congress to enact a comprehensive measure.[22] By midyear Obama, convinced that Republicans were going to vote overwhelmingly against any health reform bill, charged administration officials to pepper their public statements with criticisms of Republican intransigence and delay.[23]

As the debate over reform dragged into the early months of 2010—with Republicans having unanimously opposed versions of the health care bill in both houses of Congress—the president intensified his rhetorical assault. In his 2010 State of the Union address, Obama spoke directly to congressional Republicans, arguing, "Just saying no to everything may be good short-term politics, but it's not leadership." As he upped the rhetorical ante, the president also engaged in a series of political maneuvers to put the GOP on the spot. A ballyhooed bipartisan "health care summit" in February 2010 was less an effort to hear Republican alternatives to reform than to drama-tize Republican intransigence.[24] Scheduled in the wake of the January 20 special election in Massachusetts, the televised proceedings showed Obama engaged in a high-stakes game of political poker. By calling the GOP's hand, he hoped to prepare the public for a purely Democratic bill.

The final push for health care reform featured Obama at a series of campaign-style rallies in Missouri, Ohio, Pennsylvania, and Virginia, where the impassioned president taunted Republicans' failure to take responsibil-ity for expanding coverage and reducing health care costs.

In the immediate aftermath of Obama's multistate swing, health care reform was passed into law through a two-step process that obviated a Republican filibuster. The House passed the Senate version of the bill, and the Senate subsequently used the budget reconciliation process to remove provisions odious to House Democrats. No Republican voted for the legis-lation in either chamber. Although the Republicans' unwillingness to com-promise gave eloquent testimony to their partisan approach to legislating, Obama's leadership revealed a partisan streak of its own. The *New York Times* concluded: "Gone is the promise on which he rode to victory less than a year and a half ago—the promise of a 'postpartisan' Washington in which rationality and calm discourse replaced partisan bickering."[25] Shaped by a polarized party system, the signal legislative achievement of the president's first two years became the only major social welfare program ever to become law without a single vote from the opposition party.

New-style partisan politics also framed the debate over, and the even-tual passage of, the Wall Street Reform and Consumer Protection Act, which was enacted soon after the health care bill. Informally called Dodd–Frank after the Democrats who steered it through Congress, Sen. Christopher Dodd of Connecticut and Rep. Barney Frank of Massachusetts, the financial reform law created a new consumer protection agency within the Federal Reserve Board and gave the government power to regulate large banks and investment houses. Dodd–Frank was in the tradition of the Glass–Steagall Act, enacted during the early days of the New Deal. Until its repeal in 1998, Glass–Steagall separated savings banks from Wall Street investment firms. Cast against the flaws exposed by the unregulated securities market that both Republicans and Democrats supported until the economic implosion of fall 2008, Dodd–Frank sought to protect borrowers against abuses by mortgage and credit card lenders; to more closely regulate large banks and financial firms that were "too big to fail"; and to limit abuses of activities such as proprietary trading, hedge funds, and private equity holdings.[26]

As with health care reform, Obama sought to sell financial reform as a critical ingredient of the New Foundation. As with health care, too, Dodd–Frank passed along sharply divided partisan lines (only six congressional Republicans voted for it) and failed to win the president much credit with the public. Once again, despite legislative success, the programmatically ambitious president found it difficult to navigate a political environment characterized by bitter division in Washington and a citizenry alienated from the capital's partisan rancor.

President Barack Obama appeals for Republican support of his health care reform bill at a February 25, 2010, health care "summit."

Source: © Brooks Kraft/Corbis.

The partisan contretemps generated by the fight over health care and financial reform legislation, both of which occurred against a backdrop of stubbornly high unemployment, haunted the Democrats at the polls. In the 2010 midterm elections the voters rendered, as Obama characterized his parties' losses, a "shellacking." The Republics gained sixty-three seats in the House to reclaim control of the lower chamber—the worst defeat for a president's party in an off-year election since 1938. In the Senate, the GOP added six seats, leaving Obama and the Democrats well short of the three-fifths majority needed to enact controversial legislation. As had been the case since the emergence of the executive-centered party system, the midterm elections were a referendum on the president. The 54 percent of voters who disapproved of Obama's performance voted 85 percent to 11 percent for House Republican candidates. The elections also showed the disconnection between the polarized party system and the less polarized American public. Only 43 percent of voters had a favorable opinion of the Democratic Party, and the Republican Party fared even worse: 41 percent.[27]

We Can't Wait: Obama and the Administrative Presidency

In October 2011, Obama finally gave full vent to his frustration with the partisan opposition he suffered during his first two years as president. Responding to Republican obstruction of a jobs bill and other measures he hoped would buttress his political support and add steam to a sluggish economic recovery, the president shared a new message with a crowd in Nevada: "We can't wait for an increasingly dysfunctional Congress to do its job. Whenever they won't act, I will."[28]

The president had good reason to complain about Congress. Although the minority party in the Senate had employed aggressive partisan tactics since the Clinton administration, these maneuvers spiked during Obama's first term. Exercising the filibuster and other dilatory measures, Republicans blocked legislation as well as presidential appointments to the courts and the executive branch from reaching the floor of the Senate at unprecedented rates. From 2007 (when the Democrats regained control of the upper chamber) to 2012, Republicans threatened to filibuster on 385 occasions—equaling, in five years, the total number of filibuster threats during the seven decades from the start of World War I until the end of the Reagan administration.[29]

Obama's response—a resort to unilateralism—was symptomatic of the emergence of executive-centered partisanship. Born of the Progressive and New Deal eras, the administrative state sheltered entitlement programs like Social Security and Medicare from the vagaries of party politics and public opinion. But the expansion of programmatic liberalism in the 1960s and 1970s fractured the political order, ultimately encouraging Republican presidents to use administrative power for conservative ends. Nixon, Reagan, and George W. Bush, especially, used executive action to achieve objectives they could not achieve legislatively. In the short term, these Republican presidents were able to strengthen the GOP by meeting the demands of important party constituencies and advancing the party's ideological goals. In the long run, however, their aggressive administrative actions mired them in constitutional controversies and bitter policy disputes. By retreating to the politics of executive administration, Nixon, Reagan, and Bush implicitly admitted that their ambitions exceeded what could plausibly be achieved through legislation.

By the time Obama reached office, it no longer seemed possible for presidents to stand apart from partisan combat; more to the point, partisan polarization had come to so divide Congress and advocacy groups in Washington that the Obama administration had strong incentives to pursue its policies through the administrative presidency.[30] Obama, in fact, occasionally resorted to unilateral action as a first resort in bringing about significant policy change. In organizing the White House Office in 2009, Obama appointed a number of policy "czars" with broad authority to "cut through— or leapfrog—the traditional bureaucracy" in matters of national security, climate change, economic policy, health care, housing, and education.[31] On taking office, the president reversed a number of important domestic and foreign policies with a stroke of the pen, issuing executive orders and memoranda that reversed measures previously signed by Bush.[32]

As was the case with Reagan and Bush, many of Obama's administrative actions appealed to important party constituencies. He signed several orders reversing Bush administration policies opposed by organized labor, and he rescinded Bush's order denying funds to international family planning groups that provide abortion-related services.[33] In a move that elicited approval from environmentalists, Obama issued an order raising fuel efficiency standards on all cars and light trucks built after 2011.[34] Following through on a prominent campaign pledge, he ordered the closing of the Guantánamo Bay prison for detainees in the war on terrorism by January 2010. Closure efforts stalled when Congress, instead of acquiescing to the president's initiative, intervened to prevent any relocation of detainees to prisons within the United States.

Although the administrative actions Obama took during his first two years stoked important constituencies of the Democratic Party, the initiatives were relatively isolated and largely overshadowed by the administration's effort to reach across the aisle in Congress to get things done. After the summer of 2011, however, when Obama and congressional Republicans reached an impasse on fiscal policy and House Republicans refused to raise the debt ceiling and threatened to bring the government into default, the White House began to plot the course that led it to launch the We Can't Wait Campaign—a shift in rhetoric and policy that decisively joined partisanship and national administration. As Nancy DeParle, a deputy chief of staff assigned to lead the initiative, observed, the president determined that it was no longer enough to highlight Republican obstructionism. Facing a tough reelection in the midst of high employment and declining public support, Obama "wanted to continue down the path of being bold with Congress and flexing our muscles a little bit," thus "showing contrast with . . . a Congress that was completely stuck."[35]

During the final year of his first term, Obama took measures authorizing the Environmental Protection Agency (EPA) to implement greenhouse gas regulations that were stalled in the Senate; issued waivers releasing states from many of the requirements of No Child Left Behind, which Congress had failed to reauthorize; and bypassed the usual confirmation process by granting recess appointments to four nominees whom Senate Republicans were filibustering. Finally, Obama announced, in June 2012, an initiative—Deferred Action for Childhood Arrivals (DACA)—that granted legal status and work permits to an entire category of young undocumented immigrants, as many as 1.4 million people, who otherwise would have been subject to deportation. Obama thus elided Republican opposition to the Dream Act, the administration's bill to provide a conditional pathway to citizenship for immigrants who were brought to America illegally as children.

Obama's adroit administrative maneuver contributed to his successful reelection campaign. Prior to DACA, Hispanic activists were ambivalent about the Obama administration, which had pursued so vigorous a deportation policy that they dubbed him "deporter-in-chief." A survey of Latinos following the DACA announcement revealed a significant turning of the tide: 58 percent of respondents indicated that DACA had made them "more enthusiastic" about Obama. Only 6 percent indicated it had made them less enthusiastic.[36] Obama went on to win about 70 percent of the Latino vote in 2012.

Obama's initially hesitant but ultimately decisive action on behalf of Dreamers helped revive the spirit of the Immigration and Nationality Act of 1965 (INA), which Lyndon Johnson shepherded through Congress in the belief that the national quota system was a stain on the Great Society's dedication to civil rights and social justice. Although the INA has not traditionally been viewed as part of the civil rights revolution, and few of its champions anticipated how profoundly it would change the nation's demographic landscape, Johnson seemed to recognize that its passage was especially significant—enough so that he oversaw an elaborate signing ceremony at the base of the Statue of Liberty.[37] The massive increase in foreign-born citizens that followed in the act's wake—an increase from 9.6 million in 1965 to a record 45 million in 2015—animated the rise of an important immigration rights movement by the time of Obama's presidency. Immigration reformers viewed the creation of a path to citizenship as the civil rights cause of this generation. Although Obama was slow to embrace this cause, the combination of effective action by the Dreamers and the growing importance of the Latino vote encouraged him to make immigration reform a principal objective of his presidency.

Obama's strategy of escaping partisan gridlock by exploiting the full powers of the administrative presidency strengthened his party by servicing the demands of important constituencies and advancing the Democrats' programmatic goals. But it also advanced—indeed bestowed bipartisan legitimacy on—an executive-centered party system that threatened the integrity of political parties as collective, accountable organizations with a past and a future.

Obama's Reelection and the Perils of Partisanship

For all the controversy attending it, the health care battle, fueled by lively, sometime vitriolic town meetings throughout the country, confirmed that the recrudescence of partisanship had renewed interest in politics. Pitting Obama's OFA against the new grassroots conservative Tea Party movement, the health care battle showed that as one Democratic congressional staffer observed, "the age of apathy is over."[38] Although the president paid dearly in the coin of public opinion for the partisan nature of the battle over health care reform, his grassroots organization outperformed that of his opponent, former governor Romney, in mobilizing core supporters in 2012. The contest centered largely on the constitutional and policy conflicts aroused by health care reform.[39] That this polarizing battle between Democrats and Republicans focused on a program that both camps called "Obamacare" made clear just how executive-centered partisan conflict had become.

Obama's reelection victory testified to how his first term had polarized the country. Unlike every other two-term president since Woodrow Wilson in 1916, Obama was reelected by a smaller majority than in his initial election. Narrow as it was, however, Obama's victory was decisive. Although his popular vote margin was slim—51 percent to 47 percent—Obama achieved a comfortable Electoral College victory, 332 to 206. Moreover, his party gained eight seats in the House, narrowing the Republican majority in that chamber to 234–201. Democrats also added two seats in the Senate to extend their majority to fifty-five to forty-five, even though they had to defend twenty-three seats in the election and the Republicans only ten. Obama and the Democratic Party won these victories in the face of slow economic growth and an unemployment rate that dipped below 8 percent only a few weeks before the election. No president in the post–World War II era had been reelected with an unemployment rate that high.[40]

In covering the 2012 campaign, many pundits stressed the importance of the billions of dollars that were spent on attack ads in the mass media. But OFA's unique blend of high-tech targeting of individuals who were likely Obama supporters but unreliable voters and old-fashioned canvasing to ensure that these "lazy Democrats" would turn out appeared to provide the difference in the close election.[41] Working hand in glove with the Democratic Party and liberal advocacy groups, OFA evolved into a "well oiled machine."[42] As one volunteer put it, "Everyone was excited in 2008; in 2012 people may have been less passionate, but they worked just as hard."[43] That sense of mission continued into Obama's second term: soon after the election, OFA was recast as Organizing for Action, which was established as a nonprofit "social welfare" organization to mobilize grassroots support for the progressive causes championed by Obama in 2012—implementation of the Patient Protection and Affordable Care Act, immigration reform, LGBTQ rights, climate change legislation, and gun control.[44] The move, which removed OFA from the DNC and established it as a self-standing organization—the "Obama's Family," as many staff and volunteers self-identified—advanced the notion of a national, executive-centered Democratic Party.[45]

Just as the promise of unilateralism was illustrated by the We Can't Wait initiative, so the political perils of executive-centered partisanship were dramatically illustrated by the rocky rollout of the Patient Protection and Affordable Care Act at the outset of Obama's second term. At the president's insistence, the burden of administering the complex law fell to Nancy DeParle, the White House health care czar, who oversaw matters until she was promoted to be the president's deputy chief of staff for policy in February 2011 and the task fell to her successor, Jeanne Lambrew. The White House was in charge, but on-the-ground responsibility was the domain of the Department of Health and Human Services (HHS), especially the Centers for Medicare and Medicaid Services (CMS). The result was a fragmented process that failed to establish essential connective tissue between White House planning, bureaucratic management, and the construction of technical architecture. Adding to the chaos, Congress and the states, which were expected to play critical parts in the development of insurance marketplaces, were largely kept in the dark about controversial regulations and technical difficulties.[46] For months, nearly every news story about Obamacare's rollout concerned problems with its Web site.

The calamitous rollout of Obamacare did great damage to the reputation of the president and threatened to have serious political repercussions for his party. Although the We Can't Wait initiative, dedicated to making the president look like a strong leader in the face of fierce Republican opposition, was enthusiastically supported by congressional Democrats, the dysfunctional rollout of the president's signature program resulted in deep frustration and near rebellion. The White House blamed its furtive and uncoordinated planning on Republican hostility to Obamacare; one White House official likened the task to constructing "a complicated building in a war zone."[47] So fretful were Obama and his top advisors about GOP "sabotage" that when it became apparent that HHS and CMS were overwhelmed by administrative and technical problems, the White House created a new agency within HHS to coordinate the launching: the Center for Consumer Information and Insurance Oversight. "Oversight would be better insulated from the efforts of House Republicans," the White House reasoned, "who were looking for ways to undermine the law."[48] In the end, however, the new agency only added another layer of complexity to an already fractious process. The White House–centered administration of health care reform, according to Richard Foster, a former Medicare chief actuary who left the administration in early 2013, wrought "bad implementation" in pursuit of "short term political gains."[49]

Unrepentant, the administration delayed a number of controversial features of Obamacare until after the 2014 midterm election, including regulations requiring insurance companies to provide a core group of essential benefits, such as maternity leave and prescription drug coverage, and the so-called employer mandate, which required all but small employers to provide coverage to full-time workers. In an ironic twist of policy fate, the Republican-controlled House voted to sue President Obama over the delayed implementation of a health care reform program that GOP lawmakers had consistently opposed and repeatedly promised to repeal.[50] Criticism of the president's tinkering with his most important legislative achievement was not limited to Republicans, however. The Obama administration should not have disregarded the law's intent "without an exceptionally good reason," the *Washington Post* scolded in an editorial. "Fear of [another] midterm shellacking doesn't qualify as good reason."[51]

Obama, Partisanship, and the War on Terrorism

Obama's difficulty in navigating partisan conflicts in foreign policy offers perhaps the most striking example of how the responsibilities of the modern presidency clash with the contemporary party system. Obama inherited international commitments that pulled him away from his party's liberal base. The war on terrorism—and especially the war in Iraq—deeply divided Americans along partisan lines during Bush's presidency.[52] Obama rose to national prominence in part because of his steadfast opposition to the Iraq war, which in 2008 energized Democratic activists dissatisfied with Senator Clinton's early hawkishness. If elected, candidate Obama promised, he would "begin the phased redeployment of combat troops . . . needed for long-term success in Iraq and the security interests of the United States."[53] He also appealed to the Democratic base by pledging to close the Guantánamo Bay prison and to end the Bush administration's policy permitting torture of enemy combatants, both of which were extremely unpopular among liberals. Promising a departure from his predecessor's combative diplomatic style, which many Democrats viewed as counterproductive, Obama pledged that his administration would pursue a more multilateral foreign policy as well as engage in high-level talks with antagonists such as Iran.[54]

Even though he pleased Democrats with his campaign promises concerning Iraq, Guantánamo, and torture, not all of Obama's positions appealed to liberal activists. In fact, as a candidate he took a hawkish stance on the war in Afghanistan, pledging to order military strikes against targets in Pakistan if he received actionable intelligence that terrorists were seeking refuge within its borders. "We must refocus our efforts on Afghanistan and Pakistan—the central front in our war against al Qaeda—so that we are confronting terrorists where their roots run deepest," Obama wrote in a 2007 article in *Foreign Affairs*.[55]

After becoming president, Obama continued to steer between policies that satisfied liberal Democrats and policies that sustained the basic commitments of the national security state. In his first days in office, Obama banned the use of torture in interrogations and began efforts to close the Guantánamo Bay prison.[56] In a February 2009 announcement eagerly anticipated by Democratic critics of the war in Iraq, Obama ordered a major drawdown of forces, declaring that "our combat mission in Iraq will end" in August 2010.[57] He also made important symbolic efforts to revamp America's image in the international community, especially in the Muslim world. The president's June 2009 address at Cairo University marked a significant rhetorical departure from Bush's "with us or against us" approach to the war on terrorism. Obama vowed to "seek a new beginning between the United States and Muslims around the world, one based on mutual interest and mutual respect, and one based upon the truth that America and Islam are not exclusive and need not be in competition."[58]

The president embraced significant aspects of the war on terrorism, however. Obama retained important Bush-era military and foreign policy advisers, including Joint Chiefs of Staff chair Mike Mullen; Gen. David Petraeus, commander of American military forces in Iraq; Gen. Douglas Lute, the White House coordinator for Afghanistan and Pakistan; Nick Rasmussen, the National Security Council's senior director for terrorism; and Secretary of Defense Robert Gates, marking the first time a defense secretary had been carried over from a president of a different party.[59] Obama also appointed his more hawkish Democratic rival in 2008, Hillary Rodham Clinton, as secretary of state.

These appointments presaged critical policy decisions that disappointed civil libertarians and Democratic activists. The Obama administration essentially continued the Bush administration's practice of holding enemy combatants without trial in military prisons as well as its policy of trying at least some of them in military courts.[60] The president dramatically expanded his predecessor's use of Predator drones to assassinate suspected terrorists, including American citizens fighting for the enemy, in Afghanistan, Pakistan, and Yemen. Although Obama promised to end "extraordinary renditions" of terrorist suspects to nations likely to torture them, he did not "rule out this process in general," international relations scholar Michael Desch observed. Instead he "adopted the same less stringent criteria employed by the Bush administration to gauge the likelihood that another country will employ torture."[61]

Perhaps the most significant Bush policy that Obama adopted was the military "surge." Embracing the same strategy that his predecessor employed in Iraq during the final two years of his presidency, Obama announced in a December 2009 speech at West Point that he would send an additional thirty thousand American troops to back the beleaguered Afghan government.[62] Although the president also promised to begin drawing down American forces from Afghanistan in 2011, the slow pace of subsequent military progress imperiled this timetable.[63] Obama's approach to the Afghan war infuriated Democrats who thought that he would order an expedited withdrawal from the embattled nation. Indeed, in July 2010, 153 House Democrats, including Speaker Nancy Pelosi, voted to require the president to establish an even clearer timetable for bringing the American military effort to a close. The measure was defeated primarily on the strength of Republican votes.[64] Later that month, the House passed a $59 billion spending bill to continue financing the war in Afghanistan on a 308–114 vote. But because 102 Democrats voted against the bill, the 148 Democrats who supported it had to rely on 160 Republican votes.

Even after American soldiers killed Osama bin Laden in May 2011 and the administration began disengaging from Iraq and Afghanistan toward the end of Obama's first term, the president expanded the strategic deployment of special forces and drones in a "secret war" against suspected terrorists. Moreover, the White House joined with NATO to end the reign of Libyan dictator Colonel Muamar el-Qaddafi and then, straining credulity, argued that the War Powers Resolution, which requires the president to report to Congress when he deploys American forces, did not apply because a state of "hostilities" did not exist. Obama and his national security team claimed that the weakening of al Qaeda, including the killing of bin Laden in an Obama-approved mission in May 2011, and the overthrow of Qaddafi, were accomplished with a new approach to war that relies on multinational rather than unilateral action and surgical strikes rather than massive troop deployments. Like Obama's domestic intervention, however, this approach to national security suggested that extraordinary claims of executive authority had become a routine feature of American politics.

Executive aggrandizement continued after Obama's reelection. During the first year of his second term, the president seemed determined to take the United States off a "perpetual war footing." Sensing the country's war fatigue and noting resistance from both Democrats and Republicans to additional commitments in the Middle East, the president decided not to launch missile strikes in Syria in support of rebels fighting the autocratic regime of Bashar al-Assad, even though the brutal dictator crossed Obama's stated "red line" by using chemical weapons against civilians. With the dramatic rise of a radical group that declared itself the Islamic State during the fall of 2014, however, forbearance gave way to a muscular new course in the Middle East. The Islamic State, also known as ISIS or ISIL, was a former al Qaeda affiliate that took advantage of a civil war in Syria and the lassitude of the Iraqi government to gain territory on both sides of the Iraq–Syria border.

As the president acknowledged, his administration underestimated the danger of ISIS's incursions into Syria and Iraq; indeed, Obama initially dismissed these fighters as a "Jayvee team." But the steady advance of the self-proclaimed Caliphate and the powerful public reaction to ISIS's release of videos that graphically showed the beheading of two American journalists spurred the president to action. In a September 10, 2014, speech to the nation, Obama announced a plan to "degrade, and ultimately destroy, ISIL through a comprehensive and sustained counterterrorism strategy."[65] Two weeks later, soon after ordering air strikes on dozens of ISIS targets in Syria, the president issued an even more militant call to arms in an address to the General Assembly of the United Nations. "The once reluctant warrior," reported the *New York Times*, was "now apparently resolved to waging a twilight struggle against Islamic extremism for the remainder of his presidency."[66]

Although the air strikes on Syria had strong bipartisan support, constitutional and partisan issues lurked just beneath the surface. In his speech to the nation, Obama said he "welcomed congressional support for this effort," yet insisted he had "the authority to address the threat from ISIL." That authority, he claimed, resided in the resolution Congress passed in 2001 authorizing President Bush to use military force against those "who planned, authorized, committed or aided" the September 11 attacks. The White House argued that the resolution covered a war on ISIS because the terrorist organization is "the true inheritor of Osama bin Laden's legacy—notwithstanding the public split between al Qaeda's senior leadership and ISIL."[67]

Some legal scholars quickly dismissed the tenuous legal basis of the president's claim. Jack Goldsmith noted that if the Islamic State's "remarkably loose affiliation with Al Qaeda brings a terrorist organization under the 2001 law, then Congress has authorized the President to use force endlessly against practically any ambitious jihadist terrorist group that fights against the United States."[68] Members of Congress on both sides of the aisle also expressed concern that the president's action amounted, like the Libyan expedition, to a derogation of the War Powers Resolution. Before leaving the capital to devote their full attention to the 2014 midterm elections, Congress did hurriedly enact legislation authorizing the president to arm and train moderate Syrian rebels. But this action obviated any serious debate over what amounted to a major military offensive in Syria and Iraq.

The president took pains to ensure that the battle against ISIS would be different from the wars in Iraq and Afghanistan because it "would not involve American combat troops fighting on foreign soil." Yet the military action involved not just "a systematic campaign of airstrikes" but the deployment of 475 troops in addition to the 1,200 already there "to support Iraqi and Kurdish forces with training, intelligence and equipment." Notwithstanding the strong public sentiment to strike back against ISIS's atrocities, the failure of Congress to place limits on a new Middle East mission renewed concerns about executive power. A CNN poll revealed that more than 70 percent of Americans believed the president should seek congressional authority for military strikes against ISIS.[69] In sum, Obama's statecraft—his persistent efforts to balance post-partisan and partisan themes—brought him significant policy victories without changing the broader, politically polarized environment. Indeed, the public came to view the president in starkly partisan terms. By September 2014, in the midst of ostensibly bipartisan support for the war against ISIS, 82 percent of Democrats approved of Obama's performance as president, but only 8 percent of Republicans did. Rather than transcend partisanship, Obama's presidency reinforced, and perhaps intensified, the partisan rancor that roiled the country.[70]

Barack Obama's Fragile Legacy

As presidents since Theodore Roosevelt have trumpeted, the presidency is supposed to strengthen American democracy. But the question remains whether the executive of a vast bureaucratic state, even with the tools of instant communication, can truly be the direct representative of the people. In 1990 political scientist Robert Dahl spoke for a host of critics when he argued that in reality the modern presidency is a "pseudo-democratic institution."[71] This concern has only increased in recent years, with the gradual erosion of the constraints on executive power that Congress enacted after Watergate. It has been further accentuated, scholars and pundits fear, by a seemingly permanent war on terrorism.

In the nineteenth century, highly mobilized and localized political parties emerged to restrain presidential aggrandizement and keep the presidency "safe for democracy." But this decentralized, parties-centric system cramped the development of a national government that could ameliorate injustices at home and aggression abroad. The modern party system, in contrast, encounters an executive-centered bureaucratic state that is better suited than in the past to tackle economic insecurity, racial segregation, totalitarianism, and terrorism but lacks adequate means to foster common deliberation and public judgment, the pillars of a vital civic culture.

For all the legal and political problems associated with recent presidential management of domestic and foreign policy, Obama's two terms, in a political environment of high expectations of executive leadership and sharp partisan divisions, exposed the powerful systemic forces that are likely to roil the executive office well into the future. Although Republicans criticized many of Obama's unilateral actions, few of those actions faced serious challenge. The 112th and 113th Congresses (2011–2015) in particular illustrated the inherent difficulty of challenging presidential action. A sign of just how rancorous partisan conflict had become was the Democrats' revival of a version of the nuclear option that Republicans threatened to use during George W. Bush's second term. Toward the end of 2013, majority leader Harry Reid and the Democratic caucus changed the Senate's rules to deprive the minority of its ability to block most of President Obama's executive and judicial nominations with filibusters. The procedural change, radical as it was, did not apply to Supreme Court nominations or legislation, and the fallout from the bitter rules fight only made it more likely that Congress would remain mired in partisan gridlock.

Partisan administration is also abetted by the interest groups and social movements that shape so much rivalry between the parties. Social activists have long realized the capacity of the president to serve as a rallying force and the executive bureaucracy to be an avenue to advance their agenda in the face of fluctuating public opinion and inconsistent congressional attention.[72] Like reform-minded presidents, advocacy groups look for ways to slice through the Gordian Knot of complex constitutional forms to accomplish change. With Congress and the president divided by partisanship, activists are especially prone to set their sights on the executive bureaucracy, along with the courts, as the most promising agent of progress. Since 2010, health care activists, immigration advocates, the LGBTQ community, and environmentalists all have focused their energy on executive action rather than forlornly investing their efforts in the hollow hope of legislation.

OFA has been an important ally of partisan groups who rely on executive action and bureaucratic discretion to advance their causes. For example, just as OFA played an important part in enacting Obamacare in 2009, so was it critical to the administration's effort to rescue the shaky rollout of the program. Local OFA organizers went into their communities and assisted new enrollees in signing up for a health care plan through the state exchanges. This street-level campaign involved every active OFA member for nearly a year and a half. Volunteers promoting the Affordable Care Act's health care exchanges benefitted from many of the technological innovations that OFA developed during Obama's first term and reelection campaign. Although local expertise was often relied on to know where in their cities and towns to distribute brochures, phone-bank call lists were generated at OFA's Chicago headquarters and distributed to chapters around the country. This was an important innovation. To be sure, micro-targeting is old hat to political campaigns and policy advocacy, but it was not translated into an all-out campaign to implement a new law before OFA's work in support of Obamacare.

That OFA was built for issue advocacy and born of a political campaign endued its staff and volunteers with a sense of the stakes and the appropriate tactics. Despite a painfully slow start, enrollments in the newly established health care exchanges surpassed the Congressional Budget Office's initial expectations, reaching 7.1 million by the end of the initial open enrollment period. The White House signaled the importance of the organization's support when President Obama sent an email on September 2, 2014, titled "I hope you remember this." Reminding his personal loyalists how in the face of the Tea Party assault five years earlier, "the pundits were declaring health care reform dead," the president praised OFA staff and volunteers for snatching victory from the jaws of defeat.

Spurred by OFA's vast social media platform, the media began to broadcast more positive features of Obamacare, and public support for the program grew. Emblematic of the polarized political environment, however, the public's view of health care reform was strongly influenced by partisanship, with 73 percent of Democrats and 18 percent of Republicans supporting Obamacare by December 2013. More than anything, Obama and his OFA supporters fortified the faith of wavering liberals in the Affordable Care Act.[73]

The sharp partisan conflict that divided Congress and advocacy groups encouraged Obama's dogged pursuit of the New Foundation in the face of Republican opposition for the remainder of his presidency. This was evident in his push to remedy environmental hazards, a global initiative he defended no less ardently in his September 2014 speech to the United Nations than his actions against ISIS. By the end of 2013, the administration had given up any hope of climate change legislation and was determined to pursue green policy unilaterally. In June 2013, the Executive Office of the President issued Obama's "Climate Action Plan"—along with a memorandum directing the EPA to issue new regulations governing carbon emissions in future power plants.[74] The EPA released its proposed rule on September 20. Championed as the "first uniform national limits on the amount of carbon pollution that future power plants will be allowed to emit," the proposed rule explicitly drew on authority implied by the Clean Air Act, which was last amended in 1990. Although no amendment to the Clean Air Act had been passed in a quarter century, Congress had recognized the authority of the EPA to regulate other forms of pollution, and the Supreme Court had determined that the agency had the power to regulate carbon emissions from automobiles.[75] The Obama administration claimed that the EPA was merely applying such standards to carbon emissions from other sources.

The Obama administration's pursuit of environmental reform was extended to a global effort in 2016, when the United States joined the Paris Climate Accord, which obliged countries to slash their greenhouse gas emissions to keep global temperatures from rising to catastrophic levels. The Paris Accord, which Obama played a principal part in orchestrating, was an important breakthrough in the aftermath of the failure of a similar agreement—the Kyoto Protocol—which neither China nor the United States (under the leadership of George W. Bush) had joined. Significantly, the Obama administration joined the Paris Accord through an executive agreement, thereby obviating the need to ratify a treaty that most Senate Republicans opposed.

Like Republican presidents Reagan and George W. Bush, Obama's commitment to partisan administration revealed that modern presidents can circumvent partisan gridlock by exploiting executive power for partisan purposes.

Taking a longer historical view, however, Obama's special relationship with OFA contributed to the development of a presidential partisanship that both responds to and further undermines party organizations. But the effectiveness of this personal organization, combining a fiercely devoted activist core with a technically sophisticated campaign organization, sometimes presented the illusion that the president could campaign and govern independently of the Congress, bureaucracy, and regular party organization.

Indeed, during the 2014 midterm elections, some Democrats lamented that OFA took attention away from, rather than supported, their campaigns. The uneasy relationship between the White House and Democratic legislators underscored a long-held contention on Capitol Hill that Obama's political operation functioned purely for the president's benefit and not for his party's, an indictment that became especially bitter when the Democrats lost control of the Senate in the midterm campaign.[76] Indeed, during his eight years in office Obama presided over a greater loss of congressional seats for his party than any two-term president since World War II.[77]

In other ways, however, Obama's electoral and policy alliance with OFA greatly upgraded the Democratic Party's voter outreach by expanding the national voter file the DNC first started in 2006 under the leadership of Howard Dean. Moreover, the president's effective use of volunteers in campaigns and policy advocacy infused the party with an expanded grassroots presence. For example, the number of Democratic campaign volunteers rose from roughly 252,000 in 2004 to 2.2 million in 2012.

In August 2015, for the first time, OFA turned over the entire list of its supporters to the DNC, which national and state party leaders hoped might help their campaign efforts, not just at the presidential level but also down ballot in the 2016 campaign. This upgraded campaign capacity was joined to effective policy advocacy, as Obama and his information-age grassroots organization turned controversial issues, including immigration, gay rights, and climate change, to the Democrats' advantage.[78]

The results of the 2014 election only encouraged the White House to double down on its administrative strategy. Soon after the election, President Obama dramatically expanded his immigration deferral program. The Department of Homeland Security announced on November 20 that it was granting deportation relief to parents of legal citizens and legal permanent residents, thus bestowing protection on as many as 5 million people. Republican Speaker of the House John Boehner warned the White House that he and his partisan brethren would "not stand idle as the president undermines the rule of law in our country."

As had been the case since the Reagan years, partisan strife did not stop at the water's edge. Against strong Republican criticism that he was appeasing a leading fomenter of radical Islamic terrorism, Obama played a pivotal role in sustaining two years of grueling negotiations that finally bore fruit in the form of a 2015 agreement between the United States and western allies with Iran. The signature diplomatic achievement of the Obama presidency, the Iranian Nuclear Agreement, put strict limitations on Iran's nuclear ambitions in exchange for the lifting of stringent sanctions that had crippled Iran's economy. As was the case with the Paris Accord, Obama lacked support in the Senate to ratify the treaty. But, following the script he followed in climate change reform, the president made the United States a signatory of the seven-nation accord through an executive agreement.

The dynamics of modern presidential leadership at home and abroad illustrate the tension between executive partisanship, collective decision-making, and constitutional government. The rise of the modern presidency has placed a premium on candidate-centered campaigns and organization. More important, the contemporary office summons individuals whose ambition are best served by establishing an electoral coalition and method of governing outside of party politics. The rise of the modern presidency therefore encourages each president to exploit the full splendor of the executive office at the expense of public debate and resolution, which best takes place in Congress and the states.

In bestowing bipartisan legitimacy on the executive-centered party system, Obama continued the illusion of a presidency-centered democracy—a vision that allows presidents to get important things done but risks embroiling them in policy controversies that diminish collaboration with Congress, roils the system of checks and balances, and erodes citizens' trust in the competence and fairness of government. As Obama's heir apparent, Hillary Clinton, suffered a shocking defeat to the iconoclastic businessman and reality television star, Donald Trump, a highly disruptive politics embroiled the nation, testifying dramatically to the serious threat executive-centered partisanship poses to the fabric of American constitutional government. Trump's election also raised concerns among Democrats that much of what Obama accomplished through executive action could be undone through his successor's executive actions.

Notes

1. Obama never uttered this phrase and denied in his second State of the Union message that he expected his election to "usher in . . . some post-partisan era." "Remarks of the President in State of Union Address," http://www.whitehouse.gov/the-press-office/remarks-president-state-union-address. But other than change, the message that resonated most in his campaign was his promise to gather a coalition of Democrats, Republicans, and independents behind an agenda of sweeping change. See Jonathan Weisman, "GOP Doubts, Fears 'Post-Partisan' Obama," *Washington Post*, January 7, 2008; and Richard Cohen, "State of the Union: Obama Plays Grown Up," *Washington Post*, January 27, 2010.

2. Gary C. Jacobson, *A Divider, Not a Uniter: George W. Bush and the American People*, 2nd ed. (Boston: Longman, 2010).

3. The "ball and chain" reference comes from Thomas Stokes, *Chip Off My Shoulder* (Princeton: Princeton University Press, 1940), 503. On the regional realignments that have transformed the party system, see Nicole Mellow, *The State of Disunion: Regional Sources of Modern American Partisanship* (Baltimore: Johns Hopkins University Press, 2008).

4. Even the so-called Blue Dogs—moderate Democrats who mostly hail from southern and border states—were not nearly as powerful or obstreperous as were the southern Democrats who plagued past Democrat presidents. Rhodes Cook, "Not Your Father's Democratic Congress," *Larry Sabato's Crystal Ball*, February 19, 2009, http://www.centerforpolitics.org/crystalball/articles/frc2009021901/.

5. Ronald Brownstein, "The Clinton Conundrum," *The Atlantic*, April 17, 2015, https://www.theatlantic.com/politics/archive/2015/04/the-clinton-conundrum/431949/.

6. Michael Nelson, "The Setting: Diversifying the Presidential Talent Pool," in *The Elections of 2008*, ed. Michael Nelson (Washington, D.C.: CQ Press, 2009, pp. 1–21).

7. Elaine Kamarck, "Assessing Dean's Fifty-State Strategy in the 2006 Midterm Elections," *Forum*, 4, no. 3 (2006), http://www.degruyter.com/view/j/for.2006.4.3_2012

0105083451/for.2006.4.3/for.2006.4.3.1141/for.2006.4.3.1141.xml; and Ari Berman, "The Dean Legacy," *The Nation*, February 28, 2008.

8. Gary C. Jacobson, "Congress: the Second Democratic Wave," in Nelson, *The Elections of 2008*, 100.

9. As Jeffrey Tulis has argued, Obama's leadership style is best "understood as restorative in the sense that Obama extends and elaborates on the New Deal of 1930s and the Great Society of the 1960s, which itself was an elaboration of the New Deal." Tulis, "Plausible Futures," in *The Presidency in the Twenty First Century*, ed. Charles W. Dunn (Lexington: University Press of Kentucky, 2011), 9.

10. Barack Obama, "Remarks on the Economy," Georgetown University, April 14, 2009, http://www.whitehouse.gov/the-press-office/remarks-president-economy-georgetown-university.

11. Chuck Todd, *The Stranger: Barack Obama in the White House* (New York: Little, Brown, 2014).

12. Morton Keller, *The Unbearable Heaviness of Governing: The Obama Administration in Historical Perspective* (Stanford, Calif.: Hoover Institution Press, 2010), 11.

13. Peter Baker and David Herszenhorn, "Senate Allies Fault Obama on Stimulus," *New York Times*, January 9, 2009.

14. Carl Hulse, "Obama Team Makes Early Efforts to Show Willingness to Reach Out to Republicans," *New York Times*, January 20, 2009; Jackie Calmes and Carl Hulse, "Obama, Visiting G.O.P. Lawmakers, Is Open to Some Compromises on Stimulus," *New York Times*, January 28, 2009.

15. Jackie Calmes, "House Passes Stimulus Plan with No G.O.P. Votes," *New York Times*, January 29, 2009.

16. Sheryl Gay Stolberg and Helene Cooper, "Obama Makes Case as Stimulus Bill Clears Hurdle," *New York Times*, February 10, 2009; David M. Herszenhorn and Carl Hulse, "Deal Reached in Congress on $789 Billion Stimulus Plan, *New York Times*, February 11, 2009.

17. John Harwood, "Bipartisan Health Bill Is Possible, Leaders Say," *New York Times*, June 8, 2009; and David Herszenhorn, "Democrats Divide over a Proposal to Tax Health Benefits," *New York Times*, July 9, 2009.

18. "Executive Order Ensuring Enforcement of Abortion Restrictions in the Patient Protection and Affordable Care Act," March 24, 2010.

19. See, for example, Robert Pear and David Herszenhorn, "House Democrats End Impasse on Health Bill," *New York Times*, July 30, 2009; David Kirkpatrick, "Obama Is Taking an Active Role in Talks on Health Care Plan," *New York Times*, August 13, 2009; Sheryl Gay Stolberg, "'Public Option' in Health Plan May be Dropped," *New York Times*, August 17, 2009; and Peter Baker, "Compromising on Two Issues, Obama Gets Partial Wins," *New York Times*, December 20, 2009.

20. Adam Nagourney, "Debate Shows Obama Plays by Washington's Rules," *New York Times*, December 26, 2009.

21. Carl Hulse, "Obama Tactic Shields Health Care Bill from a Filibuster," *New York Times*, April 25, 2009.

22. Quoted in Christina Bellantoni, "Transcript: OFA's Mitch Stewart and Jeremy Bird Speak to TPMDC," Talking Points Memo, November 11, 2009, http://talkingpointsmemo.com/news/transcript-ofa-s-mitch-stewart-and-jeremy-bird-speak-to-tpmdc. For details on OFA's role in the health reform debate, see Ari Melber, "Year One of Organizing for America: The Permanent Field Campaign in a Digital Age," *techPresident Special Report*, January 2010, www.techpresident.com/ofayear1.

23. Carl Hulse and Jeff Zeleny, "Democrats Seem Set to Go It Alone on a Health Bill," *New York Times*, August 19, 2009.

24. Carrie Budoff Brown and Patrick O'Connor, "No High Hopes for Health Care Summit," *Politico*, February 9, 2010; and Carrie Budoff Brown and Glenn Thrush, "Pelosi Steeled W. H. for Health Push," *Politico*, March 20, 2010.

25. David Sanger, "Big Win for Obama, But at What Cost?" *New York Times*, March 21, 2010.

26. Keller, *The Unbearable Heaviness of Governing*, 63–64.

27. Gary Langer, "2010 Elections Exit Poll Analysis: The Political Price of Economic Pain," *ABC News*, November 3, 2010, http://abcnews.go.com/Politics/2010-midterms-political-price-economic-pain/story?id=12041739.

28. For a detailed analysis of the We Can't Wait campaign, see Kenneth S. Lowande and Sidney M. Milkis, "'We Can't Wait': Barack Obama, Partisan Polarization and the Administrative Presidency," *The Forum*, 12, no. 1 (Spring 2014): 3–27.

29. David Klaidman and Andrew Romano, "President Obama's Executive Power Grab," *The Daily Beast*, October 22, 2012, www.thedailybeast.com/newsweek/2012/10/21/president-obama-s-executive-power-grab.html.

30. Cary Coglianese, "Presidential Control of Administrative Agencies: A Debate over Law or Politics?" *Journal of Constitutional Law*, 12 (2010): 637–649; Lawrence R. Jacobs and Desmond S. King. "Varieties of Obamaism: Structure, Agency, and the Obama Presidency," *Perspectives on Politics*, 8, no. 3 (2010): 793–802; and Theda Skocpol and Lawrence R. Jacobs, "Accomplished and Embattled: Understanding Obama's Presidency," *Political Science Quarterly*, 127, no. 1 (2012): 1–24.

31. Michael D. Shear and Ceci Connolly, "Obama Assembles Powerful West Wing," *Washington Post*, January 8, 2009.

32. Sheryl Gay Stolberg, "Great Limits Come with Great Power, Ex-Candidate Finds," *New York Times*, January 25, 2009.

33. David Stout, "Obama Moves to Reverse Bush's Labor Policies," *New York Times*, January 31, 2009; and Andrea Stone, "Abortion Foes Find New Climate: Obama Repeats Commitment to Right to Choose," *USA Today*, January 23, 2009.

34. Suzanne Goldenberg, "Obama Presses for Tougher Controls on US Car Emissions," *The Guardian*, January 27, 2009.

35. DeParle cited in Charlie Savage, "Shift on Executive Power Lets Obama Bypass Rivals, *New York Times*, April 22, 2012, http://www.nytimes.com/2012/04/23/us/politics/shift-on-executive-powers-let-obama-bypass-congress.html?r=0.

36. "New Report: 2012 Elections Offer Takeaways for 2013 Immigration Debate," *America's Voice*, January 3, 2013, http://americasvoice.org/research/new-report-2012-elections-offer-takeaways-for-2013-immigration-debate-2/.

37. Daniel Tichenor, "The Overwhelming Barriers to Immigration Reform," *The Atlantic*, May 25, 2016; and Daniel Tichenor, *Dividing Lines: The Politics of Immigration Control in America* (Princeton: Princeton University Press, 2002). On uneasy but critical alliance between Obama and the immigration rights movement, see Sidney M. Milkis and Daniel J. Tichenor, *Rivalry and Reform: The Modern Presidency, Social Movements and the Transformation of American Politics* (Chicago: University of Chicago Press, 2018), chap. 7.

38. Personal interview with Democratic congressional staff member, July 19, 2009.

39. The Patient Protection and Affordable Care Act came before the Supreme Court in the midst of the 2012 campaign. In a landmark decision, *National Federation of Independent Business v. Sebelius* (567 U.S. 2012), a 5–4 majority upheld the individual mandate, the linchpin of the legislation, which required most Americans to maintain a minimum level of health insurance for themselves and their dependents. To the surprise of most pundits and public officials, Chief Justice John Roberts joined the four liberal justices on the Court in upholding this key provision. Nevertheless, Roberts's ruling may have long-term consequences that constrain the federal government's power over the economy and states.

The chief justice argued that the mandate was not a proper exercise of the Constitution's commerce power, although he was willing to sanction it as a tax, and he weakened the most redistributive feature of the legislation—the expansion of Medicaid—claiming that this change could not be forced on the states. Roberts's decision was generally praised by Democrats but not accepted by Republicans, who made the repeal of the Affordable Care Act the cornerstone of the 2012 election.

40. See Michael Nelson, ed., *The Elections of 2012* (Washington, D.C.: CQ Press, 2013).

41. Molly Ball, "Obama's Edge: The Ground Game That Could Put Him over the Top," *The Atlantic*, October 24, 2012, http://www.theatlantic.com/politics/archive/2012/10/obamas-edge-the-ground-game-that-could-put-him-over-the-top/264031/. For a detailed analysis of OFA and its contribution to the Obama presidency, see Sidney M. Milkis and John W. York, "Managing Alone: Barack Obama, Organizing for Action and Policy Advocacy in the Digital Era," paper presented at the Annual Meeting of the American Political Science Association, August 28–September 1, 2014, Washington, D.C.

42. Personal interview with OFA volunteer, December 4, 2012. For a detailed account of how OFA combined sophisticated targeting and old-fashioned canvassing, see Sasha Issenberg, "Obama Does It Better," *Slate*, October 29, 2012, http://www.slate.com/articles/news_and_politics/victory_lab/2012/10/obama_s_secret_weapon_democrats_have_a_massive_advantage_in_targeting_and.single.html.

43. Personal interview, December 3, 2012.

44. Email message from OFA volunteer, January 8, 2013.

45. Most scholars and journalists have cited Obama's relatively limited use of executive orders to discount the significance of his administrative politics. But these analyses overlooked the growing importance of unilateralism by other, less-formal means, such as memoranda and waivers, which Obama used to an unprecedented degree. For example, during the first five years of his presidency, George W. Bush issued 79 memos and 208 executive orders; during his first five years, Obama issued 162 memos and 171 executive orders (tabulated using the digitalized *Federal Register*: http://www.federalregister.gov).

46. Amy Goldstein and Juliet Eilperin, "How Political Fear Was Pitted against Technical Needs, *Washington Post*, November 2, 2013, http://www.washingtonpost.com/politics/challenges-have-dogged-obamas-health-plan-since-2010/2013/11/02/453fba42-426b-11e3-a624-41d661b0bb78_story.html.

47. Cited in ibid.

48. Ibid.

49. Foster, cited in ibid.

50. The House sued the president over the delay of the employer mandate. Jeremy W. Peters, "House Votes to Sue Obama for Overstepping Powers, *New York Times*, July 30, 2014, http://www.nytimes.com/2014/07/31/us/politics/house-votes-along-party-lines-to-sue-obama.html?emc=eta1.

51. "The Obama Administration Has a Mandate on the Health Care Law Too," editorial, *Washington Post*, February 11, 2014, http://www.washingtonpost.com/opinions/the-obama-administration-has-a-mandate-on-the-health-care-law-too/2014/02/11/f001df36-9361-11e3-84e1-27626c5ef5fb_story.html. For a detailed analysis of the partisan maneuvers in the wayward implementation of the Affordable Care Act, see Lowande and Milkis, "'We Can't Wait': Barack Obama, Partisan Polarization and the Administrative Presidency."

52. Jacobson, *A Divider, Not a Uniter*.

53. Quote is from Barack Obama, "My Plan for Iraq," *New York Times*, July 14, 2008. On the relationship between Obama's antiwar stance and his popularity among Democrats, see Gary Jacobson, "George W. Bush, the Iraq War, and the Election of Barack Obama," *Presidential Studies Quarterly*, 40 (2010): 212.

54. Peter Baker, "Obama's War over Terror," *New York Times Magazine*, January 17, 2010.

55. Barack Obama, "Renewing American Leadership," *Foreign Affairs*, July/August 2007, 9.

56. Scott Wilson, "The Making of a Wartime Commander in Chief," *Washington Post*, January 19, 2010; and Charlie Savage, "Closing Guantánamo Fades as a Priority," *New York Times*, June 25, 2010.

57. "President Obama Said Friday He Plans to Withdraw Most U.S. Troops from Iraq by the End of August 2010," *CNN.com*, February 23, 2009.

58. Barack Obama, "Remarks by the President on a New Beginning," Cairo University, Cairo, Egypt, June 4, 2009.

59. Peter Baker, "Obama's War over Terror," *New York Times Magazine*, January 17, 2010.

60. Charlie Savage, "No Terror Evidence against Some Detainees," *New York Times*, May 28, 2010.

61. Michael C. Desch, "The More Things Change, the More They Stay the Same: The Liberal Tradition and Obama's Counterterrorism Policy," *PS: Political Science and Politics*, 43 (2010): 426.

62. Barack Obama, "Remarks by the President in Address to the Nation on the Way Forward in Afghanistan and Pakistan," United States Military Academy, West Point, New York, December 2009.

63. Peter Baker and Mark Landler, "Setbacks Cloud U.S. Plans to Get Out of Afghanistan," *New York Times*, June 14, 2010; and Peter Baker, "With Shift in Afghanistan, Talk Turns to Exit," *New York Times*, June 28, 2010.

64. David Sanger, "Afghan Deadline Is Cutting Two Ways," *New York Times*, July 21, 2010.

65. Statement by President on ISIL, September 10, 2014, http://www.whitehouse.gov/the-press-office/2014/09/10/statement-president-isil-1.

66. Mark Landler, "In U.N. Speech, Obama Vows to Fight ISIS 'Network of Death,'" *New York Times*, September 24, 2014, http://www.nytimes.com/2014/09/25/world/middleeast/obama-syria-un-isis.html.

67. Krishnadev Calamur, "Obama Has Support for Syria Strikes, but Are They Legal?" *NPR*, September 25, 2014, http://www.npr.org/blogs/parallels/2014/09/25/351433505/obama-has-support-for-syria-strikes-but-are-they-legal.

68. Goldsmith, cited in ibid.

69. Bill Schneider, "ISIS Debate Colored by Iraq War Votes," *Inside Politics*, September 2014.

70. "Presidential Approval Ratings: Barack Obama," *Gallup*, www.gallup.com/poll/116479/barack-obama-presidential-job-approval.aspx. Partisan loyalists disagreed strongly about the likely outcome of the ISIS campaign. By two to one (54–27 percent), Democrats were more concerned that the United States would "go too far in getting involved." By more than two to one (66–27 percent), Republicans were concerned that the U.S. "would not go far enough." Schneider, "ISIS Debate Colored by Iraqi War Votes."

71. Robert Dahl, "The Myth of the Presidential Mandate," *Political Science Quarterly*, 105 (1990): 355–372.

72. Sidney M. Milkis, Daniel J. Tichenor, and Laura Blessing, "The Modern Presidency, Social Movements and the Transformation of American Politics," *Presidential Studies Quarterly*, 43, 2013: 641–670.

73. For a full discussion of OFA's role in the health care reform, see Sidney M. Milkis and John Warren York, "Barack Obama, Organizing for Action, and Executive-Centered Partisanship," *Studies in American Political Development*, 31, no. 1 (April 2017): 1–23.

74. "Power Sector Carbon Pollution Standards," *Federal Register*, 78, no. 126 (July 1, 2013); and "The President's Climate Action Plan," Executive Office of the President (June, 2013).

75. *Massachusetts v. Environmental Protection Agency*, 549 U.S. 497 (2007).

76. The Republicans picked up nine seats in the Senate and thirteen in the House. The GOP majority in the Senate became 54–46; its 247–188 edge in the House gave the Republicans the largest majority it has enjoyed since 1948.

77. Between 2008 and 2015, Democrats lost 13 Senate seats, 913 state legislative seats, 11 governorships, and 32 state legislative chambers. The only president in the past seventy-five years who came close was Dwight Eisenhower, who witnessed a similar decline for the GOP during his presidency. Juliet Eilperin, "Obama Who Once Stood as a Party Outsider, Now Works to Strengthen Democrats, *Washington Post*, April 25, 2016, https://www.washingtonpost.com.

78. Ibid.

CHAPTER 16

The Trump Presidency and Resilience of Constitutional Government

Donald J. Trump's election as president in 2016 seemed nothing less than astonishing. At each turn of the electoral calendar, from June 16, 2015, when Trump announced he was running, until well into the evening of Election Day—November 8, 2016—political analysts of every stripe were confident that he would not succeed. The world's leading political betting firm made him a 100-to-1 long shot on the day of his announcement. The Huffington Post refused for months to "report on Trump's campaign as part of [our] political coverage. Instead we will cover his campaign as part of our entertainment section."[1] One prominent political scientist whose statistical model forecast that any Republican nominee would win because the economic and political fundamentals were so favorable to the GOP decided that Trump was such a bad candidate that the model did not apply.[2]

Viewed historically, the roots of Trump's election become more visible. To be sure, all forty-four of his predecessors were experienced officeholders: senators, governors, vice presidents, generals, and cabinet members. In the quarter century after World War II, senators and vice presidents (most of whom had been senators) dominated presidential elections because Cold War–era voters trusted the federal government and valued experience dealing with national security issues. Then, in the aftermath of the Vietnam War and the Watergate scandal, the electorate turned to state governors, who were experienced in governing but untainted by the incompetence and corruption many voters now associated with a Washington-based political career: Jimmy Carter in 1976, Ronald Reagan in 1980, Bill Clinton in 1992, and George W. Bush in 2000.

The ascendant Tea Party movement that helped the Republican Party win control of the House of Representatives in 2010 and the Senate in 2014, however, was not just anti-Washington but antigovernment in all its forms. As a candidate who had never held public office, Trump appealed to many voters as an outsider from the business world who would "drain the swamp" in Washington.[3] "The problem with politicians," he told a rally, "[they're] all talk and no action. It's true. All talk, and it's all bullshit."[4] Trump's wealth became a major part of his allure when he ran for president. "Do you want someone who gets to be president and that's literally the highest-paying job he's ever had?"[5]

Trump was more than a businessman; he was also a celebrity. After years in the media spotlight for self-glorifying business books like *Trump: The Art of the Deal*, controversial statements on late-night and radio and television talk shows, and much-publicized affairs and marriages with glamorous women, he proved a natural when NBC signed him in 2004 for its new prime-time program *The Apprentice*. Trump improvised his lines while advancing his image as the epitome of entrepreneurial success and glamor. The show and its successor, *Celebrity Apprentice*, attracted large viewing audiences for fourteen years.

Trump's celebrity status was enhanced by his willingness to launch outrageous charges in person, on the air, and eventually on Twitter. Controversy served him well in the new media environment in which cable news networks competed feverishly for viewers and new forms of social media enabled candidates to connect directly with voters. From the start both liberal MSNBC and conservative Fox News found that all-Trump-all-the-time programming (harshly critical from the former, slavishly devoted from the latter) sent their ratings skyward. Twitter also became a vehicle for Trump to ridicule his rivals and discredit critics.

As on *The Apprentice*, where "you're fired" became his catchphrase, not "you've got the job," Trump was able to inject negative epithets into the national discourse without ever attempting to inject a positive one in the style of FDR's New Deal or JFK's New Frontier. Notoriously, he was one of the most prominent advocates of the birther conspiracy theory that alleged Barack Obama was not born in the United States and, therefore, a consti-tutionally fraudulent president. Trump's peddling of this racially charged conspiracy helped pave the way for his incendiary presidential campaign, during which he indelibly branded his Democratic opponent, former sec-retary of state Hillary Rodham Clinton, as "Crooked Hillary" and led chants of "Lock her up!" at campaign rallies after Clinton was nominated by her party. Nor did Trump spare Republican rivals Ted Cruz and Marco Rubio, whom he dubbed "Lyin' Ted" and "Liddle Marco" (Trump's spelling).[6] He discredited critical media coverage as "fake news."

Trump also understood something that his rivals and other party leaders did not: most Republican voters did not share their brand of con-servatism. For years, Republican leaders pursued an agenda that favored free trade, reduced spending on Social Security and Medicare, and a path to legal status for undocumented immigrants. Many rank-and-file Republican voters favored none of these things. In parallel 2014 surveys of Republican voters and elites, 62 percent of voters but only 26 percent of elites said that spending on Social Security should be increased. Seventy-two percent of voters said that "immigrants and refugees coming to the U.S." pose a "critical threat" to the country, compared with 22 percent of elites. By vowing to protect Social Security and Medicare, deport illegal immigrants, and introduce protectionist trade policies, Trump simply met many Republican voters where they were.[7] He would not only "build a great, great wall on our southern border," he promised, but also "have Mexico pay for that wall."[8] Trump preached a conservative nationalism that had been building in the Republican Party since the late 1960s, one tinged with nativist and isolationist strains that had a long history in the United States.

Nationally, blue-collar whites, who roughly correspond to the category "non-college educated" in polls, began defecting from the Democratic Party during the Nixon years. They tipped the balance to Trump over Clinton by turning out to vote at a higher rate than in 2012 and giving him 66 percent of their votes. Their support enabled Trump to carry enough normally Democratic states such as Wisconsin, Michigan, and Pennsylvania—keystones of the Democrats' supposed "Blue Wall"—to win a 304–227 Electoral College victory even while running 2.9 million behind Clinton in the national popular vote.[9] Equally important, 81 percent of white evangelical Christians, who enlisted as the foot soldiers of the conservative Republican base during the Reagan and George W. Bush administrations, supported the thrice-married, casino-owning, foul-mouthed Trump in response to his promise that in contrast to Clinton, he would appoint pro-life Supreme Court justices.

Taking Office

In many ways, Trump was fortunate to take office when he did. Although the world had its share of problems when his term began on January 20, 2017, they were ongoing, not new or urgent. The domestic economy had been growing, slowly but steadily, for all but one of the previous twenty-three quarters. The annual rate of inflation was about 2 percent, and unemployment had recently dipped below 5 percent. Interest rates on mortgages and car and student loans also were low. The percentage of Americans who regard themselves as middle- or upper-class reached 62 percent, a greater share than before the 2008–2009 economic meltdown.[10] The stock market was booming: from a modern nadir of 6,547 in March 2009, the Dow Jones Industrial Average nearly tripled to 18,332 by Election Day. No crises that threatened the nation's security or prosperity marred the world stage. Unlike all of his recent Republican predecessors during the past two-thirds of a century, Trump took office as the head of a united party government, with a GOP majority in both the House of Representatives and the Senate.

In other ways, however, Trump's ascent to the White House was ill-starred. Newly elected presidents normally enjoy a postelection increase in public approval that represents the vote of confidence granted to anyone who attains the office. In the history of polling from Dwight D. Eisenhower to Barack Obama, every president's initial job approval rating exceeded his share of the popular vote in the election that brought him to power.[11] But Trump's brutalist election campaign ensured that he would not have a "honeymoon" period at all. His Gallup approval rating the week after his inauguration was 45 percent, the lowest ever recorded for a new president.[12] In contrast to every other modern president, it never reached 50 percent.

Complicating the challenges Trump faced, his lack of knowledge about the presidency and the Constitution was as unprecedented in the history of the office as his lack of governing experience or broad-based early support. The new president had at best a dim understanding of the sharing of power mandated by the Constitution, both between the state and federal governments and among the branches within the federal government. A week before the election, Trump oddly promised that he would convene a special session of Congress as soon as he was sworn in, even though Congress is always in session at that time of year.[13] At a July 8 meeting with House Republicans, he professed his devotion to the Constitution; he had taken an oath to "preserve, protect, and defend" by saying of the document, "I want to protect Article I, Article II, Article XII—go down the list."[14] (There are seven articles, not twelve, much less a longer "list.") Weeks after Hurricane Maria wracked the Virgin Islands, Trump referred to "the president of the Virgin Islands," which, like all American states and territories, actually has a governor. The president of the United States is the Virgin Islands' president.[15]

Trump's particular brand of experience in business was at best dimly relevant to the challenges of the presidency. Unlike the heads of publicly traded corporations, who oversee large-scale operations and, even more to the point, share power with shareholders and boards of directors, Trump spent decades heading moderately sized private companies that developed real estate and casinos. As such he had grown used to acting on his own surrounded by a handful of family members and loyal subordinates.

In addition, unlike many business leaders who read widely in history and politics, Trump professed not to be a reader. Examples of his ignorance about the office he held abounded. Andrew Jackson, Trump said, "was really angry that he saw what was happening in regard to the Civil War."[16] (Jackson died sixteen year before the war.) Speaking of Abraham Lincoln, Trump asked, "Most people don't even know he was a Republican. Right? Does anyone know?"[17] (Every Republican who has ever claimed membership in the "party of Lincoln" does, which is pretty much every Republican.) "Frederick Douglass," Trump declared, as if speaking of a living person, "is an example of somebody who's done an amazing job."[18] After mentioning William McKinley to a crowd in Youngstown, Ohio, he wondered, "Does anybody know who the hell he is?"[19] President McKinley's birthplace is twelve miles away.

Although Trump's complete absence of experience in government made his need for a successful transition period greater than that of any previous president, he wasted much of the ten weeks between election and inauguration tossing aside the months of planning and research his team had done. On May 9, 2016, Trump had appointed Governor Chris Christie of New Jersey to lead an intensive transition planning process that would generate a list of able candidates for each appointed position in the White House and executive branch and help Trump flesh out his campaign promises with detailed advice from policy experts. On November 11, three days after the election, the president-elect fired Christie and "threw six months of work in the garbage can."[20] As a result, the new president took office knowing little about what the executive branch does or who could run it on his behalf. When it comes to future presidential transitions, the political scientist John Burke concluded, "Donald Trump's experience will likely provide the textbook case on what not to do."[21]

Forming the Administration

An axiom of staffing for presidents who lack experience in the federal government is to stock the White House with people who have that experience and then rely on their judgment. Trump took a different approach. The result was that a president who had never spent a day in office was surrounded by advisers who had never spent a day in office—with consequences that were all too predictable.

One consequence of Trump's lack of relevant experience was that he filled most White House positions by drawing from the small circle of people with whom he first became acquainted during his election campaign. Although the White House Office has tended to be an extension of the president's campaign family since the Kennedy administration, Trump's network was unprecedentedly small and fractious. It included Republican National Committee chair Reince Priebus as chief of staff, foreign policy adviser Gen. Michael Flynn as national security adviser, campaign spokesman Sean Spicer as press secretary, and senior campaign strategist Steve Bannon—the former executive chairman of the "Alt Right" web-based news site, Breitbart—as senior political strategist. Not knowing these individuals well, Trump also brought his daughter Ivanka Trump and her husband, Jared Kushner, into the West Wing as free-floating advisers.

Other than Trump's family members, none of these appointments worked out. Priebus was denied real authority to direct and discipline the rest of the staff. Spicer was undermined by Trump's barely concealed scorn for his handling of the press.[22] Flynn lasted only three weeks and later pled guilty to lying to the FBI. Bannon was out after seven months. Lines of responsibility were notoriously unclear in the Trump White House. Factions formed based on ideological differences and personal rivalries. Staff members leaked disparaging comments about each other to the press corps. A general air of chaos prevailed. By the end of Trump's second hundred days as president, the White House had seen the firing or resignation of his first national security adviser, chief of staff, deputy chief of staff, chief strategist, press secretary, and other aides, notably two communications directors. By July 2018, three-quarters of the president's top aides had left the White House (as compared with 41 percent and 17 percent who left the George W. Bush and Obama administrations, respectively, during the first 18 months of their first terms).[23]

As a former general and the administration's effective first secretary of homeland security before becoming White House chief of staff after six months, John Kelly had the stature his predecessor lacked in Trump's eyes. But as Kelly and others found, the long-term reining in of a seventy-one-year-old man who rose high in the business and entertainment worlds and was elected president by doing things in a loose, personal, and spontaneous way was not easy to accomplish. Longtime Trump associate Roger Stone warned: "General Kelly is trying to treat the president like a mushroom. Keeping him in the dark and feeding him shit is not going to work. Donald Trump is a free spirit."[24] Accordingly, Kelly's relationship with Trump deteriorated with the passage of time and the president's growing resentment of Kelly's efforts to rein in his more impulsive tendencies.

Trump was equally unfamiliar with the talent pool from which presidents usually draw cabinet members and their high-ranking subordinates. In filling the most important executive positions, Trump initially was drawn to people who had succeeded in domains he respected—business (ExxonMobil chief executive Rex Tillerson as secretary of state, investor Steven Mnuchin as secretary of the Treasury), and the military (four-star army General James Mattis as secretary of defense, generals Flynn and H. R. McMaster as his first and second national security advisers)—as well as to the small set of Republican politicians who had supported him in the election, notably Sen. Jeff Sessions as attorney general.

Most of Trump's other cabinet appointees were members of Congress or political figures whose names he got from Vice President Mike Pence, a former member of Congress.[25] Pence was exceptionally well wired in established conservative circles, and his recommendations reflected that. As a result, several cabinet nominees were actively hostile to their departments and agencies. As a House member from Georgia, for example, Tom Price strongly opposed the Affordable Care Act; as secretary of the Department of Health and Human Services (HHS), Obamacare was part of his jurisdiction. Trump's nominee for secretary of the interior, Representative Ryan Zinke of Montana, was less interested in preserving the 500 million acres of mostly western federal land that the department manages than in opening parts of it to mining, grazing, and oil and gas exploration. Scott Pruitt, whom Trump appointed as director of the Environmental Protection Agency (EPA), sued to overturn EPA regulations multiple times as attorney general of Oklahoma.

As with his staff, collisions occurred between Trump and his cabinet, whose experience leading highly structured corporate and military organizations clashed with his improvisational management style. Early tensions arose between the president and Secretary of State Tillerson, whom Trump fired after barely a year and, especially, with Attorney General Sessions, whom he wanted to fire for recusing himself from any Justice Department investigation of Russia's role in fostering Trump's election. In an Oval Office meeting in May 2017, Trump called Sessions an "idiot" and demanded that he resign.[26] Sessions stubbornly remained, and Republican senators tied the president's hands by making clear their reluctance to confirm any nominee chosen to replace him.

Trump's main problem in forming his administration, however, was his own slowness in filling most of the hundreds of subcabinet positions that department heads rely on to help lead their organizations. After a half year in office, Trump had failed to nominate candidates for 379—more than two-thirds—of 566 key positions in the executive branch, hampered by a selection process that valued loyalty above competence. Yet on the eve of a twelve-day trip to Asia in November 2017, Trump said, "I'm the only one that matters. . . . I'm a business person, and I tell my people, when you don't need to fill slots don't fill them," a fine sentiment for the hands-on leader of a small operation but, for the president, a certain formula for bureaucratic inertia.[27] Trump did confess, "This is more work than in my previous life. I thought it would be easier."[28]

Trump's Administrative Presidency

In the modern era, presidents—especially those whose party controls Congress—usually have relied on executive orders, proclamations, and other unilateral actions as the primary means of pursuing their goals only when their efforts to secure legislation have failed. To be sure, unilateral presidential action became an indispensable feature of an emerging executive-centered partisanship during the George W. Bush and Obama years, fueled in no small part by their having to face an uncooperative Congress as soon as at least one of its chambers was won by the other party. The sharp partisan divide was aggravated by the routine use of the filibuster by the party that did not control the White House. So far did Obama push the administrative envelope that after Republicans assumed command of the House in the 2010 elections, GOP strategists eagerly anticipated that the next president their party elected would seize the loaded administrative weapons Obama left in the Oval Office.[29] One might have expected that an aggressive administrative strategy would not have been so pivotal when the Trump administration took office under unified Republican government in 2017. Nevertheless, Trump immediately grasped administrative power, often in the service of highly controversial measures that strained his relations with congressional Republicans who remained split in the areas of free trade and immigration.

As a candidate Trump complained that Obama was "a president who can't get anything done, so he just keeps signing executive orders all over the place. . . . I want to do away with executive orders for the most part."[30] Yet instead of turning to Congress with most of his major policy initiatives—the equivalent in the world of publicly traded corporations of securing approval from a board of directors—Trump's different business experience in private companies prompted him to issue a blizzard of executive orders from the beginning. In a press release at the end of his first one hundred days in office, the White House bragged about what Trump decried during the election—namely, that he had signed more executive orders than any president since Harry S. Truman.[31]

The appeal of executive orders is that they lie within the president's own authority and thus can cut the knot of partisan gridlock. In some cases Trump's actions were effective in advancing his goals. For example, he issued a freeze on federal hiring that made exceptions for "national security or public safety," thereby allowing the parts of the executive branch that Republicans favor—namely the Departments of Defense and Homeland Security—to grow while shrinking the workforce in the domestic agencies favored by Democrats.[32] In early October 2017 the *New York Times* counted twenty-five environmental rules that the Trump administration already had overturned and twenty-seven more repeal efforts that were under way.[33]

Yet unilateral action entails certain disadvantages, which is why most presidents turn to them as a last rather than a first resort, the approach Trump took to some of Obama's orders with relish. For one thing, an order can be undone by another order by a subsequent president. For another, such actions often are of limited effectiveness. An order cannot repeal a regulation that already has undergone the Administrative Procedures Act's lengthy "notice-and-comment" process. All the order can do is launch a new, equally onerous notice-and-comment process aimed at undoing the regulation, and even then the new process must result in what the Supreme Court has called "a reasoned basis" to explain why the old regulation was wrong and the new one is right.[34] When EPA director Pruitt moved to suspend a regulation that restricts methane emissions from new oil and gas wells, for example, a federal appeals court voided his decision as "unreasonable," "arbitrary," and "capricious" and said that he would have to launch the required notice-and-comment process to have any chance of prevailing.[35]

Once again revealing his lack of knowledge and experience about government, Trump said he was "very frustrated" to learn that on criminal matters, the president was "not supposed to be involved with the Justice Department. I'm not supposed to be involved with the FBI." His frustration was chiefly rooted in the appointment of special counsel Robert Mueller to investigate Russian involvement in his campaign and in the department's unwillingness to continue "going after Hillary Clinton."[36] Mueller's investigation lasted well into Trump's first term, with indictments and guilty pleas from several campaign and White House advisers.

Trump also created ongoing problems for himself with sloppily designed orders. One week after taking office, he issued one to ban entry to the United States by visitors from seven predominantly Muslim nations. Devised entirely within the White House, with no advice from the agencies that would have to interpret and enforce it, the order created chaos at airports around the world as officers, tormented by protests at many international airports at home and abroad, tried to make sense of what it required. Federal courts quickly undid this order, as well as a revised one, ruling that they exceeded the president's legal authority and violated the First Amendment's establishment clause by discriminating against people on the basis of their religion. Only when the president issued a third order concerning travel after a thorough process that included the Departments of State and Homeland Security as well as the intelligence agencies did the courts agree to give serious consideration to its legality.[37] In June 2018, a narrow five-to-four majority of the Supreme Court ruled in *Trump v. Hawaii* that the third version passed constitutional muster by not limiting its prohibition to Muslim-dominated countries and by providing a process by which countries could remove their ineligibility.

As the recent history of the presidency has shown, the pursuit of partisan objectives through administrative action, although sometimes deemed necessary in periods of polarization, tends to denigrate the rule of law and public debate that is the sine qua non of a responsible party politics. The Reagan, Bush, and Obama presidencies foretold what became alarming during the first 18 months of the Trump presidency, namely, that the joining of presidential prerogative with partisanship creates the illusion that the executive of a vast bureaucratic state can function as a truly representative democratic leader with meaningful links to the party and the public. Instead, executive partisanship leads to a plebiscitary politics, which exposes the American people to leaders who scorn the institutional restraints that are a vital ingredient of constitutional democracy.

The Courts

Perhaps the most corrosive feature of partisan rancor has been its effect on the judiciary. The one-vote majority of Supreme Court justices that ruled in the president's favor in the travel ban case was no accident. Looming over nearly the entire 2016 election, for the first time since George Washington was chosen as president in 1789, was the certainty that if Trump were elected, he would have an immediate opportunity to nominate someone to the Court. No sooner had Justice Antonin Scalia died on February 13, 2016, then Senate Republican leader Mitch McConnell vowed that the vacancy would "not be filled until we have a new president." The Republican-controlled Senate ignored Obama's nomination of the moderately liberal appeals court judge Merrick Garland. With four Republican justices balancing the four Democratic appointees, voters knew that whoever was chosen to take Scalia's place would cast the decisive vote in many controversial cases. Trump's response as a candidate was to release two lists, carefully vetted by the conservative Federalist Society, comprising twenty-one conservative judges from which he said he promised to choose his Supreme Court nominees, an unprecedented action by a presidential candidate.

Even as Senate Democrats, still in the majority at the time, changed the chamber's rules in 2013 by removing the filibuster as a barrier to lower court nominations, they left it unaltered for Supreme Court appointments. Another check on harsh partisan judicial politics fell in early 2017. When forty-five Democrats announced their intention to oppose Trump's nomination of conservative appeals court judge Neil Gorsuch to the Court, Senate Republicans extended the filibuster ban to all appointments. Gorsuch's nomination was approved on April 7 by a vote of 54 to 45, with Republican senators unanimous in their support and Democrats voting 45 to 3 against confirmation.

When the less reliably conservative Justice Anthony Kennedy announced his retirement on June 27, 2018, Trump said, "We have to pick one that's going to be there for forty years, forty-five years." He focused his search for a new justice on judges who, like Gorsuch, were in their forties, as well as being on one of his previously published lists from the campaign, supplemented by an additional list of five that he issued in November 2017. Trump's choice to replace Kennedy, a critical liberal vote in landmark cases involving women's and LGBTQ rights, was Brett Kavanaugh, who like Gorsuch was a young and reliably conservative appeals court judge. Democrats and liberal advocacy groups, viewing Kavanaugh's appointment as portending a conservative majority that would endure for a generation, resisted it with all their means even before serious allegations of sexual misconduct surfaced on the eve of the scheduled Senate vote. The charges, which Kavanaugh denied, did not prevent his confirmation, albeit by a majority that was the narrowest (50–48) since 1881 and the most partisan (all but one Senate Republican voted for him and all but one Senate Democrat voted against him) of any confirmed nominee in history.[38]

Trump's imprint on the judiciary went beyond the highest tribunal. During the Obama presidency, Senate Democrats also preserved the "blue-slip" tradition that requires consent from both of a state's senators before the Senate Judiciary Committee will consider a nominee from that state for a federal judgeship. As a result, many Obama nominees from states with Republican senators were left to languish, leaving more than a hundred seats on lower federal courts unfilled when Trump took office.[39] McConnell indicated in 2017 that rather than allow Trump's nominees to fill these vacancies to fall by the wayside, he and his Republican colleagues would end the blue-slip tradition for appellate court judgeships while preserving it only for the district courts. The difference, he said, was that district court judges operate within a single state, whereas appeals court judges hear cases from all of the states within their circuit. The result was that the president's appellate court nominees from Democratic states such as Minnesota and Oregon were confirmed despite their senators' objections.

In contrast to the lagging pace of his executive branch nominations, Trump was relatively quick to send judicial nominees to the Senate. He was persuaded by McConnell that although officials in the executive branch serve only temporarily, judges serve for life. Judicial nominations have "consequences forty years out, depending on the age of the judge—but forty years out," Trump marveled.[40] By October 1, 2017, he had made eighteen appellate and thirty-nine district court nominations.[41] By mid-month, seven had been confirmed, compared with three at the same point in Obama's first year.[42] By July 2018, 23 appellate and 20 district court nominations had been confirmed, with dozens more awaiting votes in the Senate.[43]

Despite Trump's success with judicial nominations, the legacy of previous presidential appointments left much of the federal judiciary in opposition hands. Nine of the thirteen federal courts of appeals had Democratic-appointed majorities when Trump took office, and a solid majority of the 693 judges serving on the nation's ninety-three federal district courts were Democratic appointees. In addition, enough states and cities were in Democratic hands for their lawyers to bring suits against Trump administration policies. For example, adverse lower court judgments stymied the president's efforts to cut off federal aid to "sanctuary cities" that refused in many cases to help federal agents arrest undocumented immigrants. In June 2018, a federal district court judge in California ordered that children of illegal border crossers who were separated from their parents in response to a new administration policy of "zero tolerance" must be reunited with them.

Trump also faced lawsuits filed by nearly two hundred Democratic members of Congress and the Democratic attorneys general of Maryland and the District of Columbia urging courts to force his businesses to stop accepting payments from foreign governments. The legal basis of the suits was the Constitution's foreign emoluments clause, which forbids any

"Person holding any office of Profit or Trust" from accepting "any present, Emolument, Office or Title, of any kind whatever, from any King, Prince, or foreign State." The clauses were dusted off by the Democrats because Trump chose neither to sell his businesses when he became president nor put them into a blind trust. Instead he assigned his two adult sons to run them. Federal judges were asked to decide whether, for example, foreign governments renting rooms in the Trump International Hotel in Washington were conferring emoluments on the president. Liberal House Democrats who, responding to grassroots pressure from party activists, began seeking Trump's impeachment shortly after he was elected, listed his alleged violation of the emoluments clause as one of their grounds for seeking to remove him.

Trump and Congress

As the first newly elected Republican president since Eisenhower to enter office with GOP majorities in both the House and the Senate, Trump was expected to compile a significant record of legislative accomplishment. "Welcome to the dawn of a new unified Republican government," declared Speaker of the House Paul Ryan in January 2017, while predicting that the new Congress would quickly pass major health care, tax, and border legislation.[44] In reality, the only major bill enacted during Trump's first two years in office was a $1.5 trillion tax cut, the farthest thing from a heavy lift for a Republican president and Congress.

The Republicans' success in passing a flurry of Trump-supported deregulation bills in the early months of his presidency was the exception to this record of legislative futility that demonstrates the rule. They won vote after vote on measures passed under the Congressional Review Act (CRA) of 1996. That act granted Congress sixty legislative days (that is, days Congress is in session) to revoke new regulations issued by the executive branch, with no Senate filibusters allowed. Until 2017 it was used only once. But, seeing the CRA as a way to continue opposing Obama's policies even after he left office, Congress passed and Trump signed bills to repeal fourteen late Obama-administration regulations, including one that would have prevented Internet service providers from selling their customers' data. On May 11, 2017—less than four months into Trump's term—the deadline for using the CRA to undo Obama-era regulations was reached.

To some extent, Trump's problems with Congress lay on Capitol Hill. As was the case when Democratic presidents Clinton and Obama faced

Republican-controlled congresses, congressional Democrats embraced their role as the "party of no." In both the House and the Senate, not a single Democratic member was more conservative than the most liberal Republican member, and the ideological gap between the parties was not only clear but vast.[45] In addition, the Republican majority on Capitol Hill with which Trump was elected was, like him, experienced in opposition but not in governing. The party won control of the House in the 2010 midterm election by opposing Obama; it captured the Senate by opposing him again in 2014.

For the most part, however, Trump's problems with Congress were of his own creation. As the author of *The Art of the Deal*, Trump prided himself on his ability to sway others to do what he wanted and promised voters during the campaign that he would use his business acumen to make favorable deals for the American people. But as the political scientist George Tsebelis observed, the president cannot deal with "an alternative Congress" the way a real estate developer can choose a different lender or contractor if the one he is negotiating with refuses to meet his terms.[46] Each action sets the predicate for subsequent actions in the ongoing relationship between presidents and legislators. Inconsistent behavior undermines trust as surely as reliable behavior builds it.

From the beginning Republicans members united with the president in focusing relentlessly on their shared campaign promise to repeal and replace the Affordable Care Act (ACA). During his presidential campaign, Trump promised again and again "to end, terminate, repeal Obamacare and replace it with something really, really great that works."[47] But agreeing on what he and Congress were for was a challenge they were unprepared to meet.[48]

Although the Congressional Budget Office estimated that 23 million more people would be uninsured if an early version of the Obamacare "repeal-and-replace" bill was enacted, the House passed it in May 2017 on a 217–213 vote, with Democratic members unanimous in opposition. But when the House bill went to the Senate, Trump sent confusing signals, veering from praising it as a "great plan" that was "very, very, incredibly well-crafted" to condemning it as "mean" rather than "generous, kind, with heart."[49] Under Senator McConnell's guidance, the bill was modified so that 22 million more individuals would be uninsured. Trump's response during the week in mid-July that Senate Republicans were considering the McConnell bill was to take four positions in three days: first he supported it, then he proposed repealing the ACA without replacing it, then he suggested that Republicans "let Obamacare fail" by doing nothing, and finally he pressured Republican senators to replace it after all.[50] When no version of the bill attracted majority support, Trump tweeted: "Can you believe that Mitch McConnell, who has screamed Repeal & Replace for 7 years, couldn't get it done?"

After failing to repeal Obamacare, Trump and the Republican Congress were under enormous pressure not to fail on taxes. "The 115th Congress, if we go 0 for 2, gets a failing grade," said Rep. Mark Walker, the chair of the conservative Republican Study Committee; "I think a lot of us may not come back."[51] Fortunately for Trump, cutting taxes in ways that chiefly benefit corporations and well-to-do individuals has been at the heart of Republican orthodoxy since the Reagan era. Indeed, for a Republican Congress not to pass a tax bill during a Republican president's first year would be extraordinary. In the end, the tax bill enacted in December 2017 was substantially written by congressional Republicans but included not just reduced individual tax rates but also certain provisions that Trump explicitly emphasized: a substantial reduction in corporate taxes, preservation of the tax advantages of 401(k) retirement accounts, and a repeal of the individual mandate to purchase health insurance. He and Republicans on Capitol Hill took special pleasure in capping the deductibility of state and local taxes at $10,000, which hit the high-tax states especially hard.[52] As New York governor Andrew Cuomo noticed, the deduction of state and local taxes matters most for those living in Democratic bastions: California, New York, New Jersey, Massachusetts, and Illinois.[53]

Thus, for all his iconoclasm, Trump placed his own stamp on programmatic ambitions that had been central Republican objectives since the Reagan years. Indeed, lost amid the botched effort to repeal and replace Obamacare was a Trump executive order issued on his first day in office that instructed federal officials to ease regulations associated with the Affordable Care Act by directing agencies "to waive, defer, grant exemptions from or delay the implementation of any provision or requirement of the Act that would impose a fiscal burden."[54] The Trump administration issued waivers to state governments in an effort to transform a centerpiece of the Affordable Care Act: the extension of Medicaid benefits to those with annual incomes below 138 percent of the federal poverty level.

Almost one year after taking office, the Trump administration informed each state's Medicaid office of a new demonstration project, encouraged by Republican governors' demands. With federal permission, the new guidance allowed states to restrict Medicaid benefits for state residents who are unemployed or who do not meet standards of "community engagement." In redefining the eligible population of beneficiaries, the guidance letter represented the most significant change to the program since Congress voted to expand benefits under the Affordable Care Act. Within one day, the Centers for Medicare and Medicaid Services (CMS) approved Kentucky's plan to impose work requirements and remove 95,000 state residents from Medicaid rolls, saving an estimated $2 billion over the course of five years (a measure now under judicial challenge).

The Rhetorical Presidency

After compiling a modest legislative record during his first two years in office, Trump essentially stopped trying, paying lip service at best to promised efforts to rebuild the nation's infrastructure of highways, bridges, and airports and to clarify its immigration laws to extend legal status for the so-called Dreamers (immigrants who were brought into the country illegally as children) while building a wall along the Mexican border. As with his failed effort to repeal the ACA, when congressional Republicans struggled unsuccessfully in June 2018 to pass an immigration reform bill, Trump confused matters by sending a bewildering series of mixed messages. Within the span of a single week, he said that he supported the bill, would veto it, didn't want congressional Republicans "wasting their time" on the effort, and then supported it again. With votes from only a bare majority of Republicans and no Democrats, it failed in the House by 121–300. All the while, the Trump administration ratcheted up deportation enforcement and pursued harsh tactics such as the zero tolerance border policy, which until the administration abandoned it resulted in horrific scenes of asylum-seeking parents being separated from their children, as well as bureaucratic vetting that frustrated applications from American citizens and legal residents to sponsor the immigration of relatives to the United States. These attempts to reunify families were dismissed by the Trump administration as "chain migration."

In lieu of legislative leadership, Trump not only carried on administratively but also doubled down on public communications (an area in which he innovated and excelled) and foreign policy (an area that most presidents end up embracing because they face fewer constraints than in domestic affairs).

Trump's public communications during the 2016 presidential campaign were as effective as they were unorthodox. Most candidates for president, including Hillary Clinton and Trump's rivals for the Republican nomination, followed the standard campaign playbook: raise massive amounts of money for paid media—that is, television, radio, and web-based advertising—and thereby control their message to the voters. In unscripted events, especially televised debates, the textbook strategy was to be as script-like as possible, delivering well-rehearsed sound bites regardless of the questions that were asked.

In sharp contrast, Trump downplayed paid media, mostly because it was so easy for him to make the sort of news that attracted extensive coverage—so-called earned media. For audience-seeking news organizations, Trump was "the new, the unusual, the sensational."[55] His debate appearances during the campaign, like his speeches and interviews, were freewheeling and largely spontaneous. Knowing that Republican voters are especially distrustful of the news media, Trump unleashed attacks on "Fake News CNN, . . . NBC, CBS & NBC, . . . the failing @nytimes & @washingtonpost," and other mainstream outlets as "totally dishonest" and "scum." He made these assaults a standard feature of his mass rallies, an innovative and raw form of the plebiscitary politics that was a staple of the modern presidency since the Kennedy administration, thereby inoculating himself against news reports about his factually inaccurate statements, spotty business record, and other critical information.

In this effort to discredit the mainstream press, Trump built on a foundation laid by Republicans a half century earlier, when Richard Nixon, who preceded Trump as the voice of a "silent majority," and his supporters waged a systematic campaign to discredit the "liberal news media," especially the three broadcast networks (ABC, CBS, and NBC) that dominated the airwaves at the time and the leading eastern newspapers (especially the *New York Times* and *Washington Post*) that shaped national news coverage. In the 1980s, after the Federal Communications Commission abolished the fairness doctrine, talk radio emerged as an alternative source of news and opinion for conservative voters, followed in the 1990s by cable television's Fox News and in the 2000s by online outlets, including the Drudge Report and Breitbart. Vice President Pence hosted a talk radio program from 1995 to 1999 before running successfully for Congress in 2000. In addition to rhetorically discrediting the mainstream media, Trump steered his supporters to these sympathetic outlets.

Trump's rhetorical fusillade was amplified by his masterful and unprecedented use of a relatively new social medium: Twitter. Within the constraints of the 140-character tweet format (later expanded to 280 characters), he could send messages directly to millions of voters, who in turn forwarded them to millions more. As the journalist Michael Kruse pointed out, Trump's tweets assumed a distinctive, almost genre-like form: "a one-sentence declaration . . . followed usually by a one-word assertion of emotion: 'Weak!' 'Strong!' 'WIN!' 'Terrible!' 'Sad! 'BAD!'"[56] Trump used tweets to proclaim ("MAKE AMERICA GREAT AGAIN!") and, especially, to attack ("Hillary Clinton should have been prosecuted and should be in jail"). "Without the tweets I wouldn't be here," Trump said after taking office.[57]

As was the case during the campaign, Trump's many tweets as president tore down much more effectively than they built up. "Crooked Hillary" and "Fake News" took root in a way that "great health care" and "a great plan" did not.[58] "When somebody says something about me, I am able to go bing, bing, bing and I take care of it," Trump said.[59] No critic was immune from the president's retaliatory Twitter finger, but along with the media, African Americans seemed to rouse his special ire: Obama, NBA star Stephen Curry, *SportsCenter* host Jemele Hill, Congressional Black Caucus members John Lewis, Frederica Wilson, and Maxine Waters, and, especially, National Football League players who silently protested police brutality by refusing to stand for the pregame national anthem.

Not since Andrew Johnson's harsh attacks on his political enemies during his "Swing around the Circle"—the basis of two of the articles of impeachment brought against him—had critics complained that a president's communications style undermined the dignity and authority of his office. A former CIA analyst even described Trump's tweets as "a gold mine for every foreign intelligence agency" because they provided direct evidence of his "stress level and state of mind" as well as his "preoccupations, personality quirks, and habits."[60] Trump's response to the criticisms was to tweet "My use of social media is not Presidential—it's MODERN DAY PRESIDENTIAL."[61] By late summer 2018, Trump had more than 53 million followers on Twitter, exceeding the total number of daily subscribers (including online subscribers) to all the newspapers in the United States. "I wouldn't be here if it wasn't for social media," he reiterated.[62] No one disputed the point.

Trump's Twitter style as president mirrored his style as a candidate: he "repeated his claims incessantly and projected his own vices onto his opponents."[63] When news reports surfaced on October 29, 2017, that special counsel Robert Mueller was about to announce the first indictments in his investigation of possible collusion between Russia and the Trump campaign, Trump issued a flurry of tweets on the theme: "There is so much GUILT by Democrats/Clinton, and now the facts are pouring out. . . . Instead they look at phony Trump/Russia 'collusion,' which doesn't exist."[64] Throughout the year that followed, he returned again and again to the theme that although he and his campaign were innocent, Clinton, Mueller, and even the FBI were guilty.

To the extent that a strategy governed Trump's broader range of public communications, it was the same as for his use of Twitter: to solidify his base of mostly white Republican supporters, to change the subject when unfavorable developments dominated the news, and to discredit critical and even factual reports that displeased him. Trump's inaugural address painted a dystopian portrait of "American carnage" marked by "the crime and the gangs and the drugs," "the ravages of other countries," and closed factories "like tombstones"—similar to his campaign speeches but in sharp contrast to all fifty-seven previous inaugural addresses, each of which invoked widely shared American values and appealed for national unity.[65] Most of Trump's public speeches as president were stream-of-consciousness orations at campaign-style rallies. In contrast, not once did he deliver an address to the nation explaining and defending any of his major legislative priorities. Yet Trump succeeded in consolidating his political base, even at the cost of alienating a majority of voters. Throughout the first half of his term, about 90 percent of Republicans approved of Trump's performance as president and about 90 percent of Democrats and 60 percent of independents disapproved, leaving his overall approval rating only slightly below the 45 percent level at which he took office. In sum, Trump's first two years in office made the long-festering partisan polarization that had roiled the nation for nearly four decades more intractable and acrimonious.

Foreign Policy

In matters of foreign policy, Trump took office with no experience, little knowledge, and hardly any connections with people who did have experience or knowledge. During the campaign, he echoed the isolationist and nativist voices of past elections, such as Charles Lindbergh, who attacked Franklin Roosevelt's liberal internationalism in 1940, and Patrick Buchanan, who challenged George Bush for the Republican nomination in 1992. Using the same slogan these conservative insurgents shouted, Trump offered a series of bold statements whose theme was that although recent presidents had been inept and weak in their dealings with the rest of the world, he would put "America First," winning back jobs that had gone overseas, securing the nation's borders, avoiding feckless wars, and by drawing on his self-proclaimed dealmaking prowess, forging agreements with foreign leaders from a position of economic and military strength. Like most presidents, Trump enjoyed foreign policy, in which he got to play the statesman and commander in chief, more than domestic policy, with its tangled web of other constitutional actors and vocal grassroots demands. Comparing foreign to domestic policy, Trump said: "I want to focus on North Korea, I want to focus on Iran. . . . I don't want to focus on fixing somebody's back or their knee or something."[66]

From the start, Trump acted on some of his long-standing opinions, keeping campaign promises to withdraw the United States from the Trans-Pacific Partnership and initiate the three-year process required to leave the Paris climate accord, both of which Obama negotiated before leaving office. On other matters, however, he reined in his initial judgments. As a candidate, for example, Trump proclaimed that NATO is "obsolete" and that it was "time to get out of Afghanistan." Yet early in his first year as president, Trump declared that the United States would "strongly support NATO" ("It's no longer obsolete," he recanted) and authorized the secretary of defense to intensify the war in Afghanistan.[67]

The main explanation for Trump's early restraint in reorienting American foreign policy lay in the team of appointees with which he began his administration. Most of his initial choices were generals and business leaders whom he admired for their success in war and commerce, domains that (in contrast to civilian government service) he regarded highly. Secretary of State Tillerson came from the world of business. Secretary of Defense Mattis and National Security Advisor Michael Flynn were high-ranking generals in the U.S. Marine Corps and Army, respectively. All but Flynn were internationalists who wanted to steer Trump away from uni-lateralism and isolation. When Flynn was replaced just weeks into the administration by H. R. McMaster, another army general, the team became uniformly internationalist.

Over time, however, Trump's growing disregard for Tillerson's and McMaster's internationalism weakened their influence.[68] Aggravating tensions between them and the president were their efforts to focus his attention on the complexities attending American involvement in the world. McMaster found it especially difficult to hold Trump's interest when, based on the rigorous process he instituted to integrate the perspectives of relevant departments and agencies, he tried to brief the president on complicated foreign policy issues. "I call the president the two-minute man," said one presidential confidant; "The president has patience for a half-page."[69]

Frustrated by his dependence on them, Trump fired Tillerson and McMaster in favor of advisers who would not challenge him either intellectually or ideologically, replacing Tillerson with Mike Pompeo and McMaster with John Bolton. The change was felt immediately. For example, the initial foreign policy team twice persuaded the reluctant president to recertify an international agreement with Iran that the Obama administration orchestrated in 2015. The accord, which also included Russia, China, Germany, the United Kingdom, and France, lifted crippling economic sanctions in return for Iran accepting restrictions on and international monitoring of its nuclear program. Trump's new team indulged his desire to sever the agreement despite the complete absence of support for his position from America's allies.

Trump's policy toward North Korea exemplified his growing certainty about how the United States should conduct foreign policy. To be sure, he inherited a long record of frustration and failure. Trump's three predecessors—Clinton, Bush, and Obama—all tried to persuade the North Korean government to abandon its nuclear program, using a combination of economic incentives, economic sanctions, and diplomatic pressures. All three were unsuccessful. By the time Trump took office, North Korea had as many as sixty nuclear weapons, and in 2017 it conducted a series of provocative missile tests.

Trump's response was to engage in an extended and escalating exchange of taunts with North Korea's young leader, Kim Jong-un. Issuing over-the-top insults was nothing new for Kim's despised and impoverished government, but no American president had ever stooped to reply in kind.[70] Yet on August 8, 2017, Trump told reporters that "any more threats to the United States" by North Korea "will be met with fire and fury like the world has never seen."[71] In September, after North Korea successfully tested its largest-ever bomb, Trump used tweets to brand Kim "Rocket Man" and then "Little Rocket Man."[72] Kim replied, "I will surely and definitely tame the mentally deranged U.S. dotard with fire."

Less than a year later, Trump changed course entirely. In June 2018, he impulsively decided to meet with Kim in Singapore, granting the North Korean dictator the one-on-one meeting with the president of the United States that his nation's leaders had sought for decades. Exacting no concessions from Kim other than a vague promise to "denuclearize," Trump agreed to cancel joint military exercises with South Korea, his nation's staunch ally. Lightly briefed in advance of the meeting, as was his preference, Trump blithely assumed, despite strong evidence to the contrary, that North Korea had agreed to destroy its nuclear stockpile and cease its missile program.

Trump's controversial personal diplomacy continued a month later when he held a high-profile summit with Russian president Vladimir Putin in Helsinki, Finland. At the post-summit press conference, Trump refused to blame Russia for meddling in the 2016 election. Instead, he questioned the findings of the American intelligence community. Republicans, including those who were not part of the "Never Trump" wing of the party, were among the harshest critics of this claim. Even former speaker of the House Newt Gingrich, previously a staunch defender, decried "the most serious mistake of his presidency." The reaction forced the president into a series of awkward qualifications that failed to clarify what he actually meant to say. Coming soon after his strong criticisms of close allies at a NATO summit, many pundits and public officials expressed anguish that the president's equivocations and his personal affinity for Putin threatened to undermine defense alliances, roll back economic sanctions on Russia, or recognize its annexation of Crimea.

Conclusion

Presidential effectiveness usually grows during a president's first two years. Presidents become more surefooted in the job by doing it. They get better because they cram during the transition period, surround themselves (sometimes sooner but always later) with advisers experienced in government, and learn from their mistakes. Trump was a glaring exception to all of these general rules of the office.

"We need a truly great leader," Trump said during the campaign. "We need a leader that wrote *The Art of the Deal*."[73] Trump's confidence about his dealmaking prowess was overweening. "I deal with Steve Wynn. I deal with Carl Icahn," he boasted, referring to two well-known businessmen; "I deal with killers that blow these [politicians] away. It's not even the same category. This [politics] is a category that's like nineteen levels lower."[74]

Trump was surely right to think that striking deals—also known as forging compromises, reaching agreements, and finding common ground—is an important part of being president. The Constitution assigns the presidency few powers that are not shared with Congress or the states and reviewable by the courts.

"Deals are my art form," Trump once bragged. Yet overconfidence blinded him to the reality that unlike the desire to maximize profits that animates the private economy, the motivations of legislators, judges, lobbyists, journalists, state and local officials, and foreign heads of government are varied, complex, and subtle. In politics, unlike the cutthroat world of real estate development in which dealmaking is extremely fluid and abandoning a bargain is tolerable, a reputation for standing by one's word when reaching agreements is the coin of the realm and thereby essential to being trusted in the future.[75] Similarly, in the international arena, forsaking an agreement made by a previous president is likely to dissuade foreign governments from thinking that any deal they reach with the United States can be relied on to last.

Nor, never having dealt in the business world with shareholders or an independent board of directors, did Trump seem to fully realize that as president, other constitutional actors had to be reckoned with. The president cannot, for example, plausibly threaten to walk away when negotiations break down with Congress and find another legislature to deal with. He cannot fire and replace the several million civil servants on whom he must rely to implement his decisions. During Trump's first two years—having blown any chance for even a short honeymoon and failed to take advantage of a unified party government, relative global peace, and rising prosperity—only one important piece of legislation that he supported was enacted: a tax-cut bill, the near-inevitable consequence of electing a Republican president and Congress.

Partway through Trump's tenure in office, serious questions remained that only the passage of time can answer. Trump did not create the executive-centered partisanship that has sharply divided the parties and roiled the national resolve. However, as a team of accomplished political scientists wrote in August 2017, he has tapped into partisan antagonisms and aggressively deployed the powers of the modern presidency with such alacrity as to call into "sharp question the integrity and resilience of the American regime and the future of liberal democracy in the United States." "Is American democracy under threat?" they asked; "The answer is yes. . . . Once unthinkable scenarios now seem plausible: an unconstitutional third term in office, for example, or emergency government in the wake of a terrorist attack."[76]

Fortunately for the country, flawed as Trump is by aberrant personality defects—overweening self-centeredness, an inadequate attention span, and an inability to deal with criticism except in the angriest terms—not everything hinges on the president, even if, at age seventy-eight, assuming he could win a second term, he did somehow decide he wanted a third. The Constitution created a system of "separated institutions sharing powers" both among the three branches of the federal government and between the federal government and the states. It safeguarded the right of the people to speak, publish, petition, and assemble. The fierce resistance to the Trump presidency should give the friends of republican government hope that "vicious factionalism" has not displaced loyalty to the Constitution. From the opposition that emerged—in Congress; the courts; the bureaucracy; the states and localities; the media; and the dissent of Democrats, independents, Never Trump Republicans, and grass-roots social movements—Trump should have learned the hard lesson that most of the country has rejoiced in for more than two centuries: that the American constitutional system is well designed "to counteract ambition" when ambition aspires to roam directionless and unrestrained.[77]

Notes

1. Ryan Grim and Danny Shea, "A Note about Our Coverage of Donald Trump's 'Campaign,'" *Huffington Post*, July 17, 2015, http://www.huffingtonpost.com/entry/a-note-about-our-coverage-of-donald-trumps-campaign_us_55a8fc9ce4b0896514d0fd66.

2. Alan I. Abramowitz, "Forecasting the 2016 Presidential Election: Will Time for Change Mean Time for Trump?" *Sabato's Crystal Ball*, August 11, 2016, http://www.centerforpolitics.org/crystalball/articles/forecasting-the-2016-presidential-election-will-time-for-change-mean-time-for-trump/. For a long list of errant predictions about Trump's prospects, see Joel B. Pollak and Larry Schweikart, *How Trump Won: The Inside Story of a Revolution* (Washington, D.C.: Regnery, 2017), 2–3.

3. Trevor Hughes, "Trump Calls to 'Drain the Swamp' of Washington," *USA Today*, October 18, 2016.

4. Joshua Green, *Devil's Bargain: Steve Bannon, Donald Trump, and the Storming of the Presidency* (New York: Penguin, 2017), 117.

5. Maureen Dowd, "Liberties; Trump Shrugged," *New York Times*, November 28, 1999.

6. Ashley Parker, "'You Have to Brand People,' Donald Trump Says," *New York Times*, March 13, 2016.

7. John Sides, Michael Tesler, and Lynn Vavreck, *Identity Crisis: The 2016 Presidential Campaign and the Battle for the Meaning of America* (Princeton, NJ: Princeton University Press, 2018).

8. "Here's Donald Trump's Presidential Announcement Speech," *Time*, June 16, 2015, http://time.com/3923128/donald-trump-announcement-speech/

9. Robert Griffin, John Halpin, and Ruy Teixeira, "Democrats Need to Be the Party of and for Working People—Of All Races," *American Prospect* (Summer 2017), http://prospect.org/article/democrats-need-be-party-and-working-people%E2%80%94-all-races.

10. Frank Newport, "Middle-Class Identification in U.S. at Pre-Recession Levels," *Gallup News*, June 7–11, 2017, http://www.gallup.com/poll/212660/middle-class-identification-pre-recession-levels.aspx.

11. "Presidential Approval Ratings—Gallup Historical Statistics and Trends," *Gallup News*, http://news.gallup.com/poll/116677/presidential-approval-ratings-gallup-historical-statistics-trends.aspx.

12. Ibid.; and Frank Newport, "Trump Approval Nudges Down to New Monthly Low," *Gallup News*, June 5–11, 2017, http://www.gallup.com/poll/212120/trump-approval-edges-down-new-weekly-low.aspx.

13. George C. Edwards III, "No Deal: Donald Trump's Leadership of Congress," *Forum*, 15 (October 2017): 451.

14. Adam Liptak, "Trump vs. the Constitution," *New York Times*, November 29, 2016.

15. Aaron Blake, "Trump Botches Reference to 'President' of Virgin Islands a Day after Rick Perry Called Puerto Rico a 'Country,'" *Washington Post*, October 13, 2017.

16. Jonathan Lemire, "Trump Makes Puzzling Claim about Andrew Jackson, Civil War," *Chicago Tribune*, May 1, 2017.

17. John Wagner, "Trump: Most People Don't Know President Lincoln Was a Republican," *Washington Post*, March 22, 2017.

18. Noah Bierman, "Trump Says Frederick Douglass Did 'An Amazing Job,'" *Los Angeles Times*, February 1, 2017.

19. Peter Baker, "'People Love You': For Trump, a Welcome Respite from the Capital," *New York Times*, July 25, 2017.

20. Jane Mayer, "The Danger of President Pence," *New Yorker*, October 23, 2017.

21. John P. Burke, "The Institutional Presidency," in *The Presidency and the Political System*, ed. Michael Nelson, 11th ed. (Washington, D.C.: forthcoming, CQ Press, 2019).

22. Jim Acosta, "Trump Picks Priebus as White House Chief of Staff, Bannon as Top Advisor," *CNN*, November 14, 2016.

23. Kathryn Dunn Tempas, "With the Revelation of Marc Short's Impending Departure, President Trump Has Lost the Vast Majority of Tier One Staff Members," *FixGov*, Brookings, June 27, 2018, https://www.brookings.edu/blog/fixgov/2018/06/27/trump-has-lost-the-vast-majority-of-tier-one-staff-members/.

24. Philip Rucker and Ashley Parker, "During a Summer of Crisis, Trump Chafes against Criticism and New Controls," *Washington Post*, August 31, 2017.

25. Eliana Johnson and Andrew Restuccia, "Mike Pence's Power Play," Politico, December 4, 2016: https://www.politico.com/story/2016/12/mike-pence-power-play-trump-transition-232151; and Michael Grunwald, "How Trump Learned to Love the Swamp," *Politico*, November 9, 2017, https://www.politico.com/magazine/story/2017/11/09/donald-trump-drain-the-swamp-reversal-215808.

26. Michael S. Schmidt and Maggie Haberman, "Trump Humiliated Jeff Sessions after Mueller Appointment," *New York Times*, September 14, 2017.

27. Jesse Byrnes, "Trump on Lack of Nominees: 'I Am the Only One That Matters,'" *The Hill*, November 2, 2017, http://thehill.com/blogs/blog-briefing-room/news/358573-trump-on-lack-of-nominees-i-am-the-only-one-that-matters.

28. Christopher Mele, "Trump on Being President: 'I Thought It Would Be Easier,'" *New York Times*, April 28, 2017.

29. David Klaidman and Andrew Romano, "President Obama's Executive Power Grab," *The Daily Beast*, October 10, 2012, www.thedailybeast.com/newsweek/2012/10/21/president-obama-s-executive-power-grab.html.

30. Andrew Rudalevige, "The Presidency and Unilateral Power: A Taxonomy," in *The Presidency and the Political System*, ed. Michael Nelson, 11th ed. (Washington, D.C.: CQ Press, forthcoming 2019); and Andrew Rudalevige, "Candidate Trump Attacked Obama's Executive Orders. President Trump Loves Executive Orders," *Washington Post*, October 17, 2017.

31. Rudalevige, "The Presidency and Unilateral Power."

32. Sidney M. Milkis and Nicholas Jacobs, "'I Alone Can Fix It': Donald Trump, the Administrative Presidency, and the Hazards of Executive-Centered Partisanship," *Forum*, 15 (October 2017): 600.

33. Nadja Popovich and Livia Albeck-Ripka, "52 Environmental Rules on the Way out under Trump," *New York Times*, October 6, 2017.

34. David H. Becker, "Changing Directions in Administrative Agency Rulemaking: 'Reasoned Analysis,' the Roadless Rule Repeal, and the 2006 National Park Service Management Policies," *Environs*, 30 (December 2006), 66–99.

35. Lisa Friedman, "Court Blocks E.P.A. Effort to Suspend Obama-Era Methane Rule," *New York Times*, July 3, 2017. Mired in scandal and facing fierce opposition by environmental advocates, Pruitt was forced to resign in June of 2018, leaving his hasty efforts to change the trajectory of Obama environmental and climate change initiatives to the more careful conservative management of his successor, former coal lobbyist Andrew Wheeler.

36. Phillip Rucker and Matt Zapotosky, "Trump Breaches Boundaries by Saying DOJ Should Be 'Going after' Democrats," *Washington Post*, November 3, 2017.

37. Devlin Barrett, "White House Expands Travel Ban, Restricting Visitors from Eight Countries," *Washington Post*, September 24, 2017; and Michael D. Shear, Ron Nixon, and

Adam Liptak, "Supreme Court Cancels Hearing on Previous Trump Travel Ban," *New York Times*, September 25, 2017.

38. Nominated by James Garfield, the controversial Supreme Court nominee Stanley Matthews, who had played a critical part in the notorious Compromise of 1877, was confirmed by a 24–23 vote.

39. In the two years before Obama left office, the Senate confirmed only twenty-two judicial nominations, the fewest by any Congress since the Truman presidency.

40. Carl Hulse, "Trump and McConnell See a Way to Make Conservatives Happy," *New York Times*, October 17, 2017.

41. Editorial Board, "Trump's Excellent Judges," *Wall Street Journal*, October 1, 2017.

42. Seung Min Kim, "Trump's Judge Picks: 'Not Qualified,' Prolific Bloggers," *Politico*, October 17, 2017, http://www.politico.com/story/2017/10/17/trump-judges-nominees-court-picks-243834?jumpEdition=.

43. John Gramlich, "With another Supreme Court Pick, Trump Is Leaving His Mark on Higher Federal Courts," *FactTank*, Pew Research Center, July 6, 2018, http://www.pewresearch.org/fact-tank/2018/07/16/with-another-supreme-court-pick-trump-is-leaving-his-mark-on-higher-federal-courts/.

44. Susan Davis, "'Dawn of a New Unified Republican Government' Coming in 2017," *NPR*, December 22, 2016, http://www.npr.org/2016/12/22/505618360/-dawn-of-a-new-unified-republican-government-coming-in-2017; and Rachel Bade, "Ryan: GOP Will Replace Obamacare, Cut Taxes, and Fund Wall by August," *Politico*, January 25, 2017, http://www.politico.com/story/2017/01/republican-agenda-retreat-obamacare-wall-tax-cuts-234176.

45. As measured by DW-Nominate scores (George C. Edwards, "No Deal: Donald Trump's Leadership of Congress," *Forum*, 15 [October 2017]: 456–457).

46. George Tsebelis, "This Is Why Trump's 'Art of the Deal' Doesn't Work in Politics," *Washington Post*, March 29, 2017.

47. Ryan Koronowski, "68 Times Trump Promised to Repeal Obamacare," *ThinkProgress*, March 24, 2017, https://thinkprogress.org/trump-promised-to-repeal-obamacare-many-times-ab9500dad31e.

48. Paul Kane, "One Reason the GOP Health Bill Is a Mess: No One Thought Trump Would Win," *Washington Post*, July 6, 2017.

49. Thomas Kaplan, Jennifer Steinhauer, and Robert Pear, "Trump, in Zigzag, Calls House Republicans' Bill 'Mean,'" *New York Times*, June 13, 2017.

50. Julie Hirschfeld Davis, Thomas Kaplan, and Maggie Haberman, "Trump Demands That Senators Find a Way to Replace Obamacare," *New York Times*, July 19, 2017.

51. Paul Kane, "Paul Ryan Begins a Make-or-Break Push for Tax Legislation—and His Future," *Washington Post*, October 28, 2017.

52. "Minimizing the Economic Burden of the Patient Protection and Affordable Care Act Pending Repeal," Executive Order 13765. 20 Jan. 2017. Federal Registrar, 82, no. 14, 8351–8352.

53. Michael Greve, "Governor Cuomo Gets It, Sort Of: So Does The Donald." *Law and Liberty*, January 11, 2017, http://www.libertylawsite.org/2018/01/11/governor-cuomo-gets-it-sort-of-so-does-the-donald/.

54. "Minimizing the Economic Burden of the Patient Protection and Affordable Care Act Pending Repeal," Executive Order 13765. 20 Jan. 2017. Federal Registrar, 82, no. 14, 8351–8352.

55. Thomas E. Patterson, "Pre-Primary News Coverage of the 2016 Presidential Race: Trump's Rise, Sanders's Emergence, Clinton's Struggles," Shorenstein Center on Media, Politics and Public Policy, Harvard University, June 13, 2016.

56. Michael Kruse, "I Found Trump's Diary—Hiding in Plain Sight," *Politico Magazine,* June 25, 2017, http://www.politico.com/magazine/story/2017/06/25/i-found-trumps-diaryhiding-in-plain-sight-215303

57. Ibid.

58. Emily Badger and Kevin Quealy, "Trump Seems Much Better at Branding Opponents Than Marketing Policies," *New York Times*, July 18, 2017.

59. John Wagner, "'Bing, Bing, Bing': Trump Reveals His Thinking behind Firing off All Those Tweets," *Washington Post*, October 20, 2017.

60. Mark Moore, "Trump Goes after 'Failing' *New York Times* Again," *New York Post*, June 28, 2017; Liz Stark, "Ben Sasse Blasts Trump's Twitter Behavior: 'This Isn't Normal,'" *CNNPolitics*, June 29, 2017, http://www.cnn.com/2017/06/29/politics/sasse-trump-twitter/index.html; and Nada Bakos, "This Is What Foreign Spies See When They Read President Trump's Tweets," *Washington Post*, June 23, 2017.

61. Rebecca Morin, "Trump: My Social Media Use Is 'Modern Day Presidential,'" *Politico*, July 1, 2017, http://www.politico.com/story/2017/07/01/trump-tweets-modern-day-presidential-240170.

62. Nolan D. McCaskill, "Trump Credits Social Media for His Election," *Politico*, October 20, 2017, http://www.politico.com/story/2017/10/20/trump-social-media-election-244009; and Christiano Lima, "Trump, Obama among Big Losers in Twitter Follower Purge," *Politico*, July 12, 2018, https://www.politico.com/story/2018/07/12/trump-obama-twitter-user-purge-716874. Interestingly, former president Obama had a larger, if less trivial, following of more than 100 million.

63. Jeffrey K. Tulis, "The Two Constitutional Presidencies," in *The Presidency and the Political System*, 11th ed., ed. Michael Nelson (Washington, D.C.: CQ Press, 2017).

64. Julie Hirschfeld Davis, "Trump Tries to Shift Focus as First Charges Loom in Russia Case," *New York Times*, October 29, 2017. As it turned out, the twelve-count indictment of former Trump campaign chairman Paul Manafort and business partner Rick Gates announced on October 30 did not involve Trump's presidential campaign, but a guilty plea by George Papadopoulos, revealed the same day, did.

65. Michael Nelson, "Speeches, Speechwriters, and the American Presidency," in *The President's Words: Speeches and Speechwriting in the Modern White House*, ed. Nelson and Russell L. Riley (Lawrence: University Press of Kansas, 2010), 1–26.

66. Julia Manchester, "Trump: I Want to Focus on North Korea, Not 'Fixing Somebody's Back,'" *The Hill*, October 7, 2017, http://thehill.com/homenews/administration/354419-trump-on-health-care-block-grants-i-would-rather-focus-on-iran-north.

67. Mark Landler, "From 'America First' to a More Conventional View of U.S. Diplomacy," *New York Times*, March 1, 2017; and Thomas Gibbons-Neff, Eric Schmitt, and Adam Goldman, "A Newly Assertive C.I.A. Expands Its Taliban Hunt in Afghanistan," *New York Times*, October 22, 2017.

68. Jason Zengerle, "Rex Tillerson and the Unraveling of the State Department," *New York Times Magazine*, October 17, 2017.

69. Greg Jaffe and Philip Rucker, "National Security Adviser Attempts to Reconcile Trump's Competing Impulses on Afghanistan," *Washington Post*, August 4, 2017.

70. See, for example, William J. Perry, "North Korea Called Me a 'War Maniac.' I Ignored Them, and Trump Should Too," *Politico*, October 3, 2017, http://www.politico.com/magazine/story/2017/10/03/north-korea-war-maniac-donald-trump-215672.

71. Peter Baker and Choe Sang-Hun, "Trump Threatens 'Fire and Fury' against North Korea if It Endangers U.S.," *New York Times*, August 8, 2017.

72. Brent D. Griffiths, "Trump Tweets about North Korea's 'Rocket Man,' Dings Hillary Clinton Again," *Politico*, September 17, 2017, http://www.politico.com/story/2017/09/17/trump-tweets-about-north-koreas-rocket-man-242812; and Edith M. Lederer, "North Korea Says Trump's Latest Tweet Is a 'Declaration of War,'" *Time*, September 25, 2017.

73. Jane Mayer, "Donald Trump's Ghostwriter Tells All," *New Yorker*, July 25, 2017.

74. Joshua Green, *Devil's Bargain: Steve Bannon, Donald Trump, and the Storming of the Presidency* (New York: Penguin, 2017), 239.

75. Trump's approach to dealmaking in business did not always work. When he tried to renegotiate the terms for Frank Sinatra's concerts at his new Trump Taj Mahal Hotel and Casino in Atlantic City, Sinatra instructed his manager, "Tell him to go f— himself or give me his number and I'll do it" (Eliot Weisman and Jennifer Valoppi, *The Way We Were: My Life with Frank Sinatra* [New York: Hachette, 2017], 175).

76. Robert C. Lieberman et al., "Trumpism and American Democracy: History, Comparison, and the Predicament of Liberal Democracy in the United States," First Draft, August 29, 2017.

77. "The Federalist Papers: No. 51," Avalon Project, http://avalon.law.yale.edu/18th_century/fed51.asp.

CHAPTER 17

The Vice Presidency

Almost from the moment of its creation, the vice presidency became an easy and frequent target of political humor. Benjamin Franklin quipped that the vice president should be addressed as "Your Superfluous Excellency." Mr. Dooley, the invented character of writer Finley Peter Dunne, described the office as "not a crime exactly. Ye can't be sint to jail f'r it, but it's kind iv a disgrace. It's like writin' anonymous letters." George and Ira Gershwin's 1931 musical, *Of Thee I Sing*, featured a fictitious vice president whose name (which no one in the play could remember) was Alexander Throttlebottom. Vice President Throttlebottom spent most of his time feeding pigeons in a park and unsuccessfully trying to find two people willing to serve as references so he could get a library card.

Even some vice presidents poked fun at the office. Thomas R. Marshall, who was Woodrow Wilson's vice president for two terms, said that the vice president is like "a man in a cataleptic fit; he cannot speak; he cannot move; he suffers no pain; he is perfectly conscious of all that goes on, but has no part in it." Marshall also told the story of two brothers: "One ran away to sea; the other was elected vice president. And nothing was heard of either of them again." John Nance Garner was a fairly active vice president during the first two terms of Franklin D. Roosevelt's administration, but his pithy assessment of the office (at least the G-rated version of what he said) is probably the most frequently quoted of all: "The vice presidency isn't worth a pitcher of warm spit."[1]

Many a truth about the vice presidency has been spoken in jest. In terms of constitutional authority, the office was born weak and has not grown much stronger. But lost in all the laughter is an appreciation of the importance—ongoing for more than a century and accelerating in recent decades—of the position that the vice president occupies in the American political system.

The vice presidency is most significant when, cocoon-like, it empties itself to provide a successor to the presidency. "I am vice president," said John Adams, the first person to hold the office. "In this I am nothing, but I may be everything."[2] Nine vice presidents, nearly one-fifth of those who have served in the office, became president when the incumbent chief executive died or resigned: John Tyler, Millard Fillmore, Andrew Johnson, Chester A. Arthur, Theodore Roosevelt, Calvin Coolidge, Harry S. Truman, Lyndon B. Johnson, and Gerald R. Ford. Collectively, these successor presidents led the nation for forty-two years.

Besides its long-standing role as presidential successor, the vice presidency has become an important electoral springboard to the presidency. Seven of the twelve most recent vice presidents prior to Donald Trump's vice president, Mike Pence, were later nominated for president in their own right: Richard Nixon, Lyndon Johnson, Hubert H. Humphrey, Gerald Ford, Walter F. Mondale, George Bush, and Al Gore. In all four of the elections from 1960 to 2000 in which the president did not or could not run for reelection, the incumbent party nominated the vice president as its presidential candidate. Richard B. Cheney, who became George W. Bush's vice president in 2001, was the rare modern vice president to take office with no intention of seeking the presidency. In addition to Cheney's history of heart problems, his preference for operating outside the limelight accounted for his lack of political ambition.

Finally, recent changes in the vice presidency have given substance to the office, especially because presidents have come to regard their vice presidents as valuable, wide-ranging senior advisers. Modern vice presidents have a lot more to do than, as Vice President Marshall joked, "to ring the White House bell every morning and ask what is the state of health of the president."[3]

The vice presidency, then, both as successor and springboard to the presidency and as an institution in its own right, has become an important office. But its history is a problematic one, and not all of the problems have been solved. The history of the vice presidency may be organized usefully into four main periods: the founding period, the nineteenth century, the first half of the twentieth century, and the modern era.

The Founding Period

The vice presidency was invented late in the Constitutional Convention, not because the delegates saw any need for such an office but rather as a means to perfect the arrangements they made for presidential election and succession and, to some degree, for leadership of the Senate (see Chapter 2).

The original Constitution provided that the vice presidency would be awarded to the person who received the second-highest number of electoral votes for president. If two or more candidates finished in a second-place tie in the presidential election, the Senate would choose among them.

The only ongoing responsibility the Framers of the Constitution assigned to the vice president was to preside over the Senate, casting tie-breaking votes. The vice president's more important duty was to stand by as successor to the president in the event of the president's death, impeachment, resignation, or "inability to discharge the Powers and Duties" of the office. But the Constitution was vague about whether the vice president was to assume the office of president or only its powers and duties under these circumstances as well as about whether the succession was to last until the end of the departed president's four-year term or only until a special election could be held to choose a new president. The Constitution also left the word *inability* undefined and provided no procedure for the vice president to take power in the event the president became disabled. Finally, by giving the vice president both legislative and executive responsibilities, the Constitution deprived the office of solid moorings in either Congress or the presidency.

Although the vice presidency solved several constitutional design problems related to the presidency and the Senate, it was plagued from birth by problems of its own. First, the office's hybrid status was bound to arouse suspicion in legislative councils because it is partly executive and in executive councils because it is partly legislative. Second, the vice president's sole responsibility, to preside over the Senate, is not very important. Senators lead the Senate, not the vice president. Third, the poorly defined successor role has been an inevitable source of confusion and, at times, of tension between the president and the vice president. The fabled one "heartbeat away" that separates the vice president from the presidency is, after all, the president's. Finally, more than any other institution of the new government, the vice presidency required the realization of the Framers' hope that political parties would not develop. The office would seem less a brilliant improvisation of the Constitutional Convention than a rash one if it were occupied as a matter of course by the president's leading partisan foe.

Midway through John Adams's tenure as vice president, he lamented to his wife, Abigail, that "my country has in its wisdom contrived for me the most insignificant office that ever the invention of man contrived or his imagination conceived."[4] Little did Adams realize that during the period he served, the vice presidency was at an early peak of influence.

Because the Senate was small and still relatively unorganized, Adams was able to cast twenty-nine tie-breaking votes (still the record), guide the upper house's agenda, and intervene in debate. Adams also was respected and sometimes consulted on diplomatic and other matters by President George Washington. Moreover, having won the vice presidency by receiving the second-largest number of electoral votes for president in 1789 and 1792, it is not surprising that Adams was elected president in 1796 after Washington left office.

Adams's election as president was different from Washington's, however. The Framers' hopes notwithstanding, when two political parties, the Federalists and the Democratic-Republicans, emerged during the Washington administration, the result in 1796 was the election of Adams, the Federalist, as president, and Thomas Jefferson, the Democratic-Republicans' presidential nominee, as vice president. Adams tried to lure Jefferson into an active role in the administration by urging him to undertake a diplomatic mission to France. But Jefferson, eager to build his own party and win the presidency from Adams, would have no part of it. He justified his refusal by claiming that constitutionally the vice president is "a member of the legislative body."

By Jefferson's own testimony, that was the end of his dealings with President Adams, except on formal occasions. Adams could not plausibly complain about this. As vice president he once claimed grandiosely that the Constitution made him "Head of the Legislative," comparable to the president as "head of the Executive."[5] Jefferson did make a mark as Senate president by writing a book, *Manual of Parliamentary Practice*. Although Congress never formally adopted it, the manual became both chambers' working procedural guide for many decades. But most of Jefferson's vice presidential activities involved behind-the-scenes opposition to Adams and the Federalists. For example, he drafted a resolution for the Kentucky legislature challenging the federal government's authority to enforce the Alien and Sedition Acts. In all, Jefferson consoled himself, "The second office of this government is honorable and easy. The first is but a splendid misery."[6]

Dissatisfied with the divided partisan result of the 1796 election, in 1800 each party nominated a complete ticket and instructed its electors to cast their two votes for its presidential and vice-presidential candidates. The intention was that both candidates would be elected; the result was that neither was. After the electors filled out their ballots as instructed, Jefferson and his vice-presidential running mate, Aaron Burr of New York, ended up with an equal number of votes—for president. The House of Representatives was required to choose between them. It eventually elected

Jefferson but not before Federalist mischief-makers kept the outcome uncertain through thirty-six ballots.

One result of the election of 1800 was the Burr vice presidency. Burr's tenure was marked by bad relations between him and Jefferson (they were personally incompatible and represented different factions of the party) and by misdeeds, including a duel in which Burr shot and killed former Treasury secretary Alexander Hamilton and a treason case in which Burr was tried (and acquitted) for scheming to persuade the western states to secede and form an alliance with Spain. Another result of the election was the widespread realization that something had to be done about the Electoral College so that it could accommodate the emergence of party competition. Vice-presidential selection was the problem. An obvious solution was to require electors to vote separately for president and vice president.

In opposing the proposal for a separate ballot, some members of Congress argued that it would create a worse problem than it solved. Because "the vice president will not stand on such high ground in the method proposed as he does in the present mode of a double ballot [for president]," predicted Rep. Samuel Taggart of Massachusetts, the nation could expect that "great care will not be taken in the selection of a character to fill that office." Sen. William Plumer of New Hampshire warned that such care as was taken would be "to procure votes for the president."[7] Taggart and Plumer, who were leaders of the rapidly declining Federalist Party, also shared the widespread Federalist belief that finishing second in presidential elections offered their party its only hope of securing even a toehold in the government.[8] In truth, as the nomination of Burr indicated, the parties had already begun to degrade the vice presidency into a device for balancing the ticket geographically in the election.

In 1804 a constitutional amendment was introduced in Congress to abolish the vice presidency rather than continue it in a form diminished from its original status as the position awarded to the second-most-qualified person to be president. But the amendment failed by a vote of 12–19 in the Senate and 27–85 in the House. Instead, a different constitutional amendment was enacted. The Twelfth Amendment provides that electors, rather than voting for two persons as president, "shall name in their ballots the person voted for as President, and in distinct ballots the person voted for as Vice President." It also stipulates that if no one receives a majority of electoral votes for vice president, then "from the two highest numbers on the list, the Senate shall choose the Vice President . . . and a majority of the whole number shall be necessary to a choice." The Twelfth Amendment's final provision extends the Constitution's original age, citizenship, and residency qualifications for president to the vice president, correcting an oversight in the original Constitution.

The Vice Presidency in the Nineteenth Century

The development of political parties and the enactment of the Twelfth Amendment sent the constitutionally weak vice presidency into a tailspin that lasted until the end of the nineteenth century. Party leaders, not presidential candidates (who usually were not even present at national nominating conventions and who, if present, were expected to be seen and not heard), chose the nominees for vice president, which did not foster trust or respect between the president and the vice president once in office. Aggravating the tension were the main criteria that party leaders applied to vice-presidential selection. One criterion was that the nominee placate the region or faction of the party that was most dissatisfied with the presidential nomination, which led to numerous New York–Virginia, North–South, Stalwart–Progressive, and hard money–soft money pairings. Another criterion was that the nominee be able to carry a swing state in the general election where the presidential candidate was not sufficiently popular. This tactic failed more than it succeeded: only 45 percent of presidential candidates in the nineteenth century carried their vice-presidential running mate's home state.[9]

In addition to fostering tension within the government, ticket balancing placed such a stigma on the vice presidency that many political leaders were unwilling to accept a nomination. Daniel Webster, declining the vice-presidential place on the Whig Party ticket in 1848, said, "I do not propose to be buried until I am dead."[10] Those who were nominated and elected found that fresh political problems four years after their nomination invariably led party leaders to balance the ticket differently. No first-term vice president in the nineteenth century was nominated for a second term by a party convention. Nor, after Vice President Martin Van Buren in 1836, was any nineteenth-century vice president elected or even nominated for president.

Finally, the vice president's role as Senate president (which most vice presidents, following Jefferson's lead and for want of other duties, spent considerable time performing) became more ceremonial during the nineteenth century as the Senate took greater charge of its own affairs. John C. Calhoun, who served from 1825 to 1832, was the last vice president whom the Senate allowed to appoint its committees.

Not surprisingly, the nineteenth-century vice presidents make up a virtual rogues' gallery of personal and political failures. Because the office was so unappealing, many of the politicians who could be enticed to run for vice president were old or in bad health. George Clinton of New York, the first vice president elected under the Twelfth Amendment, was both: "an old man who is too feeble to aspire to the presidency."[11] Clinton was the first of six nineteenth-century vice presidents to die in office, all of natural causes. He was followed by Elbridge Gerry, William R. King (who took his oath of office in Cuba where he was receiving treatment for tuberculosis and where he died a month later), Henry Wilson, Thomas A. Hendricks, and Garret A. Hobart. Some vice presidents became embroiled in financial scandals. Daniel D. Tompkins was charged with keeping inadequate financial records while serving as governor of New York during the War of 1812. Schuyler Colfax and Henry Wilson were implicated in the Crédit Mobilier stock scandal of the 1870s.

Other vice presidents fell prey to personal weaknesses or political jealousies. Tompkins and Andrew Johnson were heavy drinkers. Johnson's first vice-presidential address to the Senate impressed listeners, including President Abraham Lincoln, as a drunken harangue. Van Buren's vice president, Richard M. Johnson, kept a series of enslaved women as mistresses, educating the children of one but selling another when she lost interest in him.[12] George Clinton, John C. Calhoun, and Chester A. Arthur each publicly expressed his dislike for the president with whom he served. Clinton refused to attend President James Madison's inauguration and openly attacked the administration's foreign and domestic policies. Calhoun alienated two presidents, John Quincy Adams and Andrew Jackson, by using his position as Senate president to subvert their policies and appointments. He then resigned in 1832 to accept South Carolina's election as senator. Arthur attacked President James A. Garfield over a patronage quarrel. "Garfield has not been square, nor honorable, nor truthful," he told the *New York Herald*. "It's a hard thing to say of a president of the United States, but it's only the truth."[13]

The history of the nineteenth-century vice presidency is not entirely bleak. A certain measure of comity existed between a few presidents and vice presidents, notably Jackson and Van Buren, James K. Polk and George M. Dallas, Abraham Lincoln and Hannibal Hamlin, Rutherford B. Hayes and William A. Wheeler, and William McKinley and Garret Hobart. But even in these administrations the vice president was not invited to cabinet meetings or entrusted with important tasks. What made most of the positive relationships possible was the president's respect for the vice president's advice, which was sought informally, and the vice president's effectiveness as an advocate of the administration's policies in the Senate, where vice presidents continued to spend nearly all their time.

In one area of constitutional responsibility—presidential succession—the vice presidency took a giant step forward in the nineteenth century. The succession question did not arise until 1841, when William Henry Harrison became the first president to die in office. The language of the Constitution provided little guidance about whether the vice president, John Tyler, was to become president for the remainder of Harrison's term or acting president until a special election could be held. All the delegates to the Constitutional Convention were dead, and the most complete record of the convention, which could have helped to clarify the delegates' intentions, was not readily available. As described in Chapter 2, they seem to have wanted a special election to occur. But in this uncertain situation, Tyler's claim to both the presidency and the balance of Harrison's term was accepted grudgingly. It set a precedent that the next successor president, Millard Fillmore, was able to follow without controversy. Vice President Fillmore succeeded to the presidency in 1850, after President Zachary Taylor died.

But even this bright spot in the early history of the vice presidency was tarnished. Because Tyler and Harrison came from different wings of the Whig Party, Tyler's presidency was marred by debilitating disagreements with Whig leaders in Congress and in the late president's cabinet. All but one cabinet member resigned within five months. Fillmore and the two other nineteenth-century successor presidents, Johnson and Arthur, encountered similar problems. They too had been chosen to run for vice president because they represented a faction of the party different from the presidential nominee, and each of them lost all or most of the cabinet members he inherited within two (Fillmore) to six (Arthur) months. Johnson's problems were even more dire. He was impeached by the House and came within one vote of being removed from office by the Senate. Indeed, of the four vice presidents who succeeded to the presidency in the nineteenth century, none is considered a successful president. In a recent round of presidential ratings by historians and political scientists, Johnson, Tyler, Fillmore, and Arthur were clustered among the nine worst presidents in history.[14] Nor were any of the nineteenth-century successor presidents nominated to run for a full term in their own right.

Unresolved issues of succession and disability also vexed the vice presidency during the nineteenth century. Taken together, six vice-presidential deaths, one vice-presidential resignation, and four presidential deaths left the nation without a vice president during eleven of the century's twenty-five presidential terms. President Taylor's death in July 1850 and Vice President King's in April 1853 meant that with the exception of the month that King spent in Cuba after taking the oath of office in Havana in March 1853, there was no vice president for seven consecutive years. Fortunately, no president ever died while the vice presidency was vacant.

The issue of vice-presidential responsibility in periods of presidential disability also remained unresolved. Five nineteenth-century presidents were disabled for measurable lengths of time.[15] In 1881, during the eighty days that President Garfield lay wounded before dying from an assassin's bullet, Vice President Arthur left town, unwilling to risk appearing to covet the presidency.

Perhaps the unkindest epitaph for the nineteenth-century vice presidency was written by political scientist Woodrow Wilson in his 1885 book *Congressional Government.* After spending less than a page on the vice presidency (in the chapter on "The Senate," not the chapter on "The Executive"), Wilson concluded that "the chief embarrassment in discussing this office is that in explaining how little there is to be said about it one has evidently said all there is to say."[16] Wilson's dismissive view of the vice presidency carried over into his presidency when he ran for reelection three decades later. Rejecting a suggestion that he replace Marshall on the ticket in 1916 with Secretary of War Newton Baker, Wilson said that Baker was too valuable to be wasted as vice president.[17]

Theodore Roosevelt to Harry S. Truman

The rise of mass-circulation magazines and newspaper wire services, a new style of active presidential campaigning, and alterations in the vice-presidential nominating process enhanced the status of the vice presidency during the first half of the twentieth century. In 1900 the Republican nominee, Theodore Roosevelt, became the first vice-presidential candidate (and, other than William Jennings Bryan, the Democratic nominee for president in 1896, the first member of a national party ticket) to campaign vigorously across the country. While President William McKinley waged a sedate reelection campaign, Roosevelt gave 673 speeches to 3 million listeners in twenty-four states.

The national reputation that Roosevelt gained through travel and the news media stood him in good stead when he succeeded to the presidency after McKinley was assassinated in 1901. Roosevelt was able to reverse the earlier pattern of successor presidents and establish a new one.

Unlike Tyler, Fillmore, Andrew Johnson, and Arthur, Roosevelt was nominated by his party to run for a full term as president in 1904. TR's nomination set the precedent for Coolidge in 1924, Truman in 1948, Lyndon Johnson in 1964, and Ford in 1976. His success also helps explain another new pattern that contrasts sharply with nineteenth-century practice. Starting with James S. Sherman in 1912, ten of the eleven elected vice presidents who wanted a second term were nominated for reelection.[18]

In addition to the political precedents he established, Roosevelt helped lay the intellectual groundwork for enhancing the vice presidency as an institution. In an 1896 article, he argued that the president and vice president should share the same "views and principles" and that the vice president "should always be . . . consulted by the president on every great party question. It would be very well if he were given a seat in the Cabinet, . . . a vote [in the Senate], on ordinary occasions, and perchance on occasion a voice in the debates."[19]

That said, Roosevelt was unable as vice president and unwilling as president to practice what he preached about the vice presidency. While vice president, he despaired, "I am not doing any work and do not feel as though I was justifying my existence." As for the office, it "ought to be abolished."[20] When Roosevelt became president, party leaders imposed the vice-presidential nomination of Charles W. Fairbanks on him in 1904 in the same way they forced Roosevelt's own nomination as vice president on McKinley in 1900 and for the same reason: to balance the ticket. (TR was from the progressive wing of the Republican Party, Fairbanks from the Old Guard.) Neither McKinley nor Roosevelt liked or trusted his vice president, much less assigned him responsibilities. In fact, TR often repeated the humorist Dunne's response when Roosevelt said he was thinking of going down in a submarine: "Well, you really shouldn't do it—unless you take Fairbanks with you."[21]

Still, the enhanced political status of the vice presidency soon began to make it a more attractive office to some able and experienced political leaders, including Charles G. Dawes, who had served in three administrations and shared in the 1925 Nobel Peace Prize; Charles Curtis, the Senate majority leader; and Garner, the Speaker of the House. With somewhat more talent to offer, a few vice presidents were given new responsibilities by the presidents they served. When President Wilson went to Europe in 1918 to negotiate the treaty that ended World War I, he asked Vice President Marshall to meet with the cabinet. Wilson's successor, Warren G. Harding, invited Vice President Coolidge to continue the practice as a matter of course, as has every president since Franklin Roosevelt.[22]

FDR, like Theodore Roosevelt, ran for vice president before becoming president (he lost in 1920) and wrote an article to urge that the responsibilities of the vice presidency be expanded. In the article, Roosevelt identified four useful roles that the vice president could perform: cabinet member, presidential adviser, liaison to Congress, and policy maker in areas "that do not belong in the province" of any particular department or agency.[23]

As president, Franklin Roosevelt initially had so much respect for Garner that even though the conservative Texan's nomination had been imposed on him at the 1932 Democratic convention, FDR relied on him during the first term as "a combination presiding officer, cabinet officer, personal counselor, legislative tactician, Cassandra, and sounding board."[24] Most significant, Garner served as an important liaison between Roosevelt and Congress. It was Garner's suggestion that led to the practice, which presidents continue to follow, of meeting regularly with congressional leaders as a group. Garner also undertook a goodwill mission abroad at Roosevelt's behest, another innovation that virtually all administrations have continued.

During their second term, Roosevelt and Garner had a falling-out over the president's plan to pack the Supreme Court, his support for organized labor, and other liberal policies. Garner even challenged Roosevelt's bid for a third term at the 1940 Democratic convention. The rupture between the president and the vice president set the stage for an important modification of the vice-presidential selection process that was designed to foster greater harmony between presidents and vice presidents. In 1936, at Roosevelt's insistence, the Democrats abolished their two-thirds rule for presidential nominations, which meant that to win at the convention, candidates for president and their agents no longer had to engage in as much political horse trading as they used to with the vice presidency and other administration posts. The party also abolished the two-thirds rule for vice-presidential nominations, reducing the degree of consensus needed for that decision as well. In 1940 Roosevelt completed his coup by seizing the party leaders' traditional power to determine nominations for vice president and making it his own. Roosevelt's tactic was simple: he threatened that unless the convention chose Secretary of Agriculture Henry A. Wallace for vice president (which it was loath to do), he would refuse the Democratic nomination for president.

Unlike Garner and many of his other predecessors, Wallace had never been a member of Congress, and while serving as vice president, he spent little time on Capitol Hill. But he did become the only vice president to be appointed to head a government agency. In July 1941 Roosevelt named

Wallace to chair the new Economic Defense Board, a three-thousand-member wartime preparation agency. After World War II was declared in December, it was renamed the Board of Economic Warfare and assigned major procurement responsibilities. Unfortunately, the powers and duties of Wallace's agency overlapped with those of several cabinet departments, notably State and Commerce. These overlaps generated interagency conflicts about jurisdiction and policy that weakened the war effort and undermined Wallace's authority. But because the vice president is a constitutionally independent officer whom the president cannot command or remove, Roosevelt felt compelled to abolish the warfare board, leaving Wallace embarrassed and devoid of function. In the end, what initially seemed to be a new birth of vice-presidential power turned out to be false labor. No president since Roosevelt has asked the vice president to head an executive agency.

Nevertheless, the steadily growing involvement of the vice president in executive branch activities persisted under Wallace. The vice president continued to sit with the cabinet, advise the president, and travel abroad as an administration emissary. Wallace's lack of involvement with Congress reflected another emerging characteristic of the twentieth-century vice presidency: the atrophy of the office's role as president of the Senate. In some ways, the first development explains the second. To the extent that vice presidents became more involved with the president, they had less time to spend with the Senate and less ability to win its members' trust. But changes in the Senate also help account for the decline of the vice president's constitutional responsibilities in that institution. The admission of new states increased the size of the Senate and made tie votes statistically less probable. The Senate also became more institutionalized, developing its own body of rules and procedural precedents, which the president of the Senate was expected merely to announce on the advice of the parliamentarian.

Advances in the visibility, stature, and extraconstitutional responsibilities of the vice presidency may help explain the office's improved performance of its main constitutional duty: to provide an able successor to the presidency. Historians and political scientists recently ranked three of the five twentieth-century successor presidents (Theodore Roosevelt, Truman, and Lyndon Johnson) among the top ten presidents of all time, with Ford scoring in the middle category and only Coolidge as below average.[25]

For all its progress, however, the vice presidency at midcentury remained a fundamentally weak office. Its constitutional status was substantially unaltered, although the Twentieth Amendment (1933) did establish the full successorship of the vice president-elect in the event of the president-elect's death. Ticket balancing to unite the party and increase its appeal on election day continued to dominate the selection of vice-presidential candidates. All the ambiguities of the vice president's rights and duties in times of presidential disability were still unresolved, as dramatized by the passive role Marshall felt compelled to play (for fear of being branded a usurper) during the prolonged illness of Woodrow Wilson. And tension continued to mark some presidential–vice-presidential pairings, although less frequently after FDR won for presidential candidates the right to choose their running mates.

Even the glimmerings of enhanced vice-presidential influence sometimes seemed to be no more than that. When Roosevelt ran for a fourth term in 1944, he replaced the unpopular Wallace with Sen. Harry Truman of Missouri. On inauguration day in 1945, the president's health was severely declining, and World War II was coming to a close. Yet Truman later was to say that in his eighty-two days as vice president, "I don't think I saw Roosevelt but twice . . . except at cabinet meetings."[26] Truman was at most only dimly aware of the existence of the atomic bomb, the Allies' plans for the postwar world, and the deterioration of the president's health. In this woeful state of unpreparedness, Truman succeeded to the presidency and its full range of powers and duties when Roosevelt died on April 12. He told a friend later that day, "I feel like I have been struck by a bolt of lightning."[27]

The Modern Vice Presidency

Truman's lack of preparation to succeed to the presidency in 1945, along with the subsequent development of an ongoing cold war between the United States and the Soviet Union and the proliferation of intercontinental ballistic missiles armed with nuclear warheads, heightened public concern that the vice president be a leader who is ready and able to step into the presidency at a moment's notice. Historically, six of nine presidential successions have occurred during the vice president's first eight months in office.[28] This concern has had important consequences for the selection, activities, succession, disability, and political status of the vice presidency. Since midcentury, in legal scholar Joel K. Goldstein's apt phrase, the vice presidency has "moved from Article I to Article II"—that is, from a primarily legislative office to a thoroughly executive one.[29]

On April 12, 1945, Vice President Harry Truman took the presidential oath of office as his wife and daughter looked on. Later that day he told a friend, "I feel like I have been struck by a bolt of lightning."

Source: Abbie Rowe—National Park Service, courtesy of Harry S. Truman Library.

Selection

To meet the new public expectations about vice-presidential competence, most modern presidential candidates have paid considerable attention to experience, ability, and political compatibility in selecting their running mates. Winning votes on election day is still as much the goal as in the days of old-style ticket balancing. But presidential nominees realize that voters now care more about competence and loyalty—a vice-presidential candidate's ability to succeed to the presidency ably and to carry on the departed president's policies faithfully—than they do about having all regions of the country or factions of the party represented on the ticket.[30] This realization helped create the climate for a more influential vice presidency. As Goldstein has shown, the president is most likely to assign responsibilities to the vice president when the two are personally and politically compatible and when the president believes that the vice president has talents the administration needs.[31] Because of the new selection criteria, these conditions have been met in almost every recent administration.

Little is left to chance in modern vice-presidential selection, at least when the presidential nominating contest is settled well in advance of the convention, as has been typical since 1952. Jimmy Carter set a precedent in 1976 when he conducted a careful, organized preconvention search for a running mate. Aides compiled and scrutinized a list of four hundred Democratic officeholders and then winnowed it down to seven finalists who were investigated and ultimately interviewed by Carter. Carter leaked the list of finalists to the news media, both to gauge public reaction to them and to ensure that any scandalous or embarrassing behavior would be revealed before he made his choice rather than afterward. In the end, Carter tapped Sen. Walter F. Mondale of Minnesota at the convention. Carter's model of vice-presidential selection caught on to such an extent that it is now standard operating procedure for presidential candidates, although each one has done things slightly differently and Republicans have tended to screen their finalists less publicly than Democrats.[32]

The fruits of the new emphasis on loyalty and competence and the new care invested in the selection process are evident in the roster of postwar vice-presidential nominees. The modern era has been marked by an almost complete absence of ideologically opposed running mates, and those vice-presidential candidates who differed on some issues with the head of the ticket have hastened to gloss over past disagreements and deny that any exist in the present. The record on competence is even more compelling. From 1948 to 2016 numerous vice-presidential candidates were the more experienced members of the ticket in high government office. These candidates include John Sparkman in 1952, Estes Kefauver in 1956, Lyndon Johnson and Henry Cabot Lodge in 1960, Walter Mondale in 1976, George Bush in 1980, Lloyd Bentsen in 1988, Al Gore in 1992, Richard Cheney in 2000, Joseph Biden in 2008, and Mike Pence in 2016.[33] As a six-term senator from Delaware, Biden brought more high-level experience to his party's ticket than any previous vice president, offsetting presidential nominee Barack Obama's relatively thin résumé as a less-than-one-term senator. "We needed a running mate . . . who brought some gray hair and years of experience here in Washington," said David Axelrod, Obama's chief political consultant.[34] Pence's years as governor of Indiana and a leader of his party in the House of Representatives similarly leavened concerns about Trump's inexperience in office.

To be sure, nothing guarantees that reasoned, responsible vice-presidential nominees will be chosen in every presidential election. Politicians do not always see their interests clearly. Richard Nixon, the Republican presidential nominee in 1968, was too clever by half when, acting on the theory that a relatively unknown running mate would have few enemies and cost the ticket few votes, he chose Maryland governor

Spiro T. Agnew. In 1984 Mondale seemed too eager to placate feminist groups within the Democratic Party when he selected Geraldine A. Ferraro, a three-term member of the House of Representatives with no notable foreign affairs experience, as his running mate. Similarly, George McGovern may have been overly concerned about satisfying organized labor when he picked Missouri senator Thomas Eagleton in 1972. It was revealed soon after Eagleton's nomination that he concealed from McGovern the electroshock therapy he underwent for a nervous breakdown, which led to his being dropped from the ticket.[35]

John McCain's selection of first-term Alaska governor Sarah Palin as his running mate in 2008 was another product of constituency pressures, albeit indirectly. McCain's first choice was Sen. Joseph Lieberman of Connecticut, a close friend who was the Democratic vice-presidential candidate in 2000. When Republican activists objected that awarding a place on the GOP ticket to a pro-choice Democrat would severely divide the party, McCain hastily looked for a different way of reinforcing his "maverick" image with a different kind of nontraditional choice. He tapped Palin, a woman with a reputation as a political outsider even in her own state.[36]

What seems certain is that the presidential candidate who pays insufficient attention to competence and loyalty in choosing the vice-presidential nominee will suffer for it in the election. The news media will run critical stories, the other party will air harsh commercials, and the now-traditional vice-presidential debate, which is nationally televised in prime time, may reveal the nominee as an unworthy presidential successor.[37] Vice-presidential candidates dominate the campaign news during at least two periods: when their names are announced and during the week bracketing the vice-presidential debate. A candidate for president who chooses an unimpressive running mate not only forfeits an opportunity to gain positive news coverage but also invites its opposite.[38]

In the 1988 election Bush's selection of the inarticulate Quayle may have reduced his margin of victory in the popular vote by as much as four to eight percentage points.[39] In contrast, Clinton's choice of Gore in 1992 successfully defied all the conventions of ticket balancing. Like Clinton, Gore was a southerner, a Baptist, a moderate, and a baby boomer whose intelligence and ability appealed to many voters.[40] In July 1992 a *Time–CNN* poll found that when asked, "Who do you think is more qualified to be president—Quayle or Gore?"—63 percent of respondents said Gore, and 21 percent named the incumbent vice president, Quayle.[41]

To screen potential running mates in 2000, George W. Bush established a vetting process headed by Cheney, a veteran Washington politician with experience in the House of Representatives, the corporate world, and several Republican administrations, including prominent service as President Ford's chief of staff and as secretary of defense under Bush's father. Bush accepted Cheney's criteria for an ideal nominee—someone with experience in the White House, Congress, the private sector, and as head of an executive department—and in effect dared Cheney, who had ruled himself out as a candidate, to come up with someone else who met these criteria. He couldn't and ended up agreeing to join the ticket.[42] The selection was surprising in one way because most of the speculation had centered on Bush's fellow big-state Republican governors, such as Tom Ridge of Pennsylvania and John Engler of Michigan. But in a more important way, Bush's selection of Cheney was not surprising at all. Governors who have been nominated for president—FDR in 1932, Alfred M. Landon in 1936, Thomas E. Dewey in 1944, Adlai Stevenson in 1952 and 1956, Carter in 1976, Reagan in 1980, Dukakis in 1988, Clinton in 1992, Bush himself in 2000, and Mitt Romney in 2012—almost always have chosen veteran Washington figures for vice president.[43] They have done so to reassure the voters that their own inexperience in national government, especially in foreign and economic policy, will be offset by the vice president's experience. Bush underlined this virtue of the Cheney nomination by declaring that he chose him less to help win the election than to help him govern "as a valuable partner"—a shrewd tactic for helping Bush win the election.[44]

Gore, persuaded of Warren Christopher's skill at screening potential Democratic running mates by the former secretary of state's work for Clinton in 1992 (which had led to Gore's own selection), enlisted Christopher to help in 2000. Between February and July, Christopher and Gore whittled a list of about forty names down to four, all of them senators: John Edwards of North Carolina, Bob Kerrey of Nebraska, John F. Kerry of Massachusetts, and Lieberman of Connecticut, who was added to the list at Gore's insistence. Gore wanted to make a bold choice that would help to establish him in the voters' minds as a leader in his own right, not just as President Clinton's loyal lieutenant. When the time came, no one doubted the boldness of Gore's decision to choose Lieberman, a deeply religious Jew who had publicly criticized Clinton's behavior during the Monica Lewinsky affair as "immoral."

In 2004 Democratic presidential candidate John Kerry chose his chief rival for the nomination, Sen. John Edwards, as his vice-presidential running mate. Kerry's choice of someone he had just defeated was not unusual: eight of the twenty vice-presidential nominees from 1960 to 2004 had already run for president at least once. But Kerry and Edwards often seemed uncomfortable in joint appearances and remarkably, the Kerry campaign made no effort to carry Edwards's home state of North Carolina. Four years later, Obama selected Biden, who was one of his opponents in the 2008 Democratic nominating contest. Obama's choice of the experienced Biden did him far more good than McCain's selection of the inexperienced Palin. Voters who worried about McCain's age (at seventy-two he was bidding to become the oldest person ever elected president) were especially alarmed at Palin's lack of knowledge about foreign affairs. Exit polls showed that although 66 percent thought Biden was "qualified to be president if necessary," only 38 percent thought that Palin was.[45] In 2012 former Massachusetts governor Romney energized Republican conservatives by selecting House budget committee chair Paul Ryan of Wisconsin, the party's leading fiscal conservative and one of its attractive "Young Guns."[46]

In 2016 Republican Mike Pence and Democrat Tim Kaine were the sort of running mates whom any presidential nominees might have chosen. Pence was experienced in both state and national office and enjoyed support from his party's leading social, economic, and national security conservatives, none of whom were confident that Trump shared their views on important issues. Kaine, whom Democratic presidential nominee Hillary Clinton chose, was governor of Virginia before being elected to represent his state in the Senate. Both vice presidential candidates had succeeded politically in "purple" states that were battlegrounds in the election, and both professed strong loyalty to the heads of their tickets.

A concern for competence and loyalty in the vice presidency characterized the solution Congress invented in the 1960s to a recurring problem made urgent by the challenges of the postwar era: vice-presidential vacancies. The Twenty-Fifth Amendment, ratified in 1967, established a procedure for selecting vice presidents in unusual circumstances. Before then, the vice presidency had been vacant for parts of sixteen administrations, leaving the president with no constitutionally designated successor.[47] The new amendment stated that "whenever there is a vacancy in the office of the Vice President, the President shall nominate a Vice President who shall take office upon confirmation by a majority vote of both Houses of Congress," with the two chambers voting separately. This procedure came in handy, albeit in circumstances its authors scarcely imagined, twice within a few years. In 1973 Vice President Agnew resigned as part of a plea bargain to reduce bribery charges and was replaced by Ford. In 1974 Ford became president after President Nixon resigned to avert impeachment proceedings. Ford appointed former New York governor Nelson A. Rockefeller to fill the vacated vice presidency.

Activities

Modern presidents try to reassure the nation that the vice president is prepared to succeed to the presidency at a moment's notice by keeping their vice presidents informed about most matters of state. As President Dwight D. Eisenhower remarked at a news conference, "Even if Mr. Nixon and I were not good friends, I would still have him in every important conference of government, so that if the grim reaper would find it time to remove me from the scene, he is ready to step in without any interruption."[48] In 1949, at President Truman's request, the vice president was made a statutory member of the National Security Council.[49] Vice presidents also receive full national security briefings on a regular basis.

As a further means of public reassurance, most presidents now encourage their vice presidents to stay active in prominent ways. Since FDR began the practice with Garner, presidents have sent their vice presidents abroad with growing frequency on a variety of diplomatic missions, ranging from simple expressions of American goodwill to actual negotiations. Every vice president since Garner has sat regularly with the cabinet and served, to some degree, as a legislative liaison between the president and Congress. In that capacity, they count votes on Capitol Hill, lobby discreetly, and listen to complaints and suggestions. Trump, the first president ever to take office with no previous experience of governing, leaned especially hard on Pence in this regard, as well as in choosing appointees for his administration.[50]

Alben W. Barkley, who served as vice president in the Truman administration, elevated the ceremonial duties of the office to center stage. Some of these, such as crowning beauty queens (a Barkley favorite), have been inconsequential. Others, such as college commencement addresses and appearances at events that symbolize administration goals, need not be. Nixon, serving a president who did not enjoy partisan politics, carved out new vice-presidential roles that were as insignificant as chair of a minor study commission and as important as chief public advocate of the administration's policies, leadership, and party. The advocacy role exposed the vice president to a wide range of politically important audiences, including interest groups, party activists, journalists, and the general public. Pence became the first vice president to establish his own political action committee—the Great America Committee—explicitly for the purpose of helping Republican candidates for Congress but with the added benefit of enhancing his own status within the party.

During the 1960s and 1970s vice presidents began to accumulate greater institutional resources to help them fulfill their more extensive duties. Lyndon Johnson, who served with President Kennedy, gained for the vice presidency an impressive suite of offices in the Executive Office Building, adjacent to the White House. Agnew won a line item in the executive budget. The result was to free vice presidents from their earlier dependence on Congress for office space and operating funds.

Even more significant institutional gains were registered by Ford and Rockefeller, the two vice presidents who were appointed under the Twenty-Fifth Amendment and whose agreement to serve was urgently needed, for political reasons, by the presidents who chose them. Ford, who feared becoming too dependent on a president who might well be removed from office, persuaded Nixon to increase dramatically his budget for hiring staff. The new personnel included support staff for press relations, speech writing, scheduling, and administration (which meant that vice presidents no longer had to depend on the often-preoccupied White House staff for these functions); policy staff (enabling vice presidents to develop useful ideas and advice on matters of presidential concern); and political staff (to help vice presidents protect their interests and further their ambitions). Rockefeller secured a weekly place on the president's calendar for a private meeting. He also enhanced the perquisites of the vice presidency—everything from a better airplane to serve as *Air Force Two* to an official residence (the Admiral's House at the Naval Observatory) and a redesigned seal for the office. The old seal showed an eagle at rest; the new one displayed a wingspread eagle with a claw full of arrows and a starburst at its head.[51]

The vice presidency came into full flower during Mondale's tenure in the Carter administration. As Carter's running mate in 1976, Mondale participated in the first nationally televised debate between the vice-presidential candidates. His most tangible contribution to the institution during his term as vice president was the authorization he won to attend all presidential meetings, receive full access to the flow of papers to and from the president, and occupy an office in the West Wing of the White House.[52] Most important, perhaps, Mondale demonstrated that the vice president could serve the president who selected him with unprecedented care as a valued adviser on virtually all matters of politics and public policy. Most vice presidents in the modern era had been consulted by their presidents on at least some matters—Johnson on space issues, Humphrey on civil rights, and Rockefeller on domestic policy. But no vice president ever attained Mondale's status as a wide-ranging senior counselor to the president. To perform this role most effectively, Mondale eschewed ongoing "line responsibilities" in specific policy areas. This freed him to take on occasional assignments as the president's "troubleshooter" when particular challenges arose, such as securing Senate endorsement of a nuclear arms treaty with the Soviet Union. The vice president's long experience in Washington meant that "Mondale could explain this world to Carter and defend Carter to it."[53]

Mondale's successors inherited all the institutional gains he secured in vice-presidential roles and resources. In varying degrees, they also inherited his role as senior presidential adviser while embracing the sort of line assignments he eschewed.[54] Although George Bush did not enter office enjoying the same close relationship with Ronald Reagan that Mondale had with Carter, Bush worked hard and for the most part successfully to win the president's confidence. When Bush became president, he fostered an even stronger relationship with Quayle, whom he appointed to chair the new White House Council on Competitiveness, a de facto board of regulatory review that was empowered to overturn regulations issuing from the federal bureaucracy.[55] As vice president, Bush had accepted a similar assignment from Reagan.

From the beginning, Clinton's relationship with Gore rivaled Carter's with Mondale for trust and responsibility, although strains developed when Gore ran for president in 2000, near the end of Clinton's second term. Gore became one of the administration's star players in September 1993 when he issued the fat-trimming "reinventing government" report of the National Performance Review, an assignment he took on with relish. Two months later, he soundly defeated administration critic Ross Perot in a widely watched, nationally televised debate about the proposed North American Free Trade Agreement.

In addition to handling specific assignments, Gore was one of the three or four people whose advice Clinton sought on virtually every important matter of presidential politics and policy. On one occasion in 1993, when Clinton was immobilized with doubt about how to proceed with his economic program in Congress, he asked Gore, "What can I do?" Gore replied, with considerable exasperation, "You can get with the goddamn program!" After a pause, Clinton said, "Okay."[56] According to veteran Washington reporter Elizabeth Drew, "Gore was in large measure responsible for the boldness of Clinton's economic program."[57] In 1998 a Clinton adviser listed several "areas where Al Gore makes the decisions—and the president rubberstamps[:] . . . science, technology, NASA, telecommunications, the environment, family leave, tobacco, nuclear dealings with the Russians, media violence, the Internet, privacy issues, and, of course, reinventing government."[58]

Especially during his first term, when George W. Bush was still unfamiliar with many of the issues he faced as president, Richard Cheney's responsibilities in the administration surpassed those of any vice president in history, including Mondale and Gore.[59] One reporter described Cheney's role as "war minister, über diplomat, political adviser and consigliere to President Bush."[60] Another writer noted that Cheney's voice was the final one Bush wanted to hear before making an important decision. "What does Dick think?" the president routinely asked.[61] Historian Douglas Brinkley described Cheney as "the vortex in the White House on foreign policy making. Everything comes through him."[62]

Cheney's influence was felt even before he took office, when Bush asked him to direct the transition from election to inauguration, the only time a vice president was assigned this task until Trump assigned it to Pence. Long experienced in Washington, Cheney was able to stack the administration with close associates and even secure senior White House staff status for his vice presidential chief of staff and political director. In the spring of 2001 Cheney was charged with developing the administration's energy policy initiative. After the September 11, 2001, terrorist attacks on New York City's World Trade Center and the Pentagon, he was Bush's primary adviser in formulating the war against the Taliban regime in Afghanistan, which was harboring the al Qaeda terrorists responsible for the attacks. His role in the war to topple the Saddam Hussein regime in Iraq, which was launched in 2003, was much more controversial. Cheney relentlessly pressed the case, in speeches and in private administration councils, that Saddam had stockpiled weapons of mass destruction and was cooperating with al Qaeda. Although Iraq was easily defeated by American and allied forces, neither of these justifications for the war proved accurate. Still worse, anti-American insurgents in Iraq waged guerilla warfare against the occupying forces for years to come, undermining public approval at home and abroad of Bush's performance as president as well as of Cheney's as vice president.[63]

The combination of power and unpopularity made Cheney a target in the 2008 election. "Vice President Cheney has been the most dangerous vice president we've had probably in American history," charged Biden in the vice-presidential debate, and Palin did not rise to defend him. Biden insisted that his primary job as vice president would be to advise President Obama and then to accept and defend his decisions. "Every major decision he'll be making, I'll be sitting in the room to give my best advice," Biden told the national television audience.[64] In practice, Obama handed Biden a series of specific assignments during his first two years as vice president: chairing a middle-class task force, overseeing spending on projects designed to stimulate the economy, lobbying on Capitol Hill, visiting foreign capitals, winding down the war in Iraq, and campaigning for

Democratic candidates in the 2010 midterm elections. But none of these responsibilities detracted from Biden's primary role as a wide-ranging senior adviser whom the president prized for speaking his mind. During Obama's lengthy first-year review of American policy in Afghanistan, Biden was a forceful and effective "house skeptic" about further military involvement. "He's got wisdom, he's got experience, he's blunt, and he's loyal," said Obama—"all the qualities you could ask for in a governing partner and in a vice president."[65] For all his criticism of his predecessor, "Biden followed Cheney's practice of staffing the vice president's office with ranking specialists in foreign and diplomatic policy and economic affairs."[66]

Obama and, especially, his staff were less appreciative of Biden's outspokenness in public settings. Less than a month into Obama's first term, when he was laboring to persuade Congress to pass a $814 billion economic recovery act, Biden said there was "a 30 percent chance we're going to get it wrong." In May 2012, shortly before Obama planned to announce his support for marriage equality, the irrepressible Biden—sometimes mocked as a "dopey, undisciplined Uncle Joe" on comedy shows and Web sites—stole the president's thunder by announcing on television in May that he was "absolutely comfortable" with same-sex marriage, a position that Obama was forced to endorse sooner than planned. The downside of Biden's thirty-six years in the Senate and two presidential candidacies was that he had much more experience publicly saying what he thought than deferring to anyone, even the president.[67]

During Trump's first two years in office, Mike Pence was a constant in the midst of otherwise rapid administration turnover. He took over the transition process when President-elect Trump summarily fired New Jersey governor Chris Christie. After the inauguration, chiefs of staff, national security advisers, communications directors, secretaries of state, and other high-ranking officials came and went in the volatile Trump presidency, but Pence stayed. Relying, as he had during his business career, on family members and devoted retainers, Trump valued the unflagging loyalty Pence showed, along with his experience in government and wide connections in Congress and within the Republican Party. Pence realized from the start that the price of influence within the administration would be to conceal that influence in public settings. In doing so he invoked the scathing criticism of conservative columnist George F. Will, who characterized Pence's loyalty to Trump as a "talent for toadyism and appetite for obsequiousness."[68]

Not just Pence, but every vice president realizes that the extent to which the new activities of the office translate into real influence still depends in large part on the president's perception of the vice president's ability, energy, and perhaps most important, loyalty. Because of the new vice-presidential selection criteria, this perception is more likely to be favorable today than at any time in the nation's history. And, because of the institutionalization of numerous roles and resources in the vice presidency, the vice president has a greater opportunity than ever to exert real influence on the president.

Succession and Disability

In addition to creating a procedure to fill vice-presidential vacancies, the Twenty-Fifth Amendment accomplished two other purposes that taken together expressed "a new constitutional vision" of the vice presidency as "an important institution in American government."[69] One was to state explicitly the right of the vice president to assume the presidency and serve for the remainder of the departed president's term if the president dies, resigns, or is impeached and removed. In this respect, the amendment was a formality that conferred constitutional sanction on the tradition Tyler established after President Harrison died in 1841. The other was to create a set of procedures

Jimmy Carter, right, regarded his vice president, Walter Mondale, as a valued adviser on virtually all matters of politics and public policy, a status no earlier vice president had attained. Mondale also was authorized to attend all presidential meetings and was allowed full access to the flow of papers to and from the president.

Source: The Jimmy Carter Presidential Library.

to handle situations of presidential disability. As discussed in Chapter 11, the amendment provided constitutional methods both for the president to name the vice president as acting president during a time of disability and for the vice president and a majority of the heads of the departments to make that decision if the president is unable to do so. The amendment even created a procedure to be followed if the vice president and the cabinet believe the president is disabled and the president disagrees. The vice president would become acting president, but the president would be restored to power within twenty-one days unless declared disabled by two-thirds of both the House and the Senate.

Only a few clear instances of presidential disability have arisen since the Twenty-Fifth Amendment was passed.[70] The first occurred when Reagan was shot on March 30, 1981. Some thought was given, then and in the days afterward, to naming Vice President Bush as acting president. But White House aides discouraged any such action for fear that to do so would make Reagan appear weak and confuse the nation and foreign governments.[71]

Criticism of the administration's failure to act in 1981

From the beginning, President Bill Clinton, left, relied heavily on Vice President Al Gore for advice and support.

Source: Scott Ferrell—Congressional Quarterly.

Vice President Richard Cheney, shown here with President George W. Bush, represents what many believe to be the most hands-on, active second-in-command since the start of the presidency.

Source: Scott Ferrell—Congressional Quarterly.

shaped its preparation for the second instance of presidential disability, Reagan's scheduled cancer surgery on July 13, 1985. This time Reagan did relinquish his powers and duties to Bush before going under anesthesia. Curiously, he did not explicitly invoke the Twenty-Fifth Amendment in doing so, saying instead that he was not convinced that the amendment was meant to apply to "such brief and temporary periods of incapacity" as his surgery. Still, a precedent was established, raising expectations that the Twenty-Fifth Amendment would work as intended in future administrations. This precedent was followed in 2002 and 2007 when George W. Bush cited the amendment in transferring authority to Cheney just before being anesthetized for a surgical procedure. Although the vice president was not called on to do anything during his few hours as acting president, Bush explained to the press, "We're at war and I just want to be super-cautious."[72]

Political Status

The vice president enjoys a curious political status. Until George Bush's victory in 1988, no incumbent vice president had been elected president since 1836, when Van Buren was victorious. Yet, in a marked departure from previous political history, the vice presidency has become one of the most effective stepping stones to a major-party presidential nomination. Of the modern vice presidents, Nixon, Humphrey, Mondale, Bush, and Gore were nominated directly for president, and Truman, Johnson, and Ford were nominated for a full term after succeeding to the presidency. Agnew and Rockefeller did not actively seek a presidential nomination. Cheney made clear from the start that he would not be a candidate. His decision enhanced Bush's trust that Cheney's advice was undiluted by personal political ambition but also reduced the vice president's sensitivity to public opinion, a useful quality in a close presidential adviser. Biden, who turned seventy-four in 2016, older than any elected or reelected president in history, initially eschewed presidential ambitions but later announced that he would keep his options open. He eventually decided not to run in that election but did not rule out a candidacy in 2020.

What accounts for the recent ascendancy of the vice presidency in the politics of presidential nominations? First, the two-term limit that was imposed on the president by the Twenty-Second Amendment in 1951 made it possible for the vice president to step forward as a presidential candidate during the president's second term without alienating the president. Nixon (1960), Bush (1988), and Gore (2000) all followed that path. This effect of the amendment was wholly unanticipated when it was enacted. Second, the roles that Vice President Nixon developed, with Eisenhower's encouragement, as party builder (campaigning during election years and raising funds between elections) and as public advocate of the administration and its policies uniquely situate the vice president to win friends among the party activists who influence presidential nominations. Finally, the recent growth in vice-presidential activities has made the vice presidency a more prestigious office and therefore a more plausible stepping stone to the presidency. Even the trappings of the office—the airplane, official residence, seal, Secret Service contingent, and West Wing office—testify to its prestige.[73]

Perhaps more important, in their efforts to assure the nation that they are fulfilling their responsibility to prepare for a possible emergency succession, presidents make public claims, inflated or otherwise, about the participation of the vice president in the administration. The typical modern vice president can argue plausibly, as Mondale frequently did, that the vice presidency "may be the best training of all" for the presidency. "I'm privy to all the same secret information as the president," Mondale said.

> I have unlimited access to the president. I'm usually with him
> when all the central decisions are being made. I've been through
> several of those crises that a president inevitably confronts, and
> I see how they work. I've been through the budget process. I've
> been through the diplomatic ventures. I've been through a host
> of congressional fights as seen from the presidential perspective.[74]

Yet vice presidents who are nominated by their party for president carry certain disadvantages into the fall campaign that are as surely grounded in the office as the advantages they bring to the nominating contest.[75] Indeed, some of the activities of the modern vice presidency that are most appealing to the party activists who influence nominations may repel members of the broader electorate that decides the general election. Days and nights spent fertilizing the party's grassroots with fervent, sometimes slashing political rhetoric can alienate voters who look to the presidency for leadership that unites rather than divides. Gore's blurt to a 1998 postimpeachment rally of Democratic House members that Clinton "will be regarded in the history books as one of our greatest presidents" doubtless roused the spirits of his fellow partisans, but it seemed wildly excessive to almost everyone else.[76]

Certain institutional qualities of the modern vice presidency also handicap the vice president who becomes a presidential candidate. Vice presidents must work hard to gain a share of the credit for the successes of the administration, but they can count on being attacked by the other party's presidential nominee for all of the administration's shortcomings. Such attacks allow no effective response. A vice president who tries to stand apart from the administration may alienate the president and cause voters to wonder why the criticisms were not voiced earlier, when they might have made a difference. Gore did himself no good when he spent the evening of his official announcement for president telling the *20/20* television audience that Clinton's behavior in the Monica Lewinsky affair was "inexcusable."[77]

The vice president's difficulties are only compounded when it comes to matters of public policy. For example, every time during the 2000 campaign that Gore identified a problem he wanted to solve as president, George W. Bush would chastise him for not already persuading Clinton to solve it. During their first debate, when Gore mentioned his proposal to extend prescription drug benefits to seniors, Bush replied, "Four years ago they campaigned on getting prescription drug benefits for seniors. And now they're campaigning on getting prescription drug benefits for seniors. It seems like they can't get it done."[78]

Vice presidents always can say that loyalty to the president forecloses public disagreement, but that course is no less perilous. The public that values loyalty in a vice president values other qualities in a potential president. Strength, independence, and vision are what most voters look for—the very qualities that vice presidents almost never have an opportunity to display.[79] Polls that through much of the election year showed Gore trailing Bush in the category of leadership were less about the candidates than about the vice presidency. So was the election day exit poll showing that voters who regarded strong leadership as the personal quality they wanted most in a president supported Bush by 64 percent to 34 percent.[80]

Although the political handicaps that vice presidents carry into the general election campaign are formidable, they need not be insurmountable. As with all things vice presidential, much depends on their relationship with the presidents they serve. One of the main reasons that sitting vice presidents Nixon and Humphrey lost is that their presidents were so unhelpful. When a reporter asked Eisenhower to name a single "major idea of [Nixon's] you had adopted" as president, he replied, "If you give me a week, I might think of one."[81] Johnson treated Humphrey spitefully as soon as it became clear that the 1968 Democratic convention was not going to draft the president for another term, despite his earlier withdrawal from the race.[82]

In contrast, more than a century earlier Van Buren benefited enormously from his association with President Andrew Jackson, who regarded his vice president's election to the presidency as validation of the transformation he wrought in American politics and government. Reagan was equally committed to Bush's success in 1988, putting ego aside to praise the vice president's contributions to what the president began calling the "Reagan–Bush administration." Reagan's popularity was of even greater benefit to Bush, who won the votes of 80 percent of those who approved of Reagan's performance as president.[83]

Although Clinton said in 2000 that he wished he could run for a third term (and identified Gore only as "the next best thing"),[84] he shared Jackson's and Reagan's belief that his legacy was closely tied to his vice president's political success. Gore, however, chose to distance himself from the popular Clinton, rejecting the president's repeated offers to campaign for him, which party leaders urged Gore to accept.[85] Instead of emphasizing the national prosperity that marked the Clinton–Gore years, Gore ran a populist-style campaign more appropriate for a candidate challenging an incumbent in economic hard times than for a vice president seeking to extend his party's control of the presidency in good times.

To be sure, vice presidents are not destined to lose presidential elections any more than they are destined to win presidential nominations. Before Bush was elected in 1988, Nixon in 1960 and Humphrey in 1968 each came within two percentage points of victory. In 2000 Gore won the national popular vote and came very close in the Electoral College. But the electoral tensions that vice presidents face as presidential candidates inhere in the office. As President Eisenhower once observed, "To promise and pledge *new* effort, *new* programs, and *new* ideas without appearing to criticize the current party and administration—that is indeed an exercise in tightrope walking."[86]

Conclusion

In matters of selection, activities, succession and disability, and political status, the vice presidency has come a long way, especially since 1945. But the curious electoral history of the vice presidency is a reminder that for all its progress as an institution, some weaknesses of the office endure. Although new selection criteria make the nomination of vice-presidential candidates who are qualified to be president more likely, the examples of Agnew in 1968, Eagleton in 1972, Ferraro in 1984, Quayle in 1988, and Palin in 2008 indicate that older patterns of choice are not yet extinct.

The new selection criteria may foster greater harmony in office between the president and the vice president, but they do not guarantee it. Perhaps it is not surprising that Johnson and Nixon, the two modern presidents who inflicted the greatest pain on their vice presidents, were once vice presidents themselves.[87]

Finally, although vice presidents enjoy more resources, responsibilities, and influence than ever before, they do so mainly at the sufferance of the president. The price of power for a vice president can be high—unflagging loyalty, sublimation of one's own views and ambitions, and willingness to answer to the president's beck and call. But, in view of the inherent constitutional weakness of the office, no other path to influence exists.

Notes

1. These familiar quotations about the vice presidency may be found in Michael Dorman, *The Second Man: The Changing Role of the Vice Presidency* (New York: Delacorte Press, 1968), 6–7.

2. Quoted in Paul C. Light, *Vice-Presidential Power: Advice and Influence in the White House* (Baltimore: Johns Hopkins University Press, 1984), 13.

3. Thomas R. Marshall, *Recollections* (Indianapolis, Ind.: Bobbs-Merrill, 1925), 368.

4. Quoted in David McCullough, *John Adams* (New York: Simon and Schuster, 2001), 447.

5. Joel K. Goldstein, "Constitutional Change, Originalism, and the Vice Presidency," *Journal of Constitutional Law*, 16 (November 2013): 390, 389.

6. Jon Meacham, *Thomas Jefferson: The Art of Power* (New York: Random House, 2012), 305.

7. Quoted in Joel K. Goldstein, *The Modern American Vice Presidency* (Princeton: Princeton University Press, 1982).

8. David E. Kyvig, *Explicit and Authentic Acts: Amending the U.S. Constitution, 1776–1995* (Lawrence: University Press of Kansas, 1996), 116.

9. Jody C. Baumgartner, *The American Vice Presidency Reconsidered* (Westport, Conn.: Praeger, 2006), 19.

10. Quoted in Thomas E. Cronin, "Rethinking the Vice Presidency," in *Rethinking the Vice Presidency*, ed. Thomas E. Cronin (Boston: Little, Brown, 1982), 326. Rather than being buried, Webster would have succeeded to the presidency when Zachary Taylor died in 1850.

11. Matthew Crenson and Benjamin Ginsberg, *Presidential Power: Unchecked and Unbalanced* (New York: Norton, 2007), 66.

12. Johnson was the protagonist in two other unique events in the history of the vice presidency. In the election of 1836, Virginia's Democratic electors refused to vote for Johnson because they objected to his interracial sexual extravagances. This situation left Johnson one vote short of the required electoral vote majority, so the Senate elected him by 33–16. Four years later, Johnson refused to withdraw as a candidate for the Democratic nomination for vice president, dividing the party convention to such an extent that it selected no vice-presidential candidate at all. The Democrats lost the election.

13. Quoted in Irving G. Williams, *The Rise of the Vice Presidency* (Washington, D.C.: Public Affairs Press, 1956), 66.

14. C-Span, "Presidential Historians Survey 2017," https://www.c-span.org/presidents urvey2017/?page=overall

15. The five nineteenth-century presidents who were disabled for a measurable period of time were Madison, William Henry Harrison, Arthur, Garfield, and Grover Cleveland. John D. Feerick, *The Twenty-Fifth Amendment* (New York: Fordham University Press, 1976), chap. 1.

16. Woodrow Wilson, *Congressional Government* (New York: Meridian Books, 1956), 162.

17. Joel K. Goldstein, *The White House Vice Presidency: The Path to Significance, Mondale to Biden* (Lawrence: University Press of Kansas, 2016), 20.

18. The exception was Henry A. Wallace in 1944. For a detailed historical perspective on the growing political security of vice presidents, see George S. Sirgiovanni, "Dumping the Vice President: A Historical Overview and Analysis," *Presidential Studies Quarterly*, 24 (Fall 1994): 765–782.

19. Theodore Roosevelt, "The Three Vice-Presidential Candidates and What They Represent," *Review of Reviews*, September 1896, 289.

20. Doris Kearns Goodwin, *The Bully Pulpit: Theodore Roosevelt, William Howard Taft, and the Golden Age of Journalism* (New York: Simon and Schuster, 2013), 274, 275.

21. Quoted in Williams, *Rise of the Vice Presidency*, 89.

22. Marshall's decision to accept Wilson's invitation to meet with the cabinet was made with some misgivings. Although he once described the president as "my commander-in-chief" whose "orders would be obeyed," Marshall believed that constitutionally the vice president, as president of the Senate, is a "member of the legislative branch," ill-suited to executive responsibilities. He told the cabinet he wanted it clearly understood that he was present only "informally and personally" and would "preside in an unofficial and informal way." Before his inauguration in 1925, Vice President Dawes said publicly that he would not accept an invitation from President Coolidge to meet with the cabinet, if as seemed likely, one were forthcoming. "The cabinet and those who sit with it should always do so at the discretion and inclination of the president," Dawes told reporters, overlooking the possibility that Coolidge might wish to exercise his discretion to have the vice president present. "No precedent should be established which creates a different and arbitrary method of selection." Williams, *Rise of the Vice Presidency*, 108–110, 134.

23. Franklin D. Roosevelt, "Can the Vice President Be Useful?" *Saturday Evening Post*, October 6, 1920, 8.

24. Williams, *Rise of the Vice Presidency*, 158–159.

25. C-Span, "Presidential Historians Survey 2017.

26. Quoted in Williams, *Rise of the Vice Presidency*, 219.

27. Quoted in Robert J. Donovan, *Conflict and Crisis: The Presidency of Harry S. Truman, 1945–1948* (New York: Norton, 1977), 15.

28. All but the successions of Millard Fillmore, Calvin Coolidge, and Lyndon Johnson.

29. Goldstein, "Constitutional Change, Originalism, and the Vice Presidency," 404.

30. Since 1940 ticket balancing has been of little explanatory value in accounting for vice-presidential nominations. Lee Sigelman and Paul J. Wahlbeck, "The 'Veepstakes': Strategic Choice in Presidential Running Mate Selection," *American Political Science Review*, 91 (December 1997): 862.

31. Goldstein, *Modern American Vice Presidency*, 147–148.

32. Michael Nelson, "Choosing the Vice President," *PS: Political Science and Politics*, 21 (Fall 1988): 858–868; Nelson, "The Elections: Turbulence and Tranquility in Contemporary American Politics," in *The Elections of 1996,* ed. Michael Nelson (Washington, D.C.: CQ Press, 1997), 66–70.

33. Goldstein, *Modern American Vice Presidency*, 85; updated by the authors.

34. Quoted in Jules Witcover, *Joe Biden: A Life of Trial and Redemption* (New York: HarperCollins, 2010), 413. As Chuck Todd has written, "Biden filled the 'Washington

insider' void. . . . The man who hated the backslapping nature of politics in Washington had picked the consummate backslapper to be his vice president." Todd, *The Stranger: Barack Obama in the White House* (New York: Little, Brown, 2014), 32, 34.

35. Joshua M Glasser, *The Eighteen-Day Running Mate: McGovern, Eagleton, and a Campaign in Crisis* (New Haven: Yale University Press, 2012).

36. See Dan Balz and Haynes Johnson, *The Battle for America 2008* (New York: Viking, 2009), chap. 26; and John Heileman and Mark Halperin, *Game Change: Obama and the Clintons, McCain and Palin, and the Race of a Lifetime* (New York: HarperCollins, 2010), chap. 20.

37. The debates appear to have at least a short-term effect on voter intentions. Thomas M. Holbrook, "The Behavioral Consequences of Vice-Presidential Debates," *American Politics Quarterly*, 22 (October 1994): 469–482.

38. Baumgartner, *American Vice Presidency Reconsidered*, chap. 5.

39. Michael Nelson, "Constitutional Aspects of the Elections," in *The Elections of 1988*, ed. Michael Nelson (Washington, D.C.: CQ Press, 1989), 190. For a more general treatment, see Martin P. Wattenberg, "The Role of Vice Presidential Candidate Ratings in Presidential Voting Behavior," *American Politics Quarterly*, 23 (October 1995): 504–514.

40. Michael Nelson, "The Presidency: Clinton and the Cycle of Politics and Policy," in *The Elections of 1992*, ed. Michael Nelson (Washington, D.C.: CQ Press, 1993), 125–132.

41. *National Journal*, August 8, 1992, 1862.

42. Bob Woodward, *State of Denial: Bush at War, Part III* (New York: Simon and Schuster, 2006), xiii.

43. In 1948 Dewey chose a fellow governor, Earl Warren of California, as his running mate. The ticket lost.

44. David Von Drehle, "First, Do No Harm," *Washington Post National Weekly Edition*, July 31, 2000, 9.

45. "Exit Polls," http://www.cnn.com/ELECTION/2008/results/polls/#val=USP00p4.

46. Mark Halperin and John Heilemann, *Double Down: Game Change 2012* (New York: Penguin Press, 2013), chap. 17.

47. Vice-presidential vacancies occurred seven times because the vice president died, once because the vice president resigned, and eight times because the president died.

48. *Public Papers of the Presidents* (Washington, D.C.: Government Printing Office, 1957), 132.

49. The only other task assigned to the vice president by law is to serve on the Board of Regents of the Smithsonian Institution.

50. Michael Nelson, *Trump's First Year* (Charlottesville: University of Virginia Press, 2018), chap. 3.

51. Rockefeller also headed the White House Domestic Council, an assignment that ended in failure, as did Henry Wallace's. Michael Nelson, "Nelson A. Rockefeller and the American Vice Presidency," in *Gerald R. Ford and the Politics of Post-Watergate America*, vol. 1, eds. Bernard J. Firestone and Alexej Ugrinsky (Westport, Conn.: Greenwood Press, 1993), 139–160.

52. "Walter F. Mondale's Memo to Jimmy Carter on the Role of the Vice President," in *The Evolving Presidency: Landmark Documents*, 6th ed., ed. Michael Nelson (Washington, D.C.: CQ Press, 2012), 241–247.

53. Goldstein, *The White House Vice Presidency*, 98.

54. Joel K. Goldstein, "The Rising Power of the Modern Vice Presidency," *Presidential Studies Quarterly*, 38 (September 2008): 374–389.

55. Fred Barnes, "Danny Gets His Gun," *New Republic*, June 26, 1989, 10–11; Bob Woodward and David S. Broder, *The Man Who Would Be President: Dan Quayle* (New York: Simon and Schuster, 1992).

56. Bob Woodward, *The Agenda: Inside the Clinton White House* (New York: Simon and Schuster, 1994), 281.

57. Elizabeth Drew, *On the Edge: The Clinton Presidency* (New York: Simon and Schuster, 1994), 228.

58. Richard L. Berke, "The Gore Guide to the Future," *New York Times Magazine*, February 22, 1998, 47. For additional evidence of Gore's influence, see Joseph A. Pika, "The Vice Presidency: New Opportunities, Old Constraints," in *The Presidency and the Political System*, 5th ed., ed. Michael Nelson (Washington, D.C.: CQ Press, 1998), 547–559.

59. On the Cheney vice presidency, see Michael Nelson, "Richard Cheney and the Power of the Modern Vice Presidency," in *Ambition and Division: Legacies of the George W. Bush Presidency*, ed. Steven E. Schier (Pittsburgh: University of Pittsburgh Press, 2009), 172–189; Barton Gellman, *Angler: The Cheney Vice Presidency* (New York: Penguin, 2008); Peter Baker, *Days of Fire: Bush and Cheney in the White House* (New York: Doubleday, 2013); and Joel K. Goldstein, "Cheney, Vice Presidential Power, and the War on Terror," *Presidential Studies Quarterly*, 40 (March 2010): 102–139.

60. Eric Schmitt, "The Vice President: Out Front or Low Profile, Cheney Keeps Powerful Role," *New York Times*, October 7, 2001.

61. Susan Page, "Cheney Takes 'Backseat' in a Strong Way," *USA Today*, November 16, 2001.

62. Brinkley quoted in Barbara Slavin, "Cheney Rewrites Role in Foreign Policy," *USA Today*, July 29, 2002.

63. Cheney's influence in the Bush administration and especially his role in the war on Iraq are chronicled in Bob Woodward, *Bush at War* (New York: Simon and Schuster, 2002); Woodward, *Plan of Attack* (New York: Simon and Schuster, 2004); and Woodward, *State of Denial*.

64. "Transcript: The Vice Presidential Debate," *New York Times*, October 2, 2008.

65. Witcover, *Joe Biden*, 477. Biden's role in the Afghanistan review is discussed in Bob Woodward, *Obama's War* (New York: Simon and Schuster, 2010).

66. Jules Witcover, *The American Vice Presidency: From Irrelevance to Power* (Washington, D.C.: Smithsonian Books, 2014), 504.

67. Evan Osnos "The Biden Agenda," *The New Yorker*, July 28, 2014, 40–53; and Halperin and Heilemann, *Double Down*, chaps. 4 and 14.

68. George F. Will, "Trump Is No Longer the Worst Person in Government," *Washington Post*, May 9, 2018.

69. Joel K. Goldstein, "The New Constitutional Vice Presidency," *Wake Forest Law Review*, 30 (Fall 1995): 526.

70. Reportedly, some White House aides regarded Reagan as mentally incapable in 1987. See Jane Mayer and Doyle McManus, *Landslide: The Unmaking of a President, 1984–1988* (Boston: Houghton Mifflin, 1988), vii–xi.

71. Lawrence I. Barrett, *Gambling with History: Ronald Reagan in the White House* (Garden City, N.Y.: Doubleday, 1983), chap. 7. See also Del Quentin Wilber, *Rawhide Down: The Near Assassination of Ronald Reagan* (New York: Henry Holt, 2011), esp. chaps. 12–13.

72. The White House, Office of the Press Secretary, "Remarks by the President upon Departure for Camp David," June 28, 2002.

73. As Vice President Ford remarked in 1974, "I am now surrounded by a clutch of Secret Service agents, reporters and cameramen, and assorted well-wishers. When I travel I am greeted by bands playing 'Hail Columbia' and introduced to audiences with great solemnity instead of just as 'my good friend, Jerry Ford.'" Quoted in Light, *Vice-Presidential Power*, 10.

74. Quoted in Cronin, "Rethinking the Vice Presidency," 338.

75. The following discussion is drawn from Nelson, "The Election," 55–92; and Michael Nelson, "The Curse of the Vice Presidency," *American Prospect*, July 31, 2000, 20–24.

76. Bill Turque, *Inventing Al Gore* (Boston: Houghton Mifflin, 2000), 356.

77. Ibid., 361.

78. "Transcript of Debate between Vice President Gore and Governor Bush," *New York Times*, October 4, 2000.

79. Michael Nelson, "Evaluating the Presidency," in *The Presidency and the Political System*, 7th ed., ed. Michael Nelson (Washington, D.C.: CQ Press, 2002).

80. Nelson, "The Election."

81. Jules Witcover, *Crapshoot: Rolling the Dice for the Vice Presidency* (New York: Crown, 1992), 138.

82. Nelson, *Resilient America*.

83. Nelson, "Constitutional Aspects of the Elections," 190.

84. David E. Sanger, "After 'Next Best Thing,' Clinton Carefully Praises Gore," *New York Times*, November 4, 2000.

85. David S. Broder, "Gore's Clinton Problem," *Washington Post National Weekly Edition*, October 30, 2000, 4.

86. Dwight D. Eisenhower, *Waging Peace* (Garden City, N.Y.: Doubleday, 1965), 596.

87. Paul Light calls this the "abused child syndrome." Light, *Vice-Presidential Power*, 108.

Appendix

Constitution of the United States

We the People of the United States, in Order to form a more perfect Union, establish Justice, insure domestic Tranquility, provide for the common defence, promote the general Welfare, and secure the Blessings of Liberty to ourselves and our Posterity, do ordain and establish this Constitution for the United States of America.

Article I

Section 1. All legislative Powers herein granted shall be vested in a Congress of the United States, which shall consist of a Senate and House of Representatives.

Section 2. The House of Representatives shall be composed of Members chosen every second Year by the People of the several States, and the Electors in each State shall have the Qualifications requisite for Electors of the most numerous Branch of the State Legislature.

No Person shall be a Representative who shall not have attained to the age of twenty five Years, and been seven Years a Citizen of the United States, and who shall not, when elected, be an Inhabitant of that State in which he shall be chosen.

[Representatives and direct Taxes shall be apportioned among the several States which may be included within this Union, according to their respective Numbers, which shall be determined by adding to the whole Number of free Persons, including those bound to Service for a Term of Years, and excluding Indians not taxed, three fifths of all other Persons.][1] The actual Enumeration shall be made within three Years after the first Meeting of the Congress of the United States, and within every subsequent Term of ten Years, in such Manner as they shall by Law direct. The Number of Representatives shall not exceed one for every thirty Thousand, but each State shall have at Least one Representative; and until such enumeration shall be made, the State of New Hampshire shall be entitled to chuse three, Massachusetts eight, Rhode-Island and Providence Plantations one, Connecticut five, New-York six, New Jersey four, Pennsylvania eight, Delaware one, Maryland six, Virginia ten, North Carolina five, South Carolina five, and Georgia three.

When vacancies happen in the Representation from any State, the Executive Authority thereof shall issue Writs of Election to fill such Vacancies.

The House of Representatives shall chuse their Speaker and other Officers; and shall have the sole Power of Impeachment.

Section 3. The Senate of the United States shall be composed of two Senators from each State, [chosen by the Legislature thereof,][2] for six Years; and each Senator shall have one Vote.

Immediately after they shall be assembled in Consequence of the first Election, they shall be divided as equally as may be into three Classes. The Seats of the Senators of the first Class shall be vacated at the Expiration of the second Year, of the second Class at the Expiration of the fourth Year, and of the third Class at the Expiration of the sixth Year, so that one third may be chosen every second Year; [and if Vacancies happen by Resignation, or otherwise, during the Recess of the Legislature of any State, the Executive thereof may make temporary Appointments until the next Meeting of the Legislature, which shall then fill such Vacancies.][3]

No Person shall be a Senator who shall not have attained to the Age of thirty Years, and been nine Years a Citizen of the United States, and who shall not, when elected, be an Inhabitant of that State for which he shall be chosen.

The Vice President of the United States shall be President of the Senate, but shall have no Vote, unless they be equally divided.

The Senate shall chuse their other Officers, and also a President pro tempore, in the Absence of the Vice President, or when he shall exercise the Office of President of the United States.

The Senate shall have the sole Power to try all Impeachments. When sitting for that Purpose, they shall be on Oath or Affirmation. When the President of the United States is tried, the Chief Justice shall preside: And no Person shall be convicted without the Concurrence of two thirds of the Members present.

Judgment in Cases of Impeachment shall not extend further than to removal from Office, and disqualification to hold and enjoy any Office of honor, Trust or Profit under the United States: but the Party convicted shall nevertheless be liable and subject to Indictment, Trial, Judgment and Punishment, according to Law.

Section 4. The Times, Places and Manner of holding Elections for Senators and Representatives, shall be prescribed in each State by the Legislature thereof; but the Congress may at any time by Law make or alter such Regulations, except as to the Places of chusing Senators.

The Congress shall assemble at least once in every Year, and such Meeting shall [be on the first Monday in December],[4] unless they shall by Law appoint a different Day.

Section 5. Each House shall be the Judge of the Elections, Returns and Qualifications of its own Members, and a Majority of each shall constitute a Quorum to do Business; but a smaller Number may adjourn from day to day, and may be authorized to compel the Attendance of absent Members, in such Manner, and under such Penalties as each House may provide.

Each House may determine the Rules of its Proceedings, punish its Members for disorderly Behaviour, and, with the Concurrence of two thirds, expel a Member.

Each House shall keep a Journal of its Proceedings, and from time to time publish the same, excepting such Parts as may in their Judgment require Secrecy; and the Yeas and Nays of the Members of either House on any question shall, at the Desire of one fifth of those Present, be entered on the Journal.

Neither House, during the Session of Congress, shall, without the Consent of the other, adjourn for more than three days, nor to any other Place than that in which the two Houses shall be sitting.

Section 6. The Senators and Representatives shall receive a Compensation for their Services, to be ascertained by Law, and paid out of the Treasury of the United States. They shall in all Cases, except Treason, Felony and Breach of the Peace, be privileged from Arrest during their Attendance at the Session of their respective Houses, and in going to and returning from the same; and for any Speech or Debate in either House, they shall not be questioned in any other Place.

No Senator or Representative shall, during the Time for which he was elected, be appointed to any civil Office under the Authority of the United States, which shall have been created, or the Emoluments whereof shall have been encreased during such time; and no Person holding any Office under the United States, shall be a Member of either House during his Continuance in Office.

Section 7. All Bills for raising Revenue shall originate in the House of Representatives; but the Senate may propose or concur with Amendments as on other Bills.

Every Bill which shall have passed the House of Representatives and the Senate, shall, before it become a Law, be presented to the President of the United States; If he approve he shall sign it, but if not he shall return it, with his Objections to that House in which it shall have originated, who shall enter the Objections at large on their Journal, and proceed to reconsider it. If after such Reconsideration two thirds of that House shall agree to pass the Bill, it shall be sent, together with the Objections, to the other House, by which it shall likewise be reconsidered, and if approved by two thirds of that House, it shall become a Law. But in all such Cases the Votes of both Houses shall be determined by yeas and Nays, and the Names of the Persons voting for and against the Bill shall be entered on the Journal of each House respectively. If any Bill shall not be returned by the President within ten Days (Sundays excepted) after it shall have been presented to him, the Same shall be a Law, in like Manner as if he had signed it, unless the Congress by their Adjournment prevent its Return, in which Case it shall not be a Law.

Every Order, Resolution, or Vote to which the Concurrence of the Senate and House of Representatives may be necessary (except on a question of Adjournment) shall be presented to the President of the United States; and before the Same shall take Effect, shall be approved by him, or being disapproved by him, shall be repassed by two thirds of the Senate and House of Representatives, according to the Rules and Limitations prescribed in the Case of a Bill.

Section 8. The Congress shall have Power To lay and collect Taxes, Duties, Imposts and Excises, to pay the Debts and provide for the common Defence and general Welfare of the United States; but all Duties, Imposts and Excises shall be uniform throughout the United States;

To borrow Money on the credit of the United States;

To regulate Commerce with foreign Nations, and among the several States, and with the Indian Tribes;

To establish an uniform Rule of Naturalization, and uniform Laws on the subject of Bankruptcies throughout the United States;

To coin Money, regulate the Value thereof, and of foreign Coin, and fix the Standard of Weights and Measures;

To provide for the Punishment of counterfeiting the Securities and current Coin of the United States;

To establish Post Offices and post Roads;

To promote the Progress of Science and useful Arts, by securing for limited Times to Authors and Inventors the exclusive Right to their respective Writings and Discoveries;

To constitute Tribunals inferior to the supreme Court;

To define and punish Piracies and Felonies committed on the high Seas, and Offences against the Law of Nations;

To declare War, grant Letters of Marque and Reprisal, and make Rules concerning Captures on Land and Water;

To raise and support Armies, but no Appropriation of Money to that Use shall be for a longer Term than two Years;

To provide and maintain a Navy;

To make Rules for the Government and Regulation of the land and naval Forces;

To provide for calling forth the Militia to execute the Laws of the Union, suppress Insurrections and repel Invasions;

To provide for organizing, arming, and disciplining, the Militia, and for governing such Part of them as may be employed in the Service of the United States, reserving to the States respectively, the Appointment of the Officers, and the Authority of training the Militia according to the discipline prescribed by Congress;

To exercise exclusive Legislation in all Cases whatsoever, over such District (not exceeding ten Miles square) as may, by Cession of particular States, and the Acceptance of Congress, become the Seat of the Government of the United States, and to exercise like Authority over all Places purchased by the Consent of the Legislature of the State in which the Same shall be, for the Erection of Forts, Magazines, Arsenals, dock-Yards, and other needful Buildings;—And

To make all Laws which shall be necessary and proper for carrying into Execution the foregoing Powers, and all other Powers vested by this Constitution in the Government of the United States, or in any Department or Officer thereof.

Section 9. The Migration or Importation of such Persons as any of the States now existing shall think proper to admit, shall not be prohibited by the Congress prior to the Year one thousand eight hundred and eight, but a Tax or duty may be imposed on such Importation, not exceeding ten dollars for each Person.

The Privilege of the Writ of Habeas Corpus shall not be suspended, unless when in Cases of Rebellion or Invasion the public Safety may require it.

No Bill of Attainder or ex post facto Law shall be passed.

No Capitation, or other direct, Tax shall be laid, unless in Proportion to the Census or Enumeration herein before directed to be taken.[5] No Tax or Duty shall be laid on Articles exported from any State.

No Preference shall be given by any Regulation of Commerce or Revenue to the Ports of one State over those of another; nor shall Vessels bound to, or from, one State, be obliged to enter, clear, or pay Duties in another.

No Money shall be drawn from the Treasury, but in Consequence of Appropriations made by Law; and a regular Statement and Account of the

Receipts and Expenditures of all public Money shall be published from time to time.

No Title of Nobility shall be granted by the United States: And no Person holding any Office of Profit or Trust under them, shall, without the Consent of the Congress, accept of any present, Emolument, Office, or Title, of any kind whatever, from any King, Prince, or foreign State.

Section 10. No State shall enter into any Treaty, Alliance, or Confederation; grant Letters of Marque and Reprisal; coin Money; emit Bills of Credit; make any Thing but gold and silver Coin a Tender in Payment of Debts; pass any Bill of Attainder, ex post facto Law, or Law impairing the Obligation of Contracts, or grant any Title of Nobility.

No State shall, without the Consent of the Congress, lay any Imposts or Duties on Imports or Exports, except what may be absolutely necessary for executing its inspection Laws: and the net Produce of all Duties and Imposts, laid by any State on Imports or Exports, shall be for the Use of the Treasury of the United States; and all such Laws shall be subject to the Revision and Controul of the Congress.

No State shall, without the Consent of Congress, lay any Duty of Tonnage, keep Troops, or Ships of War in time of Peace, enter into any Agreement or Compact with another State, or with a foreign Power, or engage in War, unless actually invaded, or in such imminent Danger as will not admit of delay.

Article II ·

Section 1. The executive Power shall be vested in a President of the United States of America. He shall hold his Office during the Term of four Years, and, together with the Vice President, chosen for the same Term, be elected, as follows:

Each State shall appoint, in such Manner as the Legislature thereof may direct, a Number of Electors, equal to the whole Number of Senators and Representatives to which the State may be entitled in the Congress: but no Senator or Representative, or Person holding an Office of Trust or Profit under the United States, shall be appointed an Elector.

[The Electors shall meet in their respective States, and vote by Ballot for two Persons, of whom one at least shall not be an Inhabitant of the same State with themselves. And they shall make a List of all the Persons voted for, and of the Number of Votes for each; which List they shall sign and certify, and transmit sealed to the Seat of the Government of the United

States, directed to the President of the Senate. The President of the Senate shall, in the Presence of the Senate and House of Representatives, open all the Certificates, and the Votes shall then be counted. The Person having the greatest Number of Votes shall be the President, if such Number be a Majority of the whole Number of Electors appointed; and if there be more than one who have such Majority, and have an equal Number of Votes, then the House of Representatives shall immediately chuse by Ballot one of them for President; and if no Person have a Majority, then from the five highest on the list the said House shall in like Manner chuse the President. But in chusing the President, the Votes shall be taken by States, the Representation from each State having one Vote; A quorum for this Purpose shall consist of a Member or Members from two thirds of the States, and a Majority of all the States shall be necessary to a Choice. In every Case, after the Choice of the President, the Person having the greatest Number of Votes of the Electors shall be the Vice President. But if there should remain two or more who have equal Votes, the Senate shall chuse from them by Ballot the Vice President.][6] The Congress may determine the Time of chusing the Electors, and the Day on which they shall give their Votes; which Day shall be the same throughout the United States.

No Person except a natural born Citizen, or a Citizen of the United States, at the time of the Adoption of this Constitution, shall be eligible to the Office of President; neither shall any Person be eligible to that Office who shall not have attained to the Age of thirty five Years, and been fourteen Years a Resident within the United States.

In Case of the Removal of the President from Office, or of his Death, Resignation, or Inability to discharge the Powers and Duties of the said Office,[7] the Same shall devolve on the Vice President, and the Congress may by Law provide for the Case of Removal, Death, Resignation or Inability, both of the President and Vice President, declaring what Officer shall then act as President, and such Officer shall act accordingly, until the Disability be removed, or a President shall be elected.

The President shall, at stated Times, receive for his Services, a Compensation, which shall neither be encreased nor diminished during the Period for which he shall have been elected, and he shall not receive within that Period any other Emolument from the United States, or any of them.

Before he enter on the Execution of his Office, he shall take the following Oath or Affirmation:—"I do solemnly swear (or affirm) that I will faithfully execute the Office of President of the United States, and will to the best of my Ability, preserve, protect and defend the Constitution of the United States."

Section 2. The President shall be <u>Commander in Chief of the Army</u> <u>and Navy</u> of the United States, <u>and of the Militia of the several States</u>, when called into the actual Service of the United States; he may <u>require</u> <u>the Opinion</u>, in writing, <u>of the principal Officer in each of the executive</u> <u>Departments</u>, upon any Subject relating to the Duties of their respective Offices, and he shall have Power to <u>grant Reprieves and Pardons</u> for Offences against the United States, except in Cases of Impeachment.

He shall have Power, by and with the Advice and Consent of the Senate, <u>to make Treaties</u>, provided <u>two thirds of the Senators present concur</u>; and he shall nominate, and by and with the Advice and Consent of the Senate, shall appoint <u>Ambassadors, other public Ministers and Consuls, Judges</u> <u>of the supreme Court, and all other Officers</u> of the United States, whose Appointments are not herein otherwise provided for, and which shall be established by Law: but the Congress may by Law vest the Appointment of such inferior Officers, as they think proper, in the President alone, in the Courts of Law, or in the Heads of Departments.

The President shall have Power to <u>fill up all Vacancies</u> that may happen during the Recess of the Senate, by granting Commissions which shall expire at the End of their next Session.

Section 3. He shall from time to time give to the Congress Information of the State of the Union, and recommend to their Consideration such Measures as he shall judge necessary and expedient; he may, on extraordinary Occasions, convene both Houses, or either of them, and in Case of Disagreement between them, with Respect to the Time of Adjournment, he may adjourn them to such Time as he shall think proper; he shall receive Ambassadors and other public Ministers; he shall take Care that the Laws be faithfully executed, and shall Commission all the Officers of the United States.

Section 4. The President, Vice President and all civil Officers of the United States, shall be removed from Office on Impeachment for, and Conviction of, Treason, Bribery, or other high Crimes and Misdemeanors.

Article III

Section 1. The judicial Power of the United States, shall be vested in one supreme Court, and in such inferior Courts as the Congress may from time to time ordain and establish. The Judges, both of the supreme and inferior Courts, shall hold their Offices during good Behaviour, and shall, at stated Times, receive for their Services, a Compensation, which shall not be diminished during their Continuance in Office.

Section 2. The judicial Power shall extend to all Cases, in Law and Equity, arising under this Constitution, the Laws of the United States, and Treaties made, or which shall be made, under their Authority;—to all Cases affecting Ambassadors, other public Ministers and Consuls;—to all Cases of admiralty and maritime Jurisdiction;—to Controversies to which the United States shall be a Party;—to Controversies between two or more States;—between a State and Citizens of another State;—between Citizens of different States;—between Citizens of the same State claiming Lands under Grants of different States, and between a State, or the Citizens thereof, and foreign States, Citizens or Subjects.[8] In all Cases affecting Ambassadors, other public Ministers and Consuls, and those in which a State shall be Party, the supreme Court shall have original Jurisdiction. In all the other Cases before mentioned, the supreme Court shall have appellate Jurisdiction, both as to Law and Fact, with such Exceptions, and under such Regulations as the Congress shall make.

The Trial of all Crimes, except in Cases of Impeachment, shall be by Jury; and such Trial shall be held in the State where the said Crimes shall have been committed; but when not committed within any State, the Trial shall be at such Place or Places as the Congress may by Law have directed.

Section 3. Treason against the United States, shall consist only in levying War against them, or in adhering to their Enemies, giving them Aid and Comfort. No Person shall be convicted of Treason unless on the Testimony of two Witnesses to the same overt Act, or on Confession in open Court.

The Congress shall have Power to declare the Punishment of Treason, but no Attainder of Treason shall work Corruption of Blood, or Forfeiture except during the Life of the Person attainted.

Article IV

Section 1. Full Faith and Credit shall be given in each State to the public Acts, Records, and judicial Proceedings of every other State. And the Congress may by general Laws prescribe the Manner in which such Acts, Records and Proceedings shall be proved, and the Effect thereof.

Section 2. The Citizens of each State shall be entitled to all Privileges and Immunities of Citizens in the several States.

A Person charged in any State with Treason, Felony, or other Crime, who shall flee from Justice, and be found in another State, shall on Demand of the executive Authority of the State from which he fled, be delivered up, to be removed to the State having Jurisdiction of the Crime.

[No Person held to Service or Labour in one State, under the Laws thereof, escaping into another, shall, in Consequence of any Law or Regulation therein, be discharged from such Service or Labour, but shall be delivered up on Claim of the Party to whom such Service or Labour may be due.][9]

Section 3. New States may be admitted by the Congress into this Union; but no new State shall be formed or erected within the Jurisdiction of any other State; nor any State be formed by the Junction of two or more States, or Parts of States, without the Consent of the Legislatures of the States concerned as well as of the Congress.

The Congress shall have Power to dispose of and make all needful Rules and Regulations respecting the Territory or other Property belonging to the United States; and nothing in this Constitution shall be so construed as to Prejudice any Claims of the United States, or of any particular State.

Section 4. The United States shall guarantee to every State in this Union a Republican Form of Government, and shall protect each of them against Invasion; and on Application of the Legislature, or of the Executive (when the Legislature cannot be convened) against domestic Violence.

Article V

The Congress, whenever two thirds of both Houses shall deem it necessary, shall propose Amendments to this Constitution, or, on the Application of the Legislatures of two thirds of the several States, shall call a Convention for proposing Amendments, which, in either Case, shall be valid to all Intents and Purposes, as Part of this Constitution, when ratified by the Legislatures of three fourths of the several States, or by Conventions in three fourths thereof, as the one or the other Mode of Ratification may be proposed by the Congress; Provided [that no Amendment which may be made prior to the Year One thousand eight hundred and eight shall in any Manner affect the first and fourth Clauses in the Ninth Section of the first Article; and][10] that no State, without its Consent, shall be deprived of its equal Suffrage in the Senate.

Article VI

All Debts contracted and Engagements entered into, before the Adoption of this Constitution, shall be as valid against the United States under this Constitution, as under the Confederation.

This Constitution, and the Laws of the United States which shall be made in Pursuance thereof; and all Treaties made, or which shall be made, under the Authority of the United States, shall be the supreme Law of the Land; and the Judges in every State shall be bound thereby, any Thing in the Constitution or Laws of any State to the Contrary notwithstanding.

The Senators and Representatives before mentioned, and the Members of the several State Legislatures, and all executive and judicial Officers, both of the United States and of the several States, shall be bound by Oath or Affirmation, to support this Constitution; but no religious Test shall ever be required as a Qualification to any Office or public Trust under the United States.

Article VII

The Ratification of the Conventions of nine States, shall be sufficient for the Establishment of this Constitution between the States so ratifying the Same.

Done in Convention by the Unanimous Consent of the States present the Seventeenth Day of September in the Year of our Lord one thousand seven hundred and Eighty seven and of the Independence of the United States of America the Twelfth. IN WITNESS whereof We have hereunto subscribed our Names,

George Washington,
President and deputy from Virginia.

New Hampshire:	John Langdon, Nicholas Gilman.
Massachusetts:	Nathaniel Gorham, Rufus King.
Connecticut:	William Samuel Johnson, Roger Sherman.
New York:	Alexander Hamilton.
New Jersey:	William Livingston, David Brearley, William Paterson, Jonathan Dayton.

Pennsylvania:	Benjamin Franklin,
	Thomas Mifflin,
	Robert Morris,
	George Clymer,
	Thomas FitzSimons,
	Jared Ingersoll,
	James Wilson,
	Gouverneur Morris.
Delaware:	George Read,
	Gunning Bedford Jr.,
	John Dickinson,
	Richard Bassett,
	Jacob Broom.
Maryland:	James McHenry,
	Daniel of St. Thomas Jenifer,
	Daniel Carroll.
Virginia:	John Blair,
	James Madison Jr.
North Carolina:	William Blount,
	Richard Dobbs Spaight,
	Hugh Williamson.
South Carolina:	John Rutledge,
	Charles Cotesworth Pinckney,
	Charles Pinckney,
	Pierce Butler.
Georgia:	William Few,
	Abraham Baldwin.

[The language of the original Constitution, not including the Amendments, was adopted by a convention of the states on September 17, 1787, and was subsequently ratified by the states on the following dates: Delaware, December 7, 1787; Pennsylvania, December 12, 1787; New Jersey, December 18, 1787; Georgia, January 2, 1788; Connecticut, January

9, 1788; Massachusetts, February 6, 1788; Maryland, April 28, 1788; South Carolina, May 23, 1788; and New Hampshire, June 21, 1788.

Ratification was completed on June 21, 1788.

The Constitution subsequently was ratified by Virginia, June 25, 1788; New York, July 26, 1788; North Carolina, November 21, 1789; Rhode Island, May 29, 1790; and Vermont, January 10, 1791.]

Amendments

Amendment I

(The first ten amendments were ratified December 15, 1791.)
Congress shall make no law respecting an establishment of religion, or prohibiting the free exercise thereof; or abridging the freedom of speech, or of the press; or the right of the people peaceably to assemble, and to petition the Government for a redress of grievances.

Amendment II

A well regulated Militia, being necessary to the security of a free State, the right of the people to keep and bear Arms, shall not be infringed.

Amendment III

No Soldier shall, in time of peace be quartered in any house, without the consent of the Owner, nor in time of war, but in a manner to be prescribed by law.

Amendment IV

The right of the people to be secure in their persons, houses, papers, and effects, against unreasonable searches and seizures, shall not be violated, and no Warrants shall issue, but upon probable cause, supported by Oath or affirmation, and particularly describing the place to be searched, and the persons or things to be seized.

Amendment V

No person shall be held to answer for a capital, or otherwise infamous crime, unless on a presentment or indictment of a Grand Jury, except in cases arising in the land or naval forces, or in the Militia, when in actual service in time of War or public danger; nor shall any person be subject for the same offence to be twice put in jeopardy of life or limb; nor shall be compelled in any criminal case to be a witness against himself, nor be deprived of life, liberty, or property, without due process of law; nor shall private property be taken for public use, without just compensation.

Amendment VI

In all criminal prosecutions, the accused shall enjoy the right to a speedy and public trial, by an impartial jury of the State and district wherein the crime shall have been committed, which district shall have been previously ascertained by law, and to be informed of the nature and cause of the accusation; to be confronted with the witnesses against him; to have compulsory process for obtaining witnesses in his favor, and to have the Assistance of Counsel for his defence.

Amendment VII

In Suits at common law, where the value in controversy shall exceed twenty dollars, the right of trial by jury shall be preserved, and no fact tried by a jury, shall be otherwise re-examined in any Court of the United States, than according to the rules of the common law.

Amendment VIII

Excessive bail shall not be required, nor excessive fines imposed, nor cruel and unusual punishments inflicted.

Amendment IX

The enumeration in the Constitution, of certain rights, shall not be construed to deny or disparage others retained by the people.

Amendment X

The powers not delegated to the United States by the Constitution, nor prohibited by it to the States, are reserved to the States respectively, or to the people.

Amendment XI (Ratified February 7, 1795)

The Judicial power of the United States shall not be construed to extend to any suit in law or equity, commenced or prosecuted against one of the United States by Citizens of another State, or by Citizens or Subjects of any Foreign State.

Amendment XII (Ratified June 15, 1804)

The Electors shall meet in their respective states and vote by ballot for President and Vice-President, one of whom, at least, shall not be an inhabitant of the same state with themselves; they shall name in their ballots the person voted for as President, and in distinct ballots the person voted for as Vice-President, and they shall make distinct lists of all persons voted for as President, and of all persons voted for as Vice-President, and of the number of votes for each, which lists they shall sign and certify, and transmit sealed to the seat of the government of the United States, directed to the President of the Senate;—The President of the Senate shall, in the presence of the Senate and House of Representatives, open all the certificates and the votes shall then be counted;—The person having the greatest number of votes for President, shall be the President, if such number be a majority of the whole number of Electors appointed; and if no person have such majority, then from the persons having the highest numbers not exceeding three on the list of those voted for as President, the House of Representatives shall choose immediately, by ballot, the President. But in choosing the President, the votes shall be taken by states, the representation from each state having one vote; a quorum for this purpose shall consist of a member or members from two-thirds of the states, and a majority of all the states shall be necessary to a choice. [And if the House of Representatives shall not choose a President whenever the right of choice shall devolve upon them, before the fourth day of March next following, then the Vice-President shall act as President, as in the case of the death or other constitutional disability of the President.—][11] The person having the greatest number of votes as Vice-President, shall be the Vice-President, if such number be a majority of the whole number of Electors appointed, and if no person have a majority, then from the two highest numbers on the list, the Senate shall choose the Vice-President; a quorum for the purpose shall consist of two-thirds of the whole number of Senators, and a majority of the whole number shall be necessary to a choice. But no person constitutionally ineligible to the office of President shall be eligible to that of Vice-President of the United States.

Amendment XIII (Ratified December 6, 1865)

Section 1. Neither slavery nor involuntary servitude, except as a punishment for crime whereof the party shall have been duly convicted, shall exist within the United States, or any place subject to their jurisdiction.

Section 2. Congress shall have power to enforce this article by appropriate legislation.

Amendment XIV (Ratified July 9, 1868)

Section 1. All persons born or naturalized in the United States, and subject to the jurisdiction thereof, are citizens of the United States and of the State wherein they reside. No State shall make or enforce any law which shall abridge the privileges or immunities of citizens of the United States; nor shall any State deprive any person of life, liberty, or property, without due process of law; nor deny to any person within its jurisdiction the equal protection of the laws.

Section 2. Representatives shall be apportioned among the several States according to their respective numbers, counting the whole number of persons in each State, excluding Indians not taxed. But when the right to vote at any election for the choice of electors for President and Vice President of the United States, Representatives in Congress, the Executive and Judicial officers of a State, or the members of the Legislature thereof, is denied to any of the male inhabitants of such State, being twenty-one years of age,[12] and citizens of the United States, or in any way abridged, except for participation in rebellion, or other crime, the basis of representation therein shall be reduced in the proportion which the number of such male citizens shall bear to the whole number of male citizens twenty-one years of age in such State.

Section 3. No person shall be a Senator or Representative in Congress, or elector of President and Vice President, or hold any office, civil or military, under the United States, or under any State, who, having previously taken an oath, as a member of Congress, or as an officer of the United States, or as a member of any State legislature, or as an executive or judicial officer of any State, to support the Constitution of the United States, shall have engaged in insurrection or rebellion against the same, or given aid or comfort to the enemies thereof. But Congress may by a vote of two-thirds of each House, remove such disability.

Section 4. The validity of the public debt of the United States, authorized by law, including debts incurred for payment of pensions and bounties for services in suppressing insurrection or rebellion, shall not be questioned. But neither the United States nor any State shall assume or pay any debt or obligation incurred in aid of insurrection or rebellion against the United States, or any claim for the loss or emancipation of any slave; but all such debts, obligations and claims shall be held illegal and void.

Section 5. The Congress shall have power to enforce, by appropriate legislation, the provisions of this article.

Amendment XV (Ratified February 3, 1870)

Section 1. The right of citizens of the United States to vote shall not be denied or abridged by the United States or by any State on account of race, color, or previous condition of servitude.

Section 2. The Congress shall have power to enforce this article by appropriate legislation.

Amendment XVI (Ratified February 3, 1913)

The Congress shall have power to lay and collect taxes on incomes, from whatever source derived, without apportionment among the several States, and without regard to any census or enumeration.

Amendment XVII (Ratified April 8, 1913)

The Senate of the United States shall be composed of two Senators from each State, elected by the people thereof, for six years; and each Senator shall have one vote. The electors in each State shall have the qualifications requisite for electors of the most numerous branch of the State legislatures.

When vacancies happen in the representation of any State in the Senate, the executive authority of such State shall issue writs of election to fill such vacancies: *Provided,* That the legislature of any State may empower the executive thereof to make temporary appointments until the people fill the vacancies by election as the legislature may direct.

This amendment shall not be so construed as to affect the election or term of any Senator chosen before it becomes valid as part of the Constitution.

Amendment XVIII (Ratified January 16, 1919)

Section 1. After one year from the ratification of this article the manufacture, sale, or transportation of intoxicating liquors within, the importation thereof into, or the exportation thereof from the United States and all territory subject to the jurisdiction thereof for beverage purposes is hereby prohibited.

Section 2. The Congress and the several States shall have concurrent power to enforce this article by appropriate legislation.

Section 3. This article shall be inoperative unless it shall have been ratified as an amendment to the Constitution by the legislatures of the several States, as provided in the Constitution, within seven years from the date of the submission hereof to the States by the Congress.[13]

Amendment XIX (Ratified August 18, 1920)

The right of citizens of the United States to vote shall not be denied or abridged by the United States or by any State on account of sex.

Congress shall have power to enforce this article by appropriate legislation.

Amendment XX (Ratified January 23, 1933)

Section 1. The terms of the President and Vice President shall end at noon on the 20th day of January, and the terms of Senators and Representatives at noon on the 3d day of January, of the years in which such terms would have ended if this article had not been ratified; and the terms of their successors shall then begin.

Section 2. The Congress shall assemble at least once in every year, and such meeting shall begin at noon on the 3d day of January, unless they shall by law appoint a different day.

Section 3.[14] If, at the time fixed for the beginning of the term of the President, the President elect shall have died, the Vice President elect shall become President. If a President shall not have been chosen before the time fixed for the beginning of his term, or if the President elect shall have failed to qualify, then the Vice President elect shall act as President until a President shall have qualified; and the Congress may by law provide for the case wherein neither a President elect nor a Vice President elect shall have qualified, declaring who shall then act as President, or the manner in which one who is to act shall be selected, and such person shall act accordingly until a President or Vice President shall have qualified.

Section 4. The Congress may by law provide for the case of the death of any of the persons from whom the House of Representatives may choose a President whenever the right of choice shall have devolved upon them, and for the case of the death of any of the persons from whom the Senate may choose a Vice President whenever the right of choice shall have devolved upon them.

Section 5. Sections 1 and 2 shall take effect on the 15th day of October following the ratification of this article.

Section 6. This article shall be inoperative unless it shall have been ratified as an amendment to the Constitution by the legislatures of three-fourths of the several States within seven years from the date of its submission.

Amendment XXI (Ratified December 5, 1933)

Section 1. The eighteenth article of amendment to the Constitution of the United States is hereby repealed.

Section 2. The transportation or importation into any State, Territory, or possession of the United States for delivery or use therein of intoxicating liquors, in violation of the laws thereof, is hereby prohibited.

Section 3. This article shall be inoperative unless it shall have been ratified as an amendment to the Constitution by conventions in the several States, as provided in the Constitution, within seven years from the date of the submission hereof to the States by the Congress.

Amendment XXII (Ratified February 27, 1951)

Section 1. No person shall be elected to the office of the President more than twice, and no person who has held the office of President, or acted as President, for more than two years of a term to which some other person was elected President shall be elected to the office of the President more than once. But this Article shall not apply to any person holding the office of President when this Article was proposed by the Congress, and shall not prevent any person who may be holding the office of President, or acting as President, during the term within which this Article becomes operative from holding the office of President or acting as President during the remainder of such term.

Section 2. This article shall be inoperative unless it shall have been ratified as an amendment to the Constitution by the legislatures of three-fourths of the several States within seven years from the date of its submission to the States by the Congress.

Amendment XXIII (Ratified March 29, 1961)

Section 1. The District constituting the seat of Government of the United States shall appoint in such manner as the Congress may direct:

A number of electors of President and Vice President equal to the whole number of Senators and Representatives in Congress to which the District would be entitled if it were a State, but in no event more than the least populous State; they shall be in addition to those appointed by the States, but they shall be considered, for the purposes of the election of President and Vice President, to be electors appointed by a State; and they shall meet in the District and perform such duties as provided by the twelfth article of amendment.

Section 2. The Congress shall have power to enforce this article by appropriate legislation.

Amendment XXIV (Ratified January 23, 1964)

Section 1. The right of citizens of the United States to vote in any primary or other election for President or Vice President, for electors for President or Vice President, or for Senator or Representative in Congress, shall not be denied or abridged by the United States or any State by reason of failure to pay any poll tax or other tax.

Section 2. The Congress shall have power to enforce this article by appropriate legislation.

Amendment XXV (Ratified February 10, 1967)

Section 1. In case of the removal of the President from office or of his death or resignation, the Vice President shall become President.

Section 2. Whenever there is a vacancy in the office of the Vice President, the President shall nominate a Vice President who shall take office upon confirmation by a majority vote of both Houses of Congress.

Section 3. Whenever the President transmits to the President pro tempore of the Senate and the Speaker of the House of Representatives his written declaration that he is unable to discharge the powers and duties of his office, and until he transmits to them a written declaration to the contrary, such powers and duties shall be discharged by the Vice President as Acting President.

Section 4. Whenever the Vice President and a majority of either the principal officers of the executive departments or of such other body as Congress may by law provide, transmit to the President pro tempore of the Senate and the Speaker of the House of Representatives their written declaration that the President is unable to discharge the powers and duties of his office, the Vice President shall immediately assume the powers and duties of the office as Acting President.

Thereafter, when the President transmits to the President pro tempore of the Senate and the Speaker of the House of Representatives his written declaration that no inability exists, he shall resume the powers and duties of his office unless the Vice President and a majority of either the principal officers of the executive department or of such other body as Congress may by law provide, transmit within four days to the President pro tempore of the Senate and the Speaker of the House of Representatives their written declaration that the President is unable to discharge the powers and duties of his office. Thereupon Congress shall decide the issue, assembling within forty-eight hours for that purpose if not in session. If the Congress, within twenty-one days after receipt of the latter written declaration, or, if Congress is not in session, within twenty-one days after Congress is required to assemble, determines by two-thirds vote of both Houses that the President is unable to discharge the powers and duties of his office, the Vice President shall continue to discharge the same as Acting President; otherwise, the President shall resume the powers and duties of his office.

Amendment XXVI (Ratified July 1, 1971)

Section 1. The right of citizens of the United States, who are eighteen years of age or older, to vote shall not be denied or abridged by the United States or by any State on account of age.

Section 2. The Congress shall have power to enforce this article by appropriate legislation.

Amendment XXVII (Ratified May 7, 1992)

No law varying the compensation for the services of the Senators and Representatives shall take effect, until an election of Representatives shall have intervened.

Notes

Source: The Constitution of the United States of America, as Amended, House Document No. 106–214 (Washington, D.C.: Government Printing Office, 2000).

1. The part in brackets was changed by section 2 of the Fourteenth Amendment.
2. The part in brackets was changed by the first paragraph of the Seventeenth Amendment.
3. The part in brackets was changed by the second paragraph of the Seventeenth Amendment.
4. The part in brackets was changed by section 2 of the Twentieth Amendment.
5. The Sixteenth Amendment gave Congress the power to tax incomes.
6. The material in brackets has been superseded by the Twelfth Amendment.
7. This provision has been affected by the Twenty-Fifth Amendment.
8. These clauses were affected by the Eleventh Amendment.
9. This paragraph has been superseded by the Thirteenth Amendment.
10. Obsolete.
11. The part in brackets has been superseded by section 3 of the Twentieth Amendment.
12. See the Nineteenth and Twenty-Sixth Amendments.
13. This amendment was repealed by section 1 of the Twenty-First Amendment.
14. See the Twenty-Fifth Amendment.

U.S. Presidents and Vice Presidents

President and political party	Born	Died	President's term of service	Vice president	Vice president's term of service
George Washington (F)	1732	1799	April 30, 1789–March 4, 1793	John Adams	April 30, 1789–March 4, 1793
George Washington (F)			March 4, 1793–March 4, 1797	John Adams	March 4, 1793–March 4, 1797
John Adams (F)	1735	1826	March 4, 1797–March 4, 1801	Thomas Jefferson	March 4, 1797–March 4, 1801
Thomas Jefferson (DR)	1743	1826	March 4, 1801–March 4, 1805	Aaron Burr	March 4, 1801–March 4, 1805
Thomas Jefferson (DR)			March 4, 1805–March 4, 1809	George Clinton	March 4, 1805–March 4, 1809
James Madison (DR)	1751	1836	March 4, 1809–March 4, 1813	George Clinton[a]	March 4, 1809–April 12, 1812
James Madison (DR)			March 4, 1813–March 4, 1817	Elbridge Gerry[a]	March 4, 1813–Nov. 23, 1814
James Monroe (DR)	1758	1831	March 4, 1817–March 4, 1821	Daniel D. Tompkins	March 4, 1817–March 4, 1821
James Monroe (DR)			March 4, 1821–March 4, 1825	Daniel D. Tompkins	March 4, 1821–March 4, 1825
John Q. Adams (DR)	1767	1848	March 4, 1825–March 4, 1829	John C. Calhoun	March 4, 1825–March 4, 1829
Andrew Jackson (D)	1767	1845	March 4, 1829–March 4, 1833	John C. Calhoun[b]	March 4, 1829–Dec. 28, 1832
Andrew Jackson (D)			March 4, 1833–March 4, 1837	Martin Van Buren	March 4, 1833–March 4, 1837
Martin Van Buren (D)	1782	1862	March 4, 1837–March 4, 1841	Richard M. Johnson	March 4, 1837–March 4, 1841
William. H. Harrison[a] (W)	1773	1841	March 4, 1841–April 4, 1841	John Tyler[c]	March 4, 1841–April 6, 1841
John Tyler[c] (W)	1790	1862	April 6, 1841–March 4, 1845		
James K. Polk (D)	1795	1849	March 4, 1845–March 4, 1849	George M. Dallas	March 4, 1845–March 4, 1849
Zachary Taylor[a] (W)	1784	1850	March 4, 1849–July 9, 1850	Millard Fillmore[c]	March 4, 1849–July 10, 1850
Millard Fillmore[c] (W)	1800	1874	July 10, 1850–March 4, 1853		

President and political party	Born	Died	President's term of service	Vice president	Vice president's term of service
Franklin Pierce (D)	1804	1869	March 4, 1853–March 4, 1857	William R. King[a]	March 24, 1853–April 18, 1853
James Buchanan (D)	1791	1868	March 4, 1857–March 4, 1861	John C. Breckinridge	March 4, 1857–March 4, 1861
Abraham Lincoln (R)	1809	1865	March 4, 1861–March 4, 1865	Hannibal Hamlin	March 4, 1861–March 4, 1865
Abraham Lincoln[a] (R)			March 4, 1865–April 15, 1865	Andrew Johnson[c]	March 4, 1865–April 15, 1865
Andrew Johnson[c] (R)	1808	1875	April 15, 1865–March 4, 1869		
Ulysses S. Grant (R)	1822	1885	March 4, 1869–March 4, 1873	Schuyler Colfax	March 4, 1869–March 4, 1873
Ulysses S. Grant (R)			March 4, 1873–March 4, 1877	Henry Wilson[a]	March 4, 1873–Nov. 22, 1875
Rutherford B. Hayes (R)	1822	1893	March 4, 1877–March 4, 1881	William A. Wheeler	March 4, 1877–March 4, 1881
James A. Garfield[a] (R)	1831	1881	March 4, 1881–Sept. 19, 1881	Chester A. Arthur[c]	March 4, 1881–Sept. 20, 1881
Chester A. Arthur[c] (R)	1830	1886	Sept. 20, 1881–March 4, 1885		
Grover Cleveland (D)	1837	1908	March 4, 1885–March 4, 1889	Thomas A. Hendricks[a]	March 4, 1885–Nov. 25, 1885
Benjamin Harrison (R)	1833	1901	March 4, 1889–March 4, 1893	Levi P. Morton	March 4, 1889–March 4, 1893
Grover Cleveland (D)	1837	1908	March 4, 1893–March 4, 1897	Adlai E. Stevenson	March 4, 1893–March 4, 1897
William McKinley (R)	1843	1901	March 4, 1897–March 4, 1901	Garret A. Hobart[a]	March 4, 1897–Nov. 21, 1899
William McKinley[a] (R)			March 4, 1901–Sept. 14, 1901	Theodore Roosevelt[c]	March 4, 1901–Sept. 14, 1901
Theodore Roosevelt[c] (R)	1858	1919	Sept. 14, 1901–March 4, 1905		
Theodore Roosevelt (R)			March 4, 1905–March 4, 1909	Charles W. Fairbanks	March 4, 1905–March 4, 1909

(Continued)

U.S. Presidents and Vice Presidents (Continued)

President and political party	Born	Died	President's term of service	Vice president	Vice president's term of service
William H. Taft (R)	1857	1930	March 4, 1909–March 4, 1913	James S. Sherman[a]	March 4, 1909–Oct. 30, 1912
Woodrow Wilson (D)	1856	1924	March 4, 1913–March 4, 1917	Thomas R. Marshall	March 4, 1913–March 4, 1917
Woodrow Wilson (D)			March 4, 1917–March 4, 1921	Thomas R. Marshall	March 4, 1917–March 4, 1921
Warren G. Harding[a] (R)	1865	1923	March 4, 1921–Aug. 2, 1923	Calvin Coolidge[c]	March 4, 1921–Aug. 3, 1923
Calvin Coolidge[c] (R)	1872	1933	Aug. 3, 1923–March 4, 1925		
Calvin Coolidge (R)			March 4, 1925–March 4, 1929	Charles G. Dawes	March 4, 1925–March 4, 1929
Herbert Hoover (R)	1874	1964	March 4, 1929–March 4, 1933	Charles Curtis	March 4, 1929–March 4, 1933
Franklin D. Roosevelt (D)	1882	1945	March 4, 1933–Jan. 20, 1937	John N. Garner	March 4, 1933–Jan. 20, 1937
Franklin D. Roosevelt (D)			Jan. 20, 1937–Jan. 20, 1941	John N. Garner	Jan. 20, 1937–Jan. 20, 1941
Franklin D. Roosevelt (D)			Jan. 20, 1941–Jan. 20, 1945	Henry A. Wallace	Jan. 20, 1941–Jan. 20, 1945
Franklin D. Roosevelt[a] (D)			Jan. 20, 1945–April 12, 1945	Harry S. Truman[c]	Jan. 20, 1945–April 12, 1945
Harry S. Truman[c] (D)	1884	1972	April 12, 1945–Jan. 20, 1949		
Harry S. Truman (D)			Jan. 20, 1949–Jan. 20, 1953	Alben W. Barkley	Jan. 20, 1949–Jan. 20, 1953
Dwight D. Eisenhower (R)	1890	1969	Jan. 20, 1953–Jan. 20, 1957	Richard Nixon	Jan. 20, 1953–Jan. 20, 1957
Dwight D. Eisenhower (R)			Jan. 20, 1957–Jan. 20, 1961	Richard Nixon	Jan. 20, 1957–Jan. 20, 1961
John F. Kennedy[a] (D)	1917	1963	Jan. 20, 1961–Nov. 22, 1963	Lyndon B. Johnson[c]	Jan. 20, 1961–Nov. 22, 1963
Lyndon B. Johnson[c] (D)	1908	1973	Nov. 22, 1963–Jan. 20, 1965		
Lyndon B. Johnson (D)			Jan. 20, 1965–Jan. 20, 1969	Hubert H. Humphrey	Jan. 20, 1965–Jan. 20, 1969

President and political party	Born	Died	President's term of service	Vice president	Vice president's term of service
Richard Nixon (R)	1913	1994	Jan. 20, 1969–Jan. 20, 1973	Spiro T. Agnew	Jan. 20, 1969–Jan. 20, 1973
Richard Nixon[b] (R)			Jan. 20, 1973–Aug. 9, 1974	Spiro T. Agnew[b]	Jan. 20, 1973–Oct. 10, 1973
				Gerald R. Ford[c]	Dec. 6, 1973–Aug. 9, 1974
Gerald R. Ford[c] (R)	1913	2006	Aug. 9, 1974–Jan. 20, 1977	Nelson A. Rockefeller	Dec. 19, 1974–Jan. 20, 1977
Jimmy Carter (D)	1924		Jan. 20, 1977–Jan. 20, 1981	Walter F. Mondale	Jan. 20, 1977–Jan. 20, 1981
Ronald Reagan (R)	1911	2004	Jan. 20, 1981–Jan. 20, 1985	George Bush	Jan. 20, 1981–Jan. 20, 1985
Ronald Reagan (R)			Jan. 20, 1985–Jan. 20, 1989	George Bush	Jan. 20, 1985–Jan. 20, 1989
George Bush (R)	1924		Jan. 20, 1989–Jan. 20, 1993	Dan Quayle	Jan. 20, 1989–Jan. 20, 1993
William J. Clinton (D)	1946		Jan. 20, 1993–Jan. 20, 1997	Albert Gore Jr.	Jan. 20, 1993–Jan. 20, 1997
William J. Clinton (D)			Jan. 20, 1997–Jan. 20, 2001	Albert Gore Jr.	Jan. 20, 1997–Jan. 20, 2001
George W. Bush (R)	1946		Jan. 20, 2001–Jan. 20, 2005	Richard B. Cheney	Jan. 20, 2001–Jan. 20, 2005
George W. Bush (R)			Jan. 20, 2005–Jan. 20, 2009	Richard B. Cheney	Jan. 20, 2005–Jan. 20, 2009
Barack Obama (D)	1961		Jan. 20, 2009–Jan. 20, 2017	Joseph R. Biden Jr.	Jan. 20, 2009–Jan. 20, 2017
Donald J. Trump (R)	1946		Jan. 20, 2017–	Michael R. Pence	Jan. 20, 2017–

Source: "Table 6-1 Presidents and Vice Presidents of the United States." In *Vital Statistics on American Politics 2009–2010*, edited by Harold W. Stanley and Richard G. Niemi, 233–235. Washington, DC: CQ Press, 2009, http://library.cqpress.com/vsap/vsap09_tab6-1.

Note: D—Democrat; DR—Democratic–Republican; F—Federalist; R—Republican; W—Whig.

a. Died in office.
b. Resigned.
c. Succeeded to the presidency.

Summary of Presidential Elections, 1789–2016

Year	No. of states	Candidates	Party	Electoral vote	Popular vote
1789[a]	10	George Washington	Fed.	69	—[b]
		John Adams	Fed.	34	
1792[a]	15	George Washington	Fed.	132	—[b]
		John Adams	Fed.	77	
1796[a]	16	John Adams	Fed.	71	—[b]
		Thomas Jefferson	Dem.-Rep.	68	
1800[a]	16	Thomas Jefferson	Dem.-Rep.	73	—[b]
		Aaron Burr	Dem.-Rep.	73	
		John Adams	Fed.	65	
		Charles Cotesworth Pinckney	Fed.	64	
1804	17	Thomas Jefferson	Dem.-Rep.	162	—[b]
		Charles Cotesworth Pinckney	Fed.	64	
		George Clinton			
1808	17	James Madison	Dem.-Rep.	122	—[b]
		Charles Cotesworth Pinckney	Fed.	64	
		George Clinton			
		Rufus King			
1812	18	James Madison	Dem.-Rep.	128	—[b]
		George Clinton	Fed.	89	
		Elbridge Gerry			
		Jared Ingersoll			
1816	19	James Monroe	Dem.-Rep.	183	—[b]
		Rufus King			
		Daniel D. Tompkins			

670

Year	No. of states	Candidates	Party	Electoral vote	Popular vote
		Rufus King	Fed.	34	
		John Howard			
1820	24	James Monroe	Dem.-Rep.	231[c]	—[b]
		Daniel D. Tompkins			
1824[d]	24	John Quincy Adams	Dem.-Rep.	99	113,122 (30.9%)
		John C. Calhoun			
		Andrew Jackson	Dem.-Rep.	84	151,271 (41.3%)
		Nathan Sanford			
1828	24	Andrew Jackson	Dem.-Rep.	178	642,553 (56.0%)
		John C. Calhoun			
		John Quincy Adams	Nat.-Rep.	83	500,897 (43.6%)
		Richard Rush			
1832[e]	24	Andrew Jackson	Dem.	219	701,780 (54.2%)
		Martin Van Buren			
		Henry Clay	Nat.-Rep.	49	484,205 (37.4%)
		John Sergeant			
1836[f]	26	Martin Van Buren	Dem.	170	764,176 (50.8%)
		Richard M. Johnson			
		William Henry Harrison	Whig	73	550,816 (36.6%)
		Francis Granger			
1840	26	William Henry Harrison	Whig	234	1,275,390 (52.9%)
		John Tyler			
		Martin Van Buren	Dem.	60	1,128,854 (46.8%)
		Richard M. Johnson			
1844	26	James K. Polk	Dem.	170	1,339,494 (49.5%)

(Continued)

Summary of Presidential Elections, 1789–2016 (Continued)

Year	No. of states	Candidates	Party	Electoral vote	Popular vote
		George M. Dallas			
		Henry Clay	Whig	105	1,300,004 (48.1%)
		Theodore Frelinghuysen			
1848	30	Zachary Taylor	Whig	163	1,361,393 (47.3%)
		Millard Fillmore			
		Lewis Cass	Dem.	127	1,223,460 (42.5%)
		William O. Butler			
1852	31	Franklin Pierce	Dem.	254	1,607,510 (50.8%)
		William R. King			
		Winfield Scott	Whig	42	1,386,942 (43.9%)
		William A. Graham			
1856[g]	31	James Buchanan	Dem.	174	1,836,072 (45.3%)
		John C. Breckinridge			
		John C. Fremont	Rep.	114	1,342,345 (33.1%)
		William L. Dayton			
1860[h]	33	Abraham Lincoln	Rep.	180	1,865,908 (39.8%)
		Hannibal Hamlin			
		Stephen A. Douglas	Dem.	12	1,380,202 (29.5%)
		Herschel V. Johnson			
1864[i]	36	Abraham Lincoln	Rep.	212	2,218,388 (55.0%)
		Andrew Johnson			
		George B. McClellan	Dem.	21	1,812,807 (45.0%)
		George H. Pendleton			
1868[j]	37	Ulysses S. Grant	Rep.	214	3,013,650 (52.7%)

Year	No. of states	Candidates	Party	Electoral vote	Popular vote
1872	37	Schuyler Colfax			
		Horatio Seymour	Dem.	80	2,708,744 (47.3%)
		Francis P. Blair Jr.			
		Ulysses S. Grant	Rep.	286	3,598,235 (55.6%)
		Henry Wilson			
		Horace Greeley	Dem.	—[k]	2,834,761 (43.8%)
		Benjamin Gratz Brown			
1876	38	Rutherford B. Hayes	Rep.	185	4,034,311 (47.9%)
		William A. Wheeler			
		Samuel J. Tilden	Dem.	184	4,288,546 (51.0%)
		Thomas A. Hendricks			
1880	38	James A. Garfield	Rep.	214	4,446,158 (48.3%)
		Chester A. Arthur			
		Winfield S. Hancock	Dem.	155	4,444,260 (48.2%)
		William H. English			
1884	38	Grover Cleveland	Dem.	219	4,874,621 (48.5%)
		Thomas A. Hendricks			
		James G. Blaine	Rep.	182	4,848,936 (48.2%)
		John A. Logan			
1888	38	Benjamin Harrison	Rep.	233	5,443,892 (47.8%)
		Levi P. Morton			
		Grover Cleveland	Dem.	168	5,534,488 (48.6%)
		Allen G. Thurman			
1892[l]	44	Grover Cleveland	Dem.	277	5,551,883 (46.1%)
		Adlai E. Stevenson			

(Continued)

Summary of Presidential Elections, 1789–2016 (Continued)

Year	No. of states	Candidates	Party	Electoral vote	Popular vote
		Benjamin Harrison	Rep.	145	5,179,244 (43.0%)
		Whitelaw Reid			
1896	45	William McKinley	Rep.	271	7,108,480 (51.0%)
		Garret A. Hobart			
		William J. Bryan	Dem.	176	6,511,495 (46.7%)
		Arthur Sewall			
1900	45	William McKinley	Rep.	292	7,218,039 (51.7%)
		Theodore Roosevelt			
		William J. Bryan	Dem.	155	6,358,345 (45.5%)
		Adlai E. Stevenson			
1904	45	Theodore Roosevelt	Rep.	336	7,626,593 (56.4%)
		Charles W. Fairbanks			
		Alton B. Parker	Dem.	140	5,028,898 (37.6%)
		Henry G. Davis			
1908	46	William Howard Taft	Rep.	321	7,676,258 (51.6%)
		James S. Sherman			
		William J. Bryan	Dem.	162	6,406,801 (43.0%)
		John W. Kern			
1912[m]	48	Woodrow Wilson	Dem.	435	6,293,152 (41.8%)
		Thomas R. Marshall			
		William Howard Taft	Rep.	8	3,486,333 (23.2%)
		James S. Sherman			
1916	48	Woodrow Wilson	Dem.	277	9,126,300 (49.2%)
		Thomas R. Marshall			
		Charles E. Hughes	Rep.	254	8,546,789 (46.1%)

Year	No. of states	Candidates	Party	Electoral vote	Popular vote
1920	48	Charles W. Fairbanks			
		Warren G. Harding	Rep.	404	16,133,314 (60.3%)
		Calvin Coolidge			
		James M. Cox	Dem.	127	9,140,884 (34.2%)
		Franklin D. Roosevelt			
1924[n]	48	Calvin Coolidge	Rep.	382	15,717,553 (54.1%)
		Charles G. Dawes			
		John W. Davis	Dem.	136	8,386,169 (28.8%)
		Charles W. Bryan			
1928	48	Herbert C. Hoover	Rep.	444	21,411,991 (58.2%)
		Charles Curtis			
		Alfred E. Smith	Dem.	87	15,000,185 (40.8%)
		Joseph T. Robinson			
1932	48	Franklin D. Roosevelt	Dem.	472	22,825,016 (57.4%)
		John N. Garner			
		Herbert C. Hoover	Rep.	59	15,758,397 (39.6%)
		Charles Curtis			
1936	48	Franklin D. Roosevelt	Dem.	523	27,747,636 (60.8%)
		John N. Garner			
		Alfred M. Landon	Rep.	8	16,679,543 (36.5%)
		Frank Knox			
1940	48	Franklin D. Roosevelt	Dem.	449	27,263,448 (54.7%)
		Henry A. Wallace			
		Wendell L. Willkie	Rep.	82	22,336,260 (44.8%)
		Charles L. McNary			

(Continued)

Summary of Presidential Elections, 1789–2016 (Continued)

Year	No. of states	Candidates	Party	Electoral vote	Popular vote
1944	48	Franklin D. Roosevelt	Dem.	432	25,611,936 (53.4%)
		Harry S. Truman			
		Thomas E. Dewey	Rep.	99	22,013,372 (45.9%)
		John W. Bricker			
1948[o]	48	Harry S. Truman	Dem.	303	24,105,587 (49.5%)
		Alben W. Barkley			
		Thomas E. Dewey	Rep.	198	21,970,017 (45.1%)
		Earl Warren			
1952	48	Dwight D. Eisenhower	Rep.	442	33,936,137 (55.1%)
		Richard M. Nixon			
		Adlai E. Stevenson II	Dem.	89	27,314,649 (44.4%)
		John J. Sparkman			
1956[p]	48	Dwight D. Eisenhower	Rep.	457	35,585,245 (57.4%)
		Richard Nixon			
		Adlai E. Stevenson II	Dem.	73	26,030,172 (42.0%)
		Estes Kefauver			
1960[q]	50	John F. Kennedy	Dem.	303	34,221,344 (49.7%)
		Lyndon B. Johnson			
		Richard Nixon	Rep.	219	34,106,671 (49.5%)
		Henry Cabot Lodge			
1964	50[w]	Lyndon B. Johnson	Dem.	486	43,126,584 (61.1%)
		Hubert H. Humphrey			
		Barry Goldwater	Rep.	52	27,177,838 (38.5%)
		William E. Miller			
1968[r]	50[w]	Richard Nixon	Rep.	301	31,785,148 (43.4%)

Year	No. of states	Candidates	Party	Electoral vote	Popular vote
		Spiro T. Agnew			
		Hubert H. Humphrey	Dem.	191	31,274,503 (42.7%)
		Edmund S. Muskie			
1972[s]	50[w]	Richard Nixon	Rep.	520	47,170,179 (60.7%)
		Spiro T. Agnew			
		George McGovern	Dem.	17	29,171,791 (37.5%)
		R. Sargent Shriver Jr.			
1976[t]	50[w]	Jimmy Carter	Dem.	297	40,830,763 (50.1%)
		Walter F. Mondale			
		Gerald R. Ford	Rep.	240	39,147,793 (48.0%)
		Robert Dole			
1980	50[w]	Ronald Reagan	Rep.	489	43,904,153 (50.7%)
		George H. W. Bush			
		Jimmy Carter	Dem.	49	35,483,883 (41.0%)
		Walter F. Mondale			
1984	50[w]	Ronald Reagan	Rep.	525	54,455,074 (58.8%)
		George H. W. Bush			
		Walter F. Mondale	Dem.	13	37,577,137 (40.6%)
		Geraldine Ferraro			
1988[u]	50[w]	George H. W. Bush	Rep.	426	48,881,278 (53.4%)
		Dan Quayle			
		Michael S. Dukakis	Dem.	111	41,805,374 (45.6%)
		Lloyd M. Bentsen Jr.			
1992	50[w]	Bill Clinton	Dem.	370	44,908,233 (43.0%)
		Al Gore			

(Continued)

Summary of Presidential Elections, 1789–2016 (Continued)

Year	No. of states	Candidates	Party	Electoral vote	Popular vote
		George H. W. Bush	Rep.	168	39,102,282 (37.4%)
		Dan Quayle			
1996	50[w]	Bill Clinton	Dem.	379	47,402,357 (49.2%)
		Al Gore			
		Robert J. Dole	Rep.	159	39,198,755 (40.7%)
		Jack Kemp			
2000[v]	50[w]	George W. Bush	Rep.	271	50,455,156 (47.9%)
		Richard B. Cheney			
		Al Gore	Dem.	266	50,992,335 (48.4%)
		Joseph I. Lieberman			
2004[x]	50[w]	George W. Bush	Rep.	286	62,025,554 (50.7%)
		Richard B. Cheney			
		John Kerry	Dem.	251	59,026,013 (48.3%)
		John Edwards			
2008	50[w]	Barack Obama	Dem.	365	69,459,909 (52.9%)
		Joseph R. Biden Jr.			
		John McCain	Rep.	173	59,930,608 (45.7%)
		Sarah Palin			
2012	50[w]	Barack Obama	Dem.	332	65,587,106 (51%)
		Joseph R. Biden Jr.			
2016	50[w][y]	[ED: Romney and Ryan were in 2012] Mitt Romney	Rep.	206	60,848,302 (47.3%)
		Paul Ryan			
		Donald J. Trump	Rep.	304	62,984,828 (46.1%)
		Michael R. Pence			
		Hillary Rodham Clinton	Dem.	227	65,853,514 (48.2%)
		Timothy M. Kaine			

Source: "Table 1-7 Popular and Electoral Votes for President, 1789–2008." In *Vital Statistics on American Politics 2009–2010*, edited by Harold W. Stanley and Richard G. Niemi, 17–21. Washington, DC: CQ Press, 2013, http://library.cqpress.com/vsap/vsap13_tab1-7.

Note: In the elections of 1789, 1792, 1796, and 1800, each candidate ran for the office of president. The candidate with the second-highest number of electoral votes became vice president. For elections after 1800, italic indicates vice-presidential candidates. Dem.-Rep. = Democratic-Republican; Fed. = Federalist; Nat.-Rep. = National-Republican; Dem. = Democratic; Rep. = Republican.

a. The elections of 1789–1800 were held under rules that did not allow separate voting for president and vice president.

b. Popular vote returns are not shown before 1824 because consistent, reliable data are not available.

c. Monroe ran unopposed. One electoral vote was cast for John Adams and Richard Stockton, who were not candidates.

d. 1824: All four candidates represented Democratic-Republican factions. William H. Crawford received forty-one electoral votes, and Henry Clay received thirty-seven votes. Because no candidate received a majority, the election was decided (in Adams's favor) by the House of Representatives.

e. 1832: Two electoral votes were not cast.

f. 1836: Other Whig candidates receiving electoral votes were Hugh L. White, who received twenty-six votes, and Daniel Webster, who received fourteen votes.

g. 1856: Millard Fillmore, Whig-American, received eight electoral votes.

h. 1860: John C. Breckinridge, Southern Democrat, received seventy-two electoral votes. John Bell, Constitutional Union, received thirty-nine electoral votes.

i. 1864: Eighty-one electoral votes were not cast.

j. 1868: Twenty-three electoral votes were not cast.

k. 1872: Horace Greeley, Democrat, died after the election. In the Electoral College, Democratic electoral votes went to Thomas Hendricks, forty-two votes; Benjamin Gratz Brown, eighteen votes; Charles J. Jenkins, two votes; and David Davis, one vote. Seventeen electoral votes were not cast.

l. 1892: James B. Weaver, People's Party, received twenty-two electoral votes.

m. 1912: Theodore Roosevelt, Progressive Party, received eighty-six electoral votes.

n. 1924: Robert M. La Follette, Progressive Party, received thirteen electoral votes.

o. 1948: J. Strom Thurmond, States' Rights Party, received thirty-nine electoral votes.

p. 1956: Walter B. Jones, Democrat, received one electoral vote.

q. 1960: Harry Flood Byrd, Democrat, received fifteen electoral votes.

r. 1968: George C. Wallace, American Independent Party, received forty-six electoral votes.

s. 1972: John Hospers, Libertarian Party, received one electoral vote.

t. 1976: Ronald Reagan, Republican, received one electoral vote.

u. 1988: Lloyd M. Bentsen Jr., the Democratic vice-presidential nominee, received one electoral vote for president.

v. 2000: One District of Columbia elector left the ballot blank.

w. Fifty states plus the District of Columbia.

x. 2004: One Minnesota elector voted for "John Edwards" *(sic)* for president.

y: 2016: One Texas elector voted for Ron Paul for president, and one voted for John Kasich. Three Washington electors voted for Colin Powell for president, and one voted for Faith Spotted Eagle. One Hawaii elector voted for Bernie Sanders for president.

Index

Note: Page numbers in *italics* refer to photographs. Page number followed by an 'n' refer to notes.

Grand Army of the Republic (GAR), 243
Grant, Ulysses S.
    1867 army appropriation bill
        and, 223
    military career of, 227, 228
    presidency of, 227–232
    use of veto, 229
Grayson, Cary, 310
Great Britain
    Civil War and, 230
    government of, 2–4, 34, 45, 51, 56,
        59, 70–71
    Jay Treaty, 105–108
    War of 1812, 138–140
    war with France, 98–100
    World War II and, 366
    Yalta agreements, 369–371
Great Depression, 335–341
Great Society, 416
Great War. *See* World War I
Greeley, Horace, 165, 191, 202,
        205–206, 232
Green Party, 525
Greenberg, Stanley, 496
Greenstein, Fred I.
    on Adams, 147
    on Carter, 442
    on Eisenhower, 387
    on FDR, 394 n4
    on Nixon and Reagan, 470
    on *Presidential Power* (Neustadt), 401
    on Washington, 98
Gridiron Club, 338
Grier, Robert C., 184
Guantánamo Bay prison, 566–567
Guiteau, Charles J., 240
Gulf of Tonkin Resolution, 420
Gulick, Luther, 358, 359

Hagerty, James C., 389, 404
Hale, Eugene, 267
Hamby, Alonzo L., 375, 471
Hamdan, Salam Ahmed, 536
Hamdan v. Rumsfeld, 536
Hamilton, Alexander, 76, 92
    1796 election and, 108–109
    Annapolis Convention, 10

call for national financial reform, 96–97
criticism of Adams, 111–112
death of, 613
as delegate of the Constitutional
        Convention, 18–19
on executive power, 89, 265
The Federalist papers, 72–76
on neutrality, 99–100
on the power to make treaties, 57
on the power to pardon, 56–57
qualifications for presidency, 64
on reeligibility, 44
on the right to veto, 51
as secretary of the Treasury, 90, 177
on succession, 67
support for Jefferson, 124–125, 130
Whiskey Rebellion and, 102
Hamlin, Hannibal, 615
Hancock, Winfield Scott, 238
Handlin, Oscar, 388
Hanna, Mark, 253, 263–264, 277
Harding, Warren G., *321*
    1920 election, 310, 319
    appointments of, 324
    Budget and Accounting Act (1921),
        325–327
    Congress and, 322–323
    death of, 324
    election of, 319–320
    presidency of, 321–330
    public relations and, 328–330
    removal power, 327–328
    scandals, 323–325
    vice presidency and, 618
Hargrove, Erwin C., 444, 446
Harlow, Ralph Volney, 137
Harper's Weekly, 299
Harris, Katherine, 527
Harris, Patricia Roberts, 446
Harrison, Benjamin A., 247–250
Harrison, William Henry
    death of, 171
    election of, 151, 169
    presidency of, 169–171
Harsch, Joseph C., 387
Hartford Convention, 140
Hawley, Ellis, 360

McClarty, Thomas F. "Mack," 498

McClellan, George B., 208, 210

McClure's, 269

McClurg, James, 43–44

McConnell, Mitch, 590, 592, 595

McCormack, John W., 422

McCormick, Robert, 366

McCulloch v. Maryland (1819), 159

McCurry, Michael, 508

McDonald, Eugene, 334

McDonald, Forrest, 107, 126

McDonald, John A., 231

McFarlane, Robert C., 467

McGovern, George, 624

McGovern–Fraser Commission, 425

McHenry, James, 60–61, 64, 111, 113

McKinley, William
    1896 election, 250
    death of, 263
    influence of, 321
    presidency of, 253–255
    presidential campaign of, 252–253

McKinley Tariff Act, 248

McKitrick, Eric, 12, 34, 91

McLane, Louis, 160

McMaster, H. R., 587, 600

McPherson, James M., 191

McVeigh, Timothy, 508

Meat Inspection Act, 270

media communications
    Harding and, 328–329
    party press, 166
    photo opportunities, 329
    press conferences, 333
    radio broadcasts, 334–335,
        352–353, 360
    Roosevelt on, 312 n28
    social media, 582, 597–599
    television broadcasts, 495–496, 582
    Trump and, 597
    Wilson and, 295

Medicare, 411

Mellon, Andrew, 322, 331

Mellon tax reduction plan, 331

Melnick, R. Shep, 438

Mencken, H. L., 332

Mercer, John, 49

Merriam, Charles E., 358

Merrill, Horace Samuel, 242

Merritt, E. A., 237

Merry, Robert W., 178

Mexican policy, 301–302

Mexican–American War, 177–180

Meyers, Marvin, 185 n8

Michel, Robert, 461

midnight rules, 490 n43

Miers, Harriet, 544–545

Mifflin, Thomas, 102

Miles, Edwin, 186 n40

Military Commissions Act (2006), 536

Military Reconstruction Act, 222–223

military tribunals, 202, 367, 536–537
    See also judiciary branch

militia, control of, 54

Miller, James C., 470

Milligan, Lambdin P., 202

Mills, Ogden, 352

Milosevic, Slobodan, 509, 517

Mingo Creek society, 101–102

Miroff, Bruce, 404

Mississippi Freedom Democratic Party
    (MFDP), 416

Missouri, admission of, 142–143

Missouri Compromise (1820), 143,
    192–194

Mitchell, George, 504

Mitchell, John, 434

Mnuchin, Steven, 587

Moley, Raymond, 353

Mondale, Walter F., 465, 623,
    627–628, 632

Monroe, James
    criticisms of the proposed
        constitution, 72
    election of, 122
    Monroe Doctrine, 143–145
    presidency of, 141–147
    slavery and, 132
    on term of office, 85

Monroe Doctrine, 143–145, 278–280

Montesquieu, Baron de, 47

Morison, Samuel Eliot, 258 n57

Morolla, Jennifer, 537

Morris, Dick, 506

Schlesinger, Arthur M., Jr., 408, 432
Schultz, George, 431
Schurz, Carl, 211–212
Schwarzkopf, Norman, *483*
scientific taxation, 331
Scigliano, Robert, 50
Scott, Dred, 184
Scott, Winfield, 180
Scowcroft, Brent, 479
secession, 197–199
Second Bank of the United States,
    141, 158
Second Treatise of Government (Locke), 53
Securities and Exchange Act, 356
Sedition Act (1798), 113–115, 128
Sedition Act (1918), 308
Senate
    judicial appointments and, 59
    president of, 67, 76
    qualifications for members, 63
    treaty-making power and, 57–58
separation of powers, 47–50, 94
September 11 attacks, 524, 531–533
Sessions, Jeff, 587
Seward, William H., 193, 196
sexual harassment, 486
Sharp, James Roger, 145
Sharpe, George H., 236
Shays's Rebellion, 10
Sheridan, Philip, 209
Sherman, James S., 618
Sherman, John, 235, 247
Sherman, Roger
    Connecticut Compromise, 20
    criticisms of the proposed
        constitution, 77
    New Jersey Plan and, 18
    on the power to pardon, 56
    on religion, 63
    on the right to veto, 51
    role in creating the presidency, 37, 41
    on the vice presidency, 69
Sherman, William Tecumseh, 209
Sherman Anti-Trust Act, 248–249
Sherman Silver Purchase Act, 249, 250
Shultz, George, 428
Sinclair, Harry F., 325
Sioux Indian Republican Club, *336*

slavery
    constitutional clauses on, 20–21, 24
    Emancipation Proclamation, 204–208
    Jacksonian era, 180–184
    Jefferson and, 132–133
    Missouri Compromise (1820), 143
Slonim, Shlomo, 79 n30
Smith, Jean Edward, 229, 230
Smith, Samuel, 125
Smoot–Hawley Act, 338–339
social media, 582, 597–599
Social Security, 468–469
Social Security Act (1935), 354, 357,
    361, 362
Socialist Party, 290
Sorenson, Theodore, 413
Souter, David, 486
Southeast Asia Treaty Organization
    (SEATO), 390
southern Democrats, 464
Soviet Union, 459, 480
Spain
    after the Revolutionary War, 8
    purchase of Florida, 152
Spanish-American War, 250, 254
Sparkman, John, 623
Sparks, Jared, 14
speaker of the House, Clay, Henry, 138
special sessions, 60–61
Specie Circular, 168
Species Resumption Act (1875), 229
Speed, Joshua A., 193
Spicer, Sean, 586
The Spirit of the Laws (Montesquieu), 47
Spitzer, Robert, 118 n81
spoils system, 324
Square Deal, 271
Stalin, Joseph, *364*, 369–371
Stalwarts, 232, 238
Stanton, Edwin, 222, 223, 225–226
Starr, Kenneth, *511*, 513, 517
state banks, 154, 160, 168–169
    See also economy
State of the Union address
    Harding, Warren G., 329
    Wilson, Woodrow, 296, 298, 329
states
    conflict among, 7–8